T0383855

Blockchain Technology in the Automotive Industry

Nowadays, the latest technologies can be found not only in healthcare and space application but also in hybrid supercars. Supercars and hypercars require high-performance materials with high strength, high stiffness, and light weight. For higher performance, car engines now become stronger but smaller and with lower fuel consumption (with cleaner exhaust). Currently, the automotive industry involves batch production, but in the near future, personalized and individualized automobiles with low and limited quantities can be fabricated in smart factories, which integrate all companies working in the supply chain, from manufacturing to marketing and services. In this regard, future automobiles in smart cities become more personalized (single user, limited version, personal spare parts), safer, and smarter.

Blockchain technology is the key to these future perspectives toward intelligent automobiles without any risk of safety, accident, security, theft, or traffic jam. In the current industry, blockchain technology can explore the interconnection of blockchain with other innovative technologies and trends, such as the Internet of Things (IoT) and artificial intelligence (AI), and analyzes the potential to transform business processes and whole industries if these innovations are applied jointly.

In the case of the manufacturing sector, manufacturing can provide a high return on investment. It was reported that $1 of investment in manufacturing can create ~$2.5 of economic activity. In addition, smart products should be fabricated from smart materials via the intelligent manufacturing system framework. In smart production, if the products and machines are integrated, embedded, or otherwise equipped with smart sensors and devices, the system can immediately collect the current operating parameters and predict the product quality and then communicate the optimal parameters to machines in the production line. For smart city applications, the global smart cities market size is expected to grow from USD 410.8 billion in 2020 to USD 820.7 billion by 2025 at a compound annual growth rate (CAGR) of 14.8%. For smart city applications, blockchain technology can build on decentralization, immutability, and consensus characteristics.

Additionally, intelligent wireless sensor networks can provide big information to monitor and manage the city's regular operations and services, including traffic and transportation systems, street lighting systems, power plants, water supply networks, waste management, libraries, hospitals, schools, universities, etc. A blockchain-based distributed framework can be used for automobiles in the smart city. This framework can include a novel miner node selection algorithm for the blockchain-based distributed network architecture.

This book explores how blockchain technology can be used in the automotive industry from smart manufacturing to the smart city.

Blockchain Technology in the Automotive Industry

Edited by
Ghulam Yasin, Amit Kumar Tyagi and
Tuan Anh Nguyen

CRC Press
Taylor & Francis Group
Boca Raton London New York

CRC Press is an imprint of the
Taylor & Francis Group, an **informa** business

Designed cover image: ShutterStock Images

First edition published 2025
by CRC Press
2385 NW Executive Center Drive, Suite 320, Boca Raton FL 33431

and by CRC Press
4 Park Square, Milton Park, Abingdon, Oxon, OX14 4RN

CRC Press is an imprint of Taylor & Francis Group, LLC

© 2025 selection and editorial matter, Ghulam Yasin, Amit Kumar Tyagi and Tuan Anh Nguyen; individual chapters, the contributors

ISBN: 978-1-032-58486-7 (hbk)
ISBN: 978-1-032-58485-0 (pbk)
ISBN: 978-1-003-45030-6 (ebk)

DOI: 10.1201/9781003450306

Typeset in Times LT Std
By Apex CoVantage, LLC

Contents

PART 1   *Blockchain Technology in the Automotive Manufacturing*

PART 2   *Blockchain Technology and Future Drivers' Everyday Lives*

Editors

Ghulam Yasin is a researcher in the School of Environment and Civil Engineering at Dongguan University of Technology, Guangdong, China. His expertise covers the design and development of hybrid devices and technologies of carbon nanostructures and advanced nanomaterials for real-world impact in energy-related and other functional applications.

Amit Kumar Tyagi is an assistant professor at the National Institute of Fashion Technology, New Delhi, India. Previously, from 2019 to 2022, he was an assistant professor (senior grade 2) and senior researcher at Vellore Institute of Technology (VIT), Chennai Campus, Tamil Nadu, India. He earned a PhD in 2018 at Pondicherry Central University, Puducherry, India. From 2018 to 2019, he was an assistant professor and the head researcher at Lingaya's Vidyapeeth (formerly Lingaya's University), Faridabad, Haryana, India. His supervision experience includes more than ten master's dissertations and one PhD thesis. He has contributed to several projects, such as AARIN and P3-Block, to address some of the issues related to privacy breaches in vehicular applications (such as parking) and medical cyber physical systems (MCPS). He has published over 190 papers in refereed high-impact journals, conferences and books, and some of his articles have been awarded best paper awards. Dr. Tyagi has filed more than 25 patents (nationally and internationally) in the area of deep learning, Internet of Things, cyber physical systems, and computer vision. He has edited more than 25 books and has also authored 4 books on intelligent transportation systems, vehicular ad hoc networks, machine learning, and the Internet of Things. Dr. Tyagi has received faculty research awards for 2020, 2021, and 2022 from the Vellore Institute of Technology, Chennai, India. Recently, he received a best paper award for a paper titled "A Novel Feature Extractor Based on the Modified Approach of Histogram of Oriented Gradient," at ICCSA 2020, Italy (Europe). His research focuses on next-generation machine-based communications, blockchain technology, smart and secure computing, and privacy. He is a regular member of ACM, IEEE, MIRLabs, Ramanujan Mathematical Society, Cryptology Research Society, and Universal Scientific Education and Research Network, CSI, and ISTE.

Tuan Anh Nguyen is the senior principal research scientist at the Institute for Tropical Technology, Vietnam Academy of Science and Technology, Vietnam. His research activities include smart sensors, smart networks, smart hospitals, smart cities, and advanced nanomaterials. He has edited over 55 Elsevier, 10 CRC Press, and 1 Springer books. He is the editor in chief of *Kenkyu Journal of Nanotechnology and Nanoscience.*

Contributors

P. Akshay
Chaitanya Bharathi Institute of Technology
Hyderabad, Telangana, India

Nizar M. Alsharari
Jackson State University
Jackson, Mississippi, USA

N. Arunachalam
SRM Institute of Science and Technology
Chengalpattu, Tamil Nadu, India

İsa Avcı
Karabük University
Karabük, Turkey

Ganga Bhattacharjee
Institute of Engineering and Management
Kolkata, West Bengal, India

Alberto Butera
Politecnico di Torino
Turin, Italy

Nalayini C. M.
Velammal Engineering College
Chennai, Tamil Nadu, India

Siriboon Chaisawat
School of Computer Science and Engineering
UNSW Sydney
Sydney, New South Wales, Australia

Anoy Roy Chowdhury
NSHM Knowledge Campus
Kolkata, West Bengal, India

S. Durga Devi
Chaitanya Bharathi Institute of Technology
Hyderabad, Telangana, India

Arup Kumar Dey
NSHM Knowledge Campus
Kolkata, West Bengal, India

Ting Du
Power3 Labs Ltd.
Singapore

Adel ElMessiry
WebDBTech
USA

Alfredo Favenza
Links Foundation
Torino, Italy

Valentina Gatteschi
Politecnico di Torino
Turin, Italy

S. Gnanavel
SRM Institute of Science and Technology
Chengalpattu, Tamil Nadu, India

Biswajit Gope
NSHM Knowledge Campus
Kolkata, West Bengal, India

Sangeeta Gupta
Chaitanya Bharathi Institute of Technology
Hyderabad, Telangana, India

Salil S. Kanhere
School of Computer Science and Engineering
UNSW Sydney
Sydney, New South Wales, Australia

Jeevaa Katiravan
Velammal Engineering College
Chennai, Tamil Nadu, India

Risha Khandelwal
JECRC University, Jaipur India
GLA University, Mathura, India

Öğr. Üyesi Murat Koca
Van Yüzüncü Yıl University
Van, Turkey

Bijoy Kumar Mandal
NSHM Knowledge Campus
Kolkata, West Bengal, India

Silvio Meneguzzo
University of Turin
Turin, Italy
and
University of Camerino
Camerino, Italy

Magdy El Messiry
Alexandria University
Alexandria, Egypt

Akshat Mistry
Sri Sri University
Cuttack, India

Sudhir Kumar Mohapatra
Sri Sri University
Cuttack, India

Hye-Young Paik
School of Computer Science and Engineering
UNSW Sydney
Sydney, New South Wales, Australia

K. Hrithik Pawan
Chaitanya Bharathi Institute of Technology
Hyderabad, Telangana, India

Y. Ramadevi
Chaitanya Bharathi Institute of Technology
Hyderabad, Telangana, India

K. Rohit
Chaitanya Bharathi Institute of Technology
Hyderabad, Telangana, India

S M Nazmuz Sakib
International MBA Institute
Lausanne, Switzerland
and
Dhaka International University
Dhaka, Bangladesh

Joseph Sarkis
Worcester Polytechnic Institute
Worcester, Massachusetts, USA

Godfrey Winster Sathianesan
SRM Institute of Science and Technology
Chengalpattu, Tamil Nadu, India

Claudio Schifanella
University of Turin
Turin, Italy

Elvis Gerardin Konjoh Selabi
Gran Sasso Science Institute
L'Aquila, Italy

Richa
BITS Mesra
Ranchi, Jharkhand, India

Gopalakrishnan Soundararajan
Muscat College
Muscat, Oman

Tanuj Surve
University of California
Berkeley, USA

Anupam Tiwari
GD Goenka University
Sohna, Haryana, India

Amit Kumar Tyagi
National Institute of Fashion Technology
New Delhi, India

Thanga Akilan V.
Velammal Engineering College
Chennai, Tamil Nadu, India

Yajing Wang
Shanghai GMoregalaxy Digital Technology
    Co. Ltd.
Shanghai, People's Republic of China

Yaodong Yang
Shandong Institute of Mechanical Design and
    Research
Shandong, People's Republic of China

Abdullah Yildizbasi
Worcester Polytechnic Institute
Worcester, Massachusetts, USA

Part 1

Blockchain Technology in the
Automotive Manufacturing

Part I

1 Blockchain Technology
An Introduction

Gopalakrishnan Soundararajan and Amit Kumar Tyagi

1.1 INTRODUCTION TO BLOCKCHAIN TECHNOLOGY

Blockchain technology is a decentralized and distributed ledger system that allows multiple parties to record and verify transactions in a secure and transparent manner [1]. It was originally introduced in 2008 as the underlying technology behind the popular cryptocurrency Bitcoin, but its potential applications extend far beyond digital currencies. At its core, a blockchain is a chain of blocks, where each block contains a list of transactions. These blocks are linked together using cryptographic hashes, creating an immutable and chronological record of all the transactions. Here are some key concepts and features of blockchain technology:

- *Decentralization.* Unlike traditional centralized systems that rely on a single authority or intermediary, a blockchain operates in a decentralized manner. It is maintained by a network of participants (nodes) spread across the globe who collectively validate and verify transactions.
- *Security.* Transactions in a blockchain are secured using cryptographic algorithms. Each block contains a unique digital signature or hash that is generated based on the data within the block and the hash of the previous block. Any alteration to a block would require changing subsequent blocks, making it extremely difficult to tamper with the data.
- *Transparency.* The transparency of blockchain stems from its distributed nature. Every participant in the network has a copy of the entire blockchain, and each transaction is visible to all participants. This transparency fosters trust and accountability, as anyone can verify the integrity of the data.
- *Immutability.* Once a block is added to the blockchain, it becomes virtually impossible to modify or delete the data contained within it. This immutability ensures the integrity and permanence of the recorded transactions.
- *Smart contracts.* Smart contracts are self-executing contracts with predefined rules and conditions encoded within the blockchain. They automatically enforce the terms of an agreement and execute actions when certain conditions are met. Smart contracts enable automation and eliminate the need for intermediaries in various industries.
- *Use cases.* Blockchain technology has applications in diverse fields beyond cryptocurrencies. It can be utilized for supply chain management, healthcare records management, voting systems, intellectual property protection, financial services, decentralized applications (dApps), and more. It provides a platform for secure and transparent interactions without relying on a central authority.

Note that while blockchain technology offers numerous advantages, it also has limitations, such as scalability issues, energy consumption concerns (in some consensus mechanisms), and regulatory challenges in certain jurisdictions. However, ongoing research and development are addressing these issues to enhance the technology's potential. In summary, blockchain technology has the potential to revolutionize various industries by providing secure, transparent, and efficient solutions for recordkeeping, transactions, and decentralized applications.

DOI: 10.1201/9781003450306-2

1.1.1 Definition of Blockchain

A *blockchain* is a decentralized and distributed digital ledger that records and verifies transactions across multiple computers or nodes. It is designed to be secure, transparent, and tamper-resistant. Each transaction is grouped into blocks, which are then linked together in a chronological and immutable chain using cryptographic hashes [2, 3]. This ensures that the data stored in the blockchain is resistant to modification or deletion. The blockchain technology eliminates the need for intermediaries and allows for secure peer-to-peer transactions, making it suitable for a wide range of applications beyond cryptocurrencies, such as supply chain management, identity verification, and decentralized applications.

1.1.2 Historical Background of Blockchain

The historical background of blockchain dates back to the late twentieth century and has evolved through various technological advancements. Here is a timeline of significant milestones:

- *1991.* The concept of a cryptographically secured chain of blocks was introduced by Stuart Haber and W. Scott Stornetta. They proposed the idea of using a Merkle tree structure to store document timestamps in order to prevent tampering.
- *2008.* An anonymous person or group using the pseudonym Satoshi Nakamoto published the white paper titled "Bitcoin: A Peer-to-Peer Electronic Cash System." This white paper described the Bitcoin cryptocurrency and the underlying blockchain technology. The blockchain in Bitcoin was designed as a decentralized ledger to record and verify transactions without the need for a central authority.
- *2009.* The first block, known as the *genesis block*, was mined, marking the birth of the Bitcoin blockchain. The genesis block contained the famous embedded message referencing a headline from *The Times* newspaper highlighting the intention to create a decentralized financial system.
- *2013.* Ethereum, a blockchain-based platform that introduced the concept of smart contracts, was proposed by Vitalik Buterin. Ethereum expanded the capabilities of blockchain beyond cryptocurrency by enabling developers to build and deploy decentralized applications (dApps) on its platform.
- *2015.* The Enterprise Ethereum Alliance (EEA) was formed, aiming to develop and standardize Ethereum for enterprise use cases. This initiative brought together a consortium of companies to collaborate on blockchain research and implementation.
- *2016.* The concept of permissioned or private blockchains gained prominence. Unlike public blockchains like Bitcoin and Ethereum, which are open to anyone, permissioned blockchains restrict access to a select group of participants, offering increased privacy and scalability.
- *2017.* Initial coin offerings (ICOs) gained attention as a means for blockchain-based projects to raise funds. ICOs allowed startups to issue and distribute their own digital tokens in exchange for funding, often using Ethereum's blockchain for token creation and distribution.
- *2019.* Facebook announced its plans to launch Libra (later renamed Diem), a global cryptocurrency, fueling discussions and debates around the regulation and mainstream adoption of blockchain technology.
- *2020.* Central bank digital currencies (CBDCs) started gaining traction, with several countries exploring the idea of issuing their own digital currencies using blockchain or distributed ledger technology. This development highlighted the potential of blockchain beyond cryptocurrencies.

- *2022.* Proof of stake (PoS) has replaced proof of work (PoW) as the consensus algorithm in Ethereum. The proof-of-stake beacon chain has merged with the original Ethereum mainnet. It currently exists as a single chain. Energy use for Ethereum has decreased by 99.95%.

The historical background of blockchain showcases its evolution from an idea to the development of Bitcoin and subsequent advancements in smart contracts, enterprise adoption, and exploration of new use cases. Blockchain technology continues to evolve and has the potential to reshape industries across the globe.

1.1.3 RELATIONSHIP WITH CRYPTOCURRENCIES OF BLOCKCHAIN

Blockchain technology and cryptocurrencies, particularly Bitcoin, have a close and interconnected relationship [4]. In fact, cryptocurrencies were the first and most prominent application of blockchain technology. Here is how they are related:

- *Foundation of cryptocurrencies.* Blockchain technology served as the foundational technology for the creation of cryptocurrencies. Satoshi Nakamoto's white paper on Bitcoin introduced the concept of a decentralized digital currency that operated on a blockchain. The blockchain in Bitcoin was designed to securely record and verify transactions without the need for a central authority.
- *Transaction verification.* Blockchain technology ensures the integrity and security of cryptocurrency transactions. Each transaction is recorded in a block, which is added to the blockchain through a process called mining. Miners, through computational power and consensus mechanisms, validate and verify transactions, preventing double-spending and ensuring the accuracy of the ledger.
- *Security and immutability.* Blockchain's cryptographic algorithms and decentralized nature provide a high level of security for cryptocurrencies. The immutability of the blockchain ensures that once a transaction is recorded, it is extremely difficult to alter or manipulate. This enhances trust and prevents fraudulent activities within the cryptocurrency ecosystem.
- *Distributed ledger.* Cryptocurrencies rely on a distributed ledger, which is maintained by a network of participants (nodes) across the globe. Each participant has a copy of the entire blockchain, allowing for transparency and verification of transactions. This distributed nature eliminates the need for a central authority, making cryptocurrencies resistant to censorship and control.
- *Token creation and distribution.* Many cryptocurrencies, including Bitcoin and Ethereum, were created and distributed using blockchain technology. Blockchain-based platforms provide a means for the creation of digital tokens, which represent ownership or value within the cryptocurrency ecosystem. These tokens can be used for various purposes, such as making transactions, accessing services, or participating in decentralized applications (dApps).
- *Decentralized exchanges.* Blockchain technology has also facilitated the development of decentralized exchanges (DEXs) for cryptocurrencies. DEXs operate directly on the blockchain, allowing users to trade cryptocurrencies without relying on intermediaries or centralized exchanges. This enhances security and promotes peer-to-peer transactions.

While blockchain technology and cryptocurrencies are closely intertwined, note that blockchain has expanded beyond cryptocurrencies and has applications in various industries. The technology's potential goes beyond digital currencies, enabling secure and transparent recordkeeping, supply chain management, decentralized applications, and more.

1.1.4 Organization of the Work

This work is organized as several sections which discusses the key concept in blockchain technology. The next section discusses the types of networks. Blockchain component has been discussed in the next section to provide the details about the various components involved. The benefits and challenges of blockchain technology has been considered as a very important factor and is discussed in detail in the next section. It is very important to see how blockchain technology is different from the traditional database, so the next section covers the concept. Various popular blockchain platforms in today's era are covered in the further section. Future trends and developments of the blockchain technology are discussed in the next section.

1.2 KEY CONCEPTS IN BLOCKCHAIN

1.2.1 Decentralization and Distributed Ledger

Decentralization and distributed ledger are closely related concepts in the context of blockchain technology. Let us explore each concept individually.

1.2.1.1 Decentralization

Decentralization refers to the distribution of control, authority, and decision-making across a network of participants instead of relying on a single central authority. In the context of blockchain technology, decentralization means that the power and responsibility for maintaining and verifying the blockchain are distributed among multiple participants, also known as nodes. Decentralization offers several benefits:

- *Enhanced security.* With a decentralized network, there is no single point of failure that can be targeted by malicious actors. The distribution of data and processing power across multiple nodes makes it more difficult to compromise the system, enhancing the overall security.
- *Increased resilience.* Decentralized systems are more resistant to disruptions and failures. Even if some nodes go offline or are compromised, the network as a whole can continue to function and maintain the integrity of the blockchain.
- *Elimination of single points of control.* Decentralization reduces the risk of concentration of power and control in the hands of a few entities. It promotes a more democratic and inclusive environment where participants have equal rights and influence over the network.

1.2.1.2 Distributed Ledger

A *distributed ledger* is a type of database that is replicated and synchronized across multiple nodes in a network. In the context of blockchain technology, the blockchain itself is a distributed ledger. It consists of a chain of blocks, where each block contains a set of transactions. These blocks are shared and stored across the network of participating nodes. The key characteristics of a distributed ledger are:

- *Replication.* The ledger is duplicated and stored on multiple nodes in the network. Each participant has a copy of the entire ledger, ensuring that all nodes have the same view of the data.
- *Synchronization.* The ledger is continuously updated and synchronized across all nodes. Whenever a new block is added to the blockchain, it is propagated to all participants, who validate and incorporate it into their copies of the ledger.
- *Consensus mechanisms.* Distributed ledgers rely on consensus mechanisms to ensure agreement on the state of the ledger among all participants. Consensus algorithms, such as proof of work (PoW) or proof of stake (PoS), enable nodes to collectively agree on the validity of transactions and the order in which they are added to the blockchain.

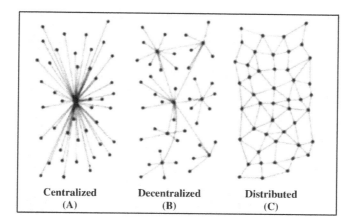

FIGURE 1.1 Structures in general.

The use of a distributed ledger in blockchain technology provides several advantages:

- *Transparency and auditability.* Since all participants have a copy of the ledger, transactions and their history are transparent and easily auditable. This promotes trust and accountability within the network.
- *Immutability.* Once a transaction is recorded on the ledger and added to the blockchain, it becomes difficult to modify or delete. The distributed nature of the ledger (see Figure 1.1), combined with cryptographic techniques, ensures the immutability and integrity of the recorded data.
- *Elimination of intermediaries.* Distributed ledgers enable direct peer-to-peer transactions without the need for intermediaries. This reduces costs, speeds up processes, and allows for more efficient and secure interactions between participants.

Decentralization and distributed ledger are fundamental aspects of blockchain technology, providing security, transparency, and resilience to the system. Together, they enable the creation of decentralized applications, trustworthy digital currencies, and a wide range of innovative solutions in various industries.

1.2.2 BLOCKS, TRANSACTIONS, AND HASHING

Blocks, transactions, and hashing are fundamental components of blockchain technology. Let us explore each of them.

1.2.2.1 Blocks

In a blockchain, a *block* is a container that holds a collection of transactions. It is the basic unit of data that is added to the blockchain. Each block typically includes a header and a body:

- *Header.* The header of a block contains metadata, such as a timestamp, a reference to the previous block in the chain (previous block's hash), and a unique identifier called a nonce. The *nonce* is a value that miners modify during the mining process to find a valid block hash.
- *Body.* The body of a block contains a set of transactions. These transactions can involve the transfer of digital assets, the execution of smart contracts, or other types of data or instructions, depending on the specific blockchain application.

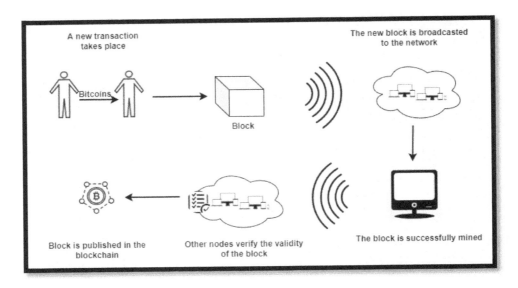

FIGURE 1.2 Workflow of blockchain.

When a new block is added to the blockchain, it is linked to the previous block, forming a chrono-logical chain of blocks (see Figure 1.2). This linking is achieved using cryptographic hashes.

1.2.2.2 Transactions

Transactions represent the actions or operations that are recorded on a blockchain. They can include various types of activities, depending on the specific blockchain's purpose. For example, in a cryp-tocurrency blockchain like Bitcoin, transactions involve the transfer of digital coins (e.g., Bitcoin) between participants. A transaction typically contains the following elements:

- *Sender and receiver addresses.* The addresses (public keys) of the sender and the recipient involved in the transaction. These addresses identify the participants on the blockchain.
- *Transaction amount.* The amount or quantity of the digital asset being transferred or exchanged.
- *Additional data.* Transactions may also include additional data or instructions, depending on the specific blockchain and its functionality. For instance, in Ethereum, transactions can include smart contract code or function calls.

1.2.2.3 Hashing

Hashing is a crucial cryptographic technique used in blockchain technology. A hash function is a mathematical function that takes an input (data) and produces a fixed-size string of characters, which is the hash output or hash value (see Figure 1.3). In the context of blockchain:

- *Transaction hash.* Each transaction within a block is hashed to create a unique identifier called the transaction hash. This hash value serves as a digital fingerprint of the transac-tion's data. It ensures the integrity and authenticity of the transaction by providing a unique identifier that cannot be reversed to obtain the original data.
- *Block hash.* The header of each block, along with the transactions it contains, is hashed to generate a block hash. The block hash uniquely identifies the block and is used to link it to the previous block in the blockchain. Altering the contents of a block would change its hash, making it detectable and preserving the immutability of the blockchain.

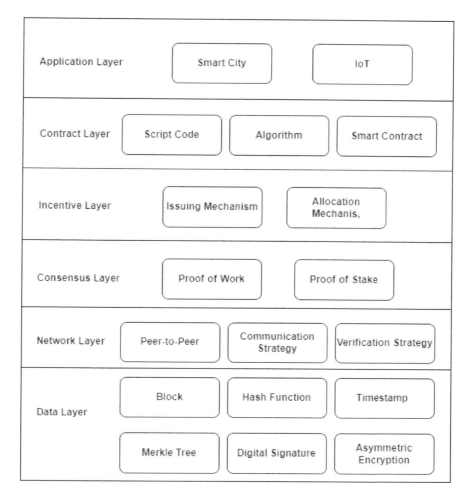

FIGURE 1.3   Architecture of blockchain.

Hashing plays a critical role in ensuring the security and integrity of the blockchain. It provides a tamper-resistant way to verify the data within blocks and maintain the chronological order of the blockchain. In summary, blocks, transactions, and hashing are interconnected elements that form the backbone of a blockchain. They enable secure and transparent recording, verification, and linking of data within the blockchain network.

1.2.3 CONSENSUS MECHANISMS

Consensus mechanisms are protocols or algorithms used in blockchain networks to achieve agreement among participants on the validity and order of transactions or blocks added to the blockchain [5, 6]. These mechanisms enable decentralized networks to reach consensus without relying on a central authority. Here are some common consensus mechanisms used in blockchain technology:

- *Proof of work (PoW)*. PoW is the consensus mechanism used in the Bitcoin blockchain. Miners compete to solve complex mathematical puzzles, requiring significant computational power. The first miner to solve the puzzle gets the right to add the next block to the blockchain. PoW ensures that the majority of participants agree on the state of the block-chain by aligning their computational power.

- *Proof of stake (PoS)*. In a PoS consensus mechanism, validators are selected to create new blocks based on their ownership or stake in the network. Validators are chosen based on the number of coins they hold or "stake" in the network. This mechanism aims to reduce the energy consumption associated with PoW and introduces a different incentive structure.
- *Delegated proof of stake (DPoS)*. DPoS is a variation of the PoS consensus mechanism that introduces a voting system to select a set of "delegates" who are responsible for validating and producing blocks. Delegates are elected by stakeholders, and they take turns in producing blocks. DPoS aims to increase the scalability of blockchain networks by reducing the number of validators and improving transaction throughput.
- *Proof of authority (PoA)*. In a PoA consensus mechanism, a set of authorized nodes or validators is chosen to create new blocks. Validators are typically known entities or organizations with a reputation to uphold. They validate transactions based on their authority in the network, providing quick transaction finality and high throughput.

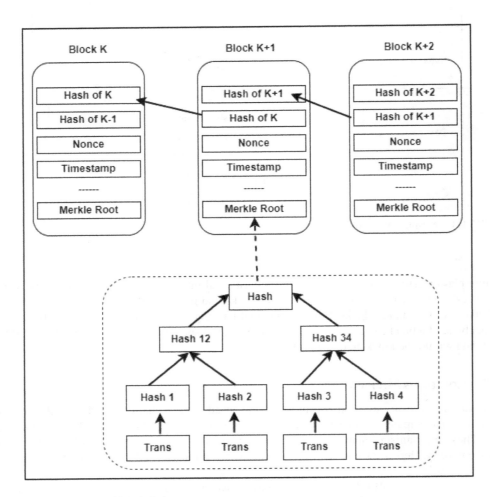

FIGURE 1.4   Structure of blockchain.

- *Practical Byzantine fault tolerance (PBFT)*. PBFT is a consensus mechanism suitable for permissioned blockchains. It allows for fast consensus among a predetermined set of validators, known as "replicas." PBFT ensures Byzantine fault tolerance, meaning, it can tolerate malicious nodes or a certain number of failures while still maintaining consensus.
- *Proof of elapsed time (PoET)*. PoET is a consensus mechanism developed by Intel. It relies on a lottery-based protocol where nodes compete to become the next block creator by waiting for a randomly assigned time period. This mechanism aims to provide energy efficiency and scalability while maintaining decentralization.

These are just a few examples of consensus mechanisms (see Figure 1.4), and new variations and hybrid models continue to emerge as blockchain technology evolves. Each mechanism has its own advantages and trade-offs in terms of security, scalability, energy efficiency, and decentralization. The choice of consensus mechanism depends on the specific goals, characteristics, and requirements of the blockchain network and its applications.

1.3 TYPES OF BLOCKCHAIN NETWORKS

1.3.1 PUBLIC, PRIVATE, AND CONSORTIUM BLOCKCHAINS

Public, private, and consortium blockchains are different types of blockchain networks [7–9] that vary in terms of their accessibility, control, and governance. Here is an overview of each type:

1.3.1.1 Public Blockchain

Public blockchains are open and permissionless networks that allow anyone to join, participate, and interact with the blockchain. They are decentralized networks that are maintained by a distributed community of nodes. Examples of public blockchains include Bitcoin and Ethereum. Key characteristics of public blockchains are:

- *Accessibility*. Public blockchains are open to anyone, and anyone can join the network, participate in transaction validation (mining), and interact with the blockchain by creating transactions or accessing data.
- *Transparency*. Public blockchains provide transparency, as all transactions and data stored on the blockchain are visible to all participants. This transparency ensures trust and accountability.
- *Decentralization*. Public blockchains are decentralized, meaning, they do not rely on a central authority. The consensus mechanisms used, such as proof of work or proof of stake, allow for distributed decision-making and validation of transactions.
- *Security*. Public blockchains leverage a large number of nodes and cryptographic mechanisms to ensure security against attacks and tampering.

1.3.1.2 Private Blockchain

Private blockchains are permissioned networks that are accessible only to a selected group of participants. These participants are typically known and have been granted permission to join the network. Private blockchains are often used by organizations for internal purposes. Key characteristics of private blockchains are:

- *Restricted access*. Private blockchains have restricted access, and participants need permission to join and interact with the network. These networks maintain a certain level of control over who can participate.

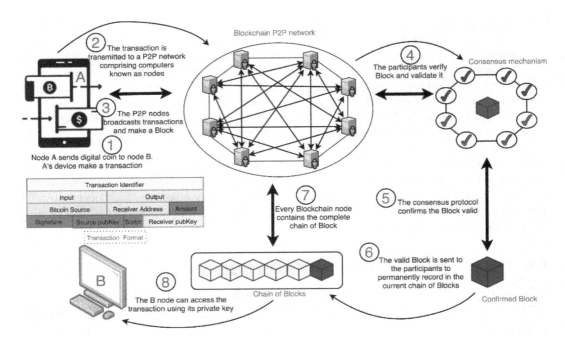

FIGURE 1.5   Creation of new block in a blockchain network.

- *Selective validation.* In private blockchains, the validation of transactions and the creation of new blocks are typically carried out by a limited number of trusted nodes or pre-approved entities (see Figure 1.5). This approach ensures faster transaction processing and greater efficiency.
- *Controlled governance.* Private blockchains are governed by the participating entities or a designated governing body, allowing for more centralized control over the network and decision-making processes.
- *Enhanced privacy.* Private blockchains provide greater privacy, as only approved participants can access and view the data and transactions stored on the blockchain.

1.3.1.3   Consortium Blockchain

Consortium blockchains, also known as federated blockchains, are a hybrid approach that combines elements of both public and private blockchains. Consortium blockchains are governed by a consortium or a group of organizations rather than a single entity. Key characteristics of consortium blockchains are:

- *Restricted membership.* Consortium blockchains have a predefined group of participants who are known and trusted entities. These participants jointly manage and validate the blockchain network.
- *Shared control.* In consortium blockchains, the consensus mechanism and governance rules are agreed upon by the consortium members. Each member has a say in the decision-making process, ensuring a more balanced control structure.
- *Increased efficiency.* Consortium blockchains offer improved scalability and transaction throughput compared to public blockchains, as the number of participants and validators is typically limited.

- *Enhanced privacy.* Consortium blockchains provide a higher level of privacy compared to public blockchains, as only approved participants have access to the blockchain data.

Consortium blockchains are often used in industries where multiple organizations need to collaborate and share data in a secure and efficient manner, such as supply chain management or healthcare.

Each type of blockchain has its own strengths and use cases, and the choice of the blockchain type depends on factors such as the desired level of transparency, privacy, control, and the specific requirements of the application or industry.

1.3.2 PERMISSIONED AND PERMISSIONLESS NETWORKS

Permissioned and *permissionless* networks are terms used to describe the access control and participation requirements in a blockchain network [8, 9]. Here is an explanation of each type:

1.3.2.1 Permissioned Blockchain Network

A *permissioned blockchain network*, also known as a private blockchain network, is a type of blockchain where access and participation are restricted to a specific group of approved entities. In a permissioned network:

- *Access control.* Participants must obtain permission or be invited by the network administrator to join the network. The network administrator or governing body has control over who can join, validate transactions, and participate in the consensus process.
- *Identity verification.* Participants in a permissioned blockchain network often need to go through an identity verification process to ensure they are known and trusted entities. This verification helps maintain the integrity and security of the network.
- *Centralized governance.* Permissioned blockchains typically have a centralized governance model, where decisions regarding the network's rules, consensus mechanisms, and upgrades are made by the governing body or a consortium of participants.
- *Enhanced privacy.* Permissioned networks often offer enhanced privacy features compared to permissionless networks. The data and transactions within the network may be visible only to the approved participants, ensuring a higher level of confidentiality.

Permissioned blockchains are commonly used in industries or scenarios where specific participants require control over the network and need to comply with regulatory or compliance requirements. Examples include consortium blockchains used in supply chain management, financial institutions collaborating on a shared ledger, or government agencies sharing data securely.

1.3.2.2 Permissionless Blockchain Network

A permissionless blockchain network, also known as a public blockchain network, is a decentralized network that allows anyone to join, participate, and interact without needing permission or approval. In a permissionless network:

- *Open access.* Anyone can download the necessary software, create an address, and participate in the network without requiring prior authorization.
- *Decentralized governance.* Permissionless blockchains typically rely on decentralized governance models, where consensus mechanisms determine the rules and decisions of the network. Consensus is achieved through mechanisms such as proof of work or proof of stake, where participants collectively validate transactions and secure the network.
- *Transparency.* Permissionless blockchains emphasize transparency, where all transactions and data stored on the blockchain are visible to anyone in the network. This transparency ensures accountability and trust among participants.

- *Security through decentralization.* Permissionless networks achieve security through the decentralized nature of the network. The distributed consensus mechanisms and a large number of nodes make it difficult for any single entity or group to manipulate or control the blockchain.
- *Anonymity.* Permissionless networks often allow participants to remain pseudonymous, using cryptographic addresses instead of real-world identities. This provides a level of privacy but also introduces challenges in terms of traceability.

Prominent examples of permissionless blockchain networks include Bitcoin and Ethereum. These networks offer open participation, public transparency, and a high level of decentralization, making them suitable for applications that prioritize censorship resistance, trustlessness, and open innovation. The choice between permissioned and permissionless blockchain networks depends on the specific requirements of an application, the desired level of control, privacy, and the intended participants of the network.

1.4 BLOCKCHAIN COMPONENTS

1.4.1 NODES AND PARTICIPANTS

In the context of blockchain technology, *nodes* and *participants* refer to the entities that are part of a blockchain network [10, 11]. Here is a breakdown of each term:

1.4.1.1 Nodes

Nodes are the individual computing devices or servers that make up a blockchain network. Each node maintains a copy of the blockchain's entire transaction history and participates in the consensus process to validate and propagate transactions across the network. Nodes play a crucial role in maintaining the integrity and security of the blockchain. There are different types of nodes in a blockchain network:

- *Full nodes.* Full nodes store a complete copy of the blockchain and independently validate all transactions and blocks. They participate in the consensus mechanism and enforce the rules of the blockchain protocol. Full nodes contribute to the decentralization and security of the network.
- *Mining nodes.* Mining nodes are a subset of full nodes that compete to solve complex mathematical puzzles through the mining process. They validate transactions and add new blocks to the blockchain. Mining nodes typically participate in consensus mechanisms like proof of work (PoW) or proof of stake (PoS) to earn rewards for their mining efforts.
- *Lightweight or SPV (simplified payment verification) nodes.* Lightweight nodes, also known as SPV nodes, do not store the entire blockchain history but rely on full nodes to verify transactions. They maintain a subset of the blockchain, typically focusing on transactions involving their own addresses or specific interests. Lightweight nodes provide a more lightweight option for users who want to interact with the blockchain without the need for extensive storage or computational resources.

1.4.1.2 Participants

Participants in a blockchain network are the individuals, organizations, or entities that engage in transactions and interact with the blockchain. Participants can have different roles and responsibilities within the network, depending on the blockchain's purpose and design. Here are a few examples:

- *Users.* Users are the individuals or entities that initiate transactions or interact with smart contracts on the blockchain. They can send and receive digital assets, access data, or execute specific operations based on the functionalities provided by the blockchain application.

- *Validators.* Validators, also known as miners or block producers, participate in the consensus process to validate transactions and create new blocks in the blockchain. Validators play a crucial role in ensuring the accuracy and security of the blockchain by verifying the integrity of transactions and adhering to the consensus rules.
- *Developers.* Developers create and maintain the software applications, smart contracts, and decentralized applications (dApps) that run on the blockchain. They contribute to the functionality and innovation of the blockchain ecosystem by building applications and improving the underlying protocols.
- *Governance entities.* In some blockchain networks, governance entities or organizations are responsible for making decisions about protocol upgrades, consensus mechanisms, and other network parameters. These entities ensure the smooth operation and evolution of the blockchain by coordinating and aligning the interests of the network participants.

Note that in public permissionless blockchains like Bitcoin or Ethereum, anyone can become a node and participate as a user, miner, or developer. In private or consortium blockchains, participation is typically limited to approved entities or members of the consortium. In summary, nodes and participants collectively form the network infrastructure and user base of a blockchain, contributing to its functionality, security, and decentralized nature.

1.4.2 SMART CONTRACTS

Smart contracts are self-executing contracts, with the terms of the agreement directly written into lines of code. They are computer programs that automatically execute and enforce the terms of a contract once predefined conditions are met. Smart contracts operate on a blockchain, allowing for trust, transparency, and automation without the need for intermediaries. Here are some key characteristics and benefits of smart contracts:

- *Automation.* Smart contracts automate the execution of contractual agreements. Once the conditions specified in the code are met, the contract is automatically enforced, eliminating the need for manual intervention and reducing human error.
- *Trust and transparency.* Smart contracts operate on a blockchain, which provides a decentralized and transparent platform for executing and recording transactions. All parties involved can view and verify the code and the outcome of the contract, ensuring trust and transparency.
- *Efficiency.* By automating contract execution, smart contracts streamline processes and reduce the time and costs associated with traditional contract management. They eliminate the need for intermediaries, paperwork, and manual verification, leading to increased efficiency.
- *Security.* Smart contracts leverage the security features of blockchain technology, such as cryptographic encryption and decentralized consensus mechanisms, to ensure the integrity and immutability of the contract. Once a contract is deployed on the blockchain, it becomes tamper-resistant and resistant to fraud or unauthorized alterations.
- *Flexibility and programmability.* Smart contracts are highly flexible and programmable. They can be designed to handle complex business logic, perform calculations, implement conditional statements, and interact with other smart contracts or external systems. This programmability allows for the creation of sophisticated decentralized applications (dApps) and opens up new possibilities for innovative business models.
- *Potential for disintermediation.* Smart contracts have the potential to remove intermediaries or middlemen from various industries. By directly executing agreements between parties, smart contracts can reduce reliance on third parties and enable peer-to-peer interactions, leading to cost savings and greater efficiency.

Note that smart contracts have a wide range of applications across industries, including finance, supply chain management, real estate, healthcare, and more. They can be used for tasks such as payment processing, asset transfers, escrow services, voting systems, and decentralized exchanges, to name a few. It is important to note that while smart contracts are highly secure and reliable within the constraints of the code, they are only as good as the code written. Careful consideration, auditing, and testing of the code are essential to avoid vulnerabilities or unintended consequences.

1.4.3 Cryptography and Digital Signatures

Cryptography and digital signatures are essential components of blockchain technology that provide security, privacy, and authenticity. Here is an overview of each:

1.4.3.1 Cryptography

Cryptography is the practice of securing communication and data by converting it into an unintelligible form and then back to its original form using cryptographic algorithms. In the context of blockchain, cryptography is used to ensure the confidentiality, integrity, and authenticity of transactions and data.

- *Encryption.* Encryption is the process of encoding information in such a way that it can only be accessed and understood by authorized parties. In blockchain, encryption is used to protect sensitive data, such as private keys, transaction details, and user identities.
- *Hash functions.* Hash functions are mathematical algorithms that take an input (data) and produce a fixed-size output (hash value). Hash functions used in blockchain, such as SHA-256 (Secure Hash Algorithm 256-bit), generate unique and irreversible hash values for data. Hash functions are used to verify the integrity of data and ensure that it has not been tampered with.
- *Digital signatures.* Digital signatures are cryptographic mechanisms used to verify the authenticity and integrity of digital documents or messages. In blockchain, digital signatures are used to prove that a transaction or a block of data was created by a specific participant and has not been tampered with during transit. Digital signatures provide non-repudiation, meaning, the sender of a transaction cannot deny sending it.

1.4.3.2 Digital Signatures

Digital signatures are a specific application of public key cryptography. They involve the use of asymmetric key pairs, consisting of a private key and a corresponding public key.

- *Private key.* A private key is a secret key known only to the owner. It is used to generate digital signatures for transactions or messages. The private key must be kept secure and should only be accessible to the owner.
- *Public key.* A public key is derived from the private key and can be freely shared with others. It is used to verify digital signatures. The public key is typically associated with a specific identity or address on the blockchain.
- *Signature generation and verification.* To generate a digital signature, the private key is used to perform a mathematical operation on the transaction data, creating a unique signature. The signature, along with the transaction, is then broadcasted to the network. Other participants can use the corresponding public key to verify the signature and ensure the authenticity and integrity of the transaction.

Digital signatures provide several benefits in blockchain, including:

- *Authentication.* Digital signatures ensure that transactions or data originated from a specific participant and have not been modified.

- *Non-repudiation*. A sender cannot deny sending a transaction if it is accompanied by a valid digital signature.
- *Integrity*. Digital signatures protect against tampering and guarantee the integrity of the transaction or data.

Hence, cryptography and digital signatures are fundamental to securing the blockchain ecosystem, preventing unauthorized access, ensuring data integrity, and enabling trust and authenticity among participants.

1.5 BENEFITS AND CHALLENGES OF BLOCKCHAIN

1.5.1 ENHANCED SECURITY AND TRANSPARENCY OF BLOCKCHAIN

Blockchain technology has the potential to revolutionize various industries by introducing transparency, security, efficiency, and trust in a decentralized manner [11–14]. Here are some potential use cases of blockchain technology across different sectors:

1.5.1.1 Finance and Banking

- *Cross-border payments*. Blockchain can enable faster, more cost-effective, and secure cross-border transactions by eliminating intermediaries and reducing settlement times.
- *Smart contracts for financial instruments*. Blockchain-based smart contracts can automate and streamline processes for issuing, trading, and settling financial instruments, such as bonds or derivatives.
- *Know your customer (KYC) and anti–money laundering (AML)*. Blockchain can facilitate secure sharing of customer data between financial institutions, reducing duplicative efforts and enhancing compliance.

1.5.1.2 Supply Chain and Logistics

- *Traceability and provenance*. Blockchain can provide end-to-end traceability of goods and raw materials, ensuring transparency and authenticity and combating counterfeiting.
- *Supply chain management*. Blockchain-based systems can improve supply chain efficiency, reduce paperwork, and enhance visibility by recording transactions and verifying documents in a tamper-resistant manner.
- *Food safety*. Blockchain can enable real-time tracking of food products, enabling swift identification and recall of contaminated or unsafe items.

1.5.1.3 Healthcare

- *Electronic health records (EHRs)*. Blockchain can securely store and share patient health records, ensuring privacy, interoperability, and data integrity across healthcare providers.
- *Clinical trials and research*. Blockchain can streamline and enhance the transparency of clinical trials, ensuring accurate recording of trial data and safeguarding against tampering.
- *Drug supply chain management*. Blockchain can track the movement of pharmaceuticals across the supply chain, ensuring authenticity, preventing counterfeit drugs, and improving drug safety.

1.5.1.4 Real Estate

- *Property ownership and title records*. Blockchain can provide a transparent and immutable record of property ownership and title transfers, reducing fraud and improving the efficiency of real estate transactions.
- *Smart contracts for rental agreements*. Blockchain-based smart contracts can automate rental agreements, ensuring transparent and self-executing terms, including rent payments and contract enforcement.

1.5.1.5   Energy and Utilities

- *Peer-to-peer energy trading.* Blockchain can enable direct peer-to-peer energy trading, allowing individuals or businesses to trade excess renewable energy and reducing reliance on centralized energy providers.
- *Grid management.* Blockchain-based systems can enhance the management and tracking of energy production, consumption, and distribution, improving grid efficiency and enabling renewable energy integration.

1.5.1.6   Government Services

- *Identity management.* Blockchain can provide a secure and decentralized identity management system, enabling individuals to have control over their personal data and streamline access to government services.
- *Voting systems.* Blockchain-based voting systems can enhance transparency, security, and auditability in elections, ensuring accurate and tamperproof vote counting.

Note that few examples of the potential use cases of blockchain technology are discussed earlier. The versatility and disruptive nature of blockchain make it applicable to a wide range of industries, promising significant improvements in efficiency, transparency, and trust in various sectors of the economy. Further, potential use cases in various industries of blockchain can be found in [15–20].

1.5.2   SCALABILITY AND ENERGY CONSUMPTION CONCERNS OF BLOCKCHAIN

Scalability and energy consumption are two important considerations when discussing blockchain technology. While blockchain offers numerous benefits, these factors have been the subject of scrutiny and ongoing research. Here is an overview of the concerns:

1.5.2.1   Scalability

Blockchain *scalability* refers to the ability of a blockchain network to handle an increasing number of transactions or users without compromising its performance. There are two main scalability challenges in blockchain:

- *Transaction throughput.* Public blockchains like Bitcoin and Ethereum have limitations in terms of the number of transactions they can process per second. Bitcoin, for example, has a limited block size and block time, resulting in a lower transaction throughput compared to traditional payment systems like credit cards. This can lead to delays and higher transaction fees during periods of high network activity.
- *Network consensus.* Consensus mechanisms used in blockchains, such as proof of work (PoW) or proof of stake (PoS), require agreement among network participants, which can be time-consuming and resource-intensive as the network grows. Achieving consensus becomes more challenging as the number of nodes and transactions increases.

To address scalability concerns, various solutions are being explored, including:

- *Off-chain scaling.* Techniques such as payment channels (e.g., Lightning Network for Bitcoin) or sidechains allow for faster and more scalable transaction processing by moving some transactions off the main blockchain.
- *Sharding.* Sharding involves partitioning the blockchain network into smaller, more manageable parts called shards, each capable of processing its own set of transactions. This can improve the overall transaction throughput.

- *Layer 2 protocols.* Layer 2 protocols, like plasma or state channels, build additional layers on top of the main blockchain to process transactions off-chain while leveraging the security of the underlying blockchain.

1.5.2.2 Energy Consumption

One criticism of blockchain technology is the significant energy consumption associated with certain consensus mechanisms, particularly proof of work (PoW). PoW requires a large amount of computational power and energy to solve complex mathematical puzzles, ensuring network security and consensus. The energy consumption concern arises from the mining process involved in PoW, where miners compete to solve these puzzles and earn block rewards. The high computational requirements lead to increased electricity consumption and carbon footprint. Efforts are being made to address this concern by exploring alternative consensus mechanisms, such as proof of stake (PoS) and variants like proof of authority (PoA) or delegated proof of stake (DPoS). These mechanisms require participants to hold or lock up tokens as a form of "stake" to validate transactions, reducing the need for extensive computational power and energy consumption. Additionally, advancements in hardware efficiency, renewable energy sources, and the development of more energy-efficient blockchains are helping mitigate the environmental impact of blockchain technology. It is important to note that scalability and energy consumption are active areas of research and development in the blockchain space. Various solutions are being explored to improve scalability, reduce energy consumption, and make blockchain technology more sustainable for widespread adoption.

1.6 BLOCKCHAIN VS. TRADITIONAL DATABASES

1.6.1 Centralized vs. Decentralized Models

Centralized and decentralized models represent two different approaches to organizing and governing systems, including technologies like blockchain. Here is an overview of the characteristics and differences between the two:

1.6.1.1 Centralized Model

In a centralized model, decision-making authority and control are concentrated in a single entity or a central authority. This central authority has the power to govern and manage the system, make decisions, and enforce rules. Some key features of a centralized model include:

- *Central authority.* There is a central entity or organization that exercises control, sets rules, and manages the system's operations.
- *Decision-making.* All major decisions are made by the central authority, which may have complete control over the system and its participants.
- *Data and information.* The central authority typically owns and controls the data and information in the system.
- *Single point of failure.* If the central authority fails or is compromised, the entire system can be at risk.
- *Efficiency and speed.* Centralized systems often offer faster processing speeds and efficient decision-making since there is a single authority making decisions.

1.6.1.2 Decentralized Model

In a decentralized model, decision-making authority and control are distributed among multiple participants or nodes in a network. There is no single central authority that exercises complete control over the system. Instead, decision-making, governance, and data management are shared among the participants. Some key features of a decentralized model include:

- *Distributed decision-making.* Decision-making authority is spread across multiple participants or nodes, typically through consensus mechanisms.
- *Governance by consensus.* Participants collectively agree on rules, protocols, and changes to the system through consensus mechanisms, ensuring a distributed decision-making process.
- *Data and information transparency.* In decentralized systems like blockchain, data and information are often transparent, visible, and accessible to all participants while maintaining privacy and security through cryptographic techniques.
- *Resilience.* Decentralized systems are more resilient to failures or attacks on individual nodes since the system's operations and data are distributed across multiple participants.
- *Trust and security.* Decentralized models aim to achieve trust and security through consensus algorithms, cryptographic techniques, and transparency.

Note that the choice between a centralized or decentralized model depends on the specific context and requirements of the system. Centralized models may offer efficiency and speed but can be susceptible to single points of failure and lack transparency. On the other hand, decentralized models promote trust, transparency, and resilience but may face challenges in scalability and decision-making. Blockchain technology, with its decentralized and distributed ledger, provides an example of a decentralized model that aims to address issues of trust, transparency, and control in various sectors. However, it is worth considering that certain applications may benefit from a hybrid model that combines elements of both centralized and decentralized approaches to strike a balance between efficiency and decentralization.

1.6.2 Trust and Data Integrity Comparisons

Trust and data integrity are crucial considerations in any system, whether it is centralized or decentralized. Here is a comparison of how trust and data integrity are approached in both models:

1.6.2.1 Centralized Model

In a centralized model, trust and data integrity rely heavily on the central authority or organization that governs the system. Participants in the system place trust in the central authority to act in their best interests and ensure the integrity of the data. Some key aspects of trust and data integrity in a centralized model include:

- *Trusted authority.* Participants trust the central authority to maintain the integrity of the system, make accurate decisions, and safeguard their data.
- *Centralized control.* The central authority has control over the system's operations, data management, and decision-making processes.
- *Data integrity measures.* The central authority typically implements measures like access controls, security protocols, and auditing processes to ensure data integrity.
- *Single point of trust.* Trust in the system relies heavily on the trustworthiness and competence of the central authority. If the central authority fails or is compromised, trust and data integrity can be at risk.

1.6.2.2 Decentralized Model

In a decentralized model, trust and data integrity are distributed among multiple participants, and mechanisms are employed to ensure trust without relying on a central authority. Blockchain technology, for example, implements several mechanisms to establish trust and data integrity. Some key aspects of trust and data integrity in a decentralized model include:

- *Consensus mechanisms.* Decentralized systems use consensus mechanisms, such as proof of work (PoW) or proof of stake (PoS), to reach agreement and validate transactions or data. These mechanisms provide trust by ensuring majority agreement among network participants.
- *Cryptographic techniques.* Blockchain utilizes cryptographic algorithms to secure and authenticate transactions and data. Techniques like digital signatures and hash functions ensure data integrity and prevent tampering.
- *Transparency and auditing.* Decentralized systems often provide transparency, allowing participants to independently verify and audit the system's operations and data. All transactions and changes to the data are recorded on the blockchain, creating an immutable and transparent ledger.
- *Trust in mathematics and protocol.* Participants trust the underlying mathematical principles and protocols of the decentralized system to ensure the accuracy and integrity of transactions and data. The reliance on cryptographic techniques and consensus algorithms provides a trust framework.
- *Redundancy and resilience.* Decentralized systems distribute data and operations across multiple nodes, making it more resilient to failures or attacks on individual nodes. The redundancy and replication of data contribute to trust and data integrity.

In summary, while both centralized and decentralized models address trust and data integrity, they do so through different mechanisms. Centralized models rely on trust in a central authority, while decentralized models establish trust through consensus mechanisms, cryptography, transparency, and redundancy. The choice between the two models depends on factors such as the level of trust desired, the need for transparency, the threat of single points of failure, and the specific requirements of the system.

1.6.3   IMPACT ON INTERMEDIARIES AND THIRD PARTIES IN REAL-LIFE SECTORS

Blockchain technology has the potential to significantly impact intermediaries and third parties in various real-life sectors by reducing their role or even eliminating the need for them in certain processes. Here is an overview of how blockchain can impact intermediaries in different sectors:

1.6.3.1   Finance and Banking

- *Payment processors.* Blockchain-based cryptocurrencies and smart contracts can enable direct peer-to-peer transactions, reducing the need for traditional payment processors and intermediaries.
- *Clearing and settlement.* Blockchain can automate and streamline the clearing and settlement processes, reducing the reliance on intermediaries such as clearinghouses and custodian banks.

1.6.3.2   Supply Chain and Logistics

- *Intermediaries in supply chain.* Blockchain can facilitate direct interaction and verification between participants in the supply chain, eliminating the need for intermediaries in processes like verification, authentication, and payment settlements.
- *Freight and customs agents.* Blockchain-based platforms can streamline documentation and tracking processes, reducing the need for intermediaries involved in freight forwarding, customs clearance, and logistics management.

1.6.3.3 Real Estate

- *Real estate agents.* Blockchain can enable peer-to-peer property transactions, removing the need for intermediaries like real estate agents or brokers in the buying and selling process.
- *Title companies.* Blockchain-based systems can provide transparent and immutable records of property ownership, reducing the reliance on title companies for verifying and managing property titles.

1.6.3.4 Intellectual Property

- Rights management agencies. Blockchain can enable direct licensing and ownership verification of intellectual property, reducing the reliance on intermediaries like rights management agencies or copyright collectives.

1.6.3.5 Insurance

- *Insurance brokers.* Blockchain can enable direct interactions between insurers and customers, eliminating the need for insurance brokers in certain cases.
- *Claims processing.* Blockchain-based smart contracts can automate and expedite claims processing, reducing the need for intermediaries in verifying and settling claims.

1.6.3.6 Energy Trading

- Energy brokers. Blockchain-based peer-to-peer energy trading platforms can enable direct trading between energy producers and consumers, reducing the reliance on energy brokers and intermediaries.

Hence, while blockchain technology has the potential to disrupt intermediaries in various sectors, its implementation and adoption may still face regulatory, legal, and operational challenges. The extent of the impact on intermediaries will vary depending on the specific use case, regulatory environment, and willingness of stakeholders to embrace decentralized systems. In some cases, intermediaries may still play a role in providing value-added services or catering to specific customer needs, even in a blockchain-enabled ecosystem.

1.7 POPULAR BLOCKCHAIN PLATFORMS IN TODAY'S ERA

1.7.1 Bitcoin and Ethereum

Bitcoin and Ethereum are two of the most well-known and widely used cryptocurrencies in the world. While they share some similarities as blockchain-based digital currencies, they have distinct features and purposes. Here is an overview of Bitcoin and Ethereum:

1.7.1.1 Bitcoin (BTC)

Bitcoin is the first and most recognized cryptocurrency, introduced by an anonymous person, or group, known as Satoshi Nakamoto in 2008. It was designed as a decentralized digital currency and a peer-to-peer payment system. Some key characteristics of Bitcoin include:

- *Store of value and digital currency.* Bitcoin is primarily used as a store of value and a medium of exchange. It allows users to securely and anonymously send and receive digital payments without relying on intermediaries like banks or payment processors.
- *Proof of work (PoW) consensus.* Bitcoin's network relies on the proof of work consensus mechanism, where miners compete to solve complex mathematical puzzles to validate transactions and add blocks to the blockchain. This process ensures network security and consensus.

- *Limited supply.* Bitcoin has a maximum supply of 21 million coins, making it a scarce asset. This controlled supply mechanism is designed to combat inflation and preserve value over time.
- *Use cases.* Bitcoin is mainly used as a digital currency for transactions, as investment, and as a store of value. It has gained popularity as a hedge against traditional financial systems and as a speculative investment.

1.7.1.2 Ethereum (ETH)

Ethereum is a blockchain platform that goes beyond being just a digital currency. It was proposed by Vitalik Buterin in late 2013 and launched in 2015. Ethereum's primary goal is to enable the development of decentralized applications (dApps) and smart contracts. Key features of Ethereum include:

- *Smart contracts and decentralized applications.* Ethereum introduced the concept of smart contracts, which are self-executing contracts with predefined rules and conditions. Developers can build and deploy decentralized applications on the Ethereum platform using these smart contracts.
- *Ether (ETH) cryptocurrency.* Ether is the native cryptocurrency of the Ethereum platform. It serves as a fuel or "gas" that powers transactions and computational operations within the Ethereum network.
- *Turing-complete programming language.* Ethereum introduced a Turing-complete programming language called Solidity, allowing developers to write complex smart contracts and build a wide range of decentralized applications with various functionalities.
- *Proof of stake (PoS) transition.* Ethereum is in the process of transitioning from the energy-intensive proof-of-work consensus mechanism to proof of stake. This transition aims to improve scalability and energy efficiency and reduce the environmental impact of the network.
- *Use cases.* Ethereum's versatility has enabled a wide range of use cases beyond digital currency, including decentralized finance (DeFi), non-fungible tokens (NFTs), decentralized exchanges, and tokenization of assets.

While Bitcoin and Ethereum both operate on blockchain technology, their primary purposes and design philosophies differ. Bitcoin is focused on being a digital currency and store of value, while Ethereum aims to provide a platform for decentralized applications and smart contracts. Both cryptocurrencies have their respective communities, use cases, and market value, contributing to the broader ecosystem of blockchain and cryptocurrencies.

1.7.2 OTHER NOTABLE BLOCKCHAIN PROJECTS

In addition to Bitcoin and Ethereum, there are numerous notable blockchain projects that have made significant contributions to the development and adoption of blockchain technology. Here are a few examples:

- *Ripple (XRP).* Ripple is a blockchain-based platform that aims to facilitate fast, low-cost international money transfers and remittances. It utilizes its native cryptocurrency, XRP, to enable liquidity and facilitate transactions between different fiat currencies.
- *Cardano (ADA).* Cardano is a blockchain platform that aims to provide a secure and sustainable infrastructure for the development of decentralized applications and smart contracts. It utilizes a peer-reviewed, research-driven approach and aims to address scalability, security, and sustainability challenges.
- *Polkadot (DOT).* Polkadot is a multi-chain blockchain platform that enables different blockchains to interoperate and share information. It aims to create a scalable and secure

ecosystem of interconnected blockchains, allowing for greater flexibility and interoperability between different projects.

- *Chainlink (LINK).* Chainlink is a decentralized oracle network that aims to connect smart contracts with real-world data and external APIs. It provides a reliable and secure way to fetch and verify off-chain data, enhancing the capabilities and functionalities of smart contracts.
- *Binance Smart Chain (BSC).* Binance Smart Chain is a blockchain platform developed by the cryptocurrency exchange Binance. It provides a scalable and low-cost environment for decentralized applications and enables the creation and management of digital assets.
- *Tezos (XTZ).* Tezos is a blockchain platform that utilizes a self-amending governance model, allowing the network to upgrade itself without the need for hard forks. It focuses on security, formal verification, and on-chain governance.
- *VeChain (VET).* VeChain is a blockchain platform that focuses on supply chain management and product authenticity. It enables businesses to track and verify the authenticity and origin of products using blockchain technology, enhancing transparency and trust in supply chain processes.
- *Filecoin (FIL).* Filecoin is a decentralized storage network that allows users to rent out their unused storage space and earn tokens in return. It aims to create a more efficient and decentralized approach to data storage and retrieval.

Hence, these are just a few examples of notable blockchain projects, and the blockchain space continues to evolve rapidly, with new projects and innovations emerging regularly. Each project aims to address different use cases, challenges, and market segments, contributing to the broader adoption and development of blockchain technology.

1.7.3 DIFFERENTIATING FEATURES AND USE CASES OF BLOCKCHAIN

Blockchain technology offers several differentiating features that set it apart from traditional systems and enable unique use cases. Here are some of the key differentiating features and their associated use cases:

Decentralization. Blockchain operates on a decentralized network of nodes, where no single entity has control over the system. This feature enables trust, transparency, and resilience. Use cases include:

- *Decentralized finance (DeFi).* Enabling peer-to-peer lending, borrowing, and trading without relying on traditional financial intermediaries.
- *Supply chain management.* Tracking and verifying the origin, authenticity, and movement of products in a transparent and tamper-resistant manner.
- *Governance and voting.* Facilitating transparent and auditable voting systems, enabling secure and verifiable elections.

Immutable and transparent ledger. Transactions recorded on a blockchain are permanent and tamper-resistant, creating an auditable and transparent history of data. Use cases include:

- *Intellectual property rights.* Establishing proof of ownership and copyright for digital assets.
- *Audit and compliance.* Providing an immutable and transparent record of transactions for auditing and regulatory purposes.
- *Charity and donations.* Ensuring transparency and accountability in charitable organizations by tracking the flow of funds.

Security and data integrity. Blockchain utilizes cryptographic techniques to secure data and transactions, ensuring their integrity and protecting against unauthorized access. Use cases include:

- *Digital identity.* Enabling secure and decentralized identity management, reducing the risk of identity theft and fraud.
- *Healthcare records.* Securing patient data and enabling controlled access to healthcare providers while maintaining privacy.
- *Supply chain traceability.* Verifying the authenticity and integrity of products, reducing the risk of counterfeit goods.

Smart contracts. Blockchain platforms like Ethereum support programmable smart contracts, which are self-executing agreements with predefined rules and conditions. Use cases include:

- *Decentralized applications (dApps).* Building decentralized applications that automate specific processes or enable new functionalities.
- *Tokenization of assets.* Creating digital representations of physical or financial assets, such as real estate or securities, enabling fractional ownership and efficient transfer.

Tokenization and cryptocurrencies. Blockchain allows the creation and management of digital tokens, enabling new forms of value exchange and incentivization. Use cases include:

- *Cryptocurrencies.* Facilitating peer-to-peer transactions and store of value, such as Bitcoin and Ethereum.
- *Reward and loyalty programs.* Creating digital tokens for customer rewards and loyalty programs, improving customer engagement and retention.
- *Tokenized assets.* Representing real-world assets, such as art, real estate, or commodities, as digital tokens for easier transfer and fractional ownership.

These differentiating features of blockchain technology enable a wide range of use cases across various industries, providing opportunities for increased efficiency, transparency, security, and new business models. The potential applications of blockchain continue to expand as the technology evolves and new innovations emerge.

1.8   BLOCKCHAIN IN PRACTICE

1.8.1   Cryptocurrency Transactions and Wallets

Cryptocurrency transactions and wallets are integral parts of the blockchain ecosystem. Let us explore how cryptocurrency transactions work and the role of wallets in securely managing cryptocurrencies:

1.8.1.1   Cryptocurrency Transactions

Few points can be discussed here:

- *Transaction creation.* A cryptocurrency transaction involves the transfer of digital assets (cryptocurrencies) from one wallet to another. To initiate a transaction, the sender's wallet generates a transaction request that includes the recipient's wallet address, the amount to be transferred, and any additional transaction data.
- *Transaction verification.* The transaction request is broadcasted to the blockchain network, where it awaits verification. Miners or validators on the network validate the transaction by confirming its legitimacy, checking for sufficient funds, and ensuring compliance with the network's rules and consensus mechanisms.

- *Transaction inclusion in a block.* Validated transactions are grouped into blocks, which are then added to the blockchain. Miners compete to solve complex mathematical puzzles through mining processes (such as proof of work), and the first miner to solve the puzzle adds a block of transactions to the blockchain. This process ensures the security and immutability of the blockchain.
- *Confirmation and finality.* After a transaction is included in a block, it receives a certain number of confirmations as subsequent blocks are added to the blockchain. The number of confirmations indicates the level of security and finality of the transaction. More confirmations increase the difficulty and cost of reversing the transaction, enhancing trust in its validity.

1.8.1.2　Cryptocurrency Wallets

Few points can be discussed here:

- *Wallet creation.* Cryptocurrency wallets are software applications that allow users to store, manage, and interact with their digital assets. Wallets generate a unique address (a combination of public and private keys) for each user to send and receive cryptocurrencies.
- *Public and private keys.* A wallet's public key is used as the recipient address for incoming transactions, while the private key is required to access and sign outgoing transactions. Public keys are openly shared, allowing others to send funds to the wallet, while private keys must be kept secure and confidential.

Wallet types. There are several types of wallets, including:

- *Software wallets.* These wallets are applications installed on computers, smartphones, or tablets, providing convenient access to cryptocurrencies.
- *Hardware wallets.* These physical devices store private keys offline, offering enhanced security and protection against online threats.
- *Web wallets.* These wallets are accessed through web browsers and are often provided by cryptocurrency exchanges or online platforms.
- *Paper wallets.* These involve printing the public and private keys on a physical medium, such as paper, for offline storage.
- *Wallet functionality.* Wallets allow users to check their cryptocurrency balances, initiate transactions, and manage their digital assets. Wallets may also support additional features, such as transaction history, address book functionality, and integration with decentralized applications.

Note that while wallets provide a means to manage and interact with cryptocurrencies, they do not actually store the digital assets. The blockchain maintains the transaction history and ownership records, while wallets provide the means to access and control the assets associated with the user's private keys. Choosing a secure and reputable wallet, implementing strong security practices (such as keeping private keys secure and using two-factor authentication), and staying vigilant against phishing attempts are crucial for the safe management of cryptocurrencies.

1.8.2　Supply Chain Management Using Blockchain

Supply chain management is a crucial aspect of many industries, and blockchain technology has the potential to revolutionize and improve the efficiency, transparency, and security of supply chain processes. Here is how blockchain can be used in supply chain management:

- *Traceability and provenance.* Blockchain enables end-to-end traceability and provenance of goods throughout the supply chain. Each step of the supply chain, from sourcing raw materials to manufacturing, distribution, and retail, can be recorded on the blockchain, creating an immutable and transparent audit trail. This allows stakeholders to verify the origin, authenticity, quality, and conditions of products.

- *Supplier verification and auditing.* Blockchain can streamline the process of supplier verification, authentication, and auditing. By recording and verifying supplier information, certifications, and compliance documents on the blockchain, organizations can ensure that suppliers meet the required standards and regulatory requirements. This reduces the risk of counterfeit products, unethical practices, and non-compliance.
- *Quality control and certifications.* Blockchain can facilitate real-time monitoring and verification of product quality throughout the supply chain. Sensors, IoT devices, and smart contracts can be integrated with the blockchain to automatically record and validate parameters such as temperature, humidity, and handling conditions. Certifications and quality assurance documents can also be stored on the blockchain for easy access and verification.
- *Supply chain financing.* Blockchain-based platforms can provide efficient and transparent supply chain financing solutions. Smart contracts can automate payment settlements and trigger automatic financing based on predefined conditions, such as goods reaching a specific checkpoint or being delivered to the buyer. This improves cash flow and reduces the reliance on traditional financing intermediaries.
- *Inventory management and demand planning.* Blockchain can enable real-time visibility and synchronization of inventory data across the supply chain. By recording inventory levels, orders, and sales on the blockchain, stakeholders can have a unified view of inventory and demand. This improves demand forecasting and inventory management and reduces inefficiencies such as stockouts or excess inventory.
- *Counterfeit prevention.* Blockchain technology can help combat the problem of counterfeit goods in the supply chain. By recording unique product identifiers, such as serial numbers or RFID tags, on the blockchain, stakeholders can verify the authenticity and integrity of products. Consumers can also scan product codes to access information about the product's journey, ensuring they are purchasing genuine items.
- *Ethical and sustainable supply chains.* Blockchain can enhance transparency and accountability in ethical and sustainable supply chain practices. By recording data related to fair trade, labor conditions, environmental impact, and certifications on the blockchain, organizations and consumers can make informed decisions and support responsible supply chains.

Implementing blockchain-based supply chain management requires collaboration and participation from all stakeholders involved. It offers benefits such as increased efficiency, reduced costs, improved trust, and enhanced customer satisfaction. However, challenges such as scalability, data privacy, interoperability, and regulatory compliance need to be addressed for the widespread adoption of blockchain in supply chain management.

1.8.3 IDENTITY VERIFICATION AND AUTHENTICATION USING BLOCKCHAIN

Identity verification and authentication are crucial processes in various industries, and blockchain technology has the potential to enhance security, privacy, and efficiency in these areas. Here is how blockchain can be used for identity verification and authentication:

1.8.3.1 Decentralized Identity (DID)

Blockchain enables the creation of decentralized identity systems, where individuals have control over their identity information and can selectively share it with trusted entities. DIDs are unique identifiers associated with an individual's digital identity. They are stored on the blockchain and can be used for authentication and authorization purposes.

- *Self-sovereign identity (SSI).* Self-sovereign identity refers to the concept of individuals having full control over their digital identity without relying on centralized authorities. Blockchain can facilitate SSI by providing a secure and tamper-resistant platform for individuals to store their identity information. Individuals can share specific attributes or proofs of their identity without revealing their entire identity.
- *Immutable identity records.* Blockchain's immutability ensures that once identity information is recorded on the blockchain, it cannot be altered or tampered with. This helps in establishing a reliable and auditable record of an individual's identity, making it difficult for fraudsters to manipulate or forge identity documents.
- *Identity verification and attestation.* Blockchain can streamline the process of identity verification and attestation by enabling trusted entities (such as government agencies or educational institutions) to issue verifiable credentials or attestations. These credentials are cryptographically signed and recorded on the blockchain, allowing quick and secure verification of an individual's identity attributes without the need for intermediaries.
- *Secure authentication.* Blockchain can enhance authentication processes by providing a decentralized and secure method for individuals to prove their identity. With blockchain-based authentication, individuals can use their private keys associated with their digital identity to authenticate themselves in various digital interactions, such as accessing online services or authorizing transactions.
- *KYC and AML compliance.* Know your customer (KYC) and anti–money laundering (AML) regulations require businesses to verify the identities of their customers. Blockchain-based identity verification systems can simplify and streamline the KYC/AML process by securely sharing verified identity attributes between different organizations, reducing redundant identity checks and enhancing compliance.
- *Privacy and data protection.* Blockchain can enhance privacy in identity verification by allowing individuals to share only the necessary attributes or proofs of their identity without revealing their full identity. Zero-knowledge proofs and selective disclosure mechanisms can be implemented on the blockchain to ensure privacy while still providing the required level of assurance to service providers.

While blockchain offers potential benefits for identity verification and authentication, it is important to consider challenges such as scalability, interoperability, legal and regulatory frameworks, and the need for user-friendly interfaces. Collaboration between stakeholders, standardization efforts, and the development of interoperable identity protocols are crucial for the widespread adoption of blockchain-based identity systems.

1.8.4 AUTOMOTIVE INDUSTRY USING BLOCKCHAIN

The automotive industry is one sector that can benefit from the adoption of blockchain technology. Here are some potential use cases and benefits of blockchain in the automotive industry:

- *Supply chain management.* Blockchain can improve transparency and traceability in the automotive supply chain. By recording every stage of the supply chain on the blockchain, including sourcing of raw materials, manufacturing processes, and distribution, stakeholders can verify the authenticity, origin, and quality of automotive parts and components. This helps in reducing counterfeit parts, improving efficiency, and ensuring compliance with industry standards and regulations.
- *Vehicle identity and history.* Blockchain can provide a tamperproof and immutable record of a vehicle's identity and history. By recording important data such as ownership records, maintenance and repair history, accident records, and mileage on the blockchain, potential

buyers can verify the accuracy of information provided by sellers, reducing the risk of fraud and providing transparency in the used-car market.

- *Vehicle life cycle management.* Blockchain can facilitate efficient management of the entire life cycle of a vehicle, from manufacturing to disposal. It can help automate processes such as warranty management, vehicle recalls, and regulatory compliance. Smart contracts can be used to automatically enforce warranty terms and conditions, ensuring a seamless and trustworthy experience for vehicle owners.
- *Vehicle data and telematics.* Blockchain can enable secure and decentralized storage and sharing of vehicle data generated by onboard sensors and telematics systems. Vehicle data, such as performance metrics, maintenance information, and driving behavior, can be recorded on the blockchain, allowing vehicle owners to maintain control over their data and selectively share it with third parties, such as insurance providers or service centers, while maintaining privacy.
- *Mobility services and payments.* Blockchain-based platforms can facilitate secure and transparent transactions for mobility services, such as car-sharing or ride-hailing. Smart contracts can automatically execute payment agreements between service providers and users, ensuring trust, transparency, and efficiency in the transaction process.
- *Intellectual property and licensing.* Blockchain can assist in managing intellectual property rights and licensing in the automotive industry. By recording patents, trademarks, and other IP-related information on the blockchain, manufacturers can protect their innovations and easily track licensing agreements, ensuring fair compensation and reducing IP infringement.

Note that implementing blockchain in the automotive industry requires collaboration between stakeholders, adherence to data privacy regulations, and the establishment of industry-wide standards. However, the potential benefits of increased transparency, efficiency, and security make blockchain an attractive technology for transforming various aspects of the automotive sector.

1.8.5 Smart Manufacturing Using Blockchain

Smart manufacturing, also known as Industry 4.0 or the Industrial Internet of Things (IIoT), is the integration of advanced technologies and data analytics into manufacturing processes to create more efficient, flexible, and automated production systems. Blockchain technology can play a significant role in enabling and enhancing smart manufacturing. Here are some potential use cases and benefits of using blockchain in smart manufacturing:

- *Supply chain management.* Blockchain can improve supply chain management in smart manufacturing by providing transparency, traceability, and accountability. It enables secure and decentralized recording of every step in the supply chain, including sourcing of raw materials, production, logistics, and distribution. This enhances visibility, reduces counterfeit products, streamlines inventory management, and ensures compliance with quality and safety standards.
- *Quality assurance and product life cycle.* Blockchain can ensure the integrity of product quality data throughout the manufacturing process. By recording quality control checks, testing results, and certifications on the blockchain, manufacturers can create an immutable and auditable record of product quality. This enhances trust, reduces disputes, and facilitates faster resolution of issues related to product recalls or warranty claims.
- *Intellectual property protection.* Blockchain can help protect intellectual property (IP) rights in smart manufacturing. By recording information related to patents, designs, and trade secrets on the blockchain, manufacturers can establish a tamperproof and

time-stamped record of their innovations. This can help in proving ownership, preventing IP infringement, and facilitating licensing or royalty agreements.

- *Interoperability and machine-to-machine communication.* Blockchain can enable secure and efficient machine-to-machine (M2M) communication and interoperability among various devices and systems in the manufacturing environment. Blockchain-based protocols can establish trust and provide a decentralized framework for devices to securely exchange data, synchronize processes, and execute transactions autonomously.
- *Smart contracts and automation.* Blockchain-based smart contracts can automate and streamline various processes in smart manufacturing. Smart contracts are self-executing contracts with predefined conditions and actions. They can be used to automate tasks such as order management, payment settlements, supply chain events, and quality control processes. This improves efficiency, reduces the need for intermediaries, and ensures compliance with agreed-upon rules and standards.
- *Data security and privacy.* Blockchain provides enhanced security and privacy for sensitive manufacturing data. With blockchain, data can be stored in a decentralized and tamperproof manner, reducing the risk of unauthorized access or manipulation. Encryption techniques and private key management further enhance data security and control, ensuring that only authorized parties can access and interact with the data.

In summary, implementing blockchain in smart manufacturing requires collaboration between manufacturers, technology providers, and other stakeholders. Interoperability standards, data governance frameworks, and addressing scalability and performance challenges are crucial considerations. However, the benefits of increased transparency, efficiency, data integrity, and trust make blockchain a promising technology for revolutionizing the manufacturing industry.

1.8.6 BANKING AND FINANCE SECTOR USING BLOCKCHAIN

Blockchain technology has the potential to revolutionize the banking and finance industry by introducing new levels of transparency, security, efficiency, and accessibility. Here are some key use cases and benefits of using blockchain in banking and finance:

- *Payments and remittances.* Blockchain can streamline cross-border payments and remittances by eliminating intermediaries, reducing transaction costs, and increasing transaction speed. Blockchain-based payment systems enable peer-to-peer transfers, real-time settlements, and secure transactions without the need for traditional banking infrastructure. This can significantly enhance financial inclusion and accessibility, especially for individuals in underserved regions.
- *Smart contracts and automation.* Blockchain's smart contract functionality allows for the automation of contract execution and enforcement. Smart contracts are self-executing agreements with predefined conditions and actions. They can automate processes such as loan origination, trade settlements, and regulatory compliance. By removing manual interventions and relying on programmable contracts, efficiency is increased, human error is reduced, and trust is enhanced.
- *Identity management and KYC.* Blockchain can simplify and enhance "know your customer" (KYC) processes for banks and financial institutions. By utilizing blockchain for identity management, customers can have more control over their personal data, selectively sharing it with authorized entities. This reduces redundant verification processes, enhances security, and improves customer onboarding experiences while complying with regulations.
- *Trade finance and supply chain finance.* Blockchain can transform trade finance and supply chain finance by improving transparency, efficiency, and trust in transactions. By

recording and verifying trade-related information, such as purchase orders, invoices, and shipping documents, on the blockchain, stakeholders can reduce fraud, streamline trade financing processes, and enable faster settlement of transactions.

- *Asset tokenization.* Blockchain enables the tokenization of various financial assets, such as stocks, bonds, real estate, and commodities. Tokenization represents ownership of these assets on the blockchain, making them more divisible, tradable, and accessible. It opens up opportunities for fractional ownership, liquidity enhancement, and streamlined asset transfer processes.
- *Auditing and regulatory compliance.* Blockchain's transparent and immutable nature can simplify auditing processes and enhance regulatory compliance in the financial sector. By recording financial transactions and activities on the blockchain, regulators and auditors can have real-time access to auditable records, reducing the need for manual reconciliation and enhancing the detection of fraudulent activities.
- *Data security and fraud prevention.* Blockchain's decentralized and cryptographic features provide enhanced security and protection against fraud. By storing data on the blockchain, financial institutions can secure sensitive customer information, prevent unauthorized access, and mitigate the risk of data breaches.

Hence, implementing blockchain in banking and finance requires collaboration between traditional financial institutions, technology providers, and regulators. Challenges such as scalability, interoperability, legal frameworks, and privacy need to be addressed. However, the potential benefits of cost reduction, increased efficiency, enhanced security, and improved financial inclusion make blockchain a disruptive force in the banking and finance industry.

1.9   FUTURE TRENDS AND DEVELOPMENTS

1.9.1   Interoperability between Blockchains

Interoperability between blockchains refers to the ability of different blockchain networks to communicate, share data, and execute transactions seamlessly. Currently, there are multiple blockchain platforms and protocols that operate independently, which can create silos of data and limit the potential of blockchain technology. Interoperability aims to overcome these limitations by enabling connectivity and collaboration between disparate blockchain networks. Here are some key approaches to achieving interoperability:

- *Cross-chain communication protocols.* Several projects and protocols focus on developing cross-chain communication protocols that allow different blockchains to exchange information and interact with each other. These protocols enable the transfer of assets, data, and messages across multiple blockchains. Examples include Polkadot, Cosmos, and Interledger Protocol (ILP).
- *Sidechains and pegged assets.* Sidechains are separate chains that are interoperable with a main blockchain. They enable the transfer of assets between the main chain and the sidechain, providing scalability and flexibility. Pegged assets, such as wrapped tokens or stablecoins, represent assets from one blockchain on another blockchain. These assets can be moved between different chains, allowing interoperability.
- *Atomic swaps.* Atomic swaps are direct peer-to-peer exchanges of cryptocurrencies between different blockchains without the need for intermediaries. They utilize smart contracts to ensure that the swap is executed only if both parties fulfill the predefined conditions. Atomic swaps enable cross-chain trading and facilitate interoperability between blockchain networks.
- *Blockchain bridges.* Blockchain bridges are mechanisms that establish a connection between two or more blockchains, allowing them to share data and assets. Bridges can be

implemented using various techniques, including relay chains, hash time-locked contracts (HTLCs), oracles, and secure multi-party computation (MPC). Bridges facilitate interoperability by enabling the transfer of assets and messages between connected blockchains.

- *Interoperability standards.* Standardization efforts play a crucial role in achieving interoperability. Various organizations and initiatives are working on developing common standards and protocols that promote interoperability between different blockchain platforms. These standards define how blockchains communicate, exchange data, and interact with each other, making it easier for developers to build interoperable solutions.

Interoperability between blockchains is still a developing field, and there are ongoing research and development efforts to address the technical and logistical challenges. Achieving seamless interoperability requires collaboration between blockchain projects, adoption of common standards, and the development of robust cross-chain communication protocols. Ultimately, interoperability enhances the utility and scalability of blockchain technology, enabling the creation of more powerful and interconnected decentralized applications and ecosystems.

1.9.2 Integration of Blockchain with Emerging Technologies (AI, IoT, AR, VR, Cloud Computing, Etc.)

Integrating blockchain with emerging technologies can unlock new possibilities and enhance the capabilities of these technologies. Here is how blockchain can be integrated with some of the prominent emerging technologies:

- *Artificial intelligence (AI).* Blockchain can enhance AI by providing a decentralized and trusted data source. Blockchain can securely store and validate data used by AI algorithms, ensuring data integrity and preventing tampering or unauthorized access. It can also enable transparent and auditable data sharing between multiple AI systems and facilitate the creation of AI models through decentralized collaborations.
- *Internet of Things (IoT).* Blockchain can address key challenges in IoT, such as data security, privacy, and interoperability. By combining blockchain with IoT, devices can securely and autonomously interact with each other, exchange data, and execute transactions. Blockchain can enable tamperproof storage of IoT device data, decentralized authentication, and peer-to-peer transactions between IoT devices.
- *Augmented reality (AR) and virtual reality (VR).* Blockchain can enhance AR and VR experiences by providing verifiable ownership and provenance of digital assets. Blockchain-based digital asset marketplaces can enable creators and users to securely trade and exchange AR/VR content, ensuring authenticity and preventing unauthorized duplication or distribution.
- *Cloud computing.* Blockchain can enhance the security and privacy of cloud computing environments. Blockchain can enable decentralized and immutable recordkeeping of cloud transactions, ensuring transparency and accountability. It can also enhance identity and access management, enabling secure and granular control over cloud resources and data.
- *Edge computing.* Combining blockchain with edge computing can enhance the security, efficiency, and privacy of edge devices and networks. Blockchain can provide decentralized consensus, enable secure data sharing and processing at the edge, and facilitate trusted interactions between edge devices and entities.
- *Big data analytics.* Blockchain can enhance big data analytics by providing a trustworthy and auditable data source. Blockchain can enable transparent and secure data sharing and incentivize data contributors through tokenization. It can also facilitate data marketplaces and decentralized data governance models, empowering individuals to control and monetize their data.

- *Machine learning (ML).* Integrating blockchain with machine learning can enhance the transparency and fairness of ML models. Blockchain can provide an immutable and auditable record of ML model training data, ensuring data integrity and preventing bias or manipulation. It can also enable decentralized and privacy-preserving federated learning approaches, where multiple parties collaborate to train ML models without sharing sensitive data.

Integrating blockchain with emerging technologies requires collaboration between different technology communities, standardization efforts, and the development of interoperable protocols. These integrations can bring numerous benefits, such as enhanced security, privacy, transparency, and decentralized governance, opening up new possibilities for innovation and transforming various industries.

1.9.3 REGULATORY AND LEGAL ISSUES TOWARD BLOCKCHAIN

The emergence of blockchain technology has presented various regulatory and legal challenges due to its unique characteristics and decentralized nature. Here are some key regulatory and legal issues that arise in relation to blockchain:

- *Jurisdiction and governance.* Blockchain operates across borders, raising questions about jurisdiction and which legal frameworks apply. Different countries have varying regulations regarding cryptocurrencies, initial coin offerings (ICOs), smart contracts, and blockchain-based activities. Establishing clear jurisdictional boundaries and developing governance models that accommodate decentralized systems is a significant challenge.
- *Data privacy and protection.* Blockchain's immutability and transparency can conflict with data privacy regulations, such as the European Union's General Data Protection Regulation (GDPR). Storing personal data on a blockchain may not align with the right to be forgotten or data rectification requirements. Solutions that balance privacy rights and blockchain transparency need to be developed.
- *Anti–money laundering (AML) and know your customer (KYC).* Blockchain-based transactions can potentially be used for illicit activities due to their pseudonymous nature. Regulators are concerned about money laundering, terrorist financing, and the lack of KYC procedures in some blockchain projects. Implementing AML and KYC measures, such as identity verification and transaction monitoring, while preserving the decentralized nature of blockchain, is a complex challenge.
- *Securities regulations.* Initial coin offerings (ICOs) and token sales have attracted regulatory scrutiny as they may fall under securities regulations. Determining whether a token qualifies as a security depends on factors such as the token's characteristics, distribution model, and investor expectations. Regulators are working to develop clear guidelines to distinguish between utility tokens and security tokens and to ensure compliance with securities laws.
- *Consumer protection.* Blockchain technology poses consumer protection challenges. Fraudulent activities, scams, and hacking incidents can occur in blockchain-based projects and cryptocurrency exchanges. Regulators are working to protect consumers by enforcing transparency, disclosure requirements, and investor education initiatives.
- *Intellectual property.* Blockchain's public and open nature can complicate intellectual property (IP) protection. Blockchain projects may involve sharing code, smart contract templates, or digital assets that raise questions about copyright, patents, and ownership rights. Clarifying IP rights in decentralized environments and ensuring adequate protection are an ongoing challenge.

- *Taxation.* The taxation of cryptocurrencies and blockchain-based activities is a complex issue. Determining the tax treatment of cryptocurrency transactions, token sales, mining activities, and decentralized finance (DeFi) protocols is still evolving, and regulations may vary across jurisdictions.

Regulators and policymakers worldwide are actively engaging with blockchain technology to strike a balance between fostering innovation and protecting the interests of users and society. Efforts are underway to establish regulatory sandboxes, develop industry standards, enhance cybersecurity measures, and create frameworks that accommodate blockchain's potential while addressing legal and regulatory challenges. Collaboration between blockchain stakeholders, industry participants, and regulators is crucial to ensure responsible and sustainable growth of the technology.

1.9.4 POTENTIAL IMPACT AND FUTURE POSSIBILITIES OF BLOCKCHAIN

Blockchain technology has the potential to have a profound impact on various aspects of our society, economy, and technology landscape. Here are some potential impacts and future possibilities of blockchain:

- *Financial inclusion.* Blockchain can provide financial services to the unbanked and under-banked populations worldwide. By enabling peer-to-peer transactions, reducing transaction costs, and eliminating the need for intermediaries, blockchain can increase access to financial services, such as payments, remittances, and lending, for individuals who are currently excluded from traditional banking systems.
- *Supply chain transparency.* Blockchain can enhance supply chain management by providing a transparent and immutable record of every transaction and movement of goods. This improves traceability, reduces counterfeiting, enhances product quality, and ensures ethical sourcing. Consumers can have verifiable information about the origin, authenticity, and journey of products, fostering trust and accountability.
- *Decentralized identity.* Blockchain-based identity systems can empower individuals with ownership and control over their personal data. Digital identities stored on the blockchain can enable secure and privacy-enhancing identity verification, simplifying authentication processes and reducing the risk of identity theft. It can also facilitate seamless cross-border identity verification and improve access to various services.
- *Voting and governance.* Blockchain can revolutionize voting systems by ensuring transparency, security, and immutability of votes. Blockchain-based voting platforms can eliminate voter fraud, increase participation, and provide an auditable trail of votes. Additionally, blockchain's decentralized governance models can enable more transparent and inclusive decision-making processes in organizations and communities.
- *Intellectual property rights.* Blockchain can transform the management and protection of intellectual property rights. By creating a tamperproof and time-stamped record of creations, blockchain can establish proof of ownership, simplify licensing, and automate royalty payments. This can revolutionize the way artists, musicians, writers, and inventors manage and monetize their creations.
- *Decentralized Internet and content distribution.* Blockchain-based decentralized protocols can disrupt the traditional centralized model of the Internet. By incentivizing content creators and consumers, blockchain can enable peer-to-peer content sharing, reduce reliance on intermediaries, and ensure fair compensation for creators. This can promote freedom of speech, protect against censorship, and foster a more open and democratic digital ecosystem.
- *Energy and sustainability.* Blockchain can play a significant role in the transition to a more sustainable energy system. By enabling peer-to-peer energy trading, tracking renewable

energy generation, and incentivizing energy conservation, blockchain can optimize energy distribution, reduce reliance on fossil fuels, and promote a decentralized and resilient energy grid.

- *Interoperability and integration.* As blockchain technology matures, the interoperability between different blockchain networks and integration with existing systems will improve. This will facilitate the seamless exchange of assets, data, and services across multiple blockchain platforms, creating a more connected and efficient ecosystem.

The future possibilities of blockchain are vast and continually evolving. However, it is important to note that realizing these possibilities requires addressing technical challenges, regulatory frameworks, scalability concerns, and ensuring widespread adoption. Collaboration between industry players, governments, and the wider community will be crucial to harness the full potential of blockchain technology and drive meaningful change across various sectors of society.

1.10 CONCLUSION

Blockchain is a cutting-edge technology with a lot of potential for both the present and the future, but it also faces a lot of obstacles that must be surmounted. This decentralized, transactional ledger storage foundation has improved and sparked innovations all around the world. It enables users to verify, safeguard/store, and synchronize the information contained in a data sheet that is being mined and worked on by numerous people. It is anticipated that blockchain would complement trusted transactions due to the large and massive possibilities of applications. The introduction of Bitcoins is what brought blockchain technology and its architecture the most attention. Blockchain is a cutting-edge technology that will undoubtedly exist and eventually have a significant impact on many important sectors. The development of this technology, which is thought to be the "heart and soul" of Web 3.0, appears to be happening far sooner than expected. Even though blockchain is frequently linked to cryptocurrencies, this is no longer the only area of interest. Among the numerous areas where blockchain has achieved revolutionary advances are the health sector, supply chain, transportation, finance, etc. The financial and insurance industries are setting the pace for the explosive growth of the blockchain business. With almost 90 countries currently investing in central bank digital currencies, it is clear from present and potential future trends that blockchain technology is changing the traditional financial system. This chapter offers a thorough analysis and assessment of what blockchain is, its architecture and structure, its development over time, its types, its uses, and the potential threats.

REFERENCES

1. Amit Kumar Tyagi and Meghna Manoj Nair. 2022. Preserving Privacy Using Distributed Ledger Technology in Intelligent Transportation System. In: *Proceedings of the 2022 Fourteenth International Conference on Contemporary Computing (IC3–2022).* Association for Computing Machinery, New York, NY, USA, pp. 582–590. doi: 10.1145/3549206.3549306.
2. Atharva Deshmukh, Disha Patil, Amit Kumar Tyagi, S.S. Arumugam and Arumugam. 2022. Recent Trends on Blockchain for Internet of Things based Applications: Open Issues and Future Trends. In: *Proceedings of the 2022 Fourteenth International Conference on Contemporary Computing (IC3–2022).* Association for Computing Machinery, New York, NY, USA, pp. 484–492. doi: 10.1145/3549206.3549289.
3. M.M. Nair and A.K. Tyagi. 2022. Preserving Privacy Using Blockchain Technology in Autonomous Vehicles. In: Giri, D., Mandal, J.K., Sakurai, K. and De, D. (eds) *Proceedings of International Conference on Network Security and Blockchain Technology. ICNSBT 2021. Lecture Notes in Networks and Systems,* vol. 481. Springer, Singapore. doi: 10.1007/978-981-19-3182-6_19.
4. H.S.K. Sheth, A.K. Ilavarasi and A.K. Tyagi. 2022. Deep Learning, Blockchain Based Multi-Layered Authentication and Security Architectures. In: *2022 International Conference on Applied Artificial Intelligence and Computing (ICAAIC),* pp. 476–485. doi: 10.1109/ICAAIC53929.2022.9793179.

5. A.A. Pandey, T.F. Fernandez, R. Bansal and A.K. Tyagi. 2022. Maintaining Scalability in Blockchain. In: Abraham, A., Gandhi, N., Hanne, T., Hong, T.P., Nogueira Rios, T. and Ding, W. (eds) *Intelligent Systems Design and Applications. ISDA 2021. Lecture Notes in Networks and Systems*, vol. 418. Springer, Cham. doi: 10.1007/978-3-030-96308-8_4.
6. D. Agrawal, R. Bansal, T.F. Fernandez and A.K. Tyagi. 2022. Blockchain Integrated Machine Learning for Training Autonomous Cars. In: *Hybrid Intelligent Systems. HIS 2021. Lecture Notes in Networks and Systems*, vol. 420. Springer, Cham. doi: 10.1007/978-3-030-96305-7_4.
7. Amit Kumar Tyagi. 2021. Analysis of Security and Privacy Aspects of Blockchain Technologies from Smart Era' Perspective: The Challenges and a Way Forward. In: *Recent Trends in Blockchain for Information Systems Security and Privacy*. CRC Press.
8. Amit Kumar Tyagi, G. Rekha and Shabnam Kumari. 2021. Applications of Blockchain Technologies in Digital Forensic and Threat Hunting. In: *Recent Trends in Blockchain for Information Systems Security and Privacy*. CRC Press.
9. S.U. Aswathy, Amit Kumar Tyagi and Shabnam Kumari. 2021. The Future of Edge Computing with Blockchain Technology: Possibility of Threats, Opportunities and Challenges. In: *Recent Trends in Blockchain for Information Systems Security and Privacy*. CRC Press.
10. I. Tibrewal, M. Srivastava and A.K. Tyagi. 2022. Blockchain Technology for Securing Cyber-Infrastructure and Internet of Things Networks. In: Tyagi, A.K., Abraham, A. and Kaklauskas, A. (eds) *Intelligent Interactive Multimedia Systems for e-Healthcare Applications*. Springer, Singapore. doi: 10.1007/978-981-16-6542-4_1.
11. A.K. Tyagi, T.F. Fernandez and S.U. Aswathy. 2020. Blockchain and Aadhaar Based Electronic Voting System. In: *2020 4th International Conference on Electronics, Communication and Aerospace Technology (ICECA)*. Coimbatore, pp. 498–504. doi: 10.1109/ICECA49313.2020.9297655.
12. Amit Kumar Tyagi, S.U. Aswathy, G. Aghila and N. Sreenath. 2021, October. AARIN: Affordable, Accurate, Reliable and Innovative Mechanism to Protect a Medical Cyber-Physical System Using Blockchain Technology. *IJIN*, vol. 2, pp. 175–183.
13. Neha Sawal, Anjali Yadav, Amit Kumar Tyagi, N. Sreenath and G. Rekha. 2019, May 15. *Necessity of Blockchain for Building Trust in Today's Applications: An Useful Explanation from User's Perspective*. SSRN. https://ssrn.com/abstract=3388558 or doi: 10.2139/ssrn.3388558.
14. Siddharth M. Nair, Varsha Ramesh and Amit Kumar Tyagi. 2021. Issues and Challenges (Privacy, Security, and Trust) in Blockchain-Based Applications. In: *Opportunities and Challenges for Blockchain Technology in Autonomous Vehicles*, p. 14. doi: 10.4018/978-1-7998-3295-9.ch012.
15. S. Mishra and A.K. Tyagi. 2019. Intrusion Detection in Internet of Things (IoTs) Based Applications Using Blockchain Technology. In: *2019 Third International Conference on I-SMAC (IoT in Social, Mobile, Analytics and Cloud) (I-SMAC)*, pp. 123–128. doi: 10.1109/I-SMAC47947.2019.9032557.
16. R. Varsha et al. 2020, January 1. Deep Learning Based Blockchain Solution for Preserving Privacy in Future Vehicles. *International Journal of Hybrid Intelligent System*, vol. 16, Issue 4, pp. 223–236.
17. V. Jayaprakash and A.K. Tyagi. 2022. Security Optimization of Resource-Constrained Internet of Healthcare Things (IoHT) Devices Using Asymmetric Cryptography for Blockchain Network. In: Giri, D., Mandal, J.K., Sakurai, K. and De, D. (eds) *Proceedings of International Conference on Network Security and Blockchain Technology. ICNSBT 2021. Lecture Notes in Networks and Systems*, vol. 481. Springer, Singapore. doi: 10.1007/978-981-19-3182-6_18.
18. Varsha Jayaprakash and Amit Kumar Tyagi. Security Optimization of Resource-Constrained Internet of Healthcare Things (IoHT) Devices Using Lightweight Cryptography. In: *Information Security Practices for the Internet of Things, 5G, and Next-Generation Wireless Networks*. doi: 10.4018/978-1-6684-3921-0.ch009.
19. A.K. Tyagi, S. Chandrasekaran and N. Sreenath. 2022. Blockchain Technology: A New Technology for Creating Distributed and Trusted Computing Environment. In: *2022 International Conference on Applied Artificial Intelligence and Computing (ICAAIC)*, pp. 1348–1354. doi: 10.1109/ICAAIC53929.2022.9792702.
20. A.K. Tyagi, D. Agarwal and N. Sreenath. 2022. SecVT: Securing the Vehicles of Tomorrow Using Blockchain Technology. In: *2022 International Conference on Computer Communication and Informatics (ICCCI)*, pp. 1–6. doi: 10.1109/ICCCI54379.2022.9740965.

2 Emerging Applications of Blockchain in the Automobile Manufacturing Process

Nizar M. Alsharari

2.1 INTRODUCTION

In the ever-evolving landscape of the automotive industry, technological advancements continue to drive innovation and revolutionize traditional manufacturing practices. Among the array of disruptive technologies, blockchain stands out as a groundbreaking solution with the potential to reshape the core pillars of automobile manufacturing (Alsharari, 2021). Originally known as the underlying technology powering cryptocurrencies like Bitcoin, blockchain has transcended its digital currency roots and emerged as a transformative force across diverse industries (Karim and Taheri, 2019). Now, the automotive sector finds itself on the precipice of a profound paradigm shift, as blockchain technology promises to revolutionize the way vehicles are designed, manufactured, and serviced (Kamath and Lobo, 2019)

The automotive industry has long embraced cutting-edge technologies to optimize production processes, enhance supply chain management, and deliver exceptional customer experiences. From robotics and artificial intelligence to the Internet of Things (IoT), every innovation has been harnessed to drive efficiency and competitiveness. As the automotive sector continues its journey toward a more sustainable and connected future, blockchain technology emerges as a transformative enabler for this ambitious vision (Karim and Taheri, 2019; Kamath and Lobo, 2019).

This chapter dives into the captivating realm of blockchain technology in automobile manufacturing, exploring its transformative potential and the myriad ways it promises to optimize every facet of vehicle production. By providing a secure, transparent, and decentralized ledger, blockchain technology is set to revolutionize supply chain management by offering real-time tracking of components and ensuring the traceability of raw materials from source to assembly line (Sharma and Dhar, 2020). The inherent characteristics of blockchain, such as immutability and transparency, contribute to an enhanced level of data integrity and security. By creating an unalterable record of transactions, blockchain mitigates the risks of counterfeit parts, fraud, and unauthorized access, thereby elevating consumer trust and confidence in the automotive products they purchase (Sharma and Dhar, 2020).

However, while the promises of blockchain technology are undoubtedly alluring, challenges persist in its widespread implementation across the automotive ecosystem. Scalability, interoperability, and regulatory compliance remain key hurdles to overcome (Walch, 2018). This chapter delves into these challenges and explores the ongoing efforts of industry stakeholders to address them, ensuring the seamless integration of blockchain into the automotive manufacturing landscape. In conclusion, the convergence of blockchain technology and automobile manufacturing represents a seismic shift that will forever redefine the industry's trajectory (Swan, 2015). By embracing this transformative technology, automotive manufacturers can unlock new levels of efficiency, transparency, and customer-centricity, setting the stage for a future of sustainable mobility and innovation.

DOI: 10.1201/9781003450306-3

2.2 DEFINE BLOCKCHAIN TECHNOLOGY

Blockchain technology is a decentralized and distributed digital ledger that records transactions and data across multiple computers or nodes in a network. It is designed to provide transparency, security, and immutability to the information stored within it. In a blockchain, each transaction or data entry, known as a block, is linked to the previous block, creating a chain of blocks. This chain forms a chronological and unalterable record of all transactions or data entries, which is stored across multiple nodes in the network. One of the key features of blockchain is its decentralized nature. The ledger is maintained and updated by a network of participants, known as nodes, rather than relying on a central authority. This decentralization ensures that no single entity has complete control over the data, making it resistant to tampering, fraud, and censorship (Niranjanamurthy et al., 2019).

Blockchain also employs cryptographic techniques to secure the data stored within it. Each block contains a unique cryptographic hash which acts as a digital fingerprint of the block's data. Any modification to the data in a block would require recalculating the hash of that block and all subsequent blocks, making it computationally infeasible to alter the blockchain's history (Politou et al., 2019). Furthermore, blockchain technology can utilize consensus mechanisms, such as proof of work (PoW) or proof of stake (PoS), to validate and agree upon the contents of the blockchain. These mechanisms ensure that participants in the network reach a consensus on the validity of transactions and the order in which they are added to the blockchain (Yadav et al., 2023).

Blockchain technology is most commonly associated with cryptocurrencies, like Bitcoin, but its potential applications extend beyond digital currencies. It can be utilized in various industries, including finance, supply chain management, healthcare, voting systems, and more, to provide transparency, security, and efficiency in recording and verifying transactions and data (Sarmah, 2018).

2.3 BLOCKCHAIN TECHNOLOGY AND AUTOMOBILE MANUFACTURING

Blockchain technology has emerged as a groundbreaking innovation with the potential to revolutionize various industries, including automobile manufacturing. Blockchain is a distributed ledger technology that enables secure, transparent, and immutable recordkeeping of transactions. It was initially introduced as the underlying technology for cryptocurrencies like Bitcoin, but its applications have extended far beyond digital currencies. Blockchain technology operates on a decentralized network of computers, known as nodes, where each node maintains a copy of the entire blockchain. Instead of relying on a centralized authority, blockchain utilizes consensus algorithms to validate and verify transactions, ensuring the integrity of the data stored on the network (Abeyratne and Monfared, 2016).

The fundamental characteristics of blockchain technology include:

- *Decentralization.* Blockchain eliminates the need for a central authority by distributing the control and verification of transactions across a network of nodes. This decentralization enhances transparency and reduces the risk of a single point of failure.
- *Transparency and immutability.* All transactions recorded on a blockchain are transparent and can be accessed by all participants. Once a transaction is added to the blockchain, it is nearly impossible to alter or tamper with the data, ensuring the immutability of the records.
- *Security.* Blockchain utilizes cryptographic algorithms to secure the data stored on the network. Transactions are bundled into blocks and linked together using cryptographic hashes, creating a chain of blocks. This makes the blockchain resistant to unauthorized modifications and fraudulent activities.
- *Smart contracts.* Blockchain platforms often support the execution of smart contracts, which are self-executing agreements with predefined conditions. Smart contracts automate and enforce the terms of an agreement, eliminating the need for intermediaries and enhancing efficiency.

2.4   APPLICATIONS OF BLOCKCHAIN IN AUTOMOBILE MANUFACTURING

Blockchain technology has the potential to transform various aspects of the automobile manufacturing industry. Here are some key applications:

- *Supply chain management.* Blockchain can provide transparency and traceability in the automotive supply chain. By recording every step of the supply chain process on the blockchain, manufacturers can ensure the authenticity and provenance of components, reduce counterfeiting risks, and improve quality control.
- *Vehicle identity and ownership.* Blockchain can be used to create a secure and tamper-proof system for verifying the identity and ownership of vehicles. Each vehicle can have a unique digital identity recorded on the blockchain, allowing for efficient transfer of ownership and reducing the risk of fraud.
- *Maintenance and service records.* Blockchain can enable a decentralized and transparent recordkeeping system for vehicle maintenance and service history. This ensures that the maintenance records are accurate, accessible, and tamperproof, enhancing trust between vehicle owners, manufacturers, and service providers.
- *Autonomous vehicle data sharing.* As autonomous vehicles generate massive amounts of data, blockchain can facilitate secure and decentralized data sharing between vehicles, manufacturers, and other stakeholders. This can enable collaborative development of autonomous driving technologies and improve road safety.
- *Car-sharing and rental services.* Blockchain can enable peer-to-peer car-sharing and rental services by providing a secure platform for transactions, identity verification, and smart contracts. This eliminates the need for intermediaries, reduces costs, and enhances trust among participants.

These are just a few examples of how blockchain technology can impact the automobile manufacturing industry. As the technology continues to evolve and mature, more innovative applications are likely to emerge, reshaping the way vehicles are manufactured, operated, and maintained.

2.5   THE OBJECTIVES OF BLOCKCHAIN TECHNOLOGY IN THE AUTOMOBILE INDUSTRY

The objectives of implementing blockchain technology in the automobile industry can vary depending on the specific use cases and stakeholders involved. However, some common objectives include (Alsharari, 2021):

1. *Enhancing transparency.* Blockchain technology can provide transparency and visibility into various aspects of the automobile industry. By recording and storing data on a decentralized ledger, stakeholders can access accurate and trustworthy information about the supply chain, vehicle history, ownership, maintenance, and more. This transparency helps build trust among participants and reduces information asymmetry.
2. *Improving security.* Security is a crucial objective in the automobile industry, and blockchain technology can contribute to enhancing the security of data and transactions. The cryptographic algorithms and decentralized nature of blockchain make it highly resistant to tampering and fraud. By utilizing blockchain for functions such as identity verification, ownership transfer, and supply chain management, the industry can mitigate risks associated with counterfeit parts, identity theft, and fraudulent activities.
3. *Streamlining supply chain processes.* The automotive supply chain is complex, involving multiple parties and processes. Blockchain technology can streamline and optimize these processes by providing real-time visibility into the movement of components, ensuring

the authenticity of parts, and automating transactional processes. By eliminating manual paperwork, reducing delays, and enhancing traceability, blockchain can improve efficiency and reduce costs in the supply chain.

4. *Facilitating efficient and secure transactions.* Blockchain technology can enable secure and efficient transactions within the automobile industry. With blockchain-based platforms, stakeholders can conduct peer-to-peer transactions, such as vehicle sales, rentals, and sharing, without the need for intermediaries. Smart contracts can automate and enforce the terms of these transactions, ensuring trust and reducing the administrative burden.

5. *Enabling data sharing and collaboration.* Data sharing and collaboration are becoming increasingly important in the automotive industry, particularly with the rise of connected and autonomous vehicles. Blockchain technology can provide a secure and decentralized platform for sharing data among vehicles, manufacturers, service providers, and other stakeholders. This collaborative approach to data sharing can accelerate the development of advanced technologies, such as autonomous driving, and drive innovation within the industry.

6. *Enhancing customer experience.* Blockchain technology has the potential to enhance the overall customer experience in the automobile industry. By ensuring the transparency and accuracy of vehicle history, maintenance records, and ownership information, customers can make more informed decisions. Additionally, blockchain-based platforms for car-sharing and rental services can provide a seamless and secure experience for customers, simplifying processes and reducing friction.

7. *Compliance and regulatory benefits.* The automobile industry is subject to various regulations and compliance requirements. Blockchain technology can facilitate compliance by providing an immutable and auditable record of transactions and activities. This can help stakeholders demonstrate adherence to regulations, streamline auditing processes, and ensure compliance with data privacy and security standards.

By aligning blockchain technology with these objectives, the automobile industry can unlock numerous benefits, including increased efficiency, improved trust, reduced costs, and enhanced innovation. However, it is essential to carefully consider the specific challenges, implementation considerations, and collaboration among stakeholders to realize the full potential of blockchain in the industry.

2.6 HISTORY FOR BLOCKCHAIN TECHNOLOGY FOR AUTOMOBILE MANUFACTURING

Blockchain technology's application in the automobile manufacturing industry is relatively new, but it has gained attention and traction in recent years. Here is a brief history of blockchain technology in the context of automobile manufacturing:

2016–2017: Initial explorations and proof of concepts. During this period, automobile manufacturers and industry players began exploring the potential of blockchain technology. Several proofs of concepts and pilot projects were initiated to test the feasibility and benefits of applying blockchain in areas such as supply chain management, vehicle identity, and ownership tracking.

2018–2019: Supply chain management and traceability. The focus shifted toward supply chain management and traceability, where blockchain technology could improve transparency and trust in the automotive supply chain. Projects and partnerships emerged, aiming to enhance the traceability of parts, components, and raw materials, reducing counterfeiting, ensuring quality control, and enabling efficient recalls.

2019–2020: Consortiums and collaborations. Automobile manufacturers and industry consortia started collaborating to accelerate blockchain adoption. Consortia, such as MOBI (Mobility Open Blockchain Initiative), were formed to develop standards, share best practices, and foster collaboration among manufacturers, suppliers, technology providers, and other stakeholders in the automotive industry. These efforts aimed to establish a common framework for blockchain implementation and accelerate its adoption across the industry.

2020–2021: Intellectual property protection and smart contracts. Blockchain's potential in protecting intellectual property and enabling smart contracts gained attention. Automobile manufacturers explored blockchain's capabilities to secure and time-stamp patents, design blueprints, and other sensitive information. Additionally, the automation and efficiency offered by smart contracts attracted interest, especially in streamlining transactions, agreements, and payments within the automotive ecosystem.

2022–present: Advancements in autonomous vehicles and mobility services. As autonomous vehicles and mobility services gained momentum, blockchain's potential in enabling secure and decentralized vehicle networks, data sharing, and trustless transactions became more apparent. Blockchain's role in coordinating autonomous vehicles, facilitating peer-to-peer car-sharing, and creating secure mobility ecosystems has been a focus for both automotive manufacturers and technology companies.

Overall, the history of blockchain technology in the automobile manufacturing industry is still evolving. While many pilot projects, proofs of concepts, and collaborations have emerged, widespread adoption is still in its early stages. As the technology matures, addressing challenges related to scalability, interoperability, privacy, and regulatory frameworks will be crucial to unlock the full potential of blockchain in automobile manufacturing.

2.7 DEVELOPMENTS OF BLOCKCHAIN TECHNOLOGY IN THE AUTOMOBILE MANUFACTURING

Blockchain technology has witnessed several developments in the automobile manufacturing industry (Alsharari, 2021). Here are some notable advancements:

1. *Supply chain integration.* Blockchain has been used to enhance supply chain integration in the automobile manufacturing sector. Manufacturers, suppliers, and other stakeholders can securely share data and track the movement of parts and components in real time. This improves transparency, reduces delays, and enables more efficient inventory management.
2. *Authentication and anti-counterfeiting.* Blockchain has been leveraged to combat counterfeiting and ensure the authenticity of automotive parts and components. By recording the history and provenance of each item on the blockchain, manufacturers can verify the legitimacy of products, reducing the risk of counterfeit parts entering the supply chain.
3. *Decentralized vehicle identity.* Blockchain enables the creation of decentralized and immutable vehicle identity records. This includes manufacturing information, maintenance records, ownership transfers, and accident history. The use of blockchain ensures the integrity and immutability of this data, providing a trustworthy source of information for manufacturers, buyers, and regulators.
4. *Smart contracts for automotive transactions.* Smart contracts on the blockchain facilitate automated and secure transactions in the automotive industry. For example, when purchasing a vehicle, smart contracts can handle ownership transfers, payments, and compliance checks, reducing paperwork and streamlining the buying process.
5. *Data sharing and monetization.* Blockchain technology allows for secure and controlled data sharing among various stakeholders. Automobile manufacturers can share vehicle

data, such as performance metrics and sensor readings, with authorized parties, like service providers or researchers. Blockchain-based platforms have emerged to facilitate the exchange of data, enabling manufacturers to monetize data while maintaining privacy and control.

6. *Autonomous vehicle networks and communication.* Blockchain can enhance the communication and coordination among autonomous vehicles. Through a decentralized network, vehicles can securely share information, such as location, speed, and intent, enabling safer and more efficient autonomous driving. Blockchain ensures the integrity and trustworthiness of the shared data, fostering collaboration and interoperability among autonomous vehicles.

7. *Collaborative development and standards.* Industry consortia and collaborations have emerged to establish standards and best practices for blockchain implementation in the automobile manufacturing sector. These efforts aim to promote interoperability, ensure data privacy, and create a common framework for blockchain adoption across the industry.

While these developments show promise, widespread adoption of blockchain technology in automobile manufacturing is still evolving. Challenges such as scalability, interoperability, regulatory frameworks, and industry-wide collaboration need to be addressed to unlock the full potential of blockchain in this sector.

2.8 STRATEGIES OF BLOCKCHAIN TECHNOLOGY IN THE AUTOMOBILE MANUFACTURING INDUSTRY

The implementation of blockchain technology in the automobile manufacturing industry offers several potential strategies that can revolutionize various aspects of the industry. Here, we will discuss these strategies in more detail and explore their implications:

1. *Supply chain transparency and traceability.* Blockchain technology can enhance supply chain transparency by providing a decentralized and immutable ledger of transactions. Manufacturers can track and verify the movement of components, parts, and raw materials throughout the supply chain, ensuring authenticity and reducing the risk of counterfeit or substandard products. This strategy promotes trust among stakeholders and enables faster identification and resolution of supply chain issues.

2. *Streamlined payments and smart contracts.* Blockchain-enabled smart contracts can automate and streamline payment processes between manufacturers, suppliers, and other stakeholders. Smart contracts are self-executing agreements that automatically enforce predefined rules when certain conditions are met. By utilizing blockchain-based payments and smart contracts, manufacturers can reduce transaction costs, eliminate intermediaries, and enhance the efficiency of financial operations.

3. *Vehicle life cycle management.* Blockchain technology can facilitate comprehensive vehicle life cycle management, including production, sales, ownership, and maintenance. By recording each vehicle's production history, ownership transfers, maintenance records, and repair information on the blockchain, manufacturers and customers can have access to an immutable and transparent vehicle history. This strategy improves trust, simplifies processes like vehicle resale, and enables proactive maintenance and warranty management.

4. *Enhanced data security and privacy.* Blockchain's cryptographic features can enhance data security and privacy in the automobile manufacturing industry. By storing data on a distributed ledger with advanced encryption techniques, manufacturers can ensure the integrity and confidentiality of sensitive information. This strategy is particularly crucial when dealing with customer data, intellectual property, and proprietary manufacturing processes.

5. *Digital identity and authentication.* Blockchain technology can enable the creation and management of digital identities for vehicles, manufacturers, suppliers, and customers. Digital identities can be used for authentication and authorization purposes, facilitating secure access to data and services. Manufacturers can leverage blockchain-based identity solutions to establish trust among stakeholders and prevent unauthorized access or tampering of critical systems.

6. *Collaborative ecosystems and innovation.* Blockchain technology fosters collaborative ecosystems among different stakeholders in the automobile manufacturing industry. By sharing data and resources on a decentralized platform, manufacturers, suppliers, service providers, and customers can collaborate more effectively. This strategy promotes innovation, enables faster product development cycles, and facilitates the emergence of new business models and services.

7. *Sustainability and carbon footprint management.* Blockchain technology can help in monitoring and managing the environmental impact of automobile manufacturing. By tracking and recording data related to carbon emissions, energy consumption, and sustainable sourcing on the blockchain, manufacturers can demonstrate their commitment to sustainability. This strategy promotes accountability, enables carbon offset programs, and aligns with growing consumer demand for eco-friendly practices.

Overall, the strategies of blockchain technology in the automobile manufacturing industry focus on enhancing transparency, efficiency, trust, and collaboration. By adopting these strategies, manufacturers can optimize supply chain operations, streamline processes, ensure data security, and create innovative solutions that address the evolving needs of the industry and its stakeholders.

2.9   BLOCKCHAIN TECHNOLOGY FOR SELF-DRIVING CAR DEVELOPMENT

Blockchain technology can play a significant role in the development and deployment of self-driving cars. Here are several ways in which blockchain can benefit the self-driving car industry:

1. *Data sharing and security.* Self-driving cars generate massive amounts of data, including sensor data, mapping information, and vehicle performance metrics. Blockchain can provide a secure and decentralized platform for sharing this data among vehicles, manufacturers, service providers, and other stakeholders. By utilizing cryptographic techniques, blockchain ensures data integrity, privacy, and protection against unauthorized access. This shared data can improve the accuracy of self-driving algorithms, enhance safety, and facilitate collaboration among different entities in the ecosystem.

2. *Autonomous vehicle coordination.* Blockchain's distributed ledger can enable secure and trustless communication and coordination among autonomous vehicles. Through blockchain, self-driving cars can exchange information, such as their location, speed, and intentions, without relying on a centralized authority. This decentralized coordination enhances safety, improves traffic flow, and enables efficient decision-making in real time.

3. *Reputation and trust systems.* Blockchain can facilitate the development of reputation and trust systems for self-driving cars. Each vehicle can have a unique digital identity recorded on the blockchain, along with a reputation score based on its past behavior and performance. This reputation score can be used to assess the reliability and safety of autonomous vehicles and inform decision-making processes, such as determining whether a vehicle should be given priority in merging or overtaking situations.

4. *Smart contracts for mobility services.* With self-driving cars being utilized in mobility services such as ride-hailing or car-sharing, blockchain's smart contract functionality can automate and secure the execution of agreements between users, service providers, and

vehicle owners. Smart contracts can handle tasks such as booking, payment processing, and service-level agreements, ensuring trust and transparency in these transactions.

5. *Over-the-air updates and maintenance.* Self-driving cars require regular software updates and maintenance to ensure optimal performance and security. Blockchain can provide a secure and auditable record of these updates, ensuring that only authorized and verified software changes are applied to the vehicles. This prevents unauthorized modifications and enhances the overall security and reliability of self-driving car systems.

6. *Insurance and liability management.* As self-driving cars become more prevalent, insurance and liability management become critical aspects. Blockchain can assist in creating transparent and tamperproof records of accidents, incidents, and other relevant data. This can facilitate the efficient and fair resolution of insurance claims, allocate liability among multiple parties, and establish a trustworthy record of events.

It is important to note that while blockchain technology offers significant benefits for self-driving car development, there are challenges to address, including scalability, privacy, standardization, and regulatory frameworks. Collaboration among industry players, researchers, and policymakers is essential to harness the full potential of blockchain in the self-driving car industry.

2.10 COMPONENTS OF BLOCKCHAIN TECHNOLOGY IN THE AUTOMOBILE INDUSTRY

Blockchain technology in the automobile industry comprises several key components that work together to enable secure and transparent operations. These components include:

1. *Distributed ledger.* The distributed ledger is at the core of blockchain technology. It is a decentralized database that maintains a continuously growing list of records, known as blocks. Each block contains a set of transactions and is linked to the previous block, forming a chain of blocks. This distributed ledger is shared and synchronized across multiple nodes in the network, ensuring consensus and data consistency.

2. *Nodes.* Nodes are individual computers or devices connected to the blockchain network. Each node maintains a copy of the entire blockchain and participates in the validation and verification of transactions. Nodes can be classified into different types, such as full nodes, which store the complete blockchain, and lightweight nodes, which rely on full nodes for transaction verification.

3. *Consensus mechanisms.* Consensus mechanisms are algorithms that enable nodes in the blockchain network to agree on the validity and order of transactions. Different consensus mechanisms, such as proof of work (PoW), proof of stake (PoS), and practical Byzantine fault tolerance (PBFT), determine how consensus is achieved. These mechanisms ensure that the majority of nodes agree on the state of the blockchain, making it difficult for malicious actors to manipulate the data.

4. *Cryptography.* Cryptography plays a crucial role in ensuring the security and integrity of blockchain technology. It involves the use of cryptographic algorithms to encrypt and decrypt data, verify identities, and secure transactions. Cryptographic techniques such as hashing, digital signatures, and public–private key pairs are employed to protect the confidentiality, authenticity, and integrity of data on the blockchain.

5. *Smart contracts.* Smart contracts are self-executing agreements that are encoded on the blockchain. They contain predefined rules and conditions, and when these conditions are met, the contract automatically executes the agreed-upon actions. Smart contracts eliminate the need for intermediaries and enable the automation of various processes, such as vehicle ownership transfer, insurance claims, and payments, based on predetermined rules.

6. *Tokens and digital assets.* In some blockchain implementations, tokens or digital assets are used to represent real-world assets or facilitate transactions within the network. In the automobile industry, tokens can be used to represent vehicle ownership, access to specific services, or incentivize participation in the ecosystem. These tokens can be traded or exchanged within the blockchain network or with external entities.

7. *Integration with IoT and other technologies.* The blockchain technology used in the automobile industry often integrates with other emerging technologies, like the Internet of Things (IoT). IoT sensors embedded in vehicles can provide real-time data that is recorded on the blockchain, enabling applications such as predictive maintenance, real-time tracking, and data-driven insights.

These components work together to create a secure, transparent, and decentralized system that can transform various aspects of the automobile industry, including supply chain management, vehicle ownership, maintenance, data sharing, and transaction settlement. By leveraging these components effectively, the automobile industry can benefit from increased efficiency, improved trust, and enhanced collaboration among stakeholders.

2.11   BLOCKCHAIN TECHNOLOGY FOR AUTOMOTIVE APPLICATION

Blockchain technology has the potential to transform various aspects of the automotive industry, offering transparency, security, and efficiency in automotive applications. At its core, blockchain is a decentralized and immutable digital ledger that records transactions and information across multiple computers or nodes. Here is an introduction to how blockchain can be applied in automotive applications (Alsharari, 2021):

1. *Supply chain management.* Blockchain can enhance transparency and traceability in the automotive supply chain. By recording every transaction related to parts, components, and raw materials, manufacturers can ensure the authenticity and provenance of each item. This helps prevent counterfeit parts, improves quality control, and enables efficient recalls if necessary.

2. *Vehicle identity and history.* Blockchain can establish a decentralized and immutable record of a vehicle's identity and history. This includes manufacturing information, maintenance records, ownership transfers, and accident history. This transparent and tamper-proof record can provide potential buyers with accurate vehicle information and combat issues like odometer fraud.

3. *Secure data sharing.* Blockchain enables secure and trusted data sharing among different entities in the automotive ecosystem. Manufacturers, suppliers, service providers, and customers can securely exchange data, such as vehicle diagnostics, performance data, and software updates. This ensures privacy and data integrity and reduces the reliance on centralized data repositories.

4. *Smart contracts for automotive transactions.* Blockchain's smart contract functionality allows for the automation and execution of predefined agreements and transactions. In the automotive industry, smart contracts can streamline processes like vehicle sales, leases, and service agreements. This reduces paperwork, eliminates intermediaries, and increases transaction efficiency.

5. *Autonomous vehicle networks.* With the rise of autonomous vehicles, blockchain can facilitate decentralized and secure communication among vehicles. Blockchain's distributed ledger can enable trustless interactions and coordination, enhancing safety and efficiency in autonomous vehicle networks.

6. *Car-sharing and mobility services.* Blockchain can support peer-to-peer car-sharing platforms and mobility services. By utilizing blockchain's transparent and secure nature, users

can verify the authenticity of vehicles, handle bookings and payments, and securely share access to vehicles without the need for intermediaries.

7. *Vehicle-to-infrastructure integration.* Blockchain technology can facilitate the integration of vehicles with infrastructure, such as charging stations and toll systems. Blockchain can securely handle transactions, authentication, and data exchange between vehicles and infrastructure, enabling seamless interactions and payments.

By leveraging blockchain technology, the automotive industry can enhance transparency, security, and efficiency across various applications. However, it is crucial to address challenges like scalability, interoperability, and regulatory considerations to fully realize the potential benefits of blockchain in the automotive sector.

2.12 LITERATURE ON BLOCKCHAIN TECHNOLOGY IN THE AUTOMOBILE MANUFACTURING INDUSTRY

Literature review discusses the application of blockchain technology in the automobile manufacturing industry. "Blockchain-Based Traceability and Anti-Counterfeiting for Automotive Parts and Accessories" by M. Tang et al. (2020) explores the use of blockchain technology to enhance traceability and anti-counterfeiting measures in the automotive parts and accessories industry. It discusses the benefits, challenges, and potential implementation strategies for utilizing blockchain in this context. "Blockchain Technology in the Automotive Industry: Potential and Challenges" by Ciotta et al. (2021) provides an overview of the potential applications of blockchain technology in the automotive industry. It discusses the challenges and opportunities associated with implementing blockchain in areas such as supply chain management, vehicle identity, data sharing, and autonomous vehicles.

"Blockchain Technology for Automotive Industry: Enabling Traceability, Privacy, and Sharing" by Huo et al. (2022). Examines the potential of blockchain technology in the automotive industry, focusing on its application in supply chain management, vehicle traceability, privacy protection, and data sharing. It discusses the benefits and challenges of implementing blockchain in the context of the automotive sector.

Kaur et al. (2024) examines the role of blockchain technology in the automotive industry, focusing on its impact on supply chain management, vehicle identity, data sharing, and autonomous vehicles. It provides insights into the potential benefits and challenges of adopting blockchain in the automotive sector. These resources should provide you with a starting point to explore the application of blockchain technology in the automobile manufacturing industry. You can access these papers through academic databases or by reaching out to the respective authors or institutions.

Blockchain technology has emerged as a potential game changer in the realm of financial inclusion. Its decentralized and transparent nature offers promising solutions to long-standing challenges faced by the unbanked and underbanked populations (Mavilia and Pisani, 2020; Casino et al., 2019; Ali et al., 2020). There are benefits of using blockchain technology in financial inclusion. Blockchain's ability to provide secure and verifiable digital identities can facilitate access to financial services for individuals lacking formal identification documents (Hernandez et al., 2019). This is particularly significant in regions such as Africa with weak or non-existent identification systems, where millions of people struggle to open bank accounts or access credit. At the same time, blockchain-based solutions have the potential to revolutionize cross-border remittances by eliminating intermediaries and reducing transaction fees and processing times (Muneeb et al., 2021). Studies have shown that blockchain-powered remittance platforms can significantly improve the speed and cost-effectiveness of international money transfers (ibid.).

In the same vein, in rural or underdeveloped regions, where traditional banking infrastructure is limited, blockchain-based financial services can serve as a bridge to financial inclusion. Blockchain enables the creation of decentralized finance (DeFi) applications, offering opportunities for peer-to-peer lending and microfinance initiatives (Yermack, 2017). However, blockchain's immutability and encryption features enhance the security of financial transactions, protecting users from potential fraud and cyberattacks (Casino et al., 2019). This heightened security can instill trust among unbanked populations and encourage them to participate in the formal financial system (ibid.).

On the other hand, different limitations and challenges have been encountered by blockchain technology in the context of financial inclusion. One of the primary challenges faced by blockchain technology in the context of financial inclusion is scalability. As the number of transactions increases, some blockchain networks may experience slower processing times and higher transaction fees (Wang et al., 2020). Addressing scalability is crucial for widespread adoption in high-volume financial systems (ibid.). Blockchain's consensus mechanisms, particularly the proof-of-work protocol, require substantial energy consumption (Ali et al., 2020). This raises concerns about the environmental impact of blockchain networks and their alignment with sustainability goals (ibid.). However, the rapidly evolving regulatory landscape surrounding blockchain and cryptocurrencies can create uncertainty for financial institutions and users (Demirgüç-Kunt and Klapper, 2018). Ambiguity in regulatory frameworks may hinder the adoption of blockchain-based financial services, deterring potential stakeholders from investing in inclusive financial initiatives.

According to Hernandez et al. (2019), blockchain technology offers the potential to revolutionize financial inclusion by enhancing access to financial services. The decentralized and transparent nature of blockchain can address critical challenges faced by the unbanked and underbanked populations, particularly in regions with weak or non-existent identification systems. By providing secure and verifiable digital identities, blockchain facilitates access to formal financial services for individuals who lack formal identification documents. Furthermore, the use of blockchain technology in cross-border remittances can significantly improve the speed and cost-effectiveness of international money transfers (Muneeb et al., 2021). Blockchain's elimination of intermediaries reduces transaction fees and processing times, making remittances more accessible and affordable for migrant workers and their families.

In conclusion, blockchain technology presents significant potential to transform financial inclusion by expanding access to financial services for underserved populations. Through its decentralized and transparent nature, blockchain can address barriers to financial inclusion, such as lack of formal identification, expensive remittance services, and limited banking infrastructure. As more research and real-world implementations continue to unfold, blockchain's impact on financial inclusion is expected to grow, shaping a more inclusive and accessible financial landscape for all. The decentralized and transparent nature of blockchain can address critical challenges in the traditional financial system (Mavilia and Pisani, 2020; Casino et al., 2019; Ali et al., 2020). However, challenges related to scalability, energy consumption, and regulatory uncertainty must be effectively tackled to realize the full potential of blockchain in promoting financial inclusion.

2.13 ROLES OF BLOCKCHAIN TECHNOLOGY IN THE AUTOMOBILE MANUFACTURING INDUSTRY

Blockchain technology plays several roles in the automobile manufacturing industry, revolutionizing various aspects of the sector. Here are the key roles of blockchain technology in automobile manufacturing:

1. *Enhanced supply chain management.* Blockchain enhances transparency and traceability in the automotive supply chain. It enables secure and transparent recording of transactions related to parts, components, and raw materials. This helps in verifying the authenticity of products, reducing counterfeiting, ensuring quality control, and facilitating efficient recalls if necessary.

2. *Secure data sharing and collaboration.* Blockchain provides a secure and decentralized platform for sharing data among different stakeholders in the automotive industry. Manufacturers, suppliers, service providers, and customers can securely exchange data, such as vehicle diagnostics, performance metrics, and software updates. This promotes collaboration, streamlines processes, and improves decision-making.

3. *Immutable vehicle identity and history.* Blockchain establishes a decentralized and immutable record of a vehicle's identity and history. It includes manufacturing information, maintenance records, ownership transfers, and accident history. This ensures the integrity and immutability of vehicle data, providing accurate and reliable information to buyers, regulators, and other relevant parties.

4. *Facilitating autonomous vehicle networks.* Blockchain technology can facilitate secure communication and coordination among autonomous vehicles. By leveraging blockchain's decentralized nature, self-driving cars can securely exchange information, such as location, speed, and intentions, without relying on a central authority. This enhances safety, improves traffic flow, and enables efficient decision-making in real time.

5. *Smart contracts for automotive transactions.* Blockchain's smart contract functionality automates and secures transactions within the automotive industry. Smart contracts can handle tasks such as vehicle sales, leases, and service agreements. By eliminating intermediaries, reducing paperwork, and ensuring transparency, smart contracts streamline transactions and improve efficiency.

6. *Establishing trust and security.* Blockchain technology enhances trust and security in the automobile manufacturing industry. The decentralized and immutable nature of blockchain ensures data integrity, reduces the risk of fraud, and provides a transparent and tamperproof record of transactions and data. This instills confidence among stakeholders and reduces the need for intermediaries.

By fulfilling these roles, blockchain technology improves transparency, efficiency, and security in the automobile manufacturing industry. However, it is important to address challenges such as scalability, interoperability, and regulatory considerations to fully realize the potential benefits of blockchain in this sector.

2.14   BLOCKCHAIN TECHNOLOGY FOR ELECTRIC VEHICLES

Blockchain technology can play a significant role in the development and adoption of electric vehicles (EVs) by addressing challenges related to charging infrastructure, battery management, renewable energy integration, and overall sustainability. Here are some specific applications of blockchain technology for electric vehicles:

1. *Charging infrastructure and payments.* Blockchain can facilitate secure and seamless payments for EV charging. By using blockchain-based smart contracts, users can automatically pay for charging services without the need for intermediaries. Additionally, blockchain can enable decentralized charging networks, allowing EV owners to easily locate and access charging stations.

2. *Grid integration and energy management.* Blockchain technology can enable efficient integration of EVs with the power grid and renewable energy sources. By using blockchain-based energy platforms, EVs can participate in demand response programs, providing grid flexibility and balancing supply and demand. Blockchain can also facilitate peer-to-peer energy trading, allowing EV owners to sell excess energy from their vehicle batteries back to the grid.

3. *Battery life cycle management.* Blockchain can enhance the management of EV battery life cycles. By recording battery information, such as manufacturing details, maintenance records, and performance data on the blockchain, transparency and trust can be ensured

throughout the battery's lifespan. This information can also help in the resale or repurposing of used EV batteries.

4. *Carbon credit and emissions tracking.* Blockchain can be used to track and verify carbon credits associated with EVs. By recording emissions data and verifying the reduction of carbon emissions through blockchain-based systems, the environmental impact of EVs can be quantified and rewarded. This can incentivize the adoption of electric vehicles and promote sustainability.

5. *Vehicle-to-grid (V2G) integration.* Blockchain technology can enable secure and decentralized vehicle-to-grid interactions. Through smart contracts and blockchain-based systems, EVs can participate in grid services, such as energy storage and load balancing. This enables EVs to act as distributed energy resources, supporting grid stability and the integration of renewable energy sources.

6. *Supply chain transparency.* Blockchain can enhance transparency and traceability in the EV supply chain. By recording manufacturing, sourcing, and logistics information on the blockchain, stakeholders can verify the origin and authenticity of EV components and ensure ethical sourcing practices.

These applications demonstrate how blockchain technology can support the growth of electric vehicles by addressing key challenges and promoting sustainability. However, it is important to consider factors such as scalability, interoperability, and regulatory frameworks when implementing blockchain solutions for electric vehicles.

2.15   BLOCKCHAIN TECHNOLOGY FOR SMART DRIVING

Blockchain technology has the potential to enhance smart driving systems by providing secure and decentralized data sharing, enabling trust and transparency, and facilitating secure and automated transactions. Here are some specific ways blockchain can be applied to smart driving:

1. *Secure and decentralized data sharing.* Blockchain can enable secure and decentralized data sharing among vehicles, infrastructure, and other stakeholders in smart driving systems. By using blockchain, vehicles can securely exchange data related to traffic conditions, road hazards, and other relevant information. This shared data can improve safety, optimize traffic flow, and enable more efficient routing.

2. *Vehicle identity and authentication.* Blockchain can establish a decentralized and immutable vehicle identity system, ensuring that vehicles are uniquely identified and authenticated. This helps prevent identity theft or tampering, reducing the risk of unauthorized access to vehicles or sensitive data. Blockchain-based vehicle identity can also facilitate secure communication and coordination among connected vehicles.

3. *Autonomous vehicle communication and coordination.* Blockchain technology can facilitate secure communication and coordination among autonomous vehicles (AVs). AVs can securely share information, such as their location, speed, and intentions, through blockchain-based systems. This decentralized communication ensures trust and enhances safety in autonomous driving environments.

4. *Smart contracts for vehicle-to-vehicle (V2V) and vehicle-to-infrastructure (V2I) transactions.* Blockchain-based smart contracts enable secure and automated transactions between vehicles and infrastructure. For example, smart contracts can facilitate automated toll payments, electric vehicle charging transactions, or insurance claims in the event of an accident. This eliminates the need for intermediaries, reduces transaction costs, and ensures transparency and trust in the process.

5. *Immutable record of driving behavior and insurance claims.* Blockchain can provide an immutable record of driving behavior, such as speed, acceleration, and adherence to traffic

rules. This data can be used by insurance companies to determine premiums or settle claims in a transparent and fair manner. Blockchain's immutability ensures the integrity of the data, reducing the potential for fraud or disputes.

6. *Privacy and data ownership.* Blockchain can empower individuals to have control over their driving and personal data. With blockchain-based systems, individuals can choose which data to share, with whom, and for what purposes. This enhances privacy and data ownership rights, giving drivers more control over their information.

It is important to note that while blockchain technology offers potential benefits to smart driving systems, there are challenges to consider, such as scalability, interoperability, and regulatory frameworks. Collaboration among industry stakeholders and the development of standards will be crucial for the successful implementation of blockchain in the smart driving ecosystem.

2.16 CONCLUSION AND FUTURE RESEARCH

The integration of blockchain technology into the realm of automobile manufacturing stands as a pivotal advancement poised to redefine the industry's landscape. The applications explored in this chapter, spanning supply chain optimization, production transparency, intellectual property protection, and aftermarket service enhancement, underscore the multifaceted benefits that blockchain brings to the table. The immutable and transparent nature of blockchain not only enhances operational efficiency by streamlining supply chain processes but also fosters trust among stakeholders through secure data sharing and collaboration. Furthermore, the technology's potential in revolutionizing intellectual property management and enabling personalized services heralds an era of innovation and customer-centricity. However, it is essential to acknowledge the challenges that lie ahead, encompassing issues of scalability, interoperability, and regulatory considerations. As the industry marches toward a future characterized by connected and autonomous vehicles, blockchain's role in safeguarding data integrity, enhancing security, and enabling seamless updates cannot be overstated. The road ahead may be paved with complexities, yet the promise of a more efficient, transparent, and secure automobile manufacturing ecosystem through blockchain remains a compelling vision worth pursuing.

Future research in the domain of blockchain technology for automobile manufacturing should prioritize addressing critical challenges and unlocking untapped opportunities for industry advancement. Investigating innovative scalability solutions, such as optimized consensus mechanisms and sharding techniques, will be crucial to ensure that blockchain networks can handle the immense data volumes inherent to the manufacturing process. Interoperability research should aim to establish standardized protocols that facilitate seamless communication between diverse blockchain networks and conventional manufacturing systems. Additionally, in-depth exploration of the legal and regulatory implications of blockchain integration, especially regarding data privacy and intellectual property, will provide essential insights for policymakers and industry stakeholders. Advancing real-time data sharing capabilities through blockchain, especially with the integration of IoT devices, could greatly enhance production transparency and decision-making processes. Lastly, research efforts should delve into the potential of blockchain to drive sustainable and energy-efficient manufacturing practices, creating a roadmap for environmentally conscious production methods within the automobile industry.

REFERENCES

Abeyratne, S. A., & Monfared, R. P. (2016). Blockchain Ready Manufacturing Supply Chain Using Distributed Ledger. *International Journal of Research in Engineering and Technology*, 5(9), 1–10.
Ali, I., Aslam, M. S., Khan, A. U., & Khan, S. U. (2020). A Comprehensive Review of Blockchain Technology: A Roadmap for Future Research Directions. *Journal of Database Management*, 31(1), 1–28.

Alsharari, N. (2021). Integrating Blockchain Technology With Internet of Things to Efficiency. *International Journal of Technology, Innovation and Management (IJTIM)*, *1*(2), 01–13.

Casino, F., Dasaklis, T. K., & Patsakis, C. (2019). A Systematic Literature Review of Blockchain-Based Applications: Current Status, Classification, and Open Issues. *Telematics and Informatics*, *36*, 55–81.

Ciotta, V., Mariniello, G., Asprone, D., Botta, A., & Manfredi, G. (2021). Integration of blockchains and smart contracts into construction information flows: Proof-of-concept. *Automation in Construction*, *132*, 103925.

Demirgüç-Kunt, A., & Klapper, L. (2018). *Financial Inclusion and Inclusive Growth: A Review of Recent Empirical Evidence*. Policy Research Working Paper, World Bank.

Hernandez, J. M. R., Skeldon, P., & Calavia, L. M. (2019). Blockchain for Identity Management: A Case Analysis of Estonia. *Journal of Theoretical and Applied Electronic Commerce Research*, *14*(2), 15–29.

Huo, R., Zeng, S., Wang, Z., Shang, J., Chen, W., Huang, T., . . . & Liu, Y. (2022). A comprehensive survey on blockchain in industrial internet of things: Motivations, research progresses, and future challenges. *IEEE Communications Surveys & Tutorials*, *24*(1), 88–122.

Kamath, A., & Lobo, S. (2019). Blockchain in Automotive Industry: The Way Forward. *International Journal of Scientific Research and Management*, *7*(1), 21–25.

Karim, M. R., & Taheri, M. R. (2019). Blockchain Technology Applications and Challenges in Smart Manufacturing. In *Advances in Manufacturing II* (pp. 261–282). Springer, Singapore.

Kaur, N., Chahal, N., Dewan, R., Singh, S., Bansal, G., Dishu, D., & Kumar, S. (2024). Blockchain: Evolution and future scope. In *Convergence of Blockchain and Internet of Things in Healthcare* (pp. 196–209). New York, USA: CRC Press.

Mavilia, R., & Pisani, R. (2020). Blockchain and Catching-Up in Developing Countries: The Case of Financial Inclusion in Africa. *African Journal of Science, Technology, Innovation and Development*, *12*(2), 151–163.

Muneeb, A., Arshad, Z., Shah, S. A. A., Hassan, S. U., & Zaman, M. A. (2021). A Comprehensive Review on Blockchain Applications in Financial Services. *International Journal of Information Management*, *56*, 102241.

Niranjanamurthy, M., Nithya, B. N., & Jagannatha, S. J. C. C. (2019). Analysis of Blockchain Technology: Pros, Cons and SWOT. *Cluster Computing*, *22*, 14743–14757.

Politou, E., Casino, F., Alepis, E., & Patsakis, C. (2019). Blockchain Mutability: Challenges and Proposed Solutions. *IEEE Transactions on Emerging Topics in Computing*, *9*(4), 1972–1986.

Sarmah, S. S. (2018). Understanding Blockchain Technology. *Computer Science and Engineering*, *8*(2), 23–29.

Sharma, P., & Dhar, P. L. (2020). Blockchain Technology for Supply Chain Management in the Automotive Industry: A Comprehensive Review. *Transportation Research Part E: Logistics and Transportation Review*, *141*, 1–17.

Swan, M. (2015). *Blockchain: Blueprint for a New Economy*. O'Reilly Media, Inc., New York, USA.

Tang, Y., Xiong, J., Becerril-Arreola, R., & Iyer, L. (2020). Ethics of blockchain: A framework of technology, applications, impacts, and research directions. *Information Technology & People*, *33*(2), 602–632.

Walch, A. (2018). The Path of the Blockchain Lexicon (and the Law). *New York University Journal of Legislation and Public Policy*, *21*, 457–480.

Wang, Q., Zhang, Y., Sun, X., Zheng, Z., & Li, Z. (2020). A Survey of Blockchain: Techniques, Applications, and Challenges. *Journal of Network and Computer Applications*, *168*, 102687.

Yadav, A. K., Singh, K., Amin, A. H., Almutairi, L., Alsenani, T. R., & Ahmadian, A. (2023). A Comparative Study on Consensus Mechanism With Security Threats and Future Scopes: Blockchain. *Computer Communications*, *201*, 102–115.

Yermack, D. (2017). Corporate Governance and Blockchains. *Review of Finance*, *21*(1), 7–31.

3 Blockchain Technology for Automobile Manufacturing

Abdullah Yildizbasi and Joseph Sarkis

3.1 INTRODUCTION

Closed-loop supply chain management encompasses both forward and reverse supply chains. The forward supply chain extends from raw material extraction to end user customer delivery, while the reverse supply chain involves collecting used products from customers, their subsequent collection, sorting, disassembly, recycling, and reuse into production or other applications. This holistic approach covers the entirety of production, distribution, collection, sorting, and reuse processes. In today's economic landscape, numerous industries strive to sustain their competitive edge by establishing economically efficient and environmentally responsible supply chains (Yildizbasi et al., 2018).

Many successful supply chain operation activities exist in the contemporary automotive industry. Manufacturers—driven by enhancing brand value in the context of growing environmental awareness and gaining competitive advantages—have implemented various technology-based initiatives over the past decade (Reddy et al., 2021). Despite these advancements, the automotive industry's supply chain is not perceived as sufficiently responsive, integrated, or transparent when compared to other sectors (Alsadi et al., 2023). The factors contributing to this perception include a multi-tiered and complex structure of suppliers and manufacturers within the supply chain, asymmetrical information flow, and transactions among organizations in the supply chain that lack traceability and transparency (Öztürk and Yildizbaşi, 2020). This context results in a deficit of trust and coordination among supply chain participants. It is currently evident that transparency, information sharing, and traceability have become pivotal distinguishing factors in the automotive industry, rendering them indispensable for effective supply chain operations (Saberi et al., 2019). To address these imperatives, establishing decentralized trust mechanisms and implementing robust tracking systems are vital steps toward ensuring seamless information connectivity among all supply chain partners (Kurpjuweit et al., 2021).

Blockchain technology, which has emerged in recent years, plays a pivotal role in closed-loop supply chain (CLSC) management and holds immense potential, particularly in terms of bolstering security, traceability, and transparency. In order to establish a transparent system, it is imperative that all transactions are meticulously recorded, a feat made possible through the implementation of blockchain technology (De Giovanni, 2022). Initially designed for financial operations, blockchain technology has since catalyzed a promising transformation in various business processes, particularly within the realm of CLSC (Goli, 2023).

Within the blockchain system, routine transactions are documented and registered by all stakeholders. The blockchain architecture stores this data in a layered block structure, ensuring a significantly higher level of security compared to conventional systems, especially with regard to safeguarding sensitive information (Filali Rotbi et al., 2022). In decentralized databases, information is encoded and stored at a robust cryptographic security level, effectively eliminating the inefficiencies often encountered in supply chain systems. This transition to blockchain offers a cost-effective and sustainable structure where all transactions are meticulously recorded (Kayikci et al., 2022). Despite the promising prospects of integrating blockchain technology into supply

DOI: 10.1201/9781003450306-4

chain applications, this integration is still in its nascent stages. There exists a substantial gap in the literature, particularly concerning its application and development phases.

The scarcity of automotive production and recycling worldwide, coupled with the multitude of firms operating within this sector, underscores the significance of understanding and advancing knowledge in this area. Blockchain applications stand as one of the key pillars in digitalization ushered in by Industry 4.0 philosophies (Zafar et al., 2022). Blockchain applications have yet to reach maturity, with new developments and knowledge emerging on a continuous basis. Consequently, numerous challenges and issues may arise during the implementation phase, encompassing aspects such as technology integration costs, stakeholder involvement, incentivization, and data storage and processing time. The shortage of skilled individuals in the blockchain field further exacerbates these challenges.

The primary focus of this chapter revolves around the analysis of studies pertaining to the integration of blockchain into closed-loop supply chain models within the automotive sector. We propose a comprehensive framework and delineate relevant research implications. To achieve this objective, we first delve into conceptual supply chain aspects, outline the challenges encountered within supply chains, and expound upon blockchain technology as a viable solution. We conduct a review of existing literature using keywords such as "supply chain," "blockchain," and "automotive supply chain." This review facilitates a current situation analysis, followed by a gap analysis. We chart a roadmap for future research, identifying key focus areas and potential research implications for integrating blockchain technology into the automotive supply chain.

3.2   SUMMARY OF PREVIOUS STUDIES

Over the last decade, blockchain technology has emerged in response to globalization and technological advances. Its integration into supply chain management has become increasingly prevalent. Blockchain technology use applications occur across diverse industries, including manufacturing, finance, healthcare, social sciences, pharmaceuticals, energy, agriculture, and food. A growing body of literature and studies reflects this trend, with a notable increase in the number of articles published on the topic in recent years.

Figure 3.1—depicting the results of a literature review using keywords such as "blockchain" and "supply chain"—underscores the substantial rise over the past five years in studies that combine

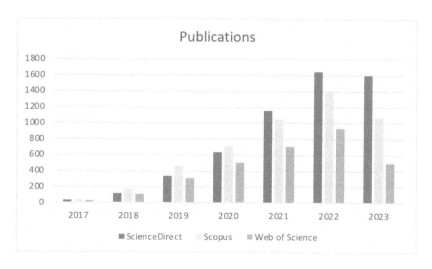

FIGURE 3.1   Evolution of the studies involving "blockchain" and "supply chain" keywords in recent years.

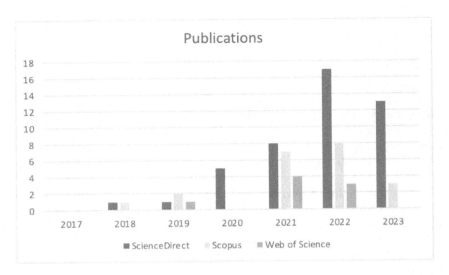

FIGURE 3.2 Evolution of the studies involving "blockchain" and "automotive supply chain" keywords in recent years.

these topics. This surge in research activity underscores the growing interest and recognition of blockchain's potential in enhancing supply chain processes.

Figure 3.2 summarizes research publications involving the keywords "blockchain" and "automotive supply chain." Figure 3.2 shows growth over the years, but a significantly smaller number of studies focusing specifically on the automotive supply chain. This shift may indicate that while blockchain technology continues to gain traction in supply chain management overall, its adoption within the automotive sector may be progressing at a slower pace or garnering less research attention.

A substantial portion of joint blockchain and supply chain literature appears to be conceptual in nature. This result suggests that many studies are exploring the theoretical and potential applications of blockchain technology in supply chains, reflecting the ongoing exploration of its capabilities and the development of innovative use cases. As blockchain technology matures and more real-world implementations are established, it is likely that the research focus will increasingly shift toward empirical studies and practical applications within supply chain management.

In accordance with the findings of Reddy et al. (2021), it is observed that the nations contributing most significantly to scholarly publications on the subject are sequenced as follows: China, the United States, the United Kingdom, and India. Furthermore, noteworthy periodicals such as *IEEE Access* and the *International Journal of Production Research* emerge as prominent disseminators of research pertaining to the keyword "blockchain."

While blockchain technology has seen significant supply chain use applications, particularly within the health and food sectors, there remains a conspicuous limit of research pertaining to the manufacturing industry and, more specifically, the automotive sector. Despite an exhaustive review of hundreds of articles, mathematical models employed in solution methodologies rarely exist, with only sporadic instances documented. There is a wealth of both qualitative and quantitative studies in blockchain supply chain application. There is a noticeable lack of research in the automotive sector.

Adoption of blockchain investigating sustainable supply chains in the automotive industry does exist (Kamble et al., 2023). This research shows the rapid adaptability of blockchain, given its dynamic nature. This adaptability is a key factor for achieving success in sustainability through blockchain integration. The automotive sector, with its extensive, network-based global supply chain requires uninterrupted and reliable stakeholder relationships. Blockchain, renowned for its traceability and transparency, is considered a multi-stakeholder technology (Zhu et al., 2022).

Taking a similar perspective, Miehle et al. (2019) developed a prototype application using the Hyperledger Fabric framework. This application aims to establish unwavering trust within the automotive industry by leveraging blockchain. Operating within the blockchain network, the application incorporates specific individuals into the system through QR codes, bridging the gap between the virtual and physical realms for companies. This approach is cost-effective.

Lu et al. (2019) also address issues of counterfeiting in the automotive supply chain and explore the impact of blockchain technology. They highlight the benefits of blockchain, such as managing product records in a distributed yet traceable ledger. However, they acknowledge challenges such as invoking multiple chain codes and ensuring privacy.

While there are numerous studies on blockchain's utility in supply chain management, many of these studies do not explore the attitudes and decisions of companies and stakeholders toward blockchain technology prior to its adoption. While the literature acknowledges the lack of information within institutions, it often overlooks the perceptions of institutions already well-versed in this transformation. Dehshiri et al. (2022) address this gap by investigating the integration of blockchain into the supply chain of an Iranian automotive company engaged in international cooperation. They engage with eight different decision-makers from various units within the company to understand the criteria that lead them to embrace blockchain transformation positively. Key criteria identified include security, demand response, and traceability.

A comprehensive systematic review of studies pertaining to the automotive industry's supply chain (Reddy et al., 2021) showed both positive and negative blockchain impacts. The review sheds light on the main challenges faced by the automotive supply chain and the role and significance of blockchain in navigating the volatile environments, uncertain outcomes, complex operational networks, and ambiguous decisions (VUCA) world.

The technological, organizational, and environmental (TOE) perspective has been used to explore the potential and existing challenges of blockchain technology in the automotive industry (Xu et al., 2022). It was found that the integration of blockchain into the automotive industry may encounter difficulties, such as technological immaturity, a lack of guidance and industry standards, non-cooperation among chain members, and legislative ambiguity. It was also found that this integration offers advantages, such as aggregating product information, securing transaction data, and establishing a reliable supply chain.

TruCert, a blockchain-based product certification system for autonomous automotive supply chains, can provide some application insight (Alsadi et al., 2023). It can address the challenges facing the automotive industry, such as lack of traceability, transparency, trust, and counterfeit items. A consortium blockchain (Hyperledger Besu) is used to record part traceability data. The findings show that by leveraging blockchain technology, TruCert can improve product quality assurance and strengthen supply chain resilience to combat risks and uncertainties.

The literature on the integration of blockchain into the automotive supply chain primarily comprises theoretical evaluations, with a dearth of concrete mathematical models. When examining blockchain studies in the automotive sector, the emphasis lies in discussing the applications within the supply chain and tools to enhance supply chain efficiency. The blockchain–supply chain relationship, while mentioned, is often presented superficially, with some articles drawing insights from case studies of major corporations. Nonetheless, mathematical models that specify the financial implications of these proposed applications on companies, particularly in terms of income, expenses, and overall financial statements, are conspicuously absent. Many articles express optimism about the potential of blockchain applications in the automotive sector but often lack empirical data or mathematical modeling to substantiate these claims.

3.3 SUPPLY CHAINS AND CURRENT PROBLEMS

Widely recognized as one of the more technologically advanced sectors, the automotive supply chain has evolved into a multifaceted ecosystem encompassing various stakeholders, including state regulatory bodies, manufacturers, suppliers, vendors, and spare parts suppliers. Despite its sophistication, the automotive supply chain faces a substantial challenge—the proliferation of counterfeit products. The estimated value of counterfeit spare parts within this industry runs into billions of dollars. These substandard components find their way into the supply chain through various channels, including online sources, and are detrimental to both original equipment manufacturers and spare parts suppliers. Consequently, dissatisfied customers emerge, and trust in the brand is eroded. Additionally, the concept of the sharing economy has become increasingly relevant within the automotive industry (Sharma et al., 2020). Counterfeiting and a sharing economy are characteristics that can benefit from blockchain capabilities, such as traceability, data reliability, and security.

Effective management of production capacity, meticulous monitoring, and real-time data recording of individual components in the supply chain can support preventive maintenance and foster sustainability within the automotive industry. These challenges have become more prevalent due to the globalized nature of the automotive supply chain. In closed-loop automotive supply chain, the complexity escalates, as it involves the additional task of tracking and recording various information, ranging from labeling parts reclaimed from returned vehicles to managing their disposal as waste. The presence of asymmetric information flow poses a significant challenge, particularly in supply chain networks, where information dissemination holds as much importance as the physical flow of products. These contexts can benefit from blockchain capabilities, including traceability and transparency.

Accurate planning necessitates the analysis of real-time data. However, the uneven exchange of information among companies in traditional supply chain management systems, coupled with the inability to monitor fluctuations, hampers the planning process and escalates costs. Establishing a smooth information flow among supply chain stakeholders is crucial not only for enhancing competitiveness within the system but also for mitigating risks and reducing expenses. Traditional supply chain systems often employ contracts to ensure and regulate information flow (Cachon and Lariviere, 2005). These contracts serve to legally bind supply chain actors, ensuring compliance with specific transaction conditions and requirements. Further efficiency in these contracts can occur through blockchain smart contracts and information processing access and efficiency.

Nevertheless, concerns persist in this regard, as these contracts frequently lack provisions that align with the principles of sustainable supply chains. Moreover, companies often work with multiple subcontractors, adding complexity to the system and leaving customers with doubts about whether sustainability requirements stipulated in the contracts are being met. While legal recourse exists in case of contract violations, pursuing such actions is typically avoided due to the associated costs and lengthy legal processes. The root cause of this issue lies in the opacity of processes, particularly in the context of global supply chain networks composed of diverse actors. Hidden elements within these networks create challenges in achieving transparency across multiple layers of the supply chain. These concealed layers may involve activities that raise concerns from social, environmental, financial, and resource perspectives. Due to the asymmetric nature of business agreements or shortcomings in traceability, many of these activities remain undisclosed throughout various supply chain processes (Öztürk and Yildizbaşi, 2020; Dutta et al., 2020; Kouhizadeh et al., 2021).

Supply chain practices and strategies are now under growing pressure to incorporate and validate sustainability concerns, encompassing environmental and social equilibrium alongside business dimensions within supply chain management (Seuring et al. 2008). Sustainability in supply chain processes has a profound impact on strategic positioning and competitiveness. Ensuring sustainability involves confirming that processes, products, and activities in the supply chain meet specific criteria (Grimm et al., 2016).

Driven by increasing consumer awareness of sustainability, there is a substantial demand for information regarding previously concealed activities (Carter and Rogers, 2008). Today's end users seek comprehensive insights into the origins of the products they incorporate into their daily lives. A mention of production location on a product label no longer satisfies either consumers or end suppliers. In the evolving landscape of supply chain processes, companies have come to recognize the value of providing customers with essential information about a product's journey to its ultimate destination (Carter and Rogers, 2008). As a result, there is a concerted effort to prioritize transparency in business processes. *Transparency*, in its essence, entails divulging all pertinent information about a product within the supply chain, accessible to both customers and supply chain stakeholders (Doorey, 2011; Egels-Zandén et al., 2015; Mol, 2015). Blockchain technology can support transparency and traceability, with data reliability and immutability across the supply chain.

Incorporating transparency into supply chain processes heightens corporate responsibility in sustainable supply chain management, propelling these companies to higher standards in social, environmental, and financial domains. Bureaucratic impediments in traditional supply chain structures also pose significant challenges. Managing intercontinental transportation entails navigating complex bureaucratic procedures. Product delays, the handling of myriad documents, errors, fraudulent activities, and accidents significantly inflate product costs and impose heavy burdens on companies. Moreover, in centralized supply chain models, adherence to contractual obligations often necessitates placing trust in third parties for transaction execution. For instance, money transfers in supply chain management contracts are often routed through banks, introducing an additional layer of intermediaries into the process. This involvement of third parties extends transaction times and escalates costs, requiring an intricate web of communication channels (Öztürk and Yildizbaşi, 2020). The immutability and traceability of information, along with transactional efficiency from blockchain systems, can mitigate these difficulties.

In transoceanic maritime transportation, the absence of digital document transfer exacerbates the supply chain management challenges. Failure to complete certain procedures can complicate product shipments considerably. Even for the simplest product shipments, approval from numerous organizations and coordination across hundreds of communication channels may be required. Considering that many companies engage in hundreds of daily shipments, the financial losses and time wastage are substantial. Current supply chains rely on information management systems, often centralized, discrete, and independently located within organizations. These supply chain processes necessitate companies to entrust their sensitive and valuable information to a single organization or intermediary (Abeyratne and Monfared, 2016). However, centralization exposes the entire system to vulnerability stemming from single points of failure, errors, corruption, or attacks (Dong et al., 2017). The automotive industry, relying on these maritime transportation modes, are directly influenced by these inefficiencies. Once again, blockchain can make these transactions and flows across the global automotive supply chain more efficient, lowering costs.

As alluded to in meeting supply chain challenges, emerging technologies with the potential to enhance global supply chain operations and bolster sustainability are on the horizon. Blockchain technology, in particular, has made significant strides in recent years and has the potential to revolutionize supply chain processes (Kshetri, 2018). Introduced an innovative approach through the development of a decentralized and cryptographic infrastructure, a blockchain payment system. This innovative approach eliminates the need for third parties, such as banks or government institutions in the financial world. Despite the promise of blockchain technology, efforts to apply and develop it for supply chain management are still in their infancy (Kshetri, 2018; Lu and Xu, 2017).

Forecasts suggest that existing supply chain relationships and consumer behaviors will undergo transformation, leading to the emergence of a more collaborative information network powered by blockchain technology (Aste et al., 2017). This technological shift will also influence consumer consumption behavior. In addition to its theoretical potential across various sectors, blockchain technology has already demonstrated its wide-reaching impact in several applications, including fraud prevention (Veuger, 2018), clinical trials (Benchoufi et al., 2017), innovative initiatives (Chen, 2018), and open production.

While blockchain technology initially gained prominence in the financial sector, the potential to make significant economic, social, and environmental impacts has not gone unnoticed. Its primary effect is the elimination of economic inefficiencies. In summary, as evidenced by responses to each of the current supply chain challenges, blockchain technology offers solutions to streamline bureaucratic processes, establish simpler and more secure operations, reduce transaction costs, eliminate human errors, and enhance efficiency in communication and interaction. Furthermore, blockchain technology enhances transparency within supply chain networks (Öztürk and Yildizbaşi, 2020).

This innovation introduces new opportunities for tracking and controlling goods, allowing for a comprehensive record of a product's history. Such transparency facilitates a more realistic consideration of sustainability within the supply chain, with traceability being crucial for both environmental and social sustainability. Blockchain technology offers extensive traceability capabilities for people, products, and vehicles, making it possible to apply sustainable supply chain principles more effectively while ensuring process transparency. Enhanced traceability in supply chain processes empowers society to make more informed choices, prompting all supply chain stakeholders to adopt a more accountable stance.

3.4   BLOCKCHAIN TECHNOLOGY

Blockchain technology is a method of securely storing transactions in distributed digital ledgers using encryption techniques (Kshetri, 2018). At its core, the blockchain functions as a decentralized database (ledger) technology where records and entries are retained for a specific duration (Tian, 2016). These transactional records are openly accessible to multiple stakeholders and can be verified at any time to ensure the accuracy of the data.

The blockchain system can be continually updated through a peer-to-peer network. When a new transaction is initiated, individuals or systems responsible for tracking these transactions, known as miners or oracles, examine the request and compute the most efficient means to resolve it. Once the transaction is verified, it is appended to the blockchain as a block. Verifiers, through proof of stake or proof of work (or other proof mechanisms), may subsequently update their ledgers to determine any inconsistencies in the transactions.

A primary advantage of blockchain lies in its dynamic database system, enabling hundreds of thousands of miners or automated agents to maintain records while incorporating the most efficient entry into the database. Once a transaction is verified, it becomes immutable, and no one can alter the records. With miners constantly scrutinizing and updating the accuracy of blocks, the system is highly resistant to cyberattacks and maintains security and reliability of data. Miners cannot collude to manipulate records, and any fraudulent activity results in expulsion from the system (Hamledari and Fischer, 2021).

While blockchain technology is often associated with cryptocurrency, it can operate independently without the need for cryptocurrency—although cryptocurrency can be used to incentivize and tokenize activities, a useful capability of blockchain technology ecosystems.

The blockchain system maintains recorded data in blocks, with each block referencing the previous one, forming a linked chain structure. Each block contains encrypted data, timestamp information, transaction details, and hash values of the preceding block (Goli, 2023). Any node connected to the blockchain network, as depicted in Figure 3.3, has the ability to observe network changes and either endorse or reject them.

When a transaction is initiated, a request is submitted to the peer-to-peer network-managed system, and this request is disseminated across the entire network. Once the request receives public approval, it is appended to the blockchain and recorded as a transaction, completing the process. The decentralized nature of the system and the requirement for consensus among multiple users contribute to the security of blockchain technology. The chain initiated by the first data entry has the potential to extend indefinitely. The data addition process commences from a single point, and all users within the chain duplicate the historical data onto their systems. Subsequently, when a new user joins the system, they generate a code that is integrated into the longest blockchain within the system at that moment, referred to as the main chain. All information within the system is mirrored across all chains (Yildizbasi, 2021).

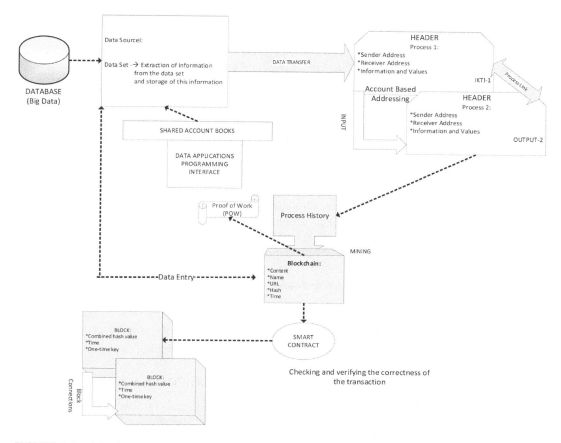

FIGURE 3.3 A basic structure showing the working principle of the blockchain system.

Blockchain technology offers a range of features and benefits that make it a preferred system for various applications, including supply chain management. These features include:

Distributed network. Blockchain operates on a decentralized network where transactions are managed without the need for a central authority. This distributed nature eliminates the need for intermediaries and fosters direct interactions among participants. While this characteristic adds to security, it can have negative environmental implications due to the energy-intensive consensus mechanisms used in public networks. Private networks often employ more-efficient algorithms with lower energy consumption (Kouhizadeh and Sarkis, 2018).

Security. Blockchain ensures data security by storing information in encrypted blocks. Each block contains a timestamp and a hash that links it to the previous block in the chain. These cryptographic structures enhance security, prevent data theft or tampering, and facilitate identity verification and secure transactions. Trust in validators is distributed across the network, increasing system security and resilience to cyberattacks (Ivanov et al., 2018).

Transparency. Blockchain maintains a copy of distributed ledgers with all authorized network participants. Every transaction and approval made on the blockchain is traceable by all participants, ensuring transparency and accountability. This transparency reduces costs, enhances product reliability, increases process efficiency, and mitigates risks by eliminating intermediaries. Smart contracts, a part of blockchain technology, further automate supply chain processes (Li et al., 2019).

Immutability. Data in the blockchain system cannot be altered without consensus from all users. Even when data is updated, the old records remain in all blocks. The system enforces stringent rules and consensus mechanisms, preventing unauthorized changes or deletions. Modifications require notifications and agreement among network members (Yildizbasi, 2021).

Smart contracts. Smart contracts are self-executing computer codes that automatically enforce contract terms and business rules. They operate without human intervention, reducing the need for trust between parties. Smart contracts are stored on the blockchain platform, eliminating intermediaries like banks or legal entities. They enable automatic and efficient execution of contractual obligations, such as payments, based on predefined conditions (Öztürk and Yildizbaşi, 2020).

Traceability. Blockchain technology allows for the tracking of physical production processes and products. This traceability is not limited to production but can extend to various processes, such as real-time tracking of shipments, patient and disease tracking, and waste tracking. Information about each stage of a product's journey is recorded, providing customers with detailed information about the product (Figorilli et al., 2018).

In addition to these features, blockchain technology supports sustainable supply chain models by offering validation, verification, accuracy, scalability, and decentralization (Kouhizadeh et al., 2021). The impact of blockchain on the different phases of the supply chain, including monitoring, analysis, evaluation, integration, and feedback, is evident in its ability to enhance transparency, traceability, and efficiency throughout the entire supply chain process.

3.5 BLOCKCHAIN INTEGRATION INTO THE AUTOMOTIVE SUPPLY CHAIN

The rapid advancement of Internet technology and the expansion of transportation options have led to an unprecedented scale of global trade in recent years. Companies now manage complex supply chain systems with numerous suppliers and customers spread across different continents. Effectively managing such large and intricate systems has become a formidable challenge for traditional supply chain models.

In classical supply chain models, a silo approach is often employed by supply chain stakeholders, focusing primarily on internal processes. This internal and siloed approach can lead to uncontrolled complexities in terms of time, cost, efficiency, and sustainability due to complex flows of information and products throughout entire supply chain networks.

The leveraging of blockchain that possesses three key foundational attributes—low cost, transparency, and security—can help address many challenges. With a blockchain-based structure, every stage of a product's journey, from manufacturing to sale, can be documented, creating a permanent and transparent product history. These capabilities have the potential to significantly reduce time delays, additional costs, sustainability concerns, amongst other strategic and operational automotive supply chain concerns.

Blockchain smart contracts enable automation of control and action processes throughout a product's journey. Conditions like transferring a specific amount of money after a product reaches a certain stage and passes certain quality controls can be executed automatically. From a customer perspective, this technology provides visibility into the product's arrival process, enabling consumers to make more informed and conscious decisions about their purchases (Zafar et al., 2022). With post-COVID difficulties in automobile supply chains, these efficiencies can be helpful in mitigating disruptions.

Figure 3.4 illustrates a conventional closed-loop supply chain (CLSC) scenario showcasing the stakeholders involved and the flow of information, materials, and financial transactions among them. The adoption of blockchain technology in such supply chain systems—of which

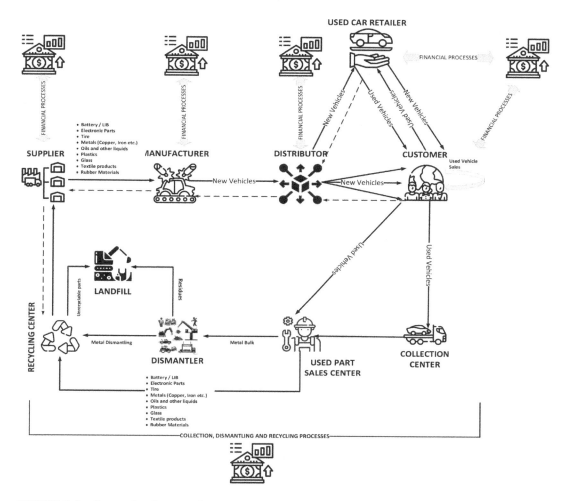

FIGURE 3.4 Conventional automotive closed-loop supply chain processes without blockchain integration.

automobile and automobile component recycling, spare parts, and resale play important roles—holds the promise of revolutionizing how these stakeholders interact, share information, and conduct transactions, ultimately leading to more efficient, transparent, and secure supply chain operations.

In contrast to the closed-loop supply chain (CLSC) flows depicted in Figure 3.4, Figure 3.5 illustrates how blockchain-integrated supply chain models enable real-time information flow, resulting in a transparent, controllable, and scalable structure for an automotive supply chain. This transformation is facilitated by the continuous and updated distribution of data within the blockchain network.

While blockchain technology is often associated with the financial sector, its applicability extends to various domains, with logistics and supply chain management encompassing a broad spectrum of these areas. Professionals in this field have come to recognize that blockchain technology represents a significant step toward reducing costs, combating smuggling and fraud, and realizing sustainability objectives more effectively. The technology achieves this by replacing asymmetric information among supply chain stakeholders with transparency (Zafar et al., 2022).

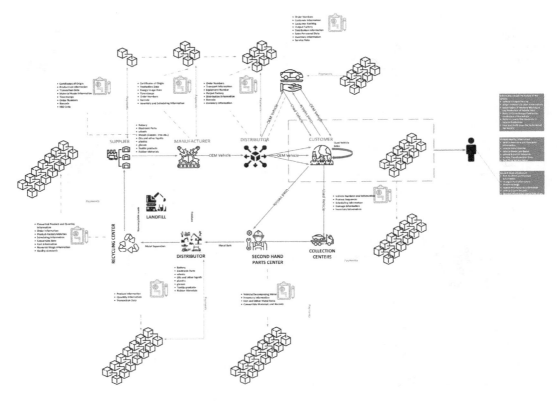

FIGURE 3.5 Blockchain technology integration in the automotive supply chain.

3.6 OUTLOOK AND FUTURE OPPORTUNITIES WITH RESEARCH IMPLICATIONS

Blockchain is a central element of emergent Industry 4.0 ecosystem technologies. It has not yet matured but holds significant potential for addressing current supply chain issues. Due to its novelty and the absence of fully established standards, there are still many aspects open to research.

There are also drawbacks even with blockchain technology advantages. These drawbacks need to be considered when designing and implementing blockchain (Yli-Huumo et al., 2016). Blockchain technology can lead to disruptive and radical changes in business processes and policies. New regulations are one of the essential aspects in the use of this technology. In addition, issues such as security, technical infrastructure, and scalability continue to remain relevant (Chiacchio et al., 2022; Yli-Huumo et al., 2016). This section explores the areas open for research from the perspective of blockchain technology in the automotive supply chain. However, these research areas have a widespread impact not only on the automotive sector but also across other sectors.

Robust encryption and privacy-preserving techniques for automotive industry blockchain applications are needed to protect proprietary information associated with permissioned blockchains. Research is needed for these techniques in practical settings, where *zero-trust* can be assumed (Collier and Sarkis, 2021). This research includes investigating advanced cryptographic methods and consensus algorithms to ensure data security and confidentiality. Exploring techniques such as homomorphic encryption and zero-knowledge proofs is essential for ensuring secure data sharing within blockchain systems (Ethirajan et al., 2021). Additionally, the development of blockchain-based access control mechanisms, incorporating fine-grained data permission settings, is crucial for managing data access and privacy effectively. Furthermore, it is imperative to conduct research into methodologies that enable the preservation of user privacy while simultaneously facilitating data transparency in blockchain applications. User privacy may also represent consumer usage of automotive vehicles, where information may be useful for design-of-vehicle purposes but may infringe on privacy rights of individuals. These efforts collectively contribute to enhancing the security, accessibility, and privacy aspects of blockchain technology in the automotive sector.

Scalability remains a challenge for blockchain in the automotive sector. Research is required to address the limitations of current blockchain architectures in handling large volumes of transactions in real time (Fraga-Lamas and Fernández-Caramés, 2019). Investigating sharding and sidechain solutions can enhance transaction processing throughput in blockchain systems (Dang et al., 2019). These approaches, along with blockchain ecosystem data storage, can alleviate scalability concerns by distributing the transaction load across multiple chains. Additionally, exploring consensus mechanisms specifically optimized for high-speed transactions is essential for achieving real-time processing capabilities in blockchain networks (Hashim et al., 2021). The development of novel techniques for data pruning and storage optimization on the blockchain can ensure efficient resource utilization while maintaining data integrity. These research efforts collectively contribute to addressing the scalability and performance challenges in blockchain technology (Okanami et al., 2022).

Another potential research area to investigate is achieving interoperability between different blockchain networks and legacy systems in the automotive industry. Research is needed to develop standards and protocols for seamless integration. Blockchain interoperability frameworks research, including cross-chain communication protocols, can foster interoperability in the automotive sector's adoption of blockchain technology (Belchior et al., 2021; Schulte et al., 2019). These frameworks facilitate seamless communication and data exchange between distinct blockchain networks.

The development of industry-wide standards for data formats and communication protocols among diverse blockchain platforms can ensure a unified and efficient ecosystem—within the automotive industry, but also affiliated industries, including petrochemical, metals, and materials.

To more fully integrate the blockchain ecosystem with other tools and technologies, such as the Internet of Things (IoT), sensors, and even robotics, research into middleware solutions that bridge the gap between blockchain and existing automotive IT systems is imperative. Enabling smooth processing, integration, and data flow can be managed by such middleware. These endeavors collectively contribute to establishing a cohesive and interoperable blockchain infrastructure within the automotive industry.

The automotive sector is subject to various regulations and standards. Research is required to ensure that blockchain solutions comply with current and emergent public policy and regulations while still providing transparency and efficiency. To promote the integration of blockchain technology in the automotive industry, there needs to be an extensive examination of the legal and regulatory frameworks relevant to this innovation (Nizamuddin and Abugabah, 2021). This analysis will provide insights into compliance requirements and potential challenges. Some of these regulations and policies will be based on environmental and sustainability dimensions; blockchain research integrating sustainability into the automotive network around carbon emissions, particulate emissions, and fuel usage standards are examples.

The development of smart contract templates and compliance mechanisms plays a pivotal role in automating regulatory adherence, streamlining processes, and ensuring transparency. Furthermore, researching decentralized identity solutions tailored for KYC (know your customer) (Kapsoulis et al., 2020) and AML (anti–money laundering) (Alarab et al., 2020) compliance is imperative. These solutions can enhance security and compliance while fostering trust in blockchain applications within the automotive sector, aligning them with regulatory standards (Upadhyay et al., 2021).

The current body of research predominantly offers conceptual frameworks and theoretical constructs for integrating blockchain into automotive supply chains, vehicle management, and other relevant areas. While these frameworks serve as a solid foundation, there is a distinct gap when it comes to empirical studies and practical applications. Real-world use cases and quantitative analyses are essential to bridge the divide between theory and practice. Researchers should actively engage with industry partners and stakeholders (a transdisciplinary approach (Bergendahl et al., 2018)) to develop and implement blockchain solutions in actual automotive environments. These practical projects can provide valuable insights into the challenges, benefits, and limitations of blockchain technology (Chan et al., 2023).

Alternatively, blockchain research conducted on the automotive supply chain also indicates that focusing exclusively on the direct integration into the automotive supply chain may yield unrealistic results and may not be practically feasible. When examining the reasons for this feasibility concern, automotive supply chain complexity comprising numerous subcomponents with their own production processes and stakeholder structures constrains blockchain functionality.

The lack of compatibility among the technological infrastructures of stakeholders in the multi-tiered automotive supply chain poses a significant obstacle to feasibility. In this context, it is clear that a broader and more holistic approach is required to effectively address the challenges of integrating blockchain into the automotive supply chain (Wiengarten et al., 2010). Stakeholder blockchain design principles need to be carefully studied to balance the need of stakeholders in this environment.

Therefore, in future studies, it is essential to consider not only the entire automotive supply chain but also the sub-suppliers and stakeholders—for example, the lithium-ion battery blockchain, engine production blockchain, and materials blockchain that feed into the automotive sector (Chen et al., 2023; Yıldızbaşı et al., 2021). Research efforts should be directed toward integrating blockchain technology into the supply chains of individual components within the automotive supply chain. This shift in focus will allow studies to progress beyond the framework level and move toward a more advanced stage. It is necessary for stakeholders to hierarchically facilitate technology adoption. By doing so, research in this direction has the potential to address the intricacies of blockchain integration more effectively within the automotive supply chain while accommodating the specific needs and structures of various component-based supply chains.

While qualitative research is valuable, such as optimization framework for understanding the nuances of blockchain adoption, quantitative studies are equally crucial (Bai and Sarkis, 2022; Goli, 2023). Empirical data and statistical analysis can quantify the impact of blockchain on factors like efficiency, cost savings, and security. In the realm of blockchain technology integration, while much attention is devoted to areas such as platform selection (Bai et al., 2021; Nanayakkara et al., 2021) and architectural layers (Mangla et al., 2022), there exists a limitation in terms of studies focusing on the system's operation and its financial implications. This dearth of research in practical blockchain aspects raises significant questions regarding its feasibility. Future studies need to place a strong emphasis on cost analysis and consider the environmental impacts through comprehensive assessments. Undertaking such analyses will not only provide valuable insights but also offer guidance for technology-based projects in transition, shedding light on the future of these endeavors. These insights set the foundation for informed decision-making and ensure that blockchain technology, with its potential benefits, is adopted sustainably and effectively. There is a compelling need for quantitative research in the blockchain domain to bridge the gap between theory and practical application.

Blockchain research should encourage collaboration between experts in blockchain technology, automotive engineering, data science, and economics. This interdisciplinary approach can lead to holistic insights and innovative solutions. Roles and interactions need to be defined, as development, implementation, and maintenance will be necessary for strategic integration of blockchain systems into the automotive supply chain.

3.7 CONCLUSION

The complex, multi-layered supply chain structure and the wide geographic scope of automotive supply chains require taking advantage of technological advances and innovative approaches to increase efficiency and competitiveness. Furthermore, the integration of blockchain technology into the closed-loop supply chain management of the automotive industry holds immense promise, providing solutions to existing challenges of transparency, security, and traceability.

While blockchain technology is still in its early stages, its potential to revolutionize automotive supply chains does exist. The journey towards full integration is fraught with challenges, including costs, stakeholder engagement, incentivization, and the need for skilled blockchain professionals. This study has sought to shed light on these gaps and provide a comprehensive framework, identifying key research implications for future investigations. Blockchain technology stands as a pivotal enabler of digital transformation within the automotive sector, and addressing the challenges outlined here will be instrumental in realizing its full potential.

REFERENCES

Abeyratne, S. A., & Monfared, R. P. (2016). Blockchain ready manufacturing supply chain using distributed ledger. *International Journal of Research in Engineering and Technology*, *5*(9), 1–10.

Alarab, I., Prakoonwit, S., & Nacer, M. I. (2020, June). Competence of graph convolutional networks for anti-money laundering in bitcoin blockchain. In *Proceedings of the 2020 5th international conference on machine learning technologies* (pp. 23–27). New York: Association for Computing Machinery.

Alsadi, M., Arshad, J., Ali, J., Prince, A., & Shishank, S. (2023). TruCert: Blockchain-based trustworthy product certification within autonomous automotive supply chains. *Computers and Electrical Engineering*, *109*, 108738.

Aste, T., Tasca, P., & Di Matteo, T. (2017). Blockchain technologies: The foreseeable impact on society and industry. *Computer*, *50*(9), 18–28.

Bai, C., & Sarkis, J. (2022). A critical review of formal analytical modeling for blockchain technology in production, operations, and supply chains: Harnessing progress for future potential. *International Journal of Production Economics*, *250*, 108636.

Bai, C., Zhu, Q., & Sarkis, J. (2021). Joint blockchain service vendor-platform selection using social network relationships: A multi-provider multi-user decision perspective. *International Journal of Production Economics*, *238*, 108165.

Belchior, R., Vasconcelos, A., Guerreiro, S., & Correia, M. (2021). A survey on blockchain interoperability: Past, present, and future trends. *ACM Computing Surveys (CSUR)*, *54*(8), 1–41.

Benchoufi, M., Porcher, R., & Ravaud, P. (2017). Blockchain protocols in clinical trials: Transparency and traceability of consent. *F1000Research*, *6*.

Bergendahl, J. A., Sarkis, J., & Timko, M. T. (2018). Transdisciplinarity and the food energy and water nexus: Ecological modernization and supply chain sustainability perspectives. *Resources, Conservation and Recycling*, *133*, 309–319.

Cachon, G. P., & Lariviere, M. A. (2005). Supply chain coordination with revenue-sharing contracts: Strengths and limitations. *Management Science*, *51*(1), 30–44.

Carter, C. R., & Rogers, D. S. (2008). A framework of sustainable supply chain management: Moving toward new theory. *International Journal of Physical Distribution & Logistics Management*, *38*(5), 360–387.

Chan, H. L., Choi, T. M., & De la Torre, D. M. (2023). The "SMARTER" framework and real application cases of blockchain. *Technological Forecasting and Social Change*, *196*, 122798.

Chen, Y. (2018). Blockchain tokens and the potential democratization of entrepreneurship and innovation. *Business Horizons*, *61*(4), 567–575.

Chen, Z., Yildizbasi, A., Wang, Y., & Sarkis, J. (2023). Circular supply chain stakeholder mapping for blockchain governance of lithium-ion battery safety. In *Academy of management proceedings* (Vol. 2023, No. 1, p. 18836). Briarcliff Manor, NY: Academy of Management.

Chiacchio, F., D'Urso, D., Oliveri, L. M., Spitaleri, A., Spampinato, C., & Giordano, D. (2022). A non-fungible token solution for the track and trace of pharmaceutical supply chain. *Applied Sciences*, *12*(8), 4019.

Collier, Z. A., & Sarkis, J. (2021). The zero trust supply chain: Managing supply chain risk in the absence of trust. *International Journal of Production Research*, *59*(11), 3430–3445.

Dang, H., Dinh, T. T. A., Loghin, D., Chang, E. C., Lin, Q., & Ooi, B. C. (2019, June). Towards scaling blockchain systems via sharding. In *Proceedings of the 2019 international conference on management of data* (pp. 123–140). New York: Association for Computing Machinery.

De Giovanni, P. (2022). Leveraging the circular economy with a closed-loop supply chain and a reverse omnichannel using blockchain technology and incentives. *International Journal of Operations & Production Management*, *42*(7), 959–994.

Dehshiri, S. J. H., Emamat, M. S. M. M., & Amiri, M. (2022). A novel group BWM approach to evaluate the implementation criteria of blockchain technology in the automotive industry supply chain. *Expert Systems with Applications, 198*, 116826.

Dong, F., Zhou, P., Liu, Z., Shen, D., Xu, Z., & Luo, J. (2017). Towards a fast and secure design for enterprise-oriented cloud storage systems. *Concurrency and Computation: Practice and Experience, 29*(19), e4177.

Doorey, D. J. (2011). The transparent supply chain: From resistance to implementation at Nike and Levi-Strauss. *Journal of Business Ethics, 103*, 587–603.

Dutta, P., Choi, T. M., Somani, S., & Butala, R. (2020). Blockchain technology in supply chain operations: Applications, challenges and research opportunities. *Transportation Research Part E: Logistics and Transportation Review, 142*, 102067.

Egels-Zandén, N., Hulthén, K., & Wulff, G. (2015). Trade-offs in supply chain transparency: The case of Nudie Jeans Co. *Journal of Cleaner Production, 107*, 95–104.

Ethirajan, M., Arasu M, T., Kandasamy, J., Kek, V., Nadeem, S. P., & Kumar, A. (2021). Analysing the risks of adopting circular economy initiatives in manufacturing supply chains. *Business Strategy and the Environment, 30*(1), 204–236.

Figorilli, S., Antonucci, F., Costa, C., Pallottino, F., Raso, L., Castiglione, M., . . . & Menesatti, P. (2018). A blockchain implementation prototype for the electronic open source traceability of wood along the whole supply chain. *Sensors, 18*(9), 3133.

Filali Rotbi, M., Motahhir, S., & El Ghzizal, A. (2022). Blockchain-based CPS and IoT in the automotive supply chain. In *Advances in blockchain technology for cyber physical systems* (pp. 155–176). Cham: Springer International Publishing.

Fraga-Lamas, P., & Fernández-Caramés, T. M. (2019). A review on blockchain technologies for an advanced and cyber-resilient automotive industry. *IEEE Access, 7*, 17578–17598.

Goli, A. (2023). Integration of blockchain-enabled closed-loop supply chain and robust product portfolio design. *Computers & Industrial Engineering, 179*, 109211.

Grimm, J. H., Hofstetter, J. S., & Sarkis, J. (2016). Exploring sub-suppliers' compliance with corporate sustainability standards. *Journal of Cleaner Production, 112*, 1971–1984.

Hamledari, H., & Fischer, M. (2021). The application of blockchain-based crypto assets for integrating the physical and financial supply chains in the construction & engineering industry. *Automation in Construction, 127*, 103711.

Hashim, F., Shuaib, K., & Sallabi, F. (2021). Medshard: Electronic health record sharing using blockchain sharding. *Sustainability, 13*(11), 5889.

Ivanov, D., Sethi, S., Dolgui, A., & Sokolov, B. (2018). A survey on control theory applications to operational systems, supply chain management, and industry 4.0. *Annual Reviews in Control, 46*, 134–147.

Kamble, S. S., Gunasekaran, A., Subramanian, N., Ghadge, A., Belhadi, A., & Venkatesh, M. (2023). Blockchain technology's impact on supply chain integration and sustainable supply chain performance: Evidence from the automotive industry. *Annals of Operations Research, 327*(1), 575–600.

Kapsoulis, N., Psychas, A., Palaiokrassas, G., Marinakis, A., Litke, A., & Varvarigou, T. (2020). Know your customer (KYC) implementation with smart contracts on a privacy-oriented decentralized architecture. *Future Internet, 12*(2), 41.

Kayikci, Y., Subramanian, N., Dora, M., & Bhatia, M. S. (2022). Food supply chain in the era of industry 4.0: Blockchain technology implementation opportunities and impediments from the perspective of people, process, performance, and technology. *Production Planning & Control, 33*(2–3), 301–321.

Kouhizadeh, M., Saberi, S., & Sarkis, J. (2021). Blockchain technology and the sustainable supply chain: Theoretically exploring adoption barriers. *International Journal of Production Economics, 231*, 107831.

Kouhizadeh, M., & Sarkis, J. (2018). Blockchain practices, potentials, and perspectives in greening supply chains. *Sustainability, 10*(10), 3652.

Kshetri, N. (2018). 1 Blockchain's roles in meeting key supply chain management objectives. *International Journal of Information Management, 39*, 80–89.

Kurpjuweit, S., Schmidt, C. G., Klöckner, M., & Wagner, S. M. (2021). Blockchain in additive manufacturing and its impact on supply chains. *Journal of Business Logistics, 42*(1), 46–70.

Li, Z., Bahramirad, S., Paaso, A., Yan, M., & Shahidehpour, M. (2019). Blockchain for decentralized transactive energy management system in networked microgrids. *The Electricity Journal, 32*(4), 58–72.

Lu, D., Moreno-Sanchez, P., Zeryihun, A., Bajpayi, S., Yin, S., Feldman, K., . . . Kate, A. (2019, April). Reducing automotive counterfeiting using blockchain: Benefits and challenges. In *2019 IEEE international conference on decentralized applications and infrastructures (DAPPCON)* (pp. 39–48). New York: IEEE.

Lu, Q., & Xu, X. (2017). Adaptable blockchain-based systems: A case study for product traceability. *IEEE Software, 34*(6), 21–27.

Mangla, S. K., Kazançoğlu, Y., Yıldızbaşı, A., Öztürk, C., & Çalık, A. (2022). A conceptual framework for blockchain-based sustainable supply chain and evaluating implementation barriers: A case of the tea supply chain. *Business Strategy and the Environment*, *31*(8), 3693–3716.

Miehle, D., Henze, D., Seitz, A., Luckow, A., & Bruegge, B. (2019, April). PartChain: A decentralized traceability application for multi-tier supply chain networks in the automotive industry. In *2019 IEEE international conference on decentralized applications and infrastructures (DAPPCON)* (pp. 140–145). Newark, CA, USA: IEEE.

Mol, A. P. (2015). Transparency and value chain sustainability. *Journal of Cleaner Production*, *107*, 154–161.

Nanayakkara, S., Rodrigo, M. N. N., Perera, S., Weerasuriya, G. T., & Hijazi, A. A. (2021). A methodology for selection of a blockchain platform to develop an enterprise system. *Journal of Industrial Information Integration*, *23*, 100215.

Nizamuddin, N., & Abugabah, A. (2021). Blockchain for automotive: An insight towards the IPFS blockchain-based auto insurance sector. *International Journal of Electrical and Computer Engineering (IJECE)*, *11*.

Okanami, N., Nakamura, R., & Nishide, T. (2022). Load balancing with in-protocol/wallet-level account assignment in sharded blockchains. *IEICE TRANSACTIONS on Information and Systems*, *105*(2), 205–214.

Öztürk, C., & Yildizbaşi, A. (2020). Barriers to implementation of blockchain into supply chain management using an integrated multi-criteria decision-making method: A numerical example. *Soft Computing*, *24*, 14771–14789.

Reddy, K. R. K., Gunasekaran, A., Kalpana, P., Sreedharan, V. R., & Kumar, S. A. (2021). Developing a blockchain framework for the automotive supply chain: A systematic review. *Computers & Industrial Engineering*, *157*, 107334.

Saberi, S., Kouhizadeh, M., & Sarkis, J. (2019). Blockchains and the supply chain: Findings from a broad study of practitioners. *IEEE Engineering Management Review*, *47*(3), 95–103.

Schulte, S., Sigwart, M., Frauenthaler, P., & Borkowski, M. (2019). Towards blockchain interoperability. In *Business process management: Blockchain and Central and Eastern Europe forum: BPM 2019 blockchain and CEE forum, Vienna, Austria, September 1–6, 2019, proceedings 17* (pp. 3–10). New York: Springer International Publishing.

Seuring, S., Sarkis, J., Müller, M., & Rao, P. (2008). Sustainability and supply chain management–an introduction to the special issue. *Journal of Cleaner Production*, *16*(15), 1545–1551.

Sharma, P. K., Kumar, N., & Park, J. H. (2020). Blockchain technology toward green IoT: Opportunities and challenges. *IEEE Network*, *34*(4), 263–269.

Tian, F. (2016, June). An agri-food supply chain traceability system for China based on RFID & blockchain technology. In *2016 13th international conference on service systems and service management (ICSSSM)* (pp. 1–6). Kunming, China: IEEE.

Upadhyay, A., Ayodele, J. O., Kumar, A., & Garza-Reyes, J. A. (2021). A review of challenges and opportunities of blockchain adoption for operational excellence in the UK automotive industry. *Journal of Global Operations and Strategic Sourcing*, *14*(1), 7–60.

Veuger, J. (2018). Trust in a viable real estate economy with disruption and blockchain. *Facilities*, *36*(1/2), 103–120.

Wiengarten, F., Humphreys, P., Cao, G., Fynes, B., & McKittrick, A. (2010). Collaborative supply chain practices and performance: Exploring the key role of information quality. *Supply Chain Management: An International Journal*, *15*(6), 463–473.

Xu, X., Tatge, L., Xu, X., & Liu, Y. (2022). Blockchain applications in the supply chain management in German automotive industry. *Production Planning & Control*, 1–15.

Yildizbasi, A. (2021). Blockchain and renewable energy: Integration challenges in circular economy era. *Renewable Energy*, *176*, 183–197.

Yildizbasi, A., Çalik, A., Paksoy, T., Farahani, R. Z., & Weber, G. W. (2018). Multi-level optimization of an automotive closed-loop supply chain network with interactive fuzzy programming approaches. *Technological and Economic Development of Economy*, *24*(3), 1004–1028.

Yıldızbaşı, A., Öztürk, C., Yılmaz, İ., & Arıöz, Y. (2021, August). Key challenges of lithium-ion battery recycling process in circular economy environment: Pythagorean fuzzy AHP approach. In *International conference on intelligent and fuzzy systems* (pp. 561–568). Cham: Springer International Publishing.

Yli-Huumo, J., Ko, D., Choi, S., Park, S., & Smolander, K. (2016). Where is current research on blockchain technology?—a systematic review. *PLoS One*, *11*(10), e0163477.

Zafar, S., Hassan, S. F. U., Mohammad, A., Al-Ahmadi, A. A., & Ullah, N. (2022). Implementation of a distributed framework for permissioned blockchain-based secure automotive supply chain management. *Sensors*, *22*(19), 7367.

Zhu, Q., Bai, C., & Sarkis, J. (2022). Blockchain technology and supply chains: The paradox of the atheoretical research discourse. *Transportation Research Part E: Logistics and Transportation Review*, *164*, 102824.

4 Car Insurance Blockchain

Nalayini C. M., Jeevaa Katiravan, and Thanga Akilan V.

4.1 INTRODUCTION

4.1.1 INSURANCE

Individuals and institutions take risk to achieve something. But with high risk comes high chances of losing. This costs the peace of mind of those who take risk. This can be eliminated by insurance companies, which is all about risk management. The insurance company shares the risk of an entity and gets a premium paid for it. It consists of two main stakeholders: the insurer and the insured. The insured pays a premium regularly to the insurer for sharing the risk. The insurer takes the risk by accepting to provide financial assistance in case of any unfortunate events [1].

The insurer collects premium from many entities to get a large amount which it uses for paying for those who encounter that unfortunate event. The insured requesting for a payout after such an event is known as insurance claim. In a society, not everyone will be broke (i.e., claim) at the same time normally. So only a few people will need to be paid out, and the remaining is the profit of the insurer.

The global insurance industry witnessed a growth of 4.5% in the year 2019, which is higher than the CAGR of 3.0% from 2010 to 2018 [2]. The data for the post-COVID period is still unclear, but the growth in life insurance has grown positively. COVID has proven the importance of insurance to all of us. According to Statista, the global insurance industry is worth USD 5 trillion as of 2020, with the United States holding nearly half of the market value [3]. The global insurance penetration stands at 6.8%, with Taiwan leading the list with 17.4%, USA with 12%, India with 4.4%, and China with 4.5% [4].

Car insurance is a type of insurance which covers financial protection against physical damage, collision, and theft [5]. It has many add-ons that focus on different parts of the car. It covers not only the vehicle and the driver but also third party. *Third party* refers to the person or asset who is affected by the driver driving the car. It is made mandatory for car owners to get a car insurance in countries like the United States, China, India [6]. Figure 4.1 shows the working of an insurance.

The global auto insurance was worth $739.30 billion in 2019 and is expected to grow at a compound annual growth rate (CAGR) of 8.5% from 2020 to 2027 [7]. It is projected to reach $1.06 trillion by 2027. However, the COVID pandemic had a significant impact on the industry, with car and home insurance losing a lot, according to Forbes [8].

Car insurance gets very little attention even though it provides financial protection at difficult times. This backlash on car insurance is attributed to many factors. Figure 4.2 shows the various factors affecting the car insurance industry.

Lack of knowledge. One of the major factors is the lack of knowledge about insurance. It is especially seen in developing countries like India. It exists even after governments have made car insurance mandatory and used various methods to spread awareness about the same.

Negative image. The industry has an overall negative image on the minds of people due to the various frauds that happen either from the insured's side or from the insurer's side. This image contradicts the actual objective of the industry, such that getting an insurance has become a risky business.

Complexity. The paper-signing process for car insurance requires a lot of documents and verification to prevent frauds. It also has a lot of plug-ins with hidden exceptions, which make it difficult to understand for the insured.

DOI: 10.1201/9781003450306-5

Car Owner takes Insurance and pays premium

Insurer collects premium and provides protection against unfortunate events

In case of accident, The insurer pays the amount to the insured

FIGURE 4.1 Working of an insurance.

FIGURE 4.2 Factors affecting car insurance.

Frauds. Insured-side fraud can be of two types, that is, soft and hard frauds. *Soft fraud* is when the insured provides wrong information during the paper-signing process without knowledge. *Hard fraud* is when the insured intentionally makes way for an insurance claim, such as staged accidents. The insurer, in response to these frauds, have made the claims process hectic to undertake.

Insurer paradigm. The insurer profits more when claims are less. These pain points are yet to be solved, since some factors impact positively on the profits of the insurer. The premium paid is also high in many countries.

Agents. Most insurance companies hire agents who are paid based on the number of insurances signed. These agents focus more on insurance registration than explaining the pitfalls in the contracts. This has affected the trust of third party agents in insurance.

Governments have an exclusive body to regulate and license insurance and re-insurance for insurance companies. These regulatory bodies ensure that the insurer does not undergo any fraudulent actions. They are established to overview the proper working of the insurance processes. Examples include CBIRC (China), IRDAI (India), EIOPA (Europe), NAIC (USA). Insurance companies work under these regulatory bodies [9]. According to AMBest, Allianz is the world's largest insurer in terms of total assets, with 1,261.9 billion in 2020, and United Health Group is the world's largest insurer in terms of net premiums written, with 201.5 billion net premiums written [10].

The insurer invests the premium in various financial instruments, like stocks, mutual funds, debentures, etc., to get a higher rate of return than simply holding it in a bank account. Hence, insurers are also institutional investors in many countries [11].

4.1.2 BLOCKCHAIN

Blockchain is a distributed ledger with blocks of data linked together using cryptographic hashes. The timestamp and the hash of the previous hash are included in the block before calculating the hash, hence ensuring connectivity between them. If one of the blocks is modified, not only will its hash be changed, but all the preceding blocks' hash will also be modified. This makes it immutable after written into a block [12]. Figure 4.3 describes the chaining of blockchain.

It is a distributed ledger technology where each node maintains a separate ledger and the ledger is updated with a transaction only after having been digitally signed by the buyer. The new nodes can be added to the network anytime with or without the permission of the existing nodes based on the type of blockchain network. The different types of blockchain used for various use cases are listed in Table 4.1.

Consensus algorithms are used to reach a consensus between the members of the network. This can be achieved in many ways, where the entity that uses more computing power gets to add the new block (proof of work), the entity that has more of an asset (proof of stake), the entity with an authority (proof of authority), etc. [13]. Figure 4.4 gives the main properties of blockchain.

Blockchain can be established in any industry where the parties do not trust each other but nevertheless work together. It also removes the middlemen involved and the costs that occur. Smart contracts enable the automatic execution of code or action when a particular condition is met. These aspects inspire people to adapt blockchain in various fields, like insurance.

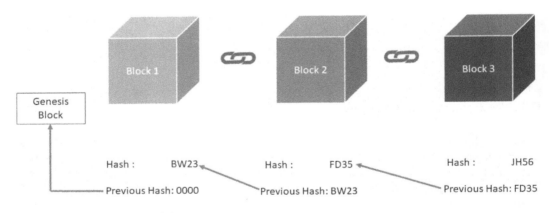

FIGURE 4.3 Blockchain chaining.

TABLE 4.1
Types of Blockchain

Public	No access restriction	Bitcoin, Ethereum
Private	Permissioned	Hyperledger
Consortium	Permissioned	Corda, Hyperledger
Hybrid	Depends	IBM Food Chain

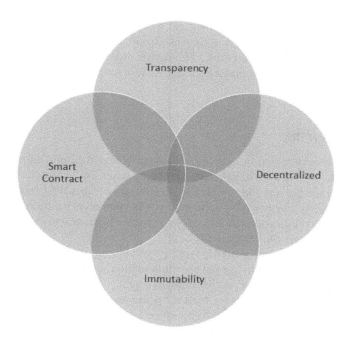

FIGURE 4.4 Properties of blockchain.

Different blockchains are developed for their own use case, and sometimes these blockchains will need to work together. It is possible to link the blockchains and transfer information and assets from one to another using blockchain bridge. It is the interface between two blockchains which needs to exchange information or assets between them.

4.2 RELATED WORKS

Friendsurance, an insurance solutions company based in Germany, is the first company to introduce peer-to-peer insurance in 2010. People form groups to get a premium into a common pool, and then this pool is used for payout to the claims. In case the pool has money at the end of the period, it is shared between the insureds [14].

Teambrella, founded in 2015, enables a Bitcoin-based peer-to-peer insurance company. Each member joins a Teambrella team and deposits funds in a special Bitcoin wallet. The funds are controlled by the team. In case of a claim, each member votes to reimburse the specific insured [15].

Blockchain Insurance Industry Initiative (B3i) is a blockchain insurance venture incorporated in 2018. It began with five major insurers, and many joined later to become 20 in 2020. It used R3 Corda for the blockchain network. It got the project of managing nuclear reinsurance in six European nuclear pools. Due to failure of further funding, it filed for bankruptcy in July 2022 [16–18].

RiskBlock Alliance is a blockchain consortium of 31 risk management and insurance companies. According to Business Insider, its blockchain solutions are aimed to reduce transaction cost and increase speed and security of data transfers. It uses R3 Corda for the blockchain for blockchain solutions [19, 20].

Lemonade Crypto Climate Coalition is a decentralized autonomous organization (DAO) which aims to protect farmers from climate change by providing insurance. It especially focuses on African farmers since they do not get weather reports prior and they lack the infra to provide affordable insurances. It is a decentralized application (dApp) on the Avalanche platform using the proof-of-stake network. This helps provide insurance coverage throughout the continent irrespective of the boundaries and increases the usage of cryptocurrencies in the African continent [21, 22].

4.3 PROPOSED WORK

The working of the network for car insurance can be broadly classified into three stages (Figure 4.5). The first stage begins with the verification of owning an asset, for example, car in the car block-chain. Then choosing the various add-ons for the car insurance as per the interests of the insured. It also provides schemes like pay-how-you-drive and pay-as-you-drive that need an extra device to be attached to the car and the info added to the car blockchain. The stage ends with the insured signing the record of accepting to get the car insured.

The second stage involves the insured paying premiums regularly, as stated in the insurance document at the first stage. Failing to pay the premium regularly affects the claim score of the insurance, which affects the payout as well as the reimbursement.

The third stage has multiple scenarios which are possible. One, in case of small accidents, information about the change of car parts needs to be added to the car blockchain to request for a payout in the insurance blockchain. Second, in case of a huge accident, the car's ownership needs to be transferred to the scrapping company in the car blockchain, after which the payout continues in the insurance blockchain. Third, when the insurance ends, reimbursement is made to the insured, taking into account the amount of payout made, claim score, etc.

It also includes usage-based motor insurance schemes, like pay-as-you-drive (PAYD) and pay-how-you-drive (PHYD) [23–27]. Instead of paying a fixed premium, these schemes determine the premium to be paid based on the driving of the insured. This reduces the premium paid by disciplined drivers, who are less probable to cause an accident.

It requires the driver to install a piece of hardware in the car that records data like distance, speed, time, acceleration, etc. and sends it through wireless connection to the cloud. The data is retrieved weekly, and the driving score is calculated and stored. Various telematic hardware manufacturers provide this solution, like Sky-meter, OnStar, Freematics, etc., and their cost and configuration [28] are given in Table 4.2.

FIGURE 4.5 Insurance process architecture.

TABLE 4.2

Telematic Manufacturers, Products, Configuration, and Cost

Manufacturer	Data	Transmission Method	Installation Cost	Monthly Cost
CarChipFleetPro	Distance, time, acceleration, speed, GPS location, fuel, engine speed	USB cable/port	$149 (plus a $395 charge for software, one per fleet); can also be used wirelessly, with a $200 base unit	None
Sky-meter	Time, distance, place, speed, acceleration of all driving, and the location and time of all parking	GPRS/CDMA (other protocols available at extra charge)	$50–$250 activation fee	$5 per month plus 5%–8% of monthly premium (depending on volume)
OnStar	Distance, speed, time, (incl. other features)	Automatic through GPS S	First year free for new GM cars (only available for GM)	$18.95 per month after one year
Freematics	Speed, distance, time, location, acceleration, engine RPM	Built-in Bluetooth Low Energy and SPP module for wireless data communication	99$ (plus $30 for GPS module, plus $10 for EMS MPU-9150 (9-axis) module)	None

Source: Design and Development of Weigh-In-Motion Using Vehicular Telematics.

4.4 IMPLEMENTATION

The various aspects of blockchain, such as distributed systems, cryptographic hashing, consensus, etc., should be developed for the specific use case, and they are integrated to work together. It requires an expertise in all these fields to develop such solutions, so many open-source communities come together to build blockchain platforms that can be easily tuned for the use case. Many insure-tech companies use R3 Corda for blockchain development, but it is mostly used in financial aspects, which have a centralized authority for management. This proves that the companies develop non-public blockchain, where these companies have an upper hand.

There are various blockchain platforms available to implement the public insurance blockchain use case. These public blockchain platforms are analyzed about their configuration in the Table 4.3.

The insurance blockchain is a public blockchain that has a public ledger to store the transactions, a native cryptocurrency, ability to execute smart contracts [29–33] (Figure 4.6). This can be best implemented using the EOSIO protocol. The EOSIO protocol is used by some major networks, like EOS and Telos Blockchain, mainly due to the "no transaction fees" policy. These networks also have their own cryptocurrencies, such as EOS and Telos, respectively.

The EOSIO protocol has various features that satisfy our car insurance blockchain. The insurance blockchain needs to be connected with the car blockchain to verify the ownership and alteration made to the car. EOSIO protocol makes this process of connection easier if the car blockchain is also based on the EOSIO protocol. This is established with the help of a unidirectional trustless blockchain bridge.

The consensus layer has delegated proof-of-stake consensus algorithm for block generation. In the algorithm, peers holding the asset (cryptocurrency) get to vote to select the miner, whose block will be added to the blockchain and rewarded for it. In EOSIO protocol, the asset holders

TABLE 4.3
Blockchain Platform

	Ethereum	Ardor	Cardano	EOS	ICON
Language	Go, C++, Rust	Java	Haskell	C++	Python
Consensus	PoW	PoS	PoS	DPoS	LFT
Block time (s)	14–15	60	20	0.5	1
Smart contract	Yes	No	No	Yes	No
Token creation	Yes	Yes	No	Yes	No
Average transaction cost	21,000 GAS	1 ARDR		Free	0.01 ICX

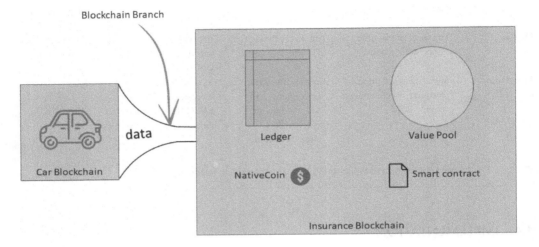

FIGURE 4.6 Insurance blockchain architecture.

vote to select 21 miners, all of which will add a new block to the blockchain. The EOSIO protocol helps in development focusing on all the five layers of the blockchain network, as shown in Figure 4.7.

4.4.1 PHYSICAL LAYER

EOSIO Virtual State Machine works on managing the current state and changes the state of the network. Its performance is the same regardless of the infrastructure on which it runs, since it is virtual. New state can be added to the network with the help of smart contracts. EOSIO has an account model that stores the values in key pairs, and these can be updated. Many public and private key pairs can be created by the owner key for various processes. The owner key is the main key that can be used to create active keys and keys for various processes. This enables the network to use separate key pairs for each process, like premium payment, claim request processing, and if the keys are found to be compromised, then the key pairs can be changed [34].

4.4.2 DATA LAYER

Any process like issue of insurance, premium payment, claim reports, and reimbursement is the transaction in the network. Every transaction is signed for verification. These transactions are then

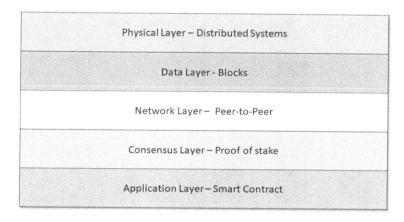

Physical Layer – Distributed Systems

Data Layer - Blocks

Network Layer – Peer-to-Peer

Consensus Layer – Proof of stake

Application Layer – Smart Contract

FIGURE 4.7 Blockchain network layers.

put in a block and added to the blockchain by the miners. The network does not charge transaction fees for the transactions made in the network, unlike many other platforms. This reduces a small cost that more occurs frequently. The network has a 5% inflation protocol to pull out transaction fees. This helps in getting the whole premium into action.

4.4.3 NETWORK LAYER

The network is a peer-to-peer network where the blocks are transported to all nodes using the gossip protocol. This model of the network prevents any entity from getting the network down. When a malicious node gossips compromised blocks into the network, it is accepted by the peers only after the chain becomes longer than other chains, which is practically hard to attain.

4.4.4 CONSENSUS LAYER

The network uses a delegated proof-of-stake (DPoS) consensus algorithm. The block time of the network is 0.5 seconds.

4.4.5 SMART CONTRACT

Smart contract focuses on executing the business logic of the network. It manages processes such as insurance registration, premium payment, claim settlement, and reimbursement. Artificial intelligence used with the smart contracts can detect fraudulent claims made [35]. It is also possible to make automatic recurring payment for premium. Separate key can be used for different processes to reduce the chance of key compromise.

Block time (ABT) is the time taken to verify the transactions in a block and produce a new block in the blockchain. Every transaction occurs only after the block containing the transaction is generated. It influences the quickness of the execution of the transactions in the network. The block times of various blockchain networks are shown in Figure 4.8

Transactions per second is calculated by dividing block size by transaction size and then dividing it by block time. It is the number of transactions the blockchain network is capable of processing. Modern payment processing systems like Visa have a throughput of 2,000 transactions per second. The earlier networks, such as Bitcoin, have high block time that reduces their TPS, as shown in Figure 4.9. Hence, a higher TPS means the network has high throughput. The TPS of different blockchain networks are shown in Figure 4.9.

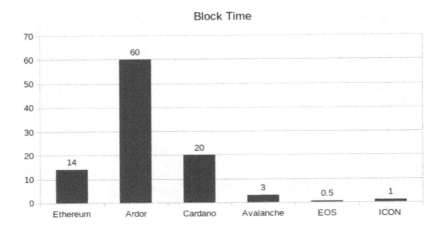

FIGURE 4.8   Block time.

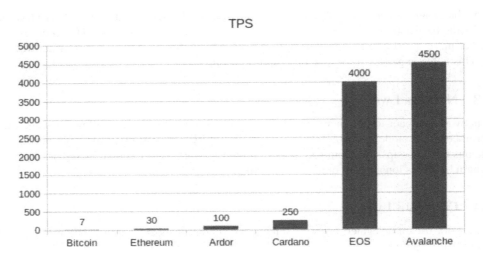

FIGURE 4.9   Transactions per second (TPS).

4.4.6   INSURANCE DETAIL

In the beginning, the premium is calculated based on the value, age, and extra fittings of the car and the add-ons selected by the insured. This premium is not fixed for the entire period, but it changes as per the driving score and the claim score of the driver. The maximum claim score can deduce the premium up to 50% [36].

The claim score can have a maximum score of 100. The various rubrics of claim score are given in Table 4.4. No claim bonus is applicable only if the insured has not made any claims in the insurance period. When the insured makes more than five payouts, the premium starts increasing directly without affecting the claim score.

The subjects given in the rubrics will be positively affected if the values are within the limits. In case any one of the values falls below or above the limits, then premium deduction is not possible and the premium rises above the nominal value.

The score of 10 points to "No claim bonus" encourages to submit for claim for smaller problems. Once the insured loses claim score, they need not exit the network but must instead try to maintain

TABLE 4.4
Claim Score Rubrics

Subject	Points
Regular premium payment	40
Driving score	20
History of claim	15
Policy length	15
No claim bonus	10
Total claim score	100

a good claim score for the next insurance, since the claim score is only for the specific insurance. This cannot be misused to create short-period insurance since the policy length will be negatively affected.

The net pay is calculated by subtracting the total payout made to the insured from the total premium paid by the insured. If the net pay is less than 25% of the total premium paid by the insured, then reimbursement is made to the insured in accordance with the claim score of the insurance.

4.5 COMPARISON

4.5.1 TRADITIONAL

The traditional insurance process involves a lot of paperwork and verification of the produced documents, which are time-consuming processes. The policies are very complicated to explain and have a lot of exceptions. The premium is mostly fixed, while few companies provide usage-based motor insurance schemes. In case of accident, these companies require the insured to follow a lot of procedure and filing of documents to get the claim for the insurance, and the claim settlement time is always in days. The insurance is centralized, and the insurance company has more control over the insurance than the insured. It also involves agent or brokers who get a commission from the insured's pockets.

4.5.2 FRIENDSURANCE

Friendsurance is a centralized P2P insurance company, and hence, the insured should trust the company in terms of insurance. Traditional insurance companies are present in the process and get a portion of the insured's pay. Disagreement within the peer group causes tensions in the group. The claims are delayed, but not to the extent of the traditional process.

4.5.3 TEAMBRELLA

Teambrella does not require the insured to trust the company but the peers in the network. It becomes a challenge when a group of fraudsters has majority over a small team; they could deny real claims and accept the fraudulent claims. In large teams, not everyone will be active, so it pays the teammate for voting from the insured's pockets.

4.5.4 PROBLEMS

The insurance blockchain is focused on providing decentralized peer-to-peer insurance, where insurance is provided for the sole purpose of providing financial protection to the insured. It is designed to increase the value that the insured obtains from the insurance. Yet it still has some problems which need to be rectified.

The network requires to use the native cryptocurrency for all purposes, but cryptocurrencies are unstable assets. These currencies fluctuate about 1–15% in a day and thus affect the value the insured puts into the network.

Premium is calculated from the value of the car in the native currency, but if the currency loses value within the insurance period, this makes it unfeasible for the insured to be protected financially. Even if the amount is reimbursed, the value of it is reduced.

The network solely relies on the car blockchain for car ownership and car damage verification, but if that blockchain is compromised, then it is impossible to prevent the flow of fraudulent activities.

4.6   CONCLUSION

In this chapter, a car insurance blockchain implemented using EOSIO software demonstrates the potential benefits of blockchain technology in the car insurance industry. The three-stage process begins with ownership verification, add-ons selection, and premium calculation, which became instant processes with the connection of the car blockchain. The second phase involves the regular payment of premiums to maintain claim score to reduce the premium paid. The third phase encompasses various scenarios, such as major and minor accidents, during which the insured requests claim, which is verified with the car blockchain, and payout is processed as per claim score immediately. If the insured contributed more to the blockchain than claims, then reimbursement is made in accordance with the claim score.

The insurance blockchain requires the car blockchain to be updated for processing any claims, thereby encouraging the users to update the current state of the car. This increases the scope of the car blockchain by managing the changes made to the car, hence providing more information about the asset to the buyer. A car service provider can access the car blockchain and intimate the user about the parts that are past their lifetime.

This insurance blockchain network focuses on removing the complexities and middlemen involved in the insurance processes, thereby increasing the benefit of the insured. It also aims to introduce new technologies in the insurance industry that increases the efficiency of the insurance process.

REFERENCES

1. K.H. Borch, A. Sandmo, K.K. Aase, *Economics of Insurance*. https://books.google.co.in/books?hl=-en&lr=&id=aDujBQAAQBAJ&oi=fnd&pg=PP1& dq=insurance&ots=LnhoKO3yKv&sig=ALsfEaEO qbHGxtJpwzps0FdxTkA&redir_esc=y#v=onepage&q=insurance&f=false.
2. *Global Insurance Pools Statistics and Trends: An Overview of Life, P&C, and Health Insurance.* www.mckinsey.com/industries/financial-services/our-insights/global-insurance-pools-statistics-and-trends-an-overview-of-life-p-and-c-and-health-insurance.
3. *Forecast of the Global Insurance Market in 2021 and 2022, With Forecasts from 2023 to 2026.* www.statista.com/statistics/1192960/forecast-global-insurance-market/.
4. *Life and Non-Life Insurance Penetration in Selected Countries and Territories Worldwide in 2020 and 2021.* www.statista.com/statistics/381174/insurance-penetration-in-selected-countries-worldwide/.
5. Stephanie Blows, Rebecca Q. Ivers, Jennie Connor, Shanthi Ameratunga, Robyn Norton, "Car Insurance and the Risk of Car Crash Injury." *Accident Analysis & Prevention*, vol. 35, no. 6, pp. 987–990, 2003. ISSN 0001-4575, https://doi.org/10.1016/S0001-4575(02)00106-9.
6. *Vehicle Insurance.* https://en.wikipedia.org/wiki/Vehicle_insurance.
7. *Global Auto Insurance Market to Garner $1.06 Trillion by 2027, at 8.5% CAGR.* www.globenewswire.com/news-release/2020/10/21/2111986/0/en/Global-Auto-Insurance-Market-to-Garner-1-06-Trillion-by-2027-at-8-5-CAGR.html.
8. *How Coronavirus May Affect Home and Renter Insurance.* www.forbes.com/sites/dimawilliams/2020/03/28/how-coronavirus-may-affect-home-and-renter-insurance/?sh=128f7443133b.

9. V. Chatzara, "FinTech, InsurTech, and the Regulators." In: Marano, P., Noussia, K. (eds), *InsurTech: A Legal and Regulatory View. AIDA Europe Research Series on Insurance Law and Regulation*, vol. 1. Springer, Cham, 2020. https://doi.org/10.1007/978-3-030-27386-6_1.

10. *AM Best Ranks UnitedHealth Group and Allianz as World's Largest Insurers.* https://news.ambest.com/presscontent.aspx?altsrc=14&refnum=27525.

11. John Breckenridge, James Farquharson, *Ruth Hendon the Role of Business Model Analysis in the Supervision of Insurers.* https://papers.ssrn.com/sol3/papers.cfm?abstract_id=2416239.

12. Satoshi Nakamoto, *Bitcoin: A Peer-to-Peer Electronic Cash System.* https://bitcoin.org/bitcoin.pdf.

13. G. Nguyen, K. Kim, "A Survey About Consensus Algorithms Used in Blockchain." *Journal of Information Processing Systems*, vol. 14, no. 1, pp. 101–128, 2018. https://doi.org/10.3745/JIPS.01.0024.

14. S. Da Chishti, J. Barberis, D. Pietroni, "Assessing the Long-Term Viability of the Insurance Peer-to-Peer Business Model." In: Chishti, S., Barberis, J. (eds), *The InsurTech Book*. 2018. https://doi.org/10.1002/9781119444565.ch46.

15. A. Paperno, V. Kravchuk, E. Porubaev, *Teambrella: A Peer to Peer Insurance System.* https://policy.report/Resources/Whitepapers/feb3ffac-837f-4027-bc4d-e405c01a0434_WhitePaper777.pdf.

16. *Blockchain: B3i Consortium to Cease Operations.* www.atlas-mag.net/en/category/regions-geographiques/monde/blockchain-b3i-consortium-to-cease-operations.

17. *Industry's Blockchain Project, B3i, Ceases to Trade After Filing for Insolvency.* www.insurancejournal.com/news/international/2022/07/29/677926.htm.

18. *Major Insurers Pull the Plug on B3i Insurance Blockchain Consortium.* www.ledgerinsights.com/major-insurers-pull-the-plug-on-b3i-insurance-blockchain-consortium/.

19. *RiskBlock Alliance Launches Canopy Blockchain Framework.* www.businessinsurance.com/article/20180912/NEWS06/912323950/The-Institutes-RiskBlock-Alliance-launches-Canopy-blockchain-framework-R3CEV-LLC.

20. *RiskBlock's Blockchain Targets Entire Insurance Industry.* www.ledgerinsights.com/riskblock-blockchain-insurance-industry/.

21. *Introducing the Lemonade Crypto Climate Coalition.* www.lemonade.com/blog/crypto-climate-coalition/.

22. *Lemonade to Use Blockchain to Deliver "Affordable and Instantaneous" Climate Insurance.* www.reinsurancene.ws/lemonade-to-use-blockchain-to-deliver-affordable-and-instantaneous-climate-insurance/.

23. Yiyang Bian, Chen Yang, J. Leon Zhao, Liang Liang, "Good Drivers Pay Less: A Study of Usage-Based Vehicle Insurance Models." *Transportation Research Part A: Policy and Practice*, vol. 107, pp. 20–34, 2018. ISSN 0965-8564, https://doi.org/10.1016/j.tra.2017.10.018.

24. S. Arumugam, R. Bhargavi, "A Survey on Driving Behavior Analysis in Usage-Based Insurance Using Big Data." *Journal of Big Data*, vol. 6, no. 86, 2019. https://doi.org/10.1186/s40537-019-0249-5.

25. G. Meyers, I.V. Hoyweghen, " 'Happy Failures': Experimentation with Behaviour-Based Personalisation in Car Insurance." *Big Data & Society*, vol. 7, no. 1, 2020. https://doi.org/10.1177/2053951720914650.

26. P. Francois, T. Voldoire, "The Revolution that did not Happen: Telematics and Car Insurance in the 2010s." *Big Data & Society*, vol. 9, no. 2, 2022. https://doi.org/10.1177/20539517221142033.

27. N. Milanović, M. Milosavljević, S. Benković, D. Starčević, Ž. Spasenić, "An Acceptance Approach for Novel Technologies in Car Insurance." *Sustainability*, vol. 12, no. 24, p. 10331, December 2020. doi: 10.3390/su122410331.

28. Sivaramalingam Kirushanth, Boniface Kabaso, "Design and Development of Weigh-In-Motion Using Vehicular Telematics." *Journal of Sensors*, vol. 2020, Article ID 7871215, p. 22, 2020. https://doi.org/10.1155/2020/7871215.

29. V. Gatteschi, F. Lamberti, C. Demartini, C. Pranteda, V. Santamaría, "Blockchain and Smart Contracts for Insurance: Is the Technology Mature Enough?" *Future Internet*, vol. 10, no. 2, p. 20, February 2018. doi: 10.3390/fi10020020.

30. M. Raikwar, S. Mazumdar, S. Ruj, S. Sen Gupta, A. Chattopadhyay, K.-Y. Lam, "A Blockchain Framework for Insurance Processes." In: *2018 9th IFIP International Conference on New Technologies, Mobility and Security (NTMS)*, Paris, France, 2018, pp. 1–4. doi: 10.1109/NTMS.2018.8328731.

31. P. Tasca, "Insurance Under the Blockchain Paradigm." In: Treiblmaier, H., Beck, R. (eds), *Business Transformation Through Blockchain*. Palgrave Macmillan, Cham. 2019. https://doi.org/10.1007/978-3-319-98911-2_9

32. D. Popovic, C. Avis, M. Byrne, C. Cheung, M. Donovan, Y. Flynn, C. Fothergill, Z. Hosseinzadeh, Z. Lim, J. Shah, "Understanding Blockchain for Insurance Use Cases." *British Actuarial Journal*, vol. 25, p. e12, 2020.

33. F. Lamberti, V. Gatteschi, C. Demartini, M. Pelissier, A. Gomez, V. Santamaria, "Blockchains Can Work for Car Insurance: Using Smart Contracts and Sensors to Provide On-Demand Coverage." In: *IEEE Consumer Electronics Magazine*, vol. 7, no. 4, pp. 72–81, July 2018. doi: 10.1109/MCE.2018.2816247.

34. *EOS Whitepaper*. www.allcryptowhitepapers.com/eos-whitepaper/.

35. Luca Maiano, Antonio Montuschi, Marta Caserio, Egon Ferri, Federico Kieffer, Chiara Germanò, Lorenzo Baiocco, Lorenzo Ricciardi Celsi, Irene Amerini, Aris Anagnostopoulos, "A Deep-Learning–Based Antifraud System for Car-Insurance Claims." *Expert Systems with Applications*, vol. 231, p. 120644, 2023. ISSN 0957-4174, https://doi.org/10.1016/j.eswa.2023.120644.

36. Mihaela David, "Auto Insurance Premium Calculation Using Generalized Linear Models." *Procedia Economics and Finance*, vol. 20, pp. 147–156, 2015. ISSN 2212-5671, https://doi.org/10.1016/S2212-5671(15)00059-3.

5 Blockchain Technology for Car Insurance

Anupam Tiwari

5.1 INTRODUCTION

5.1.1 BLOCKCHAIN

Blockchain is a decentralized, distributed ledger technology that caters a way to store and share data in a transparent, secure, and tamperproof way [1]. It is cardinal to cryptocurrencies like Bitcoin, but in recent times, a multitude of use cases is being seen which go far beyond just digital currencies.

At its center, a blockchain is an appending list of records inside blocks of certain fixed sizes that are linked and secured using cryptography. Simply, to understand, each block contains a set of transactions, a timestamp, and a unique cryptographic hash that links it to the previous block. This makes a chain of blocks, which makes the name "blockchain." The blocks are distributed and replicated across peer-to-peer connected computers on network, which means that no individual entity or user has control over the network, making it a true decentralized system. When a transaction is made, it is first validated by the network's nodes, which are computers connected to the blockchain network. These nodes use complex algorithms to verify the transaction and ascertain that it is legitimate. Once the transaction is verified, it is bunched up with other transactions and added to the block. This entails that if someone attempts to change any part of a block, the hash of that block will alter, which will annul all concomitant blocks in the chain. This makes it nearly impossible to tamper with the data stored on the blockchain in current computing processing environs known.

5.1.2 MERKLE TREES

A Merkle tree (or hash tree) is a data structure used in blockchain technology (BCT) to expeditiously and securely verify the integrity of given data [2]. The structure of a Merkle tree is established on a binary tree, where each leaf node represents a piece of data or transaction in a blockchain. The tree is constructed by hashing pairs of nodes together, creating a parent node, and then hashing pairs of parent nodes together, going on until there is only one hash left, which is called the Merkle root. The Merkle root is thus a single hash that symbolizes the entire tree, and it is stacked in the header of the block in the blockchain. By using a Merkle tree, *it is possible to verify that a particular piece of data is part of a larger set of data, without having to store all the data on the blockchain.* This is important because it *allows for more efficient storage and verification of data*, which is essential in a blockchain, where large amounts of data need to be stored and verified.

To understand the Merkle tree basics, see Figure 5.1, which is explained here:

- *Datasets.* We have eight datasets, labeled as Data 1, Data 2, Data 3, Data 4, Data 5, Data 6, Data 7, and Data 8.
- *Hashing datasets.* Each dataset is individually hashed, resulting in eight hashes: H1, H2, H3, H4, H5, H6, H7, and H8. These hashes serve as unique representations of their corresponding datasets.

DOI: 10.1201/9781003450306-6

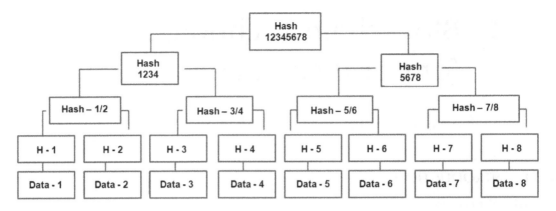

FIGURE 5.1   Merkle tree for an understanding.

- *Pairwise hashing.* Hashes are grouped in pairs and combined to create new hashes. Specifically, H1 and H2 are combined to form Hash 1/2, H3 and H4 are combined to form Hash 3/4, H5 and H6 are combined to form Hash 5/6, and H7 and H8 are combined to form Hash 7/8.
- *Second-level pairwise hashing.* Similar to the previous step, the second-level hashes (Hash 1/2, Hash 3/4, Hash 5/6, and Hash 7/8) are paired and combined to generate two new hashes. Hash 1/2 and Hash 3/4 are combined to form Hash 1234, and Hash 56 and Hash 78 are combined to form Hash 5678.
- *Root hash.* Finally, the two second-level hashes (Hash 1234 and Hash 5678) are combined to create the root hash, denoted as H12345678. This root hash represents the entire set of data and serves as a compact, cryptographic proof of the integrity of all the original datasets. *Root hash (H12345678)* is the key component in a Merkle tree. By comparing the root hash with a known or expected value, one can efficiently verify whether the datasets within the tree have been tampered with or remain intact. Additionally, this hierarchical structure allows for efficient verification of specific datasets within the tree without needing to traverse the entire tree.

The primary and peculiar advantage of Merkle root is that it can be used to verify a particular transaction as being part of the larger set of transactions, and that, too, without having to store all the transactions on the ledger.

5.1.3 Consensus

Consensus is the most interesting part of any public blockchain and is much complex mathematically [3]. It is attained in a blockchain network through a process called mining that ensures that all nodes in a network agree on the current state of the blockchain. There are multiple types of consensus algorithms, and they are mostly enabled on solving complex mathematical problems to add new blocks to the blockchain.

When a new block is appended to the blockchain, it must be verified by all nodes in the network to ascertain that it is legitimate. To do this, each node ensures the proof of work that was used to figure out the mathematical problem that appropriated the block to be indexed in the chain. If the proof of work is valid and legitimate, the block is added to the blockchain, and all nodes update their copy of the blockchain to include the new block. The process of mining involves competing against other nodes in the network to solve the mathematical problem first. The first node to solve

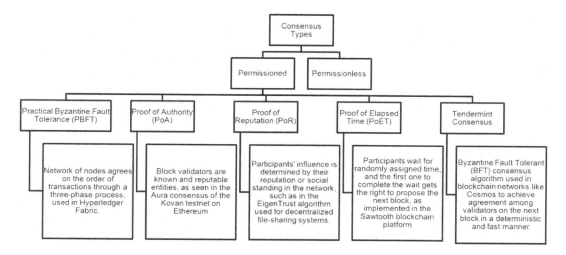

FIGURE 5.2   Well-known consensus algorithms.

the problem is rewarded with a certain amount of cryptocurrency, such as Bitcoin, and is known as the block reward, and it is an incentive for nodes to invest computing efforts in the mining action and secure the blockchain.

Mining is a resource-intensive process that requires substantial computing and processing power [4], which is why many P2P nodes in the network work together in mining pools. By pooling their computing resources, nodes can solve the mathematical problems faster and increase their chances of earning the block reward. In proof-of-work mechanism, nodes compete against each other to solve a mathematical problem that demands a significant amount of computational power. The first node to solve the problem is rewarded with the block reward, and the new block is added to the blockchain. While this is explained in simpler terms, there are more concepts to it, like mempool, difficulty level, etc., but for a basic understanding, this is it to suffice [5].

While proof of work [6] is a dependable and secure way to attain consensus in a blockchain, it has several drawbacks. First is being energy-intensive that demands a significant amount of computing power, which makes it pricy to take part in the mining process. Second, it can be sluggish and inefficient at times, as nodes must compete against each other to solve the mathematical problem, which can lead to delays and high transaction fees.

To address these issues, a multitude of alternative consensus mechanisms has been developed, such as proof of stake and delegated proof of stake. These mechanisms work by permitting nodes to vote on the validity of new blocks, rather than contending against each other to solve mathematical problems.

In proof of stake, nodes are selected to verify new blocks based on the amount of cryptocurrency they hold [7]. In delegated proof of stake, nodes are selected to verify new blocks based on the number of votes they receive from other nodes in the network. As on date, there are more than 50 consensus algorithms working around different ways to accomplish consensus, with efficient, non-efficient, and hybrid ways. Figure 5.2 shows brief details on some well-known permissioned blockchain consensus algorithms. The figure only shows details of permissioned types since in the car insurance, for almost all use cases, permissionless consensus may not be a preferred option.

Consensus and mining are critical components of BCT that ensure the security and reliability of the blockchain. While the proof-of-work mechanism used in Bitcoin and other early blockchains are efficient, newer genre consensus mechanisms, such as proof of stake and delegated proof of stake, offer up alternatives that are more energy-efficient and cost-effective.

5.1.4 SEQUENCE BLOCKCHAIN PROCESS

Although BCT can be classified like private or public or permissionless or permissioned with distinct architectures, the sequence presented in what follows provides a broad overview of a typical blockchain operation:

- *Creation of transaction.* User creates a transaction containing data to be recorded on the blockchain.
- *Validation of transaction.* Transaction is broadcast to the network of nodes, which validate its authenticity and integrity.
- *Block formation.* Once the transaction is validated, it is combined with other validated transactions to form a block.
- *Verification of block.* Block is then broadcast to the network, where each node verifies its authenticity and adds it to its copy of the blockchain.
- *Consensus.* A network of nodes uses a consensus algorithm to agree on the order and content of the blocks, ensuring that all copies of the blockchain are synchronized and are set the same, verified by hashes.
- *Addition of block.* Once consensus is reached, the block is added to the blockchain, making the data it contains permanent and immutably recorded.
- *Mining and incentivization.* In public or permissionless blockchain networks, a process called mining is used to add new blocks to the blockchain. This incentivizes network participation and ensures the security and integrity of the blockchain.
- *Accessing the blockchain.* Users can access the blockchain through a variety of interfaces, such as wallets or APIs, explorers [8] to view, send, or receive transactions.

5.2 CAR INSURANCE

Car insurance is a type of insurance coverage that provides financial protection to vehicle owners against possible losses and liabilities ensuing from fortuities, theft, or other covered events involving their vehicles [9]. It is a contract agreement between the vehicle proprietor and an insurance company, where the owner bears regular premiums in exchange for coverage and financial compensation in the event of defined risks. Car insurance typically offers several types of coverage, including:

- *Liability coverage.* Protects the policyholder from legal liabilities for bodily injury or property damage caused to others in an accident where the policyholder is at fault.
- *Collision coverage.* Assists pay for the repair or replacement of the policyholder's vehicle if it is damaged in a hit/accident with another vehicle or object.
- *Comprehensive coverage.* Provides protection against damage to the policyholder's vehicle resulting from events other than collisions, such as theft, vandalism, natural disasters, or falling objects.
- *Uninsured/underinsured motorist coverage.* This assists to compensate the costs if the policyholder is involved in an accident with a driver who either has no insurance or has insufficient insurance to cover the damages.

5.2.1 PROCESSES FROM THE COMPANY PERSPECTIVE

- *Research.* Insurance companies research and analyze market trends to build up insurance products that meet customer demands and remain competitive.
- *Underwriting.* Insurance companies use actuarial and risk assessment tools to assess the risks affiliated with providing insurance coverage to a particular driver or vehicle. This involves examining a variety of factors, including the driver's age, driving history, vehicle type, and other risks.

TABLE 5.1

Few Alarming Statistics in Insurance Industry

Ser. No.	Description of Statistic Figure	Stats
(a)	Total cost of insurance fraud (non-health insurance) estimates [10]	$40 billion per year
(b)	Percentage of those who say they were victims but never reported their suspicions (i.e., under-reporting of claims) [11]	29%
(c)	Drivers who lied to their insurer [12]	20%
(d)	Percentage of insurance claims that are fraudulent [13]	Between 10% and 20%
(e)	Damage to auto insurers annually by insurance scams [14]	$29 billion
(f)	Average observed deceitful insurance claim in the UK in 2021 [14]	£12,283
(g)	Percentage of insurance industry respondents who await to improve the loss ratio thanks to new technologies [14]	59%
(h)	Insurance fraud costs which an average US family bears in the form of increased premiums [14]	Between $400 and $700 a year
(i)	Deliberately initiated car fires in the United States in 2020	8,898
(j)	Ordinary American family expense on car insurance annually	Around $1,575
(k)	Percentage of insurance companies who have appointed a fraud investigation team	85%
(l)	Projected compound annual growth rate (CAGR) of the insurance fraud detection industry	17.4% between 2021 and 2026
(m)	Percentage of insurers who use algorithms to flag suspicious claims	10%
(n)	Damage amount in 2021 motor vehicle insurance scams in the UK [14]	Totaling £577 million

- *Policy creation.* Once the underwriting process is complete, the insurance company makes a policy document that schemes the terms and conditions of the coverage, including the premium, deductibles, and coverage limits.
- *Premium collection.* Insurance companies collect premiums from customers either up front or on a recurring basis, such as monthly or yearly.
- *Claims handling.* Insurance companies cover claims when customers meet with an accident or damage to their vehicle. The claims process involves verifying the validity of the claim, ascertaining the extent of the damages, and allowing for compensation established on the terms and conditions of the policy.
- *Risk management.* Insurance companies engage in ongoing risk management activities to extenuate risks associated with providing insurance coverage. This includes monitoring market trends, analyzing claim data, and correcting premiums and coverage limits as required.
- *Regulatory compliance.* Insurance companies must abide by with a variety of state and federal regulations related to insurance products, pricing, and marketing. This calls for ongoing monitoring and compliance activities to assure that the company remains in conformity with all applicable regulations.
- *Customer service.* Insurance companies provide customer service to policyholders to assist with policy questions, claims, and other issues that may come up. This includes providing support through various channels, such as phone, email, or online chat.

5.2.2 UNDERSTANDING THE CURRENT CHALLENGES IN CAR INSURANCE

Empathizing with the current challenges in car insurance is crucial for acknowledging the possible benefits that BCT can bring to the industry. Here are some key challenges that subsist in the traditional car insurance model:

- *Inefficiencies in the traditional car insurance model.* The traditional car insurance model involves multiple intermediates, such as brokers, agents, and middlemen, that lead to a complex and long-drawn procedure. This often ensues in inevitable delays and inefficiencies in policy issuance, claims processing, and final resolution. The manual paperwork and legacy systems involved in the traditional model chip in to these inefficiencies.
- *Fallacious activities and claim altercates.* Activities, such as faux claims, staged accidents, and exaggerated damage approximates, are substantial challenges in car insurance. These activities lead to financial losses for insurers and higher premiums for policyholders. Moreover, claim disputes between insurers and policyholders often arise due to discarding renditions of policy terms, coverage limits, or liability. Resolving these disputes can be lengthy and pricey for both parties.
- *Lack of transparence and trustfulness between insurers and policyholders.* There is often a lack of transparency and trust between insurers and policyholders in the traditional car insurance model. Policyholders may feel that insurers do not have their best concerns at heart, surmising hidden fees, unjust claim abnegations, or slanted probes. Insurers, on the other hand, face challenges in verifying the authenticity of the information provided by policyholders. This lack of transparency and trust can strain the insurer–policyholder relationship.

Table 5.1 brings to fore few important statistics related to car and general insurance challenges to concerned industry and clients.

5.3 CAR INSURANCE AND BLOCKCHAIN

By utilizing blockchain technology, insurance companies can efficaciously deal with the existing challenges within the realm of car insurance [15]. One notable solution is the ability to track claims in an unprecedented manner simply by accessing a shared trusted ledger. For instance, with the use of blockchain technology, a car insurance provider can intimately monitor the driving record and conduct of their policyholders, enabling them to tailor their policies accordingly. This way, if a driver engages in reckless and rash behavior, they will be unable to deceitfully claim eligibility for certain premiums or bonuses.

BCT can help to almost decimate fraudulent claims in the insurance industry, since all information related to a claim, such as the policyholder's identity, the nature of the loss, and the amount of the claim, would be stored on a shared ledger. This would make it much harder for fraudsters to present fake claims, as they would need to break into multiple systems in order to do so.

In addition, BCT can help to better the efficiency and transparency of the insurance claims process. This is because all parties involved in a claim, such as the policyholder, the insurer, and the reinsurer, would have access to the same common information. This would help speed up the claims process and abbreviate the risk of errors. A recent study by PwC found that 66% of insurance executives believe that blockchain will have a substantial impingement on their industry within the next five years.

5.4 HOW BCT ADDRESSES THE CHALLENGES

5.4.1 Immutable and Transparent Transaction Records

- *Immutable transaction records.* In a blockchain, transactions are indexed in blocks, which are linked together in a sequential and unchangeable manner. Once a transaction is added to the blockchain, it cannot be altered or tampered with. This immutability assures that all transaction records, such as policy issuance, premium payments, and claims settlements, are securely stored and cannot be modified retrospectively. The immutability of BCT helps forestall fallacious activities and allows for an authentic source of truth for all parties involved.

- *Transparency and auditability.* Every transaction recorded on a blockchain is transparent and visible to all participants in the network, which ensures that all stakeholders, including insurers, policyholders, and regulatory authorities, can get at the same set of information in real time. It decimates information asymmetry and enhances trust between the parties. This is possible through blockchain explorers, which show each transaction with times details to everyone interested to know. Policyholders can verify the accuracy of their policy terms, premiums paid, and claims history, while insurers can ensure that the information provided by policyholders is coherent and binding [16].
- *Consensus mechanisms.* Blockchain networks rely on consensus mechanisms, such as proof of work, proof of stake, etc., to validate and verify transactions. Consensus mechanisms ensure that all participants agree on the validity of transactions before they are added to the blockchain. This decentralized consensus process eliminates the need for a centralized authority or intermediaries to validate transactions, reducing the potential for manipulation or bias. It thus enhances the integrity and reliability of the transaction events, fostering trust among participants.

5.4.2 ENHANCED SECURITY AND FRAUD PREVENTION

- *Decentralized and distributed nature.* The distributed nature of BCT makes it highly resistant to hacking or manipulation. Unlike centralized systems that have a single point of failure, blockchain's distributed architecture ensures that no single entity can change or control the entire network. This decentralization enhances the security of car insurance transactions and mitigates the risk of data breaches or unauthorized access.
- *Cryptographic algorithms.* Blockchain utilizes cryptographic algorithms to secure transactions and protect data. Thus, each transaction is enabled on cryptographic hashes, making it extremely difficult for malicious actors to alter the data without detection. Additionally, digital signatures are used to authenticate and verify the identity of participants in the network. These cryptographic measures ensure the integrity and confidentiality of car insurance data, reducing the risk of fraud and unauthorized access.
- *Enhanced verification and authentication.* BCT provides mechanisms for verifying and authenticating data and identities. Policyholders' information, vehicle history, and claims data can be securely stored on the blockchain, creating a reliable and tamperproof source of information. This reduces the risk of fraudulent claims or false information being furnished by policyholders. Insurance companies can cross-verify information against trusted sources on the blockchain, such as vehicle registration databases or repair records, assuring the accuracy and genuineness of claims.

5.4.3 SMART CONTRACTS FOR AUTOMATED CLAIMS PROCESSING

- *Definition of smart contracts.* Smart contracts are self-executing agreements coded with predefined rules and conditions [16]. They are built on BCT platforms and automatically enforce the terms and conditions of the insurance policy. Smart contracts eliminate the need for manual intervention and streamline the claims process.
- *Automated claims validation.* Smart contracts can be programmed to validate claims automatically based on predefined conditions. For example, if a policyholder's claim conforms to the specified criteria, such as the occurrence of an addressed event and submission of required documents, the smart contract can activate the claims settlement process (see Figure 5.3). By automating this validation process, smart contracts save time and reduce the potential for errors or bias in claims assessment.

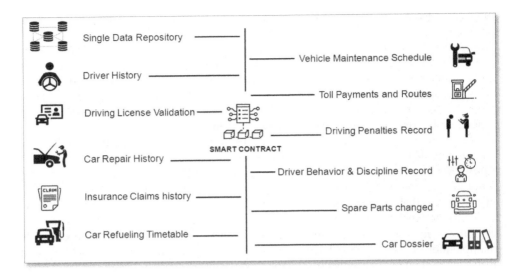

FIGURE 5.3 Inherent advantages of smart contract for car insurance.

- *Transparency and efficiency.* Smart contracts can again provide transparency and visibility into the claims process. Policyholders can track the progress of their claims in real time, ensuring transparency and building trust in the system. Insurers benefit from increased efficiency, as the automated nature of smart contracts reduces the manual effort involved in claims processing. Each smart contract executed on the BCT platform generates an event transaction ID which is time-stamped and visible on the blockchain ledger.
- *Faster claims settlement.* Smart contracts facilitate faster claims settlement as once the predefined conditions are met, the smart contract automatically actuates the release of the due claim amount to the policyholder. This decimates delays associated with manual claims assessment to enable quicker and smoother settlements.
- *Fraud detection and prevention.* Smart contracts contribute to fraud detection and prevention in car insurance. Any attempt to submit fraudulent claims that do not meet the predetermined criteria would be identified by the smart contract, reducing the risk of fraudulent activities.
- *Lower administrative costs.* By automating claims processing, removing mediators and third parties through consensus [16], smart contracts abbreviate administrative costs for insurance companies. Manual claims assessment and settlement involve significant paperwork, coordination, and administrative overhead. Smart contracts eliminate much of this manual effort, ensuing in cost savings and increased operational efficiency.

5.4.4 IMPROVED DATA ACCURACY AND INTEGRITY

- *Cross-verification and trusted sources.* BCT appropriates cross-verification of data against trusted sources. For example, insurance companies can access and validate policyholder information against official databases, such as vehicle registration records or driver's license databases. By leveraging blockchain's transparent and immutable nature, insurers can verify the authenticity and accuracy of data, reducing the risk of hinging on incorrect or falsified information.
- *Secure data sharing and privacy.* Enables controlled and secure data sharing between insurers, policyholders, and other stakeholders, while protecting personal and confidential information.

- *Streamlined data reconciliation.* Traditional car insurance processes often involve multiple intermediates and manual data reconciliation, leading to potential errors and variances. With blockchain, all parties share a common, immutable dataset, bringing down the need for manual reconciliation and the affiliated risks of human error. This streamlined data reconciliation process enhances the accuracy and consistency of the shared data.

5.5 EXPLORING THE USE CASES OF BCT IN CAR INSURANCE

5.5.1 POLICY ISSUANCE AND MANAGEMENT ON THE BLOCKCHAIN

Car policy issuance and management on the blockchain revolutionize the traditional processes, offering streamlined operations, enhanced transparency, and improved efficiency. By leveraging blockchain technology, insurers can automatize respective steps, abbreviating the need for manual intervention and paperwork. Smart contracts play a vital role in policy issuance by executing predefined rules and conditions, ensuring accurate and reliable policy creation, verification, and updates.

For example, Insurwave, a collaborative effort between EY and Maersk [17], utilizes blockchain for marine insurance. The platform digitizes and automates the entire insurance value chain, including policy issuance, premium payments, and claims management, and thus imparts peculiar BCT characteristics to the complete processes involved.

Another noteworthy instance is the partnership between AIG and IBM to create multinational insurance policies using blockchain [18]. The BCT-based solution offers better policy management for companies operating in multiple countries, facilitating streamlined policy issuance and coordination across different jurisdictions. It ensures consistent policy terms, reduces administrative complexities, and provides a transparent audit trail.

5.5.2 CLAIMS MANAGEMENT AND SETTLEMENT

Claims management and settlement of car insurance are a crucial area where BCT extends substantial benefits. By leveraging BCT, insurers can streamline the claims process, enhance transparency, and improve the efficiency of settlements. Here are few existing examples of BCT use cases in car insurance claims:

- One example is the collaboration between B3i and Swiss Re [19], where they have developed a BCT-enabled solution for addressing complex insurance claims. The platform alleviates real-time data sharing and automates claims processing, enabling quicker and more accurate resolutions.
- Another example is the use of BCT by Fizzy, a subsidiary of AXA, for flight delay insurance [20]. The platform automatically asserts flight data from reliable sources and triggers claims payments based on preset conditions, obviating the need for manual claims assessment.

5.5.3 VERIFICATION OF VEHICLE HISTORY AND OWNERSHIP

Verification of vehicle history and ownership is a significant use case of BCT in the car insurance industry. Here are some examples of BCT use cases for vehicle history and ownership verification:

- One example is the partnership between BMW and VeChain, where they have developed VerifyCar [21], a blockchain-based solution to verify the authenticity of vehicle parts and maintenance records. This ascertains transparency and trust in the vehicle's history, corroborating insurance underwriting and claims judgment.

- Another example is **Mobility Open Blockchain Initiative (MOBI)**, which recently released "Vehicle Identity Standard" (VID II):
  - Collaborative Industry Effort
    - MOBI [22] has brought out the second version of its "Vehicle Identity Standard," VID II.
    - Leading companies in the automotive industry are getting together on this project, with **BMW** and **Ford** chairmanning the working group.
  - MOBI's Objective
    - To boost the adoption of blockchain standards in the mobility sector, aspiring to raise transportation efficiency and affordability.
  - Vehicle Identity I (VID I)
    - MOBI's initial version, VID I, acts as a "birth certificate" for vehicles.
    - VID I laid the foundation for future use cases, such as tracking a vehicle's history, including ownership changes, repairs, insurance claims, and odometer readings.
  - VID II Enhancements
    - Release of VID II represents an evolution of the "Vehicle Identity Standard."
    - Builds upon the foundation established by VID I and introduces additional functionalities and improvements.

5.5.4 Usage-Based Insurance and Telematics Data

Usage-based insurance (UBI) and telematics data play a crucial role in car insurance, and BCT offers innovative solutions for leveraging this data securely and efficiently. Here are some examples of BCT use cases in UBI and telematics data:

- The collaboration between Metromile and Ford [23] is one example where they utilize BCT to enable UBI based on real-time vehicle data. BCT securely records and verifies the vehicle's mileage, facilitating accurate premium calculations and personalized insurance coverage.
- One other example is the partnership between InsurePal and Toyota [24], where they leverage blockchain to create a peer-to-peer insurance platform. Telematics data collected from Toyota vehicles is securely indexed on the blockchain, providing reasonable and tailor-made insurance premiums established on actual driving behavior.

5.5.5 Addenda Blockchain for Enhancing Motor Insurers' Efficiency

One recent example would be to discuss the Addenda blockchain [25], which facilitates reconciliation of motor recovery receivables among insurers. Following are the key points in brief:

- XA Group, a UAE-based global provider of automotive aftermarket services, has brought out Addenda, a blockchain-based solution.
- Enables insurers to conciliate motor recovery receivables between each other. In simple terms, this aids insurance companies to determine and resolve the payments they need to receive from one another for motor vehicle repairs, which causes the process of reconciliation to be transparent and more effective.
- Facilitates to ease, concentrate, and handle communications between insurers during the motor claims recovery process.
- Plans to integrate existing products into the platform to raise its potentialities and provision for seamless communication between insurers, brokers, repairers, and customers.
- Extends a real-time and shared view of policy data and documentation among insurers, providing visibility into the approval and reconciliation process during recovery claims.

5.6 CURRENT WORKS AND PECULIAR USE CASES

Paper [26] contribution lies in the introduction of a new use case that utilizes BCT to establish a vehicle insurance ledger for sharing insurance records. Their research also encompasses:

- Design of digital assets
- Smart contract automation
- Interaction design
- Providing a comprehensive model for the proposed solution

By leveraging blockchain, they suggest to capture insurance details in a collaborative environment involving multiple actors and stakeholders, facilitating transparency and trust among all participants. The authors highlight the possible gains of incorporating connected cars and telematics in the automotive industry. They accentuate that the data compiled from connected cars can be worthy for manufacturers, insurance companies, vehicle owners, and governments. Insurance companies, in particular, can exploit this technology to extend discounts based on voluntarily rendered reliable information. The tamper-free nature of blockchain ensures the integrity of records, forbidding unauthorized modifications. The proposed system serves with a reliable driving history record for an extended period. Individuals can present their public keys or signatures to new insurance companies to secure better discounts. Additionally, the blockchain records can assist courts in cases involving driver behavior patterns. By extending the functionality of the blockchain with other data sources, the system can also record alcohol levels and log detailed event data for further analysis.

[27] introduces a novel application of BCT in vehicle insurance management. The authors propose a vehicle insurance ledger built on blockchain for sharing insurance records. The work contribution includes the indexing of digital assets, smart contract automation, and interaction design. Key highlights of the paper are discussed:

- Connected cars can render valuable data for manufacturers, insurance companies, vehicle owners, and governments.
- System enables insurance companies to offer discounts based on reliable data.
- Blockchain records serve as a reliable driving history repository and can be used for years to come.
- Generated ledger can facilitate young driver programs, driver's license renewals, and interstate highway moves.
- Blockchain records can serve as evidence in legal cases related to driver behavior patterns.
- Future directions include exploring the potential of connected cars and telematics in the automotive industry.
- Further possibilities include recording alcohol levels, event logs, and conducting detailed analysis, as bought out in [26].

Paper [28] introduces a novel personalized car insurance (PCI) schema that pertains to data transparency and privacy in auto insurance. The suggested work leverages a consortium blockchain to achieve both privacy preservation and transparency. Initially, a blockchain is established by a group of consortium members, enabling insurance companies (ICs) to deploy insurance contracts on the blockchain. To preserve privacy, a verifiable and privacy-preserving driving behavior evaluation protocol is designed. This protocol utilizes techniques such as partially homomorphic encryption and zero-knowledge proofs. By interacting with ICs through the contracts, drivers can securely share their driving data while keeping it encrypted. ICs can then examine the encrypted data to evaluate driving behavior and find out appropriate insurance premiums. To enhance security and prevent fraud, a third-party auditor (TPA) is authorized by car drivers and ICs to audit the encrypted driving data stored. The auditing process is prototyped as a recursive inspection game, where the TPA minimizes the number of audits required to detect data fraud and penalize malicious drivers, following the principles of Nash equilibrium [29]. This auditing mechanism ensures that the majority of the collected driving data is unbiased. The paper thus provides formal simulation-based security analysis and offers a robust solution that guarantees data privacy, transparency, and security.

[30] presents a blockchain-based framework for auto insurance claims and adjudication (B-FICA) oriented for connected and automated vehicles (CAVs). The model B-FICA ensures access control through partitions, effectively forbidding unauthorized access to data essential for evidence. Moreover, it constitutes a dynamic validation protocol to forbid tampering with the evidence. The authors provide a demonstration of B-FICA's effectiveness by describing a likely scenario and illustrating how evidence is generated and processed. The paper includes an in-depth security analysis, which showcases the mechanisms employed by B-FICA to meet design requirements and defy various malicious actions from potential liable entities. Other key highlights of the paper include the following:

- Security analysis highlights B-FICA's mechanisms for following design requirements and resilience against malicious actions.
- Simulation results indicate that B-FICA importantly reduces processing time compared to existing approaches.
- B-FICA enhances the credibleness of the judgment model for CAVs and extenuates the risk of data misuse at a marginal cost.
- Renders comprehensive information for decision-makers and demonstrates the interaction between entities in the adjudication model.
- It mentions future work could include carrying out attestation protocols for data correctness, reliability, and integrity in evidence submitted by CAVs.
- Authors foresee the potential applicability of B-FICA variations to other liability scenarios, such as home or health insurance, too.

The authors [31] have delivered a comprehensive analysis of the different solutions, their benefits, and linked challenges, aiming to gain a more recondite apprehension of the insurance industry and blockchain adoption. The primary contribution of this research is the introduction of a new use case involving the creation of a vehicle insurance ledger using BCT to facilitate the sharing of insurance records. Few of the other key points are enumerated here:

- *Future research direction.* Explore connected cars and telematics in the auto industry.
- *Opportunities for stakeholders.* Manufacturers, insurance companies, vehicle owners, and governments.
- *Value of collected data.* Enables insurance companies to offer deductions and discounts based on reliable information.
- *Persistent driving history.* Blockchain records serve as a comprehensive and reliable driving history.
- *Benefits for individuals.* Present public keys/signatures for better discounts, verify driver maturity and authentication.
- *License exchange facilitation.* Transferability of blockchain records between states.
- *Use in court cases.* Valuable in legal matters related to driver behavior patterns.
- *Potential use cases.* Recording alcohol levels, capturing full event logs for analysis.

In [32], a cyber infrastructure design and prototyping solution for vehicle insurance applications is proposed, combining IoT and blockchain technologies. The work demonstrates a trustworthy and cooperative network among drivers, transport operators, and insurance companies on a P2P design. The solution covers key design considerations in architecture, service definition, and the integration of "on-chain" and "off-chain" services. A hybrid blockchain scheme integrating both permissioned (Hyperledger) and public (Ethereum) blockchain networks is proposed to derive their respective advantages. Key points from the paper follow:

- Dynamic pricing is a key aspect of the proposed solution, where the vehicle's riding status decides the insurance premium based on indexed information.
- The concept of dynamic pricing holds potential for emerging applications in the transportation sector, such as car-sharing and effected insurance.
- On-chain information, including trip duration and timestamps, allows for fair distribution of insurance fees among drivers with assigned time slots for car use in car-sharing apps.
- Increasing presence of car-sharing apps has incited the exploration of more rational business models to conform to the evolving demands of the vehicle insurance industry.
- Prototype platform is implemented to recognize the cyber infrastructure design, comprising backend services and front-end web-based UIs to satisfy application features.
- Comprehensive experimental case study using real-world transportation trip data has been conducted to evaluate performance under various configurations, considering practical deployment considerations.
- Suggestions for further performance enhancements are provided, including module-based design, to incorporate more realistic insurance models aligned with practical policies.
- Experimental evaluation highlights the potential for performance enhancement through the utilization of in-memory databases instead of CouchDB for data storage.

In [33] work, a blockchain-based decentralized framework for usage-based insurance (UBI) and incentives in intelligent transportation systems (ITS) is proposed. The traditional approach to vehicular insurance relies on analyzing driver behavior history to determine premiums, but with the increasing number of vehicles on the road, there is a need for a more innovative and efficacious approach. UBI, based on telematics, calculates premiums based on current driver behavior, providing a transparent and personalized insurance model. Key work derivates of the work [33] are mentioned as follows:

- BTC framework is developed utilizing temporary addresses for private communication on the public blockchain.
- Generic algorithm is designed to incentivize safer driving practices through performance-based incentives and insurance discounts.
- Smart contracts enhance system availability and ensures non-repudiation of credit scores and insurance discounts.
- Proposed framework benefits insurers, insured individuals, original equipment manufacturers (OEMs), and legal authorities.
- Enables secure firmware updates for OEMs and facilitates efficient investigation by legal authorities.
- Feasibility and effectiveness of the framework are demonstrated through a test bed experiment.
- Experimental results validate the practicality and potential benefits of the proposed blockchain-based approach in the context of vehicular insurance.

Figure 5.4 shows a generic architecture layout for a car insurance enabled on blockchain with distributed storage like IPFS.

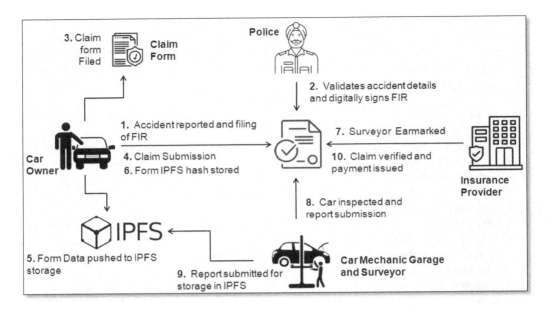

FIGURE 5.4   Generic architecture with a blockchain-enabled car insurance.

5.7   CURRENT GAPS AND CHALLENGES

- *Data integration.* Integrating data from various sources into a blockchain network can be challenging. The car insurance industry relies on data from multiple parties, such as car manufacturers, telematics devices, repair shops, and government agencies. Ensuring seamless integration and standardization of data formats is crucial for accurate risk assessment and premium calculation.
- *Data storage.* While in this chapter it has been mentioned multiple times that data will be stored in blockchain, any blockchain is not meant for storing data but is only important from imparting its implicit characteristics of immutability, security, transparency, etc. This happens because, with increase of data size, blockchains get bloated, effecting into low transaction-per-second speeds. So where is the data stored? For this, multiple works are proposing offline storage in distributed protocols like IPFS, which will take care of storage, while the effected transaction hashes are stored in blocks of blockchain.
- *Privacy and data protection.* While blockchain provides transparency and immutability, privacy concerns arise when dealing with sensitive personal information. Striking the right balance between transparency and privacy is essential. Implementing privacy-enhancing technologies, such as zero-knowledge proofs or private channels, can help protect sensitive data while still leveraging the benefits of blockchain technology. Another alternative is to create private blockchains with granular permission controls of access of information of transaction
- *Regulatory frameworks.* The legal and regulatory landscape surrounding BCT is still evolving. Car insurance companies need to navigate subsisting regulations and adapt them to the blockchain context. Clear guidelines and frameworks for compliance, data protection, and smart contract execution are necessary to ensure the widespread adoption of blockchain in the insurance industry. This will be complex in a global scenario, with contradicting approaches to legal regulations country-wise.
- *Scalability and performance.* Blockchain networks, particularly public ones, confront scalability and performance challenges. Processing a high volume of transactions related

to car insurance policies, claims, and premium calculations necessitates efficient consensus mechanisms and network scalability. Solutions like sharding, sidechains, IPFS, or layer-2 protocols can help address these limitations.

- *Interoperability.* Interoperability between different blockchain platforms and existing legacy systems is crucial for the adoption of BCT in the car insurance industry. This will be a major challenge once a blockchain-enabled car insurance ecosystem is in place. Ensuring seamless data exchange and consolidation between disparate systems can raise efficiency and cut down complexity for insurers, policyholders, and other stakeholders.
- *Education and awareness.* BCT is still relatively new, and there is a need for education and awareness among industry professionals, regulators, and consumers.
- *Cost and infrastructure.* Implementing BCT demands investment in infrastructure, including nodes, storage, and computational resources. The initial setup and ongoing maintenance costs should be carefully considered, especially for smaller insurance companies. Collaborative efforts, industry partnerships, or cloud-based blockchain solutions can help mitigate these barriers.
- *Standardization and collaboration.* Establishing industry standards and fostering collaboration among insurers, technology providers, and other stakeholders are essential for the widespread adoption of blockchain in car insurance. Standardization can ensure interoperability, data consistency, and efficient integration across the industry, rearing trust and raising the value of BCT-based solutions [34].

5.8   ADVANCING CAR INSURANCE: AI AND BLOCKCHAIN AT THE FOREFRONT

Looking forward to the future of car insurance and the growth of "generative large language multimodal models" (GLLMMs) [35], the combination of these technologies with blockchain generates a multitude of exciting hypotheses. Few of these potential advancements are mentioned thus:

- Enhanced risk assessment through multimodal data fusion
- Personalized policies powered by multi-dimensional representations
- Innovative claims processing through multimodal insights
- Seamless user interaction via language and media integration
- Trust and transparency with blockchain-backed multimodal models
- Decentralized data sharing for collective risk pools
- AI-driven automation and fraud detection
- Personalized risk assessment
- Fraud detection and prevention
- Automated claims processing
- Usage-based insurance (UBI)
- Predictive maintenance
- Decentralized insurance pools
- Parametric insurance solutions
- Autonomous vehicle insurance
- Customer support and interaction
- Data privacy and consent management

The coalescing of AI and blockchain in car insurance admits revolutionary possibilities, extending better efficiency, transparency, and personalized solutions. With the integration of generative large language multimodal models and blockchain, the future hopes for intelligent and customer-centric insurance advancements, translating risk assessment, customer interactions, and claims management for the benefit of all stakeholders.

5.9 CONCLUSION

BCT presents a paradigm shift in the realm of car insurance. Throughout this chapter, we have delved into the ways in which BCT addresses the inherent challenges faced by car insurance companies, as well as the diverse use cases it offers. The immutable and transparent nature of blockchain transaction records stands as the pivotal advantage. By securely recording transactions in a sequential and unalterable manner through the use of Merkle trees, BCT establishes an incontrovertible source of truth for critical processes, such as policy issuance, premium payments, and claims settlements.

Furthermore, BCT enhances security and thwarts fraudulent activities through its decentralized architecture and cryptographic mechanisms. The deployment of smart contracts endues automated claims processing, importantly cutting the need for manual intervention and streamlining operations. This automation, coupled with improved data accuracy and integrity, contributes to optimized car insurance workflows and an elevated customer experience.

When exploring specific use cases, blockchain proves highly beneficial in the realm of claims management and settlement. The verification of vehicle history and ownership can be seamlessly executed, effectively mitigating the risk of fraudulent claims. Notably, the fusion of usage-based insurance (UBI) and telematics data [36] becomes a potent tool for exact risk assessment and premium calculation, fostering equitable and personalized insurance offerings.

Nevertheless, it is essential to acknowledge and address the current gaps and challenges impeding the widespread adoption of blockchain in car insurance. The integration of data from multiple sources, privacy and data protection concerns [37], regulatory frameworks, scalability, storage, and interoperability necessitate concerted efforts for resolution and advancement.

Despite these challenges, the transformative potential of blockchain in car insurance remains substantial. It is imperative for the industry to collaborate, innovate, and proactively solve problems to deduce the full potential of blockchain technology. By doing so, car insurance companies can elevate their operational efficiency, enhance customer satisfaction, and cultivate a secure and transparent ecosystem for all stakeholders affected. As BCT continues its evolution, it becomes increasingly evident that it has the capacity to reshape the future of car insurance, propelling the industry toward a more efficient, equitable, and technologically driven landscape.

REFERENCES

1. Z. Zheng, S. Xie, H. Dai, X. Chen and H. Wang, "An Overview of Blockchain Technology: Architecture, Consensus, and Future Trends," *2017 IEEE International Congress on Big Data (BigData Congress)*, Honolulu, HI, USA, 2017, pp. 557–564, doi: 10.1109/BigDataCongress.2017.85.
2. H. Liu, X. Luo, H. Liu and X. Xia, "Merkle Tree: A Fundamental Component of Blockchains," *2021 International Conference on Electronic Information Engineering and Computer Science (EIECS)*, Changchun, China, 2021, pp. 556–561, doi: 10.1109/EIECS53707.2021.9588047.
3. D. Mingxiao, M. Xiaofeng, Z. Zhe, W. Xiangwei and C. Qijun, "A Review on Consensus Algorithm of Blockchain," *2017 IEEE International Conference on Systems, Man, and Cybernetics (SMC)*, Banff, AB, Canada, 2017, pp. 2567–2572, doi: 10.1109/SMC.2017.8123011.
4. D. Rusovs, S. Jaundālders and P. Stanka, "Blockchain Mining of Cryptocurrencies As Challenge and Opportunity For Renewable Energy," *2018 IEEE 59th International Scientific Conference on Power and Electrical Engineering of Riga Technical University (RTUCON)*, Riga, Latvia, 2018, pp. 1–5, doi: 10.1109/RTUCON.2018.8659867.
5. M. Saad, L. Njilla, C. Kamhoua, J. Kim, D. Nyang and A. Mohaisen, "Mempool Optimization for Defending Against DDoS Attacks in PoW-Based Blockchain Systems," *2019 IEEE International Conference on Blockchain and Cryptocurrency (ICBC)*, Seoul, Korea (South), 2019, pp. 285–292, doi: 10.1109/BLOC.2019.8751476.
6. C. Gupta and A. Mahajan, "Evaluation of Proof-of-Work Consensus Algorithm for Blockchain Networks," *2020 11th International Conference on Computing, Communication and Networking Technologies (ICCCNT)*, Kharagpur, India, 2020, pp. 1–7, doi: 10.1109/ICCCNT49239.2020.9225676.

7. W. Y. Maung Maung Thin, N. Dong, G. Bai and J. S. Dong, "Formal Analysis of a Proof-of-Stake Blockchain," *2018 23rd International Conference on Engineering of Complex Computer Systems (ICECCS)*, Melbourne, VIC, Australia, 2018, pp. 197–200, doi: 10.1109/ICECCS2018.2018.00031.

8. H. Kuzuno and C. Karam, "Blockchain Explorer: An Analytical Process and Investigation Environment for Bitcoin," *2017 APWG Symposium on Electronic Crime Research (eCrime)*, Scottsdale, AZ, USA, 2017, pp. 9–16, doi: 10.1109/ECRIME.2017.7945049.

9. M. J. Wang, C. H. Wen and L. Lan, "Modelling Different Types of Bundled Automobile Insurance Choice Behaviour: The Case of Taiwan," *Geneva Papers on Risk and Insurance. Issues and Practice*, vol. 35, 2010, pp. 29–308, doi: 10.1057/gpp.2010.5.

10. S. Coleman, "Car Insurance Statistics 2022," *Bankrate*, no date. Available at: www.bankrate.com/insurance/car/fraud-facts-statistics/ (Accessed: 23 July 2023).

11. Fraud Stats, *InsuranceFraud.org.*, 2023. Available at: https://insurancefraud.org/fraud-stats/ (Accessed: 23 July 2023).

12. Insurance Fraud, *FBI*, 2010. Available at: www.fbi.gov/stats-services/publications/insurance-fraud (Accessed: 23 July 2023).

13. Insurance Fraud Stats & How to Avoid IT, *Valuepenguin*. Available at: www.valuepenguin.com/auto-home-insurance-fraud (Accessed: 23 July 2023).

14. M. Lazic, *Insurance Fraud Statistics—Amazing Facts and Numbers*, 2023. Available at: https://legaljobs.io/blog/insurance-fraud-statistics/ (Accessed: 23 July 2023).

15. C. Huang, W. Wang, D. Liu, R. Lu and X. Shen, "Blockchain-Assisted Personalized Car Insurance With Privacy Preservation and Fraud Resistance," *IEEE Transactions on Vehicular Technology*, vol. 72, no. 3, March 2023, pp. 3777–3792, doi: 10.1109/TVT.2022.3215811.

16. F. Lamberti, V. Gatteschi, C. Demartini, M. Pelissier, A. Gomez and V. Santamaria, "Blockchains Can Work for Car Insurance: Using Smart Contracts and Sensors to Provide On-Demand Coverage," IEEE Consumer Electronics Magazine, vol. 7, no. 4, July 2018, pp. 72–81, doi: 10.1109/MCE.2018.2816247.

17. Mrinmoyee, "EY and Guardtime Launch Blockchain Platform for Marine Insurance," *Ship Technology*, 2018. Available at: www.ship-technology.com/news/ey-guardtime-launch-blockchain-platform-marine-insurance/ (Accessed: 29 July 2023).

18. AIG Pilots First Multinational Insurance Policy Using Blockchain, *Asia Insurance Review*, 2017. Available at: www.asiainsurancereview.com/Magazine/ReadMagazineArticle?aid=39584 (Accessed: 29 July 2023).

19. L. Gallin, "B3I Conceptually Interesting, but Required End-to-End View: Swiss Re Execs," *Reinsurance News*, 2022. Available at: www.reinsurancene.ws/b3i-conceptually-interesting-but-required-end-to-end-view-swiss-re-execs/ (Accessed: 29 July 2023).

20. AXA Goes Blockchain with Fizzy: AXA, *AXA.com.*, 2017. Available at: www.axa.com/en/news/axa-goes-blockchain-with-fizzy (Accessed: 29 July 2023).

21. Airck, Crypto, "BMW Showcases Blockchain Car Mileage App on Vechainthor," *PolkaVerse*, 2021. Available at: https://polkaverse.com/4474/bmw-showcases-blockchain-car-mileage-app-on-ve-chain-thor-18528 (Accessed: 29 July 2023).

22. Andreas Freund, "Home—Mobi: The New Economy of Movement," *MOBI*, 2023. Available at: https://dlt.mobi/ (Accessed: 29 July 2023).

23. B. Wire, "Metromile and Ford Team Up to Bring Highly Personalized Car Insurance to Ford Owners," *Benzinga*, 2020. Available at: www.benzinga.com/pressreleases/20/09/b17368014/metromile-and-ford-team-up-to-bring-highly-personalized-car-insurance-to-ford-owners (Accessed: 29 July 2023).

24. Politecnico di torino, *A Business Model for Vehicle Insurance Based on Blockchain Smart-Contracts*, 2018. Available at: https://webthesis.biblio.polito.it/7727/1/tesi.pdf (Accessed: 29 July 2023).

25. G. Olano, "Xa Group Rolls Out Blockchain-Based Motor Insurance Platform," *Insurance Business Asia*, 2022. Available at: www.insurancebusinessmag.com/asia/news/auto-motor/xa-group-rolls-out-blockchainbased-motor-insurance-platform-422141.aspx (Accessed: 29 July 2023).

26. M. Demir, O. Turetken and A. Ferworn, "Blockchain Based Transparent Vehicle Insurance Management," *2019 Sixth International Conference on Software Defined Systems (SDS)*, Rome, Italy, 2019, pp. 213–220, doi: 10.1109/SDS.2019.8768669.

27. F. Lamberti, et al. "Blockchains Can Work for Car Insurance: Using Smart Contracts and Sensors to Provide on-Demand Coverage," *IEEE Consumer Electronics Magazine*, vol. 7, no. 4, 2018, pp. 72–81, doi: 10.1109/mce.2018.2816247.

28. C. Huang, W. Wang, D. Liu, R. Lu and X. Shen, "Blockchain-Assisted Personalized Car Insurance With Privacy Preservation and Fraud Resistance," *IEEE Transactions on Vehicular Technology*, vol. 72, no. 3, March 2023, pp. 3777–3792, doi: 10.1109/TVT.2022.3215811.

29. L. Yan, "The Application of Nash Equilibrium in Trust Model of Deterministic Wireless Sensor Network," *2014 Enterprise Systems Conference*, Shanghai, China, 2014, pp. 284–288, doi: 10.1109/ES.2014.55.

30. C. Oham, R. Jurdak, S. S. Kanhere, A. Dorri and S. Jha, "B-FICA: Blockchain Based Framework for Auto-Insurance Claim and Adjudication," *2018 IEEE International Conference on Internet of Things (iThings) and IEEE Green Computing and Communications (GreenCom) and IEEE Cyber, Physical and Social Computing (CPSCom) and IEEE Smart Data (SmartData)*, Halifax, NS, Canada, 2018, pp. 1171–1180, doi: 10.1109/Cybermatics_2018.2018.00210.

31. M. Demir, O. Turetken and A. Ferworn, "Blockchain Based Transparent Vehicle Insurance Management," *2019 Sixth International Conference on Software Defined Systems (SDS)*, Rome, Italy, 2019, pp. 213–220, doi: 10.1109/SDS.2019.8768669.

32. Z. Xiao et al., "Blockchain and IoT for Insurance: A Case Study and Cyberinfrastructure Solution on Fine-Grained Transportation Insurance," *IEEE Transactions on Computational Social Systems*, vol. 7, no. 6, December 2020, pp. 1409–1422, doi: 10.1109/TCSS.2020.3034106.

33. P. K. Singh, R. Singh, G. Muchahary, M. Lahon and S. Nandi, "A Blockchain-Based Approach for Usage Based Insurance and Incentive in ITS," *TENCON 2019–2019 IEEE Region 10 Conference (TENCON)*, Kochi, India, 2019, pp. 1202–1207, doi: 10.1109/TENCON.2019.8929322.

34. L. Yan, "The Application of Nash Equilibrium in Trust Model of Deterministic Wireless Sensor Network," *2014 Enterprise Systems Conference*, Shanghai, China, 2014, pp. 284–288, doi: 10.1109/ES.2014.55.

35. A. Barua, M. U. Ahmed and S. Begum, "A Systematic Literature Review on Multimodal Machine Learning: Applications, Challenges, Gaps and Future Directions," *IEEE Access*, vol. 11, 2023, pp. 14804–14831, doi: 10.1109/ACCESS.2023.3243854.

36. P. K. Singh, R. Singh, G. Muchahary, M. Lahon and S. Nandi, "A Blockchain-Based Approach for Usage Based Insurance and Incentive in ITS," *TENCON 2019–2019 IEEE Region 10 Conference (TENCON)*, Kochi, India, 2019, pp. 1202–1207, doi: 10.1109/TENCON.2019.8929322.

37. P. K. Singh, "Artificial Intelligence With Enhanced Prospects by Blockchain in the Cyber Domain," *Lecture Notes in Electrical Engineering*, 2022, pp. 513–525, doi: 10.1007/978-981-16-8248-3_43.

6 Blockchain for Smart Vehicular Communications

*S. Gnanavel, N. Arunachalam, and
Godfrey Winster Sathianesan*

6.1 INTRODUCTION

Blockchain is a new technology of immutable and distributed ledger that aids in the copy of transactions and the tracking of property throughout a big business network. A tangible investment (a house, a car, money, and land) can be made, as can an intangible investment (intellectual property, copyrights, branding, and patents,). In blockchain, any of the values can be recorded and sold, its low risk and costs for everyone involved. It is significant because it offers immediate, full, and shareable transparent data. We can track orders, accounts, payments, production, and other things in blockchain network. we can see all transaction details end-to-end. Members share a single version of the truth, which gives you more trust and opens up new possibilities. The blockchain protocol state is displayed in Figure 6.1.

6.1.1 Key Definitions in Blockchain Technology

Node. This term refers to the block's owner.
Transaction. The act of moving anything from point A to point B.
Block. Set of transactions.
Miners. They expend energy to make blocks and are compensated by block rewards plus transaction costs.
Block reward. The miner receives any newly produced coins from each block.
Transaction fees. The small fraction of the transaction value that goes to the miner is known as a transaction fee.

6.1.2 Types of Blockchain

There are many distinct varieties of blockchain; let us concentrate on the following three most common.

6.1.2.1 Public Blockchain

Public blockchain is accessible to all users, as the name implies. There are no access limitations; therefore, anyone with access to the Internet can conduct transactions and carry out validations (using the consensus protocol). No single authority may conduct the action on a public blockchain. Anyone is free to read, write, or audit information on a public blockchain. The public blockchain is still accessible to the general public, fully disclosing all acts made there. So it makes sense to doubt the legitimacy of a public blockchain. You might wonder how accountable such a public blockchain is in the absence of any authority or management. How are decisions reached? There are countless questions that cross people's minds, and the public blockchain contains the solution. Public blockchain uses a decentralized compromise mechanism like proof of work (POW) and

DOI: 10.1201/9781003450306-7

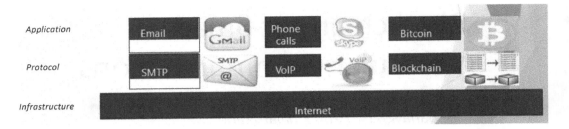

FIGURE 6.1 Blockchain protocol.

proof of stake (POS) to carry out any decision-making. Numerous real-world blockchain instances are available. A few of the coins on the list are Bitcoin, Ethereum, Monero, Dash, and Litecoin. Blockchain became popular among the tech community thanks to Bitcoin technology. These three factors account for public blockchain:

- Anybody can get the code and run a public node on their own device. They may validate every network transaction and participate in the consensus process. The public can freely choose which blocks to add and what size they should be.
- As long as the transactions are valid, anyone can transact in the network.
- Using a block explorer, anybody can access or read transactions.

The most significant implication of open blockchain in any firm is that anyone can disrupt business models. It also minimizes the cost of running decentralized apps because no server or system administrators are required. Isn't it fascinating?

6.1.2.2 Private Blockchain

The private blockchain, as the name implies, is kept secret within the community and requires consent to access. Furthermore, the private blockchain acts as a private property of an individual or organization to fulfil a certain job function established by them. Unlike public blockchain, private blockchain has an authorized individual or in charge who oversees network communication, and one cannot join the privateblockchain network unless he is a permission user. The participant should be invited by network administrators to complete validations and transactions. And he will be in charge of granting network access to read or write. The consensus is based on the whims of the network's central controller. As a result, a private blockchain is usually recommended for corporate organizations. It works well for businesses that want to carry out certain operations using blockchain technology. However, when compared to public blockchain, the comfort zone in terms of level of control is frequently perceived to be minimal.

6.1.2.3 Consortium or Federated

It is a combination of private and public blockchain features. It is also known as a federated blockchain. However, it differs in that many organizational members collaborate on a decentralized network.

6.1.3 Benefits of Blockchain

- *Greater trust*
- *Greater security*
- *More efficiency*

6.1.4 APPLICATION OF BLOCKCHAIN

- Money transfer in real time
- The sharing economy
- Education credentials, criminal records
- Land registries
- Financial services: securities clearing, syndicated loans
- Airlines: registration, re-booking, discounts, and loyalty programs
- Voting
- Controlling the supply chain
- Audit logs
- Global supply chain: automotive recalls and fake airbags
- Secure document storage: property deed, auto title
- Birth registrations
- Payment channels: Starbucks or for broadband use
- Subsidy distribution/crowdfunding
- Healthcare: EMRs, insurance claims, genomic research

6.1.5 VEHICULAR NETWORK

Vehicular networks (VANETs) provide urban monitoring and data sharing in a variety of transportation contexts. Vehicular networks lack the traditional limits of WSNs, such as power, bandwidth, and memory constraints, allowing for more accurate sensing and data collecting (see Figure 6.2). Furthermore, automobiles may contain sensors that are not frequently found in handheld devices used in PSNs. Coverage is another essential characteristic of VANETs. Vehicles traverse the city via streets and lanes. As this mobility spreads, vehicular networks will be able to collect the specifics of numerous cities. All these characteristics combine to make VANETs an important data source that supplements data gathered from PSNs in order to better comprehend urban phenomena. Automotive applications can be employed in a variety of situations. VANETs, for example, must monitor a variety of events, such as potholes, traffic congestion, car accidents, and the presence of animals on the road. As a result, we give studies in this area that focus on three key issues: recording general traffic incidents, using data from VANETs to analyze people's practices, and studying traffic congestion. We also talk about the numerous obstacles that come with these issues.

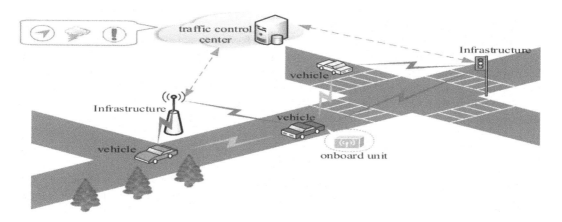

FIGURE 6.2 Blockchain with Vehicular adhoc networks.

Modern vehicles have undergone remarkable advancements, characterized by their speed, sophistication, and efficiency. These developments encompass numerous and extensive communication network and electronic control units (ECUs), facilitating a revolutionary driving experience. This includes capabilities such as remote locking and unlocking of vehicles, as well as keyless start and off for the vehicle. Recently, auto industry engineers have competed not only on physical vehicle designbut also on engine power and performance. In Nevada, Florida, and California, Google's driverless cars are also legal. As a result, it is just a matter of time before self-driving cars improve driver safety. This new technology is available in newer cars, and some of these functions and settings are also available in older cars. This one-of-a-kind driving experience functionality is provided by hundreds of terabytes of code in the vehicle's ECUs. But how about the security features? We live in the twenty-first century, and we are no longer surrounded by automated autos; instead, thanks to recent technological breakthroughs, computers on wheels are now available.

These technologies can be used to develop protocols for a wide range of safety equipment and vehicles, such as forward collision warnings, autonomous emergency braking, and car-to-vehicle communication. In the future, we may see fully automated vehicles. Within the realm of intelligent transportation systems (ITS), vehicle communication relies on ad hoc networks, including technologies such as dedicated short-range communication (DSRC), wireless access vehicular environment (WAVE), and cellular networks. However, these communication methods do not ensure secure data transmission. Currently, vehicular communication application security protocols are based on antiquated cellular and IT security technologies that are incompatible with ITS applications. Many researchers, on the other hand, are working to develop a general security mechanism for ITS [1].

6.1.6 Purpose of Vehicle Network Communication

Data centers are incorporated into systems that connect vehicles to networks to provide reliable admission and continuous statement. The vehicle can connect to high-latency cellular networks and the cloud to receive continuous broadcast notifications of traffic and road updates. For instance, well-known smartphone applications like Google Maps and Waze gather current traffic information to aid drivers in navigating their routes. The V2N network also allows for the communication of vehicles with one another. However accurate the information on traffic updates and navigation provided by third-party applicationsmay be, their technology has its limitations. Vehicles might rely on the good judgment of others to provide direction for an often-unexpected phenomenon on the road. Vehicles can communicate directly with one another to exchange data about their location, speed, and status. The direct communication between vehicles made possible by useful technology like intersection movement assist (IMA)and left-turn assist (LTA)increases road safety. When making a left turn or moving through an intersection, you can communicate with other motorists to warn them of potential collisions [2].

To prevent potential accidents, the vehicle-to-network systems can also direct pedestrian devices, also known as V2P. Traffic lights get signals from V2N that instruct them to alter their lights at predetermined intervals. For instance, it has an impact on how rapidly the signal changes during the day's set periods or when vehicles drive over pavement sensors. Delivering vital enabling technologies that will improve safety, decrease incidents, and reduce the effects of traffic congestion is the objective of connected cars.

6.1.7 Advancement of Smart Vehicular Communications

The area of vehicular communications, which also includes the infrastructure for roadside communications, is growing. Advances in wireless communications make it possible for infrastructure and vehicles to exchange information in real time. This has led to applications that enhance vehicle security and passenger Internet connectivity. Attempts are being made to standardize vehicular communication to make driving safer, more ecologically friendly, and easier. The Internet of

Vehicles (IoV) is one of the alluring innovations that transformed the automotive services industry. IoV is the fundamental idea behind autonomous and intelligent vehicles. Vehicles can communicate both inside and outside the car thanks to several wireless networking options. Through these connectivities, the car can communicate with other vehicles and its surroundings. The development of technologies related to IoV and connected cars will make autonomous driving possible, which is a novel automotive service [3,4].

Smart road infrastructures interact with the environment to carry out certain functions, like sensor cameras and traffic signals. The activities these devices take change based on how many vehicles and people are parked in each lane. To cut down on traffic as much as possible, the time it might take to clean up each route is calculated. Like that, these signals are sent over V2N to notify you of changes in the road's state, accidents, and other abnormalities. The cars have access to the following data through V2N: When you are going to proceed through a red light, you will receive warnings, and notifying drivers when a pedestrian is going to cross or when the crosswalk button has been touched. It can also warn drivers that a nearby emergency vehicle is approaching and show the traffic [3, 4].

6.1.8 BLOCKCHAIN APPLICATION FOR SMART VEHICULAR COMMUNICATIONS

VANETs have undergone a transformation inside the paradigm of distributed ledger technology (DLT). Applications built on the blockchain for vehicle-to-vehicle (V2V) leverage the blockchain services. Although not all the most often requested applications are included, it does cover many of them. In the V2V area, accident investigationsand insurance are significant applications for blockchain since they can make use of all the blockchain services. Blockchains firstly allow for the acquisition of dynamic insurance policies via payments and smart contracts. Users can buy considerably more specialized plans, such as insurance that simply covers the time spent driving. As a result, insurance providers may experience a reduction in risk and be able to better tailor premiums to specific driving scenarios, which could result in cost reductions for many consumers [4]. People continually produce data, including while driving. Vehicle data may be used to create extremely accurate maps, among other things. Blockchain technology can assist in resolving these issues. Payments made via blockchain can be used to purchase data. Specialized procedures are required to lower transaction fees, because individual sensor readings are typically worth relatively little. Smart contracts can also be utilized to benefit from more complicated pricing schemes. Reputation management strategies can also be used to address this issue to guarantee the accuracy of the data, offer purchasers small loans, and further [4, 5].

The transport sector faces a significant problem in figuring out how to cut carbon emissions. A cap-and-trade system, wherein people and businesses are allocated a set allocation of carbon credits, entitling them to a particular quantity of emissions, is a recommended technique for emissions reduction. If someone uses more of their allotment than they are allowed, they must buy credits from people who do not use their entire allotment. For efficiency, resiliency, and user-friendliness, all this can be tracked on a blockchain. Such a program might make use of each of the blockchain's services. Payment services and exchange smart contracts have the potential to facilitate the purchase and sale of credits, while robust identity and reputation services could play a crucial role in identifying the organizations deserving of carbon credits. Evidently, payments made using blockchain technology are possible. For parking, ride-sharing, and tolls. Blockchains have several benefits over conventional systems. First, because blockchains are open-source, many parties can charge and pay for these services using a single shared interface. Due to the option to sell parking spaces or available transportation, more cars and parking spaces are available and are used. Additionally, it makes it possible for towns of all sizes to establish toll systems that would not otherwise be viable [5].

Next, V2V includes communications from vehicles to power grids (V2G). Electric vehicles (EVs) can interface with proposed networks. With electric grids to buy electricity and even sell power back to the grid or to other vehicles to guarantee a steady supply of energy. By dispersing power sources, they first aid in the development of a stronger power grid. The capacity to drive supply to meet demand through incentive-compatible pricing schemes also promotes stability. It is possible to make it simple for any user to make and accept payments using blockchain technology, enabling a larger pool of players. Additionally, by utilizing microtransactions and smart contracts, it is possible to offer more dynamic pricing structures [4, 5].

6.1.9 FUTURES OF SMART VEHICULAR COMMUNICATIONS

Numerous problems, such as traffic congestion and accidents, frequently take priority over the transportation industry. Despite this, there has been an evolution in vehicle collaboration in recent years. Increasing road safety is the main goal, which tries to foresee probable hazardous situations. As vehicle-to-vehicle (V2V), infrastructure-to-vehicle (V2I), and everything-to-vehicle (V2X), its aim is to provide communication models that cars can use in a variety of application scenarios. The implementation of ITS technologies on roadways around the world is a key priority for the near future. Thus, to get the funding required for the modernization of the whole road system, most of the national governments will need to establish public–private partnerships. To implement the Internet of Things (IoT) successfully, new ITS technologies are needed for a more seamless integration with current mobile networks or software-defined networks (SDN) used, thereby generating increasingly complex services. These networks must be used in ITS applications to determine their broadest applicability and practical execution. ITS technologies will need to be implemented on less-used roads in order to cover the whole road network of each state. When the network is overwhelmed, device-to-device (D2D) communications and next-generation mobile communication technologies, including 5G, may be employed to ensure coverage. Additionally, the utilization of social networks and crowdsourcing strategies could be a significant help in ITS applications for resource management. Large private corporations, on the other hand, will have the ability to manage huge volumes of data from connected mobile devices and autos, with the aim of launching new marketing and sales initiatives [5].

One of the innovations that can be utilized to improve traffic in smart cities, urban areas, and on the highway is the employment of smart automobiles. Smart vehicles' development calls for multimedia services for the passengers as well as mobile communication services to guarantee safety. The intelligent transportation system must incorporate these services. Data communication services are provided by 5G vehicular network technology for intelligent transportation systems. The fundamental technology that must be in place to serve data communication traffic from sensors to the cloud is 5G networks offering broadband communication services. 5G networks are a smart city enabler. The 5G service has three primary use cases: the IoT that makes use of numerous devices, such as sensors and actuators, uses massive machine-type communications (mMTC); multimedia and mobile communication employ enhanced mobile broadband (eMBB); then, for transport services, ultrareliable and low-latency communications (URLLC) are employed. Cities will become smarter and more connected thanks to the development of 5G wireless technology, with better infrastructure, smarter objects, and smarter transportation. The benefit of 5G technology is its ability to utilize network function virtualization (NFV) to link and interact with existing networks. A centralized cloud system, distributed cloud, and mobile cloud are all used in the vehicular network architecture of smart city services. The fog computing node in this network architecture can offer mobile services for intelligent vehicles and multimedia apps for passengers [19].

6.2 RELATED WORKS

Advanced wireless network designs and applications with a focus on automotive networks are covered by Mario Gerla et al. ALOHA, CSMA, and related extensions were just a couple of the significant multi-access technologies that were created in the 1970s, with an emphasis on analytical models. They recognized the requirement for routing and topology maintenance for these vehicle networks in addition to the test bed implementations and studies that led to ALOHANET.

This is a crucial direction of growth for the automotive industry, as the integration of advanced digital and networking technologies into autos is growing rapidly and is currently making it possible for the types of applications we have described, using stationary, abstract content sources and stores like parked cars. These stationary vehicles may join together to build a MANET without moving, making routing simple. However, when parked cars leave their parking place, network routing must be updated. Using public buses as dependable roving servers along a well-known route is another extension. Mobile devices and aerial sensors are used by vehicular networks to map the area. Body area sensor networks work with VANET alerts to keep track of the driver's vital indicators within the car, measures to take in case the motorist slips and crashes. Vehicular networks provide geo-location-aware applications and social networks by utilizing the multitude of services offered by current smartphones [1].

For blockchain used in V2V and V2I communication in the dynamic nature of traffic, Madhusudan Singh et al. handle the issues of identification, trust, and verification. You must wait a few minutes for additional blocks with more information to come in Bitcoins. Mobile vehicles, however, do not have the luxury of taking their time acknowledging communications. Additionally, the volume of transactions in the case of vehicles is extraordinarily high in comparison to a cryptocurrency network.

Consequently, a perfect intelligent vehicle blockchain should possess two characteristics: it must be somewhat real-time, and it should be able to manage a lot of message traffic without slowing down. To address these issues, they unveiled a new blockchain algorithm. First, the difficulty of mining a block is adjusted to be so low that it only takes 2 to 3 seconds to complete. In order to divide the blockchain into many parallel chains, each of which provides a distinct geographic region and/or direction of movement, LDB branching is secondly implemented. By incorporating these ideas into an intelligent vehicle, blockchain can build and maintain a live network with minimal message authentication delay and good performance even under stress. Similar to Bitcoin, the idea of IVTP has been put up for intelligent vehicles to assess the reliability of other vehicles. There are numerous potentials created by the usage of blockchain in intelligent vehicles [6].

Using blockchain technology, Madhusudan Singh et al. introduced a reward-based intelligent vehicle communication that is not for the specific services that other researchers had previously suggested. To enhance the secrecy of IVs, they have offered crypto IV-TP. Fast and secure communication between IVs is provided via IV-TP. Discovering a thorough history of IV interaction is also beneficial. Data from IV communications is kept in the VC for as long as the user desires. The communication history and reputation of the IV are accessible to all authorized organizations (hospitals, insurance companies, police, etc.) in the event of any accident, as well as at home via the VC [7].

According to Chao Wang et al., all vehicles connected to the Internet under the Internet of Vehicles (IoV) future vision add blockchain technology for additionalsupport for critical vehicle information at a minimal cost. A distributed ledger known as blockchain technology successfully solves the issue that a centralized IoV architecture has. Although the integration of blockchain technology and IoVs has already been investigated in a number of studies, many features of these applications have not been taken into account.

We therefore present a thorough discussion and comparison of recent studies on blockchain applications, concentrating on fusing blockchain technology with IoV, based on the introduction of core IoV and blockchain principles [8].

The fundamentals of blockchain and recent initiatives to apply blockchain in automotive IoT are explained by Chunrong Peng et al. After covering current approaches and open technology, they highlight upcoming study areas for problems, blockchain, and automotive IoT. Both "how to improve automotive IoT protocols to support blockchain" and "how to design an efficient blockchain system to meet application requirements in automotive IoT" are topics they cover [9].

El-hacen Diallo originally adapted the VANET environment's PoW (proof-of-work) consensus process, in which RSUs (roadside units) keep a decentralized database of traffic statistics. The plan is then assessed while harmful cars are present. The findings demonstrate that the suggested method permits a safe and decentralized road traffic database at the level of RSUs. They then use the PBFT technique for voting-based consensus mechanism to reduce blockchain latency in response to their findings. The location of the origin of the traffic event determines the dynamic selection of the traffic data. Finally, we provide a new approach to blockchain replication between RSUs. This plan offers a trade-off between replication frequency and blockchain latency. The performance of the simulation is improved by minimizing validates (i.e., RSUs). Finally, they provide a trust model to lower the number of moderators without sacrificing the fairness and decentralization of block creation. We formalize and assess this trust model while taking into account several scenarios involving malicious RSUs. The outcomes demonstrate how well the suggested model reduces the set of estimators [10].

The dynamic selection of the traffic data validates is based on where the traffic event originated. They offer a novel approach for blockchain replication among RSUs. With this strategy, replication frequency and blockchain latency are traded off. By decreasing validates (also known as RSUs), the simulation's performance is enhanced. Finally, they offer a trust architecture that allows for a reduction of moderators without compromising block creation's fairness and decentralization. Based on geographic distance and RSUs, this trust model automatically assembles a team of moderators for each blockchain block. They formalize and evaluate this faith model while allowing for various RSU-related harmful scenarios. The results show how effectively the suggested model narrows the collection of estimators for bad [10].

A new blockchain-based framework is proposed by Vidya Krishnan and colleagues to provide a private and secure vehicle communication model. This system additionally verifies communication auditability using blockchain transaction records and data integrity utilizing hashes in transactions. Vehicles in this work can be confident that the data they get come from a trustworthy node. The use of blockchain technology for vehicle communication has the advantage that it helps prevent the majority of cyberattacks, including eavesdropping and man-in-the-middle attacks. Verifying the signature makes it simple to identify content changes in transactions. With the public key technique, privacy is mostly established [11].

For the Internet of Vehicles, TianhongSu et al. suggest a blockchain privacy protection mechanism. To guarantee the privacy of security information, they implement secure user registration, an effective key management system, blockchain-based two-way authentication, a secret key mechanism based on anonymous communication technology, and random numbers, between the vehicle and the service provider. To avoid central failure issues, the system makes use of blockchain's decentralization feature [12].

A decentralized IoT solution for vehicle communication (DISV) was introduced by Rateb Jabbar et al. It combines three fundamental layers to investigate the use of blockchain for IoV communication. On Ethereum's testnet, an intelligent contract prototype was utilized. This study examined a few solution attributes, such as integrity, security, and availability, to determine whether blockchain is a trustworthy and secure method of IoV communication. According to the findings, DISV can be regarded as a real-time application and a remedy for the primary problems associated with vehicle-to-X (V2X) communication, such as security, centralization, and lack of privacy. Additionally, it makes it easier for vehicles, infrastructure, and other participants in intelligent transportation systems to collaborate and exchange data. Additionally, DISV can be seen as a crucial part of advanced driver-assistance systems (ADAS), which can increase mobility and traffic safety [13].

A blockchain-based data security solution for automotive networks is presented by Naseem us Sehar et al. There is a trade-off between ensuring security and expediting communication distribution in vehicle networks powered by blockchain. The security of the blockchain network will be significantly greater if the consensus method is based on the utilization of the miner's enormous resources, including time, computing power, storage, and currency. But tighter security may result in worse performance. It is also important to keep in mind that adding more transactions to a block can extend the time used for block formation and propagation. An increase in confirmed transactions was seen along with the rise in vehicle-generated transactions [14].

To explain "blockchain-enabled VANET architecture" by Muhammad Saad et al., this review's emphasis on the significance of blockchain's fundamental qualities in other sectors is a noteworthy contribution. In that review, a particular VANET was chosen to demonstrate the possibilities of blockchain technology. Decentralized DLT-based vehicle networks can also use this design. In light of blockchain technology, various VANET and IoT procedures, including handoffs, handshaking, and data transfer, are examined. Professionals still need to deal with interoperability, scalability, and storage-related technological issues. Last but not the least, this study offers a classification of publications based on the findings. Theoretical, simulational, and experimental studies demonstrate the scarcity of blockchain-enabled pilot programs. Therefore, practitioners should take into account practical implementation for a more concrete implementation of blockchain in diverse sectors. An overview of current research on the IoT chain that is enabled by blockchain is provided in this paper for future work.

The experiment could start leveraging Narrowband IoT (NB-IoT) technologies for high mobility, low power consumption, and low latency as part of future work on blockchain-based VANETs that are 5G-enabled. This study could result in the use of blockchain technology across a range of industries, including door-to-door vaccination and the conveyance of healthcare via blockchain, both of which can be used to combat pandemic-like conditions. Future applications of this study may be useful for managing isolation and contact tracking in IoT. The decentralized architecture that is being presented can be expanded to provide sophisticated travel management systems for drones and autonomous vehicles [15].

In their assessment of blockchain solutions, Wendong Chen et al. discuss how pseudonymization, permission management, ring signature techniques, and other methods might be used to deliver a variety of vehicular services while maintaining privacy. Location identity and data privacy are the three categories they use to categorize the literature. They assign grades based on the blockchain platform and architecture each one employs. Each individual privacy protection field was identified through classification to have fairly developed privacy-protection technology. To fulfil the low-computation and low-latency needs of IoV, many blockchain-based privacy-preserving solutions have started integrating other cutting-edge technology. In order to encourage and motivate academics interested in this area to perform additional study, we outline key concerns and future research paths in this area [16].

Youssef De Genoury and others research the available IoV solutions and suggest a SISIV framework in a report. Use is made of a deep learning framework and a focus strategy based on GCNs. Blockchain technology is used by SISIV to protect data transfer between nodes. The branch-and-bound method is additionally utilized to figure out the deep learning model's higher parameters. Four networked car datasets created to forecast different traffic statistics were used to validate SISIV. The findings demonstrate that, in terms of prediction rate, F-measure, and identified attacks, SISIV performs better than the baseline solutions.

The research done for this paper opens up a number of new directions for future investigation. IoV has improved in a number of operational areas; however, users of such systems continue to face serious security issues. High security should be ensured when data is retrieved and transmitted from users' devices for traffic forecasting. Associative learning has also been the subject of contemporary research. Given the amount of devices running at the edge of such IoV networks, applying the deep learning techniques examined in this study in a federated learning environment is beneficial. The lack of data for training graph convolution neural networks is a weakness of this study. It will be crucial for future research to examine data augmentation methods, particularly when using a formative adversarial network [17].

A blockchain-based data security solution for car networks is offered by Naseem Us Sehar et al. The transportation system can be transformed by incorporating blockchain technology into vehicle networks, which can also bring a wide range of applications that can be created on top of the blockchain. There are compromises between offering security and instantly distributing messages in blockchain-based vehicular networks. The security of the blockchain network will be significantly greater if the consensus method is built on using the miner's enormous resources, including time, computing power, storage, and currency. But tighter security may result in worse performance. It is also important to keep in mind that a block's propagation and creation times will increase as the number of transactions in the block rises. Confirmed transactions have increased together with the quantity of transactions generated by automobiles [18].

6.3 TECHNOLOGY DISCUSSION

In the growth of vehicular communications, self-contained motor vehicles, and intelligent transportation systems during the past ten years, the automotive industry has seen enormous changes. These technologies are possible thanks to recent advancements in hardware, software, and communication systems that have led to the development of various applications and standards. Modern cars come equipped with innovative technologies that detect potential driving issues and improve the driving experience. In a networked environment, V2V communication is used to reduce traffic congestion and improve passenger safety.

6.3.1 EXISTING TECHNOLOGY

The concept of integrating smart vehicles and the developments in automobile automation result in positive effects, such as a reduction in traffic fatalities and congestion. However, incorporating a chain of automation into the attack surface will broaden the attack surface and expose automotive security to malicious intrusion. To ensure genuine and authentic communication, only vehicles having a correct and verifiable record will be permitted to exchange messages on the blockchain network. Aside from the danger of collusion attacks, the usage of blockchain in smart car privacy necessitates enormous storage and scalability limits. With the increasing integration of computing and communication technology into automobiles, vehicular networks are emerging as a feasible solution for long-term urbanization. Vehicular networks are concerned with the development and administration of ad hoc wireless networks made up of moving cars and a small piece of stationary communication infrastructure [19].

6.3.2 ADVANCED TECHNOLOGY

VANETs provide communication networks by combining specialized short-range networks and conventional cell phone technologies. The Third Generation Partnership Project recently specified 5G technology, which is now being deployed globally. 5G communication technology is poised to revolutionize a wide range of application industries. 5G will considerably improve vehicle network capabilities and meet vehicular network needs for extremely high peak data, sustainable data rates, and low latency, while also enhancing security, communication cost, network reliability, and connectivity energy efficiency. The recognition of vehicle networks as one of the most important applications for 5G led to the creation of 5G-enabled VANETs. A wave of new vehicle network services and businesses is anticipated to be made possible by the combination of 5G technology and VANETs. To ensure safe car authentication, an undisputed record, and message integrity of vehicle reputation, a few initiatives, in particular, employ blockchain to manage trust in 5G-enabled autonomous vehicle systems. Vehicle network systems must handle data storage in an acceptable manner, carry out transactions in a highly secure manner, and employ non-interference networks. Blockchain is revolutionizing a wide range of industries as its popularity grows. Blockchain technology is becoming more and more popular as more application fields want to capitalize on its security, immutability, costsaving, quick processing capabilities, and transparency. Several industries can now enhance their current systems or completely redesign them thanks to blockchain technology. Blockchain, for instance, has made it possible for IoT systems to increase the quality of their services while still adhering to security regulations. Blockchain is being used by a number of initiatives to manage trust in 5G-enabled autonomous vehicle systems, guaranteeing message integrity, secure car authentication, and an unquestionable vehicle reputation record. Systems for vehicle networks need to handle data storage effectively and ensure secure transactions and interference-free networks. Blockchain is a viable candidate alternative for 5G car network systems due to its immutability, tamperproofness, and inherent security [20].

6.3.3 Data Security Issues

With its present use in car networks, blockchain technology can offer a smart transportation system that is decentralized, dependable, and secure, without the need for a middleman. Data security and authenticity are improved in automotive networks through the use of blockchain technology [21]. In the Internet of Vehicles (IoV), blockchain can offer security for electric vehicles (EV).

The efficient use of energy resources can also be ensured by blockchain technology, which has the ability to greatly improve energy efficiency, reduce management costs, and so on. As a result, its incorporation into the IoV concept makes it possible for EVs to exchange energy in a safe, automatic, and independent manner. IoV is one of the many fields and applications where blockchain has the potential to be quite helpful. Decentralization, transparency, immutability, improved security, anonymity, cost reduction, and autonomy are some characteristics of this new technology [22].

In the context of smart energy grids, blockchain has recently emerged as a revolutionary technology that enables secure and trustworthy P2P energy exchange. A reliable, transparent, and decentralized record of all information and transactions pertaining to energy production and consumption might be created thanks to the characteristics of blockchain. System automation and efficiency are increased by blockchain integration, while security, privacy, and dependability are also increased [22]. The IoV's use of blockchain offers the future Internet the possibility to address security vulnerabilities, like interruption, single point of failure, and availability problems. This is because all peer nodes functioning in the network can synchronize and replicate data on the blockchain. As a result, the IoV services can continue to function normally even if one or more nodes fail. Blockchain technology is based on sophisticated cryptographic algorithms to preserve common security and privacy characteristics. Blockchain in particular encourages enhanced security and privacy within IoV networks through encryption. Particularly, many researches have looked into blockchain as a privacy-preserving mechanism for energy storage, privacy protection, and trusted data sharing. All these things are conceivable, including identity management, malicious attack prevention, safe V2G payment mechanisms, secure tariff choice, and encrypted vehicular communication. Blockchain improves the security of the IoV. The cryptographic methods, combined with the consensus procedure, provide data immutability. It would be extremely impossible to amend or delete an energy transaction after it has been added to the blockchain network, creating a very secure and robust foundation for IoV services and applications. Blockchain's immutability may help prevent data manipulation and tampering while also enabling reliable audits. All organizations can generally access public blockchain, which is permissionless. The implementation of blockchain enhances the IoV's security. Data immutability is provided by the cryptographic techniques, along with the consensus process. After being added to the blockchain network, it would be virtually impossible to change or remove an energy transaction, which would create a very secure and reliable foundation for IoV services and applications [22].

6.3.4 Future Technologies

6.3.4.1 Blockchain-Adopted VANET Applications

Studies have implied on blockchain-adopted IoTs which were said to be appropriate on specific domains in the following sections, amidst its instant deployment that would fundamentally transform the perception of future directions [23].

6.3.4.2   Asset Tracking

It is difficult to comply with authorities who want to ensure efficient asset movement. Data can be stored on shared ledgers during a product's life cycle with the assistance of blockchain-enabled VANETs. The relevant government agencies, consignees, producers, and shippers may receive the ledger information. With the cutting-edge capability of cost-effectiveness, blockchain technology is simple to adopt, secure, and transparent in asset management [23].

6.3.4.3   Data Science and Management

Blockchain technology can be used to create data science and management apps that provide tamperproof operation and maintenance data. In order to avoid prediction anomalies, it helps to maintain data sciences and data integrity. For further compliance and administration, the appropriate authorities may also be given access to the trusted data modifications and ledger [23].

6.3.4.4   Solid Waste Management

Researchers have examined trash management strategies based on blockchain and VANET to advance rubbish-collecting practices in poor cities. Truck routing, monitoring, waste collection, and transportation of the recycling of specific types of rubbish are the main elements of waste management models. Researchers suggest clever waste collecting, recycling, and disposal algorithms [23].

6.3.4.5   Contact Tracing and Social Distancing

Keeping social distance is the only way to stop pandemics. An international consortium, including Google and Apple, supports the decentralized form of contact tracking to preserve openness and privacy. In order to maintain privacy, openness, and security, researchers have examined contact tracing methods supported by blockchain and IoT.

6.4   CONCLUSION AND FUTURE WORK

This chapter summarizes a systematic evaluation and analysis based on diverse study investigations that address the problems that may arise with blockchain and IoT, particularly VANETs. This chapter makes a significant contribution by highlighting the importance of blockchain in various fields due to its intrinsic properties. For the different potentials of blockchain technology, the field of VANETs was chosen for this assessment. For vehicle networks based on DLT, the decentralized architecture was also derived. The specific mechanisms of VANETs and the IoT are also examined in the context of blockchain technology, such as data communication. Prospective users can also sort through the applications' difficulties, restrictions, and open problems. Practitioners still need to address the technological problems associated with storage, scalability, and interoperability. Studies on 5G network–enabled blockchain-based VANETs with high mobility, low latency, and low power consumption using NB-IoT technologies can start as part of the next effort. This research may also lead to the adoption of blockchain technology across a range of industries, including healthcare delivery for door-to-door vaccinations that can be tailored to combat pandemic-like conditions.

REFERENCES

1. Gerla, Mario, and Leonard Kleinrock, "Vehicular networks and the future of the mobile internet." *Computer Networks* 55, no. 2(2011):457–469.ISSN 1389-1286, https://doi.org/10.1016/j.comnet.2010.10.015.
2. Nadeem Ahangar, M., Qasim Z. Ahmed, Fahd A. Khan, and Maryam Hafeez, "A survey of autonomous vehicles: Enabling communication technologies and challenges." *Sensors* 21, no. 3 (2021): 706. https://doi.org/10.3390/s21030706.
3. Arena, Fabio, and Giovanni Pau, "An overview of vehicular communications." *Future Internet* 11, no. 2 (2019): 27. https://doi.org/10.3390/fi11020027.
4. Wang, Chao, Xiaoman Cheng, Jitong Li, Yunhua He, and Ke Xiao, "A survey: Applications of blockchain in the internet of vehicles." *Eurasip Journal of Wireless Communication and Networking* 2021 (2021): 77. https://doi.org/10.1186/s13638-021-01958-8.

5. Meijer, James, Panagiotis Michalopoulo, Shashank Motepalli, Gengrui Zhang, Shiquan Zhang, Andreas Veneris, and Hans-Arno Jacobsen, "Blockchain for V2X: Applications and architectures."*IEEE Open Journal of Vehicular Technology* 3 (2022): 193–209. https://doi.org/10.1109/OJVT.2022.3172709.

6. Singh, Madhusudan, and Shiho Kim, "Branch based blockchain technology in intelligent vehicle."*Computer Networks* 145 (2018): 219–231.ISSN 1389-1286, https://doi.org/10.1016/j.comnet.2018.08.016.

7. Singh, Madhusudan, and Shiho Kim, "Intelligent vehicle-trust point: Reward based intelligent vehicle communication using blockchain." ArXiv. /abs/1707.07442 (2017).

8. Wang, Chao, Xiaoman Cheng, Jitong Li, et al., "A survey: Applications of blockchain in the internet of vehicles." *EURASIP Journal on Wireless Communications and Networking* 2021 (2021): 1–16.

9. Peng, Chunrong, Celimuge Wu, Liming Gao, Jiefang Zhang, Kok-Lim Alvin Yau, and Yusheng Ji, "Blockchain for vehicular internet of things: Recent advances and open issues." *Sensors* 20, no. 18 (2020): 5079.

10. Diallo, El-hacen, "Study and design of blockchain-based decentralized road traffic data management in VANET (Vehicular Adhoc NETworks)." Thèse soutenue à Paris-Saclay, le 1 Avril 2022.

11. Koduri, Rajesh, Sivaprasad Nandyala, and Mithun Manalikandy, Secure Vehicular Communication Using Blockchain Technology. No. 2020-01-0722. SAE Technical Paper (2020).

12. Su, Tianhong, Sujie Shao, Shaoyong Guo, and Min Lei, "Blockchain-based internet of vehicles privacy protection system." *Wireless Communications and Mobile Computing* 2020 (2020): 1–10.

13. Jabbar, R., M. Kharbeche, K. Al-Khalifa, M. Krichen, and K. Barkaoui, "Blockchain for the internet of vehicles: A decentralized IoT solution for vehicles communication using ethereum." *Sensors* 20 (2020): 3928. https://doi.org/10.3390/s20143928

14. Sehar, Naseem Us, Osman Khalid, Imran Ali Khan, Faisal Rehman, Muhammad A.B. Fayyaz, Ali R. Ansari, and Raheel Nawaz, "Blockchain enabled data security in vehicular networks." *Scientific Reports* 13, no. 1 (2023): 4412.

15. Saad, Muhammad, Muhammad Khalid Khan, and Maaz Bin Ahmad, "Blockchain-enabled vehicular ad hocnetworks: A systematic literature review." *Sustainability* 14, no. 7 (2022): 3919.

16. Chen, Wendong, Haiqin Wu, Xiao Chen, and Jinfu Chen, "A review of research on privacy protection of internet of vehicles based on blockchain." *Journal of Sensor and Actuator Networks* 11, no. 4 (2022): 86.

17. Djenouri, Y., A. Belhadi, D. Djenouri, G. Srivastava, and J.C.-W. Lin, "A secure intelligent system for internet of vehicles: Case study on traffic forecasting." In *IEEE Transactions on Intelligent Transportation Systems*. https://doi.org/10.1109/TITS.2023.3243542.

18. Sehar, N.U., O. Khalid, I.A. Khan, et al., "Blockchain enabled data security in vehicular networks." *Scientific Reports* 13, no. 4412 (2023). https://doi.org/10.1038/s41598-023-31442-w.

19. Smys, S., and Haoxiang Wang, "Security enhancement in smart vehicle using blockchain-based architectural framework." *Journal of Artificial Intelligence and Capsule Networks* 3, no. 2 (2021): 90–100. https://doi.org/10.36548/jaicn.2021.2.002.

20. Bendechache, Malika, Takfarinas Saber, Gabriel-Miro Muntean, and Irina Tal, "Application of blockchain technology to 5G-enabled vehicular networks: Survey and future directions." *DORAS DCU Online Research Access Service* 20, no. 10.

21. Sehar, Naseem us, Osman Khalid, Imran Ali Khan, Faisal Rehman, Muhammad A.B. Fayyaz, Ali R. Ansari, and Raheel Nawaz, "Blockchain enabled data security in vehicular networks." *Scientific Reports* 13, no. 1 (2023): 4412.

22. Kapassa, Evgenia, Marinos Themistocleous, Klitos Christodoulou, and Elias Iosif, "Blockchain application in internet of vehicles: Challenges, contributions and current limitations." *Future Internet* 13 (2021): 313. https://doi.org/10.3390/fi13120313

23. Saad, Muhammad, Muhammad Khalid Khan, and Maaz Bin Ahmad, "Blockchain-enabled vehicular ad hoc networks: A systematic literature review."*Sustainability* 14 (2022): 3919. https://doi.org/10.3390/su14073919.

7 Blockchain Technology for Automobile Sales and Leasing

Magdi El Messiry and Adel ElMessiry

7.1 INTRODUCTION

Blockchain technology has emerged as a disruptive force in recent years, holding the potential to revolutionize various industries. One sector that stands to greatly benefit from blockchain is the automotive industry. In 2021, the global automotive market size reached 2.73 trillion USD and is projected to reach 3.27 trillion USD by 2028, exhibiting a compound annual growth rate (CAGR) of 3.01%. Around 85.4 million motor vehicles are produced globally every year. This interactive chart shows the share of each world region for the 2007–2022 period. Note that, among all vehicles produced, China produces total 32%, followed by Europe 12% and North America at 18% [1, 2].

The automobile industry has been a pioneer in adopting advanced technologies to enhance efficiency, safety, and overall user experience. In recent years, blockchain technology has emerged as a disruptive force with the potential to transform various sectors, including the automotive industry. Blockchain, originally designed as the underlying technology for cryptocurrencies like Bitcoin, is a decentralized, distributed ledger system that allows secure and transparent recordkeeping [3].

This chapter delves into the diverse applications of blockchain technology in the automobile industry, exploring its impact on supply chain management, vehicle traceability, autonomous vehicles, and more.

Originally developed as the foundation of cryptocurrencies, blockchain's decentralized and immutable nature has found practical applications far beyond the financial sector. Already, blockchain technology is being utilized by various automotive companies, as outlined in the following.

Instances of automotive companies leveraging blockchain technology [4–6]:

- **BMW** uses blockchain to track its vehicles' status, so customers can always access accurate information about their cars.
- **Ford** has partnered up with IBM and Sweetbridge in order to launch a blockchain-based platform that will allow for parts procurement and supply chain management.
- **Toyota** teamed up with the Massachusetts Institute of Technology (MIT) to investigate blockchain-based methods of securely managing vehicle data.
- **Volvo** uses blockchain technology to ensure the safety and quality of its products across the entire supply chain. This technology reduces recall risk and helps ensure that components meet strict requirements.
- **Audi** uses blockchain to manage customer data and provide personalized experiences for drivers. If you want to create automotive software for your business, you must take assistance from an experienced automotive software development company.
- **Honda** uses blockchain technology to secure vehicle data, allowing driver performance evaluations to improve road safety.
- **Volkswagen** uses blockchain technology to increase the efficiency of its supply chains. Volkswagen can cut expenses and shorten the time it takes to commercialize new goods thanks to this technology.
- **Tesla** uses blockchain technology to trace its lithium-ion batteries' origins to reduce costs and ensure quality control.

DOI: 10.1201/9781003450306-8

- **Mercedes-Benz** uses blockchain to detect fraud and manage identity, protecting its customers against cyberattacks.
- **General Motors** uses blockchain technology to secure vehicle data and provide personalized customer experiences.
- **NIO**, a Chinese electric vehicle manufacturer, was reportedly working on a project involving blockchain technology to track and verify used car histories.
- **ZF Friedrichshafen** (ZF), a German automotive supplier, was exploring blockchain for supply chain optimization and counterfeit part prevention.
- **Bosch**, a global supplier of technology and services, was researching the use of blockchain in various industrial applications, including the automotive sector.
- **Renault** has been involved in a pilot project called "Blockchain My Car" in collaboration with Microsoft and VISEO. The project aimed to provide transparency in the maintenance and repair history of used cars.
- **Porsche** has been exploring blockchain technology for verifying the authenticity of spare parts and optimizing the supply chain.
- **Toyota** is a member of the MOBI consortium as well. They have been researching blockchain technology for various use cases, including vehicle data sharing and supply chain transparency.
- **Jaguar Land Rover** had announced a partnership with IOTA Foundation to explore blockchain technology's potential to reward vehicle owners for sharing driving data and enabling smart city initiatives.

IBM, while not an automotive manufacturer, has been working with various companies in the automotive sector to implement blockchain solutions [7]. Their blockchain platform has been used for supply chain optimization and other applications.

It is important to note that the level of involvement and specific initiatives of these companies may have changed since this last update. To get the most up-to-date information about companies applying blockchain technology in their automotive productions, I recommend checking recent news articles, official company announcements, and reports from industry sources.

These examples show that many companies already use blockchain in the automotive industry to improve operations and deliver better customer experiences. We can expect more companies to join the trend as technology advances and unlock even greater potential from blockchain-based technologies.

Blockchain technology comprises a distributed ledger of records or a database encompassing all events executed or shared by participating entities [8].

Blockchain differentiates itself from other technologies through four distinct attributes:

- Decentralization
- Security
- Auditability
- Smart execution

At a more elevated level, the operation of a blockchain unfolds as follows:

- An entity intending to record an event transmits a transaction to its peers within the network.
- Following verification and scrutiny of the received transaction by a majority of network peers, the transaction gains approval in accordance with the established regulations adhered to by blockchain participants.
- Multiple peers uphold a record of the sanctioned transaction, bolstering resistance against attacks and enhancing reliability in the presence of node or equipment failures.

- Transactions are typically grouped into blocks, each linked to the preceding block via a hash function of its contents, thereby establishing a chain of interdependence among the blocks and forming a series of interconnected records.
- An arbitrary contract can be deployed in the form of instructions on each network node, executing autonomously upon fulfillment of predetermined conditions.

This chapter explores how blockchain is reshaping the automobile industry, revolutionizing various aspects of manufacturing, supply chain management, vehicle ownership, and data security.

Blockchain technology introduces a transparent and tamper-resistant supply chain management system for the automobile industry. Manufacturers, suppliers, and dealers can record every step of the production and distribution process on the blockchain. This increased visibility ensures better accountability, reduces counterfeit parts, and expedites recalls or maintenance services. Smart contracts integrated into the blockchain enable automated execution of agreements, streamlining transactions and reducing costs [9].

7.2   DEFINITION AND PRINCIPLES OF BLOCKCHAIN

Blockchain is a distributed ledger technology that operates through a network of nodes, where each node holds a copy of the entire ledger. Transactions are grouped into blocks cryptographically linked in chronological order, creating a chain of blocks. Its core principles of decentralization, transparency, immutability, and consensus form the basis for its widespread adoption.

7.3   HOW BLOCKCHAIN WORKS

The chapter delves into the technical workings of blockchain, explaining concepts such as cryptographic hashing, consensus mechanisms (proof of work, proof of stake, etc.), and smart contracts, which play a vital role in revolutionizing the automobile industry [10].

Blockchain's immutable nature enables the creation of a comprehensive vehicle history database, recording every crucial detail from manufacturing to ownership transfers. Potential buyers can access this decentralized repository, ensuring the authenticity of the vehicle's history and eliminating the risk of purchasing stolen or fraudulently altered vehicles. This added transparency builds trust and confidence among buyers and sellers in the pre-owned car market [11, 12].

7.3.1   IMMUTABLE VEHICLE HISTORY

Blockchain enables the creation of a tamperproof vehicle history record, providing potential buyers with accurate information about a vehicle's maintenance, accidents, and ownership history. This not only builds trust between buyers and sellers but also reduces the prevalence of fraudulent practices in the used car market.

7.3.2   VEHICLE IDENTITY AND AUTHENTICATION

With blockchain-based vehicle identities, cars can be uniquely identified on the network, preventing identity theft and unauthorized modifications. Additionally, this technology paves the way for secure vehicle-to-vehicle (V2V) and vehicle-to-infrastructure (V2I) communication essential for the development of autonomous vehicles.

7.3.3   SUPPLY CHAIN FINANCE AND PAYMENTS

Blockchain technology can facilitate efficient and secure financial transactions within the automobile supply chain (see Figure 7.1). It enables quicker and more transparent payments between manufacturers

Buyer purchases something

Buyer pays
lender later

Supplier requests
early payment

Lender pays supplier less fee

FIGURE 7.1   Supply chain example.

and suppliers, ensuring smoother cash flow and reducing delays in production. Additionally, block-chain-powered cryptocurrencies could revolutionize vehicle purchases by allowing direct peer-to-peer transactions, eliminating the need for intermediaries and reducing transaction costs.

7.3.4   DECENTRALIZED MOBILITY SERVICES

Peer-to-peer car-sharing. Blockchain enables peer-to-peer car-sharing platforms, where vehicle owners can directly rent out their cars to others. Smart contracts manage rental agreements, payment processing, and access control, making the process secure and autonomous.

Micropayments for services. Blockchain facilitates seamless micropayments for various in-car services, like entertainment, navigation, and charging. This creates new revenue streams for manufacturers and service providers while giving consumers more control over the services they access.

Data privacy and security. The advent of autonomous vehicles brings forth challenges related to data privacy and security. Blockchain provides a decentralized solution for storing and sharing data generated by autonomous cars, ensuring that sensitive information remains secure and accessible only to authorized parties. Moreover, the decentralized nature of blockchain enhances data reliability and integrity, vital for safe and efficient autonomous driving.

Protecting connected vehicle data. As vehicles become more connected and data-driven, block-chain ensures the security and privacy of sensitive information. By decentralizing data storage and granting vehicle owners control over their data-sharing preferences, blockchain mitigates data breaches and unauthorized access.

Securing autonomous vehicles. In the context of autonomous vehicles, blockchain enhances cybersecurity by safeguarding communication networks, protecting vehicle-to-cloud data transmissions, and preventing potential hacking attempts.

7.3.5   SMART CONTRACTS

Smart contracts enable the automation of routine vehicle services and maintenance tasks. When integrated with the vehicle's system, these self-executing contracts can schedule maintenance appointments, order parts, and process payments automatically when specific conditions are met.

This automation improves vehicle performance, reduces downtime, and enhances the overall user experience.

7.3.6 Mobility as a Service

Blockchain can revolutionize the concept of mobility as a service (MaaS) by providing a decentralized platform for users to access and pay for various transportation services seamlessly. By integrating different modes of transportation into a single blockchain-based ecosystem, MaaS becomes more efficient and cost-effective, encouraging the use of shared transportation options and reducing traffic congestion [13].

Blockchain's transparent and immutable ledger can be leveraged to track the electric vehicle (EV) battery life cycle, ensuring responsible disposal and recycling. By promoting sustainability and environmental consciousness, blockchain technology contributes to the broader goal of reducing the automobile industry's carbon footprint, overcoming challenges and future perspectives. While blockchain offers immense potential for the automobile industry, there are challenges that need to be addressed, such as scalability, interoperability, and regulatory compliance.

As of our last knowledge update in September 2021, several automotive manufacturers and companies are exploring the use of blockchain technology in various aspects of the automotive industry [14]. Blockchain technology offers benefits, such as enhanced transparency, data security, and streamlined supply chain processes. Some of the potential use cases for blockchain in the automotive industry include:

- *Supply chain management.* Blockchain can be used to create a transparent and secure supply chain network. It allows tracking the movement of components and parts from suppliers to manufacturers, helping to prevent counterfeiting and ensure the authenticity of parts.
- *Vehicle history and maintenance.* Blockchain can record and securely store vehicle history, including maintenance records, accident history, and ownership changes. This can help potential buyers make informed decisions and improve the resale value of vehicles.
- *Digital identity and authentication.* Blockchain can be used to create a digital identity for vehicles, ensuring that only authorized parties have access to vehicle data and features. This could enhance security and enable new functionalities, such as secure vehicle-to-vehicle communication.
- *Shared mobility and payments.* Blockchain can facilitate secure and transparent payments for services like ride-sharing and parking. It can also enable peer-to-peer car-sharing platforms with secure transactions and access control.
- *Energy and charging infrastructure.* Blockchain can play a role in managing electric vehicle (EV) charging stations, optimizing energy usage, and enabling seamless billing and payment systems.
- *Licensing and intellectual property.* Blockchain can help track and protect intellectual property rights related to automotive innovations, such as patents, designs, and software.

While there were various pilots, partnerships, and initiatives exploring blockchain technology in the automotive sector, widespread adoption was still in its early stages as of 2021 [15].

Major automotive manufacturers and tech companies are often involved in collaborations and consortia to develop and test blockchain solutions.

This chapter explores possible solutions to these obstacles and envisions a future where blockchain technology is deeply integrated into the automobile industry, revolutionizing the way we manufacture, use, and interact with vehicles.

- *Scalability and energy efficiency.* The chapter discusses the challenges associated with blockchain's scalability and energy consumption and explores potential solutions and alternative consensus mechanisms.

- *Collaborative efforts and standards.* The adoption of blockchain in the automobile industry requires collaboration among stakeholders and the establishment of industry-wide standards to ensure interoperability and efficiency.
- *Future applications and possibilities.* Finally, the chapter explores the potential future blockchain applications in the automobile industry, such as autonomous vehicle fleets, mobility-as-a-service platforms, and cross-border transactions.

This chapter introduces a protocol called Vehicle Ownership, Leasing, and Rental Blockchain Protocol (VOLR BP), which utilizes blockchain and non-fungible tokens (NFTs) to create digital replicas of vehicles. These digital twins enable the secure and transparent transfer of ownership, leasing, and rental transactions. The VOLR BP aims to address existing challenges in vehicle ownership and streamline the processes involved in vehicle leasing and rental, ultimately fostering increased trust, efficiency, and decreased administrative overhead [16].

7.4 CHALLENGES OF THE AUTOMOTIVE INDUSTRY

While the potential of blockchain technology to revolutionize the automotive industry is vast, it is important to recognize that the road to implementation is not without its challenges. As with any disruptive innovation, there are obstacles that must be addressed to fully harness the benefits of blockchain in the automotive sector. The fundamental attributes of blockchains, encompassing their decentralized character, transparency, and unchangeability, position them ideally to tackle the intricate challenges that automobile manufacturers encounter regularly. Concurrently, solutions rooted in blockchain have the capacity to yield tangible advantages for consumers, empowering them to trace the entire chronicle of a specific vehicle and introducing user-friendly methods to engage with post-purchase service providers. There is a wide array of potential uses for blockchain within the automotive realm. Let us explore a few of the avenues through which this technology can bring advantages to the industry [17].

This chapter explores the key challenges that the industry faces when applying blockchain technology.

7.4.1 SCALABILITY AND PERFORMANCE

Blockchain networks, especially public ones like Ethereum, can suffer from scalability and performance issues. The automotive industry involves massive amounts of data, such as supply chain information, vehicle histories, and real-time data from autonomous vehicles [18]. Scaling blockchain networks to accommodate such data volumes and ensuring high-speed transaction processing are significant challenges that require innovative solutions.

7.4.2 INTEROPERABILITY

The automotive industry is a complex ecosystem with numerous stakeholders, each using different systems and databases. Integrating blockchain into this environment requires seamless interoperability with existing technologies. Ensuring that blockchain networks can communicate with legacy systems, third-party applications, and other blockchains is a formidable challenge that requires standardization efforts [19].

7.4.3 DATA PRIVACY AND SECURITY

While blockchain is lauded for its security features, challenges still exist, particularly in managing off-chain data and private information [20]. The automotive industry handles sensitive data, including personal information, vehicle performance data, and proprietary designs. Balancing transparency with data privacy and security concerns is a delicate task that requires careful design of permissioned blockchain systems.

7.5 REGULATORY AND LEGAL COMPLEXITIES

Blockchain's decentralized nature can clash with regulatory requirements that mandate centralized oversight and control. Legal challenges arise when determining liability in case of disputes, adhering to data protection laws, and defining jurisdiction in decentralized transactions. Striking a balance between blockchain's inherent attributes and regulatory compliance is a puzzle that needs to be solved [21].

7.6 ADOPTION AND RESISTANCE TO CHANGE

Introducing blockchain technology involves cultural and organizational shifts. Resistance to change, particularly among well-established industry players, can hinder widespread adoption. Convincing manufacturers, suppliers, dealerships, and consumers to embrace new processes and technologies requires education and overcoming skepticism about the benefits of blockchain.

7.7 COST AND INFRASTRUCTURE

Implementing blockchain technology demands substantial investments in terms of infrastructure, development, and maintenance. Small- and medium-sized players in the automotive industry might find it challenging to allocate resources for blockchain integration. Moreover, creating and maintaining a secure and resilient blockchain infrastructure can be costly, deterring some stakeholders from full-scale adoption.

7.8 ENERGY CONSUMPTION

Many blockchain networks, especially those relying on proof-of-work consensus mechanisms, are criticized for their energy-intensive operations. Given the automotive industry's increasing focus on sustainability, integrating blockchain could be seen as counterproductive if it leads to excessive energy consumption. The industry must explore consensus mechanisms that are more energy-efficient.

7.9 EDUCATION AND SKILL GAP

Blockchain technology is relatively new, and expertise in its application is still evolving. The automotive industry needs professionals with a deep understanding of both blockchain and the intricacies of the industry. Bridging the education and skill gap to build a workforce capable of developing and managing blockchain solutions is a challenge that requires a long-term commitment.

As the automotive industry gears up to embrace the potential of blockchain technology, it must also tackle these multifaceted challenges head-on [22]. Overcoming these obstacles demands collaboration, innovation, and a patient approach. Addressing scalability, interoperability, security, regulatory compliance, adoption hurdles, costs, energy consumption, and skills shortage will determine the extent to which blockchain transforms the industry. By navigating these challenges, the automotive sector can drive toward a future where blockchain enhances transparency, efficiency, and trust across the entire value chain.

The global economy greatly depends on the automotive industry, as it offers transportation solutions to individuals, businesses, and various sectors. Nevertheless, conventional methods of owning, leasing, and renting vehicles have suffered from inefficiencies, a lack of transparency, and trust problems. These obstacles have generated a demand for innovative solutions that can optimize operations, increase security, and enhance the overall customer journey.

Over the past few years, blockchain technology has gained recognition as a promising solution that has the potential to tackle these issues effectively. By offering a transparent, secure, and

FIGURE 7.2 Sustainability triple bottom.

decentralized framework, blockchain can revolutionize the management of vehicle ownership, leasing, and rental transactions [23]. In the past, the only available method for managing waste and ensuring quality was through centralized control of the supply chain. However, with the growth of blockchain (distributed ledger technology) [24], decentralized control became a means of improving the quality and speed of supply chains while eliminating waste and reducing economic costs [25]. Treiblmaier makes the case that only blockchain applications can satisfactorily address and improve the "triple bottom lines" of the supply chain's goals for social, economic, and environmental sustainability, as shown in Figure 7.2.

7.10 VEHICLE OWNERSHIP, LEASING, AND RENTAL BLOCKCHAIN PROTOCOL VOLR BP

There are many issues with how vehicles are now owned, leased, and rented. The hazards associated with fraud, forgery, and a lack of transparency in ownership records are significant for both buyers and sellers. The administrative burden and the complexity of paperwork involved in transferring ownership result in delays, errors, and higher costs. In the case of leasing, trust issues emerge due to the lack of transparency in lease terms and limited flexibility for lessees. Rental services face challenges in verifying the eligibility of renters, tracking vehicle usage, and settling payments efficiently. These problems hinder the growth and efficiency of the automotive industry, necessitating a robust and reliable solution [26–33].

7.10.1 PROPOSED SYSTEM

The blockchain-based protocols for vehicle ownership, leasing, and rental (VOLRP) have the following primary goals:

7.10.1.1   Enhance Transparency and Trust

The protocol intends to eradicate fraud, forgery, and errors in ownership records while establishing a transparent and unchangeable ecosystem for car ownership, leasing, and renting. For all parties, the protocol offers a reliable and impenetrable platform by utilizing blockchain technology.

7.10.1.2   Streamline Procedures

The goal of the BVOLRP is to simplify the paperwork needed for leasing contracts, rental agreements, and transfers of vehicle ownership. The protocol lowers paperwork, gets rid of middlemen, and enables quicker, more effective transactions by automating activities and using smart contracts.

7.10.1.3   Enhance Privacy and Security of Data

The protocol focuses on enhancing security methods to safeguard confidential information. The BVOLRP protects personal and financial data, lowering the likelihood of data breaches and identity theft through cryptographic methods and access control systems.

7.10.1.4   Promote Cost and Efficiency Savings

By minimizing paperwork, eliminating manual verification procedures, and decreasing administrative costs, BVOLRP seeks to increase operating efficiency. All parties involved—manufacturers, dealerships, lessors, lessees, and rental service providers—save money as a result of this.

7.11   PROMOTE PEER-TO-PEER TRANSACTIONS

7.11.1   CHALLENGES IN PEER-TO-PEER TRANSACTIONS IN THE AUTOMOBILE INDUSTRY

In the ever-evolving landscape of the automobile industry, the concept of peer-to-peer (P2P) transactions has gained traction as a promising alternative to traditional dealership-based sales. P2P transactions offer the potential to revolutionize how vehicles are bought and sold, fostering a sense of community and empowerment among buyers and sellers. However, beneath the surface lies a range of challenges that must be addressed to ensure the smooth and secure functioning of P2P transactions in the automobile industry. The main challenges in peer-to-peer transactions in the automobile industry include a lack of trust between buyers and sellers, difficulty in verifying the condition of the vehicle, and issues with financing and insurance [34].

7.11.1.1   Trust and Transparency

One of the primary challenges in P2P transactions is establishing trust between buyers and sellers, who are often strangers to each other. In traditional dealership models, buyers rely on established brands and reputation to ensure the legitimacy of the transaction. In a P2P setting, verifying the authenticity of the vehicle, its condition, and ownership history becomes paramount. The lack of a trusted intermediary may result in apprehension, fraud, or disputes that can negatively impact the credibility of the P2P model.

7.11.1.2   Vehicle History and Provenance

Understanding the complete history of a vehicle is crucial for buyers to make informed decisions. However, verifying a vehicle's history in a P2P transaction can be challenging. The absence of reliable documentation, tampering of odometer readings, and undisclosed accidents or repairs can lead to a disparity in the perceived and actual value of the vehicle, ultimately affecting buyer confidence and satisfaction.

7.11.1.3   Payment Security

P2P transactions often involve significant amounts of money changing hands directly between individuals. This creates opportunities for fraudulent activities, such as payment scams, where buyers might not receive the vehicle after making the payment or sellers might not receive the agreed-upon amount. Ensuring secure payment methods and escrow services becomes crucial to prevent financial losses and disputes.

7.11.1.4   Legal and Regulatory Compliance

The automobile industry is subject to numerous regulations and legal requirements that differ from region to region. P2P transactions can complicate compliance with these regulations, especially when it comes to title transfers, emissions standards, safety inspections, and tax implications. Ensuring that both buyers and sellers adhere to legal obligations becomes a complex challenge in a decentralized P2P framework.

7.11.1.5   Vehicle Inspection and Quality Assurance

In traditional dealerships, vehicles undergo inspections and quality assurance processes to ensure they meet certain standards before being sold. In a P2P transaction, ensuring the vehicle's condition and authenticity becomes the responsibility of the parties involved. The lack of standardized inspection protocols and mechanisms to verify the vehicle's condition can lead to dissatisfaction and disputes among buyers and sellers.

7.11.1.6   Dispute Resolution

Disputes are inevitable in any business transaction, and P2P transactions are no exception. In the absence of a centralized entity overseeing the transaction, resolving disputes becomes complex. Establishing a clear mechanism for dispute resolution and arbitration that is both efficient and unbiased is essential to maintain trust and protect the interests of all parties involved.

7.11.2   Privacy and Security

P2P transactions involve sharing personal information and data, creating potential vulnerabilities for identity theft, fraud, and cyberattacks. Ensuring the security of sensitive information while facilitating necessary communication between buyers and sellers is a delicate balance that requires robust cybersecurity measures.

The potential for P2P transactions to disrupt and reshape the automobile industry is undeniable. However, the challenges associated with establishing trust, verifying vehicle history, ensuring payment security, complying with regulations, conducting inspections, and resolving disputes cannot be ignored. Addressing these challenges requires a collaborative effort from industry stakeholders, including technology developers, regulatory bodies, and consumers, to create a framework that enables secure, transparent, and efficient P2P transactions while safeguarding the interests of all parties involved. Only by navigating these challenges can P2P transactions truly live up to their potential in revolutionizing the automobile buying and selling experience.

Peer-to-peer vehicle sharing is envisioned by the protocol, giving users the option to directly lease or rent vehicles from other owners. BVOLRP increases the sharing economy in the car industry by doing away with middlemen and offering a safe platform for trustless transactions. By reaching these goals, VOLRP hopes to revolutionize the car ownership, leasing, and rental landscape, revolutionizing the way vehicles are transacted, and economic and environmental sustainability.

7.11.2.1   Proposed Architecture for a Protocol

The technology used by VOLR blockchain to create digital twins of automobiles transforms how vehicles are represented and managed on the blockchain by generating distinctive digital twins in the form of non-fungible tokens (NFTs). This process begins at the manufacturer's end through their digital wallet, ensuring the creation of a secure and tamperproof representation of the vehicle's information.

7.12 DIGITAL WALLET FROM THE MANUFACTURER

7.12.1 Challenges in Peer-to-Peer Transactions in the Automobile Industry

The concept of peer-to-peer (P2P) transactions has gained traction across various industries, including the automobile sector. P2P transactions involve the direct exchange of goods or services between individuals without the need for intermediaries. While P2P transactions offer the promise of efficiency, cost savings, and convenience, the automobile industry faces several challenges in implementing and managing such transactions. This chapter delves into the problems associated with P2P transactions in the automobile industry and explores potential solutions.

7.12.1.1 Lack of Trust and Transparency

P2P transactions in the automobile industry often involve significant sums of money, making trust and transparency paramount. Unlike transactions involving dealerships, where a certain level of regulation and accountability is established, P2P transactions lack such safeguards. Buyers and sellers may be concerned about hidden defects, misrepresented information, or fraudulent activities. The absence of a trusted intermediary can lead to disputes and a lack of recourse in case of issues.

7.12.1.2 Verification and Documentation

When dealing with P2P transactions, verifying the authenticity of both the vehicle and the parties involved becomes a challenge. Proper documentation, including ownership records, maintenance history, and legal agreements, is essential to ensure a smooth transfer of ownership. However, obtaining and validating these documents independently can be time-consuming and complex, especially when dealing with different jurisdictions and regulatory requirements.

7.12.1.3 Payment Security

Managing payments in P2P transactions poses a significant challenge. Traditional payment methods such as cash or bank transfers may carry risks of fraud, and buyers and sellers may be wary of sharing financial information. Moreover, determining the authenticity of the funds and ensuring they are transferred securely can be difficult without an established financial intermediary.

7.12.1.4 Liability and Recourse

In the event of a dispute or disagreement between parties involved in a P2P transaction, the lack of a central authority to mediate and enforce agreements can complicate matters. Establishing liability for issues arising post-transaction, such as undisclosed defects or undisclosed loans, becomes intricate. Resolving such disputes often requires legal action, which can be time-consuming and expensive.

7.12.1.5 Vehicle Inspection and Evaluation

Evaluating the condition of a vehicle accurately is challenging in P2P transactions. Sellers may exaggerate the condition of the vehicle, and buyers may not have the technical expertise to assess its true value and state. The lack of professional inspection services and standardized evaluation processes can lead to disagreements and dissatisfaction.

7.12.1.6 Regulatory Compliance

P2P transactions in the automobile industry must adhere to various regulatory requirements, including vehicle registration, tax payment, emissions standards, and safety regulations. Ensuring compliance with these regulations without the guidance of a dealership or regulatory agency can be daunting for individuals involved in P2P transactions.

7.12.1.7   Security and Privacy Concerns

Conducting P2P transactions involves sharing sensitive information, such as personal details, identification documents, and financial data. Without proper cybersecurity measures, there is a risk of data breaches and identity theft, further eroding trust in the process [35].

7.12.2   SOLUTIONS

To address these challenges, the automobile industry can explore several solutions:

- *Blockchain technology.* Utilizing blockchain's transparency and tamperproof nature can enhance trust and transparency in P2P transactions. It can securely store ownership records, maintenance history, and transaction details, reducing the risk of fraud.
- *Third-party platforms.* Trusted third-party platforms can facilitate P2P transactions by providing authentication, documentation, and payment services. These platforms can offer an intermediary role while still maintaining the benefits of P2P transactions.
- *Professional inspection services.* Establishing professional vehicle inspection services can ensure accurate evaluation of vehicles, providing both buyers and sellers with reliable information.
- *Smart contracts.* Implementing smart contracts can automate transaction processes, ensuring that ownership transfers and payments are executed only when predefined conditions are met.
- *Education and awareness.* Educating consumers about the benefits, risks, and best practices of P2P transactions can empower them to make informed decisions and navigate the challenges.

While P2P transactions hold promise in the automobile industry, they also bring forth a range of challenges related to trust, transparency, security, and regulation. Addressing these challenges requires a combination of technological innovations, regulatory reforms, and consumer education. As the industry evolves, finding effective solutions to these problems will be essential to unlock the full potential of P2P transactions while safeguarding the interests of all stakeholders involved.

The digital twin creation process is started by the maker, who is outfitted with a digital wallet that is integrated with the VOLR blockchain. This digital wallet acts as a safe place to store, manage, and communicate with the NFTs that stand in for automobiles.

7.13   VEHICLE IDENTIFICATION NUMBER (VIN)

What issues may arise when creating a vehicle identification number (VIN)?

Creating a vehicle identification number (VIN) might seem like a straightforward process, but it involves several challenges and considerations due to its critical role in uniquely identifying vehicles. Here are some of the problems that can arise in creating a VIN.

7.13.1   UNIQUENESS

Each VIN must be unique to a specific vehicle, which becomes increasingly challenging as the number of vehicles on the road grows. Ensuring that no two vehicles share the same VIN is essential to prevent confusion, fraud, and legal issues.

7.13.2   INTERNATIONAL STANDARDS

VINs are used worldwide, and there are different standards and regulations for VIN formats in different regions. Creating a VIN that adheres to the standards of various countries while maintaining its uniqueness can be complex.

7.13.3 Length and Format

VINs are typically composed of 17 characters, which include both letters and numbers. These characters represent various information about the vehicle, such as the manufacturer, model year, plant of assembly, and more. Balancing the need for encoding information and keeping the VIN a manageable length can be a challenge.

7.13.4 Avoiding Confusion

Certain characters, like "I," "O," and "Q," are often omitted from VINs to avoid confusion with the numbers "1" and "0." This avoidance of potentially ambiguous characters while maintaining readability adds complexity to VIN creation.

7.13.5 Compatibility with Existing Systems

When creating a VIN, manufacturers must ensure compatibility with their existing systems and databases. This includes integrating VINs with inventory management, registration, insurance, and maintenance tracking systems.

7.13.6 Counterfeiting and Fraud

A valid and properly constructed VIN is crucial to prevent counterfeiting and fraud. If a VIN is not properly generated or authenticated, it could lead to stolen vehicles being resold, incorrect identification, or vehicles with altered histories.

7.13.7 Consistency in Data Entry

VINs are often manually entered into various systems, which increases the likelihood of human error. Inconsistent data entry, misspellings, or transpositions can lead to issues in identifying and tracking vehicles accurately.

7.13.8 Changing Regulations

Regulations related to VINs, their structure, and information encoded can change over time. Manufacturers need to keep up with these changes to ensure compliance and accurate representation of vehicle details.

7.13.9 Use in Emerging Technologies

As vehicles become more connected and integrated with emerging technologies like blockchain and IoT, VINs might need to be compatible with these systems for secure data sharing and verification.

7.13.10 Data Privacy and Security

VINs contain sensitive information about a vehicle's history, including ownership, maintenance, and accidents. Ensuring the security and privacy of this data is essential to protect consumers from identity theft and unauthorized access.

Creating a vehicle identification number involves overcoming various challenges related to uniqueness, international standards, format, consistency, fraud prevention, and evolving regulations. Manufacturers must navigate these complexities to ensure that each vehicle is properly identified and tracked throughout its life cycle while adhering to industry standards and legal requirements.

While creating a vehicle identification number (VIN) may appear straightforward, a range of challenges exists that manufacturers and regulatory bodies must address to maintain accuracy, consistency, and effectiveness in vehicle identification. Addressing these challenges is vital for ensuring the integrity of the automotive industry's data systems.

The merits of creating a vehicle identification number (VIN) extend far beyond simple identification. VINs are essential tools that enable accurate tracking, documentation, and communication throughout the life cycle of a vehicle. Their role in safety, compliance, transparency, and efficiency makes them a cornerstone of the modern automotive industry.

The vehicle's manufacturer obtains its vehicle identification number (VIN), a special number that sets it apart from other vehicles. The brand, model, manufacturing year, and serial number—along with other vital details—are all included in the vehicle identification number (VIN).

7.14   DIGITAL TWIN MINTING

Digital twin minting in the automobile industry refers to the creation and utilization of digital replicas of physical vehicles and their components. These digital twins can provide a range of benefits to the industry, revolutionizing various aspects of vehicle design, manufacturing, testing, and maintenance [36].

Here are some of the merits of using digital twin minting in the automobile industry.

7.14.1   PRODUCT DEVELOPMENT AND DESIGN

Digital twin minting enables manufacturers to create virtual representations of vehicles and their components. This allows for rapid prototyping, design iterations, and simulations before any physical prototypes are built. Design flaws and inefficiencies can be identified and corrected early in the development process, reducing costly revisions and delays.

7.14.2   ACCELERATED INNOVATION

With digital twin minting, engineers and designers can experiment with new materials, features, and technologies in a virtual environment. This accelerates the innovation process by enabling rapid testing and validation of ideas without the need for physical manufacturing and assembly.

7.14.3   IMPROVED MANUFACTURING PROCESSES

Digital twins can be used to simulate and optimize manufacturing processes, such as assembly lines and robotic automation. Manufacturers can identify bottlenecks, optimize workflows, and improve efficiency, leading to reduced production costs and shorter time to market.

7.14.4   QUALITY ASSURANCE AND TESTING

Digital twins allow for comprehensive testing of vehicle components and systems in a virtual environment. This ensures that vehicles meet safety, performance, and regulatory standards before physical production begins. It also reduces the need for extensive physical testing, saving time and resources.

7.14.5   PREDICTIVE MAINTENANCE

Once a vehicle is in operation, digital twins can be used to monitor its performance in real time. This enables manufacturers and service providers to predict maintenance needs, identify potential issues before they escalate, and optimize maintenance schedules, ultimately increasing vehicle uptime and reducing downtime.

7.14.6 Personalization and Customization

Digital twin minting supports the creation of personalized and customized vehicles by allowing customers to visualize and configure their vehicles virtually. This enhances the buying experience and ensures that customers get the exact specifications they desire.

7.14.7 Supply Chain Optimization

Digital twins can be extended to the supply chain, enabling manufacturers to track the status and location of components and materials. This transparency improves supply chain management, reduces delays, and enhances overall production efficiency.

7.14.8 Sustainability and Environmental Impact

By optimizing vehicle designs and manufacturing processes in a digital environment, manufacturers can reduce waste and minimize the environmental impact of physical production. Digital twin minting supports sustainable practices by identifying opportunities for lightweighting and efficient resource utilization.

Data-driven insights. Digital twin minting generates a wealth of data that can be analyzed to gain insights into vehicle performance, usage patterns, and customer preferences. Manufacturers can use this data to refine their products, anticipate customer needs, and make informed business decisions.

7.14.9 Remote Diagnostics and Support

In the case of vehicle issues, digital twins enable remote diagnostics and troubleshooting. Manufacturers and service centers can analyze the virtual twin to identify problems, offer solutions, and guide technicians in resolving issues efficiently [37–39].

In conclusion, digital twin minting brings a multitude of benefits to the automobile industry by transforming how vehicles are designed, manufactured, tested, and maintained. The use of digital twins accelerates innovation, improves efficiency, enhances quality, and supports sustainability, ultimately contributing to a more agile, customer-centric, and technologically advanced automotive sector.

The manufacturer's digital wallet starts the minting procedure to produce a corresponding NFT, which serves as the vehicle's digital twin on the VOLR blockchain, using the VIN as a reference. The metadata and attributes of the vehicle are encoded into the NFT during the minting process to guarantee its legitimacy.

7.15 ATTRIBUTES AND METADATA

Using attributes and metadata in the automobile industry can offer several benefits that enhance various aspects of vehicle design, manufacturing, marketing, sales, and customer experience. *Attributes* refer to specific characteristics or features of a product, while *metadata* provides additional context and information about those attributes. Here are some of the merits of using attributes and metadata in the automobile industry.

7.15.1 Product Differentiation

Attributes and metadata allow manufacturers to highlight unique features and characteristics of their vehicles. This differentiation can help vehicles stand out in a competitive market, attract customers, and create a strong brand identity.

7.15.2 Customization and Personalization

Attributes and metadata enable customers to customize and personalize their vehicles according to their preferences. Whether it is selecting specific features, colors, or configurations, customers can create a vehicle that aligns with their individual tastes and needs.

7.15.3 Efficient Search and Comparison

Attributes and metadata provide a structured way to categorize and describe vehicles. This allows customers to search for vehicles based on specific criteria and easily compare different models, aiding in informed decision-making.

7.15.4 Improved Marketing and Advertising

Detailed attributes and metadata support more targeted and effective marketing campaigns. Manufacturers can tailor their messaging to specific customer segments, highlighting features that resonate with different demographics.

7.15.5 Regulatory Compliance

Attributes and metadata help ensure that vehicles meet regulatory standards and requirements. By accurately documenting relevant characteristics, manufacturers can demonstrate compliance with safety, emissions, and other regulatory guidelines.

7.15.6 Supply Chain Management

Attributes and metadata are valuable in managing the supply chain. They help track components and materials, ensuring that the right parts are used in the production process and that inventory is managed effectively.

7.15.7 Quality Assurance and Inspection

Detailed metadata can assist in quality control and inspection processes during manufacturing. Manufacturers can use metadata to trace the origin of components, track production stages, and ensure consistent quality across vehicles.

7.15.8 Vehicle Maintenance and Service

Attributes and metadata support efficient vehicle maintenance and service. Service centers can access detailed information about a vehicle's specifications, components, and history, allowing for accurate diagnosis and timely repairs.

7.15.9 Data-Driven Decision-Making

Attributes and metadata generate data that manufacturers can analyze to gain insights into customer preferences, trends, and usage patterns. This data-driven approach informs product development, marketing strategies, and business decisions.

7.15.10 Enhanced Customer Experience

Attributes and metadata contribute to an enriched customer experience. Detailed information empowers customers with comprehensive knowledge about the vehicles they are considering, helping them make informed choices.

7.15.11 Life Cycle Management

Throughout a vehicle's life cycle, attributes and metadata play a role in tracking changes, updates, and modifications. This ensures that accurate and up-to-date information is available for resale, leasing, or other transactions.

7.15.12 Connectivity and IoT Integration

In the era of connected vehicles and the Internet of Things (IoT), attributes and metadata are vital for managing vehicle data and communication. They enable seamless integration with digital platforms and smart technologies.

Leveraging attributes and metadata in the automobile industry offers a range of merits that enhance efficiency, customer experience, marketing, and compliance. Their role in categorizing, describing, and tracking vehicles supports various functions across the industry, from manufacturing to sales to post-purchase services.

The digital twin of the vehicle's NFT is connected to a wide range of metadata and attributes. The VIN, make, model, manufacturing year, color, mileage, maintenance history, and any other pertinent details deemed necessary by the manufacturer or according to industry standards are included in this data. Digital twin technology exhibits a broad spectrum of applications, permeating numerous technological domains, with the anticipation of extending into various other fields as technology advances. As a result, the significance of the digital twin concept has escalated across several business sectors [40].

7.16 BLOCKCHAIN INTEGRATION

Integrating blockchain technology into the automobile industry offers numerous merits that can transform various aspects of the sector [41–46]. Blockchain's decentralized, transparent, and secure nature has the potential to revolutionize processes, enhance customer experience, and address longstanding challenges. Here are some of the key merits of using blockchain integration in the automobile industry.

7.16.1 Transparency and Trust

Blockchain provides an immutable and transparent ledger that records every transaction and event in the vehicle's life cycle. This transparency enhances trust among all stakeholders, including manufacturers, dealerships, customers, and regulatory authorities. The entire history of a vehicle, from manufacturing to ownership changes, can be easily verified, reducing fraud and providing a trustworthy source of information.

7.16.2 Supply Chain Management

Blockchain enables a transparent and traceable supply chain for automotive components and parts. Manufacturers can track the origin, manufacturing processes, and distribution of each component, ensuring the authenticity and quality of parts. This reduces the risk of counterfeit or substandard parts entering the supply chain.

7.16.3 Ownership and Provenance

Blockchain facilitates accurate and tamperproof recording of vehicle ownership changes. This streamlines the process of buying and selling vehicles, reducing administrative complexities and preventing issues like title fraud and odometer tampering.

7.16.4 SMART CONTRACTS FOR TRANSACTIONS

Smart contracts, self-executing digital agreements, automate processes such as vehicle purchases, transfers of ownership, and leasing. These contracts eliminate intermediaries, reducing transaction costs and enhancing the efficiency of deals between parties.

7.16.5 SECURE VEHICLE DATA SHARING

Blockchain ensures secure and controlled sharing of vehicle-related data between stakeholders. Manufacturers, service providers, and insurers can access specific data with the vehicle owner's consent, improving the accuracy of services and enabling data-driven decisions.

7.16.6 ENHANCED RECALL MANAGEMENT

Blockchain simplifies and accelerates safety recalls by providing a real-time, traceable record of affected vehicles. Manufacturers can quickly identify affected units and communicate recall information directly to owners, improving response times and reducing risks.

7.16.7 AFTERMARKET PARTS AUTHENTICATION

Blockchain can verify the authenticity of aftermarket parts and components. By maintaining a record of each part's origin and history, it becomes easier for consumers and service centers to identify genuine parts, reducing the risk of substandard or counterfeit replacements.

7.16.8 DATA SECURITY AND PRIVACY

Blockchain's cryptographic protocols enhance data security and privacy, reducing the risk of data breaches and unauthorized access to sensitive information. Vehicle owners can control who has access to their data and grant permission for specific purposes.

7.16.9 IoT INTEGRATION AND CONNECTED VEHICLES

As vehicles become more connected and generate extensive data, blockchain can ensure secure and standardized communication between vehicles and infrastructure. This enables secure and efficient vehicle-to-vehicle (V2V) and vehicle-to-infrastructure (V2I) communication.

7.16.10 CARBON CREDIT TRACKING AND SUSTAINABILITY

Blockchain can track carbon credits and monitor emissions reduction efforts across the automotive industry. This ensures transparency in sustainability initiatives, allowing manufacturers to accurately measure and report their environmental impact.

In conclusion, blockchain integration offers a range of merits for the automobile industry, from transparency and traceability to security and efficiency. By addressing long-standing challenges and creating new opportunities, blockchain has the potential to reshape how vehicles are manufactured, sold, maintained, and experienced.

The manufacturer's digital wallet communicates with the VOLR blockchain after the NFT is created in order to safely keep the NFT that represents the digital twin. The digital twin of the car is guaranteed to be immutable and transparent thanks to the integration because it joins the decentralized ledger.

7.17 OWNERSHIP AND TRANSFERABILITY

Applying blockchain technology to ownership and transferability in the automobile industry brings a multitude of merits that can significantly enhance the processes of buying, selling, and transferring vehicle ownership. Blockchain's unique characteristics, including immutability, transparency, and security, address many of the challenges and complexities associated with traditional ownership transfer methods. Here are some of the key merits of using blockchain for ownership and transferability in the automobile industry.

7.17.1 Immutable Ownership Records

Blockchain creates an unalterable and transparent record of ownership changes. Each transfer of ownership is securely recorded on the blockchain, providing an indisputable history of the vehicle's ownership journey. This eliminates the risk of fraud, forgery, and disputes related to ownership history.

7.17.2 Enhanced Transparency

Blockchain's decentralized and transparent nature ensures that all parties involved in the transaction have access to the same information. This transparency reduces information asymmetry, creating a level playing field for buyers, sellers, and regulatory authorities.

7.17.3 Tamperproof Title History

The blockchain's tamperproof ledger prevents unauthorized modifications to ownership records. Any attempt to alter or manipulate ownership information is immediately detectable, ensuring the accuracy and integrity of the title history.

7.17.4 Streamlined Transactions

Ownership transfers on blockchain can be executed through smart contracts, automating the process without the need for intermediaries. Buyers and sellers can interact directly, reducing administrative burdens, delays, and associated costs.

7.17.5 Elimination of Intermediaries

Traditional ownership transfers often involve intermediaries such as notaries, legal representatives, and government agencies. Blockchain eliminates the need for these intermediaries, making transactions more efficient and cost-effective.

7.17.6 Global Accessibility

Blockchain transcends geographical boundaries, allowing ownership transfers to occur seamlessly across jurisdictions. This is particularly beneficial for cross-border transactions and international sales, simplifying the complex process of complying with different legal systems.

7.17.7 Rapid Ownership Changes

Blockchain enables almost instantaneous updates to ownership records. This is especially useful for time-sensitive situations, like buying a vehicle with an expiring temporary registration or facilitating quick sales.

7.17.8 Enhanced Security and Privacy

Ownership information stored on the blockchain is encrypted and secure, reducing the risk of unauthorized access and data breaches. Vehicle owners have greater control over their data, sharing only the necessary information during transfers.

7.17.9   TRUST IN SECONDHAND MARKETS

In the used car market, blockchain can provide buyers with accurate and reliable ownership histories. This builds trust between buyers and sellers, facilitating transactions and mitigating concerns about hidden issues.

7.17.10   REDUCED ADMINISTRATIVE COSTS

The automated nature of blockchain ownership transfers reduces administrative overhead. Governments and regulatory authorities can also benefit from streamlined processes and reduced paperwork.

7.17.11   IMPROVED RESALE VALUE

Vehicles with verifiable and transparent ownership histories are more attractive to potential buyers. Blockchain-verified ownership can lead to higher resale values, benefiting both sellers and buyers.

Applying blockchain to ownership and transferability in the automobile industry offers numerous merits that enhance transparency, security, efficiency, and trust in the ownership transfer process. By revolutionizing the way ownership records are managed, blockchain has the potential to reshape how vehicles change hands and contribute to a more streamlined and secure automobile market.

The VOLR blockchain ecosystem allows for the transfer of the NFT, which stands for the digital twin of the vehicle, from the manufacturer's digital wallet to other stakeholders, like dealers or customers. The blockchain keeps track of every transfer, making the ownership history transparent and auditable.

The digital twin creation method offers a trustworthy and traceable representation of the vehicle's information by minting NFTs using the vehicle VIN and safely storing them on the VOLR blockchain. This facilitates effective vehicle ownership, leasing, and rental operations by allowing numerous stakeholders to access accurate and unchangeable records of the vehicle's history. It also increases transparency and confidence, as seen in Figure 7.3.

7.18   OPERATION OF PROTOCOLS

By utilizing smart contracts, which represent the terms and conditions of these transactions, the VOLR blockchain protocol accelerates the processes for buying, leasing, and renting vehicles. These automated, secure exchanges between parties made possible by smart contracts guarantee openness, effectiveness, and conformity to predetermined terms. As seen in Figure 7.3, when payments are not made on time, the related NFT can be revoked by the smart contract, adding another layer of enforcement.

7.18.1   PURCHASING A VEHICLE

Smart contracts offer a wide range of benefits across various industries, including the automobile sector. These self-executing digital agreements automatically enforce terms and conditions when predefined conditions are met. Here are some of the key benefits of smart contracts:

- *Automation.* Smart contracts automate the execution of agreements, reducing the need for manual intervention. This streamlines processes, eliminates paperwork, and ensures accuracy in fulfilling contractual obligations.
- *Trust and transparency.* Smart contracts are recorded on a blockchain, which provides transparency and immutability. Parties involved can trust that the terms will be executed as programmed, minimizing the need for intermediaries and reducing the risk of disputes.

- *Security.* Smart contracts use cryptographic techniques, making them highly secure and resistant to tampering. The decentralized nature of blockchain enhances security, making it difficult for malicious actors to manipulate the contract.
- *Accuracy and error reduction.* Human errors in contract execution can lead to disputes and inefficiencies. Smart contracts follow predefined rules, reducing the likelihood of errors in interpreting or executing the terms.
- *Cost savings.* By automating processes and reducing the need for intermediaries, smart contracts can lead to significant cost savings. Traditional contract management involves administrative costs, legal fees, and third-party intermediaries that smart contracts can eliminate or reduce.
- *Speed and efficiency.* Smart contracts operate in a digital environment, enabling instant execution of terms when conditions are met. This eliminates delays associated with manual processes and paper-based agreements.
- *Accessibility.* Smart contracts can be accessed and executed from anywhere with an Internet connection. This is particularly valuable for international transactions and parties in different geographical locations.
- *Elimination of intermediaries.* Traditional contracts often require intermediaries, such as lawyers, notaries, and escrow services. Smart contracts can replace these intermediaries, reducing associated costs and delays.
- *Immutable audit trail.* All actions and transactions related to a smart contract are recorded on the blockchain, creating an immutable audit trail. This transparency enables parties to trace the history of the contract's execution.
- *Versatility.* Smart contracts can be applied to a wide range of use cases beyond basic financial transactions. They can automate complex multi-party agreements, such as supply chain contracts, insurance claims, and voting systems.
- *Trustless transactions.* The trust is embedded in the code and cryptographic mechanisms of smart contracts, reducing the need for parties to trust each other. This trustless nature enhances security and reduces the risk of fraudulent activities.
- *Real-time updates.* Smart contracts can be designed to update in real time based on external events or changing conditions. This dynamic nature allows contracts to adapt to evolving circumstances.
- *Data integrity.* Smart contracts rely on accurate data inputs. The immutability of blockchain ensures that data used in the contract remains unchanged and tamperproof.

The system consists of:

- *Creation of smart contracts.* A smart contract is generated on the VOLR blockchain when a buyer wants to buy a car. The information on the buyer and seller, the vehicle's features, the purchase price, and the terms of payment are all included in this smart contract.
- *Payment validation.* The smart contract keeps track of the payment schedule that the buyer and seller have established. The smart contract will cause specified actions, such as sending payment reminders or applying fines if the buyer fails to make the necessary payments on time.
- *NFT transfer.* When the buyer completes the transaction in accordance with the terms, the smart contract instantly moves the corresponding NFT, which represents the digital twin of the car, from the seller's wallet to the purchaser's wallet to the buyer's wallet, indicating the transfer of ownership.

Smart contracts offer benefits that encompass automation, security, cost savings, efficiency, transparency, and trust in various industries, including the automobile sector (see Figures 7.3 and 7.4).

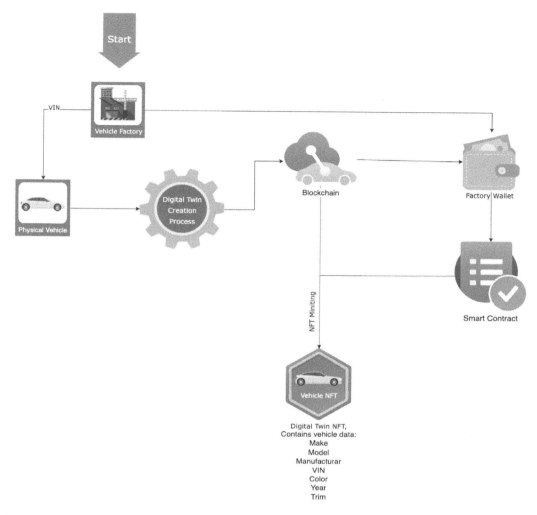

FIGURE 7.3   Proposed solution architecture.

By revolutionizing contract management, smart contracts have the potential to streamline processes and transform the way agreements are executed and enforced.

7.18.2   VEHICLE LEASE

A smart contract for automobile lease can streamline the leasing process, automate payments, and ensure transparent execution of the lease agreement. Here is how a smart contract for automobile lease might work:

Initialization

- The leaser (owner of the vehicle) and the lessee (individual or business leasing the vehicle) agree on the terms of the lease, including lease duration, monthly payment, mileage limit, and any other relevant conditions.

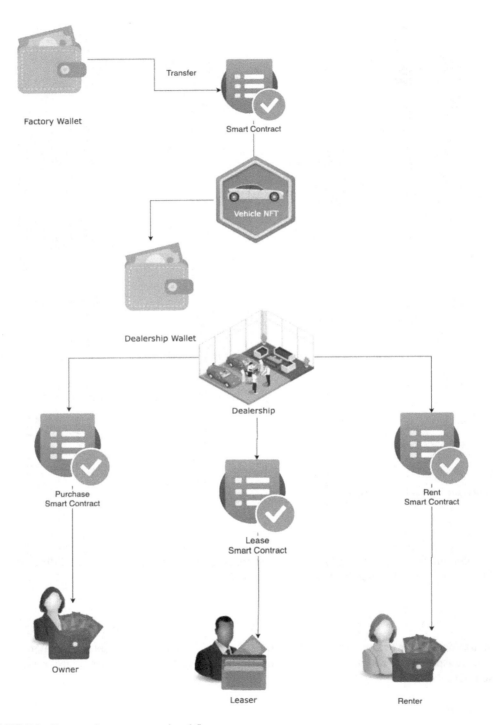

FIGURE 7.4   Proposed system operational flow.

Contract Creation

- A smart contract is created on a blockchain platform. The contract includes the terms of the lease, payment schedule, mileage tracking, and other relevant details.

Verification

- Both parties verify their identities on the blockchain platform to ensure the integrity of the contract.

Monthly Payments

- The smart contract automatically deducts the agreed-upon monthly lease payment from the lessee's designated wallet. This can be done using cryptocurrencies or digital tokens.

Mileage Tracking

- The smart contract tracks the vehicle's mileage using various data sources, such as GPS systems or odometer readings. If the vehicle exceeds the agreed-upon mileage limit, the contract can automatically trigger additional charges or adjustments to the payment schedule.

Maintenance and Repairs

- The contract can include provisions for routine maintenance and repairs. When maintenance is due, the lessee is notified, and the cost can be factored into the payment schedule or paid separately using the smart contract.

Early Termination

- If either party wishes to terminate the lease early, the smart contract can facilitate the process. Terms and penalties for early termination can be programmed into the contract.

End of Lease

- When the lease term ends, the smart contract triggers a final payment, which may include any outstanding charges or adjustments based on mileage.

Return of Vehicle

- If the vehicle is to be returned at the end of the lease, the smart contract can facilitate the return process. Any inspections and evaluations can be recorded on the blockchain to ensure transparency.

Ownership Transfer

- If the lessee chooses to purchase the vehicle at the end of the lease, the smart contract can facilitate the transfer of ownership. The contract can automatically adjust the final payment to account for the purchase price.

Dispute Resolution

- In the event of disputes, the smart contract's transparent and tamperproof record can serve as a source of truth, simplifying resolution processes.

Data Privacy

- Personal and financial information is encrypted and secure on the blockchain, enhancing data privacy and security.

Efficiency and Cost Savings

- By automating payment collection and contract execution, the smart contract reduces administrative overhead, mitigates human errors, and saves time for both parties.

Trust and Transparency

- The transparent nature of the blockchain ensures that both parties can trust that the terms of the lease will be executed as programmed.

Using a smart contract for automobile lease not only modernizes the leasing process but also enhances security, efficiency, and transparency for both lessors and lessees. It eliminates the need for intermediaries, reduces administrative burdens, and facilitates smoother lease management.

- *Establishing a smart contract.* In a scenario involving car leasing, the lessor and lessee create a smart contract on the VOLR blockchain. The lease's tenure, monthly payment amount, mileage limitations, and any other duties are all described in the contract's terms and conditions. The smart contract keeps track of the lessee's recurring monthly lease payments. The smart contract may impose fines, send notifications, or carry out other specified actions if the lessee fails to make the payments on time.
- *NFT and usage tracking.* The digital counterpart of the vehicle's NFT stays in the lessor's wallet for the duration of the lease. The smart contract keeps track of the vehicle's usage, including miles and maintenance, to make sure the predetermined terms are followed. The smart contract keeps track of the lessee's recurring monthly lease payments. The smart contract may impose fines, send notifications, or carry out other specified actions if the lessee fails to make the payments on time.
- *NFT and usage tracking.* The digital counterpart of the vehicle's NFT stays in the lessor's wallet for the duration of the lease. The smart contract keeps track of the vehicle's usage, including miles and maintenance, to ensure adherence to the agreed-upon conditions.
- *Lease termination.* The smart contract automatically ends the lease when the agreed-upon term expires. The car can be returned by the lessee, and the NFT ownership can be returned to the lessor's account if all conditions have been satisfied.

7.18.3 VEHICLE RENTAL

A smart contract for automobile lease can streamline the leasing process, automate payments, and ensure transparent execution of the lease agreement. Here is how a smart contract for automobile lease might work:

Initialization

- The leaser (owner of the vehicle) and the lessee (individual or business leasing the vehicle) agree on the terms of the lease, including lease duration, monthly payment, mileage limit, and any other relevant conditions.

Contract Creation

- A smart contract is created on a blockchain platform. The contract includes the terms of the lease, payment schedule, mileage tracking, and other relevant details.

Verification

- Both parties verify their identities on the blockchain platform to ensure the integrity of the contract.

Monthly Payments

- The smart contract automatically deducts the agreed-upon monthly lease payment from the lessee's designated wallet. This can be done using cryptocurrencies or digital tokens.

Mileage Tracking

- The smart contract tracks the vehicle's mileage using various data sources, such as GPS systems or odometer readings. If the vehicle exceeds the agreed-upon mileage limit, the contract can automatically trigger additional charges or adjustments to the payment schedule.

Maintenance and Repairs

- The contract can include provisions for routine maintenance and repairs. When maintenance is due, the lessee is notified, and the cost can be factored into the payment schedule or paid separately using the smart contract.

Early Termination

- If either party wishes to terminate the lease early, the smart contract can facilitate the process. Terms and penalties for early termination can be programmed into the contract.

End of Lease

- When the lease term ends, the smart contract triggers a final payment, which may include any outstanding charges or adjustments based on mileage.

Return of Vehicle

- If the vehicle is to be returned at the end of the lease, the smart contract can facilitate the return process. Any inspection and evaluation can be recorded on the blockchain to ensure transparency.

Ownership Transfer

- If the lessee chooses to purchase the vehicle at the end of the lease, the smart contract can facilitate the transfer of ownership. The contract can automatically adjust the final payment to account for the purchase price.

Dispute Resolution

- In the event of disputes, the smart contract's transparent and tamperproof record can serve as a source of truth, simplifying resolution processes.

Data Privacy

- Personal and financial information is encrypted and secure on the blockchain, enhancing data privacy and security.

Efficiency and Cost Savings

- By automating payment collection and contract execution, the smart contract reduces administrative overhead, mitigates human errors, and saves time for both parties.

Trust and Transparency

- The transparent nature of the blockchain ensures that both parties can trust that the terms of the lease will be executed as programmed.

Using a smart contract for automobile lease not only modernizes the leasing process but also enhances security, efficiency, and transparency for both lessors and lessees. It eliminates the need for intermediaries, reduces administrative burdens, and facilitates smoother lease management.

7.18.4 Smart Contract for Vehicle Rental

A smart contract for vehicle rental can revolutionize the rental process by automating reservations and payments and ensuring transparency in the terms and conditions of the rental agreement. Here is how a smart contract for vehicle rental might work:

Reservation

- A customer selects the desired rental vehicle, pickup and return dates, and any additional services (such as insurance or accessories).

Smart Contract Creation

- A smart contract is created on a blockchain platform, detailing the rental terms, payment schedule, pickup and return locations, and other relevant information.

Identity Verification

- Both the rental company and the customer verify their identities on the blockchain platform, ensuring that only authorized parties are involved in the transaction.

Payment

- The customer's digital wallet is connected to the smart contract. The contract automatically deducts the rental fee and any additional charges, such as insurance or fuel, from the customer's wallet.

Security Deposit

- The contract can hold a security deposit in the customer's wallet until the vehicle is returned and inspected. This deposit is automatically refunded if the vehicle is returned in satisfactory condition.

Pickup and Return

- When the pickup date arrives, the smart contract generates a unique digital key that grants the customer access to the vehicle. This key is encrypted and time-limited, enhancing security.

Mileage Tracking

- The smart contract can track the vehicle's mileage throughout the rental period. If the vehicle exceeds a predetermined mileage limit, the contract can automatically adjust the final payment.

Extensions and Early Returns

- If the customer wants to extend the rental or return the vehicle early, the smart contract can facilitate these changes. The contract adjusts the payment schedule accordingly.

Damage Reporting and Claims

- In case of damage to the vehicle, the smart contract can guide the customer through the process of reporting the damage and initiating an insurance claim if applicable.

Vehicle Inspection

- Upon return, the vehicle is inspected. The results of the inspection are recorded on the blockchain, ensuring transparency in the condition assessment.

Refunds and Disputes

- If there are no issues, the security deposit is automatically refunded to the customer's wallet. In case of disputes, the blockchain's transparent record can serve as evidence for resolution.

Data Privacy and Security

- Personal and financial information is securely stored on the blockchain, reducing the risk of data breaches.

Streamlined Administration

- The automated nature of smart contracts reduces administrative burdens for both the rental company and the customer.

Trust and Transparency

- The transparent and tamperproof nature of the blockchain ensures that both parties can trust that the terms of the rental agreement will be executed as programmed.

Using a smart contract for vehicle rental simplifies the process, enhances security, and fosters a more efficient and trustworthy rental experience. It eliminates paperwork, reduces manual intervention, and ensures that all aspects of the rental are transparently recorded for both the rental company and the customer.

- *Smart contract creation.* When a vehicle is rented out, a smart contract is created on the VOLR blockchain, detailing the terms and conditions of the rental agreement. This includes the rental duration, rental fee, payment schedule, and any penalties for late returns or damages.
- *Payment verification.* The smart contract verifies the renter's payment schedule. If the renter fails to make the required payments on time, the smart contract can impose penalties, trigger reminders, or initiate actions based on the agreed-upon terms.
- *NFT transfer and usage tracking.* The NFT representing the vehicle's digital twin remains with the rental service provider until the rental period ends. The smart contract tracks the vehicle's usage, ensuring compliance with rental terms, and facilitates real-time tracking of the vehicle's location and condition.
- *Rental conclusion.* When the rental period concludes, the smart contract finalizes the agreement. If all obligations have been met, the renter returns the vehicle, and the NFT ownership is transferred back to the rental service provider's wallet. By utilizing smart

contracts, the VOLR blockchain protocol automates and enforces the terms and conditions of vehicle purchase, lease, and rental transactions. The inclusion of NFTs as digital twins ensures transparent ownership records, while the smart contract's ability to revoke the NFT in case of nonpayment adds an additional layer of security and enforcement to these transactions.

7.19   THE APPLICATIONS OF THE BLOCKCHAIN IN THE AUTOMOTIVE INDUSTRY: MERITS AND FUTURE APPLICATIONS

The integration of blockchain technology into the automotive industry has ushered in a new era of innovation and transformation. The merits of blockchain's transparency, security, and decentralization have revolutionized key processes, leading to enhanced efficiency, reduced fraud, improved customer experiences, and streamlined operations. From supply chain management to vehicle ownership, blockchain has made significant contributions to various facets of the industry.

Blockchain's ability to create secure, tamperproof records has improved traceability and authenticity in the supply chain, ensuring the quality and origin of components. In ownership and transferability, blockchain has introduced transparency and efficiency, simplifying transactions and reducing disputes. Moreover, the implementation of smart contracts has automated processes, eliminating intermediaries, and providing trustless execution of agreements.

Looking to the future, blockchain's potential in the automotive industry is even more promising. As connected and autonomous vehicles become mainstream, blockchain can ensure secure communication and data sharing among vehicles, infrastructure, and stakeholders. Vehicle data monetization, where users can share their vehicle data securely and receive compensation, holds potential for changing the dynamics of data ownership. Moreover, blockchain's role in electric vehicle (EV) charging infrastructure could enable seamless payments, interoperability, and optimization of charging stations. Additionally, as sustainability gains importance, blockchain could aid in tracking carbon credits, improving the environmental impact of the automotive industry. However, challenges remain, including regulatory hurdles, scalability concerns, and the need for industry-wide collaboration. Standardization and interoperability will be crucial to fully realizing the benefits of blockchain across the automotive ecosystem.

In conclusion, the applications of blockchain in the automotive industry have reshaped traditional practices and paved the way for a more efficient, transparent, and secure future. The merits witnessed so far, along with the potential for further innovation, highlight blockchain's pivotal role in shaping the next phase of automotive evolution. By embracing this technology, the industry is poised to redefine mobility, ownership, and connectivity for generations to come.

The Blockchain Vehicle Ownership, Leasing, and Rental Protocol (BVOLRP) presented in this chapter demonstrates the potential of blockchain technology and non-fungible tokens (NFTs) in revolutionizing the automotive industry. By addressing the challenges associated with vehicle ownership, leasing, and rental, BVOLRP offers a robust and innovative solution that enhances transparency, trust, and operational efficiency. This protocol offers significant potential to revolutionize the automotive industry by introducing greater transparency, security, and efficiency in vehicle ownership, leasing, and rental processes. By leveraging the power of blockchain technology, this protocol addresses several key challenges and provides numerous benefits to all stakeholders involved. The benefits of BVOLRP extend beyond individual transactions and extend to the broader automotive ecosystem. The protocol presents opportunities for peer-to-peer vehicle sharing, promoting collaborative consumption, and expanding the sharing economy within the industry. By eliminating intermediaries, reducing costs, and increasing efficiency, BVOLRP has the potential to reshape the automotive landscape and unlock new possibilities for individuals, businesses, and emerging mobility services.

However, it is important to note that the widespread adoption of the Blockchain Vehicle Ownership, Leasing, and Rental Protocol faces a few challenges. Firstly, regulatory frameworks and legal standards need to adapt to accommodate the decentralized nature of blockchain-based transactions. Governments and authorities must establish guidelines to ensure compliance, consumer protection, and liability in this new paradigm.

In conclusion, the Blockchain Vehicle Ownership, Leasing, and Rental Protocol holds immense promise for transforming the way we own, lease, and rent vehicles. By leveraging the decentralized and transparent nature of blockchain technology, this protocol can provide secure and efficient solutions, foster trust among participants, and enable a more inclusive and sustainable automotive industry. However, addressing regulatory challenges, ensuring scalability, and promoting interoperability will be crucial for its widespread adoption and long-term success.

REFERENCES

1. Alippi, C., Bogdanovic, A., Roveri, M.: Big data analytics for secure industrial internet of things-driven automotive systems. *IEEE Transactions on Industrial Informatics* 13(4), 1995–2004 (2017).
2. ACEA.AUTO.: *(Online).* www.acea.auto/figure/motor-vehicle-production-by-world-region/ [Accessed August 8, 2023].
3. Han, Hongdan, Shiwakoti, Radha K., Jarvis, Robin, Mordi, Chima, Botchie, David.: Accounting and auditing with blockchain technology and artificial intelligence: A literature review. *International Journal of Accounting Information Systems* 48, 100598 (March 2023).
4. Scaling Parrots.: *Scalability and new business in the world of blockchain (online) blockchain and automotive: Examples of applications.* www.scalingparrots.com/en/blockchain-and-automotive-examples/.
5. EU Blockchain Observatory & Forum.: *(Online) blockchain applications in the automotive sector.* www.eublockchainforum.eu/news/blockchain-applications-automotive-sector.
6. MSRcosmos.: *(Online) examples of automotive companies.* www.msrcosmos.com/blog/blockchain-technology-in-automotive-industry/.
7. Kuiper, Jon.: *(Online) blockchain brings visibility to the finished vehicle supply chain.* www.ibm.com/blog/blockchain-brings-visibility-to-the-finished-vehicle-supply-chain/.
8. Alqarni, M.A., Alkatheiri, M.S., Chauhdary, S.H., Saleem, S.: Use of blockchain-based smart contracts in logistics and supply chains. *Electronics* 12, 1340 (2023). https://doi.org/10.3390/electronics12061340.
9. Kannengießer, N., Lins, S., Sander, C., Winter, K., Frey, H., Sunyaev, A.: Challenges and common solutions in smart contract development. *IEEE Transactions on Software Engineering* 48, 4291–4318 (2021).
10. Hornyak, Oliver, Alkhoury, George.: Smart contracts in the automotive industry. *Vehicle and Automotive Engineering 3, Proceedings of the 3rd VAE2020*, Miskolc, Hungary, October 2020. https://doi.org/10.1007/978-981-15-9529-5_13.
11. Harvard Business Review.: *(Online) customer data: Designing for transparency and trust.* https://hbr.org/2015/05/customer-data-designing-for-transparency-and-trust.
12. Digital Dealer.: (Online) transparency in the car buying process. *Digital Dealer Conference*, Las Vegas, October 17–19 (2023). https://digitaldealer.com/latest-news/transparency-in-the-car-buying-process/.
13. Auer, Sophia, Nagler, Sophia, Mazumdar, Somnath, Mukkamala, Raghava Rao.: Towards blockchain-IoT based shared mobility: Car-sharing and leasing as a case study. *Journal of Network and Computer Applications* 200, 103316 (April 2022).
14. Papoutsoglou, Iordanis, Livitckaia, Kristina, Votis, Konstantinos, Francis, Kate Elizabeth, Barata, Martim Taborda.: *Blockchain applications in the automotive sector; a thematic report prepared by The European Union blockchain observatory & forum.* www.eublockchainforum.eu/sites/default/files/reports/eubof_automotive_2022_FINAL.pdf.
15. Agi, Maher A.N., Jha, Ashish Kumar.: Blockchain technology in the supply chain: An integrated theoretical perspective of organizational adoption. *International Journal of Production Economics* 247, 108458 (May 2022).
16. ElMessiry, Adel, ElMessiry, Magdi, ElMessiry, Kenzy.: Vehicle ownership, leasing, and rental blockchain protocol VOLR BP. In Q. Wang, J. Feng, L.J. Zhang (Eds.), *Blockchain – ICBC 2023*, Vol. 14206. Springer. https://doi.org/10.1007/978-3-031-44920-8_9.
17. Dutta, P., Choi, T.M., Somani, S., Butala, R.: Blockchain technology in supply chain operations: Applications, challenges and research opportunities. *Transportation Research Part E: Logistics and*

Transportation Review 142, 102067 (October 2020). https://doi.org/10.1016/j.tre.2020.102067. Epub 2020 September 29. PMID: 33013183; PMCID: PMC7522652.

18. Reddy, Kotha Raj Kumar, Gunasekaran, Angappa, Kalpana, P., Raja Sreedharan, V., Arvind Kumar, S.: Developing a blockchain framework for the automotive supply chain: A systematic review. *Computers & Industrial Engineering* 157, 107334 (July 2021).

19. Schulte, S., Sigwart, M., Frauenthaler, P., Borkowski, M.: Towards blockchain interoperability. In *International Conference on Business Process Management*. Springer, 3–10 (2019).

20. Going, Mongetro, Bertelle, Cyrille, Duvallet, Claude.: Secure access control to data in off-chain storage in blockchain-based consent systems. *Mathematics* 11(7), 1592 (2023). https://doi.org/10.3390/math11071592.

21. Ganne, E.: Blockchain's practical and legal implications for global trade and global trade law. In M. Burri (Ed.), *Big Data and Global Trade Law*. Cambridge University Press, 128–159 (2021). https://doi.org/10.1017/9781108919234.009.

22. Giannaros, Anastasios, Karras, Aristeidis, Theodorakopoulos, Leonidas, Karras, Christos, Kranias, Panagiotis, et al.: Autonomous vehicles: Sophisticated attacks, safety issues, challenges, open topics, blockchain, and future directions. *Journal of Cybersecurity and Privacy* 3(3), 493–543 (2023). https://doi.org/10.3390/jcp3030025.

23. Syed, Toqeer Ali, Siddique, Muhammad Shoaib, Nadeem, Adnan, Alzahrani, Ali, Jan, Salman, Khattak, Khan, Muazzam, A.: A novel blockchain-based framework for vehicle life cycle tracking: An end-to-end solution. *IEEE Access* 8, 111043–111063 (2020).

24. El Messiry, M., ElMessiry, A.: Blockchain framework for textile supply chain management. In *International Conference on Blockchain*. Springer, 213–227 (2018).

25. Alcarria, R., Robles, T., Sanchez, L.: Blockchain for secure electric vehicle charging management. In *Proceedings of the 20th Conference on Innovation in Clouds, Internet and Networks and Workshops*. IEEE, 351–356 (2017).

26. Alippi, C., Bogdanovic, A., Roveri, M.: Big data analytics for secure industrial internet of things-driven automotive systems. *IEEE Transactions on Industrial Informatics* 13(4), 1995–2004 (2017).

27. ElMessiry, M., ElMessiry, A.: Blockchain framework for textile supply chain management. In *International Conference on Blockchain*. Springer, 213–227 (2018).

28. Elmessiry, A., Bridgesmith, L.: *A Call for an Artificial Intelligence Constitution*. SSRN, 4120592 (2022).

29. Accenture.: *Blockchain Technology in the Automotive Industry*. Tech. Rep. (2018).

30. Deloitte.: *Blockchain in the Automotive Industry*. Tech. Rep. (2018).

31. Wang, H., Wang, Y., Zeadally, S., Liu, R.: Blockchain-enabled electric vehicles in smart grids: A comprehensive review. *IEEE Transactions on Intelligent Transportation Systems* 20(6), 2224–2238 (2019).

32. Muduli, K., Raut, R., Narkhede, B.E., Shee, H.: Blockchain technology for enhancing supply chain performance and reducing the threats arising from the COVID-19 pandemic. *Sustainability* 14, 3290 (2022). https://doi.org/10.3390/su14063290.

33. Kang, J.M., Kim, J.S., Kim, J.K.: A secure and efficient vehicle data sharing scheme using blockchain in vanets. *IEEE Transactions on Industrial Informatics* 14(6), 2671–2680 (2018).

34. Surjandy, Meyliana, Warnars, Harco Leslie Hendric Spits, Abdurachman, Edi.: The benefit and challenge of blockchain technology for tracing automotive component: A simulation test. *International Journal of Recent Technology and Engineering (IJRTE)* 8(4), 2277–3878 (November 2011).

35. Cremer, F., Sheehan, B., Fortmann, M., Kia, A.N., Mullins, M., Murphy, F., Materne, S.: Cyber risk and cybersecurity: A systematic review of data availability. *Geneva Papers on Risk and Insurance. Issues and Practice* 47(3), 698–736 (2022). https://doi.org/10.1057/s41288-022-00266-6. Epub 2022 February 17. PMID: 35194352; PMCID: PMC8853293.

36. Chong, Anna Louraine.: *(Online) digital twin in automotive industry*. www.linkedin.com/pulse/digital-twin-automotive-industry-louraine-chong/.

37. D'Amico, R.D., Addepalli, S., Erkoyuncu, J.A.: Industrial insights on digital twins in manufacturing: Application landscape, current practices, and future needs. *Big Data and Cognitive Computing* 7, 126 (2023). https://doi.org/10.3390/bdcc7030126.

38. D'Amico, R.D., Addepalli, S., Erkoyuncu, J.A.: Industrial insights on digital twins in manufacturing: Application landscape, current practices, and future needs. *Big Data and Cognitive Computing* 7, 126 (2023). https://doi.org/10.3390/bdcc7030126.

39. Singh, Maulshree, Fuenmayor, Evert, Hinchy, Eoin P., Qiao, Yuansong, Murray, Niall, Devine, Declan.: Digital twin: Origin to future. *Applied System Innovation* 4(36), 1–20 (2021).

40. Digital Twins in the Automotive Industry.: *The Road toward Physical-Digital Convergence*. www.researchgate.net/publication/361810179_Digital_Twins_in_the_Automotive_Industry_The_Road_toward_Physical-Digital_Convergence [Accessed August 22, 2023].
41. Habib, G., Sharma, S., Ibrahim, S., Ahmad, I., Qureshi, S., Ishfaq, M.: Blockchain technology: Benefits, challenges, applications, and integration of blockchain technology with cloud computing. *Future Internet* 14(11), 341 (2022). https://doi.org/10.3390/fi14110341.
42. Xia, J., Li, H., He, Z.: The effect of blockchain technology on supply chain collaboration: A case study of Lenovo. *Systems* 11, 299 (2023). https://doi.org/10.3390/systems11060299.

Part 2

---

*Blockchain Technology and
Future Drivers' Everyday Lives*

8 Applications of Blockchain for Future Mobility

Arup Kumar Dey, Biswajit Gope, and Bijoy Kumar Mandal

8.1 INTRODUCTION: MOBILITY AND ITS FUTURE PROSPECTS

The term "mobility" denotes the ability to move or travel freely and comfortably. With the progress of automation, artificial intelligence, the Internet of Things (IoT), e-commerce, battery technology, and blockchain, people seek to have customized transportation solutions that cater to their individual preferences and requirements. In response to this trend, consumers are now utilizing services that are in harmony with their unique lifestyle choices while moving between various destinations [1].

The use of personal cars as the primary mode of transportation will decrease gradually in the next few years. This is due to the limited usage time of most cars, which has led to the emergence of new options for vehicle access. Nowadays, car owners and renters can pay for access to a mobility service instead of buying a car outright and letting it remain unused for an extended period. Various car-sharing systems are in use globally, whereby the companies running these systems do not have permanent rental sites. Additionally, these systems are expanding to incorporate commercial fleets to enhance capacity utilization and lower expenses. Even though they no longer own cars, individuals anticipate a customized mobility experience. They aspire for vehicles that operate like their personal devices, allowing them to enjoy their preferred entertainment and access information, make purchases, reserve accommodations, and even monitor their well-being [2]. Consumers with discerning tastes now anticipate personalized interactions owing to their familiarity with industries like retail, where customization and tailored choices are commonplace. With the growing software integration in vehicles, a more significant opportunity exists to enhance the digital in-car experience through personalization. By gathering individual data, cars can provide people's desired customized experience. As a result, the vehicle can function as an intelligent device that transports them. Nevertheless, ensuring secure and dependable data protection is critical for these in-car personalized experiences to become feasible. In the future [3], a secure ledger built on blockchain technology can effectively handle vehicle data, personal preferences, and transactions [4].

8.2 BLOCKCHAIN: CHARACTERISTICS AND APPLICATIONS

A decentralized digital ledger known as a *blockchain* is responsible for recording and authenticating transactions across a network of multiple computers or nodes. The system utilizes cryptographic algorithms to guarantee transparency, security, and the unchangeable nature of the data it contains. Each transaction, or "block," is linked to the previous one through a unique cryptographic hash, forming a chain. Its key characteristics include [5]:

- *Decentralization.* Blockchain operates on a distributed network, eliminating the need for central authority and providing increased resilience against single points of failure.
- *Transparency.* Every transaction recorded on the blockchain is visible to all participants, promoting trust and accountability within the network.
- *Immutability.* Immutability guarantees a permanent and tamper-resistant record of all transactions on the blockchain, as they cannot be modified or erased once they have been recorded.

DOI: 10.1201/9781003450306-10

- *Security.* Blockchain utilizes cryptographic algorithms to secure transactions, making it highly resistant to hacking and fraud.
- *Smart contracts.* Blockchain can execute self-executing contracts, called smart contracts, automating the execution and enforcement of agreements.
- *Efficiency.* By removing intermediaries and streamlining processes, blockchain can enhance efficiency, reduce costs, and accelerate transaction settlement.
- *Traceability.* Each transaction on the blockchain is traceable, enabling transparent audit trails and improved supply chain management.
- *Privacy.* While transactions are transparent, blockchain also allows for selective privacy and confidentiality by controlling access to specific information.

These characteristics make blockchain a promising technology with diverse applications beyond cryptocurrencies, including supply chain management, financial services, healthcare, and more.

8.2.1 Ensuring Reliable and Protected Transmission of Data

A secure ledger facilitated by blockchain technology could manage vehicle data, personal preferences, and transactions. The distributed ledger would be shared among individuals and institutions, providing all participants with trust, transparency, and audibility [6]. Authorized participants would share each data associated with an event or transaction in real time after time-stamping and appending it to the previous record. As agreed-upon rules among participants would govern the addition of documents, no individuals could tamper with them. This would create an unbreakable chain of trust for the data.

Regarding personal mobility, blockchain technology could identify the digital identity of a driver, a rider, and a car. It could link a specific car's unique configuration and preferences to an individual's identity and transfer them to any car they drive. For instance, if drivers prefer a Mercedes today and switch to driving a Honda tomorrow, their preferences for horsepower, entertainment, and insurance rates would follow them to the new vehicle [7].

8.2.2 Smart Contracts and Novel Business Models

With blockchain technology, micropayments for charging, tolls, and parking can be managed and linked to the identities of both the driver and the specific car. This enables new business models, such as pay-per-mile, as it allows for secure identification of who was using a vehicle at a particular time. Insurance companies can also calculate rates based on mileage and driver behavior, incentivizing individuals to drive better to avoid high insurance costs. Moreover, blockchain can hold business logic as smart contracts, expanding provider services beyond company borders. Current car-sharing operations are limited as they depend on third-party organizations [8]. With smart contracts, more companies can offer services such as recharging, cleaning, and keeping the pool of cars operational. Automation and decentralization of the process can be achieved through innovative contract technology. Management of a driver's profile is essential due to its valuable dataset, and security, authentication, and privacy are crucial to blockchain-enabled services. Companies must govern and monitor the blockchain network for ethical and regulatory reasons.

8.2.3 Vehicular Communication

The use of blockchain technology could potentially enhance vehicular communication, which is a significant factor in the realm of smart mobility. Secure key-sharing schemes using blockchain technology are under development for facilitating communication between various devices or vehicles [9]. The participants in a vehicular network experience significant fluctuations, leading to a lack of knowledge and trust among members. This situation poses a risk of malicious vehicles joining the network and spreading false or unreliable information. In a vehicular network, it can be challenging for vehicles to assess the reliability and authenticity of the messages they receive [10]. Blockchain-based technology creates a safe and reliable communication environment by enabling network users to gather trust values from other users and use them to evaluate the veracity of messages received. Another challenge is persuading users of a vehicular network to contribute information, which is addressed by adding credit point–based systems. These programs encourage networked automobiles to share traffic data while maintaining privacy [11].

8.2.4 POWER TRADING

Finding charging stations so that their cars can be recharged is one of the biggest problems that EV owners have. Unlike conventional gasoline or diesel pumps, EV charging infrastructure is not as extensively distributed or as easily accessible. When traveling long distances, this lack of charging choices causes EV owners ongoing concern, particularly if there are no charging stations nearby. They must thus carefully plan their routes, taking into account the power range of their vehicles, sunset times, and the accessibility of charging stations at their final destination. This restriction seriously slows down the adoption of EVs on a worldwide scale and turns away many prospective customers [12]. If corporations or governments take action, overcoming this problem would hasten the adoption of EVs. Peer-to-peer (P2P) EV charging on the blockchain is one idea that might help with the issue of charging outlets being available. This idea entails EV charging utilizing power trading and blockchain technology.

Electric vehicle (EV) owners have the option to possess their own charging stations, enabling them to conveniently charge their cars at their own discretion. Blockchain apps facilitate the exchange of electricity among vehicle owners, who can lend their personal EV chargers to those in need. Specialized Internet platforms enable peer-to-peer (P2P) charging, allowing owners to share their chargers with others when not in use. Noteworthy examples of blockchain-based platforms for EV charging systems include Share&Charge, Chargemap, Aerovironment, and EasyPark. EV owners utilize these systems to digitally pay for the electricity they consume [13].

As a result, when traveling, EV owners can locate and utilize nearby private chargers if their battery runs out. By participating in secure power trading facilitated by blockchain technology, owners of personal EV charging stations can increase the utilization of their stations. This ensures the safety of power transfers and financial transactions for all parties involved. The implementation of blockchain technology can contribute to the expansion of available charging stations. Furthermore, P2P EV charging requires minimal additional investment since it leverages existing infrastructure that would otherwise remain unused. Companies that invest in creating such infrastructure can gain a competitive advantage as EVs become more widespread [14]. Tesla, for instance, has made substantial investments in EV charging infrastructure to enhance customer convenience.

In the future, smart cities can integrate these energy-sharing platforms into their smart grid systems. This integration would help manage and direct electric power to the most needed areas. Using blockchain for EV-related operations effectively resolves the most significant challenge of owning EVs. By doing so, blockchain technology is vital in expediting the global adoption of electric-powered vehicles [15].

8.2.5 CREATION OF DIGITAL VEHICLE PASSPORTS FOR BUYING AND SELLING OF USED EVS

Before considering buying a secondhand electric vehicle (EV), buyers need to be aware of some crucial facts. These facts include the vehicle's mileage, accident history, servicing habits, interior and electric battery condition, and the effectiveness of safety features, like the electronic brake force distribution (EBD), airbags, anti-lock braking system (ABS), hill descent control (HDC), electronic stability program (ESP), and others.

Blockchain-based applications offer a solution for sellers of pre-owned electric vehicles (EVs) to generate a digital "passport" for each car, addressing the need to verify essential details. These applications permit buyers to confirm relevant information about any EV available in the used car market. Third-party experts can also validate the data related to a specific vehicle. Buyers can access authenticated information regarding used EVs by scanning a QR code on the seller's app using their phone. Blockchain technology safeguards the records kept within these applications and renders them immune to tampering. Although the general public often associates blockchain solely with cryptocurrencies, its applications extend to various industries, such as healthcare, banking, insurance, and supply chain management. Multiple sectors utilize blockchain-based applications, employing shared features such as decentralization, data security, and transparency [16]. Implementing blockchain-based applications in the electric vehicle (EV) sector can improve safety for EV networks and associated data.

8.3 ASSESSING THE RELEVANCE OF BLOCKCHAIN TECHNOLOGY IN THE AUTOMOTIVE SECTOR

The challenges the stakeholders face can be grouped under three domains: data management, operations management, and finance management [17].

8.3.1 DATA MANAGEMENT

All stakeholders must use the same set of reference data. Several business network stakeholders now maintain the reference data, updating it via email or paper when information changes. A distributed recordkeeping system is required, and it must be shared throughout the company network's users. This allows each business network member to have a personal copy of the distributed ledger. A work history, a job card, or the tracking numbers for a spare component are a few examples of this data.

By storing all the data in a distributed ledger, it is possible to restrict who may alter the data and who can access it after it has been changed, making the process far more dependable. Since the automobile business spans several sectors, nations, and legal jurisdictions, maintaining reference data using a single dataset may be pretty effective. Benefits include lessening mistakes, enhancing real-time access to crucial data, and facilitating routine procedures for adding, modifying, and removing data pieces [18].

Regulatory compliance auditing, similar to regular auditing, involves a complex process due to the dispersal of data and transactions across multiple locations and control by various parties. The approval and verification of transactions by business network members enhance trust within the network. Additionally, the use of a consistent business procedure by all participants in the network further strengthens this trust (see Figure 8.1).

To enhance reliability, one can consolidate all the data into a distributed ledger, which limits data editing and viewing permissions once modifications are made. This overall process becomes more dependable. By utilizing privacy services in a blockchain implementation, the immutability of the blockchain is maintained, ensuring tamperproof records and controlling data visibility within the business network (ensuring appropriate confidentiality among subsets of participants). In a permissioned blockchain, stakeholders can determine which ledger components are visible based on their relevance and mode of operation. Consequently, an audit trail is generated, enabling verification of ownership and exchanges that have occurred within the business network since the inception of the blockchain [19]. These transactions remain immutable due to consensus, provenance, immutability, and the inclusion of business logic as a smart contract within the blockchain.

8.3.2 OPERATIONS MANAGEMENT

Operations management inefficiency is likely the most pervasive across sectors due to the limited adoption of supply chain risk management solutions. Traceability in the supply chain has previously been managed using technology like RFID. A new age of end-to-end openness in the system is

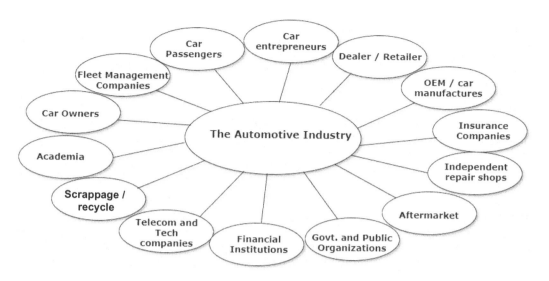

FIGURE 8.1   Main stakeholders in the automotive industry.

enabled by blockchain technology, allowing stakeholders to communicate information swiftly and confidently across a strong and trustworthy network. Additionally, implementing intelligent contracts reduces transaction costs since a reliable contract is administered without the participation of third parties. For instance, all production data on the whereabouts of each asset or component of a subsystem may be recorded as it travels from the producer to the point of integration into an automobile. This network of different stakeholders might become more integrated and linked as a result of the standard set of referenced data. If suitable, supply chain information may additionally contain intelligent manufacturing techniques (such as the precise computer-aided machine programming module used to create the item or other elements). As a consequence, it ensures the traceability of an asset over its entire life. It is clear that this traceability has advantages. The whole supply chain becomes much more successful since it is simple to ascertain who has held each item or where it has gone, which increases trust [20].

The supply chain may also include information about creative production methods that ensure an asset's traceability throughout the course of its life. These advantages of traceability are clear. The whole supply chain becomes much more successful since it is simple to ascertain who has held each item or where it has gone, which increases trust.

To prevent the need for a thorough cross-fleet review or recall in the event of failure, it should be emphasized that diagnosing the incident or figuring out which subsystems or components were involved may be quickly addressed. This is particularly true if anything requires the use of many vehicles or spare components to remedy it (such as a maintenance project or an insurance claim) [21].

To prevent the need for a thorough cross-fleet review or recall in the event of failure, it should be emphasized that diagnosing the incident or figuring out which subsystems or components were involved may be quickly addressed. This is particularly true if anything requires the use of many vehicles or spare components to remedy it (such as a maintenance project or an insurance claim). The following operational benefits will thus arise from incorporating blockchain into a system for handling transactions.

Transactions could change from taking a few days to happening very instantaneously [22]. The whole firm network may be made more productive by getting rid of expensive middlemen with overhead. Distributed ledger and privacy services are in charge of the blockchain components, guarding against manipulation, fraud, or cyberattacks within the corporate network. Additionally, since everyone uses the same procedure to keep their registers updated and their business operations operating, the trust may actually increase inside the corporate network.

8.3.3 FINANCIAL MANAGEMENT

These services include cross-border import and export systems, finance, leasing, and letters of credit in the automobile sector. Cross-border transactions that include buying and selling depend heavily on letters of credit. The banks and the many counterparties who stand in for the buyer and the seller in the business network exchange and sign various unique individual papers. Additionally, smart contracts may facilitate verification processes in automobile finance, such as document review, risk assessment, and loan approval, directly on a vehicle lease. IoT devices may be used in conjunction with financial and logistical activities. For instance, when a pallet of products enters a warehouse and passes through an RFID scanner. This RFID event can automatically verify that the goods have reached the end user and are in good condition (for example, if the assets were delivered in the specified humidity requirements, tilt, or other parameters). As a result, the seller can withdraw a portion of the letter of credit [23]. The execution time is decreased to practically real time by these automated methods. As a result, they significantly cut costs and risks for all parties involved in the transaction—the seller, the buyer, and the correspondent banks. This method might be used for additional financial arrangements and international import and export systems.

8.4 ADVANCED BLOCKCHAIN-BASED APPLICATIONS

According to its primary functionalities, blockchain is used by the automobile sector in a variety of ways (see Figure 8.2). These activities include transactions, which include dynamic registry and payments infrastructure, identity management, smart contracts, and recordkeeping, which includes static registry [24].

Through business network contacts and agreements that create a flow of goods and services, the automobile industry creates wealth. An open market is something like an auto auction. An example

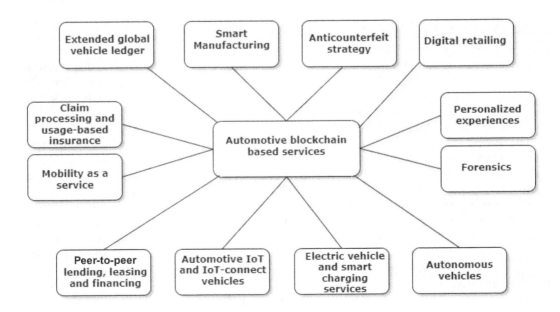

FIGURE 8.2 Application of blockchain in different sectors of the automobile industry.

of a private call would be supply chain finance. In every situation, the several parties that make up the business network trade assets. Physical assets (like a car) and intangible assets are two categories of assets. Intangible assets are divided into three categories: financial, intellectual, and digital. Financial assets include things like bonds, intellectual property like patents, and digital assets like software. The automobile sector interacts with several stakeholder groups [25].

8.4.1 EXTENDED GLOBAL VEHICLE LEDGER

A ledger that securely stores, updates, tracks, and communicates data (such as a car's maintenance history or ownership history) in real time is considered an extended global vehicle ledger. With the help of a blockchain service provider, manufacturers may establish a different ledger for the network of original equipment manufacturers (OEMs) to monitor and regulate logistics (such as problems with replacement parts quality and authenticity). The register may compile data on a car's past from many sources and charge people for access to the information. The platform might be developed to accept payment for services (such as fixing a car or getting or giving car data to/from a third party) [26].

8.4.2 SMART MANUFACTURING

Blockchain in software-based manufacturing may improve productivity and quality control while lowering warranty costs, inventory management, ownership problems, maintenance, and recycling duties. For example, it makes version management simpler [27].

8.4.3 ANTI-COUNTERFEITING

Blockchain and the Internet of Things (IoT) may provide a powerful method of preventing fraud. On the one hand, counterparties may alter the products' status throughout their lifespan, from the point of origin to the end of the sale. On the other hand, sensors may be put to assets to monitor their real-time position and status, such as if a shipment meets the estimated time of arrival (ETA) or if each component pallet is transported from the original equipment supplier (OES). To prevent odometer fraud, it is possible to suggest a solution employing an in-car connection to communicate vehicle mileage data to its digital logbook regularly. If manipulation is detected, the displayed mileage and the recorded distance may be compared via an app. Additionally, a car owner may track the miles of their vehicle on a blockchain and acquire an accuracy certificate that might be used to guarantee selling terms [28].

8.4.4 DIGITAL RETAILING AND PERSONALIZED CUSTOMER EXPERIENCE

In the age of online purchasing and personalized customer experiences, loyalty and reward programs may serve as consumer incentives. In this use scenario, it may be possible to monitor consumer purchases and give loyalty points that can be converted into cash within the shareholder loyalty network using a blockchain-based and cutting-edge contract-based solution. For the whole network, the points are instantly updated and shown (for instance, as a discount) [29].

8.4.5 CLAIM PROCESSING AND USAGE-BASED INSURANCE

Multiple parties are involved in claims, especially when using complicated insurance instruments. Currently, the driver is responsible mainly for accidents; however, when it comes to autonomous cars, other players in the automotive ecosystem, such as automakers, software suppliers, service providers, or vehicle owners, must also be considered. For instance, allowing insurance companies access to driving information to show safe driving practices may lower a motorist's insurance cost. Data gathered, like braking habits and speed, may be utilized to prevent fraud [30].

This is how the system would operate. The insurance provider would first construct a cloud-based personal account with each automobile's public and private keys. The business requires a personal statement to know the policyholder's true identity. A secure database would be used to store the public key. The car would utilize the public and private keys for each future interaction with the insurance provider. As a result, the vehicle retains data about driving habits in the cloud that the insurance provider may use to provide services [31]. The in-car storage might house a blockchain with specific crucial data (like the vehicle's location). The car may automatically submit a claim by providing the necessary information to the insurance provider in the event of an accident.

8.4.6 MaaS (Mobility as a Service)

The groundbreaking idea of "mobility as a service" (MaaS) is actively changing how consumers access transportation. Through a single platform, people are given the capacity to easily and quickly plan, reserve, and pay for a variety of transportation services. MaaS combines many forms of transportation, including taxis, ride-sharing services, trains, buses, and more, into a single, seamless system. MaaS improves travel routes, lessens traffic, and boosts overall efficiency using cutting-edge technology, including mobile applications, real-time data, and clever algorithms. With various transportation alternatives and the ability to make selections based on their requirements and preferences, the user is in charge of this live instance of MaaS [32].

8.4.7 Peer-to-Peer Lending, Leasing, and Financing

Peer-to-peer models provide a corporate structure that links the parties concerned, conducts "know your customer" (KYC) checks before leasing a car, maintains the lease agreement, and automates the payment.

Platforms based on blockchain will use secure connections and get rid of data threats. The data that was gathered may be utilized for analytics and for keeping tabs on customer behavior (KYC) while renting or leasing an automobile [33].

8.4.8 Connected Services

Through the use of preconfigured contracts that are recorded and carried out on the blockchain, vehicle owners may easily acquire infotainment or other services, like parking and tolls. To execute wireless remote software updates and ensure consistency, blockchain technology has another potential use. Specifically, between the service provider and service center, the supply chain only has a limited impact on this concentrated, non-scalable operation at the moment. Furthermore, because only the original equipment manufacturer (OEM) is authorized to carry out these functions, there are privacy issues connected to the authentication of connections and update downloads. Direct communication between the car and the OEM can put the driver's privacy at risk, including data on their actions and whereabouts. A decentralized end-to-end data interchange, including OEMs, service centers, automobiles, and assembly lines, would be possible with the use of blockchain technology [34]. This strategy would protect user privacy, keep a current history, and enable open verification of the software's legitimacy.

8.4.9 Automotive IoT and IoT-Connected Vehicles

The use of the IoT paradigm in automobiles makes it feasible to gather a lot of data [35]. For instance, on-board diagnostics (OBD) connectors that provide access to vehicle diagnostic data are included in the majority of cars made in the previous ten years. Another significant breakthrough is the introduction of event data recorders (EDRs), which gather event data in response to circumstances like a sudden decrease in speed. Connecting sensors and equipment over an approved mobile network enables data collection related to driving events (such as distance and speed), safety events (such as notifications for spare component replacements), and maintenance events (such as annual service). The owner of the automobile may be a party to the shared ledger, where this information is exchanged. Remote device monitoring and control are made possible by IoT apps, which provide insightful, real-time data. Blockchain and IoT technologies can track, process, and make device-to-device transactions easier.

8.4.10   Autonomous or Self-Driving Vehicles

Since human mistake causes most auto accidents, a computer would make the best driver since it can employ intricate algorithms to identify the best course of action. Advanced IoT capabilities, navigation systems, and computer vision technologies are all included in autonomous cars, allowing them to operate with little human interaction. Using blockchain as the underlying communication method would ensure the reliability and trustworthiness of these systems.

8.4.11   Forensics

Forensics increasingly considers a vehicle's operational history and design. Among the interested parties are insurance companies and law enforcement involved in murder, burglary, and accident occurrence investigations. Both insurers and companies that provide cars to their employees for usage during work hours have expanded their use of forensics in recent years. In the case of an incident or accident, autonomous and IoT-connected vehicles capture a ton of data that may be crucial to large manufacturers, service providers, drivers, or insurance companies. The ability to collect information from inside and around the vehicles has the potential to impact the forensics sector significantly.

Blockchain technology can offer several advantages to the electric vehicle (EV) industry, including lowering production expenses, developing a seamless and convenient charging network, and generating reliable and validated EV "passports" [36].

The utilization of blockchain technology in future mobility has vast potential to transform the transportation industry. Blockchain technology has the vast potential to transform the transportation industry in future mobility by utilizing it. By adopting blockchain, the transportation industry can achieve numerous advantages, such as heightened security, transparency, and decentralization. This paves the way for a wide range of mobility enhancements, encompassing vehicle ownership, sharing, infrastructure development, and data management.

One notable blockchain application in future mobility involves establishing secure and reliable platforms for peer-to-peer vehicle sharing. Blockchain maintains immutable records of ownership, maintenance history, and usage data, fostering transparency and trust between vehicle owners and renters. This facilitates the growth of sharing economies and promotes efficient utilization of resources.

Furthermore, blockchain can advance smart cities and interconnected transportation systems. Its utilization allows for secure and decentralized traffic data management, enabling real-time route optimization, congestion alleviation, and overall transportation efficiency improvement. Blockchain-powered payment systems and smart contracts streamline transactions and ensure seamless interoperability between different mobility services.

Blockchain's capability to create tamperproof and auditable records also opens up opportunities for automated vehicle identity verification, supply chain management, and maintenance tracking [37]. This ensures the integrity and authenticity of data across the entire mobility ecosystem. Blockchain technology can reshape how we navigate our world, enhancing convenience, sustainability, and trust within the ever-evolving realm of mobility.

REFERENCES

1. *Industry 4.0 Project Official Web Page*. Available online: www.bmbf.de/de/zukunftsprojekt-industrie-4-0-848.html (Accessed on 3 August 2018).
2. Blanco-Novoa, Ó., Fernández-Caramés, T. M., Fraga-Lamas, P., Vilar- Montesinos, M. A. "A Practical Evaluation of Commercial Industrial Augmented Reality Systems in an Industry 4.0 Shipyard", *IEEE Access*, vol. 6, pp. 8201–8218, 2018.
3. Fraga-Lamas, P., Fernández-Caramés, T. M., Blanco-Novoa, Ó., Vilar-Montesinos, M. A. "A Review on Industrial Augmented Reality Systems for the Industry 4.0 Shipyard", *IEEE Access*, vol. 6, pp. 13358–13375, 2018.
4. Fernández-Caramés, T. M., Fraga-Lamas, P., Suárez-Albela, M., Vilar-Montesinos, M. "A Fog Computing and Cloudlet Based Augmented Re-ality System for the Industry 4.0 Shipyard", *Sensors*, vol. 18, p. 1798, 2018.
5. Fraga-Lamas, P., Fernández-Caramés, T. M., Castedo, L. "Towards the Internet of Smart Trains: A Review on Industrial IoT-Connected Railways", *Sensors*, vol. 17, no. 6, no. 1457, pp. 1–44, June 2017.
6. Frost & Sullivan. *Digital Transformation of the Automotive Industry Digitalization Spending to Grow Rapidly to $82.01 Billion in 2020*. Available online: https://store.frost.com/digital-transformation-of-the-automotive-industry.html (Accessed on 3 August 2018).
7. Tapscott, D., Tapscott, A. *Cummings J. Blockchain Revolution: How the Technology Behind Bitcoin is Changing Money, Business, and the World*. Random House, LLC, 2016.
8. Fernández-Caramés, T. M., Fraga-Lamas, P. "Design of a Fog Computing, Blockchain and IoT-Based Continuous Glucose Monitoring System for Crowdsourcing mHealth", in *Proceedings of the 5th International Elec-tronic Conference on Sensors and Applications*, 15–30 November 2018.
9. World Economic Forum. "Deep Shift Technology Tipping Points and Societal Impact", *Survey Report*, September 2015. Available online: http://www3.weforum.org/docs/WEF_GAC15_Technological_Tipping_ Points_report_2015.pdf (Accessed on July 2018).
10. Hernández-Rojas, D. L., Fernández-Caramés, T. M., Fraga-Lamas, P., Escudero, C. J. "Design and Practical Evaluation of a Family of Lightweight Protocols for Heterogeneous Sensing Through BLE Beacons in IoT Telemetry Applications", *Sensors*, vol. 18, no. 1, p. 57, December 2017.
11. Froiz-Míguez, I., Fernández-Caramés, T. M., Fraga-Lamas, P., Castedo, L. "Design, Implementation and Practical Evaluation of an IoT Home Automation System for Fog Computing Applications Based on MQTT and ZigBee-WiFi Sensor Nodes", *Sensors*, vol. 18, 2018.
12. Hernández-Rojas, D. L., Fernández-Caramés, T. M., Fraga-Lamas, P., Escudero, C. J. "A Plug-and-Play Human-Centered Virtual TEDS Architecture for the Web of Things", *Sensors*, vol. 18, p. 2052, 2018.
13. Blanco-Novoa, O., Fernández-Caramés, T. M., Fraga-Lamas, P., Castedo, L. "A Cost-Effective IoT System for Monitoring Indoor Radon Gas Concentration", *Sensors*, vol. 18, 2018.
14. Fernández-Caramés, T. M., Fraga-Lamas, P. "Towards The Internet of Smart Clothing: A Review on IoT Wearables and Garments for Creating Intelligent Connected E-Textiles", *Electronics*, vol. 7, 2018.
15. Zheng, Z., Xie, S., Dai, H., Chen, X., Wang, H. "An Overview of Blockchain Technology: Architecture, Consensus, and Future Trends", in *Proceedings of the IEEE International Congress on Big Data (BigData Congress)*, Honolulu, United States, 25–30 June 2017, pp. 557–564.
16. Puthal, D., Malik, N., Mohanty, S. P., Kougianos, E., Das, G. "Everything You Wanted to Know About the Blockchain: Its Promise, Components, Processes, and Problems", *IEEE Consumer Electronics Magazine*, vol. 7, no. 4, pp. 6–14, July 2018.
17. Karafiloski, E., Mishev, A. "Blockchain Solutions for Big Data Challenges: A Literature Review", in *Proceedings of the IEEE International Conference on Smart Technologies*, Ohrid, Macedonia, 6–8 July 2017.
18. Ahram, T., Sargolzaei, A., Sargolzaei, S., Daniels, J., Amaba, B. "Blockchain Technology Innovations", in *Proceedings of the IEEE Technology & Engineering Management Conference (TEMSCON)*, Santa Clara, United States, 8–10 June 2017.
19. Conoscenti, M., Vetrò, A., De Martin, J. C. "Blockchain for the Internet of Things: A Systematic Literature Review", in *Proceedings of the IEEE/ACS 13th International Conference of Computer Systems and Applications (AICCSA)*, Agadir, Morocco, 29 November–2 December 2016.
20. Yli-Huumo, J., Ko, D., Choi, S., Park, S., Smolander, K. "Where is Current Research on Blockchain Technology?—A Systematic Review", *PLoS One*, vol. 11, no. 10, pp. 1–27, 2016.
21. Swan, M. *Blockchain: A Blueprint for a New Economy*. First Edition. O'Reilly Media, January 2015.

22. Christidis, K., Devetsikiotis, M. "Blockchains and Smart Contracts for the Internet of Things", *IEEE Access*, vol. 4, pp. 2292–2303, May 2016.

23. Jesus, E. F., Chicarino, V. R. L., de Albuquerque, C. V. N., Rocha, A. A. de A. "A Survey of How to Use Blockchain to Secure Internet of Things and the Stalker Attack", *Security and Communication Networks*, April 2018.

24. Fernández-Caramés, T. M., Fraga-Lamas, P. "A Review on the Use of Blockchain for the Internet of Things", *IEEE Access*, vol. 6, pp. 32979–33001, 2018.

25. Dai, F., Shi, Y., Meng, N., Wei, L., Ye, Z. "From Bitcoin to cybersecurity: A Comparative Study of Blockchain Application and Security Issues", in *Proceedings of the 4th International Conference on Systems and Informatics (ICSAI)*, Hangzhou, China, 2017, pp. 975–979.

26. Sukhodolskiy, I., Zapechnikov, S. "A Blockchain-Based Access Control System for Cloud Storage", in *Proceedings of the IEEE Conference of Russian Young Researchers in Electrical and Electronic Engineering (EIConRus)*, Moscow, Russia, 2018, pp. 1575–1578.

27. DeCusatis, C., Zimmermann, M., Sager, A. "Identity-Based Network Security for Commercial Blockchain Services", in *Proceedings of the IEEE 8th Annual Computing and Communication Workshop and Conference (CCWC)*, Las Vegas, NV, USA, 2018, pp. 474–477.

28. Mylrea, M., Gourisetti, S. N. G. "Blockchain for Smart Grid Resilience: Exchanging Distributed Energy at Speed, Scale and Security", in *Proceedings of the Resilience Week (RWS)*, Wilmington, DE, USA, 2017, pp. 18–23.

29. Fraga-Lamas, P. "Enabling Technologies and Cyber-Physical Systems for Mission-Critical Scenarios", PhD dissertation, Dept. Electrónica y Sistemas, Univ. A Coruña, A Coruña, Spain, 2017.

30. Zhao, Y., Li, Y., Mu, Q., Yang, B., Yu, Y. "Secure Pub-Sub: Blockchain-Based Fair Payment With Reputation for Reliable Cyber Physical Systems", *IEEE Access*, vol. 6, pp. 12295–12303, 2018.

31. Rawat, D. B., Njilla, L., Kwiat, K., Kamhoua, C. "iShare: Blockchain-Based Privacy-Aware Multi-Agent Information Sharing Games for Cybersecurity", in *Proceedings of the International Conference on Computing, Networking and Communications (ICNC)*, Maui, HI, USA, 2018, pp. 425–431.

32. Ortega, V., Bouchmal, F., Monserrat, J. F. "Trusted 5G Vehicular Networks: Blockchains and Content-Centric Networking", *IEEE Vehicular Technology Magazine*, vol. 13, no. 2, pp. 121–127, June 2018.

33. Zyskind, G., Nathan, O. "Decentralizing Privacy: Using Blockchain to Protect Personal Data", in *Proceedings of the IEEE Secur. Privacy Workshops (SPW)*, San Jose, CA, USA, May 2015, pp. 180–184.

34. Giungato, P., Rana, R., Tarabella, A., Tricase, C. "Current Trends in Sustainability of Bitcoins and Related Blockchain Technology", *Sustainability*, vol. 9, no. 12, p. 2214, 2017.

35. Decker, C., Wattenhofer, R. "Information Propagation in the Bitcoin Network", in *Proceedings of the IEEE 13th Int. Conf. Peer-Peer Comput. (P2P)*, Trento, Italy, September 2013, pp. 1–10.

36. Kasemsap, K. "Mastering Intelligent Decision Support Systems in Enterprise Information Management", in Management Association (Ed.), *Intelligent Systems: Concepts, Methodologies, Tools, and Applications* (pp. 2013–2034). IGI Global.

37. Park, S., Aslam, B., Turgut, D., Zou, C. C. "Defense Against Sybil Attack in the Initial Deployment Stage of Vehicular Ad Hoc Network Based on Roadside Unit Support", *Security and Communication Networks*, vol. 6, no. 4, pp. 523–538, 2013.

38. Nakamoto, S. *Bitcoin: A Peer-to-Peer Electronic Cash System.* Available online: https://bitcoin.org/bitcoin.pdf (Accessed on 3 August 2018).

39. Sato, M., Matsuo, S. "Long-Term Public Blockchain: Resilience Against Compromise of Underlying Cryptography", in *Proceedings of the IEEE European Symposium on Security and Privacy Workshops*, Vancouver, Canada, 31 July-3 Ago. 2017.

9 Digital Vehicle Passport through Blockchain

Siriboon Chaisawat, Hye-Young Paik, and Salil S. Kanhere

9.1 INTRODUCTION

Connected autonomous vehicles (CAVs) employ sensors and onboard software to perceive their surroundings and make real-time driving decisions with minimal human intervention. Exchanging data among CAVs and with road infrastructure allows groups of vehicles to collaborate on shared objectives, improving transportation safety and enhancing efficiency in traffic management [1]. Furthermore, the data generated by CAVs offer businesses the opportunity to extract insights [2], supporting the creation of personalized services for vehicle users, streamlining cross-organizational operations, and promoting informed decision-making toward environmental sustainability practices.

Digital vehicle passport (DVP) is an emerging concept highlighted in the roadmaps of leading automobile manufacturers as an essential component of future vehicle models [3–5]. As discussed in [6], it serves as a single repository that collects data and history relating to a vehicle, bound to a physical vehicle through a unique identification reference. It serves as a trusted source for verifying the identity and data of the vehicle. As vehicle systems evolve toward greater autonomy and connectivity, the need for DVP becomes increasingly apparent. DVP aims to support systematic management and promote the utilization of vehicle data, while also prioritizing the protection of sensitive information and controlling access to prevent the risk of privacy breaches and data misuse.

This chapter aims to explore various aspects related to the creation of the DVP. Section 9.1 provides a definition, background concepts, and technologies. Section 9.2 dives into the vehicle life cycle. We introduce key actors and activities involved in each phase of the life cycle, identifying necessary data, capabilities, and features for the DVP. Current development progress and related works from the industry and academic research will be discussed in Section 9.3. Lastly, Section 9.4 discusses design considerations and addresses challenges for the development of the DVP.

9.1.1 WHAT IS A DIGITAL VEHICLE PASSPORT

A digital vehicle passport (DVP) serves as a digital logbook that comprehensively captures the complete life cycle of a vehicle. Figure 9.1 illustrates the conceptual model of DVP and its connections with physical vehicles, data input sources, and other entities in the vehicle ecosystem. Data in the DVP are inputted from data sources such as vehicle sensors or OEMs and are collaboratively updated and maintained by stakeholders. They can be grouped into the following main categories:

- *Identity data.* Such as the vehicle identification number (VIN), model, and year of manufacturing.
- *Operation data.* Collected from onboard sensors, telematics systems equipped in the vehicle, or manually inputted by the service center during check-ups.
- *History records.* Collected from stakeholders involved in the vehicle's life cycle, such as ownership records, insurance, maintenance history, and compliance data.

Bridging the physical vehicle to the DVP requires a combination of hardware and software designed to facilitate secure vehicle authentication and access to digital documents. Ensuring the authenticity

DOI: 10.1201/9781003450306-11

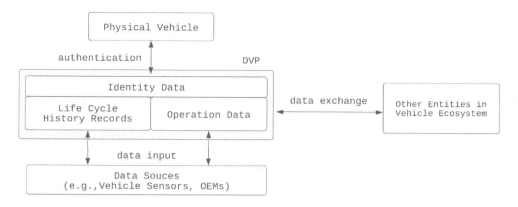

FIGURE 9.1 Conceptual model of DVP and interactions with external entities.

of the connection and the accuracy of data synchronization between the physical vehicle and the corresponding digital data store enables the DVP to function as a trusted data source for verifying the identity and data of vehicles.

To support the future of interconnected and autonomous vehicles, DVP should be capable of facilitating interactions and data exchanges with other entities in vehicle networks, as well as stakeholders throughout the vehicle's life cycle. It is, therefore, essential to adopt a uniform approach to data management, incorporating security and privacy mechanisms to ensure proper control of data usage.

9.1.2 Importance of Digital Vehicle Passport

The need for DVP arises from the problems in current vehicle data management practices, which are siloed and isolated. This leads to data being repetitive, fragmented, and not current. This results in high costs for data reconciliation. The lack of comprehensive, trusted, and unified data sources obstructs the verification and investigation processes in vehicle-related procedures [7, 8].

Another issue is the usage of manual logbooks, which are prone to missing, corrupted, and falsified data [6]. For instance, the manual process of entering data into information systems, often controlled by states or government entities, is easily prone to mistakes. A small error, especially with vehicle identification numbers (VINs), can result in a series of consequences that further complicates the vehicle data management landscape [9].

The existence of DVP will provide numerous benefits to vehicle users and stakeholders by offering data visibility and data provenance [10]. For vehicle owners, the DVP can contribute to safety improvements, such as tracking recalled parts, improving a vehicle's resale value by providing verifiable usage records that boost the trust of potential buyers. For the service centers, convenient access to vehicle operational data and service history is also beneficial for vehicle repairment, allowing for precise problem diagnosis. For transportation authorities, DVP helps facilitate the process of vehicle compliance verification, such as safety and emission standards, streamlines administrative tasks like vehicle registration and taxation, and promotes cross-agency cooperation by enabling uniform access to vehicle information. For automotive manufacturers, data from the DVP can support efficient supply chain management, foster research and development on vehicle features, improve the service qualities and customer experiences, and drive the creation of new service models.

DVP also serves as an enabler for revolutionizing future mobility and transportation. With vehicle data digitally stored and managed through DVP, the emergence of a data marketplace will enable vehicle data to be traded and utilized by businesses. Advancements in data analytics enable the extraction of valuable insights from the large volume of data for the creation of personalized services [2]. For example, in-vehicle infotainment systems can utilize driver preference data to suggest route plans and media content. Combined with location data, this allows the service to offer location-based suggestions, such as nearby events or advertisements for businesses in the area [11]. Usage-based insurance (UBI) is another potential business model where driving data is collected to construct a driver's profile, allowing the creation of personalized insurance plans based on the potential risk of accidents. Vehicle operation data can be monitored and linked to service centers to offer predictive maintenance. Analyzing data allows suggestions for potential maintenance needs or replacement of critical parts before they break down. In addition to individual benefits, vehicle data exchange can significantly contribute to smart city development. For instance, smart charging of electric vehicles (EVs) uses battery health in combination with vehicle usage data to suggest optimal charging times, stations, and reservation of charging slots. Charging data can be shared with the intelligent grid infrastructure, supporting more efficient energy management. Additionally, vehicle data facilitates traffic management strategies like platooning, increasing road utilization by forming groups of vehicles that closely follow each other. Trusted trip standards established by MOBI [12], integrate vehicle identity and trusted location data, supporting pay-per-use infrastructure and offering incentives for the usage of green transportation alternatives. The potential of vehicle data also extends to fleet management. Businesses that own fleets can access data to plan and optimize routes, reduce fuel consumption, and improve overall efficiency. In addition to supporting authorized user access, DVP can be used to enable trusted connections among vehicles, particularly in circumstances that require collaboration. For example, in intersection management scenarios, vehicles can verify their peers and share trajectory data to create efficient scheduling plans. Similarly, in cases of emergencies or accidents, vehicles can quickly collaborate to respond to the incident, provide investigative authorities with access to recorded evidence, and facilitate the efficient resolution of the situation. Overall, these advancements require DVP as a foundational building block for transformative progress in the field of mobility.

9.1.3　Related Systems and Technologies

This part discusses related concepts and systems that share similarities with DVP and introduces the technologies that empower the development of DVP.

9.1.3.1　Digital Product Passport

The concept of DVP derives from the digital product passport (DPP), which began to gain attention after the European Commission announced the EU Green Deal [13]—an agenda aiming to make Europe the first climate-neutral continent. One of the important parts of this agenda is the circular economy action plan (CEAP) [14], which provides a framework for enhancing sustainability and circularity throughout a product's life cycle. The DPP is seen as an essential tool for enabling these goals by allowing comprehensive tracking of product data from its beginning to its end of life. The data captured in the digital passport consists of performance and operation data generated from the product itself and from stakeholders' input.

As displayed in Figure 9.2, a study [15] defined the high-level purposes of DPP into nine categories, such as providing product comparisons, empowering consumers to make more informed decisions toward sustainable choices, promoting sustainable business practices, and enabling regulatory bodies to utilize this data for future policymaking.

The concept of DPP leads to a number of succeeding project implementations. The Building Information Modelling (BIM)–based material passport [16, 17] was developed on BIM software with the help of field experts with the aim of collecting all material data used in building construction. This enables a fine-grained assessment of environmental impact, supports design decisions, and ensures compliance with regulations in building construction. Formed in response to the EU Battery Regulation [18], the Battery Pass consortium [19] has developed a comprehensive

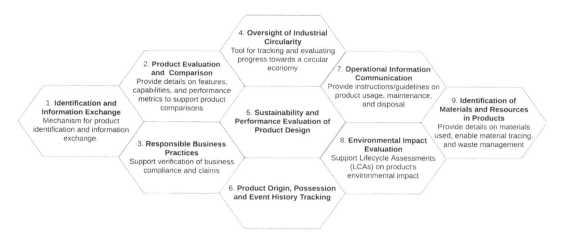

FIGURE 9.2 High-level purposes of DPP categorized in [15].

guideline for the design and development of a digital battery passport (DBP). The emphasis is on usage circularity and tracing carbon footprints, covering all aspects in the design considerations of the DBP, such as data requirements, technical design, defining responsibility and liability, and more. Circthread [20], funded by the European Union's Horizon 2020 program, creates a platform to connect all information about resources and products throughout the life cycle. It serves as a valuable tool for stakeholders, promoting circular usage and reducing waste and pollution. The project focuses on data collection and management, information exchange, and circularity use cases.

These are some of the examples of projects demonstrating that DPP can be adapted to a wide range of application areas, where its capabilities and data may be adjusted to meet the specific requirements of each use case.

9.1.3.2 Blockchain

One of the key technologies underlying the creation of digital passports is blockchain, which facilitates trusted collaboration among stakeholders in vehicle life cycle. As a kind of distributed ledger technology (DLT), blockchain addresses several challenges posed by centralized databases, including asymmetric data perceptions and vulnerability to single points of failure. It maintains a growing list of blocks containing validated transaction records. Each block is time-stamped and linked to the previous block through a cryptographic hash derived from its contents and the previous block's hash, forming an immutable chain. For a new transaction to be validated and appended to the block, all nodes in the network must agree on the validity of the transactions, which can be achieved through a consensus mechanism. Recorded transactions can be publicly verified, providing trust and transparency to all participants in the network. Altering a transaction in a blockchain requires recomputation of the hashes of all subsequent blocks. Given that the network of nodes is decentralized and continuously expanding, performing modifications on recorded data is computationally infeasible. This allows the identity data and the critical status features of a vehicle to be maintained immutably, aiding in verification in instances such as regulatory processes, maintenance checks, or accident forensics.

Smart contracts are sets of logic that run decentrally on blockchain nodes, facilitating the unbiased execution of processes and allowing intermediaries to be eliminated. This can be beneficial for various activities, such as vehicle ownership transfer or insurance claims. The architecture and properties of blockchain supports the emergence of Web3, empowering individuals to have control over every aspect of their own data, in contrast to the conventional client–server web model. With its distinct characteristics, such as transparency, security, and decentralized control, blockchain has gained interest for adoption in the automotive industry and related research fields. Section 9.3 provides details on the current work being conducted in this area.

9.1.3.3 Digital Twins

A digital twin is a virtual representation of a physical object or system that continuously receives data from the physical counterpart, such as sensor data and performance data, to enable simulations, predictions, and optimizations on the virtual instance before implementing such changes to the physical object. While digital twins and digital passports share similarities in terms of collecting, storing, and managing data of an asset, they differ in their data depth and interaction. A digital passport is designed to provide a broad overview of the object; thus, it requires the collection of various aspects of data from the object itself and external actors. On the other hand, digital twins demand more detailed and real-time data, typically focusing on specific aspects of an object. While digital passports are primarily intended to facilitate human interaction, digital twins primarily interact with software systems to learn and provide data feedback to analytics systems.

9.1.3.4 Personal Data Stores

The concept of a personal data store (PDS) has been leveraged in EU-funded projects to develop digital passports and decentralized data exchange models, such as CircThread [20] and Mobility Data Spaces [21]. PDS has emerged as a solution to address the challenges in the current centralized Internet model, where users often have limited or no control over their data. It is described as a user-centric model that enables data owners to define data usage policies and ensures that value is derived from the data obtained by the owner. In addition to empowering users, PDS also offers significant benefits for businesses and industries by providing access to a wide range of personal-related data that was previously difficult or even illegal to obtain. The analysis of these data will allow for obtaining personal insights, which further leads to the creation of new data-driven services. Several implementations of PDS have been developed to establish a standardized approach for user authentication, data storage, management, and sharing of personal data. One of the implementations is SOLiD (Social Linked Data) [22], introduced by MIT, which leverages linked data principles to create a decentralized web. Another implementation is the IDS Reference Architecture Model (IDS RAM) [23], which was developed and maintained by the International Data Spaces Association (IDSA). Built upon the EU's open standards and emphasizing data sovereignty, the model aims to facilitate the implementation of trusted data exchanges in various application areas.

9.1.3.5 Industry-Wide Information Exchange Systems

The concept of a digital passport shares similarities with various global data exchange systems designed for the automotive industry. For instance, the International Material Data System (IMDS) [24] is a global database used for managing material information in the automotive industry. Both concepts aim to enhance operational efficiency and support data collaboration among various entities. As a result, both systems need to present accurate and verifiable information. Given that there are multiple parties involved in data management, transparency and trust are essential factors in their design.

However, they differ in terms of scope and application. Digital passports focus more on in-depth individual object data and related activities, enabling the validation of individual-level compliance and assessment. In contrast, data exchange systems, which are not intended for public access, often employ business terminology and focus on collective units rather than individual units. In sum, the data exchange systems aim to align with industrial application workflows, in contrast to the digital passport, which leans more towards end-user usage and comprehension.

9.2 UNDERSTANDING VEHICLE LIFE CYCLE AND IDENTIFYING REQUIREMENTS OF DVP

In order to identify the data and requirements needed for designing a DVP, it is necessary to build a comprehensive understanding of the key activities and actors associated with each phase in the vehicle life cycle.

9.2.1 Phases, Activities, and Actors in the Vehicle Life Cycle

The vehicle life cycle can be segmented into three phases, with several terms often used interchangeably to represent each stage. The first is the "beginning of life" (BOL), also known as the production phase. This phase encompasses all activities related to the production stages, including research, design, production, and testing. Following this is the "middle of life" (MOL), or the use phase, which begins after the vehicle is manufactured and continues until the end of its usage. The final stage is the "end of life" (EOL), which is also referred to as the dismantling or recycling phase. In each stage, there are various activities involved. Figure 9.3 illustrates the relationship between these activities and the corresponding phases in the vehicle life cycle.

9.2.1.1 Activities in Vehicle Life Cycle

- *Manufacturing.* During the manufacturing phase, raw materials are transformed into vehicle parts and assembled. This process involves design and production and undergoes quality and standard checks.
- *Distribution.* In the distribution phase, the completed vehicles are distributed to dealerships for sale.
- *Sales and ownership.* Initial sales typically occur at dealerships, and vehicle ownership is registered with public authorities. Used cars, on the other hand, can be resold through various channels, which involve additional processes such as inspections and ownership transfers.

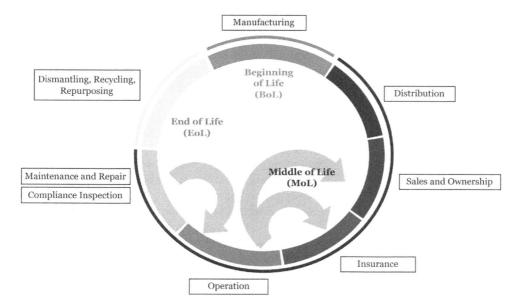

FIGURE 9.3 Phases and key activities in vehicle life cycle.

- *Insurance.* Insurance is integral to the vehicle life cycle, as owners acquire insurance policies to cover potential incidents. Premiums can vary based on factors such as vehicle age, accident history, vehicle type, and driving behavior.
- *Operation.* The operation phase involves the day-to-day usage of the vehicle. Usage patterns can inform maintenance needs and can impact insurance premiums and resale values.
- *Maintenance and repair.* Maintenance and repair are crucial for ensuring the proper functioning and longevity of the vehicle. Regular check-ups are performed, and necessary repairs or replacements are made if any components are found to be malfunctioning during inspections.
- *Inspection and compliance.* Vehicles are required to undergo mandatory inspection and compliance to confirm safety and emission standards compliance at authorized centers.
- *End of life.* The end-of-life stage involves dismantling or recycling of vehicle parts. The entire process is overseen and regulated by the government to minimize environmental impact.

9.2.1.2 Actors in Vehicle Life Cycle

Based on the activities in the vehicle life cycle, the related actors can be identified as follows:

- *Automotive OEM manufacturers.* Oversee production, ensure compliance with safety regulations, and manage after-sales services like recalls and warranties.
- *Distributors and dealerships.* Use manufacturing data to manage inventory, forecast demand, and provide detailed vehicle information to potential buyers. They facilitate vehicle registration and, in the case of resale, may require access to vehicle history for legal checks, accurate pricing, and pre-resale maintenance.
- *Vehicle owners.* Handle the purchase, registration, and insurance of the vehicle. They need to ensure the vehicle receives proper maintenance and complies with regulatory policies. Besides that, owners have the authority to sell the vehicle or grant driving permissions to others.
- *Vehicle drivers/users.* May or may not be the same as vehicle owners. Responsible for operating the vehicle, maintaining fuel levels, reporting issues, and obeying traffic rules. They may have access to some data generated during driving but cannot make significant decisions related to the vehicle.
- *Insurance companies.* Provide insurance policies linked to vehicle identification and ownership data. They use accident claim history and other accessible risk factor data to adjust policy prices and suggest plans.
- *Service centers and mechanics.* Recommend maintenance schedules, conduct inspections, carry out repairs, and use manufacturing data for diagnosing issues. Certain authorized service centers can also conduct mandatory vehicle inspections, including safety and emission tests, as required by state or national regulations.
- *Transportation authorities.* Establish regulations and ensure compliance at all stages of a vehicle's life cycle. During the BOL phase, they ensure that the vehicle's manufacturing processes meet safety and environmental standards. In the MOL phase, they ensure vehicles are in proper operating conditions through routine inspections, such as safety and emissions checks. At the EOL stage, they oversee safe vehicle disposal and recycling to promote circularity in material usage and minimize environmental impact. Additionally, they handle administrative tasks like vehicle registrations and ownership transfers, while also monitoring any legal violations to ensure overall road safety.
- *Dismantling and recycling centers.* Utilize manufacturing data to correctly identify and categorize a vehicle's components and materials before carrying out appropriate treatments, such as repurposing, recycling, or disposal. They ensure that all processes are carried out in compliance with national and state regulations.

- *Technology providers.* The emergence of data marketplaces will facilitate the trading and exchange of vehicle data. This will allow service providers, such as data analytics firms, to offer new models of vehicle services, such as personalized in-vehicle infotainment tailored to user preferences.

9.2.2 IDENTIFYING ESSENTIAL DATA IN DVP

Based on the previously identified processes and actors, the essential data to be captured by the DVP can be classified into three categories: vehicle identity data, operational data, and life cycle history records, as depicted in Figure 9.1. Considering that a vehicle comprises various parts, each with distinct life cycle activities and data, creating a dedicated category for maintaining references to parts' passports will facilitate efficient management. This is important because vehicle parts can be removed or replaced multiple times over the vehicle's lifespan. The data categories in the DVP are illustrated in Figure 9.4, detailed as follows:

- *Vehicle identity data.* This category includes identification data and attributes that are unique to an individual vehicle. Typically, identity data remains constant over time. Examples include the vehicle identification number (VIN), a globally unique code assigned to every motor vehicle upon manufacture that is physically present on the vehicle, and the license plate number, a unique combination of numbers and letters issued to a vehicle by transportation authorities upon its registration. Registration information, such as the name and address of the owner, the issuing state, and the vehicle's registration expiration date, is also part of identity data. Any indirect identification data, such as year, make, model, color, or other unique features, is also included in this category.
- *Life cycle history records.* This category includes data related to processes and related actors in each phase of the vehicle life cycle. Starting from the BOL, which includes production data, the MOL encompasses records of vehicle ownership, insurance, maintenance, and repair, as well as compliance certifications. Finally, EOL data includes details on the repurposing, recycling, or dismantling of vehicle components.

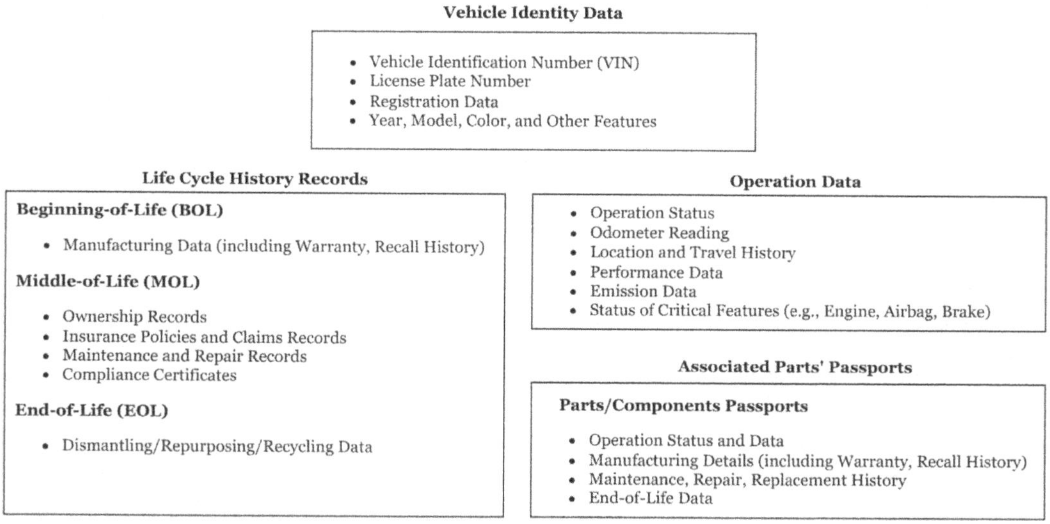

Vehicle Identity Data

- Vehicle Identification Number (VIN)
- License Plate Number
- Registration Data
- Year, Model, Color, and Other Features

Life Cycle History Records

Beginning-of-Life (BOL)

- Manufacturing Data (including Warranty, Recall History)

Middle-of-Life (MOL)

- Ownership Records
- Insurance Policies and Claims Records
- Maintenance and Repair Records
- Compliance Certificates

End-of-Life (EOL)

- Dismantling/Repurposing/Recycling Data

Operation Data

- Operation Status
- Odometer Reading
- Location and Travel History
- Performance Data
- Emission Data
- Status of Critical Features (e.g., Engine, Airbag, Brake)

Associated Parts' Passports

Parts/Components Passports

- Operation Status and Data
- Manufacturing Details (including Warranty, Recall History)
- Maintenance, Repair, Replacement History
- End-of-Life Data

FIGURE 9.4 Data categories in DVP.

- *Operation data.* This category consists of operation and performance data collected from the vehicle's equipped sensors and interpreted by installed software. Examples of data recorded include engine status, energy consumption, trip history, driving behavior, and vehicle-to-vehicle and vehicle-to-infrastructure communication logs.
- *Associated parts' passports.* Different vehicle components may have distinct life cycles, which include manufacturing information, maintenance history, changes in ownership, and specific end-of-life treatment requirements. Storing the data associated with each component in separate passports facilitates systematic management and efficient data access. Therefore, it is essential to capture the references and relationships to the part passports within the DVP design.

9.2.3 Capabilities and Features of DVP

9.2.3.1 Data Storage

The primary function of DVP is to offer comprehensive records of vehicle data, encompassing various types, such as real-time sensor data, stakeholder-related information, and static vehicle identity details. Each data type necessitates distinct handling models to ensure efficient management.

Considering about the storage location, local storage, situated within vehicles or stakeholder servers, delivers fast accessibility and heightened privacy by limiting external access and reducing reliance on networks. However, it comes with limitations, such as limited capacity, susceptibility to tampering, and uncertain data availability. On the other hand, remote storage options, such as cloud solutions, offer increased data availability and scalability. However, they depend on network connectivity, which can expose data to security risks like man-in-the-middle attacks and eavesdropping.

The architecture of the storage is also important to consider. Centralized storage consolidates data in a single location, which simplifies data management and enforcement of security protections. Nonetheless, it faces vulnerabilities through single points of failure and raises privacy concerns due to the centralized control over sensitive data. In contrast, decentralized storage involves a network of storage devices spread across multiple locations, enhancing system resilience by eliminating single points of failure and offering the ability to detect unauthorized data manipulation. However, the trade-offs include higher costs, complexity, and performance degradation due to extensive use computing and storage resources, as well as more complicated setup and management processes which require specialized personnel.

9.2.3.2 Data Verification, User Authentication, and Authorization

For external verifiers to ensure data authenticity and integrity, the DVP should incorporate data verification methods. These include using public key infrastructure (PKI) for asymmetrically encrypted data, ensuring only recipients with the private key can access the content. Digital signatures, using private keys for signing data, allow anyone to verify the public key owner and confirm data authenticity. A hash function, which converts data to fixed-size values or digests, is also useful as it can ensure that small changes in the data are detected, allowing the data recipient to confirm its authenticity.

To prevent unauthorized access, the DVP must ensure only authorized users enter the system. User authentication schemes can be implemented by adopting standard methods, such as OAuth, which allows third-party services to exchange user data without requiring user credentials; OpenID Connect, built on top of OAuth 2.0, which verifies identity and provides basic user profiles; and new standards for decentralized identity (DID), which give users control over their identity data. Depending on the confidentiality level needed and other systems requirements, other authentication techniques can also be employed, such as single sign-on (SSO), which enables a single login for accessing multiple services, and multi-factor authentication, which requires multiple credentials for identity verification. To provide digital proofs about entities, verifiable credentials (VC) standards can be applied for user authentication and data verification.

Authorization is crucial for controlling access to resources for authenticated users. Therefore, developing DVP must consider implementing certain policies. For example, role-based access control (RBAC) ties permissions to specific user roles, and attribute-based access control (ABAC) determines access based on user attributes.

9.2.3.3 Stakeholder Collaboration Infrastructure

Stakeholder collaboration is pivotal for keeping the digital passport current and utilized. A study [15] introduced the digital product passport ecosystem (DPPE) as a "system of systems" (SoS), where a network of organizations and technologies collaborates to share product data to promote the creation of additional value for the economy and environment. The key to promoting stakeholder collaboration consists of having an adaptive and robust infrastructure that supports the expansion and evolution of the mobility ecosystem. To foster stakeholder trust, actions related to data should be transparent, auditable, and executed according to the data owner's agreed terms. Formal liability agreements must also be established to clearly define responsibilities, rights, and duties associated with data sharing. Since stakeholders may operate on diverse IT systems, the system should support integration by adopting standard data formats and protocols, ensuring interoperability among heterogeneous IT environments. Regulatory support is also crucial for addressing any legally related actions and encouraging widespread adoption in the long term. Lastly, incentives—whether financial, reputation-based, or privileged access grants—can increase stakeholder participation, improve the quality of contributions, and foster positive engagement.

9.3 CURRENT DEVELOPMENT ON DVP

This section presents recent progress from both the industry and research sectors that introduce blockchain as an underlying technology to support DVP development. Additionally, it discusses collaborative projects that aim to develop a decentralized platform to foster the creation and promote the long-term sustainability of the ecosystem.

9.3.1 INDUSTRY PARTNERSHIP PROJECTS FOR DVP DEVELOPMENT

A number of automotive companies have partnered with technology companies to develop DVP, with varying focuses on usage applications, resulting in differences in the type of data collected and the scope of development. Partnered with VeChain, BMW has developed a decentralized application project called VerifyCar [4], which aims to create a tamperproof data store of vehicle usage history. The VeChainThor blockchain is utilized to store only the digital fingerprint, enabling external parties to verify the authenticity of the vehicle data, while the raw data itself is stored locally on the vehicle. Similarly, Renault Group has partnered with Microsoft and VISEO to develop a digital car maintenance book [5], aiming to consolidate vehicle data and provide drivers with more control over their data, while also enabling service providers to leverage the data to offer services with improved quality and enhanced experiences for vehicle users. MG has partnered with Koinearth to develop a digital passport for their new SUV model, MG Astor [3]. This passport records driving data, such as fuel consumption, and also allows users to input details such as maintenance services. These records are accessible through MG's app, where users can selectively share them with external service providers or trusted entities. The Passport for Connected Car (PCC) [25] is an initiative aimed at developing a blockchain-based system to store vehicle life cycle information. This system allows vehicle owners to manage their data privately and securely. PCC is also designed to support industry collaboration by introducing token incentives to encourage stakeholders to maintain and improve the quality of data on the network. carVertical is a collaborative project between Hyundai AutoEver and Blocko, focused on developing a blockchain platform to store used-vehicle records [26]. The comprehensive reports on vehicle history allow potential buyers to verify that the vehicle they intend to purchase is safe from potential fraud, such as the reselling of stolen vehicles.

Similarly, Carnomaly [27], in partnership with the National Motor Vehicle Title Information System (NMVTIS), not only provides a database of vehicle profiles but also offers a decentralized finance solution for peer-to-peer lending and streamlined processes for buying and selling vehicles.

9.3.2 FORMATION OF AN INITIATIVE FOR THE DEVELOPMENT OF DATA EXCHANGE INFRASTRUCTURE

Several initiatives have actively contributed to the development of the digital mobility ecosystem by focusing on crucial digital infrastructure and promoting engagement among automotive players. Projects such as VinChain [28], PCC [25], and CarBlock [29] are working on creating a data marketplace platform that implements standards and mechanisms to support trustworthy data exchange, bringing together various players in the vehicle value chain. Token economy is one of the mechanisms introduced to incentivize data contributions, allowing contributors to gain access to data insights and other privileged services. The Mobility Open Blockchain Initiative (MOBI) working group has developed the Vehicle Identity Standard [30], which aims to create a verifiable link to a digital document containing vehicle data. The group has been focusing on technical specifications and developing use cases that align with business requirements. GAIA-X [31], a European initiative, plays a significant role in shaping the future of mobility by focusing on the development of a federated data infrastructure. The GAIA-X MoveID project [32], under the Gaia-X 4 Future Mobility initiative, aims to establish a decentralized digital identity infrastructure to enable trusted communication and support peer-to-peer transactions in future V2X use cases. The development relies on the concept of self-sovereign identity, enabling decentralized control over individual credentials and private information. Another GAIA-X project is GAIA-X 4 PLC-AAD [33], which focuses on creating an open and distributed data ecosystem that supports data exchange throughout the product life cycle. This project's goal is to support suppliers and manufacturers in the development of automated and networked driving functions. Digital twins will be used to facilitate the design, development, and testing processes due to the complexity involved in combining hardware and software. Linked to the GAIA-X project, Catena-X [34], founded by leading automotive manufacturers, suppliers, and technology companies, aims to improve collaboration among entities in the automotive value chain by developing a standardized framework for self-sovereign data exchange. Lastly, the Mobility Data Space [21], supported by the German government, aims to create a community for sharing mobility data. This project focuses on establishing secure and decentralized ecosystems that facilitate uniform data access between the public and private sectors. Extending the open architecture model proposed by International Data Spaces Association (IDSA) [35], the project prioritizes data sovereignty by enabling data providers to define and control the conditions for data usage.

9.3.3 RESEARCH STUDIES ADDRESSING CHALLENGES IN DVP DEVELOPMENT

A number of research studies have begun to focus on addressing the limitations of introducing blockchain to DVP. These studies can be categorized into different areas, as follows:

9.3.3.1 Design and Integration

Blockchain, in combination with a decentralized file system, has been explored in many studies for storing vehicle's life cycle data. A paper [36] presents the development of a decentralized application (dApp) with the integration of InterPlanetary File System (IPFS), where access to the data is managed through a defined list of authorized users. However, the proposed design only considers input data generated solely from the vehicle. Without considering data from stakeholders, the model may result in an incomplete data perspective. Another research study [37] also focuses on the development of a blockchain-based framework to record a vehicle's life cycle data. Once a vehicle is registered, a digital "car book" is created on the blockchain, allowing authorized stakeholders to collaboratively access and edit data. To enhance data privacy protection, a hybrid cryptographic protocol is proposed in [38] to offer fine-grained data management. This protocol allows for the dynamic modification of access capabilities and the list of authorized users. To address limitations in handling a large number of participants and services in [37], the study [38] emphasizes a scalable design through the introduction of a shared data structure and workflow. Another study [39] presents the use of non-fungible tokens (NFTs) to represent the unique information of individual vehicles. This allows a vehicle's history and ownership to be transparently tracked, eliminating issues regarding information asymmetries in secondhand vehicle trading. Once vehicles are purchased, the ownership of the NFT will automatically be transferred.

9.3.3.2 Data Access and Privacy

A study [40] addresses security concerns in the vehicle network, emphasizing the risks associated with data manipulation, particularly emission data, due to economic incentives and regulatory policies. In response to these concerns, the study leverages blockchain for the development of self-sovereign identities (SSI) for IoT device identification and introduces zero-knowledge proof (ZKP) to protect sensitive information. The results of the work allow for the creation of a trusted framework that automates vehicles' emissions certification according to standards and regulations. Besides the issue of data trust, another significant concern in data exchange is the potential for bias in data verification. Typically, once an agreement for data exchange is made on-chain, the raw data is then transmitted off-chain to the recipient to ensure data privacy. Considering this scenario, the study [6] highlights the issue that data providers, rather than users, often have the privilege of making the final decision in disputes arising from data verification failures. To tackle this problem, the study proposes a data verification method using consistent commitment encryption (CCE) that allows encrypted data to be publicly verified on-chain, ensuring fairness in data verification without confidential information being exposed.

9.3.3.3 Data Storage

Having a secure system for recording data generated from autonomous vehicles is essential for determining post-accident responsibilities. In contrast to the amount of data generated from different vehicle sensors, the vehicle storage capacity is limited; thus, secure and efficient approaches for persistently storing critical data are needed. To tackle the challenges, a paper [41] introduces a solution that combines blockchain with the IPFS, where raw data is stored on IPFS while references are added to the blockchain. This approach allows related stakeholders to validate vehicle-generated data during post-accident analysis. Focusing on similar scenario and issues as the previous study, the Block4Forensic (B4F) framework [8] is introduced, providing a lightweight privacy-aware blockchain through the design of a fragmented ledger. This enables each stakeholder to retain only relevant data, reducing storage overhead while maintaining privacy.

9.4 LEVERAGING BLOCKCHAIN IN DVP DEVELOPMENT: DESIGN CONSIDERATIONS AND CHALLENGES

This section discusses the structure of DVP, highlighting the benefits and challenges in incorporating blockchain into the design.

Figure 9.5 displays the interactions between entities in the DVP ecosystem and illustrates both the layers composing DVP and the service components provided by the blockchain. DVP is built upon four foundational layers. The first is the data layer, where private vehicle data is maintained. Above this is the data access control layer, which manages user access permissions and data usage policies. Next is the integration layer, which incorporates standards to support connections to external data input sources. The final layer is the communication layer, which establishes secure connections for data exchanges between DVPs and other entities within the vehicle network. The following are details of each layer:

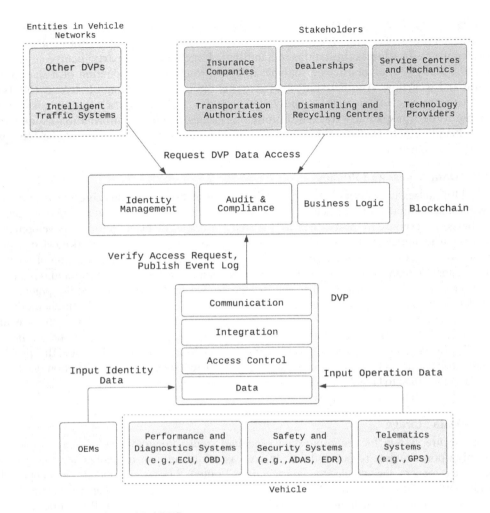

FIGURE 9.5 Blockchain-enabled DVP ecosystem.

1. *Data layer.* This layer focuses on storing vehicle information. As illustrated in Figure 9.4, vehicle-related data can be classified into five categories: vehicle identity data, life cycle history records, operational data, and associated parts' passport references. As this data contains private and personal information, access to and usage of the data must be restricted to specific parties and permitted only with the consent of the data owner(s). For instance, vehicle operation data, which includes traveling locations, belongs to the driver who was operating the vehicle at the time the data was recorded. Thus, to request access to this data, consent must be obtained from them.

2. *Access control layer.* This layer focuses on managing user permissions and policies associated with groups of data or resources from the data layer. To accomplish this, mechanisms for user authentication and authorization must be implemented to verify user identities and validate permissions during access attempts. One approach to defining access permissions is the utilization of role-based access control (RBAC), which involves associating permissions with specific roles; for instance, vehicle owners, manufacturers, and insurance companies might each have different types of access permissions, such as view-only, edit, or delete. Moreover, certain actions may be permitted only under specific

circumstances, necessitating conditional access policies. For example, dismantling entities might be allowed to add end-of-life treatment data only after a vehicle is designated for disposal. In some cases, actions may be permitted only with the consent of the data owner, such as the deletion of specific data entries. Therefore, it is essential to clearly define the scope of development to identify the appropriate supporting mechanisms that need to be implemented.

3. *Integration layer.* This layer serves as a bridge, facilitating the connection between external data sources and DVP. To ensure consistency across all interfacing sources, a standard data format and connection protocol must be established. The authenticity and permissions associated with the data sources must also be verified through authentication and authorization processes conducted in the access control layer. A number of methods can be adopted to support integration; one of the most prevalent is the use of application programming interfaces (APIs). To further enhance security, techniques such as sessions, access tokens, and end-to-end data encryption can be employed.

4. *Communication layer.* This layer facilitates the establishment of secure connections and data exchanges among DVPs and other entities within vehicle networks. Unlike traditional communication systems that rely on centralized intermediaries and are susceptible to data tampering, deploying DVPs in a blockchain network allows for direct peer-to-peer (P2P) interactions. Confidentiality of messages can be achieved through encryption using the recipient's public key, ensuring that only the intended recipient, who possesses the corresponding private key, can decrypt the message. Moreover, the authenticity and integrity of the messages are preserved through the use of digital signatures.

Incorporating blockchain can offer unified identity management, ensuring that DVPs are interacting with trustworthy entities. Activities on the network are verified before being added to immutable chain, providing transparent audit trails that foster trust and accountability in the system. Moreover, blockchain can facilitate automating business processes through decentralized execution logic or smart contracts, which facilitate activities such as transferring ownership without the need for intermediaries. Details on how blockchain can benefit DVP development are as follows:

1. *Identity management.* Blockchain can facilitate the registration of vehicles and the entities involved in vehicle networks. This registration process utilizes the vehicle's identification data, and once registered to the network, the registration data is added on the blockchain, available for public verification. The registration process involves the generation of a public and private key pair by trusted certificate authorities (CAs). This key pair can be used to secure data transmission by encrypting the message and ensuring the authenticity of messages through signing, fostering trust among the interacting parties. Using blockchain for identity management allows the registered identities to be recognized and referenced across different platforms, streamlining interactions across various business processes, enhancing efficiency, and reducing the potential for fraud.

2. *Audit and compliance.* All activities related to DVPs are published as time-stamped transactions, which are then validated against agreed-upon network rules or policies before being added to a block. Each block may contain multiple transactions and is managed using a Merkle tree structure, which facilitates efficient verification processes to ensure the integrity of recorded transactions. Hash functions are used to form a cryptographic linkage between blocks, ensuring the correct order and that no blocks are altered or deleted. Overall, these mechanisms make blockchain an attractive solution for providing transparent and auditable trails of activities, which can enhance the level of trust among stakeholders.

3. *Business logic.* Blockchain offers smart contracts, which are self-executing pieces of logic that run on decentralized blockchain nodes. This mechanism allows for the automation of

business processes, eliminating the need for intermediaries or human intervention, which is error-prone. Smart contracts also offer transparency, as participants in the network can review the logic to ensure trustworthiness in execution. The use of smart contracts can provide numerous benefits by automating various activities related to vehicles. For example, a transfer of vehicle ownership can occur once purchase payments are confirmed. For a smart contract to be executed, the nodes in the network must reach consensus on the validity of transactions. One of the consensus mechanisms is Proof of Stake (PoS), where nodes are selected based on the number of tokens they hold. The greater the number of tokens staked, the higher the chance of being selected to validate a block. The selected validators are then rewarded once the validation process is completed.

9.4.1 BLOCKCHAIN CHALLENGES

Despite the benefits that blockchain offers, there are several limitations, discussed in the following, that need to be considered prior to incorporating it into DVP.

- *Data storage.* Storing data on-chain offers a high level of security since the data is replicated across multiple network nodes. However, this approach consumes significant resources, which limits the scalability of the system. An alternative approach is to store data off-chain while maintaining references on the chain, offering greater scalability, especially when handling large or dynamic datasets. It is also appropriate for managing private or personal data as it facilitates more flexible data management, allows data to be erased, and supports deployment of additional protective mechanisms. However, off-chain storage may encounter issues related to centralization attacks, which can result in data corruption and unavailability. Decentralized file storage systems, such as IPFS, have been designed to address the concerns of centralized file storage. They can provide a higher level of security and availability through cryptographic hashing and data replication across a network of multiple storage nodes. In the context of DVP, this storage type is suitable for storing critical indicator data, which is essential in situations requiring indisputable evidence, such as determining liability in vehicle accident scenarios. However, due to the decentralized nature of this storage system, access performance might be slower compared to centralized systems.
- *Latency and scalability.* Transactions in blockchain require validation through a consensus mechanism to ensure their authenticity and adherence to defined rules. However, this process creates delays, leading to bottlenecks in transaction processing. Furthermore, once transactions are verified and added to a block, the block is then propagated across the network to ensure that each node perceives the updated state. With the increasing number of transactions, it is challenging for blockchain to effectively manage the growing workload while maintaining performance and cost efficiency.
- *Computation cost.* Blockchain relies on consensus among nodes to validate transactions. The consumption of computational resources largely depends on the chosen consensus mechanism, which can vary in terms of security, speed, and energy consumption. For instance, the proof-of-work (PoW) mechanism involves multiple nodes competing to solve a complex mathematical puzzle, ensuring that only valid transactions are added to the chain. While this mechanism offers a high level of security—since attacking it would require control of more than 50% of the mining power—the speed of transaction validation is slow, and it consumes a substantial amount of processing energy.
- *Data privacy.* After transactions are recorded on the blockchain, they can be verified by any network participant, ensuring transparency and fostering trust within the group. However, this transparency also exposes transaction details, such as information about creators and recipients, potentially allowing for the analysis of transaction patterns and

their linkage to real-world identities. Selecting the appropriate type of blockchain, therefore, is essential in improving privacy within the network. Public blockchains offer a high level of transparency, but they also reveal transaction details to the public. In contrast, private blockchains are restricted to a specific group of participants, providing a high level of privacy but introducing some obscurity due to the limited number of nodes and participants involved. Permissioned blockchains strike a balance between the two, permitting only approved participants to engage in transactions while maintaining a moderate level of transparency and privacy. Apart from the type of blockchain, several mechanisms have been proposed to enhance privacy within the network without compromising transparency. For instance, mixing techniques can help obscure the sources and destinations of transactions by aggregating multiple transactions into one. These approaches can be considered in the DVP design to balance transparency and privacy effectively.

9.5 CONCLUSION

Connected autonomous vehicles will be key in revolutionizing the future of transportation, enhancing safety and efficiency in traffic management, increasing the utilization of vehicles and road infrastructure, and promoting sustainable practices to mitigate environmental impact. Collecting and managing a vehicle's life cycle data has become essential, enabling users and stakeholders to extract insights from the data for informed decision-making and the development of new business services. The concept of DVP has emerged to serve as a tool for the collection, management, and control of a vehicle's life cycle data, as well as to provide a standardized method for sharing data among related entities. Although this concept has been explored in the automotive industry and research studies, it remains in its infancy, necessitating further collaboration and contributions. Since DVP relies on data collaboration among multiple parties, leveraging blockchain in its design can address key concerns such as data security, transparency, and trust among entities. However, limitations such as privacy and scalability still exist, along with significant consumption of computing and storage resources, highlighting opportunities for future improvements in this area.

REFERENCES

1. L. Ye and T. Yamamoto, "Evaluating the impact of connected and autonomous vehicles on traffic safety," *Physica A: Statistical Mechanics and Its Applications*, vol. 526, p. 121009, 2019.
2. McKinsey Company, "Unlocking the full life-cycle value from connected-car data," 2021. [Online]. Available: www.mckinsey.com/industries/automotive-and-assembly/our-insights/unlocking-the-full-life-cycle-value-from-connected-car-data. [Accessed 20 06 2023].
3. Ledger Insights, "MG to launch car with blockchain digital passport," 2021. [Online]. Available: www.ledgerinsights.com/mg-to-launch-car-with-blockchain-digital-passport/. [Accessed 20 06 2023].
4. BMW AG, "How blockchain automotive solution can help drivers," 2019. [Online]. Available: www.bmw.com/en/innovation/blockchain-automotive.html. [Accessed 20 06 2023].
5. VISEO, "Groupe Renault innovates with VISEO and Microsoft on the blockchain," [Online]. Available: www.viseo.com/en/north-america/groupe-renault-innovates-viseo-and-microsoft-blockchain. [Accessed 23 06 2023].
6. I. Afia, H. S. Galal, R. AlTawy and A. M. Youssef, "vPass: Publicly verifiable fair exchange protocol for vehicle passports," in *2023 IEEE International Conference on Blockchain and Cryptocurrency (ICBC)*, 2023.
7. R. Rak and D. Kopencova, "Actual issues of modern digital vehicle forensic," *Internet of Things and Cloud Computing*, vol. 8, 2020.
8. M. Cebe, E. Erdin, K. Akkaya, H. Aksu and S. Uluagac, "Block4Forensic: An integrated lightweight blockchain framework for forensics applications of connected vehicles," *IEEE Communications Magazine*, vol. 56, pp. 50–57, 2018.
9. R. Rak, "Analysis of VIN errors in information systems, causes, consequences and solutions," in *Proceedings of 1st International Conference on Structural Damage Modelling and Assessment*, Singapore, 2021.

10. MOBI, "Blockchain for vehicle identity," 2021. [Online]. Available: https://dlt.mobi/wp-content/uploads/2022/06/MOBI-VID0001WP2021-Version-2.0-1.pdf. [Accessed 20 06 2023].
11. A. Sporrer, "Autonomous cars will drive advertising," 2018. [Online]. Available: www.linkedin.com/pulse/autonomous-cars-drive-advertising-adam-sporrer. [Accessed 20 06 2023].
12. MOBI, "MOBI trusted trip," 2021. [Online]. Available: https://dlt.mobi/trusted-trip. [Accessed 20 06 2023].
13. European Commission, "A European Green Deal," 2019. [Online]. Available: https://commission.europa.eu/strategy-and-policy/priorities-2019-2024/european-green-deal. [Accessed 20 06 2023].
14. European Commission, "Circular economy action plan," 2020. [Online]. Available: https://environment.ec.europa.eu/strategy/circular-economy-action-plan. [Accessed 20 06 2023].
15. M. R. N. King, P. D. Timms, and S. Mountney, "A proposed universal definition of a Digital Product Passport Ecosystem (DPPE): Worldviews, discrete capabilities, stakeholder requirements and concerns," *Journal of Cleaner Production*, vol. 384, p. 135538, 2023.
16. M. Honic, I. Kovacic, G. Sibenik and H. Rechberger, "Data- and stakeholder management framework for the implementation of BIM-based material passports," *Journal of Building Engineering*, vol. 23, pp. 341–350, 2019.
17. M. Honic, I. Kovacic and H. Rechberger, "Concept for a BIM-based material passport for buildings," *IOP Conference Series: Earth and Environmental Science*, vol. 225, p. 012073, January 2019.
18. European Commission, "Proposal for a regulation of the European Parliament and of the council concerning batteries and waste batteries, repealing directive 2006/66/EC and amending regulation (EU) No 2019/1020," 2019. [Online]. Available: https://eur-lex.europa.eu/legal-content/EN/TXT/?uri=CELEX%3A52020PC0798. [Accessed 20 06 2023].
19. Battery Pass Consortium, "Battery pass," 2023. [Online]. Available: https://thebatterypass.eu/. [Accessed 25 07 2023].
20. European Commission, "Building the digital thread for circular economy product, resource & service management," 2023. [Online]. Available: https://cordis.europa.eu/project/id/958448. [Accessed 25 06 2023].
21. Fraunhofer Institute for Transportation and Infrastructure Systems, "Mobility data space—secure data space for the sovereign and cross-platform utilization of mobility data," 2022. [Online]. Available: www.mobility-data-space.de/content/dam/ivi/mobility-data-space/documents/Mobility_Data_Space_2022_EN.pdf. [Accessed 25 07 2023].
22. SOLiD, "SOLiD: Your data, your choice. Advancing web standards to empower people," [Online]. Available: https://solidproject.org/. [Accessed 20 06 2023].
23. International Data Spaces Association, "IDS reference architecture model," 2019. [Online]. Available: https://internationaldataspaces.org/wp-content/uploads/IDS-Reference-Architecture-Model-3.0–2019.pdf. [Accessed 20 06 2023].
24. DXC Technology, "International material data system," 2023. [Online]. Available: https://public.mdsystem.com/en/web/imds-public-pages/home. [Accessed 25 07 2023].
25. The Blockchain Group, "The passport for connected car (PCC)," [Online]. Available: www.theblockchain-group.com/cas/the-digital-car-passport/. [Accessed 20 06 2023].
26. SiliconANGLE Media Inc, "Hyundai taps the blockchain to track used cars, with help from Blocko," 2019. [Online]. Available: https://siliconangle.com/2019/04/25/hyundai-taps-blockchain-track-used-cars-help-blocko/. [Accessed 20 06 2023].
27. Carnomaly, "CARNOMALY—practical blockchain solutions for buying, selling, and owning a car," [Online]. Available: https://carnomaly.io/. [Accessed 25 07 2023].
28. VINchain, "VINchain—decentralized vehicle history," 2023. [Online]. Available: https://vinchain.io/. [Accessed 20 06 2023].
29. CarBlock, "A global transportation data protocol with decentralized applications," 2018. [Online]. Available: www.allcryptowhitepapers.com/wp-content/uploads/2018/11/Carblock.pdf. [Accessed 25 07 2023].
30. MOBI, "MOBI vehicle identity (VID)," 2021. [Online]. Available: https://dlt.mobi/standards/vid. [Accessed 20 06 2023].
31. Gaia-X, "A federated and secure data infrastructure," 2023. [Online]. Available: https://gaia-x.eu/. [Accessed 20 06 2023].
32. K. Meinke, "An introduction to moveID," 2022. [Online]. Available: https://moveid.org/2022/08/16/introduction-of-gaia-x-4moveid/. [Accessed 20 06 2023].
33. Automotive Solution Center for Simulation e.V., "Gaia-X 4 PLC-AAD," [Online]. Available: www.gaia-x4plcaad.info/. [Accessed 20 06 2023].

34. Catena-X Automotive Network e.V., "Catena-X," [Online]. Available: https://catena-x.net/en/vision-goals. [Accessed 25 07 2023].

35. International Data Spaces Association, "The role of IDS for the European data economy," 2019. [Online]. Available: https://internationaldataspaces.org/wp-content/uploads/dlm_uploads/IDSA-digital-summit-international-statements-neutral.pdf. [Accessed 20 06 2023].

36. H. Ye and S. Park, "Reliable vehicle data storage using blockchain and IPFS," *Electronics*, vol. 10, 2021.

37. K. L. Brousmiche, T. Heno, C. Poulain, A. Dalmieres and E. Ben Hamida, "Digitizing, securing and sharing vehicles life-cycle over a consortium blockchain: Lessons learned," in *2018 9th IFIP International Conference on New Technologies, Mobility and Security (NTMS)*, 2018.

38. K. Leo Brousmiche, A. Durand, T. Heno, C. Poulain, A. Dalmieres and E. Ben Hamida, "Hybrid cryptographic protocol for secure vehicle data sharing over a consortium blockchain," in *2018 IEEE International Conference on Internet of Things (iThings) and IEEE Green Computing and Communications (GreenCom) and IEEE Cyber, Physical and Social Computing (CPSCom) and IEEE Smart Data (SmartData)*, 2018.

39. A. Butera, V. Gatteschi, F. G. Pratticò, D. Novaro and D. Vianello, "Blockchain and NFTs-based trades of second-hand vehicles," *IEEE Access*, vol. 11, pp. 57598–57615, 2023.

40. S. Terzi, C. Savvaidis, K. Votis, D. Tzovaras and I. Stamelos, "Securing emission data of smart vehicles with blockchain and self-sovereign identities," in *2020 IEEE International Conference on Blockchain (Blockchain)*, 2020.

41. L. Gerrits, R. Kromes and F. Verdier, "A true decentralized implementation based on IoT and blockchain: A vehicle accident use case," in *2020 International Conference on Omni-layer Intelligent Systems (COINS)*, 2020.

10 On-Chain Decentralized Identity through Blockchain Technology

Ganga Bhattacharjee, Anoy Roy Chowdhury,
and Bijoy Kumar Mandal

10.1 INTRODUCTION

In the digital age, identity has become an increasingly important issue. With the rise of online transactions and interactions, the need for secure and reliable identity verification has become critical. Traditional methods of identity verification, such as usernames and passwords, have proven to be inadequate in providing adequate security [1]. In this chapter, we will explore on-chain decentralized identity through blockchain technology.

10.2 THE BASICS OF BLOCKCHAIN TECHNOLOGY

Blockchain technology is a decentralized and distributed ledger system that allows multiple parties to maintain a tamper-resistant and secure record of transactions or information. It gained popularity with the advent of Bitcoin, the first cryptocurrency, in 2009. The underlying concept of a blockchain is the creation of a transparent and trustless system where data is stored in a chain of blocks, each containing a list of transactions or data records.

A blockchain is essentially a chain of blocks, where each block contains a list of transactions. These blocks are linked together in chronological order, creating a permanent and immutable record of transactions.

There are two main types of blockchain: public and private. Public blockchains are open to anyone and allow for anyone to participate in the network [2]. Private blockchains are restricted to a specific group of users and are often used by businesses for internal purposes.

Here are some key features and aspects of blockchain technology:

- *Decentralization.* Unlike traditional centralized systems, blockchain operates on a network of computers (nodes) that collaborate to validate and record transactions. There is no single central authority or intermediary controlling the entire network.
- *Transparency.* Every transaction on a blockchain is visible to all participants in the network. This transparency helps build trust and accountability.
- *Immutability.* Once a block is added to the blockchain, it becomes extremely difficult to alter or delete the data within it. This immutability ensures the integrity and security of the recorded transactions.
- *Consensus mechanisms.* To validate and agree on the state of the blockchain, nodes in the network use various consensus mechanisms. The most well-known consensus mechanism is proof of work (PoW), used by Bitcoin, but there are other mechanisms, like proof of stake (PoS), delegated proof of stake (DPoS), and more.
- *Security.* Blockchain uses cryptographic techniques to secure transactions and ensure that only authorized parties can access and modify the data [3].

DOI: 10.1201/9781003450306-12

- *Smart contracts.* Smart contracts are self-executing agreements with the terms of the contract directly written into lines of code. They run on the blockchain and automatically execute when predefined conditions are met.
- *Use cases.* While initially popularized for cryptocurrencies, blockchain technology has diverse applications. It can be used in supply chain management, voting systems, healthcare, identity verification, real estate, finance, and many other sectors where transparency, security, and efficiency are essential.
- *Challenges.* Despite its potential, blockchain faces challenges, such as scalability, energy consumption (in the case of PoW), regulatory uncertainties, and interoperability with existing systems.

Blockchain technology is a powerful tool that has the potential to transform the way we conduct transactions and recordkeeping. Its decentralized and transparent nature makes it ideal for applications that require secure and tamperproof recordkeeping; as blockchain is an emerging technology, we can expect to see more innovative and transformative use cases in the future.

10.3 THE PROBLEM WITH TRADITIONAL IDENTITY VERIFICATION

Traditional identity verification methods, such as usernames and passwords, social security numbers, and government-issued identification cards, have been used for decades to verify a person's identity. While these methods have been effective to some extent, they are not without their flaws.

There are several problems associated with traditional identity verification methods, including:

- *Costly and inefficient.* Traditional identity verification methods are often time-consuming and expensive, requiring extensive manual verification and validation processes.
- *Centralized control.* Traditional identity verification methods are often controlled by centralized authorities, such as governments and corporations, which can lead to a lack of privacy and control over personal information.
- *Lack of interoperability.* Traditional identity verification methods are often incompatible with each other, making it difficult to transfer and verify identity information across different systems and platforms.

Blockchain technology can provide a solution to the problems associated with traditional identity verification methods. By leveraging the decentralized and secure nature of blockchain technology, individuals can have more control over their personal information and protect themselves from security risks and data breaches.

Blockchain technology can provide the following benefits for identity verification:

- *Decentralized control.* The decentralized nature of blockchain allows individuals to have more control over their personal information and protect their privacy.
- *Increased security.* Blockchain technology cryptographic algorithms that are used to verify transactions.
- *Interoperability.* Blockchain technology can provide a universal standard for identity verification, making it easier to transfer and verify identity information across different systems and platforms.
- *Cost-efficiency.* Blockchain technology can streamline the identity verification process, reducing the need for expensive manual verification and validation processes.

Traditional identity verification methods have significant flaws that can compromise personal information and lead to identity theft. Blockchain technology provides a solution to these problems by leveraging its decentralized and secure nature. By using blockchain technology for identity verification, individuals can have more control over their personal information and protect themselves from security risks and data breaches [4].

10.4 WHAT IS ON-CHAIN DECENTRALIZED IDENTITY?

On-chain decentralized identity refers to a system where an individual's identity information is stored on a blockchain, allowing for a secure and decentralized way to verify their identity. On-chain decentralized identity removes the need for centralized authorities, such as governments or corporations, to verify an individual's identity. Instead, individuals can control their own identity information and share it with others as they see fit.

How does on-chain decentralized identity work? On-chain decentralized identity works by leveraging the blockchain's ability to provide a tamperproof and immutable record of transactions. Each individual's identity information is stored on the blockchain in the form of a digital identity, which is a unique identifier that can be used to verify their identity. This digital identity is linked to the individual's public key on the blockchain, which is used to sign transactions and verify their identity.

When an individual needs to verify their identity, they can provide their digital identity and public key to the requesting party [5]. The requesting party can then verify the individual's identity by checking the digital identity on the blockchain and verifying that it is linked to the correct public key.

Benefits of on-chain decentralized identity. On-chain decentralized identity provides several benefits, including:

- *Decentralized control.* On-chain decentralized identity removes the need for centralized authorities to verify an individual's identity, giving individuals more control over their own identity.
- *Interoperability.* On-chain decentralized identity can provide a universal standard for identity verification, making it easier to transfer and verify identity information across different systems and platforms.
- *Immutable record.* On-chain decentralized identity provides a tamperproof and immutable record of identity transactions, ensuring that identity information is secure and accurate.

On-chain decentralized identity provides a secure and decentralized way to verify an individual's identity, removing the need for centralized authorities and giving individuals more control over their own identity information. By leveraging the blockchain's ability to provide a tamperproof and immutable record of transactions, on-chain decentralized identity provides increased privacy, decentralized control, interoperability, and an immutable record of identity transactions.

10.5 ADVANTAGES OF ON-CHAIN DECENTRALIZED IDENTITY

Let us explore the advantages of on-chain decentralized identity and how it can benefit individuals and organizations.

- *Increased privacy and security.* One of the main advantages of on-chain decentralized identity is increased privacy and security. Traditional identity verification methods often rely on centralized authorities to store and verify identity information, which can be vulnerable to security breaches and data theft. On-chain decentralized identity, on the other hand, stores identity information in a decentralized manner on the blockchain, making it less vulnerable to attacks and data breaches. Additionally, the use of cryptographic algorithms in the blockchain ensures that transactions are secure and tamperproof.

- *Control over personal information.* On-chain decentralized identity provides individuals with greater control over their personal information. With traditional identity verification methods, individuals often have to share their personal information with centralized authorities, which can lead to a loss of privacy and control over their information [6]. On-chain decentralized identity, however, allows individuals to control their own identity information and decide who they want to share it with. This provides individuals with greater privacy and control over their personal information.
- *Improved efficiency.* On-chain decentralized identity can also improve efficiency by streamlining the identity verification process. Traditional identity verification methods often involve extensive manual verification and validation processes, which can be time-consuming and costly. On-chain decentralized identity, however, can automate the verification process through the use of smart contracts and blockchain technology, reducing the need for manual processes and improving efficiency.
- *Interoperability.* On-chain decentralized identity can also provide interoperability, making it easier to transfer and verify identity information across different systems and platforms. With traditional identity verification methods, identity information is often incompatible with different systems, making it difficult to transfer and verify information across different platforms. On-chain decentralized identity, however, provides a universal standard for identity verification, making it easier to transfer and verify information across different systems and platforms.
- *Trust and transparency.* On-chain decentralized identity can also improve trust and transparency in the identity verification process. With traditional identity verification methods, there is often a lack of transparency in the verification process, making it difficult to know how identity information is being used and shared. On-chain decentralized identity, however, provides a transparent and tamperproof record of identity transactions, ensuring that individuals have visibility into how their information is being used and shared.

On-chain decentralized identity provides several advantages, including increased privacy and security, control over personal information, improved efficiency, interoperability, and trust and transparency. By leveraging blockchain technology, on-chain decentralized identity can provide a more secure, efficient, and decentralized way to verify identity, benefiting individuals and organizations alike.

10.6 USE CASES FOR ON-CHAIN DECENTRALIZED IDENTITY

Let us explore some of the potential use cases for on-chain decentralized identity.

- *Identity verification.* One of the most obvious use cases for on-chain decentralized identity is for identity verification. With traditional identity verification methods, individuals often have to share their personal information with centralized authorities, which can be vulnerable to security breaches and data theft. On-chain decentralized identity, however, provides a more secure and private way to verify identity information, with individuals in control of their own personal information.
- *Financial services.* On-chain decentralized identity can also be used in financial services, such as in the process of "know your customer" (KYC) compliance [7]. KYC requirements often involve extensive manual verification and validation processes, which can be time-consuming and costly. On-chain decentralized identity, however, can automate the verification process through the use of smart contracts and blockchain technology, reducing the need for manual processes and improving efficiency.

- *Healthcare.* On-chain decentralized identity can also be used in healthcare, providing patients with greater control over their own health records. By storing health records on the blockchain, patients can control access to their records and share them with healthcare providers as needed, without having to worry about the privacy and security concerns associated with centralized data storage.
- *Government services.* On-chain decentralized identity can also be used in government services, such as voting or applying for government benefits. By using on-chain decentralized identity, governments can reduce the risk of fraud and identity theft while also providing citizens with greater privacy and control over their personal information.
- *Supply chain management.* On-chain decentralized identity can also be used in supply chain management, providing a more transparent and secure way to track goods and materials throughout the supply chain [8]. By using on-chain decentralized identity, organizations can ensure the authenticity and provenance of goods and materials, while also improving supply chain efficiency.
- *Education.* On-chain decentralized identity can also be used in education, providing students with greater control over their own educational records. By storing educational records on the blockchain, students can control access to their records and share them with potential employers or educational institutions without having to worry about the privacy and security concerns associated with centralized data storage.

On-chain decentralized identity provides a range of potential use cases, including identity verification, financial services, healthcare, government services, supply chain management, and education. By leveraging the security, privacy, and transparency benefits of blockchain technology, on-chain decentralized identity has the potential to revolutionize how we think about identity verification and data storage.

10.7 CHALLENGES AND LIMITATIONS OF ON-CHAIN DECENTRALIZED IDENTITY

While on-chain decentralized identity has the potential to revolutionize the way we think about identity verification and data storage, there are several challenges and limitations that must be considered. In this chapter, we will explore some of the key challenges and limitations associated with on-chain decentralized identity.

- *Scalability.* One of the biggest challenges associated with on-chain decentralized identity is scalability. Blockchain networks are currently limited in their capacity to process large amounts of data quickly and efficiently, which can be a major challenge when it comes to identity verification, especially in high-volume use cases, such as financial services or government services.
- *Interoperability.* Another challenge associated with on-chain decentralized identity is interoperability. Different blockchain networks often have different standards and protocols for managing identity information, which can make it difficult to transfer data between different networks. This can be a major limitation when it comes to using on-chain decentralized identity in complex multi-party use cases, such as supply chain management.
- *User adoption.* On-chain decentralized identity relies on users being willing to manage their own identity information, which can be a significant barrier to adoption. Many individuals may not feel comfortable managing their own identity information or may not have the technical knowledge or resources to do so effectively.
- *Legal and regulatory challenges.* On-chain decentralized identity also presents legal and regulatory challenges, particularly in the context of data protection and privacy laws.

While blockchain technology provides a high degree of security and transparency, it can also make it difficult to comply with existing legal and regulatory frameworks.

- *Security and privacy.* Finally, on-chain decentralized identity presents security and privacy challenges that must be carefully managed. While blockchain technology provides a high degree of security, it is still vulnerable to certain types of attacks, such as 51% attacks or double-spending attacks. Additionally, on-chain decentralized identity presents unique privacy challenges, as blockchain networks are designed to be transparent and public, which can make it difficult to protect sensitive identity information.

On-chain decentralized identity presents a range of challenges and limitations that must be carefully considered and managed. While blockchain technology provides a range of benefits when it comes to security, transparency, and privacy, it also presents scalability, interoperability, user adoption, legal and regulatory, and security and privacy challenges. Addressing these challenges will be essential for realizing the full potential of on-chain decentralized identity.

10.8 SOLIDITY: THE FUTURE OF WRITING CONTRACTS IN ETHEREUM NETWORK

Ethereum has been making waves in the world of cryptocurrencies since its inception in 2015. However, the smart contracts are programmed using Solidity, a high-level programming language that Ethereum specifically designed for writing smart contracts on the Ethereum network.

The benefits of using Solidity are numerous. One of the key advantages is its ability to automate the enforcement of contractual obligations. Solidity contracts can execute automatically, without the need for an intermediary to enforce the terms of the agreement. The elimination of intermediaries reduces costs and increases efficiency, making it an ideal tool for creating decentralized applications.

Solidity is also being used in a variety of industries, from finance and healthcare to supply chain management and more. In the finance industry, Solidity can be used to create smart contracts that automate the process of issuing and trading securities, making it faster, cheaper, and more secure. In healthcare, Solidity can be used to create smart contracts that ensure the privacy and security of patient data. In supply chain management, it can be used to create smart contracts that track the movement of goods from manufacturer to consumer.

As the Ethereum network continues to grow, Solidity is becoming an increasingly important tool for developers looking to create dApps. Whether you are a seasoned developer or just starting out, Solidity is a valuable language to learn.

If you are interested in learning more about Solidity and how it can be used to write contracts on the Ethereum network, there are plenty of online resources available. The Ethereum Foundation offers a variety of tutorials and documentation, and there are also a number of online courses and tutorials available.

Moreover, the future of contracts on the Ethereum network is bright, and Solidity is at the forefront of this exciting new technology. As more industries adopt blockchain technology, the demand for developers with experience in Solidity increases. With Solidity, developers can write smart contracts that are secure, transparent, and self-executing, making it an ideal tool for creating decentralized applications.

In conclusion, Solidity is a powerful tool for developers looking to create decentralized applications and smart contracts on the Ethereum network. With its ability to automate the enforcement of contractual obligations, eliminate intermediaries, and reduce transaction costs, it is poised to revolutionize the way we think about contracts and agreements. The use of Solidity is a significant step toward a more transparent, secure, and efficient future.

10.9   SOLIDITY CONTRACT TO STORE ON-CHAIN DECENTRALIZED IDENTITY

To write a Solidity contract for decentralized identity, you first import the required libraries and interfaces. Then you define a struct to store identity details, like name, email, and image URL.

You can define mappings from addresses to identity structs to store the identity details for each user.

You define functions for users to set and update their identity details. These functions should only be callable by the owner of that address.

```
-----
pragma solidity ^0.8.0;

import "@openzeppelin/contracts/access/Ownable.h";

contract DecentralId is Ownable {

  struct Identity {
        string name;
        string email;
        string imageUrl;
  }

  mapping (address => Identity) public identities;

  function setIdentity (string memory _name, string memory _email, string
memory _imageUrl) public onlyOwner {

        identities [msg. sender] = Identity (_name, _email, _imageUrl);
  }

  }
--------------
```

This contract allows a user to set their on-chain decentralized identity details by calling the setIdentity () function.

10.10   WHY WE SHOULD USE ETHEREUM FOR STORING OUR DECENTRALIZED IDENTITY

In today's digital age, where online transactions are becoming more and more prevalent, the need for a secure and reliable identity management system has become increasingly important. A decentralized identity system offers a secure, tamperproof way to manage identity, ensuring that personal information is not controlled by a single entity or vulnerable to hacking.

Ethereum blockchain is one of the popular platforms that can be used to store decentralized identity on-chain. Ethereum's unique features make it a great choice for decentralized identity management. In this book, we will explore why Ethereum is a great platform for decentralized identity management and how it can help us create a more secure and trustworthy identity system that can be used by everyone.

10.10.1   SECURITY

One of the primary reasons to use Ethereum for decentralized identity management is its security. Ethereum uses cryptographic algorithms to ensure tamperproof data storage, making it an ideal platform for storing sensitive identity information. The decentralized nature of the platform ensures that the data cannot be modified or tampered with by a single entity [8]. This means that the identity data stored on Ethereum is secure and cannot be easily hacked or stolen.

10.10.2 DECENTRALIZATION

Another advantage of using Ethereum for decentralized identity management is its decentralization. Ethereum is a decentralized platform, meaning, that there is no central authority that controls the network. This ensures that the identity data cannot be controlled by a single entity and is not vulnerable to censorship or manipulation. This is important because it means that no one can control or manipulate the data to their advantage, ensuring a fair and transparent system for everyone.

10.10.3 INTEROPERABILITY

Ethereum is compatible with other blockchain platforms, which makes it easy to integrate decentralized identity data with other blockchain-based applications. This interoperability ensures that decentralized identity data stored on Ethereum can be easily accessed and used by other platforms, making it a versatile solution for decentralized identity management. This means that the identity data stored on Ethereum can be used in a variety of applications, from financial services to healthcare, making it a valuable asset for individuals and businesses alike.

10.10.4 TRANSPARENCY

Finally, Ethereum's transparency ensures that all transactions are recorded on the blockchain, making it easy to audit the decentralized identity data. This transparency ensures that the data is being used in a transparent and accountable manner. This means that anyone can access the data and verify its accuracy, ensuring that the system is fair and trustworthy.

10.11   WHAT ARE ATTESTATIONS IN DECENTRALIZED IDENTITY?

Attestations in decentralized identity (DID) refer to the process of verifying and validating certain claims or attributes about an individual or entity within a decentralized identity system. Attestations provide a means to establish trust and credibility by having trusted third parties or authorities vouch for the accuracy and authenticity of the claims made by a DID subject.

In a DID ecosystem, individuals or entities can make claims about themselves, such as their name, age, address, educational qualifications, or any other attribute. These claims can be self-asserted or derived from other sources. However, to establish trust and enable interoperability, these claims need to be verified by trusted parties.

Attestations act as digital credentials that verify the claims made by a DID subject. They are issued by trusted issuers, often called attestation authorities, that are recognized within the ecosystem. These issuers could be institutions, organizations, or individuals that have the authority to validate specific attributes.

When a claim needs to be attested, the DID subject presents the relevant information to the attestation authority for verification. The attestation authority then performs the necessary checks and verification processes to ensure the accuracy and validity of the claim. Once verified, the attestation authority generates a digitally signed attestation, which includes the verified claim, along with additional metadata, such as the expiration date, issuance timestamp, and the public key of the issuer.

The attestation is then associated with the corresponding DID and can be stored on a distributed ledger or any other decentralized storage system. The DID subject can then present this attestation whenever they need to provide proof of their claims to relying parties within the decentralized identity ecosystem. Relying parties can independently verify the attestation by digital signature and the issuer's public key.

In summary, *attestations* in decentralized identity are the digitally signed credentials issued by trusted authorities to validate the claims made by individuals or entities within a decentralized identity system. They help establish trust, interoperability, and verifiability of identity attributes.

10.11.1 What Are Decentralized Identifiers?

Decentralized identifiers (DIDs) are a core component of the decentralized identity (DI) framework. DIDs provide a method for creating and managing globally unique identifiers for entities such as individuals, organizations, or devices in a decentralized and self-sovereign manner.

Unlike traditional identifiers, such as usernames or email addresses, which are often controlled by centralized authorities, DIDs are designed to be independent of any central authority or single point of control. They enable individuals to have control over their own digital identities and how their identity information is shared and accessed.

DIDs are typically represented as unique strings, such as "did:example:123456789abcdefghi," and are designed to be resolvable, meaning, they can be looked up in a decentralized manner to retrieve associated metadata or public keys. Resolving a DID involves querying a DID resolver, which is responsible for retrieving and providing the relevant information associated with the DID.

DIDs are created using a combination of cryptographic techniques to ensure uniqueness, security, and tamper resistance. They are typically based on public key cryptography, where a pair of cryptographic keys is generated: a private key and a corresponding public key. The public key is associated with the DID and can be used for cryptographic operations, such as verifying digital signatures.

10.12 COMPONENTS OF DECENTRALIZED IDENTIFIERS

10.12.1 Public Key Infrastructure

Public key infrastructure (PKI) is a system of technologies, protocols, and procedures used to establish, manage, and distribute digital certificates, public keys, and other cryptographic credentials. PKI enables secure communication and authentication in various applications, including secure email, web browsing, virtual private networks (VPNs), and digital signatures.

When a user wants to establish a secure connection or verify the authenticity of a digital certificate, their system checks the certificate's digital signature, validity period, and the certificate's trust chain up to a trusted root certificate. If the checks pass, the user can trust the authenticity of the entity and establish secure communication.

PKI plays a crucial role in ensuring the confidentiality, integrity, and authenticity of digital communications by enabling secure encryption, digital signatures, and trust verification through the use of digital certificates.

10.12.2 Decentralized Data Stores

Decentralized data stores refer to systems or architectures where data is stored and distributed across multiple nodes or participants in a decentralized network, without reliance on a central authority or single point of control. These data stores are designed to provide increased resilience, fault tolerance, and data availability compared to traditional centralized data storage systems.

In decentralized data stores, data is typically distributed and replicated across multiple nodes in a peer-to-peer (P2P) network. Each node in the network contributes storage capacity and acts as both a provider and a consumer of data. This distributed nature eliminates the need for a central server or database, reducing the risk of a single point of failure and enabling data to be accessed and stored in a more resilient and censorship-resistant manner.

Decentralized data stores offer advantages such as data availability, fault tolerance, data sovereignty, and resistance to censorship. They can be particularly beneficial in scenarios where trust, resilience, and data integrity are crucial, such as in decentralized applications (dApps), content sharing, distributed file storage, or when there is a need to avoid reliance on centralized infrastructure.

10.13 USING DECENTRALIZED IDENTIFIERS AND ATTESTATIONS TO ENABLE DECENTRALIZED IDENTITY

Decentralized identifiers (DIDs) and attestations play crucial roles in enabling decentralized identity (DI) by providing the necessary infrastructure and mechanisms for self-sovereign identity, trust establishment, and verifiability within decentralized systems. Here is how they contribute to decentralized identity.

Decentralized identifiers (DIDs). DIDs provide a way to create unique identifiers for individuals, organizations, or devices in a decentralized manner. DIDs are independent of any central authority, allowing individuals to have control over their own digital identities. DIDs enable the following:

- *Self-sovereign identity*. DIDs empower individuals to manage their own identity information and control how it is shared, eliminating reliance on centralized identity providers. Individuals can create their own DIDs, associate their personal data with them, and use them across various applications and services.
- *Portability and interoperability*. DIDs can be used across different platforms, services, and ecosystems, facilitating interoperability. Individuals can carry their DIDs across multiple applications, asserting their identity attributes and establishing trust without the need for redundant identity verification processes.
- *Privacy and data minimization*. DIDs enable selective disclosure of identity attributes, allowing individuals to share only the necessary information without revealing unnecessary personal data. By controlling the flow of their identity information, individuals can protect their privacy and minimize data exposure.

Attestations. Attestations are digitally signed credentials issued by trusted parties or authorities within a decentralized identity system. Attestations validate the claims made by individuals or entities and enable trust establishment and verifiability. Attestations contribute to decentralized identity in the following ways:

- *Trust and credibility*. Attestations are issued by trusted issuers, such as institutions or organizations, which vouch for the accuracy and authenticity of the claims made by a DID subject. By relying on attestations from trusted authorities, decentralized identity systems can establish trust and credibility in the attributes and claims associated with DIDs.
- *Verifiable credentials*. Attestations act as verifiable credentials that can be presented by individuals to relying parties. Verifiable credentials are digitally signed and can be independently verified, enabling relying parties to authenticate the identity attributes without relying on a centralized authority. This facilitates secure interactions and transactions between different entities within the decentralized identity ecosystem.
- *Selective disclosure and proof presentation*. Attestations provide a mechanism for individuals to selectively disclose specific claims or attributes in a controlled and verifiable manner. Individuals can present attested credentials or proofs to relying parties, proving their identity attributes without revealing unnecessary personal information, promoting privacy and data protection.

By combining DIDs and attestations, decentralized identity systems enable individuals to have control over their identities, establish trust through verifiable credentials, and selectively share identity attributes as needed. These technologies empower individuals, promote privacy, and reduce reliance on centralized identity providers, fostering a more secure, user-centric, and interoperable identity ecosystem.

10.14 TYPES OF ATTESTATIONS IN DECENTRALIZED IDENTITY SYSTEMS

In decentralized identity systems, various types of attestations can be used to verify and validate different types of identity attributes or claims. The specific types of attestations may vary depending on the implementation or requirements of the decentralized identity ecosystem. Here are some common types of attestations:

- *Self-attestations.* Self-attestations are claims made by the individuals themselves about their own identity attributes. These claims are self-asserted, without external verification. Self-attestations can be useful for attributes that do not require external validation or when individuals have direct knowledge and control over the claimed attributes.
- *Social attestations.* Social attestations involve the validation of identity attributes by trusted individuals or social connections within a decentralized network. These trusted parties can vouch for the accuracy of certain attributes based on their personal knowledge or relationship with the individual. Social attestations can be used to verify attributes such as reputation, endorsements, or affiliations.
- *Professional attestations.* Professional attestations involve verification of identity attributes related to professional qualifications, certifications, or licenses. Trusted professional bodies or organizations can issue attestations to validate an individual's expertise, education, or professional achievements.
- *Institutional attestations.* Institutional attestations are issued by trusted institutions, such as universities, employers, or government agencies, to verify specific identity attributes. These attestations can validate attributes like educational degrees, employment history, or official identification documents.
- *Government attestations.* Government attestations involve verification and validation of identity attributes by governmental authorities. These attestations can include identity documents like passports, driver's licenses, or national identification cards issued by government agencies.
- *Device attestations.* In the context of IoT (Internet of Things), device attestations verify the identity or integrity of connected devices within a decentralized identity ecosystem. These attestations ensure that the device is genuine, is trusted, and has not been tampered with.

It is important to note that the types of attestations and their availability may depend on the specific decentralized identity framework or ecosystem being used. The attestation authorities, issuers, and the level of trust associated with each type of attestation can vary in different decentralized identity implementations.

10.14.1 SOULBOUND TOKENS AND IDENTITY

Soulbound tokens are unique digital assets that represent ownership or proof of authenticity for a particular item. While Soulbound tokens can be associated with various types of digital assets, their connection to decentralized identity is often related to the concept of verifiable ownership and identity verification.

In the context of decentralized identity, soulbound tokens can be used to establish a link between a digital identity and a specific digital asset or item. By associating a soulbound token with a decentralized identifier (DID), it becomes possible to prove ownership or control of that token, and thus the associated asset, as part of an individual's verifiable credentials.

10.15 VERIFIABLE CREDENTIALS AND DECENTRALIZED IDENTIFIERS

Decentralized identifiers (DIDs) and *verifiable credentials* are two essential components of decentralized identity (DI) systems that work together to enable self-sovereign identity, privacy, and secure data sharing. Here is how DIDs and verifiable credentials relate to each other.

Decentralized identifiers (DIDs). DIDs provide a unique and globally resolvable identifier for individuals, organizations, or devices in a decentralized manner. DIDs are independent of any central authority and give individuals control over their own digital identities. DIDs enable the following:

- *Self-sovereign identity.* DIDs empower individuals to manage their own identity information and control how it is shared. Individuals can create their own DIDs, associate their personal data with them, and use them across various applications and services.
- *Portability and interoperability.* DIDs can be used across different platforms, services, and ecosystems. They facilitate interoperability by enabling individuals to carry their DIDs across multiple applications, asserting their identity attributes, and establishing trust without redundant identity verification processes.
- *Privacy and selective disclosure.* DIDs enable selective disclosure of identity attributes. Individuals can control the flow of their identity information and share only the necessary attributes without revealing unnecessary personal data.

Verifiable credentials. Verifiable credentials are digitally signed credentials that provide verifiable proof of identity attributes or claims. Verifiable credentials can be associated with DIDs and enable the following:

- *Credential issuance.* Trusted issuers can issue verifiable credentials, which include identity attributes or claims, and digitally sign them. These credentials can be associated with the corresponding DIDs of individuals or entities.
- *Proof presentation.* Individuals can present verifiable credentials to relying parties as proof of their identity attributes or claims. Relying parties can independently verify the credentials' authenticity and integrity by checking the digital signature and associated issuer's trust.
- *Selective disclosure and minimal disclosure proofs.* Verifiable credentials enable selective disclosure of specific attributes or claims in a controlled manner. Individuals can share only the necessary information while minimizing the exposure of their personal data.

The combination of DIDs and verifiable credentials allows individuals to have control over their identities, establish trust through verifiable proofs, and selectively share identity attributes as needed. DIDs provide the foundation for unique and decentralized identifiers, while verifiable credentials offer the means to attest and verify identity attributes in a secure and privacy-enhancing manner within the decentralized identity ecosystem.

10.15.1 DECENTRALIZED AUTHENTICATION?

Decentralized authentication refers to the process of verifying and validating the identity of individuals or entities in a decentralized manner without relying on a central authority or single point of control. Figure 10.1 discusses the module for the verifiable credential flow. It involves using decentralized identity (DI) technologies and principles to authenticate users and establish trust within a decentralized ecosystem. Here is an overview of decentralized authentication:

- *Self-sovereign identity.* Decentralized authentication aligns with the concept of self-sovereign identity, where individuals have control over their own digital identities. Users can

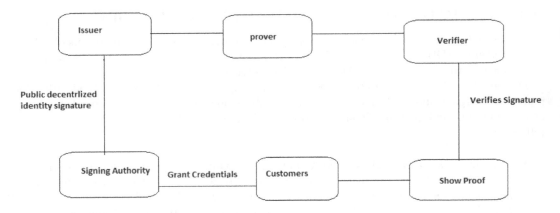

FIGURE 10.1 The verifiable credential flow.

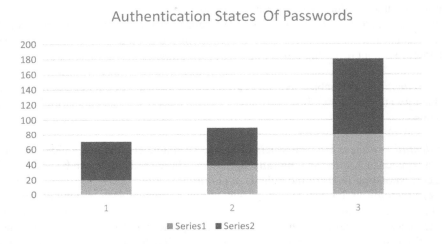

FIGURE 10.2 State of password and authentication security behavior.

create and manage their unique identifiers, such as decentralized identifiers (DIDs), and assert their identities without depending on centralized identity providers.
- *Decentralized identity infrastructure.* Decentralized authentication leverages the infrastructure and mechanisms provided by decentralized identity systems. This includes the use of cryptographic techniques, such as public key cryptography, to create and manage identity credentials, digital signatures, and secure communication channels.

1. *Verifiable credentials.* Verifiable credentials play a crucial role in decentralized authentication. Figure 10.2 discusses about the digitally signed credentials that attest to specific identity attributes or claims. Verifiable credentials can be issued by trusted parties, such as institutions or organizations, and associated with the individual's DID. These credentials can be presented to relying parties for authentication and verification purposes.
2. *Selective disclosure.* Decentralized authentication enables individuals to selectively disclose specific identity attributes or claims as needed. Figure 10.2 describes the features where instead of sharing their entire identity information, users can provide only the

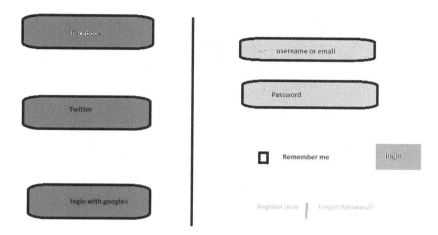

FIGURE 10.3 User interface for login credentials.

relevant attributes to different service providers, enhancing privacy and minimizing the exposure of personal data.

3. *Distributed trust networks.* Figure 10.3 describes how the decentralized authentication relies on distributed trust networks, where trust is established through consensus and cryptographic mechanisms. Trust can be built based on verifiable credentials issued by trusted entities and the use of decentralized consensus algorithms, such as blockchain, to validate and verify identity-related transactions.

4. Interoperability and portability. Decentralized authentication promotes interoperability and portability across different applications and services. Since it is not tied to a specific centralized identity provider, individuals can use their decentralized identity credentials across multiple platforms and ecosystems, reducing the need for redundant identity verification processes.

Further, Figure 10.3 also describes decentralized authentication, which provides individuals with greater control over their identities, enhances privacy and security, and reduces reliance on centralized authorities for authentication. By leveraging decentralized identity technologies and principles, decentralized authentication offers a more user-centric, resilient, and privacy-preserving approach to identity verification in the digital world.

10.16 IMPORTANCE OF DECENTRALIZED IDENTITY

Decentralized identity (DI) is important for several reasons, as it addresses various challenges and offers numerous benefits in the digital landscape. Here are some key reasons that decentralized identity is significant.

10.16.1 PRIVACY AND CONTROL

Decentralized identity puts individuals in control of their own personal data and identity information. In Figure 10.4, a "decentralized authentication interface" describes the module to enable the users to manage and share their identity attributes selectively, reducing the risk of personal information being collected, stored, and potentially abused by centralized entities. DI empowers individuals to determine when, how, and with whom their identity information is shared, enhancing privacy and giving users greater autonomy.

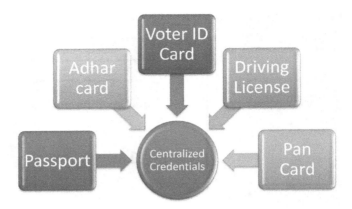

FIGURE 10.4 Decentralized identity of personal information.

10.16.2 SELF-SOVEREIGN IDENTITY

Decentralized identity aligns with the concept of self-sovereign identity, allowing individuals to assert their digital identities without reliance on centralized authorities or identity providers. Users can create their own unique identifiers, such as decentralized identifiers (DIDs), which they can use across various platforms, services, and ecosystems. Self-sovereign identity puts individuals in the driver's seat, granting them ownership and control over their digital identities.

10.16.3 INTEROPERABILITY AND PORTABILITY

Decentralized identity promotes interoperability and portability of identity credentials across different systems, platforms, and applications. With decentralized authentication interface standards and protocols, as shown in Figure 10.4, individuals can carry their identity credentials and verifiable proofs across multiple services without the need for redundant identity verification processes. This improves user experience, reduces friction, and enables seamless interactions in a connected digital environment.

10.16.4 TRUST AND SECURITY

Decentralized identity employs cryptographic techniques and distributed trust mechanisms to establish and validate identities. It reduces the risk of identity theft, impersonation, and fraud by enabling individuals and entities to verify identities through trusted attestations, digital signatures, and secure communication channels. Decentralized identity systems enhance trust and security in digital transactions, mitigating the reliance on centralized intermediaries and reducing vulnerabilities to single points of failure.

10.16.5 INCLUSION AND EMPOWERMENT

Decentralized identity has the potential to address identity gaps and empower individuals who lack traditional forms of identification, such as refugees, marginalized communities, or those without official documents. In Figure 10.4, the decentralized identity of personal information discusses how DI enabled individuals to assert their identities and access services, participate in the digital economy, and exercise their rights even without traditional identity credentials. It fosters inclusivity, reducing barriers to entry and expanding opportunities for underserved populations.

10.16.6 DATA BREACH RESILIENCE

Centralized databases containing personal data are attractive targets for hackers. Decentralized identity reduces the risk of massive data breaches since personal information is distributed across multiple nodes in a decentralized network. By eliminating central points of vulnerability, decentralized identity enhances data breach resilience and reduces the potential impact of data breaches on individuals' identities and privacy.

Overall, decentralized identity offers individuals greater control, privacy, security, and inclusivity in the digital world. By leveraging cryptographic techniques, distributed networks, and user-centric principles, decentralized identity systems redefine how identities are managed, shared, and verified, shifting power back to individuals while fostering a more trusted, secure, and user-friendly digital environment.

10.17 AN OVERVIEW OF DECENTRALIZED IDENTITY PROJECTS

Decentralized identity (DI). Decentralized identity of personal information, as show in Figure 10.4, is an initiative that aims to develop and implement systems, protocols, and standards for self-sovereign identity and decentralized identity management. These projects focus on empowering individuals, enhancing privacy, and promoting user-centric control over digital identities. Here is an overview of some notable decentralized identity projects (see Figures 10.5 and 10.6).

Microsoft decentralized identity. Microsoft's Identity Overlay Network (ION) is a decentralized identity project built on the Bitcoin blockchain. Figure 10.4 discusses the aims to enable decentralized identifiers (DIDs) and verifiable credentials to be anchored and resolved in a decentralized and scalable manner.

Hyperledger Indy, a decentralized identity system to prove true credentials, as shown in Figure 10.1, as a part of the Linux Foundation's Hyperledger Project, is an open-source project that provides a decentralized identity platform for creating and managing DIDs, verifiable credentials, and related identity components. Decentralized identity system to verify the users, as shown in Figure 10.2, discusses on interoperability and privacy-enhancing features. The module contains a centralized authority to issue centralized identity to the customers which are controlled by other

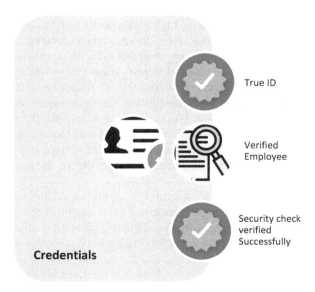

FIGURE 10.5 Decentralized identity systems to prove true credentials.

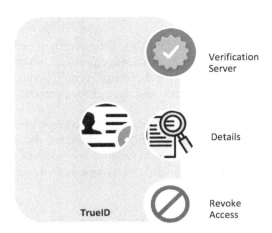

FIGURE 10.6   Decentralized identity system to verify the users.

users or any other third-party user. The centralized authority holds a major power than the other identities which are in the same association. Centralized identity leads to decomposition to generate separate identities, which enables storing the data in a cylindrical data warehouse, thereby giving authority to service providers than users. To control this, only the authorized users are given credentials to access all the data. Here, the same users with the common credential get logged into multiple websites of the same domain with a secured network channel. This identity helps the users remember less of the login credentials and, meanwhile, be able to access multiple web services.

10.18   CONCLUSIONS

The Decentralized Identity Foundation (DIF) is a consortium of organizations and individuals working on decentralized identity standards, protocols, and interoperability. DIF focuses on creating open-source technologies and promoting cross-industry collaboration to advance the field of decentralized identity.

The system in IOT works in a centralized network of digital integrated environment. Blockchain is one of the efficient technologies to provide high-end security to IOT-based systems to enable the concept of dynamic storage of data to enable end-to-end transmission of data traversal to provide product tracing and monitoring. Algorithms are designed to facilitate the throughput of transaction. High-level security is provided in blockchain to identify fraud that proves to be extremely efficient, as it provides data verification and a register-like structure. Further, blockchain is encouraged to create and collaborate on an intrusion-detection algorithm where the codes are interchanged through the journey of the entire exchange of data. Blockchain is used to solve the risk associated with the code exchange by maintaining integrity and transparency of data storage in different databases.

Blockchain plays a very important role in preserving the ACID property for RFIDs with mutual authentication of ultra-weight light to authenticate RFID protocol. Hence, blockchain is used to build trust in open environment.

We have tried to implement the security standards through blockchain method with the reference of existing components, along with some features and attributes inherited and further extended to describe the decentralized identity standards. The security build with blockchain technology proves to be robust as compared to other technologies, which have been proven to some extent in this book chapter.

We culminate by noting that developing on-chain decentralized identity with further extension of privacy and security algorithms should be encouraged for future development of blockchain technology.

REFERENCES

[1] Yaga, D., P. Mell, N. Roby, and K. Scarfone. *Blockchain Technology Overview*. https://doi.org/10.6028/nist.ir.8202

[2] Zheng, Z., Xie, S., Dai, H., Chen, X., & Wang, H. 2017. *An Overview of Blockchain Technology: Architecture, Consensus, and Future Trends*. Honolulu, HI, USA: IEEE. https://doi.org/10.1109/bigdatacongress.2017.85

[3] Saberi, S., M. Kouhizadeh, J. Sarkis*, and L. Shen. 2019. Blockchain technology and its relationships to sustainable supply chain management. *International Journal of Production Research* 57 (7): 2117–2135. https://doi.org/10.1080/00207543.2018.1533261.

[4] Crosby, M., P. Pattanayak, S. Verma, and V. Kalyanaraman. 2016. Blockchain technology: Beyond bitcoin. *Applied Innovation* 2: 6–9.

[5] Anghinolfi, D., R. Montemanni, M. Paolucci, and L. M. Gambardella. 2011. A hybrid particle swarm optimization approach for the sequential ordering problem. *Computers & Operations Research* 38 (7): 1076–1085.

[6] Barski, C., and C. Wilmer. 2016. The blockchain lottery: How miners are rewarded—CoinDesk. *CoinDesk RSS*. CoinDesk, 23 Nov. Web. 03 May 2016.

[7] Lee, T. B. 2015. Bitcoin's value is surging. Here are 5 charts on the growing bitcoin economy. *Vox*, N.p., 03 Nov. Web. 03 May 2016.

[8] Driscoll, S. 2013. How bitcoin works under the hood. *Imponderable Things*. 14 Jul. Web. 03 May 2016.

11 Charging Stations for E-Cars through Blockchain

Akshat Mistry and Sudhir Kumar Mohapatra

11.1 INTRODUCTION

Blockchain-powered EV charging is a game-changing technology with the potential to transform the electric vehicle market. It facilitates secure and transparent peer-to-peer energy transfers by using blockchain's decentralized nature, improving charging efficiency and empowering EV owners. We will look at the impact of blockchain-powered EV charging and its role in creating the future of sustainable mobility in this post.

The world is moving toward a low-carbon economy, and electric vehicles (EV) are an essential part of this transition. As EVs become more affordable and accessible, their sales are expected to grow exponentially, with a recent report by Bloomberg NEF estimating that EV sales will increase from 2.7 million in 2020 to 56 million by 2040. However, for EVs to reach their full potential, a reliable and efficient charging infrastructure is necessary.

Blockchain technology has emerged as a promising solution to address the challenges of scaling up the EV charging infrastructure. *Blockchain* is a decentralized, distributed ledger that records transactions in a secure and transparent manner. It has the potential to revolutionize the way we charge our EVs by providing a more efficient, secure, and transparent charging infrastructure.

India is one country that has recognized the potential of blockchain technology in the EV space. Despite accounting for only 0.5% of the global EV market, the Indian automobile industry is one of the fastest-growing markets for EVs, according to a 2019 white paper by the World Economic Forum. However, the lack of a robust charging infrastructure has been a significant barrier to EV adoption in India.

To address this challenge, the Indian government has set a target of installing 10,000 EV charging stations by 2022. However, a recent report by the CEEW Centre for Energy Finance suggests that India would need around 29 lakh public charging stations by 2030 to support EV adoption under the base case target of NITI Aayog. This highlights the urgent need for a scalable and reliable charging infrastructure.

Blockchain can help address this challenge by providing a decentralized and secure platform for managing EV charging stations. By leveraging blockchain, EV owners can securely access and pay for charging services, while charging station owners can securely manage and monetize their charging infrastructure. Additionally, blockchain can help reduce the operational costs of charging stations by automating billing and payment processes.

In this chapter, we will explore the key features of blockchain technology and its potential to revolutionize the way we charge our EVs. We will also examine the current state of EV charging infrastructure in India and how blockchain can help address the challenges of scaling up the charging infrastructure. By the end of this chapter, readers will gain a better understanding of how blockchain can help accelerate the adoption of EVs, by providing a scalable, secure, and transparent charging infrastructure.

11.1.1 SIMPLIFIED SETUP AND APPROVAL PROCESS

Blockchain technology can streamline the setup process for new EV charging infrastructure. By leveraging self-contract approval and registration mechanisms, blockchain eliminates the need for

DOI: 10.1201/9781003450306-13

cumbersome paperwork and reduces the time required for installation. Through smart contracts and distributed ledger technology, the entire process becomes more transparent and efficient.

11.1.2 Automated Payments and Billing

The integration of blockchain enables automated payments and billing for EV charging services. By eliminating manual billing processes, blockchain ensures accurate and transparent transactions. Smart contracts can be utilized to automatically initiate payment upon completion of charging, reducing friction for both users and operators. Moreover, blockchain's immutability guarantees a secure and tamperproof payment ecosystem.

11.1.3 Transparent Management of Complaints and Infrastructure Damage

Blockchain provides a transparent and accountable system for managing complaints and infrastructure damage in EV charging stations. Through distributed ledger technology, each reported issue is recorded immutably, creating an audit trail that facilitates timely resolutions. The transparent nature of blockchain instils trust among users and operators, enhancing the overall user experience.

11.1.4 Coordinated Access to Charging Services

In scenarios where a particular charging station is unavailable, blockchain can coordinate with nearby stations to ensure continuous access to charging services. Through smart contracts and decentralized coordination mechanisms, EV owners can seamlessly be redirected to operational stations, minimizing inconvenience. This coordination is enabled by blockchain's distributed nature and real-time updates on station availability.

11.1.5 Ensuring Maintenance and Reliability

Blockchain technology plays a vital role in ensuring the maintenance and reliability of EV charging infrastructure. By imposing penalties on infrastructure owners for poor maintenance and user redirection, blockchain incentivizes timely repairs and upkeep. Through automated monitoring and predefined criteria, blockchain fosters a culture of proactive maintenance, resulting in a reliable and efficient charging network.

11.1.6 Incentivizing Infrastructure Maintenance

Blockchain enables the incentivization of charging station owners for maintaining the quality of infrastructure. By defining criteria such as uptime targets, cleanliness, and customer service, blockchain automates the reward process. Owners who meet or exceed these criteria receive incentives, encouraging them to invest in infrastructure maintenance and deliver exceptional user experiences.

11.1.7 Promoting EV Adoption and Market Growth

The integration of blockchain technology in EV charging infrastructure enhances reliability, transparency, and user satisfaction. A well-maintained and coordinated charging network instils confidence in EV owners, spurring further adoption. As the charging infrastructure improves, the overall market for EVs grows, benefiting manufacturers, users, and the environment.

This chapter sheds light on the potential of blockchain technology in revolutionizing EV charging infrastructure. It covers various aspects of the proposed model, which combines multiple functionalities into a single blockchain solution, unlike dedicated blockchains for individual fields. The chapter also acknowledges the existing literature and solutions that have explored the application of blockchain in the EV industry.

Several areas within the EV industry have already witnessed proposed implementations of blockchain technology. These include power grid management, electrical supply management, and automated billing systems. By leveraging blockchain, these solutions aim to enhance the efficiency and transparency of operations, promoting the seamless integration of EV charging infrastructure with existing electrical systems. The proposed model in this chapter goes beyond these individual applications, offering a comprehensive approach that encompasses all aspects of EV charging infrastructure management within a single blockchain framework.

Furthermore, a literature review is conducted to provide insights into the existing blockchain-based solutions in the context of the EV industry. This review highlights the benefits and challenges encountered in previous studies and implementations. By drawing upon this body of research, the chapter provides a comprehensive understanding of the current state of blockchain adoption in EV charging infrastructure management.

It is important to acknowledge that successful implementation of blockchain in real-world scenarios requires careful consideration of technical, regulatory, and operational factors. Collaboration among various stakeholders, including government bodies, charging station operators, and technology providers, is crucial to ensure the seamless integration of blockchain technology and maximize its potential benefits. Ongoing research and development efforts will continue to address challenges and refine the proposed model. With a collaborative and innovative approach, blockchain holds the promise of significantly transforming the EV charging landscape and driving widespread adoption of electric vehicles.

11.2 LITERATURE REVIEW

Sharma et al. explore the existing protocols for anonymous auctions using blockchain technology [1]. The focus is on preserving bidder privacy and achieving verifiability in auction systems. The review highlights the use of cryptographic techniques such as zero-knowledge proofs, smart contracts, and public bulletin boards in maintaining bid confidentiality and integrity. However, the reviewed literature mainly addresses bid confidentiality, leaving room for the development of protocols ensuring bidder anonymity.

In response to this gap, the authors propose a new protocol that offers anonymity and verifiability in sealed-bid auctions. The protocol utilizes designated verifier ring signature (DVRS), commitment, and public key encryption (PKE) techniques. By leveraging these cryptographic building blocks, the protocol allows bidders to keep their identities and bid values secret, while the overall auction process remains publicly verifiable. Additionally, the protocol minimizes trust in the auctioneer's influence, ensures bid binding to prevent modifications, and provides a means for resolving disputes.

The contribution of this research lies in the introduction of a generic protocol that addresses the need for bidder anonymity in blockchain-based auctions. The protocol expands upon existing cryptographic techniques and offers a comprehensive solution for achieving privacy and verifiability. Future research in this area can build upon this protocol to further enhance the security and fairness of anonymous auction systems.

Chen et al. examine the existing research on sealed-bid auctions in the context of electronic auctions (e-auctions) [2]. While e-auctions offer advantages such as efficiency and expanded market reach, they also present challenges related to trust, collusion, and privacy. The review highlights the need for auction designs that achieve decentralization, privacy preservation, collusion resistance, and public verifiability. Various cryptographic techniques, including comparable encryption, homomorphic encryption, and secure multi-party computation, have been proposed to address these challenges. However, most existing solutions either compromise bid privacy or lack public verifiability and resistance to collusion. The review emphasizes the importance of simultaneously achieving these key features and identifies a research gap in the literature. Furthermore, the review introduces the potential of smart contracts in blockchain technology to enhance security and scalability in e-auctions. The proposed blockchain-based sealed-bid auction scheme leverages the properties of blockchain, zero-knowledge proofs, and anonymous veto networks to achieve bid price privacy, public verifiability, and decentralization. The scheme is evaluated based on its design goals, and experiments conducted on a simulated Ethereum test network demonstrate its efficiency and practicality. This literature review contributes to the advancement of secure and privacy-preserving e-auctions, providing insights for researchers and practitioners in the field.

Liu et al. propose an urgency-first charging (UFC) scheduling policy and a reservation-based CS-selection scheme to address the challenges of long charging time and uneven distribution of charging stations (CSs) for electric vehicles (EVs) [3]. The UFC policy prioritizes EVs based on their charging urgency, calculated using their charging demand and remaining parking duration. The CS-selection scheme selects the optimal CS with the minimum trip duration, considering real-time charging status and EVs' reservations. Simulation results demonstrate the advantages of the proposed schemes in improving user experience by shortening trip duration and fully charging more EVs before departure. The paper also discusses related works in EV charging scheduling and CS selection.

Flocea et al. proposes a custom reservation algorithm to address the limitations of the OCPP (open charge point protocol) standard for electric vehicle (EV) charging stations [4]. The algorithm generates reservation intervals based on the charging station's reservation and transaction history. The paper discusses the current state of EV adoption, challenges in finding available charging points, and the need for reservations for long-distance trips. It also reviews related work on congestion prevention, optimal distribution of energy resources, and reservation algorithms. The proposed algorithm aims to optimize the distribution of available charging resources, minimize queueing times, and increase user satisfaction. The solution is independent of the OCPP reservation method and operates through a central system, authorizing only the reservation creator to start the charging transaction.

Viziteu et al. proposes a solution for addressing multiple issues related to EV charging scheduling, such as congestion management, advance scheduling, and optimized trip planning [5]. The solution utilizes reinforcement learning algorithms and considers factors such as battery charge level, trip distance, available charging stations, and average speed. The novelty of the proposed solution lies in the scenario simulator that generates labelled datasets for training the algorithm. The paper discusses related work in the field, including studies on reinforcement learning, optimization strategies, and congestion management. The methodology section describes the implementation of the DQN reinforcement learning algorithm for smart reservation of charging points.

Zhong et al. discusses the challenges faced by current blockchain systems, including high transaction costs, network congestion, and low transaction rates [6]. To address these issues, a new payment scheme called the secure versatile light payment (SVLP) system is proposed. The SVLP system offers security comparable to existing blockchain systems while significantly reducing power consumption. It supports flexible payment and refunding processes, promotes divisibility in the denomination, and enables off-chain and offline transactions. The abstract highlights the practicality and versatility of the SVLP system and outlines its contributions, including a new payment system model, a modular construction, and a formal security analysis. Overall, the SVLP system provides a practical and efficient solution to enhance transaction speeds and scalability in blockchain systems.

Blockchain technology has shown potential in various areas beyond just cryptocurrencies [7–11]. Here is a bit more detail on how blockchain is being used in each of the areas mentioned:

Blockchain in healthcare. It can help in securely storing and sharing patient data, ensuring data integrity, and providing a transparent and auditable record of medical transactions and treatments.

Transfer contracts and wills. Blockchain can streamline the transfer of ownership for various assets like real estate and facilitate the execution of contracts and wills, ensuring transparency and reducing the need for intermediaries.

Supply chain management. Blockchain can enhance transparency and traceability in supply chains by recording every step in a product's journey. This helps prevent fraud, ensure quality control, and improve efficiency.

Protection of copyright and royalties. Blockchain provides a way to time-stamp and secure intellectual property rights. It can help track digital content usage, ensure proper attribution, and automate royalty distribution.

Voting. Blockchain can offer secure and transparent voting systems that help prevent voter fraud and ensure the integrity of election results. Each vote is recorded on the blockchain, making manipulation more difficult.

Cryptocurrency. The most well-known use case, cryptocurrencies like Bitcoin and Ethereum are built on blockchain technology, enabling secure and decentralized digital transactions.

Internet of Things (IoT). Blockchain can enhance the security and interoperability of IoT devices by providing a decentralized and tamperproof ledger for device communication and data exchange.

Asset administration. Blockchain can be used for tracking ownership and provenance of physical and digital assets, making transactions more efficient and secure, whether it is real estate, art, or even virtual items in video games.

These use cases highlight the potential of blockchain technology to provide transparency, security, and efficiency across various industries. However, it is important to note that while blockchain offers promising solutions, it also comes with its own set of challenges, such as scalability, energy consumption, and regulatory considerations. The implementation and success of blockchain projects often depend on various factors, including the specific use case, technology maturity, and broader adoption within the industry.

11.3 PROPOSED BLOCKCHAIN-BASED FRAMEWORK

11.3.1 BIDDING MECHANISM FOR NEW EV INFRASTRUCTURE PROJECT CONTRACT

The proposed architecture presented in this chapter serves as a high-level conceptual representation of the intricate e-bidding blockchain-based solutions (see Figure 11.1). It is important to note that the encryption algorithm and architecture described herein are subject to potential replacement by industry-standard techniques, as outlined in the literature review section. As the field of e-auctions continues to evolve, advancements in cryptographic methodologies may lead to the adoption of more robust and established practices. Researchers and practitioners are encouraged to refer to the literature review section for up-to-date information on the industry-standard techniques and to consider their applicability to their specific use cases.

This chapter presents an innovative approach to secure and privacy-preserving bidding processes through the integration of a semi-public blockchain solution. In this proposed system, bidders actively participate as nodes within the blockchain network, ensuring transparency and accountability throughout the process.

To protect the confidentiality of individual bid amounts, a robust homomorphic encryption technique is employed. *Homomorphic encryption* is a cryptographic method that allows computations to be performed on encrypted data without decrypting it. Bidders encrypt their quoted values using homomorphic encryption before submitting them to the blockchain. This technique ensures that bid amounts remain hidden from other participants, preserving privacy and preventing bid manipulation.

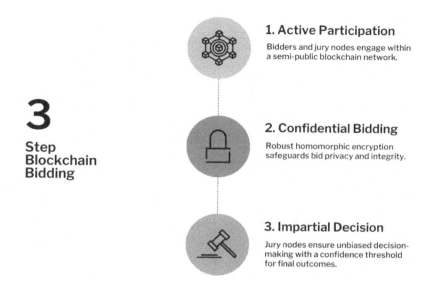

1. Active Participation

Bidders and jury nodes engage within a semi-public blockchain network.

2. Confidential Bidding

Robust homomorphic encryption safeguards bid privacy and integrity.

3. Impartial Decision

Jury nodes ensure unbiased decision-making with a confidence threshold for final outcomes.

3

Step
Blockchain
Bidding

FIGURE 11.1   The proposed model for bidding mechanism for new EV infrastructure.

At the conclusion of the bidding period, a consensus mechanism is triggered to determine the winning bid. Leveraging the power of homomorphic comparison, the encrypted bids are evaluated without revealing the actual bid amounts, guaranteeing fairness and privacy. Homomorphic comparison allows for comparisons to be made on encrypted data, enabling the identification of the smallest bid without disclosing the precise amounts. This process ensures that bidders cannot deduce each other's bid amounts or manipulate the system based on bid information.

To enhance the decision-making process and minimize conflicts, a select group of jury nodes is strategically included within the blockchain network. These nodes contribute to an unbiased consensus and assist in resolving any discrepancies that may arise during the determination of the winner. A predefined confidence threshold is utilized to ascertain the validity of the final decision, ensuring a high level of confidence in the outcome.

To uphold the integrity of the system, severe penalties are imposed on nodes found to have manipulated data or arrived at incorrect conclusions. This acts as a deterrent against fraudulent activities and reinforces the trustworthiness of the bidding process. Such penalized nodes are also barred from future bidding activities to maintain the integrity of future competitions.

In this proposed system, the identities of bidders are safeguarded using unique bidder IDs or cryptographic hashing techniques. The encrypted bids are sorted based on their values without revealing the actual amounts (see Figure 11.2). Only the winning bidder is informed of their successful bid by decrypting the amount using their private key, provided by the winner themselves. This ensures that the winner's identity and bid amount remain confidential, while other participants remain unaware of the winning bidder and their bid amount, preserving privacy and maintaining the overall integrity of the bidding process.

This research offers a comprehensive and secure solution for conducting bidding processes by harnessing the potential of blockchain technology, homomorphic encryption, and consensus mechanisms. By providing confidentiality, fairness, and accountability, this approach addresses key challenges faced in traditional bidding systems and lays the foundation for a trusted and efficient bidding environment. The integration of homomorphic encryption ensures that bid amounts remain hidden, while enabling accurate comparisons and decision-making, making it well-suited for this solution.

Blockchain Bidding Process Simplified

Bidders & Jury Nodes

o Bidders participate, while jury nodes monitor transactions in a semi-public blockchain network.

Secure Bidding

o Bidders use robust encryption for confidential bid submission via blockchain.

Consensus & Privacy

o Homomorphic encryption ensures confidentiality during bid evaluation, aided by impartial jury nodes.

Confidence in Outcomes

o A predefined threshold authenticates final decisions, penalizing data manipulation for system integrity.

Bidder Anonymity

o Bidder identities remain confidential throughout, preserving privacy.

Accurate Comparisons

o Encrypted bids are sorted by value for precise evaluation while safe guarding confidentiality.

Triumphant Bidder

o The successful bidder is discreetly informed and can access decrypted bid amount using their private key.

Transparent Conclusion

o The official winner is declared, ensuring a secure and meticulous process.

FIGURE 11.2   Simplified components of blockchain bidding process.

11.3.2 Automatic Smart Pre-Reservation System for Long-Route EV Rides

An efficient and reliable charging infrastructure is crucial for supporting long-distance travel in the ever-growing electric vehicle (EV) market. However, the lack of coordination between EV owners and charging stations poses a significant challenge when planning long-route trips. To overcome this issue, we propose an innovative automatic smart pre-reservation system for long-route EV rides which utilizes blockchain technology to enhance the coordination and optimization of charging infrastructure (see Figure 11.3).

This chapter presents a comprehensive solution comprising multiple layers. At the forefront, a user-friendly client application acts as an information hub, leveraging intelligent route suggestion algorithms to provide real-time alerts for routes lacking adequate charging facilities. The application streamlines decision-making processes while intricate calculations occur on the blockchain, ensuring accuracy and efficiency.

The core blockchain architecture forms the second layer of our proposed system, incorporating a sophisticated custom smart reservation algorithm (to be detailed in the literature review section) while eliminating the need for manual searches using geospatial tools to find nearby charging

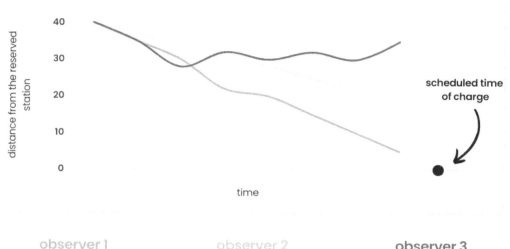

observer 1

It is highly probable to arrive punctually due to factors such as the anticipated rate of slope decline and the presence of a negative slope.

observer 2

There is a lower likelihood of being punctual. This is attributed to the fact that, despite having a negative slope, the rate of decline does not meet the expected standard.

observer 3

Displays entirely random behavior and is highly improbable to adhere to the scheduled charging time.

FIGURE 11.3 The criteria for meeting the scheduled time of charge.

infrastructure. This integration empowers the system to intelligently reserve appropriate charging ports at designated stations along the planned route, considering waiting time as a critical factor. By harnessing the transparency, immutability, and decentralized nature of blockchain technology, our system enhances the reliability and efficiency of charging infrastructure allocation.

Moreover, building upon the existing ideas highlighted in the literature review section, we introduce a dynamic remapping of the port reservation process. This advanced functionality effectively addresses challenges posed by heavily congested charging infrastructure. The system holds users accountable by imposing penalties for failing to adhere to scheduled charging times, ensuring fairness. Additionally, it employs dynamic remapping techniques at less-crowded stations, flexibly reassigning charging ports based on users' travel patterns to optimize resource utilization.

To further enhance adaptability, our system introduces the concept of semi-reserved ports. While certain ports are initially reserved for specific users, they can be allocated to other EV owners in urgent need of charging when the station experiences increased traffic.

Furthermore, our system recognizes the presence of on-site charging ports at the charging stations, which cannot be reserved or prebooked. These on-site ports cater to spontaneous trips or local EV owners who require immediate charging without prior planning. By considering both reserved ports and on-site ports, our system maximizes the utilization of available charging resources and minimizes penalties for users encountering unexpected delays or unforeseen circumstances.

While users maintain the freedom to customize their charging plans and modify reservations according to their preferences, our system implements a balanced approach. Excessive and urgent customizations may incur fines, discouraging misuse of the system while still allowing reasonable flexibility.

By combining the power of blockchain technology and intelligent algorithms, our proposed automatic smart pre-reservation system revolutionizes the planning and coordination of long-route EV rides. It streamlines the reservation process, optimizes charging infrastructure utilization, reduces waiting time, and enhances the overall user experience, contributing to the growth of sustainable transportation networks (see Figure 11.4). This groundbreaking system represents a significant advancement in the field, providing valuable insights for researchers, policymakers, and industry practitioners in the realm of smart transportation systems.

Streamlined Electric Vehicle Charging Reservation Process

1. Streamlined User Experience

o Users engage with an intuitive client application, acting as a central information hub. Intelligent route suggestion algorithms evaluate multiple variables, issuing real-time alerts for routes with insufficient charging infrastructure.

2. Blockchain Synergy

o The core blockchain framework seamlessly incorporates a sophisticated, tailor-made smart reservation algorithm, obviating the need for manual searches via location-based services. The blockchain executes intricate calculations, ensuring immediate and accurate decision-making.

3. Efficient Port Allocation

o The system judiciously reserves suitable charging ports at designated stations along the preplanned route, factoring in waiting times as a pivotal consideration.

4. Adaptive Port Remapping

o Expanding upon concepts elucidated in the literature review, the system integrates a dynamic remapping technique to address challenges presented by heavily congested charging infrastructure. Users who deviate from their designated charging schedule may incur penalties, fostering equity and responsibility.

5. Resource Optimization

o In less congested stations, dynamic remapping strategies flexibly reassign charging ports based on users' travel patterns, optimizing resource utilization. The system maximizes the utilization of available charging infrastructure, while minimizing penalties for users facing unexpected delays or unforeseen circumstances.

6. Semi-Reserved Ports

o The system introduces the concept of semi-reserved ports initially designated for specific users. During periods of heightened traffic, these ports can be reallocated to other EV owners with urgent charging needs.

7. On-Site Charging Ports

o The system recognizes the existence of on-site charging ports at certain stations, which cannot be reserved or prebooked. These on-site ports cater to spontaneous trips or local EV owners requiring immediate, unplanned charging.

8. Customization and Flexibility

o Users retain the freedom to personalize their charging plans and adjust reservations in line with their preferences. However, excessive, and last-minute customizations may incur fines to deter system misuse, while permitting reasonable adaptability.

FIGURE 11.4   Streamlined electric vehicle charging reservation process.

11.3.2.1   Challenges with Pre-Reservation Methodology

The arrival time at the station can fluctuate due to traffic conditions, user choices like detours or selecting alternative routes, vehicle-related concerns, and unforeseeable events, such as accidents or tire punctures. Consequently, the model needs to account for uncertainty and emulate the actions of a typical user in exceptional scenarios. Achieving such behavior may necessitate intricate logic but might still not perfectly replicate a real individual's actions.

11.3.3   ENHANCED PAYMENT FRAMEWORK

The proliferation of electric vehicles (EVs) has prompted the need for innovative approaches to enhance the charging infrastructure and payment systems. In this chapter, we propose an integration of the enhanced automated payment system (EAPS) into the existing secure versatile light payment (SVLP) mechanism to address the challenges faced by current payment systems.

The SVLP system is a new payment scheme that offers security comparable to existing blockchain systems while significantly reducing power consumption. However, to further enhance the SVLP system and accommodate the evolving needs of the electric vehicle market, we introduce two new modes of payment through the EAPS integration: wallet auto-debit and a first-pay-then-charge model.

The wallet auto-debit mode enables users to link their payment wallets directly to the SVLP system, facilitating seamless and automatic deduction of charging costs. This mode simplifies the payment process for EV owners, enhancing their charging experience.

Additionally, the first-pay-then-charge model introduces a novel approach where users make a payment up front before initiating the charging process. This model ensures that EV owners have sufficient balance in their wallets to cover the charging costs, reducing the risk of incomplete transactions and optimizing the charging infrastructure utilization.

Furthermore, we propose incorporating a personalized charging rate calculator algorithm into the SVLP system through the EAPS integration. This algorithm considers the profitability for both the charging infrastructure providers and EV owners, enabling them to negotiate and establish charging rates that align with their unique requirements. By incorporating this algorithm into the payment system, we promote fairness, transparency, and trust among stakeholders.

Through the integration of the EAPS into the SVLP system, we present a practical and efficient solution to enhance transaction speeds, scalability, and user experience in the charging ecosystem. This integration fosters collaboration, maximizes profitability for providers, and contributes to the continued growth and sustainability of the electric vehicle industry.

For further details on the secure versatile light payment (SVLP) system, please refer to the literature review section of this document.

11.3.3.1   Models of Payment

11.3.3.1.1   Wallet Auto-Debit Model

The wallet auto-debit mode simplifies the payment process by enabling users to register their payment wallets with the SVLP system (see Figure 11.5). When an EV owner connects their vehicle to a charging station, the system automatically identifies the user and calculates the charging cost based on various factors. Subsequently, the system deducts the calculated cost from the user's registered payment wallet, ensuring a seamless and hassle-free experience.

11.3.3.1.2   First-Pay-Then-Charge Model

The first-pay-then-charge model offers an alternative approach for EV owners who either have insufficient balance in their payment wallets or prefer not to set up wallet functionalities

Process Workflow

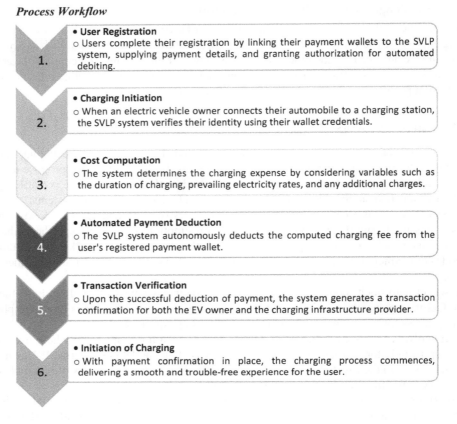

1.
- **User Registration**
  o Users complete their registration by linking their payment wallets to the SVLP system, supplying payment details, and granting authorization for automated debiting.

2.
- **Charging Initiation**
  o When an electric vehicle owner connects their automobile to a charging station, the SVLP system verifies their identity using their wallet credentials.

3.
- **Cost Computation**
  o The system determines the charging expense by considering variables such as the duration of charging, prevailing electricity rates, and any additional charges.

4.
- **Automated Payment Deduction**
  o The SVLP system autonomously deducts the computed charging fee from the user's registered payment wallet.

5.
- **Transaction Verification**
  o Upon the successful deduction of payment, the system generates a transaction confirmation for both the EV owner and the charging infrastructure provider.

6.
- **Initiation of Charging**
  o With payment confirmation in place, the charging process commences, delivering a smooth and trouble-free experience for the user.

FIGURE 11.5 Wallet auto-debit model workflow.

(see Figure 11.6). Upon connecting their vehicle to a charging station, EV owners select this model, prompting the SVLP system to initiate direct payment method. Then the system guides them to make a payment through the registered payment method before initiating the charging process. Once the payment is successfully processed, the system confirms the transaction, enabling the EV owner to proceed with the charging process with the assurance that the charging costs are covered in advance.

11.3.4 Personalized Charging Rate Calculator Algorithm

In the proposed integration of the enhanced automated payment system (EAPS) into the existing secure versatile light payment (SVLP) mechanism, a significant aspect of enhancement lies in the ability to offer customizable, personalized rate calculation mechanisms. This feature enables both private sectors and EV owners to customize the rate calculation process according to their specific needs.

For private sectors, the integration of custom logic for rate calculation provides the flexibility to incorporate their unique business models and pricing strategies. This customization allows private sectors to deploy their proprietary algorithms and decision-making processes, aligning the rate calculation with their specific goals and objectives. Alongside this customizability, the system also provides a baseline rule-based rate calculation model, ensuring a standardized approach for rate determination.

On the other hand, EV owners or clients can benefit from personalized pricing options tailored to their individual preferences and requirements. The system offers the capability to generate

Process Workflow

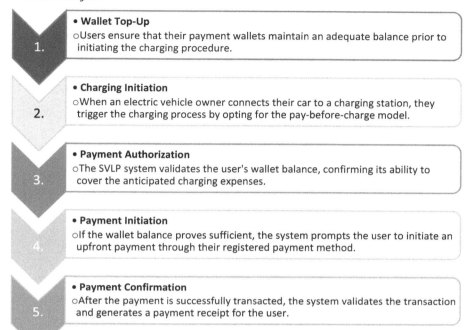

1. • **Wallet Top-Up**
   o Users ensure that their payment wallets maintain an adequate balance prior to initiating the charging procedure.

2. • **Charging Initiation**
   o When an electric vehicle owner connects their car to a charging station, they trigger the charging process by opting for the pay-before-charge model.

3. • **Payment Authorization**
   o The SVLP system validates the user's wallet balance, confirming its ability to cover the anticipated charging expenses.

4. • **Payment Initiation**
   o If the wallet balance proves sufficient, the system prompts the user to initiate an upfront payment through their registered payment method.

5. • **Payment Confirmation**
   o After the payment is successfully transacted, the system validates the transaction and generates a payment receipt for the user.

6. • **Charging Onset**
   o With payment confirmation secured, the SVLP system grants the EV owner permission to commence the charging process, guaranteeing that the associated costs are pre-funded.

FIGURE 11.6   First-pay-then-charge model workflow.

personalized prices or costs based on factors such as charging demand, time of use, loyalty programs, or any other relevant parameters. This personalized approach empowers EV owners to optimize their charging expenses, select the most cost-effective options, and align the charging experience with their specific needs.

By offering these two forms of personalization, the integrated EAPS and the SVLP system create a dynamic and adaptable environment for all stakeholders involved in the charging ecosystem. Private sectors can leverage their expertise and strategies to determine competitive pricing models, while EV owners can enjoy a charging experience that is tailored to their preferences and budget.

It is worth noting that the implementation of personalized rate calculation mechanisms for private sectors and EV owners builds upon existing research and industry practices (see Figure 11.7). The literature review section provides in-depth insights into various approaches, algorithms, and studies related to personalized rate calculation in the context of electric vehicle charging. Researchers and practitioners are encouraged to explore these references for a comprehensive understanding of the available techniques and their applicability to specific use cases.

By integrating personalized rate calculation mechanisms, the EAPS and the SVLP system contribute to a more customer-centric and efficient charging ecosystem. The flexibility provided to private sectors and the customization options offered to EV owners foster a mutually beneficial environment, promoting competitiveness, satisfaction, and sustainability in the electric vehicle industry.

Features Summarised

┌───┐
│ **Charging Rate Negotiation** │
├───┤
│ ○ EV owners and charging infrastructure providers engage in a negotiation process to establish customized charging rates. │
└───┘

┌───┐
│ **Algorithm Incorporation** │
├───┤
│ ○ The integration of the personalized charging rate calculator algorithm, a component of the Enhanced Automated Payment System (EAPS), considers various factors, including electricity expenses, infrastructure upkeep costs, and profit margin preferences for both stakeholders. │
└───┘

┌───┐
│ **Rate Computation** │
├───┤
│ ○ Utilizing the mutually agreed-upon parameters, the algorithm computes a charging rate that is specific to the EV owner and the charging infrastructure provider involved in the transaction. │
└───┘

┌───┐
│ **Transparency and Concurrence** │
├───┤
│ ○ The SVLP system presents the computed charging rate to both parties for review and mutual consent, thereby promoting transparency and building trust within the charging ecosystem. │
└───┘

┌───┐
│ **Rate Implementation** │
├───┤
│ ○ Following consensus, the system seamlessly integrates the negotiated charging rate into the payment framework, enabling precise cost calculations and equitable compensation for infrastructure providers. │
└───┘

FIGURE 11.7 Financial layer components summarized.

11.3.5 Overall Architecture

The blockchain-based EV charging solution we have designed is a comprehensive system that comprises several key components, each playing a pivotal role in ensuring the efficiency and reliability of electric vehicle charging infrastructure (see Figure 11.8).

At the core of this system is the reservation management component, which acts as the orchestrator of charging resources. It employs a sophisticated adaptive port re-mapping algorithm that dynamically reallocates charging ports based on real-time demand and usage patterns. This algorithm optimizes resource allocation, guaranteeing that charging ports are utilized effectively. Situated alongside is the decision-making layer, serving as the brain of the system. This layer harnesses data from diverse sources to make informed decisions regarding port assignments, scheduling, and user preferences. It ensures that EV owners enjoy optimal charging experiences. Simultaneously, the resource optimization layer takes care of the nitty-gritty, focusing on factors like waiting times, congestion, and infrastructure maintenance, all to ensure that charging resources are distributed efficiently and equitably.

To complement the reservation management component, the payment framework offers a robust and secure payment system. It boasts the payment models layer, allowing for flexible payment options such as wallet auto-debit and first-pay-then-charge models. Additionally, the transaction verification layer employs blockchain technology to guarantee transparent and tamperproof financial transactions. Meanwhile, the rate negotiation layer fosters fair rate agreements, promoting trust within the ecosystem by empowering EV owners and infrastructure providers to customize charging rates.

Integrating EV charging infrastructure with the broader power grid is a key focus of the power grid management component. It encompasses critical aspects such as overload management to

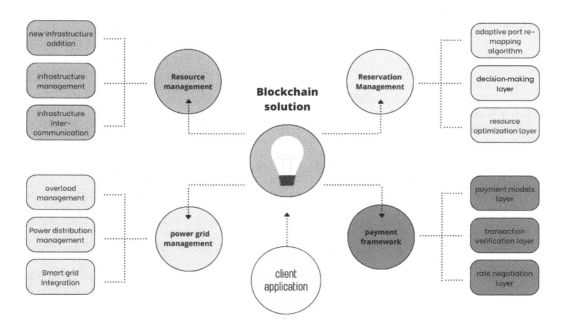

FIGURE 11.8 Overall architecture.

prevent grid disruptions, power distribution management for efficient electricity allocation, and smart grid integration, enhancing grid reliability and enabling demand response. This component acknowledges the pivotal role EV charging plays in the broader energy landscape.

Finally, the resource management component oversees the growth and maintenance of EV charging infrastructure. It comprises layers for new infrastructure addition, addressing the expansion of charging infrastructure, and infrastructure management, which ensures the ongoing functionality and reliability of deployed charging stations. The infrastructure inter-communication layer facilitates seamless information exchange between charging stations and external systems, enabling efficient coordination.

In sum, our blockchain-based solution is a holistic approach to electric vehicle charging, bringing together cutting-edge technology and meticulous resource management to offer a seamless, secure, and efficient charging experience for both EV owners and service providers.

11.4 CONCLUSION

The proposed blockchain-based architecture represents a transformative shift in the EV charging landscape. By leveraging blockchain's security, transparency, and efficiency, combined with innovative features like bidding mechanisms, pre-reservation systems, and enhanced payment frameworks, this architecture addresses the complex challenges of EV charging while fostering a user-centric and sustainable ecosystem.

It is crucial to acknowledge that the successful implementation of this architecture requires collaboration among stakeholders, including government bodies, charging station operators, and technology providers. Continuous research and development efforts will refine and optimize the proposed model, maximizing its potential benefits.

In conclusion, this architecture holds the promise of significantly transforming the EV charging landscape, promoting widespread adoption of electric vehicles, and contributing to a greener and more sustainable future.

REFERENCES

1. Sharma, Gaurav, et al. "Anonymous fair auction on blockchain." In *2021 11th IFIP International Conference on New Technologies, Mobility and Security (NTMS)*. IEEE, 2021.
2. Chen, Biwen, et al. "SBRAC: Blockchain-based sealed-bid auction with bidding price privacy and public verifiability." *Journal of Information Security and Applications* 65 (2022): 103082.
3. Liu, Shuohan, et al. "Reservation-based EV charging recommendation concerning charging urgency policy." *Sustainable Cities and Society* 74 (2021): 103150.
4. Flocea, Radu, et al. "Electric vehicle smart charging reservation algorithm." *Sensors* 22.8 (2022): 2834.
5. Viziteu, Andrei, et al. "Smart scheduling of electric vehicles based on reinforcement learning." *Sensors* 22.10 (2022): 3718.
6. Zhong, Lin, et al. "A secure versatile light payment system based on blockchain." *Future Generation Computer Systems* 93 (2019): 327–337.
7. Aggarwal, S., et al. "Blockchain for smart communities: Applications, challenges, and opportunities." *Journal of Network and Computer Applications* 144 (2019): 13–48.
8. Arias, M.B., et al. "Electric vehicle charging demand forecasting model based on big data technologies." *Applied Energy* 183 (2016): 327–339.
9. Chen, L., et al. "Blockchain based searchable encryption for electronic health record sharing." *Future Generation Computer Systems* 95 (2019): 420–429.
10. Ben-Sasson, E., et al. Zerocash: Decentralized anonymous payments from bitcoin. In *2014 IEEE Symposium on Security and Privacy*, pages 459–474. IEEE, 2014. DOI: 10.1109/SP.2014.36.
11. Blass, E.-O. and F. Kerschbaum. Strain: A secure auction for blockchains. In *ESORICS*, volume 11098 of LNCS, pages 87–110. Springer, 2018.

12 To Build a Shared Charging Network for Electric Vehicles Based on Blockchain Technology

Yajing Wang, Yaodong Yang, and Ting Du

12.1 INTRODUCTION

12.1.1 Rapidly Growing Electric Vehicle Market

With the continuous deterioration of the natural environment, people have become increasingly concerned about carbon emissions and global environmental changes. In light of this, electric vehicles (EVs) have gradually taken center stage, becoming the primary way of transportation. This has led to rapid growth in the electric vehicle market, with data indicating a substantial share of new car users being EV users in recent years in China, the United States, and Europe. Over the past five years, the annual average growth rate of global electric vehicle sales has exceeded 20%. In some countries, regulations have even been enacted to require the complete phase-out of traditional gasoline-powered cars from the market, as shown in Table 12.1.

As of the end of 2021, the sales of new energy vehicles (NEVs) in Europe reached approximately 2.3 million units, showing a year-on-year growth of about 70%. In the United States, NEV sales reached 630,000 units, marking a year-on-year increase of 114%. The International Energy Agency (IEA) predicts that by 2030, Europe and the United States will see NEV sales reach 7.3 million units and 3.1 million units, respectively [1]. In 2021, among the top three European countries with the highest NEV penetration rates, Norway led the pack with a penetration rate exceeding 86%. Norway's NEV sales amounted to 153,000 units, with a year-on-year growth of 44.5%. Sweden achieved a penetration rate of 45%, with sales of 47,000 units, marking a year-on-year growth of 70.5%. Finland had a penetration rate of 30.8%, with sales of 30,300 units and year-on-year growth of 73.3%. In the same year, NEV sales in the United States reached approximately 640,000 units, showing a remarkable year-on-year increase of 114.2%, but the penetration rate remained at only 4.44%.

In comparison, China's automobile sales for the first ten months of 2022 reached 21.97 million units, accounting for 33% of global sales and ranking first in the world. China's sales of new energy vehicles (NEV) reached 6.884 million units, a year-on-year growth of 61.6%, representing 63.6% of the global NEV sales of 10.824 million units. This is a significant increase from the 53.0% share in 2021.

If we extrapolate this trend, the global sales of NEV are projected to reach 52.12 million units by 2030, with an estimated global NEV stock of around 300 million vehicles. In comparison, as of 2022, the global automobile stock stood at 1.446 billion vehicles, with annual sales of 810.5 million units. Clearly, this projection is conservative, indicating that the revolution in clean energy transfer is still in its early stages. The emergence of greener and more sustainable transportation will be a vast and expansive journey in the years to come.

DOI: 10.1201/9781003450306-14

TABLE 12.1
Forbidden Sale of Fuel Vehicle Timetable

Country	Forbidden Sale of Gasoline-Powered Vehicle Time (year)
Norway	2025
Germany	2030
Netherlands	2030
India	2030
Scotland	2032
France	2040
UK	2040

12.1.2 INADEQUATE INFRASTRUCTURE HINDERS THE EV MARKET

Electric vehicles are gradually replacing traditional gasoline-powered vehicles, signaling that new methods of energy replenishment will replace the widely distributed gas station currently in use. However, traditional commercial charging piles are primarily controlled by centralized businesses, such as China's State Grid, resulting in high operational costs. For EV users, using these charging piles is expensive, and there are limited access ports.

The inadequate development of new energy infrastructure has consistently been one of the major concerns for consumers when it comes to purchasing electric vehicles, which hinders the expansion of the electric vehicle market. A survey conducted in China (among over 1,000 consumers) revealed that the primary reasons cited by respondents for not purchasing electric vehicles were the scarcity of public charging facilities and safety concerns, accounting for 25% and 20%, respectively.

In early 2022, Consumer Reports surveyed over 8,000 American respondents, revealing that 61% of those surveyed expressed concerns regarding the charging infrastructure [2].

In recent years, as electric vehicle battery capacities have increased, pure electric driving ranges have also improved. To extend the driving range, automakers have been adding larger batteries to their EVs, which have helped alleviate "range anxiety" but has also brought forward the issue of "charging anxiety." Therefore, the charging dilemma has been considered the "last mile" challenge in the promotion of electric vehicles. Developing charging infrastructure is crucial in addressing consumers' concerns about EV range limitations (range anxiety) and is essential for the widespread adoption of electric vehicles.

12.1.3 VEHICLE-TO-CHARGING-PILE RATIO—A KEY INDICATOR

The term "vehicle-to-charging-pile ratio" refers to the ratio between the number of new energy vehicles and the number of charging piles. The vehicle-to-charging-pile ratio is a key metric for assessing the level of charging infrastructure development [3]. A lower ratio implies a more abundant supply of charging piles, making charging more convenient. In theory, the satisfaction of new energy vehicle owners with the charging network should be directly proportional to the decrease in the vehicle-to-charging-pile ratio. However, in practice, this ratio is not the sole metric to address "range anxiety." The application of new energy vehicles in the "last mile" is much more complex than simply having a 1:1 vehicle-to-charging-pile ratio. The key factors affecting the user experience of charging piles are whether the layout of charging piles is reasonable and whether the operational efficiency can meet the needs of users. These considerations are what truly impact the usability of charging piles.

What is the current situation globally regarding this indicator? As of the end of 2021, the United States had a total of 2.3 million new energy vehicles with 130,000 public charging piles, resulting in a public-vehicle-to-charging-pile ratio of 18:1. If we further break down these 130,000 public charging piles, there were approximately 110,000 AC chargers and only 20,000 DC fast chargers.

In Europe, the NEV stock reached 5.5 million vehicles, with 330,000 public charging piles, resulting in a public-vehicle-to-charging-pile ratio of 16.7:1. Among these, there were approximately 300,000 AC chargers and around 30,000 DC fast chargers. It is important to note that the vehicle-to-charging-pile ratio varies significantly among European countries. While the demand for NEVs is high, the construction of charging piles has progressed relatively slowly, leading to disparities in the vehicle-to-charging-pile ratio.

According to data from the International Energy Agency, the average vehicle-to-charging-pile ratio in the European Union in 2021 was 14:1. However, some European countries, such as Germany, the United Kingdom, Spain, and Sweden, had vehicle-to-charging-pile ratios exceeding 20:1. France and Italy also had ratios exceeding 10:1. Norway, despite having a high penetration of NEVs, faced a significant charging infrastructure gap, resulting in a vehicle-to-charging-pile ratio of 33.6:1.

The situation in China deserves a detailed analysis. In 2022, driven by both policy and market, China continued to experience explosive growth in the field of new energy vehicles. China's NEV production and sales reached 7.058 million and 6.887 million units, respectively, maintaining its global leadership for the eighth consecutive year. This represented year-on-year growth of 96.9% and 93.4%, with a market share of 25.6%, an increase of 12.1 percentage points from the previous year. By the end of 2022, the cumulative NEV stock in China reached 13.1 million units, accounting for 3.14% of the total automotive fleet of 417 million vehicles. In 2022, the number of charging piles for NEVs in China grew by nearly 100%. The charging infrastructure reached a total of 5.2 million units, with approximately 650,000 of them being public charging piles and over 1.9 million being private charging facilities. When calculated against the total NEV stock of 13.1 million units, China achieved an impressive vehicle-to-charging-pile ratio of 2.519:1 by the end of 2022. According to the "Electric Vehicle Charging Infrastructure Development Guidelines (2015–2020)," the target for China is to achieve a 1:1 vehicle-to-charging-pile ratio by 2020, which means one NEV has one charging pile [4]. While China has not reached this goal yet, it reflects the forward-looking and ambitious nature.

However, the calculated vehicle-to-charging-pile ratio in this manner is far from reflecting the real experience of new energy vehicle owners. For instance, by the end of 2022, there were 13.1 million NEVs and 5.2 million charging piles in China, with 3.4 million of them being private charging piles. Due to the exclusive nature of private charging piles, as many as 9.7 million NEVs without private charging piles can only rely on 1.8 million public charging piles for service. For these 9.7 million NEV users, the vehicle-to-charging-pile ratio is not 2.5:1 but 5.4:1. To make matters worse, over the past decade, the installed 1.8 million public chargers have exhibited a variety of models, specifications, with some poorly located and underutilized. Some remain out of service due to poor maintenance or improper use. The annual decline in the vehicle-to-charging-pile ratio is merely an illusion, and for charger-less vehicles, the challenge of charging has not been alleviated.

12.1.4   CHALLENGES FOR EV CHARGING

With the increasing popularity of electric vehicles, the electric vehicle charging industry is rapidly expanding. Currently, the global charging pile has entered a period of rapid growth. As the number of electric vehicles surges, there is a growing demand for charging infrastructure that is multi-network, convenient, and readily accessible. In 2021, hundreds of thousands of new charging piles were installed worldwide. According to data from the International Energy Agency, by the end of 2020, there were already 740,000 charging piles globally, compared to 500,000 in the previous year. Additionally, IEA data shows that in 2021, global EV sales increased by 60% compared to the previous year [1]. In 2021, the global charging pile market reached several billion dollars and is poised for rapid growth. According to forecasts by Market-and-Market, the charging pile market is expected to have an average annual growth rate of over 25% from 2020 to 2025.

However, this industry is still in its early stages and faces some challenges that need to be addressed.

12.1.4.1   Lack of Charging Infrastructure

Currently, the number of charging piles and the charging network are insufficient to support the future development of the EV industry. While EV manufacturers have made significant efforts in the development of charging piles and some medium-sized charging networks have been established through the initiatives of companies like Tesla, ChargePoint, and the New Energy Vehicle Industry Alliance, the density of these charging piles remains low in many regions, particularly in rural areas [5]. Due to the lack of charging infrastructure, electric vehicle owners find it challenging to undertake long-distance travel, and range anxiety limits the use of electric vehicles. There is a general dissatisfaction with the completeness of the charging network.

12.1.4.2   Slow Charging Speed of Current Charging Technology

While fast-charging technology has made advancements, it still appears slow in comparison to refueling traditional internal combustion engine vehicles. Slow charging speeds result in extended wait times for electric vehicle owners, limited single-pile charging capacity, and can negatively impact the overall user experience.

12.1.4.3   Different Charging Standards and Connectors by Various Vehicle Manufacturers

Charging piles operated by different manufacturers lack uniform standards and have limited functionality, high costs, and varying quality. The lack of standardization makes it difficult for charging pile operators to serve a wide range of electric vehicles, potentially resulting in a sub-optimal experience for electric vehicle owners.

12.1.4.4   High Cost

The cost of charging equipment, installation, and maintenance remains high, especially for fast-charging piles. This high cost can make it challenging for charging pile operators to recoup their investments and generate profits. In June 2021, Open Miles New Energy Technology Co. Ltd. conducted testing in China on nearly 80,000 charging piles and over 6,000 charging piles across six key expressways and 33 core new energy vehicle sold cities. Unfortunately, the test results were disappointing, revealing that approximately 40% of the charging piles were not operational. Within this 40%, about 12.7% were attributed to hardware issues, meaning, the charging piles could not function properly, while around 27% were related to operational problems, involving multiple interaction barriers that prevented users from charging.

The emergence of blockchain technology holds the potential to address the aforementioned issues. Blockchain, as a distributed and trusted ledger, involves interactions among different stakeholders and is suitable for resolving trust issues among these stakeholders or serving as a trusted third-party platform to address user trust issue. In the shared charging field mentioned earlier, blockchain conducts open, transparent, and real-time accounting of charging activities, with results maintained by multiple parties and immutable. This effectively resolves trust frictions among multiple parties, creating a trust environment for charging piles (CPs), benefiting operators, private CP owners, and platform users (such as drivers) [6].

Some teams are already trying to combine blockchain with charging network.

He and others have designed a blockchain-based shared charging architecture that leverages blockchain to create a trust environment involving various stakeholders, including private pile owners, CP operators, and EV users. This architecture enables fast searching, automated execution of multi-party contracts, secure computation of contract contents, and reputation-based incentive mechanisms, providing high-quality billing services [6]. Jian Ping proposed a two-stage electric vehicle charging coordination mechanism that reduces the additional burden on the distribution system operator by satisfying both the total charging demand and charging benefits [7]. Chao Liu proposed a profit proof-of-benefit consensus mechanism using the online revenue generation algorithm on a blockchain platform to manage electric vehicle charging and discharging loads, ensuring that all EVs can be charged [8]. Here, we have also designed a blockchain-based sharing charging pile system that uses DID to verify the identity of participants, ensuring the trustworthiness of system members.

12.2 A BLOCKCHAIN-BASED SHARED CHARGING PILES NETWORK

12.2.1 System Architecture

The blockchain-based shared charging pile system is built on blockchain as the underlying technology, utilizing the InterPlanetary File System (IPFS) as the user data storage, confirming user identities through DIDs, and linking four user roles—EV charging pile manufacturers, public charging piles operators, private charging pile owners, and charging pile users (e.g., EV drivers)—to form a network, thus supporting the seamless operation of the entire system, as shown in Figure 12.1.

12.2.2 Advantages of Blockchain Technology

In this solution, blockchain serves as the foundational layer within the charging piles system. Firstly, it can be used to create and manage a distributed charging network, facilitating data sharing and collaboration among various nodes and participants. This approach helps to better coordinate and optimize the electric vehicle charging system, establish more shareable charging piles, reduce node access barriers, and enhance user convenience. Secondly, blockchain technology can be utilized to

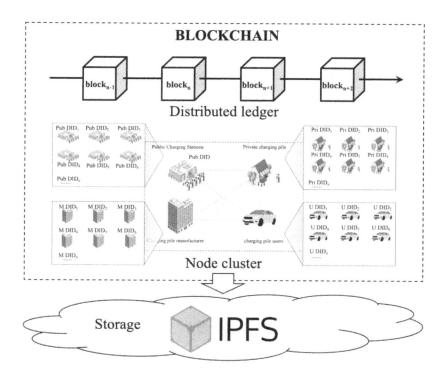

FIGURE 12.1 Architecture of the shared charging piles system based on a blockchain.

record billing information for each charging session and payment. The involvement of smart contracts ensures the automatic execution of each transaction, enhancing the transparency and security of the entire transaction history, and expediting transaction processing times.

12.2.3 INTERPLANETARY FILE SYSTEM

IPFS is a modular suite protocol designed for organizing and transmitting data, which is guided by design principles rooted in content addressing and peer-to-peer networking [9]. In other words, IPFS is a peer-to-peer distributed file system, a content-addressed, versioned, and peer-to-peer hypermedia transfer protocol capable of permanently storing a vast amount of files. In this study, a substantial amount of charging data submitted by users is stored using IPFS. To ensure data privacy, the design of storage nodes in this network is based on multiple nodes forming a node cluster to safeguard the privacy of registered data storage.

12.2.4 DIDs

DIDs stands for "decentralized identifier." In the definition provided by W3C, a DID is a novel, verifiable, decentralized digital identity designed to represent entities created and controlled by subjects, such as individuals, organizations, devices, things, data models, and abstract entities [10]. Unlike typical federated identifiers, the design of DIDs allows them to be separated from centralized registries, identity providers, and certificate authorities. Specifically, while other parties may be used to assist in discovering information related to DIDs, this design enables DID controllers to prove control over them without the need for permission from any other party. DID are uniform resource identifiers that link DID subjects to DID documents, serving as a means to achieve trustless interactions between subjects and documents, as depicted in Figure 12.2.

To better manage community members' information, becoming a member of the distributed charging network involves three stages: DID registration, DID login, and DID authentication.

After DID registration, the interaction between the DID and the DID subject is achieved through a verifiable and distributed means—the DID identifier. DID authentication can confirm whether a user's identity meets the requirements of the charging community before successful registration and can verify the user's identity information when needed. A DID identifier can be resolved into

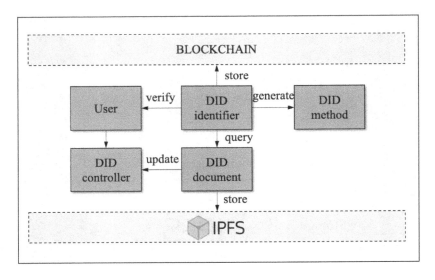

FIGURE 12.2 Schematic diagram of DID architecture.

a DID document, which may include all authentication attributes of the DID subject and undergo data authenticity verification by the DID subject management committee. Its primary function is to ensure the credibility of the DID subject's identity. The members of such committee must include four categories of roles: charging pile manufacturers, public charging piles owners/operators, private charging pile owners, and charging pile users. Each of these four categories elects multiple highly active nodes to form this management committee. The committee re-elects its members on a daily, weekly, or monthly basis to ensure fairness.

12.2.5 PARTICIPANTS' ROLES

As mentioned earlier, the construction of the distributed charging pile community involves four categories of roles: charging pile manufacturers, public charging piles owners/operators, private charging pile owners, and charging pile users. Each role category includes multiple nodes, collectively forming a distributed charging-sharing community. Charging pile manufacturers are primarily responsible for producing EV charging piles, which can be purchased in batches for use in public CPs or by private individuals. Public CPs are similar to gas station and mainly provide public travel services. Private CPs are purchased privately and placed near residences for individual convenience in personal travel, and charging pile users are individuals with charging needs. The establishment of the distributed charging community allows these four participating roles to efficiently and quickly meet their respective needs, thereby ensuring the construction and development of the community.

12.3 SYSTEM DESIGN

12.3.1 MODULES OF A DISTRIBUTED EV CHARGING NETWORK

The following introduces the main functional modules of the EV charging blockchain system.

12.3.1.1 DID Subject Management Committee

The DID subject management committee is mainly responsible for the authentication, registration, and data uploading of user role applications to ensure the authenticity of the registration data of distributed charging community members.

12.3.1.2 DID Certification and Register

EV charging pile manufacturer A, in order to become a member of the distributed charging community node, must undergo DID registration. The specific process is shown in Figure 12.3. Firstly, charging pile manufacturer A provides the necessary data for the application, such as individual qualifications of the manufacturer, business license, legal representative, registered address, and company size, bundled into a registration dataset <A>, and initiates a DID registration request.

Verification node N_1 is the first to receive the DID registration request, and it is important to note that the verification nodes $N = [N_1, N_2, N_3, . . .]$ are any nodes in the subject management committee that receive the registration request first. Upon receiving the DID registration request, registration dataset A is parsed, resulting in the creation of a DID registration document <MDID document>$_{regist}$. A DID registration vote broadcast is initiated within the subject management committee. The subject management committee receives the broadcast, verifies the <MDID document>$_{regist}$, and casts votes for confirmation. Once the number of nodes that vote in favor of the registration request exceeds 3/4, the registration request is considered approved. Verification node N1, upon receiving the approval command, first creates a DID identifier for charging pile manufacturer A (the identifier generation rules are explained later). Next, it generates a key pair for charging pile manufacturer A, updates the content of <MDID document>$_{regist}$, and generates the MDID document <MDID document>. Finally, the MDID document <MDID document> is stored in the IPFS permanent storage managed by the private node. The MDID document <MDID

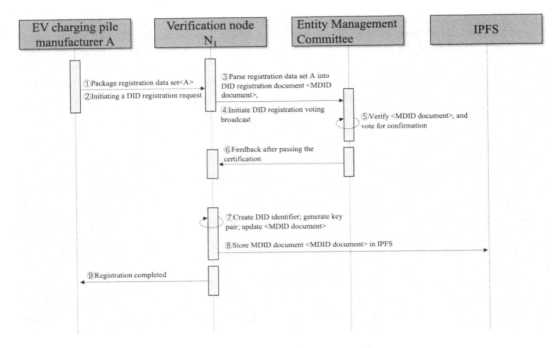

FIGURE 12.3 EV charging pile manufacturer registration sequence diagram.

document> includes {qualification, business license, legal person, registered funds, enterprise scale, pub key}, signifying a successful registration. If the subject management committee identifies any anomalies in the registration information, the registration request will not be approved, and charging pile manufacturer A will need to modify the registration dataset and resubmit the registration request. In this chapter, IPFS is chosen as the storage medium for private data of role subjects. EV charging pile manufacturer A can connect as one of the distributed charging pile community nodes upon successful registration. The MDID of the EV charging pile manufacturer subject is MDID = [$MDID_1$, $MDID_2$, $MDID_3$, . . . , $MDID_n$].

When public charging piles owners register, they are also required to submit various qualification proofs, such as charging pile establishment qualifications, certificates of eligibility, registered addresses, and other relevant credentials. Upon successful verification, they become one of the nodes in the group role of public charging piles, Public EV charging station Pub DID = [Pub DID_1, Pub DID_2, Pub DID_3, . . . , Pub DID_n].

Private charging pile owners need to submit data such as the charging pile installation location, charging pile compliance certificate, and installation license certificate when registering. Role group of private charging pile owners Pri DID = [Pri DID_1, Pri DID_2, Pri DID_3, . . . , Pri DID_n].

Submitting data for CP users is simpler than the first three types of roles, but they also need to prove their legal identity, role group of users UDID = [$UDID_1$, $UDID_2$, $UDID_3$, . . . , $UDID_n$].

In addition to this, users have the option to register multiple identities within the community. However, in order to prevent congestion caused by excessive transactions, users must choose one identity as their primary identity to participate in broadcasting transactions and bookkeeping. They can only use other identities for transactions when needed.

DID login.

After the role registration is completed, the logged-in subject (hereinafter referred to as a node) can detect the situation in the community in real time after logging in at the front end of the system and interact with other nodes in real time to maintain the normal operation of the system.

The verification node serves as one of the nodes within the DID subject management committee.

```
DID identifier setting rules: did:gxcdz:<method id>
<method id>:Pub did/Pri did/mdid/udid:SHA256{SHA256<DID document>}
```

12.3.2 User Charging Procedure

When a CP's user node has only one identity, the charging process is as follows (see Figure 12.4).

EV drivers $UDID_1$ can connect vehicles to platforms; during the driving process, the platform continuously monitors the vehicle's battery level. When the battery level drops below 20%, the platform initiates a charging alert to the user's end node. Upon receiving the charging alert, the user initiates a charging request through the platform's front end. The platform recommends information about available charging piles (including public CPs and private CPs) with shorter driving distances based on the user's current location. If the user selects the nearest Pub CPs node Pub DID_1, there are multiple CPs in public CPs = [CP_i, CP_{ii}, CP_{iii}, . . . , CP_x]. The central processor selects an available CP. Taking the selected idle charging pile I as an example, the user can lock the CP_i. The locking process begins with the user selecting the estimated time of arrival at the public CPs. The platform initiates a 15-minute lock starting from the estimated arrival time and sends a charging pile locking request to the public CPs node Pub DID_1 on the platform side①. Upon receiving the user's locking request, the Pub DID_1 platform automatically triggers a smart contract to verify CP_i, checking if it is in an idle state. If it is verified as idle, the platform automatically approves the user's locking request②. After the locking request is approved, the smart contract automatically generates an initial transaction authentication ID for the process③. When the user arrives at CP_i as scheduled, they click the Arrival button. Once the platform confirms the user's location via GPS, it immediately

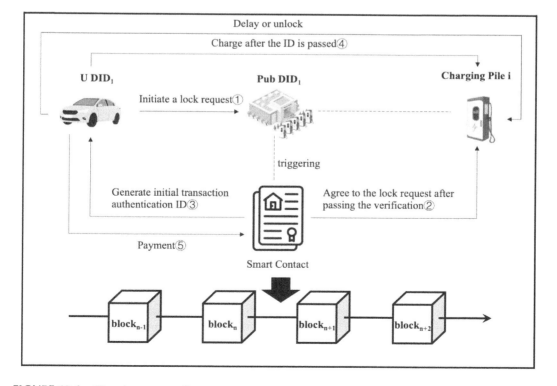

FIGURE 12.4 Charging process diagram.

sends the initial transaction authentication ID. After the user's vehicle and CP_i authentication IDs are confirmed, charging begins directly④. Upon completion of charging, the charging pile determines the transaction amount based on the user's electricity usage. The user makes the payment to complete the transaction or can choose automatic payment⑤. If the user has not arrived after 15 minutes, the smart contract sends a message to unlock CP_i and notifies the user. If the user receives the notification and decides to delay their arrival, they can click a delay command. The delay time will be included in the charges, and payment can be made after completing the charging. If the user cancels the locking delay, the smart contract automatically unlocks CP_i, destroys the initial transaction authentication ID, and sets CP_i back to idle mode, allowing other users in need of charging to select and lock it. If the user chooses a nearby available private CP Pri DID_1, the main difference from the preceding process is that only this private CP Pri DID_1 needs to be verified. The user prioritizes the lock time period, initiates a locking request for private CP Pri DID_1, and the platform triggers a smart contract upon receiving the request. The contract verifies and approves the locking request, generating a transaction token, and the subsequent process follows as described earlier.

When a charging pile user node has multiple community identities, there are two scenarios for handling this. In the first scenario, the user needs to change the system interface to switch to the charging pile user identity interface for charging. When the charging pile user node has completed the identity switch, there are two charging situations: in the first case, the primary identity of the node is a charging pile supplier, and the secondary identity is a charging pile user. Switching to the secondary identity allows charging to proceed as described earlier. In the second scenario, if the primary identity of the node is a pile owner, there is no need to charge for charging at their own charging pile. However, when charging at other charging piles, the charging process is conducted as described earlier.

12.3.3 Smart Contract

Smart contracts are a set of digital protocols composed of code, jointly created by multiple nodes on a blockchain, and they provide explicit rules for the rights and obligations of parties involved. Contracts can encode predefined rules and are enforced by consensus protocols. Once the contract activation conditions are triggered by a user, the contract instructions are executed and cannot be altered [1, 11]. The smart contracts in the blockchain-based shared charging pile system involve complex and delicate operations, such as authorization, pricing, and transactions. The specific process of contract deployment includes the following steps:

First, members of the distributed charging sharing community engage in discussions and write contract code.

Next, the written contract code is compiled into bytecode that can be read by the blockchain and deployed to the blockchain. Each time a user initiates a charging request, the contract code is called and executed. After the contract execution is completed, the transaction result is updated on the blockchain.

In fact, the deployment process of smart contracts is also a process of transactions being recorded on the blockchain. It includes four steps: transaction initiation, broadcasting, packaging, and recording on the blockchain. The specific transaction process will be detailed in the following sections.

12.3.4 Transaction Process

After user $UDID_1$ completes CP_i charging in Pub CPs Pub DID_1, the contract will obtain the amount to be paid based on the delay time T and output power E. After confirming the transaction type, transaction authentication ID, and transaction amount, the user fills in the private key to confirm the transaction. The contract packages this transaction *TX1* (including the user's signature (<sig>) and the user's public key (<PubK(user)>)), and initiates the transaction. The transaction is sent to the distributed charging sharing community node network. The node that first receives this transaction

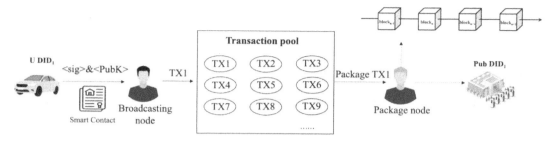

FIGURE 12.5 Charging process.

message (referred to as the broadcasting node in the following text) initiates broadcasting within the community and places the transaction in the transaction pool. The accounting node begins verifying transaction *TX1*, and after verifying the signature, the accounting node packages transaction *TX1* along with a batch of transactions into a block, generating a new block number. It then initiates accounting broadcasting. Other nodes receive the broadcast, and all nodes in the network compare the locally synchronized block number information. They batch-process the log event information based on the block number range and the contract addresses configured locally for listening. The log information is processed according to transaction types, including registration transactions and charging transactions. After processing is complete, local logs are updated, and blocks are synchronized, completing the transaction's inclusion in the blockchain. The specific process is illustrated in Figure 12.5.

12.3.5 INCENTIVE AND EVALUATION

When the CP user completes a charging transaction, it needs to make a payment, which includes the charging fee and the incentive fee. The charging fee is calculated based on the CP's delayed locking time and the electricity consumption during the charging session. The design of the incentive fee is intended to promote community activity. The charging fee is provided to CP owners, including both private CP and public CPs, while the incentive fee is distributed to broadcasting nodes and accounting nodes.

In addition to this, broadcasting nodes and accounting nodes earn points every time they complete broadcasting and accounting tasks. Typically, one task yields 1 point. During the points redemption period, broadcasting nodes and accounting nodes have the opportunity to convert their accumulated points into cash, thus generating income.

After the CPU transaction is completed, it can be evaluated, and different levels of points rewards are given based on the evaluation level. The evaluation content can include charging time, service attitude, and so on. When a user gives a positive evaluation to the transaction, the charging pile owner can earn 1 point, while no points are awarded for neutral or negative evaluations. Points owners can earn additional income or benefit through point redemption.

12.3.6 SAFETY INSPECTION FOR CPS

In the future, both the public charging piles and the charging piles purchased by private owners are equipped with solar charging panels. These panels are continuously connected to the charging pile's energy storage system to charge the pile. Additionally, they are also connected to the grid to ensure an adequate power supply for the charging pile.

CPs are equipped with a central processor that can monitor the availability and health status of each one. To ensure timely attention to the health status of the CPs, each CP is fitted with an automatic safety detection device. At regular intervals (which can be defined by the CP owner), these devices perform automatic hardware safety checks. The results of these checks are then transmitted back to the central processor. Specifically, during a safety check, if a CP's hardware is functioning normally, it outputs a result of 1. If any abnormalities are detected, it outputs a result of 0 and records the hardware issues. These records are then sent to the central processor. The central processor receives and categorizes the results, compiling a list of CPs with abnormalities, along with their respective fault locations, denoted as a set $F = \{F1, F2, F3, \ldots, Fn\}$. This information is then relayed to the CP owners. Upon receiving the abnormal detection results, CP owners can initiate hardware repair transaction requests with the community's supplier nodes. The transaction process has been described in detail in the previous sections. Additionally, in cases where CPs are damaged, CP owners can directly initiate purchase transactions to replace the damaged CPs.

12.4 CONCLUSION

This chapter presents a blockchain-based charging pile system for electric vehicles. By establishing a distributed charging network that connects four key roles—users (drivers), piles manufacturers, public CP owners/operators, and private CP owners—and employing decentralized identity verification for registered users, the system enables efficient, secure, and trustworthy charging processes. When the user's charging account has sufficient balance, they can directly make online reservations for a charging pile and simply arrive on time to commence charging. The system leverages distributed ledgers to record every charging order, rewarding nodes with points through broadcasting and accounting. It provides an incentive mechanism, allowing accounting nodes to redeem points for benefits, thus encouraging node participation in maintaining the overall system. This system aims to solve the current challenges in EV charging scenario, reducing charging costs and achieving efficient EV charging.

REFERENCES

[1] EVI. *IEA, 2021*, pp. 1–101, Global EV Outlook, 2021, https://iea.blob.core.windows.net/assets/ed5f-4484-f556-4110-8c5c-4ede8bcba637/GlobalEVOutlook2021.pdf. Accessed 04 Oct. 2023.

[2] David Butler, et al. "More Americans would 'definitely' get electric vehicles, consumer reports survey shows." *More Americans Would "Definitely" Get Electric Vehicles*, Consumer Reports Survey Shows, Consumer Reports, 14 Nov. 2022, www.consumerreports.org/media-room/press-releases/2022/07/more-americans-would-definitely-get-electric-vehicles-consumer/. Accessed 04 Oct. 2023.

[3] Zhongyang Yang. "Charging piles should be built and managed." *Economic Daily News*, 7 Oct. 2022, pp. 1–1. Accessed 04 Oct. 2023.

[4] PRC National Development and Reform Commission. *National Development and Reform Commission, 2015*, pp. 1–28, Guidelines for the Development of Electric Vehicle Charging Infrastructure, 2015–2020, www.gov.cn/xinwen/site1/20151117/89061447751624822.pdf. Accessed 04 Oct. 2023.

[5] Jian-hua Liu, et al. "Innovation model analysis of new energy vehicles: Taking Toyota, Tesla and BYD as an example." *Procedia Engineering* 174 (2017): 965–972. Accessed 04 Oct. 2023.

[6] Yunhua He, et al. "A trusted architecture for EV shared charging based on blockchain technology." *High-Confidence Computing* 1.2 (2021): 100001. Accessed 04 Oct. 2023.

[7] Ping Jian, et al. "A two-stage autonomous EV charging coordination method enabled by blockchain." *Journal of Modern Power Systems and Clean Energy* 9.1 (2020): 104–113. Accessed 04 Oct. 2023.

[8] Chao Liu, et al. "Proof-of-benefit: A blockchain-enabled EV charging scheme." *2019 IEEE 89th Vehicular Technology Conference (VTC2019-Spring). IEEE* (2019): 1–6. Accessed 24 Sept. 2023.

[9] IPFS. "What is IPFS." *IPFS Docs*, IPFS, 2 Oct. 2023, docs.ipfs.tech/concepts/what-is-ipfs/#defining-ipfs. Accessed 04 Oct. 2023.

[10] Manu Sporny, et al. "Decentralized identifiers (DIDs) v1.0." *W3C,* 19 July 2022, www.w3.org/TR/did-core/. Accessed 04 Oct. 2023.

[11] Shuai Wang, et al. "An overview of smart contract: Architecture, applications, and future trends." *2018 IEEE Intelligent Vehicles Symposium (IV). IEEE* (2018): 108–113. Accessed 24 Sept. 2023.

13 Blockchain Technology for Ride- and Car-Sharing Apps

Tanuj Surve and Risha Khandelwal

13.1 INTRODUCTION

The objective of this chapter proposal is to delve into the realm of car- and ride-sharing apps and their transformative impact on transportation. Companies such as Uber and Careem have transformed the way we travel by putting simple, on-demand transportation at our fingertips. This proposal also looks into integrating blockchain technology, a decentralized and transparent platform, with these innovative apps. By investigating the connection between blockchain and car-sharing services, we may learn how this technology improves efficiency and cost-effectiveness. We will look at real-world examples of how blockchain is already being used in the industry. We hope to uncover the future possibilities and ramifications of blockchain technology in the field of transportation and car-sharing through this investigation.

13.2 DEFINING CAR-SHARING APPS

Car-sharing apps have emerged as revolutionary platforms that have transformed how we travel and commute within cities (Mounce & Nelson, 2019). Uber and Careem, two business titans that have changed the concept of mobility, are among the most notable companies in this industry. Let us embark on a journey of discovery to identify the relevance and influence of these car-sharing apps to comprehend their essence.

Uber, a global phenomenon linked with ease and mobility, has used technology to disrupt the traditional taxi sector (Mohamed, Rye, & Fonzone, 2020). Uber, at its heart, is a platform that links riders and drivers, connecting the supply and demand for transportation services. With a few taps on their cell phones, users can easily order a trip, sending a driver to pick them up and carry them to their desired destination.

But what distinguishes Uber from traditional taxis? Uber sprang onto the scene with innovation, introducing the notion of ride-sharing and revolutionizing the way people commute. Ride-sharing allows numerous customers traveling in the same direction to share a car, effectively splitting the trip cost and making transportation more accessible and economical. This surge of innovation has revolutionized commuting convenience and flexibility, allowing customers more control over their travel experiences.

Similarly, Careem, which is primarily present in the Middle East, has built a name for itself in the car-sharing market by providing a variety of transportation options suited to the demands of its consumers (Liyanage, Dia, Abduljabbar, & Bagloee, 2019). Individuals can use the Careem app to book rides and connect with drivers in the Careem network. Careem's success stems from its dedication to offering dependable and safe travel solutions, with client happiness as the cornerstone of its service.

The distinguishing features of car-sharing apps like Uber and Careem go beyond sheer convenience. These platforms have come to represent the sharing economy, cultivating a sense of community and connection among riders and drivers. These apps have changed our perceptions of ownership and mobility by utilizing technology to create a seamless interface. Users no longer

DOI: 10.1201/9781003450306-15

have to rely simply on personal vehicles or traditional taxis; they can now obtain transportation on demand, enabling them to experience a new level of freedom and flexibility.

The advantages of car-sharing apps for riders are numerous. These technologies' convenience and accessibility allow people to travel in their cities with ease. Users have more choice and control over their transportation experiences because of real-time tracking, transparent pricing, and a range of travel options. Furthermore, car-sharing applications have helped reduce traffic congestion and the environmental effect of transportation by encouraging shared rides and lowering the number of privately owned automobiles on the road.

Drivers who partner with car-sharing applications benefit from an increase in economic possibilities. Drivers can earn money on a flexible schedule by converting their automobiles into income-generating assets. Car-sharing apps connect drivers with potential passengers, providing a dependable and secure source of revenue. This burst of economic empowerment has resulted in a dynamic workforce capable of adapting to fluctuating demand, making transport services readily available when and when they are required.

13.3   HOW CAR-SHARING APPS HELP US

Car-sharing apps like Uber and Careem have impacted how we navigate and commute inside cities, providing a plethora of perks that improve our daily lives (Liyanage, Dia, Abduljabbar, & Bagloee, Flexible Mobility On-Demand: An Environmental Scan, 2019). These cutting-edge platforms offer convenience, flexibility, safety, sustainability, economic opportunities, and community connections, making them indispensable modern transportation tools.

Car-sharing apps provide unparalleled convenience and efficiency. We may easily request a trip and have a driver arrive at our place with a single tap on our cell phones. This eliminates the need for us to wait in long lines or look for parking spaces, saving us important time and energy on our daily commutes. Transportation arrangements are simplified by the easy booking process and real-time information.

Car-sharing apps give us more flexibility and independence (Dowling, Maalsen, & Kent, 2018). They give transport solutions that can be tailored to our specific demands and schedules. These apps are available 24/7, catering to our different mobility needs, whether it is a morning commute, a late-night outing, or an impromptu vacation. The ability to request trips on-demand provides a level of convenience that traditional modes of transportation cannot always match.

Car-sharing apps prioritize safety and security. These platforms employ stringent driver screening procedures and provide services like real-time tracking and trip-sharing. Users can access driver information, such as ratings and reviews, to make informed judgments and feel confident about their chosen ride. This emphasis on safety gives comfort throughout the journey, assuring a safe transit experience.

Car-sharing apps contribute to a more sustainable future from an environmental standpoint. These apps help reduce traffic congestion and lower carbon emissions by increasing shared transportation and lowering the number of independently owned automobiles on the road. The increased emphasis on carpooling choices encourages more efficient use of existing transportation resources, which benefits both the environment and the community by reducing traffic congestion and pollution.

Car-sharing apps have also changed the economic landscape by giving drivers new revenue prospects. Individuals can earn extra money by driving for these platforms using their vehicles. Drivers can choose their schedules because of the flexible working hours, which provide a valuable income stream that fits their lifestyle. This economic empowerment has created new opportunities for people looking for flexible work or extra income.

Car-sharing apps also generate a sense of community and connection among riders and drivers. The rating and review systems foster mutual respect and accountability, ensuring that all participants have a positive experience. The interactions between the driver and the passengers build a supportive environment, promoting professionalism and excellence in service. Users frequently value the social connections they make during rides, which builds a feeling of community inside the app's ecosystem.

13.4 BLOCKCHAIN TECHNOLOGY

Blockchain technology has emerged as a game-changing breakthrough with the potential to transform multiple industries and redefine how we communicate, transact, and trust in the digital world. *Blockchain*, at its core, is a decentralized and transparent digital ledger that records transactions across several computers or nodes. This technology provides a new paradigm of trust, security, and immutability, paving the way for unprecedented possibilities in finance, supply chain management, healthcare, and other fields.

To grasp the essence of blockchain technology, one must first understand its fundamental concepts. The blockchain relies on a distributed network of nodes to validate and record transactions (Rodrigo, Perera, Senaratne, & Xiaohua, 2018). Each transaction, also known as a block, is cryptographically connected to the previous block, producing a chain of blocks and giving rise to the term "blockchain." This cryptographic link protects the data's integrity and immutability, making it nearly difficult to alter or tamper with the information held within the blockchain.

Decentralization is one of the most important aspects of blockchain technology. Unlike traditional systems, which rely on a central authority to verify and approve transactions, blockchain works on a peer-to-peer network, with each participating node having a copy of the complete blockchain (Sarode, Poudel, Shrestha, & Bhalla, 2021). This decentralized structure eliminates the need for intermediaries and central authority, lowering the danger of single points of failure and improving transaction security and transparency.

Transparency is another distinguishing quality of blockchain. The data stored on the blockchain is public to all network participants, allowing every transaction and update to the ledger to be traced and audited. Because it allows for the verification of transaction history and assures that all parties have access to the same information, this transparency encourages confidence among participants, reducing the need for third-party intermediaries to establish trust.

Blockchain technology also introduces the concept of consensus processes, which are used to validate and agree on the ledger's state (Li, Sforzin, Fedorov, & Karame, 2017). To secure agreement among nodes on the authenticity of transactions, different blockchain networks use different consensus algorithms, such as proof of work (PoW) or proof of stake (PoS). Consensus mechanisms not only protect the network from bad actors but also allow the blockchain to operate efficiently and reliably.

Blockchain technology has a wide range of possible applications. Blockchain has the potential to revolutionize payments, remittances, and cross-border activities in the financial sector by enabling faster, cheaper, and more secure value transfers. Blockchain can streamline procedures and decrease costs by eliminating intermediaries and lowering the need for manual reconciliation.

Furthermore, blockchain technology has the potential to improve supply chain management by allowing for end-to-end visibility and traceability of commodities. Stakeholders can follow the origin, validity, and path of items by documenting every transaction and movement on the blockchain, ensuring transparency and eliminating fraud and counterfeiting.

Blockchain technology can potentially help the healthcare business by securely storing and sharing patient information and medical data. Blockchain technology has the potential to improve data privacy, interoperability, and patient consent management, allowing for easy and secure access to medical information while retaining confidentiality and security.

As blockchain technology advances, efforts are being made to address scalability, energy consumption, and regulatory challenges. Layer-2 solutions and consensus algorithm innovations, for example, seek to improve blockchain network scalability, allowing them to handle a higher volume of transactions. In addition, investigations into renewable energy sources and more efficient consensus algorithms aim to lessen the environmental impact of blockchain energy use.

13.5   THE LINK BETWEEN BLOCKCHAIN TECHNOLOGY AND CAR-SHARING SERVICES

With its decentralized and transparent nature, blockchain technology has the potential to change car-sharing businesses like Uber and Careem by increasing efficiency, lowering prices, and building trust among users and drivers. The use of blockchain in car-sharing apps adds a new degree of security, immutability, and accountability to transactional operations, which benefits both service providers and customers (Auer, Nagler, Mazumdar, & Mukkamala, 2022).

The increased security and trust provided by blockchain technology is one of the key advantages of employing it in car-sharing services. The decentralized nature of blockchain ensures that transaction records are disseminated across various network nodes, making it harder for shady actors to corrupt or tamper with the data. Blockchain technology protects the integrity of transaction records by using cryptographic methods, making them essentially immutable once published on the blockchain. This level of protection fosters confidence among users and drivers, alleviating concerns about fraud, disputes, and data manipulation.

A further manner in which blockchain technology affects car-sharing services is by lowering costs and increasing efficiency. Traditional payment methods entail the use of intermediaries, such as banks or payment processors, which add transaction fees and delays. Car-sharing apps can eliminate intermediaries and promote direct transactions between consumers and drivers by exploiting blockchain's peer-to-peer nature. This not only lowers transaction costs but also allows for speedier settlement times, boosting overall payment process efficiency. Furthermore, car-sharing apps can automate certain components of the transaction, such as fare calculations and revenue distribution, by utilizing smart contracts, which are self-executing agreements stored in the blockchain, thereby improving the process and eliminating administrative overhead.

The use of blockchain technology in car-sharing services also allows for the inclusion of novel features, such as secure and transparent identification verification. Users can use blockchain to have their digital identities securely preserved on the blockchain, ensuring privacy and control over personal information. This enables more rapid and reliable verification processes, increasing the platform's trustworthiness and lowering the danger of identity fraud.

In addition, blockchain technology can make it easier to incorporate reputation systems within car-sharing apps. A transparent and immutable record of prior interactions is generated by storing user and driver ratings and reviews on the blockchain. This reputation system rewards positive behavior and encourages users and drivers to be accountable. When picking a driver based on their reputation score, users may make better-informed decisions, while drivers are incentivized to offer outstanding service to preserve or enhance their ratings. This trust-building mechanism improves the platform's overall experience and reliability.

Blockchain technology has the potential to enable the development of decentralized car-sharing services. These platforms would be regulated by a consensus method in which rules, pricing, and policies would be decided collaboratively by the community of users and drivers. Because blockchain is decentralized, no single entity influences the platform, encouraging a more democratic and inclusive ecosystem. This concept encourages increased participation and ownership among members, giving them the ability to define the future of the car-sharing service they use.

While incorporating blockchain technology into car-sharing services has obvious benefits, issues such as scalability, privacy, and regulatory compliance must be addressed. To support the high demand and usage patterns of car-sharing services, blockchain networks must handle a significant volume of real-time transactions. Privacy concerns about sharing personal data on a transparent blockchain must also be addressed to ensure the proper balance of transparency and privacy is reached. Furthermore, regulatory frameworks for the use of blockchain technology in car-sharing services must be devised to ensure compliance with existing laws and regulations.

13.6 HOW BLOCKCHAIN TECHNOLOGY ENHANCES EFFICIENCY AND COST-EFFECTIVENESS IN CAR-SHARING SERVICES

The incorporation of blockchain into car-sharing services has the potential to significantly improve the efficiency and cost-effectiveness of these platforms. Car-sharing services can streamline operations, decrease expenses, and offer a more seamless experience for both consumers and drivers by exploiting the unique capabilities of blockchain, such as decentralization, transparency, and automation.

The elimination of intermediaries is one important way in which blockchain technology improves efficiency and cost-effectiveness in car-sharing services. Banks or payment processors are frequently used in traditional payment systems, which introduce transaction costs and delays. These intermediaries function as trustworthy third parties to enable transactions between users and drivers, increasing the process's complexity and expense. Car-sharing apps can eliminate the need for intermediaries by using blockchain's decentralized nature, enabling direct peer-to-peer transactions. Because there are no intermediate fees to pay, this direct engagement lowers transaction costs, making the service more cost-effective for users.

Furthermore, blockchain technology has the potential to automate several components of the car-sharing process, enhancing efficiency and decreasing administrative overhead. Smart contracts are self-executing agreements maintained on the blockchain that may automate functions like fare computation, revenue distribution, and dispute settlement. When a user books a ride via a car-sharing app, a smart contract can automatically calculate the cost based on established factors like distance and time. Once the ride is done, the fare is automatically withdrawn from the user's digital wallet and distributed to the driver, with no manual involvement or reconciliation required. This automation minimizes not only human mistakes but also the requirement for extra workers to execute these jobs, enhancing efficiency and lowering operational costs.

The transparency and immutability of transaction data are another way blockchain technology improves efficiency in car-sharing services. Every transaction on the blockchain is transparent and visible to all network participants, ensuring a shared source of truth (Javaid, Haleem, Singh, Suman, & Khan, 2022). This transparency creates trust among users and drivers since they can verify the accuracy of transaction data and have faith in the system's integrity. Because blockchain is immutable, once a transaction is recorded, it cannot be changed or tampered with, providing an auditable trace of every transaction. This decreases the risk of fraud or conflicts, because all parties have access to the same information and can trust the integrity of the recorded data.

Blockchain technology offers secure and rapid identification verification, which is critical in car-sharing services to ensure both user and driver safety. Traditional identity verification systems frequently include the exchange of sensitive personal information, which might expose users to security risks. Users' digital identities can be securely preserved on the blockchain, decreasing the danger of data breaches and identity theft. These digital identities may be cryptographically confirmed, making identity verification more efficient and reliable without compromising privacy. Blockchain technology facilitates speedier onboarding of new users and drivers by automating the identity verification process, improving the overall efficiency of the car-sharing platform.

Furthermore, because blockchain technology is decentralized, it allows for the development of decentralized car-sharing platforms in which decision-making is dispersed among the community of users and drivers. Traditional car-sharing systems frequently have centralized decision-making processes, with a single body dictating rules, pricing, and policies. This centralized approach has the potential to impede innovation and flexibility. Car-sharing platforms can incorporate democratic governance models by using blockchain's decentralization, in which members have a role in decision-making via consensus methods. This decentralized governance enables more efficient and fast decision-making processes, allowing the car-sharing platform to adapt to changing user and driver demands and preferences.

To summarize, the integration of blockchain technology into car-sharing services significantly improves efficiency and cost-effectiveness. Blockchain technology optimizes the operations of car-sharing platforms by eliminating intermediaries, automating jobs using smart contracts, ensuring the transparency and immutability of transaction records, enabling safe identity verification, and embracing decentralized governance. These improvements result in lower costs, simpler operations, more trust, and a better overall customer experience. As blockchain technology evolves and matures, we can anticipate future breakthroughs that will enable even greater efficiency benefits and cost savings in the car-sharing business and beyond.

13.7   LIVE EXAMPLES OF BLOCKCHAIN TECHNOLOGY IN CAR-SHARING SERVICES

Blockchain technology can transform the car-sharing industry by increasing efficiency, lowering prices, and building trust between users and drivers. While blockchain adoption in car-sharing services is still in its early phases, multiple actual examples demonstrate this technology's transformative power in improving the overall experience for both service providers and customers.

Share&Charge. Share&Charge is a blockchain-based technology that seeks to transform electric vehicle (EV) charging infrastructure and enable peer-to-peer charging. The platform makes use of blockchain to make transactions between EV owners and charging station operators safer and more transparent. Share&Charge eliminates the need for intermediaries by leveraging smart contracts and the decentralized nature of blockchain, making the charging process more efficient and cost-effective. EV owners can use digital tokens to access charging stations and pay for services, which are securely recorded on the blockchain. This decreases transaction costs and eliminates the complications associated with traditional payment systems, benefiting both EV owners and charging station operators.

DOVU. DOVU is a blockchain-powered platform that incentivizes and pays users for sharing mobility-related data. The platform's goal is to build a decentralized marketplace for mobility-related data, allowing users to monetize their data while maintaining privacy control. DOVU may integrate with existing car-sharing apps and use blockchain to securely record and verify data such as trip details, mileage, and usage patterns in the context of car-sharing. This information can then be utilized to provide personalized services, optimize fleet management, and reward environmentally responsible driving behavior. DOVU offers openness, efficiency, and user empowerment within the car-sharing ecosystem by rewarding data sharing via blockchain.

Arcade City. Arcade City is a peer-to-peer ride-sharing company that uses blockchain technology to enable direct transactions between riders and drivers. Arcade City eliminates the need for intermediaries by exploiting blockchain's transparency and security capabilities, allowing users to negotiate fares and payment terms directly. The platform automates the payment process with smart contracts, ensuring quick and secure transactions. Arcade City gives drivers the ability to set their rates and build a reputation based on consumer feedback, creating a feeling of community and trust. Arcade City's usage of blockchain technology provides a decentralized ride-sharing paradigm in which consumers have greater influence over the entire transaction process.

La'Zooz. La'Zooz is a decentralized carpooling platform that connects drivers and riders travelling in the same direction using blockchain technology. The platform uses the transparency and trustworthiness of blockchain to deliver a safe and efficient carpooling experience. La'Zooz stores ride data on the blockchain, such as routes, lengths, and split fees, creating an auditable and immutable record of transactions. This not only increases user trust but also allows for fair and transparent fee distribution. La'Zooz's use of blockchain lowers the need for intermediaries, making carpooling more cost-effective for both drivers and riders.

Oaken Innovations. Oaken Innovations is a blockchain-based firm that aspires to build a decentralized car-sharing platform for autonomous vehicles. The platform makes use of blockchain technology to facilitate secure and transparent transactions between vehicle owners and renters. Oaken

Innovations automates the entire car rental process, from identity verification to payment settlement, by employing smart contracts. This decreases administrative overhead, eliminates the need for intermediaries, and improves car-sharing's overall efficiency. In addition, blockchain integration protects the integrity and immutability of transaction records, fostering confidence and transparency in the car-sharing ecosystem.

These real-world examples show how blockchain technology has the ability to revolutionize car-sharing services. Blockchain improves efficiency, lowers costs, and increases trust within the car-sharing ecosystem by eliminating intermediaries, automating procedures, ensuring transparency, and boosting security. We can expect additional ideas that will revolutionize the way we share and access transportation services as more organizations and startups investigate the possibilities of blockchain in the transportation business.

13.8 LEVERAGING BLOCKCHAIN FOR COST REDUCTION IN MULTI-PASSENGER CAR-SHARING

When multiple people share a ride, blockchain technology has the potential to lower costs in car-sharing services like Uber. Cost reduction can be achieved by leveraging blockchain through enhanced efficiency, trust, and equitable cost-sharing methods.

One way blockchain can cut expenses is by optimizing the rider–driver matching process. Due to the decentralized nature of blockchain, car-sharing services can connect riders directly with drivers, removing the need for intermediaries (Duy, Hien, Hien, & Pham, 2018). Blockchain enables more direct and efficient interactions by eliminating middlemen, such as traditional ride-sharing firms. This simplified approach minimizes administrative costs and ensures that a larger amount of the fare is paid directly to the driver, resulting in cheaper costs for both the rider and the driver.

The transparency of blockchain also plays an important role in cost reduction. All transaction data are securely maintained and shared among participants when a ride is booked and logged on the blockchain. Because all parties can access and verify the details of the ride, this transparency fosters confidence and responsibility. Riders can rest assured that the fare is distributed evenly among the passengers, ensuring an equal cost-sharing agreement. Blockchain transparency reduces disputes and eliminates the need for costly third-party resolution methods, resulting in overall cost reductions.

Smart contracts, which are self-executing agreements recorded on the blockchain, can be made easier to implement using blockchain. Smart contracts enable riders to split costs in an automated and accurate manner. A smart contract can automatically calculate the fee for each passenger based on predetermined parameters, such as distance travelled or time spent in the car when three passengers share an Uber journey. This technology replaces manual computations and guarantees that each rider pays their fair portion. Blockchain technology, through the use of smart contracts, streamlines the cost-sharing procedure, eliminates administrative costs, and ensures transparency and accuracy in dividing the ride cost.

Through incentives and loyalty programs, blockchain technology can incentivize cost reduction. As a reward for riders who choose to share their rides with others, car-sharing services can use blockchain-based tokens or cryptocurrencies. Riders can earn tokens that can be used to offset future ride expenses or unlock additional perks by engaging in the cost-sharing model. This encourages users to take shared rides more frequently, potentially saving money for both the riders and the platform. The capacity of blockchain to design and manage reward systems gives a low-cost approach to encouraging and promoting ride-sharing within the car-sharing service.

The usage of blockchain in car-sharing services allows for the development of decentralized platforms. *Decentralization* means that decision-making processes are disseminated among the community of users and drivers rather than being centralized. This democratic approach ensures that the car-sharing platform's rules and policies are democratically set and aligned with the interests of the participants. Decentralized governance models decrease bureaucracy, cut wasteful expenditures, and enable quicker decision-making, resulting in an efficient and cost-effective car-sharing business.

13.9   PROPONENTS OF BLOCKCHAIN TECHNOLOGY

Blockchain technology has acquired substantial attention and recognition, attracting the support of a wide range of advocates who are confident in its ability to transform numerous industries. These blockchain proponents, also known as blockchain enthusiasts or advocates, are united by a shared vision of a decentralized future that empowers people, improves security, and promotes transparency.

The open-source community is a major proponent of blockchain technology. The open-source nature of blockchain promotes collaboration and creativity, drawing developers, technologists, and enthusiasts from all over the world. These individuals are interested in leveraging blockchain's capabilities to develop decentralized applications (dApps), smart contracts, and other solutions that have the potential to reinvent industries such as finance, supply chain management, healthcare, and others. These proponents drive the evolution of the technology and push for its wider implementation by contributing to open-source projects and encouraging the adoption of blockchain.

Another group of proponents include industry experts and thought leaders who recognize blockchain's disruptive power. These people come from a variety of disciplines, including finance, technology, academia, and entrepreneurship. They recognize that blockchain can alter existing processes and open up new avenues for innovation. These proponents promote awareness of blockchain's benefits and push for its adoption into various sectors through educating the public, participating in conferences, publishing research papers, and sharing ideas.

Blockchain technology is also popular among entrepreneurs and startups. They see blockchain as a tool for disrupting established sectors, developing decentralized business models, and empowering individuals. Blockchain is being used by startups to address inefficiencies, lower costs, and deliver novel solutions. These entrepreneurs are accelerating the adoption and acceptance of blockchain technology by developing blockchain-based platforms, applications, and services. They demonstrate real-world use cases that demonstrate the usefulness and promise of blockchain in tackling complicated problems.

Privacy advocates are also proponents of blockchain technology. They understand the value of data privacy and management in the digital age. The intrinsic characteristics of blockchain, such as encryption, immutability, and decentralized storage, open up new avenues for preserving personal information. Proponents of privacy see blockchain as a tool to empower individuals by allowing them to govern their data, eliminating the need for centralized authorities, and lowering the danger of data breaches and unauthorized access. They advocate for the creation of privacy-focused blockchain technologies that place a premium on user sovereignty and data protection.

Furthermore, advocates for social impact are supporters of blockchain technology. They are optimistic about the technology's ability to address societal issues, such as financial inclusion, supply chain transparency, and identity verification. Blockchain can give people in underserved areas access to financial services, enable fair trade practices, and assure product authenticity. Proponents of social impact are actively working to use blockchain to effect positive change and promote social equality.

Government agencies and policymakers are also avid proponents of blockchain technology. Recognizing the potential benefits of blockchain technology, governments are investigating how to use it to improve public services, expedite processes, and increase transparency. Government supporters want to build regulatory frameworks that stimulate innovation while also striking a balance between pushing blockchain usage and reducing risks. These proponents hope to establish an enabling environment for blockchain technology to thrive by partnering with industry stakeholders.

13.10 CHALLENGES OF BLOCKCHAIN TECHNOLOGY

While blockchain technology has enormous potential to alter numerous industries, it also confronts several challenges on its way to widespread adoption. These challenges vary from technical restrictions to legislative hurdles, and overcoming them calls for careful navigation and creativity.

Scalability is one of the key issues of blockchain technology. Blockchain networks, particularly public ones like Bitcoin and Ethereum, have constraints when it comes to handling a high number of transactions at the same time. The decentralized structure of blockchain necessitates consensus among network participants, resulting in slower transaction processing times and increased energy consumption. To address scalability difficulties and boost the transaction throughput of blockchain networks, scaling options such as layer-2 protocols and sharding approaches are being investigated. Overcoming scalability issues will be critical for blockchain technology to support the amount of adoption required for widespread implementation.

Interoperability is another key challenge in the blockchain realm. At present, separate blockchain networks frequently operate independently, resulting in data silos and impeding seamless communication and data transfer between networks. Standards and protocols for interoperability among blockchain platforms are being created, enabling efficient and safe data transfer. Overcoming interoperability issues is critical for maximizing blockchain technology's potential benefits and facilitating seamless integration with current systems and networks.

Blockchain technology is also subject to regulatory scrutiny. Blockchain operates outside traditional regulatory frameworks due to its decentralized and transnational nature, causing uncertainties and legal complications. In the context of blockchain, governments and regulatory agencies are debating how to address concerns such as identity verification, data privacy, taxation, and consumer protection. Striking a balance between encouraging innovation and ensuring compliance with existing laws and regulations is a difficult task that demands coordination between industry stakeholders and the government. Creating clear and adaptable legislative frameworks will lay the groundwork for the widespread implementation of blockchain technology.

In the blockchain arena, security is a major issue. While blockchain has intrinsic security characteristics like immutability and cryptographic techniques, it is not without flaws. Bugs in smart contracts, hacker attempts, and concerns with private key management have resulted in high-profile security breaches and financial losses. As blockchain technology evolves, it is critical to prioritize strong security measures and do rigorous audits and testing of smart contracts and blockchain implementations. To address increasing risks and weaknesses, ongoing research and innovation in the field of blockchain security are required.

Usability and user experience are barriers to blockchain adoption. For general consumers, the complexity of blockchain technology, particularly the administration of cryptographic keys and wallets, is a barrier to entry. Improving the user interface, increasing wallet security, and simplifying the process of connecting with blockchain-based applications are all crucial to ensuring wider user acceptance. User-friendly interfaces, intuitive designs, and improved education and support resources will all help to overcome these usability difficulties.

13.11 CONCLUSION

To conclude, this chapter proposal has investigated the use of blockchain technology in the context of car-sharing services. We defined car-sharing apps throughout the proposal, highlighted how these companies benefit customers, and gave an overview of blockchain technology and its connection to car-sharing. We investigated how blockchain technology improves efficiency and cost-effectiveness by lowering transaction costs, optimizing procedures, and increasing participant trust. Car-sharing firms can revolutionize their operations by integrating blockchain technology, making them more efficient, cost-effective, and user-centric.

REFERENCES

Auer, S., Nagler, S., Mazumdar, S., & Mukkamala, R. R. (2022). Towards blockchain-IoT based shared mobility: Car-sharing and leasing as a case study. *Journal of Network and Computer Applications*, *200*, 103316.https://doi.org/10.1016/j.jnca.2021.103316

Dowling, R., Maalsen, S. and Kent, J.L. (2018). Sharing as sociomaterial practice: Car sharing and the material reconstitution of automobility. *Geoforum*, 88, pp. 10–16. https://doi.org/10.1016/j.geoforum.2017.11.004.

Duy, P. T., Hien, D. T. T., Hien, D. H., & Pham, V. H. (2018, December). A survey on opportunities and challenges of Blockchain technology adoption for revolutionary innovation. In *Proceedings of the 9th International Symposium on Information and Communication Technology* (pp. 200-207). https://doi.org/10.1145/3287921.3287978.

Javaid, M., Haleem, A., Singh, R.P., Suman, R. and Khan, S. (2022). A review of Blockchain Technology applications for financial services. *BenchCouncil Transactions on Benchmarks, Standards and Evaluations*, 2(3), p. 100073. https://doi.org/10.1016/j.tbench.2022.100073.

Li, W., Sforzin, A., Fedorov, S., & Karame, G. O. (2017, April). Towards scalable and private industrial blockchains. In *Proceedings of the ACM workshop on blockchain, cryptocurrencies and contracts* (pp. 9-14). https://doi.org/10.1145/3055518.3055531.

Liyanage, S., Dia, H., Abduljabbar, R. and Bagloee, S. (2019). Flexible mobility on-demand: An environmental scan. *Sustainability*, 11(5), p. 1262. https://doi.org/10.3390/su11051262.

Mohamed, M.J., Rye, T. and Fonzone, A. (2020). The utilisation and user characteristics of Uber services in London. *Transportation Planning and Technology*, 43(4), pp. 424–441. https://doi.org/10.1080/03081060.2020.1747205.

Mounce, R. and Nelson, J.D. (2019). On the potential for one-way electric vehicle car-sharing in future mobility systems. *Transportation Research Part A: Policy and Practice*, 120, pp. 17–30. https://doi.org/10-.1016/j.tra.2018.12.003.

Rodrigo, M., Perera, S., Senaratne, S. and Xiaohua, J. (2018). Blockchain for construction supply chains: A literature synthesis. Best Value IT for Construction View Project; Android Disaster Resilience Network View Project.in proceedings of the conference ICEC-PAQS Conference 2018 in Sydney

Sarode, R.P., Poudel, M., Shrestha, S. and Bhalla, S. (2021). Blockchain for committing peer-to-peer transactions using distributed ledger technologies. *International Journal of Computational Science and Engineering*, 24(3), p. 215. https://doi.org/10.1504/ijcse.2021.115651.

14 Blockchain for Cybersecurity
Architectures and Challenges

İsa Avcı and Öğr. Üyesi Murat Koca

14.1 INTRODUCTION

Blockchain technology has emerged as a promising solution for addressing cybersecurity challenges [1, 2]. This chapter explores the various applications of blockchain in the field of cybersecurity, focusing on its potential to enhance data integrity, identity management, threat intelligence sharing, and secure communication. The chapter also delves into the architectural aspects of blockchain-based cybersecurity solutions and discusses the challenges and limitations associated with their implementation. Furthermore, it provides insights into the prospects and research directions in this rapidly evolving domain.

The necessity for strong cybersecurity measures is becoming more and more important as the digital world grows [3]. Traditional security solutions often fall short in combating evolving cyber threats. Blockchain technology, originally designed for secure and decentralized transactions in cryptocurrencies, has gained traction as a disruptive force in the realm of cybersecurity [4]. They explore the potential applications of blockchain in addressing cybersecurity challenges and provide an in-depth analysis of the architectural aspects and challenges associated with implementing blockchain-based solutions.

Data integrity is a fundamental aspect of cybersecurity. Manipulation or unauthorized modifications of data can have severe consequences for organizations and individuals [5]. Blockchain technology offers a decentralized and tamper-evident platform for maintaining data integrity. They discuss the utilization of blockchain to ensure the integrity of critical data, such as digital certificates, logs, and transaction records. Also, they explore the mechanisms for data verification, consensus algorithms, and smart contracts that contribute to establishing trust and ensuring data integrity.

Identity theft and unauthorized access remain significant challenges in the cybersecurity landscape. Blockchain-based identity management systems provide a novel approach to tackling these issues. It delves into the concept of self-sovereign identity (SSI), where users have control over their data and can selectively share it with trusted entities [6]. They explore the architecture and mechanisms of blockchain-based identity systems and discuss the potential to enhance authentication and authorization processes while preserving privacy and security.

Sharing threat intelligence among organizations is crucial for collective defense against cyber threats. However, barriers such as trust, privacy concerns, and data integrity hinder effective information sharing. Blockchain technology presents a decentralized and transparent framework for the secure sharing of threat intelligence [7]. They explore the potential of blockchain in enabling secure and privacy-preserving threat intelligence-sharing platforms. Also, they discuss the architecture and protocols for information exchange and highlight the role of blockchain in establishing trust among participants.

Securing communication channels and IoT devices is a pressing concern in the era of interconnected systems. Blockchain's decentralized nature and cryptographic mechanisms offer opportunities for secure communication and IoT device management [8]. They examine the application of blockchain in securing communication channels, including secure messaging, peer-to-peer

DOI: 10.1201/9781003450306-16

networks, and secure overlay networks. They also explore the integration of blockchain with IoT devices to establish trust, enhance security, and enable secure data exchange.

Implementing blockchain-based cybersecurity solutions poses various architectural considerations and challenges. It provides insights into the design considerations for building secure and scalable blockchain architectures. This study discusses scalability issues, privacy and confidentiality concerns, and interoperability challenges. Furthermore, it addresses the trade-offs between decentralization and performance, highlighting the need to balance security requirements with practical considerations.

Blockchain technology is continually evolving, and its potential for cybersecurity applications is far-reaching. This study provides an outlook on prospects and emerging research directions in the field. Yang and Li discuss the integration of emerging technologies such as artificial intelligence, machine learning, and zero-knowledge proofs with blockchain to enhance cybersecurity capabilities [9]. They also highlight the importance of interdisciplinary collaborations and standardization efforts to accelerate the adoption of blockchain in cybersecurity.

This chapter explores the architectures and challenges associated with using blockchain for cybersecurity. It discusses different blockchain architectures, such as public, private, and consortium blockchains, and their applications in enhancing cybersecurity. We also highlight the benefits and limitations of leveraging blockchain for cybersecurity, including decentralization, transparency, data integrity, and scalability challenges. Furthermore, we delve into the challenges that organizations must address when implementing blockchain for cybersecurity, including technical, governance, legal, and adoption challenges. Finally, we present case studies showcasing real-world applications of blockchain in cybersecurity and outline future directions and research opportunities in this domain. By understanding the architectures and challenges of blockchain for cybersecurity, organizations can make informed decisions about implementing this technology to fortify their security defenses.

14.2   WHAT IS BLOCKCHAIN AND HOW IT WORKS

Blockchain is a distributed and decentralized database. Blockchain is a structure in which time-stamped data is chained and recorded in blocks. Each block is linked by a "hash," which is a unique identifier for the data contained in the block. This ensures the security and integrity of the blockchain. The blockchain works like a ledger shared by many nodes in the network. A *node* collects new transactions, combines these transactions into a block, and sends the created block to other nodes. Published blocks are validated and accepted by the nodes [10, 11].

Generating and validating a block is usually based on consensus algorithms. The most widely used consensus algorithm is known as proof of work (PoW). PoW works by having nodes solve certain math problems. Once a block is verified, it is added to the end of the chain and forms the basis for the next block to be created. This process ensures the continuous growth of the blockchain. Blockchain technology has great potential to ensure the reliability, transparency, and durability of transactions. Lightweight blockchain applications could potentially be used in finance, supply chain management, healthcare, energy, and many other industries. Issues such as privacy, security, scalability, and regulation are key issues that need to be addressed when developing lightweight blockchain technology [12].

14.3   BASIC COMPONENTS AND FUNCTIONING OF BLOCKCHAIN

Blockchain consists of three main components: blocks, transactions, and distributed networks. These transactions are combined into a single block. Each block is linked by a "hash," which is the unique validator of the previous block (see Figure 14.1). Blockchains are shared between nodes in a decentralized network. Each node collects and verifies new transactions and communicates

How to blockchain works ?

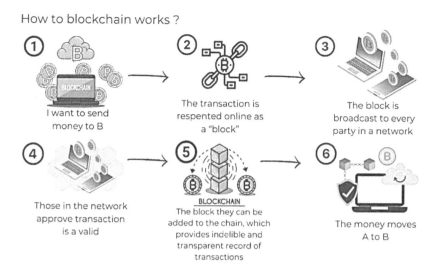

① I want to send money to B

② The transaction is respented online as a "block"

③ The block is broadcast to every party in a network

④ Those in the network approve transaction is a valid

⑤ BLOCKCHAIN
The block they can be added to the chain, which provides indelible and transparent record of transactions

⑥ The money moves A to B

FIGURE 14.1 Blockchain working example.

with other nodes to create blocks [13]. The reliability, integrity, and durability of blockchains are ensured by the process of connecting blocks and verifying transactions within a decentralized network. Blockchain technology thus creates a secure database, allowing transactions to be conducted securely without the need for a central authority or a trusted third party. Once a block is verified, it is added to the end of the chain and forms the basis for the next block to be created. Blockchain technology has great potential to ensure the reliability, transparency, and durability of transactions. Lightweight blockchain applications could potentially be used in finance, supply chain management, healthcare, energy, and many other industries. Issues such as privacy, security, scalability, and regulation are key issues that need to be addressed when developing lightweight blockchain technology [14].

14.4   ARCHITECTURE OF BLOCKCHAIN TECHNOLOGY

Blockchain architecture consists of a certain number of blocks. Each block receives headers from the block's previous block and next block. In addition, each block keeps the previous state and the current state in the block. Figure 14.2 shows that block k-1 saves transaction ID, public key, and signature information.

Blockchain architecture generally has four types of usage methods: public, hybrid, private, and consortium (see Figure 14.3). Public types are models without any central structure [15]. Hybrid types are generally structures that can be controlled by an authority, and some processes are unauthorized. Private types are structures controlled by an authority. Consortium types are structures that can be controlled by a group.

14.5   DIFFERENCES BETWEEN CENTRALIZED AND
DECENTRALIZED STRUCTURES

The differences between centralization and decentralization have important implications in many areas. *Centralization* refers to a structure in which power, control, and decision-making are concentrated in a specific central authority. On the other hand, decentralized structures refer to a structure or a distributed network in which power, control, and decision-making are distributed among

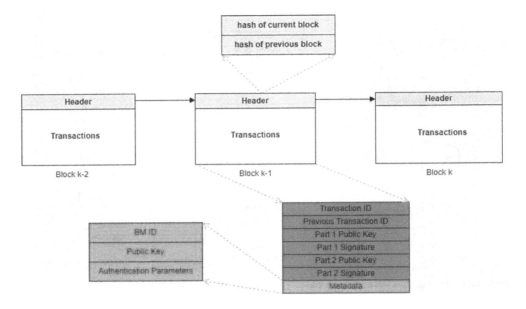

FIGURE 14.2   Blocks in blockchain technology.

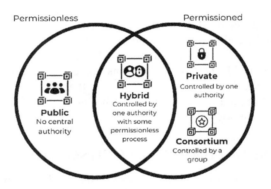

FIGURE 14.3   Types of blockchain structures.

individuals. In this type of structure, decisions are made primarily by participants, and resources are managed through a distributed system, usually a blockchain. A decentralized structure, unlike centralization, has a structure where data and resources are distributed and shared over a wider network [16, 17].

Centralization can provide more centralized control by consolidating control and power, but it can also present weaknesses in terms of security and resilience (see Figure 14.4). Decentralized structures have the potential to provide security and resilience through a broader participant base, but decision-making and implementation costs can be more complex. Understanding the difference between centralization and decentralization is an important issue that can impact the future of operations and management in many industries. In a distributed structure, multi-directional communication is provided between data centers, and it is possible to communicate with each data center from more than one data center.

Central   **Decentralized**   **Distributed**

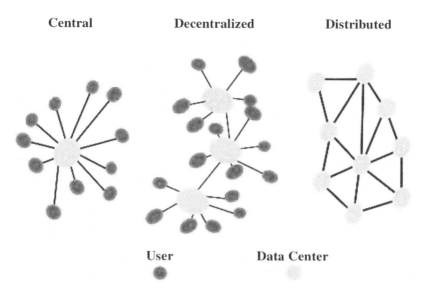

User   Data Center

FIGURE 14.4   Examples of centralized, decentralized, and distributed structures in blockchain.

14.6   SECURITY MECHANISMS OF THE BLOCKCHAIN

Blockchain technology uses a variety of mechanisms to ensure security. The first is the "proof of work" (PoW) algorithm, which is a mathematical proof of work. PoW requires solving a specific problem to create blocks. PoW is used to verify and add blocks to the chain (see Figure 14.5).

This algorithm improves network security and makes it harder to change blocks backward. Blockchain also uses a consensus mechanism called "consensus." Consensus allows nodes to agree on the validity of blocks. Consensus algorithms are based on certain rules for blocks to be accepted and added to the chain. For example, the "proof of stake" (PoS) algorithm uses assets held by nodes to validate blocks (see Table 14.1). These distributed consensus mechanisms offer alternative methods for securing the blockchain. Another security mechanism is the cryptographic protection of data on the blockchain.

The hash is a unique validator of the block, and changing a block requires recalculating all blocks (see Figure 14.6). Finally, blockchain networks are often distributed. In this way, blockchain provides benefits such as secure data storage, reliable transactions, and reduced vulnerabilities. In

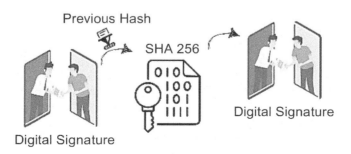

FIGURE 14.5   Proof of work (PoW).

TABLE 14.1
Differences between PoW and PoS

Proof of Work (PoW)	Proof of Stake (PoS)
Computing power	Invested amount
More competition	More efficiency
Pooling power	Pooling stakes
Lack of scale	Coin hoarding

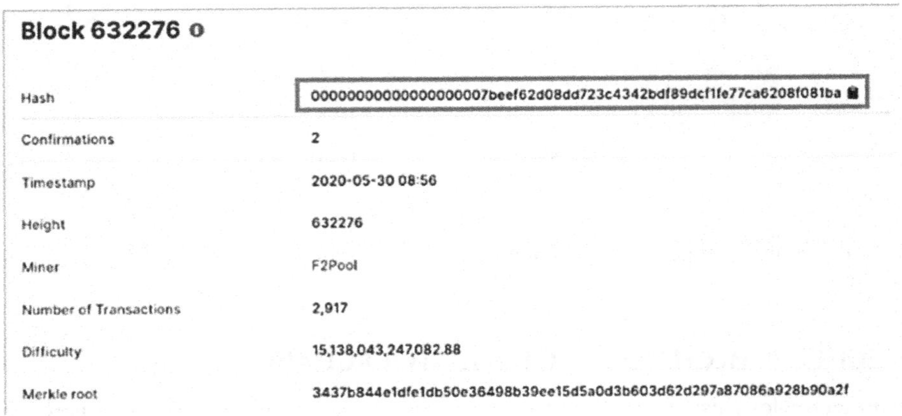

Block 632276 ⓘ

Hash	0000000000000000007beef62d08dd723c4342bdf89dcf1fe77ca6208f081ba 🖿
Confirmations	2
Timestamp	2020-05-30 08:56
Height	632276
Miner	F2Pool
Number of Transactions	2,917
Difficulty	15,138,043,247,082.88
Merkle root	3437b844e1dfe1db50e36498b39ee15d5a0d3b603d62d297a87086a928b90a2f

FIGURE 14.6   Block node data.

this way, blockchains have become the technology of choice in critical use cases, such as secure data storage, reliable transactions, and mitigating vulnerabilities [18]. Challenges such as security mechanism complexity and energy consumption should also be considered, so they should be carefully considered when designing and using blockchain applications.

14.7   BLOCKCHAIN ARCHITECTURES FOR CYBERSECURITY

Blocks are foundational building blocks of the blockchain and consist of a header and content. The block body will consist solely of transactions created in the form of a Merkle tree or proposed for inclusion in blocks. There are four primary categories of blockchains: public, private, hybrid, and consortium [19]. The features of the blockchain architecture depend on these types.

14.7.1   Public Blockchain

The public blockchain is the first form of blockchain technology. This is where cryptocurrencies such as Bitcoin emerged and contributed to the proliferation of distributed ledger technology (DLT), eliminating the issues associated with centralization, such as decreased security and a lack of transparency. Instead of storing information, DLT distributes it across a peer-to-peer network [20]. Its decentralized nature necessitates some methods for validating the data's authenticity. This method is a consensus algorithm in which blockchain participants concur on the present state of the distributed ledger. Proof of work (PoW) and proof of stake (PoS) are two prevalent consensus protocols. Public blockchains are accessible without permission restrictions. They can utilize a variety of consensus mechanisms; however, scalability can be challenging due to the increasing demands of a large user base, and Bitcoin and Ethereum are exemplary cases.

14.7.2 PRIVATE BLOCKCHAIN

Participants can only join a private blockchain network via an invitation that verifies their identity and other pertinent information. The network operator(s) or a clearly defined set of protocols implemented by the network via smart contracts or other automatic authentication methods perform authentication [20]. It is a blockchain with restricted access that is typically reserved for commercial entities. Hyperledger Fabric is among the most prominent private blockchains.

14.7.3 HYBRID BLOCKCHAIN

A hybrid blockchain combines public and private blockchains. The public blockchain validates transaction data using a blockchain consensus mechanism because it is open and accessible [21]. The information is then stored on a private blockchain, which only authorized users can access. This consolidation strikes a balance between transparency, privacy, and security for a variety of applications in the finance, governance, and supply chain management sectors.

14.7.4 CONSORTIUM BLOCKCHAIN

Consortium blockchain, also known as unified blockchain, resembles hybrid blockchain in that it combines private and public blockchain characteristics. But things change when multiple members of an organization collaborate on a decentralized network [22]. A consortium blockchain is essentially a private blockchain with restricted access to a specific group, eradicating the risks associated with a network controlled by a single entity. Consensus procedures in a consortium blockchain are managed by predetermined nodes. A validation node initiates, validates, and receives transactions. Nodes can initiate or receive transactions.

14.7.5 COMPARATIVE ANALYSIS OF ARCHITECTURES

In general, blockchains are designed for specific applications where multiple forms of user access or engagement are supported. Whether public, private, hybrid, or consortium, each blockchain network has distinct advantages and disadvantages that will largely dictate its optimal application and help you choose the best one [23]. The advantages, disadvantages, and ideal uses of each of these platforms are shown in Table 14.2.

TABLE 14.2
Differences between the Four Main Blockchain Architectures

Differences	Public Blockchains	Private Blockchains	Hybrid Blockchains	Consortium Blockchains
Advantages	Independence Transparency Trust	Access control Performance	Access control Performance Scalability	Access control Scalability Security
Disadvantages	Performance Scalability Security	Trust Auditability	Transparency Upgrading	Transparency
Usage zones	Cryptocurrency Document Validation	Supply chain Asset Ownership	Medical records Real estate	Banking Research Supply chain

14.8 APPLICATIONS OF BLOCKCHAIN IN CYBERSECURITY

Blockchain continues to penetrate every aspect of our lives today. The most well-known application is in cryptocurrency financial applications. However, apart from cryptocurrencies, many other application areas, such as energy trading, healthcare, supply chain, manufacturing, identity management, e-government, etc., are based on blockchain technology. Blockchain acts in a distributed structure and provides a service by allowing data sharing among other peer/neighbor connections without a central authority. In this complex structure, each block contains the cryptographic hash of the previous block. We will explain the applications in this structure as follows.

14.8.1 SECURE DIGITAL TRANSACTIONS

Blockchain is a system designed to establish trust in a networked environment through the secure transmission of data using a distributed, decentralized ledger system. It grants access to information to all designated nodes or members who can record, share, and view encrypted transaction data on blockchains. To mitigate the risks of fraud and cyberattacks, blockchain security must be a comprehensive risk management system.

As the data structures of blockchain technology are based on consensus, cryptography, and decentralized principles, they contain inherent security features. Each new information block is linked to all previous information blocks, making it nearly impossible to alter. Additionally, a consensus mechanism (authorized users) confirms and accepts every transaction in a block, ensuring that each transaction is accurate and valid. Consequently, there is no single point of failure, and users are unable to modify transaction records.

14.8.2 DATA INTEGRITY AND AUDITING

Data accuracy and integrity maintenance are top security priorities. Therefore, the most popular cryptographic function in proof of work is hash. The hashing computations are extremely simple, whereas the reverse is extremely difficult to compute. The miner of the blockchain network creates and publishes a new block whenever it discovers a solution for a hash that matches certain properties. Each participant joining the network can verify the validity of the last block that matches the network's required properties.

Blockchain generates a self-verifiable, transparent, and immutable ledger; it enables the creation of smart contracts without the need for a notary public, and all these objectives are met with the utmost dependability and accessibility. It is a new paradigm that guarantees the deterministic execution of a contract and the integrity of the data in a ledger without the intervention of a third party and with complete guarantees.

14.8.3 IDENTITY AND ACCESS MANAGEMENT

Identity management includes processes, policies, and technologies to ensure that only authorized users have access to technology resources. Numerous extant digital identity management systems have drawbacks, such as the risk of data breaches, a poor user experience, and a lack of control over user data.

Increasing data security, accelerating verification/authentication processes, preventing identity fraud, reducing costs, creating an auditable audit trail, automating processes, facilitating data conformance, and enhancing identity accessibility are some of the benefits of blockchain identity management.

Increasing numbers of use cases across industries and sectors, including healthcare, financial services, supply chain, Web3, and retail, are amenable to blockchain identity management. On the blockchain, no personally identifiable information (PII) should be stored.

14.8.4 Supply Chain Security

On a blockchain network, anonymous parties conduct encrypted transactions following a predefined protocol. The use of blockchain technology in the supply chain is one of this technology's emerging applications. Because blockchain transactions are encrypted with the initiator's private key (or the user's digital signature), they are tamper-resistant. Each participant in supply chains with multiple counterparties has a unique digital signature [24]. The user's digital signature serves as protection for transactions like purchase orders. Similar to a supplier, the recipient entity can verify that the purchase order originated from a legitimate customer. Because every transaction in a supply chain is added as a block to the blockchain, it is impossible to falsify a transaction. The blockchain leaves a transaction audit trace that is unalterable, trustworthy, and sequential. There are hundreds of counterparties and thousands of transactions in complex supply channels. Adopting blockchain technology necessitates garnering the trust of partners, which is a difficult but necessary task for businesses, as each partner must transact over a blockchain-based network.

14.9 BENEFITS AND LIMITATIONS OF BLOCKCHAIN FOR CYBERSECURITY

Blockchain maintains a secure, decentralized ledger. Therefore, blockchain can ensure the veracity and safety of data records without requiring a third party. With these characteristics, it provides an exceptional benefit. By performing these operations, it was unable to accomplish the desired pace, performance, high costs, and data integrity.

14.9.1 Benefits

- *Decentralization and immutable records.* The decentralization of the blockchain means that any network member can verify the data recorded on the blockchain. Therefore, the public can trust the network. On the other hand, a traditional database is centralized and does not support transparency. Users cannot verify information at any time, and the administration makes a selected dataset public.
- *Transparency and auditability.* Verifying a blockchain and auditing the digital assets held on the chain provide a significant security advantage. Due to the decentralized nature of the blockchain, all transactions can be viewed transparently by utilizing a personal node or blockchain explorers, which enable anyone to view the live transactions. Each node has its copy of the chain, which is updated whenever new blocks are added and confirmed. This means that you can follow a blog wherever it goes if you so choose. In the past, exchanges have been compromised, resulting in the loss of substantial quantities of cryptocurrencies. Although hackers are anonymous except for their wallet addresses, the cryptocurrencies they steal are readily traceable due to the public nature of their wallet addresses on the blockchain.
- *Enhanced data integrity.* The data stored on the blockchain is immutable and permanent; it cannot be altered or deleted, ensuring that the technology satisfies the Food and Drug Administration's (FDA) ALCOA concept for master data integrity. The term *ALCOA* is an acronym containing several FDA-defined principles. It signifies **a**ttribution, **r**eadability, **c**urrentness, **o**riginality, and **a**ccuracy [25].

Creating versions of edited documents, verifying that different versions of the same file are identical, and inspecting and signing them concurrently are all blockchain features that can be used to resolve data security concerns. When a block is added to the blockchain, the original version of that block is assigned a hash value, recorded in a data block, and distributed to all nodes in the blockchain's structure. By comparing the hash number they receive with the hash stored on the blockchain, various parties with access to this file can verify the integrity of these blocks.

When there are multiple instances of a document, such as agreements that require multiple signatures, you can also monitor the order of actions performed on the document by examining the change records documented in the file's metadata. In addition, this ensures that the document is in its most recent version and that all copies distributed to various departments are identical.

14.9.2 LIMITATIONS

- *Scalability challenges.* Typically measured in transactions per second (TPS), *scalability* is the capacity of a system, network, or process to handle an increasing volume of work, activity, or transactions. It is optimal for blockchain developers to attain vast scope without compromising security. However, this procedure becomes more difficult as blockchain popularity and the number of transactions to be processed increase.
- *Regulatory and compliance considerations.* Compliance with specific regulations can be enhanced by utilizing blockchain technology, but its implementation presents significant obstacles. Blockchain technologies may expose the blockchain network operator and/or network participants to legal and regulatory ambiguity, as many governments and regulators are still attempting to comprehend blockchain and determine whether certain laws need to be updated to manage decentralization appropriately. Essentially, the current dual challenge for blockchain network participants is to ensure compliance with current regulations while minimizing as much as possible the business risks associated with potential regulatory environment changes.
- *Energy consumption.* Blockchain technology has a significant problem with energy consumption. Due to mining, the blockchain's energy consumption is quite high. This is because each newly deployed node immediately connects to every other node, creating a distributed, continuously updated ledger. Each blockchain solution operates differently. For instance, Bitcoin miners compete to officially record and verify a transaction in exchange for Bitcoin. Bitcoin miners use a great deal of energy to solve intricate cryptographic and mathematical problems to verify these transactions. In private or permissioned blockchain networks with fewer nodes, these issues do not exist.

14.10 CYBERSECURITY THREATS IN BLOCKCHAIN APPLICATIONS

14.10.1 SYBIL ATTACKS

Sybil attack is an attacker's attempt to dominate the system by creating multiple fake accounts on the blockchain. These accounts are digital identities used to establish a trusted relationship between regular users or other nodes. A Sybil attack causes the attacker to compromise the integrity and security of the blockchain by controlling fake accounts [26]. With Sybil attack, an adversary can manipulate the transaction verification process using false identities and even double-spend on the blockchain. Sybil attacks can undermine the network by targeting the blockchain's consensus mechanism. Such attacks can be launched with minimal expense and have the potential to seize control of the majority of the network. Therefore, they represent a significant hazard to the blockchain's security. The following measures can be taken to prevent Sybil attacks:

- *Authentication.* In this procedure, each user is authenticated, and only users who have been authenticated are permitted to join the blockchain network. This precludes Sybil attacks because an assailant cannot join the network unless all their identities are verified, even if they have multiple identities.
- Proof of work (PoW). In this method, competition is made between users who have to make a transaction for each block. To do this, users must have sufficient computing power.

This makes it difficult for an attacker to create many identities because he must have sufficient computational power for each identity.

- *Proof of stake (PoS)*. In this method, users must have a certain amount of cryptocurrency to join the network. This makes it difficult for an attacker to create many identities, because he must have enough cryptocurrencies for each identity.
- *Voting*. Users vote to approve or deny blockchain modifications. This makes it difficult for an adversary to alter the blockchain, as any change must be approved by the network's majority.
- *Decentralization*. Preventing the decentralization of the blockchain network makes it difficult for an attacker to dominate the network. Having more local nodes outside the center makes it more difficult for attackers to dominate the network, as a large portion of the network must be controlled for an attacker to dominate the network.

14.10.2 DDoS Attacks

A DDoS attack is a type of cyberattack, also known as a "denial of service attack." During a DDoS attack, a large number of requests are sent to the targeted service, concentrating traffic. This heavy traffic disrupts the normal operation of the service, and the service becomes unusable. A DDoS attack on a blockchain network is a type of attack that overwhelms the network with a large volume of traffic or requests, overloading its capacity to process transactions and slowing the network down or rendering it completely unusable [27].

DDoS attacks on the blockchain can slow down the system or disrupt the service by preventing a node from working, affecting its ability to process transactions on the blockchain or verifying it correctly. In a DDoS attack on a blockchain network, attackers often hijack large numbers of computers or devices, generating a high volume of traffic and making it difficult for the network to distinguish legitimate requests from malicious ones. Such an attack could disrupt the normal functioning of the blockchain network and prevent users from accessing or transacting the network. Preventing DDoS attacks on a blockchain network requires a multi-pronged approach, including implementing anti-DDoS measures, load balancing, decentralization, using robust consensus algorithms, and regular auditing. The main methods of preventing DDoS attacks are as follows:

- *Implementing anti-DDoS measures*. It is important to implement anti-DDoS measures, such as firewalls, intrusion detection systems, and traffic analysis tools, to detect and block malicious traffic. These measures can help prevent DDoS attacks on a blockchain network by filtering out malicious traffic, allowing only legitimate traffic to pass through.
- *Load balancing*. Load balancing is used to distribute the traffic among multiple servers, to distribute the traffic evenly over the network, and to avoid overloading a single server. This can help prevent DDoS attacks, as the network can handle high traffic volumes without overloading it.
- *Decentralization*. Decentralization is the core principle of blockchain technology and can help prevent DDoS attacks. By spreading the network across multiple nodes, the network becomes more resistant to attacks, as there is no central point of failure.
- *Consensus algorithms*. These algorithms are used to verify transactions in a blockchain network. By using a consensus algorithm such as PoS (proof of stake), which is more resistant to DDoS attacks rather than PoW (proof of work), the blockchain network can become more resistant to DDoS attacks.
- *Regular audit*. Regular auditing of the blockchain network can help identify weak spots that attackers can exploit. Identifying and resolving these vulnerabilities can help make the network more secure and less susceptible to DDoS attacks.

14.10.3   51% ATTACKS

A 51% attack on a blockchain is an attack in which a single entity or group of entities controls more than 50% of the network's computing power (hash rate). This allows the attacker to invalidate transactions, double-spend coins, or prevent other miners from adding new blocks to the blockchain to disrupt the blockchain. With more than 50% of the network's computing power, an attacker can create a new blockchain that essentially separates from the original blockchain and corrupts the coins or the network by rewriting the transaction history. This type of attack is considered a significant threat to the security of the blockchain network, as it weakens the decentralized and trust-based nature of the technology. The 51% attack takes its name from the percentage of computing power required to perform the attack [28].

With a 51% attack, an attacker can:

- *Reverse transactions.* An attacker can spend their money twice, reversing already-confirmed transactions. This may result in financial loss for other users who receive approved transactions accepted by other users in good faith.
- *Obstructing the confirmation of transactions.* The assailant possesses the capability to immobilize funds on the blockchain, so obstructing the verification of transactions made by other users.
- *Generating new blocks.* By controlling the majority of the hash rate, the attacker can generate new blocks faster than the rest of the network and create a new blockchain that is fundamentally incompatible with the original.

These 51% attacks are a serious threat to the security and integrity of a blockchain network because they can cause a loss of trust in the network and have a significant financial impact on users.

The following measures can be taken to prevent 51% attacks on a blockchain network:

- *Increasing the network hash rate.* By increasing the overall hash rate of the network, it becomes more difficult for a single entity to control 51% of the network's computing power.
- *Implementing proof-of-stake consensus.* Proof-of-stake (PoS) is an alternative consensus mechanism that does not rely on computational power to validate transactions. Instead, users deposit cryptocurrencies as collateral to participate in the consensus process, making it more difficult for a single entity to control the network.
- *Applying multi-algorithm consensus.* Multi-algorithm consensus involves using different algorithms to verify transactions on the network, making it more difficult for a single entity to control the network by dominating a single algorithm.
- *Regular monitoring of network activity.* By monitoring network activity regularly, suspicious behavior that could lead to a 51% attack can be detected and dealt with in advance.
- *Network management and decentralization.* Providing a decentralized network and strong governance structures can also help prevent 51% attacks, by distributing power and decision-making among a large and diverse stakeholder group.

14.11   CONCLUSION

Blockchain technology has the potential to revolutionize the field of cybersecurity by addressing critical challenges related to data integrity, identity management, threat intelligence sharing, and secure communication. This chapter explored the various applications of blockchain in cybersecurity and discussed the architectural aspects and challenges associated with their implementation. As blockchain continues to evolve, researchers, practitioners, and policymakers need to collaborate to unlock its full potential in building secure and resilient cyber infrastructures. As a result of studies showing that data storage using blockchain is safer than other existing methods, storing data on the blockchain has become popular. Thanks to blockchain, transfers can be made easily by eliminating intermediary institutions (states, banks, etc.), data can be accessed at any time without a time limit, it is used as a shopping tool in some countries, and blockchain mining can be done easily with only electricity and the necessary hardware infrastructure. It has played a major role in the development of the blockchain network. However, the use of blockchain, especially on the side of cryptocurrencies, has increased the appetite of attackers. As a result, they try to manipulate the network and change the data as they wish. This makes it necessary to ensure the security of data in the blockchain infrastructure, which is expanding day by day, train the necessary qualified personnel, and be prepared for possible attacks. Finally, it is necessary to constantly audit the blockchain network and be careful against new attack techniques. As the digital landscape expands, the need for robust cybersecurity measures becomes increasingly critical.

REFERENCES

[1] A.S. Rajasekaran, M. Azees, F. Al-Turjman, A comprehensive survey on blockchain technology, *Sustainable Energy Technologies and Assessments.* 52 (2022) 102039. https://doi.org/10.1016/J. SETA.2022.102039.

[2] H. Han, S. Fei, Z. Yan, X. Zhou, A survey on blockchain-based integrity auditing for cloud data, *Digital Communications and Networks.* 8 (2022) 591–603. https://doi.org/10.1016/J.DCAN.2022.04.036.

[3] S. Mahmood, M. Chadhar, S. Firmin, Cybersecurity challenges in blockchain technology: A scoping review, *Human Behavior and Emerging Technologies.* 2022 (2022) 1–11. https://doi.org/10.1155/2022/7384000.

[4] T. Kim, J. Ochoa, T. Faika, H.A. Mantooth, J. Di, Q. Li, Y. Lee, An overview of cyber-physical security of battery management systems and adoption of blockchain technology, *IEEE Journal of Emerging and Selected Top Power Electronics.* 10 (2022) 1270–1281. https://doi.org/10.1109/JESTPE.2020.2968490.

[5] R. Akter, M. Golam, V.S. Doan, J.M. Lee, D.S. Kim, IoMT-Net: Blockchain-integrated unauthorized UAV localization using lightweight convolution neural network for internet of military things, *IEEE Internet of Things Journal.* 10 (2023) 6634–6651. https://doi.org/10.1109/JIOT.2022.3176310.

[6] U. Cali, M. Fogstad Dynge, M. Sadek Ferdous, U. Halden, Improved resilience of local energy markets using blockchain technology and self-sovereign identity, *2022 IEEE 1st Global Emerging Technology Blockchain Forum: Blockchain and Beyond, IGETblockchain.* 2022 (2022). https://doi.org/10.1109/ IGETBLOCKCHAIN56591.2022.10087157.

[7] D. Puthal, N. Malik, S.P. Mohanty, E. Kougianos, C. Yang, The blockchain as a decentralized security framework [future directions], *IEEE Consumer Electronics Magazine.* 7 (2018) 18–21. https://doi. org/10.1109/MCE.2017.2776459.

[8] K.M. Giannoutakis, G. Spathoulas, C.K. Filelis-Papadopoulos, A. Collen, M. Anagnostopoulos, K. Votis, N.A. Nijdam, A blockchain solution for enhancing cybersecurity defence of IoT, *Proceedings—2020 IEEE International Conference on Blockchain, Blockchain 2020.* (2020) 490–495. https://doi. org/10.1109/BLOCKCHAIN50366.2020.00071.

[9] X. Yang, W. Li, A zero-knowledge-proof-based digital identity management scheme in blockchain, *Computer Security.* 99 (2020) 102050. https://doi.org/10.1016/J.COSE.2020.102050.

[10] N. Buchmann, C. Rathgeb, H. Baier, C. Busch, M. Margraf, Enhancing breeder document long-term security using blockchain technology, *Proceedings—International Computer Software and Applications Conference.* 2 (2017) 744–748. https://doi.org/10.1109/COMPSAC.2017.119.

[11] R. Hutt, *All you need to know about blockchain, explained simply,* World Economic Forum (2016). www. weforum.org/agenda/2016/06/blockchain-explained-simply/ (accessed July 31, 2023).

[12] S.S. Sarmah, Understanding blockchain technology, *Computer Science and Engineering.* 8 (2018) 23–29. https://doi.org/10.5923/j.computer.20180802.02.

[13] Coding Bootcamps Blockchain Training, *Ethereum architecture and components* (2023). www.coding-bootcamps.com/blog/ethereum-architecture-and-components.html (accessed July 31, 2023).

[14] K.K. Vaigandla, R. Karne, M. Siluveru, M. Kesoju, Review on blockchain technology : Architecture, characteristics, benefits, algorithms, challenges and applications, *Mesopotamian Journal of CyberSecurity.* 2023 (2023) 73–84. https://doi.org/10.58496/MJCS/2023/012.

[15] D.E. O'Leary, Configuring blockchain architectures for transaction information in blockchain consortiums: The case of accounting and supply chain systems, *Intelligent Systems in Accounting, Finance and Management.* 24 (2017) 138–147. https://doi.org/10.1002/ISAF.1417.

[16] A.R. Sai, J. Buckley, B. Fitzgerald, A. Le Gear, Taxonomy of centralization in public blockchain systems: A systematic literature review, *Information Processing & Management.* 58 (2021) 102584. https://doi. org/10.1016/J.IPM.2021.102584.

[17] C. Liu, Z. Li, Comparison of centralized and peer-to-peer decentralized market designs for community markets, *IEEE Transactions on Industry Applications.* 58 (2022) 67–77. https://doi.org/10.1109/TIA.2021.3119559.

[18] E. Günen, En Sade Anlatımla Blockchain Nedir, Nasıl Çalışır? *Cointelegraph* (2020). https://tr.cointelegraph.com/news/a-simple-explanation-of-what-is-blockchain-and-how-its-works (accessed July 31, 2023).

[19] Y. Yohan, Proof of work: What is it, and how does it figure into bitcoin halving? *Forkast News* (2023). https://forkast.news/proof-of-work-what-is-it-bitcoin-halving/ (accessed July 31, 2023).

[20] R. Kumar Kaushal, N. Kumar, S. Narayan Panda, N. Adeeb Ali Abdu, Z. Wang, R. Stephen, A. Alex, A review on BlockChain security, *IOP Conference Series: Materials Science and Engineering.* 396 (2018) 012030. https://doi.org/10.1088/1757-899X/396/1/012030.

[21] E.H. Abualsauod, A hybrid blockchain method in internet of things for privacy and security in unmanned aerial vehicles network, *Computers and Electrical Engineering.* 99 (2022) 107847. https://doi.org/10.1016/J.COMPELECENG.2022.107847.

[22] Y. Wang, A. Zhang, P. Zhang, H. Wang, Cloud-assisted EHR sharing with security and privacy preservation via consortium blockchain, *IEEE Access.* 7 (2019) 136704–136719. https://doi.org/10.1109/ACCESS.2019.2943153.

[23] C. Campbell, What are the 4 different types of blockchain technology? *TechTarget* (2023). www.techtarget.com/searchcio/feature/What-are-the-4-different-types-of-blockchain-technology (accessed August 2, 2023).

[24] V. Hassija, V. Chamola, V. Gupta, S. Jain, N. Guizani, A Survey on supply chain security: Application areas, security threats, and solution architectures, *IEEE Internet of Things Journal* 8 (2021) 6222–6246. https://doi.org/10.1109/JIOT.2020.3025775.

[25] Purdie, Florine P, Data integrity and compliance with CGMP guidance for industry. *Draft Guidance* (2016). www.fda.gov/Drugs/GuidanceComplianceRegulatoryInformation/Guidances/default.htm (accessed August 2, 2023).

[26] S. Aggarwal, N. Kumar, Attacks on blockchain, *Advances in Computers.* 121 (2021) 399–410. https://doi.org/10.1016/BS.ADCOM.2020.08.020.

[27] R. Chaganti, B. Bhushan, V. Ravi, The role of Blockchain in DDoS attacks mitigation: Techniques, open challenges and future directions (2022). https://arxiv.org/abs/2202.03617v1 (accessed August 2, 2023).

[28] C. Ye, G. Li, H. Cai, Y. Gu, A. Fukuda, Analysis of security in blockchain: Case study in 51%-attack detecting, *Proceedings—2018 5th International Conference on Dependable Systems and Their Applications, DSA 2018.* (2018) 15–24. https://doi.org/10.1109/DSA.2018.00015.

15 Enabling Citizen Sustainable Behaviors in Urban Mobility through Blockchain and Tokenization

Silvio Meneguzzo, Elvis Gerardin Konjoh Selabi,
Alfredo Favenza, Valentina Gatteschi,
and Claudio Schifanella

15.1 INTRODUCTION

Urban mobility remains a pressing issue that cities globally grapple with, presenting an array of challenges that include but are not limited to traffic congestion, air pollution, and parking shortages (Javier & NOMMON, n.d.). These challenges have far-reaching implications, affecting both environmental sustainability and the quality of life in urban areas. The transportation sector, a significant part of urban mobility, is a leading contributor to greenhouse gas emissions, thereby exacerbating climate change (IPCC, 2018; Nallet, 2018).

Traditional methods to mitigate these challenges, such as subsidies for using public transportation or penalties for excessive emissions, have had limited success (Gössling & Hall, 2022). These approaches often fail to bring about the behavioral changes needed for a sustainable transformation of urban mobility. Therefore, there is an increasing consensus among policymakers and researchers alike that innovative solutions are required. These solutions should not only be effective but also equitable, promoting citizen participation and encouraging virtuous behaviors in urban mobility.

In this context, blockchain technology and tokenization emerge as promising avenues for innovation. Blockchain, initially conceptualized for the cryptocurrency Bitcoin, is a distributed ledger technology that offers secure, transparent, and immutable recording of transactions (Nakamoto, 2008). Its decentralized nature eliminates the need for a central authority, thereby reducing the risk of fraud and manipulation. Tokenization, on the other hand, involves the representation of physical assets or services as digital tokens on a blockchain (Swan, 2015). These tokens can serve as a medium to incentivize and reward behaviors that contribute to sustainable urban mobility.

For instance, mobility services like car-sharing or ride-sharing can be tokenized to create a reward system. Users can earn these tokens by engaging in sustainable practices, such as reducing carbon emissions, using electric vehicles, or opting for public transport over personal cars. These tokens can then be exchanged for various benefits, like discounts on future rides, thereby creating a positive feedback loop that encourages sustainable behavior (White, Habib, & Hardisty, 2019).

The integration of blockchain technology ensures that this token-based incentive system is secure, transparent, and immutable. Users can earn and exchange tokens on a decentralized platform without the need for intermediaries or a centralized authority. This not only streamlines the process but also adds a layer of trust and transparency, as all transactions are publicly recorded on the blockchain.

DOI: 10.1201/9781003450306-17

In the forthcoming chapters, we will delve deeper into the multifaceted benefits and challenges of employing blockchain technology and tokenization in urban mobility, with a particular focus on the automotive industry. We aim to provide a comprehensive analysis that includes technical requirements for implementing such a system, its potential impact on user behavior, sustainability, and overall urban mobility. Furthermore, we will explore the regulatory landscape and policy implications, offering recommendations for stakeholders involved. By examining these aspects, this chapter aims to contribute to the ongoing discourse on sustainable urban mobility, offering a novel perspective on how blockchain technology and tokenization can serve as catalysts for change.

15.2 THE STATE OF URBAN MOBILITY

15.2.1 Traffic Congestion

Traffic congestion is an enduring and pervasive issue in contemporary urban environments, causing a domino effect of challenges that go beyond simple inconvenience. According to a study by Schrank, Eisele, and Lomax (2021), the repercussions of congestion are multifaceted, leading to increased travel times, higher fuel consumption, and a consequent rise in greenhouse gas emissions.

In the United States, the economic impact of traffic congestion is particularly alarming. Estimates indicate an annual cost exceeding $160 billion, a figure that encompasses 3.1 billion gallons of wasted fuel and nearly 7 billion extra hours of travel time (Somuyiwa, Fadare, & Ayantoyinbo, 2015). This economic burden is not just a standalone issue but is part of a larger, more complex problem exacerbated by demographic shifts. Population growth and urban sprawl are putting additional stress on already-overburdened transportation infrastructures, making the problem of congestion even more severe (Arnott & Small, 1994). The issue of traffic congestion is not merely a logistical or economic problem; it is a complex challenge that intersects with environmental sustainability and quality of life. As urban areas continue to grow and evolve, the traditional methods of addressing congestion are proving to be increasingly inadequate. This underscores the need for innovative solutions that can tackle the issue in a more holistic manner, taking into account its various economic, environmental, and social dimensions.

15.2.2 Air Pollution

Air pollution stands as a critical environmental and public health issue in urban landscapes globally. The World Health Organization (WHO) reports that over 90% of the world's population resides in areas where air quality falls below WHO guidelines, leading to approximately 4.2 million premature deaths annually (WHO, 2020). The transportation sector is a significant contributor, accounting for about 23% of global energy-related CO_2 emissions and 18% of all anthropogenic emissions of NOx, a key precursor to ozone and particulate matter (PM) (IEA, 2023a)

15.2.2.1 Vehicle Emissions and Their Components

Vehicles emit a complex cocktail of pollutants, the composition of which depends on various factors, such as vehicle type, age, fuel quality, and driving conditions (Zhang & Batterman, 2013). These pollutants include:

CO. Carbon monoxide (CO) is a colorless, odorless gas resulting from incomplete combustion. High concentrations can lead to headaches, dizziness, and impaired cognitive functions. It is particularly dangerous because it interferes with the blood's ability to carry oxygen (US EPA, 2020).

NOx. Nitrogen oxides (NOx) are highly reactive gases that contribute to ozone formation, acid rain, and respiratory issues. They are formed when nitrogen and oxygen in the air react at high temperatures in the engine. NOx emissions are a significant concern in urban areas, where traffic density is high (EPA U., 2021).

PM. Particulate matter (PM) can penetrate deep into the lungs and bloodstream, causing various health issues, such as asthma and cardiovascular diseases. PM is categorized based on its size into PM10 and PM2.5, with the latter being more harmful due to its ability to penetrate deeper into the respiratory system (Block & Calderón-Garciadueñas, 2009; IEA, 2023b).

VOCs. Volatile organic compounds (VOCs) can react with NOx to form ozone and PM and can also cause various health issues ranging from eye irritation to cancer. VOCs are emitted not only from vehicle exhaust but also from fuel evaporation and other vehicle-related activities (Graedel, 1992; USEPA, 2022).

Ozone. Formed when NOx and VOCs react in sunlight, ozone can damage lung tissues and aggravate respiratory diseases. While ozone high in the atmosphere protects us from ultraviolet rays, at ground level, it is an air pollutant that causes health problems (US EPA, 2021).

15.2.2.2   Health and Environmental Impacts of Air Pollution

The health impacts of air pollution are well-documented, affecting various bodily systems and leading to a range of diseases (Pannia, 2023). These include respiratory diseases like asthma and COPD, cardiovascular diseases such as hypertension and heart failure, and neurological conditions like Alzheimer's and Parkinson's diseases (Block & Calderón-Garciadueñas, 2009).

Air pollution also has significant environmental impacts. It contributes to climate change by altering the radiative balance of the atmosphere. Pollutants like CO2, methane, and nitrous oxide are greenhouse gases that trap heat in the atmosphere. Other pollutants like PM and ozone can have both warming and cooling effects (IPCC, 2018). Additionally, air pollution can lead to ecosystem degradation by affecting biodiversity and the functioning of plants and animals (Lovett et al., 2007).

It also has material consequences, causing corrosion and erosion of buildings, monuments, and other infrastructures, thereby affecting their longevity and aesthetic value (Graedel, 1992).

15.2.2.3   Distributional Effects of Air Pollution

Air pollution's impact is not uniformly distributed. Factors like meteorology, topography, and land use contribute to its spatial and temporal variability (Zhang & Batterman, 2013). Moreover, certain demographic groups, such as children, the elderly, and people of color, are more vulnerable due to various socio-economic and health-related factors (Bell & Ebisu, 2012).

For instance, children and the elderly are more susceptible due to their immature or weakened immune and respiratory systems. They are also more exposed to air pollution due to their higher breathing rates and outdoor activities (EPA, 2018).

Gender and racial disparities also exist; women and people of color are generally more vulnerable due to a range of socio-economic and health-related factors. Women, for example, are more likely to use public transportation, thereby increasing their exposure (Clancy, Goodman, Sinclair, & Dockery, 2002).

15.2.3   Parking Shortages

Urban mobility is a complex issue that encompasses various challenges, one of which is the persistent problem of parking shortages. The scarcity of parking spaces in urban areas has far-reaching implications, affecting not only the efficiency of the transportation system but also contributing to environmental degradation. The phenomenon of "cruising," where drivers roam streets in search of parking, exacerbates traffic congestion and increases vehicle emissions (Shoup, 2006).

The economic costs of parking shortages are also significant. According to a study by INRIX, the average American driver spends 17 hours per year searching for parking, which costs the US economy approximately $73 billion annually (INRIX, 2023). This economic burden extends to businesses as well, as customers who cannot find parking are less likely to return, affecting revenue and local economies (Anderson & de Palma, 2004).

The environmental impact of parking shortages is another critical concern. Cruising for parking contributes to increased fuel consumption and emissions of greenhouse gases and other pollutants. A study in Brooklyn found that cruising for parking produced 730 tons of carbon dioxide per year in one small 15-block area (Weinberger et al., 2010). This is a significant addition to the already-high levels of emissions produced by the transportation sector, which is responsible for approximately 28% of greenhouse gas emissions in the United States (EPA U., 2021).

Technological solutions, such as smart parking systems, have been proposed to mitigate the impact of parking shortages. These systems use sensors and real-time data analytics to provide drivers with information on available parking spaces, thereby reducing the time spent cruising (Abadi, Rajabioun, & Ioannou, 2015). However, the adoption of these systems has been slow and inconsistent, often due to high implementation costs and lack of public awareness (Vanheusden, van Dalen, & Mingardo, 2022).

Moreover, the issue of parking shortages intersects with broader urban planning and policy considerations. For instance, the allocation of urban space for parking is often at odds with other important uses, such as green spaces, pedestrian areas, and public transportation infrastructure (Chester, Horvath, & Madanat, 2010). Therefore, addressing parking shortages requires a multifaceted approach that considers not only technological solutions but also urban planning strategies and policy interventions (Guo & Ren, 2013).

15.2.4 CONTRIBUTION TO CARBON EMISSIONS AND CLIMATE CHANGE

The transportation sector is an increasingly significant contributor to global carbon emissions and, consequently, climate change. According to the International Energy Agency (IEA), the sector was responsible for 27% of global greenhouse gas emissions in 2020, with road vehicles being the primary contributors (IEA, 2023a). This is an alarming increase from the 24% contribution reported in 2014 (Sims et al., 2014). The emissions from transportation are primarily carbon dioxide, released when fossil fuels are burned. This greenhouse gas plays a pivotal role in trapping heat in the Earth's atmosphere, leading to global warming.

The ramifications of global warming are far-reaching and multifaceted. Rising sea levels, more frequent and severe weather events, and shifts in plant and animal life are among the most pressing concerns. For instance, the thermal expansion of oceans and the melting of polar ice caps, both consequences of global warming, contribute to rising sea levels. This poses a direct threat to coastal communities and can lead to saltwater intrusion into freshwater supplies. Furthermore, the increased frequency of extreme weather events—heat waves, droughts, floods, and storms—has devastating impacts on human life, property, and infrastructure.

The rapid growth in transportation emissions is particularly concerning. Between 1990 and 2020, global transportation emissions surged by 50%, driven by factors such as population growth, economic expansion, and urbanization (IEA, 2023a). This trajectory is unsustainable and demands immediate intervention.

Several strategies can be employed to curb transportation emissions. Investment in public transportation, walking, and biking infrastructure can provide more sustainable alternatives to individual car use. The promotion of electric vehicles (EVs) and other zero-emission vehicles can also make a significant difference. Unlike traditional vehicles, EVs do not produce tailpipe emissions, substantially reducing their impact on climate change. Cleaner fuels and more efficient engines can further mitigate the environmental impact of the transportation sector.

Policy interventions are crucial in this context. Implementing tax incentives for electric vehicles, subsidizing public transportation, and investing in pedestrian-friendly infrastructure are examples of how policy can drive change. These measures not only reduce emissions but also encourage a cultural shift toward more sustainable transportation behaviors.

The transportation sector's growing contribution to carbon emissions and climate change is a critical issue that intersects with various aspects of urban mobility. While technological advancements offer promising solutions, they must be complemented by robust policy interventions to achieve meaningful impact. The urgency of the situation calls for a multi-pronged approach that involves stakeholders at all levels, from individual citizens to global organizations.

15.3 TRADITIONAL INCENTIVE SYSTEMS

15.3.1 SUBSIDIES

Subsidies are monetary incentives provided to individuals or organizations to encourage specific behaviors, such as the use of sustainable transportation options. In urban mobility, these financial incentives often target the promotion of public transit and electric vehicles. For instance, many cities offer discounted fares for public transportation, aiming to alleviate traffic congestion and minimize air pollution. Similarly, tax incentives for electric vehicles are designed to make them more financially accessible, contributing to a reduction in greenhouse gas emissions.

Subsidies have long been employed as a policy tool to encourage the adoption of more sustainable modes of transportation, such as electric vehicles (EVs) and public transit (Gillingham & Palmery, 2014). Governments offer financial incentives like tax breaks, rebates, or direct subsidies to lower the up-front cost of EVs (Sierzchula, Bakker, Maat, & Van Wee, 2014). However, the effectiveness of these subsidies is a subject of debate. While they have led to an increase in EV adoption rates in some regions (Hardman, Chandan, Tal, & Turrentine, 2017), they often benefit higher-income households that would have purchased EVs even without the subsidy (Diamond, 2009).

15.3.2 PENALTIES

Penalties are financial punishments that are imposed on individuals or organizations for engaging in certain behaviors. In the context of urban mobility, penalties are often used to discourage the use of private vehicles and other unsustainable transportation modes. Penalties, such as congestion pricing and high-emission zone fees, aim to discourage the use of fossil fuel-powered vehicles in urban areas (Eliasson, 2014). These measures have shown some success in reducing traffic congestion and emissions in cities like London and Stockholm (Duranton & Turner, 2011). However, they can also be regressive, disproportionately affecting lower-income households who cannot afford to switch to cleaner alternatives (Bento, Goulder, Jacobsen, & Von Haefen, 2009).

15.3.3 EFFECTIVENESS AND LIMITATIONS

Both subsidies and penalties have shown mixed results in changing user behavior toward more sustainable mobility options (Graham-Rowe, Skippon, Gardner, & Abraham, 2011). One of the key limitations is the lack of long-term effectiveness. Subsidies often lead to a temporary spike in sustainable behavior, which wanes once the financial incentives are removed. Penalties, on the other hand, can lead to unintended consequences, such as increased traffic in areas not subject to fees (Small & Yan, 2001).

15.3.4 SUMMARY

Traditional incentive systems, while well-intentioned, have limitations in their ability to induce lasting behavioral changes for sustainable urban mobility. These limitations highlight the need for innovative approaches that can address the shortcomings of existing systems and engage citizens more effectively in sustainable practices.

15.4 BLOCKCHAIN TECHNOLOGY: A BRIEF OVERVIEW

15.4.1 INTRODUCTION

Blockchain technology, initially conceptualized for Bitcoin, has evolved far beyond its original application to offer secure, transparent, and tamperproof transactions across a multitude of sectors, including urban mobility (Khan et al., 2021). Operating on a decentralized peer-to-peer network, it offers a robust platform that is resistant to fraud and data manipulation (Xie et al., 2019)

15.4.2 KEY FEATURES

15.4.2.1 Decentralization

One of the cornerstone features of blockchain is its decentralization. Unlike traditional centralized systems, where a single entity has control, blockchain operates on a network of nodes with no central authority. This architecture not only enhances security but also democratizes the control and verification of transactions, making the system more resilient to fraudulent activities and single points of failure.

15.4.2.2 Transparency

Transparency is another defining feature of blockchain technology. Every transaction is recorded on a public ledger, accessible to anyone who wishes to inspect it. This level of transparency is unprecedented in traditional systems and is particularly beneficial in applications that require a high degree of auditability, such as governmental operations and financial systems (Javed et al., 2022).

15.4.2.3 Immutability

Immutability in blockchain is achieved through cryptographic hashing and consensus algorithms. Once a transaction is verified and added to a block, altering this information would require an unrealistic amount of computational power, making the data virtually tamperproof. This feature is crucial for applications that require the secure and permanent recording of data, such as legal contracts, property deeds, and identity verification (Xie et al., 2019).

15.4.3 APPLICATIONS IN URBAN MOBILITY

15.4.3.1 Tokenization of Mobility Services

Tokenization in the context of urban mobility involves representing physical assets or services, such as car-sharing or ride-sharing, as digital tokens on a blockchain. Users can earn these tokens by engaging in sustainable behaviors, such as reducing carbon emissions or using eco-friendly transportation options. These tokens can then be exchanged for various rewards, thereby incentivizing sustainable practices in urban mobility.

15.4.3.2 Decentralized Vehicle Monitoring and Management

Blockchain technology can be leveraged to create decentralized systems for real-time vehicle tracking and management. Such systems can provide a wide range of functionalities, from basic location tracking to more complex features like predictive maintenance and usage-based insurance. This not only enhances the efficiency of vehicle sharing and rental services but also contributes to road safety and sustainability (Javed et al., 2022).

15.4.3.3 Secure and Efficient Payment Systems

Payment systems based on blockchain technology can offer a more secure and efficient alternative to traditional methods. By eliminating intermediaries and offering direct peer-to-peer transactions, blockchain can significantly reduce transaction costs and processing times, thereby improving the overall user experience in urban mobility services (Xie et al., 2019).

15.4.4 CHALLENGES AND LIMITATIONS

15.4.4.1 Scalability

One of the most pressing challenges facing blockchain technology is scalability. The decentralized nature of blockchain networks often results in slower transaction speeds and higher costs, especially as the network grows. This is a significant hurdle for applications that require rapid and high-volume transactions (Xie et al., 2019).

15.4.4.2 Complexity

Blockchain technology is often criticized for its complexity, which can be a barrier to its widespread adoption. The technical intricacies involved in developing and deploying blockchain-based solutions can be daunting, requiring specialized knowledge and expertise.

15.4.4.3 Regulatory Uncertainty

The regulatory landscape for blockchain technology is still evolving, leading to a degree of uncertainty that can be a deterrent for businesses and investors. The lack of clear guidelines and standards can make it risky to invest in blockchain-based applications, particularly in sectors that are heavily regulated (Javed et al., 2022).

Despite these challenges, blockchain technology holds significant promise for revolutionizing urban mobility. Its unique features offer new avenues for incentivizing sustainable behaviors, enhancing operational efficiency, and reducing costs, thereby contributing to the creation of a more sustainable and equitable urban mobility ecosystem (Xie et al., 2019).

15.5 TOKENIZATION: A PRIMER

15.5.1 DEFINITION AND CONCEPT

Tokenization represents a paradigmatic shift in asset management and ownership, fundamentally altering how we interact with financial and non-financial assets. By converting the rights to an asset into a digital token on a blockchain, tokenization creates a digital twin of the asset, encapsulating its value and ownership rights into a digital format (Swan, 2015; Nakamoto, 2008). This digital representation is not merely a facsimile but a fully functional asset that can be transferred, traded, or integrated into complex financial instruments via smart contracts. Smart contracts are self-executing contracts with the terms of the agreement between buyer and seller being directly written into lines of code, thereby automating and streamlining the transaction process (Szabo, 1997).

The transformative power of tokenization lies in its ability to abstract and digitize real-world assets, making them easily transferable and divisible without compromising the asset's intrinsic value or integrity. For example, a valuable artwork could be tokenized to allow multiple people to own fractions of it, thereby democratizing access to art investment. This is particularly impactful in sectors like real estate, where the high cost of entry often precludes widespread participation. Tokenization can break down these barriers, allowing for fractional ownership and investment from a broader demographic (Merkle, 2016).

Blockchain technology serves as the foundational infrastructure for tokenization, offering a secure, transparent, and immutable environment for digital transactions. Unlike traditional databases, which are centralized and controlled by a single entity, blockchain is decentralized and distributed across a network of computers (Zheng, Xie, Dai, Chen, & Wang, 2018). This decentralization ensures that no single entity has unilateral control over the entire blockchain, thereby providing a level of security and trust that is often lacking in centralized systems.

Moreover, the blockchain's immutable ledger ensures that once a token is created, its ownership and transaction history can be transparently traced back, reducing the risk of fraud or unauthorized alterations (Nakamoto, 2008). This feature is not just a technological nicety but a fundamental requirement for the secure and transparent functioning of tokenized assets. It ensures that the digital representation of the asset remains a true reflection of its real-world counterpart, both in terms of its value and its ownership history. Furthermore, the blockchain's cryptographic algorithms ensure that each transaction is securely encrypted, providing an additional layer of security. This cryptographic security, combined with the network's decentralized validation process, makes blockchain an ideal platform for the secure and transparent management of tokenized assets (Buterin, 2020). Tokenization is not merely a technological innovation but a transformative process that has the potential to revolutionize asset management and ownership. By leveraging the robust, secure, and transparent infrastructure provided by blockchain technology, tokenization offers a new paradigm for asset ownership and investment. It democratizes access to various asset classes, enhances liquidity, and provides an unprecedented level of security and transparency. As such, the symbiotic relationship between tokenization and blockchain technology is poised to redefine the landscape of asset management, offering new opportunities and challenges for investors, regulators, and stakeholders alike.

15.5.2 Types of Assets and Services That Can Be Tokenized

Tokenization, the process of converting rights to an asset or service into a digital token on a blockchain, has emerged as a disruptive force in asset management and financial services format (Swan, 2015; Nakamoto, 2008). This transformative technology has the potential to democratize access to a variety of asset classes, enhance liquidity, and provide an unprecedented level of security and transparency. The scope of tokenization is vast, encompassing a wide range of assets and services, each with its unique characteristics and implications for tokenization.

Financial assets are perhaps the most straightforward candidates for tokenization. Stocks, bonds, and other securities can be tokenized to facilitate easier and more transparent trading. Tokenization can break down the barriers to entry for retail investors by allowing for fractional ownership of high-value assets (Mougayar, 2016). This democratization of financial markets could potentially lead to a more equitable distribution of wealth and opportunity. Moreover, tokenized securities can be easily integrated into decentralized finance (DeFi) platforms, providing additional avenues for yield generation and risk management (Schär, 2021).

Real estate is another asset class that stands to benefit significantly from tokenization. The high cost of real estate investments often precludes widespread participation. Tokenization can mitigate this by allowing for fractional ownership, thereby lowering the minimum investment requirement (Merkle, 2016). This not only democratizes access to real estate investment but also enhances the liquidity of these traditionally illiquid assets. Furthermore, tokenization can simplify the complex and cumbersome process of real estate transactions, from due diligence to title transfer, by automating these processes through smart contracts (Szabo, 1997).

Intellectual property, including patents, copyrights, and even brand equity, can also be tokenized to enable fractional ownership and revenue sharing. This could open new avenues for creators to monetize their work and for investors to participate in the economic success of intellectual property (Tapscott & Tapscott, 2016).

In the realm of services, tokenization can be applied to healthcare records, educational credentials, and even identities. This streamlines administrative processes and reduces the risk of fraud (Zheng, Xie, Dai, Chen, & Wang, 2018). More abstract concepts like carbon credits and voting rights can also be tokenized, offering new mechanisms for civic engagement and environmental conservation (Reijers, O'Brolcháin, & Haynes, 2016).

Beyond traditional assets, services such as data storage, computational power, and bandwidth can also be tokenized. This could lead to decentralized networks for cloud computing and data storage, where users can rent out their unused resources in exchange for tokens (Zohar, 2015).

Tokenization is not without its challenges, including regulatory uncertainty, technological complexity, and issues related to compliance and governance (Government, 2015). However, the potential benefits, from democratizing asset ownership to enhancing liquidity and transparency, make it a compelling avenue for innovation and investment.

Tokenization has the potential to revolutionize the way we think about asset ownership and investment. By leveraging the robust, secure, and transparent infrastructure provided by blockchain technology, tokenization can democratize access to a wide range of assets and services, from stocks and real estate to intellectual property and computational resources. As this technology continues to mature, it is likely to redefine the landscape of asset management, offering new opportunities and challenges for investors, regulators, and stakeholders alike (Catalini & Gans, 2020).

15.5.3 BENEFITS OF TOKENIZATION

Tokenization, the act of converting rights to an asset or service into a digital token on a blockchain, has emerged as a groundbreaking paradigm in the digital transformation of various industries (Swan, 2015; Nakamoto, 2008). This section aims to provide an in-depth exploration of the multifaceted benefits that tokenization brings to the table, supported by empirical evidence and academic discourse.

- *Liquidity enhancement.* Liquidity is often cited as one of the most compelling advantages of tokenization. Traditional assets like real estate, art, and even certain financial instruments are often illiquid, meaning, they cannot be easily converted into cash without a substantial loss in value. Tokenization mitigates this by enabling fractional ownership, allowing smaller investors to buy "shares" in these assets (Fisch, 2019). This fractionalization democratizes investment opportunities and creates a more dynamic and liquid market, thereby attracting a broader range of investors and increasing the asset's market value (Schär, 2021; Ahmadjee, Mera-Gómez, Bahsoon, & Kazman, 2022).
- *Cost-effectiveness.* The traditional asset-trading and management landscape is fraught with inefficiencies, including high transaction fees and cumbersome paperwork. Tokenization, by its very nature, eliminates the need for intermediaries such as brokers, custodians, and notaries, thereby significantly reducing transaction costs (Mougayar, 2016). Furthermore, the advent of smart contracts allows for the automation of complex legal and financial processes, such as compliance checks and dividend distribution, which further reduces administrative overhead (Swan, 2015; Buterin, 2020).
- *Accessibility and democratization.* Tokenization has the potential to democratize investment and ownership. Traditional investment opportunities are often restricted by financial, geographical, and regulatory barriers. Tokenization obliterates these barriers by enabling global access to asset ownership (Tapscott & Tapscott, 2016). This is particularly impactful in emerging markets and for marginalized communities, where access to investment opportunities is often limited by the constraints of traditional financial systems.
- *Programmability.* The concept of tokenization, particularly its programmable aspect, is poised to bring about a seismic shift in the financial landscape. This feature allows for the creation of "smart assets," which are digital tokens embedded with specific conditions and logic that enable them to autonomously execute a wide array of actions (Zheng, Xie, Dai, Chen, & Wang, 2018). These smart assets can execute a wide range of actions autonomously, from dividend payments to voting rights, and even more complex operations

like asset-backed lending or dynamic pricing models (Catalini & Gans, 2020; Morkunas, Paschen, & Boon, 2019).

The implications of this programmability for the financial system are manifold and transformative. One of the most immediate benefits is the increased efficiency and automation it brings to asset management and trading. Traditional financial systems often involve cumbersome and time-consuming processes, which can be streamlined through the use of smart assets. These digital tokens can automate many of the tasks that would otherwise require human intervention, thereby reducing operational costs and speeding up transaction times.

Another significant advantage is the reduced risk of fraud and error. In traditional systems, the complexity and manual nature of transactions often leave room for mistakes and fraudulent activities. However, the self-executing nature of smart contracts, which are the building blocks of smart assets, minimizes these risks. These contracts automatically execute when predefined conditions are met, leaving little room for manual error or manipulation.

Transparency and accountability are also greatly enhanced through the use of smart assets. All transactions involving these assets are recorded on a blockchain, providing a transparent and immutable record of ownership and activity. This level of transparency is unprecedented in traditional financial systems and can act as a deterrent against fraudulent activities and abuse, thereby instilling greater confidence among participants in the financial ecosystem.

The programmability of tokens also paves the way for new and innovative investment opportunities. For example, it enables the creation of fractional ownership models for high-value assets like real estate or fine art, which have traditionally been accessible only to wealthy investors. This democratizes investment opportunities and allows for greater participation from a broader demographic. Additionally, smart assets can be used to develop new types of investment funds, risk management strategies, and other financial products that were not feasible under traditional financial systems.

Specific applications of this technology are already emerging across various sectors. In the realm of securities, for instance, smart assets are being used to create tokenized versions of traditional financial instruments, like stocks, bonds, and derivatives. This not only makes these assets more accessible but also simplifies the trading process. In the lending sector, smart assets enable the creation of asset-backed lending platforms, where borrowers can use their tokenized assets as collateral, and smart contracts manage the lending and repayment processes automatically. Furthermore, the rise of decentralized finance (DeFi) is largely facilitated by smart assets, which are used to create a wide range of decentralized financial products and services, from exchanges and lending platforms to derivatives markets.

- *Tokenizing intangible assets and services.* Beyond tangible assets, tokenization extends to intangible assets and services. For instance, healthcare records, educational credentials, and even personal identities can be tokenized to streamline administrative processes and reduce fraud (Zheng, Xie, Dai, Chen, & Wang, 2018). This has profound implications for data privacy and identity management in the digital age.
- *Tokenizing social and environmental credits.* Tokenization also offers innovative mechanisms for civic engagement and environmental conservation. Concepts like carbon credits and voting rights can be tokenized, thereby creating transparent and immutable systems for social and environmental impact (Reijers, O'Brolcháin, & Haynes, 2016).

Tokenization is not merely a technological innovation; it is a multifaceted revolution that has the potential to redefine the very fabric of how we understand ownership and investment. Its benefits are manifold, from enhancing liquidity and reducing costs to democratizing access and enabling unprecedented programmability. As blockchain technology continues to evolve, the scope and impact of tokenization are set to expand exponentially, offering a plethora of opportunities and challenges for investors, regulators, and society at large.

15.6 BLOCKCHAIN AND TOKENIZATION IN URBAN MOBILITY

15.6.1 TOKENIZING MOBILITY SERVICES (CAR-SHARING, RIDE-SHARING)

The transformative potential of blockchain technology has been a subject of extensive research and practical applications across various domains. One of the most intriguing possibilities lies in the tokenization of mobility services. *Tokenization*, in this context, refers to the use of blockchain technology to create digital tokens that represent a unit of value or a set of permissions within a specific ecosystem (Mougayar, 2016). Traditional mobility services have often been plagued by inefficiencies, ranging from payment frictions to the underutilization of assets. The centralized nature of these services also raises concerns about data privacy and monopolistic practices (Shaheen, Cohen, & Zohdy, 2016). Tokenization, facilitated by blockchain's decentralized architecture, offers a paradigm shift. By converting rights or privileges such as the right to use a car for a certain period into digital tokens, blockchain provides a secure, transparent, and more efficient method of interacting with mobility services. Mobility services, such as car-sharing, ride-sharing, bike-sharing, or public transport, are becoming increasingly popular and convenient modes of transportation in urban areas. These services offer various benefits for users, such as lower costs, greater flexibility, reduced congestion, and lower emissions. However, these services also face several challenges, such as high operational costs, low utilization rates, complex payment systems, and regulatory uncertainties (Vanheusden, van Dalen, & Mingardo, 2022). Tokenization is a process that can address some of these challenges by converting the rights to use or access mobility services into digital tokens on a blockchain. A *token* is a digital representation of an asset or a unit of value that can be transferred, traded, or integrated into smart contracts. A blockchain is a distributed ledger that records and verifies transactions in a secure, transparent, and immutable way (Swan, 2015; Nakamoto, 2008).

The token economy can significantly enhance user experience and operational efficiency. For instance, a user could earn tokens by opting for eco-friendly rides or carpooling, and these tokens could be used for future rides or traded in a decentralized marketplace. This not only incentivizes sustainable practices but also adds a layer of gamification that could attract and retain users (Fagnant & Kockelman, 2018). On the operational side, tokenization can streamline the payment process by eliminating intermediaries, thereby reducing costs and increasing transaction speed (Tapscott & Tapscott, 2016). One critical advantage of tokenization is its potential to foster interoperability between various transportation modes. Currently, each form of public transport or sharing service operates in isolation, with its own ticketing and payment systems. A token-based system could serve as a universal medium of exchange, enabling seamless transition from a subway to a shared bike or car, all under a single payment umbrella (Hensher, 2017). This could be particularly impactful in congested urban areas, where multimodal commuting is often the most efficient way to travel. The transparent and immutable nature of blockchain transactions could significantly enhance trust among all stakeholders. This is crucial in shared mobility contexts, where trust deficits can significantly impede adoption. For example, the blockchain could be used to transparently and immutably log service quality metrics or vehicle maintenance records, thereby providing users with verifiable information to make more informed choices (Pelgander, Öberg, & Barkenäs, 2022). The road to full-scale implementation is fraught with challenges. Regulatory frameworks around tokenization and blockchain are still evolving, and there are significant technical challenges related to scalability and data privacy that need to be addressed (Maurer, Nelms, & Swartz, 2013). The transition to a token-based system would require substantial investment in technology and infrastructure, not to mention the need for a cultural shift among users and service providers toward adopting this new model (Glaser, 2017).

Tokenization can enable new business models and value propositions for mobility services, such as:

- *Fractional ownership.* Tokenization can allow users to own fractions of mobility assets, such as cars or bikes, and share the benefits and costs of their use. This can increase the affordability and accessibility of mobility services, as well as the efficiency and utilization of mobility assets. For example, Togg is a global mobility technologies and ecosystem provider that offers digital asset custody wallets for users to own fractions of vehicles and benefit from their use cases (Metaco).
- *Peer-to-peer exchange.* Tokenization can allow users to exchange mobility tokens directly with each other without intermediaries or centralized platforms. This can reduce the transaction costs and frictions of mobility services, as well as increase the trust and transparency among users. For example, Helbiz is a decentralized peer-to-peer platform that allows users to rent electric scooters using blockchain-based tokens (Helbiz).
- *Dynamic pricing.* Tokenization can allow users to pay for mobility services based on dynamic and flexible prices that reflect the supply and demand of mobility tokens. This can optimize the allocation and management of mobility resources, as well as incentivize users to adopt more sustainable travel behavior. For example, DOVU is a blockchain-powered reward platform that allows users to earn and spend tokens for sharing mobility data or using eco-friendly transport modes (DOVU).
- *Integrated mobility.* Tokenization can allow users to access multiple mobility services through a single application or interface using interoperable tokens. This can enhance the convenience and user experience of mobility services, as well as facilitate the modal shift and integration of different transport modes. For example, MaaS Global is a "mobility as a service" provider that allows users to plan and pay for various transport options using a subscription-based token system (MaaS Global).

15.6.2 Earning Tokens for Virtuous Behaviors

The integration of blockchain technology into urban mobility solutions has opened up innovative avenues for incentivizing sustainable and efficient transportation behaviors. One of the most transformative applications of this technology is the tokenization of *virtuous behaviors*, which can be broadly defined as actions that contribute to the overall sustainability and efficiency of the urban mobility ecosystem.

Tokenization in this context refers to the issuance of digital tokens on a blockchain network as a reward for engaging in specific behaviors. These tokens serve as a form of digital currency that can be used within the ecosystem for various purposes, such as paying for services or accessing premium features. The concept is rooted in behavioral economics, which suggests that individuals are more likely to engage in desired behaviors if they are provided with immediate, tangible rewards (Thaler & Sunstein, 2008). Traditional methods of incentivization, such as tax breaks or discounts, often suffer from issues of delayed gratification and low visibility, making them less effective in motivating immediate behavioral changes (Kahneman & Tversky, 2018).

The immediacy and transparency of blockchain-based tokens can serve as a powerful motivator for individuals to adopt more sustainable transportation habits. For example, a user who chooses to take public transportation instead of driving a personal car could be instantly rewarded with tokens. These tokens could then be used to pay for future rides, thereby creating a positive feedback loop that encourages continued use of public transportation. The blockchain's transparent and immutable nature ensures that these transactions are secure, traceable, and resistant to fraud, thereby building trust among users (Ostrom, 2015).

Moreover, the utility of these tokens can be extended to encourage a wide range of virtuous behaviors. For instance, tokens could be earned for carpooling, thereby incentivizing individuals to share rides and reduce the number of vehicles on the road. Similarly, tokens could be awarded for using bicycles or even walking, thereby promoting healthier and more environmentally friendly modes of transportation. Advanced implementations could even use smart contracts to automate these rewards based on real-time data, such as the current air quality index, thereby dynamically incentivizing behaviors that contribute to environmental sustainability (Buterin, 2014).

The tokenization system can also serve as a powerful tool for reducing reliance on traditional, less-sustainable systems. By offering immediate, tangible rewards, blockchain-based tokens can make sustainable options more attractive than their traditional counterparts. For example, the cost savings from using tokens earned by taking the bus or train could make these options more financially appealing than driving a personal car. Similarly, the tokens earned from carpooling could be used to access premium parking spaces, thereby providing a direct, immediate benefit that offsets the inconvenience of sharing a ride.

Furthermore, the tokens could be designed to have additional utility within a broader ecosystem, thereby increasing their value and appeal. For example, they could be exchanged for goods and services in a marketplace, converted into other cryptocurrencies, or even cashed out into fiat currency. This added utility makes the tokens more than just a tool for incentivization; they become a versatile asset that can be used in various ways, thereby encouraging more users to earn and use them (Pelgander, Öberg, & Barkenäs, 2022).

However, the implementation of such a system is not without challenges. The primary concern is the potential for fraud or abuse. Ensuring that tokens are awarded for genuine virtuous behaviors requires robust verification mechanisms, which could be provided by IoT devices or other forms of digital authentication (Christidis & Devetsikiotis, 2016). Additionally, the blockchain network itself must be scalable to handle a large number of transactions, especially if the system gains widespread adoption. Various solutions, such as layer-2 protocols or alternative blockchain architectures, have been proposed to address these scalability issues (Poon & Buterin, 2017).

The concept of earning tokens for virtuous behaviors in the realm of urban mobility presents a compelling use case for blockchain technology. By leveraging the principles of behavioral economics and the unique capabilities of blockchain, such as transparency, security, and automation, a token-based system can serve as an effective tool for promoting sustainable and efficient transportation behaviors. While challenges remain, particularly in the areas of verification and scalability, the potential benefits of such a system in fostering a more sustainable and efficient urban mobility ecosystem are significant.

Table 15.1 provides a comprehensive comparison of various methods aimed at incentivizing sustainable and efficient transportation behaviors. Each method is evaluated based on several criteria: the mechanism of incentive, pros and cons, scalability, technology required, and token utility, where applicable.

Traditional methods like tax incentives and discounts on public transport primarily rely on financial mechanisms. While they are straightforward and have been in use for years, they often require complex administrative procedures and may not provide immediate rewards to the users. Their scalability is generally high, but they lack the technological innovation that could make them more effective and engaging.

Loyalty points and gamification introduce a psychological element to the incentive mechanism. These methods are generally more engaging and can be tailored to individual behaviors. However, they may require a digital platform and may not sustain user interest in the long term. Their scalability varies, and they often do not offer any token utility.

Blockchain-based methods, on the other hand, offer a blend of financial and reward-based incentives. They are immediate, transparent, and secure, fostering trust among users. These methods are highly scalable but require a robust technological infrastructure, including blockchain and Internet of Things (IoT) technologies (Abbas et al., 2021). The token utility in blockchain methods is generally high, offering users various ways to use or exchange their rewards, thereby increasing the attractiveness of these options.

TABLE 15.1

Comparative Analysis of Incentive Methods for Sustainable Mobility and Transportation

Method	Mechanism of Incentive	Pros	Cons	Scalability	Technology Required	Token Utility
Tax incentives	Financial	Long-term impact, government-supported	Delayed gratification, complex paperwork	High	None	None
Discounts on public transport	Financial	Immediate, easy to implement	Limited impact, cost to service providers	Medium	None	None
Loyalty points	Reward-based	Encourages repeat behavior, easy to understand	Limited to specific services, low engagement	Medium	Digital platform	None
Gamification	Psychological	Engaging, builds community	May lose interest over time	Low	App	None
Blockchain tokens (public transport)	Financial/ reward-based	Immediate, transparent, secure	Requires tech infrastructure, scalability issues	High	Blockchain, IoT	High
Blockchain tokens (carpooling)	Financial/ reward-based	Encourages ride-sharing, reduces cars on road	Requires user adoption, trust issues	High	Blockchain, IoT	High
Blockchain tokens (cycling)	Financial/ reward-based	Promotes healthy behavior, eco-friendly	Requires IoT for tracking, limited scope	Medium	Blockchain, IoT	Medium
Blockchain tokens (walking)	Financial/ reward-based	Promotes health, zero emissions	Limited impact on transport ecosystem	Low	Blockchain, IoT	Low
Real-time dynamic pricing	Financial	Adapts to demand, can reduce congestion	Complex to implement, can be expensive	High	Dynamic algorithms	None
Congestion pricing	Financial	Effective in reducing peak-time traffic	Unpopular, can be seen as a tax	High	Sensors, cameras	None

Real-time dynamic pricing and congestion pricing are more systemic approaches that aim to manage demand and reduce congestion. While effective, they can be complex to implement and may require significant technological infrastructure. They also do not offer any form of token utility, making them purely financial mechanisms.

While traditional methods have their merits, blockchain-based incentivization schemes offer a multifaceted approach that can be both engaging and effective. They do, however, require a more complex technological setup and a willingness from users to adopt new technologies. As the world moves towards more integrated and intelligent transportation systems, the role of advanced technologies like blockchain is likely to become increasingly significant.

Table 15.2 delineates the contrasting dimensions between traditional systems and blockchain-based systems, specifically focusing on aspects relevant to mobility and payment services. It aims to provide a multifaceted evaluation to guide stakeholders in the mobility and payment sectors in making informed decisions about adopting either of these technological paradigms.

15.6.3 Secure Management and Exchange of Tokens

Secure management and token exchange within the mobile ecosystem are integral to the success of any blockchain-based incentive program. The advent of blockchain technology has revolutionized

TABLE 15.2

Comparative Dimensions of Traditional and Blockchain-Based Systems in the Context of Mobility and Payment Services

Dimension	Traditional Systems	Blockchain-Based Systems
Payment systems	Centralized, often requiring intermediaries like banks	Decentralized, peer-to-peer transactions without the need for intermediaries
Data transparency	Limited; data controlled by single entities	High; blockchain ledgers transparent and can be audited
Security	Vulnerable to single points of failure	Enhanced security due to cryptographic techniques and decentralized architecture
User incentives	Limited scope for rewarding sustainable or shared mobility	Tokenization allows for a wide range of incentives, including tokens for eco-friendly behavior
Interoperability	Low; each service provider with its own system	High; blockchain can integrate different modes of transport into a single payment and information system
Trust	Relies on brand reputation and centralized reviews	Enhanced through immutable records and smart contracts
Efficiency	Can be bogged down by administrative overhead	Streamlined operations due to the elimination of intermediaries and automated smart contracts
Scalability	Dependent on the capacity of centralized servers	High; blockchain networks designed to be scalable
Data ownership	Controlled by service providers	Could be controlled by users, enhancing privacy and data security
Regulatory compliance	Requires extensive paperwork and is often slow to adapt to new regulations	Smart contracts can be programmed to automatically comply with existing and new regulations
Fraud prevention	Dependent on centralized security measures	Enhanced through cryptographic verification and consensus algorithms
Real-time updates	May suffer from delays due to centralized processing	Near-instantaneous due to decentralized processing
Cost	Can be high due to administrative and intermediary fees	Generally lower due to the absence of intermediaries and lower administrative costs.
Accessibility	May require multiple accounts and platforms for different services	Single platform could provide access to multiple services
Customization	Limited by the capabilities of centralized systems	High; smart contracts can be customized to meet individual needs
Environmental impact	Difficult to track and incentivize	Easier to track and incentivize through token rewards for sustainable actions.
Dispute resolution	Often manual and time-consuming	Automated through smart contracts, saving time and reducing conflicts
Service availability	May be limited to specific geographic areas	Potentially global, as blockchain networks are not confined to specific locations.

the way we think about data integrity, transparency, and security. This is especially true for mobility services, where token exchange can serve multiple purposes, such as paying for tickets, rewarding sustainable behavior, and exchanging data between stakeholders, different, including commuters, service providers, and urban planners (Nakamoto, 2008).

The decentralized nature of blockchain ensures that no single entity has control over the entire system, reducing the risk of fraud or manipulation (Maurer, Nelms, & Swartz, 2013). Each transaction is recorded on multiple nodes in the network, making it nearly impossible to modify past transactions. This is important for the mobility sector, where secure and transparent token exchanges can facilitate a wide range of services from ride-sharing to public transportation and even pedestrian reward programs.

Smart contracts, self-executing contracts whose terms are written directly in code, further enhance the security and efficiency of these transactions (Szabo, 1997). For example, a smart contract can automatically perform a token transfer from the commuter's account to the service provider's account once the journey is complete. This not only reduces transaction time but also eliminates the need for intermediaries, thereby reducing costs and potential failure points (Christidis & Devetsikiotis, 2016).

However, securely managing these tokens is not without challenges. One of the main concerns is the risk of "double spending," where users may attempt to use the same token for multiple services. Blockchain effectively solves this problem through consensus algorithms, validating transactions across multiple nodes before it is recorded on the blockchain.

Another concern is user privacy and anonymity. While blockchain records are transparent, they are also pseudonymous, meaning, the identities of parties can be masked with digital signatures. This is especially important in the context of mobility services, where users may not want their travel habits and behaviors to be publicly revealed. Zero-knowledge proofs, a cryptographic method, can prove the validity of a transaction without revealing transaction details, thereby ensuring user privacy.

The utility of the token is another aspect that requires secure and efficient management. In the mobile ecosystem, tokens can serve many purposes beyond paying for tickets. They can be used to encourage sustainable behaviors, such as carpooling, using public transport, or even walking. Tokens can also be exchanged for other services or traded on various platforms. This multi-utility aspect makes the token more attractive to users but also requires a robust and secure governance system to manage the complexity of various transactions (Tapscott & Tapscott, 2016)

Secure token management and exchange is critical to the success of blockchain-based mobile ecosystems. While blockchain provides strong solutions for integrity, transparency, and security in transactions, challenges such as double spending, user privacy, and token utility need to be addressed effectively. As mobile services continue to grow, the integration of blockchain technology can provide a secure, efficient, and transparent system for token management and exchange, promoting a sustainable and more user-friendly mobile environment.

15.6.4 CASE STUDIES OR EXAMPLES: THE CITYCOIN PROJECT

The complexity of urban mobility, characterized by traffic congestion, air pollution, and noise pollution, poses significant challenges for cities around the world. These issues have far-reaching implications for public health, environmental sustainability, and economic growth. Blockchain technology, combined with tokenization, offers a promising path to addressing these challenges by promoting sustainable behaviors among citizens. This section explores the transformative potential of blockchain and tokenization in urban mobility, focusing on decentralized systems that support sustainable transport options.

15.6.4.1 System Overview

In the proposed decentralized framework, the first step for users is to create an account on the platform. This is more than just a simple registration; it is the gateway to a new ecosystem of sustainable mobility. During this account creation process, users would specify their preferred methods of sustainable transportation, which could range from bicycles and electric scooters to public transportation like buses and trains.

Once the account is created, the system will automatically generate a unique blockchain wallet for each user. This wallet serves as the user's identity within the blockchain network and is crucial for the tokenization process. The wallet is also tied to a smart contract, known as the account abstraction contract (AAC) (Buterin, 2021). The AAC is a pivotal element in the system, as it signs the UserOperations. In simpler terms, it validates and records each sustainable action taken by the user, such as taking a bus ride or cycling to work, and converts these actions into transactions on the blockchain.

After the AAC is set up, the system is ready to award tokens for sustainable actions. The process of earning tokens is automated and highly accurate, thanks to GPS tracking and vehicle sensors. For example, if a user opts to ride a bicycle for a short commute, the GPS on the user's smartphone or on the bicycle itself would track the distance covered. Similarly, if the user takes public transportation, sensors on the bus or train could detect the user's entry and exit, thanks to a QR code or RFID tag linked to their account. These data points are then sent to the AAC, which validates them and triggers the token award process.

The tokens earned are not just digital gimmicks; they have real-world utility. They can be redeemed for a variety of rewards aimed at further promoting sustainable behavior. For instance, accumulated tokens could offer discounts on future public transportation tickets, reduced rates on bike or scooter rentals, or even special offers at local businesses that are partners in this sustainability initiative. The idea is to create a virtuous cycle where sustainable actions lead to rewards, which, in turn, make it easier and more attractive to continue making sustainable choices.

The utility and finality of the tokens in this decentralized framework extend beyond just incentivizing individual users to adopt sustainable transportation methods. The tokens can serve as a valuable asset for various stakeholders, including transportation companies, local businesses, and even governmental bodies focused on environmental sustainability.

For transportation companies, these tokens can essentially function as a form of advertising or customer acquisition. By offering discounts or other incentives to token holders, these companies can attract more riders, thereby increasing their overall revenue. In this sense, the tokens serve a dual purpose: they encourage sustainable behavior among citizens while also driving business for the transportation companies. The tokens, therefore, become a form of currency that these companies are willing to "buy" in exchange for increased ridership and, by extension, increased income.

Local businesses and service providers can also participate in this ecosystem by accepting these tokens in exchange for goods or services. Much like transportation companies, these businesses benefit from increased patronage by being part of a system that rewards sustainable behavior. For them, buying and accepting these tokens is an investment in both community goodwill and their own long-term customer base.

Government bodies, particularly those focused on environmental sustainability, can play a pivotal role in this token ecosystem. Governments can mandate or incentivize environmentally focused companies and organizations to buy these tokens. The rationale behind this is that the overall system aims to reduce environmental impact by promoting sustainable transportation. Companies can "buy" these tokens and "burn" them, essentially taking them out of circulation, as a way to offset their own environmental impact. This could be integrated into a broader environmental credits system where companies are rewarded by the government for their contributions to sustainability efforts. The more tokens a company buys and burns, the more benefits or credits it could receive from the government.

In this way, the token becomes more than just a tool for encouraging sustainable individual behavior; it becomes a valuable asset within a larger ecosystem aimed at promoting sustainability. It creates a virtuous cycle involving multiple stakeholders, each of whom has a vested interest in both promoting and benefiting from sustainable urban mobility. This multifaceted utility of the token, backed by the security and transparency of blockchain technology, makes it a powerful instrument for driving meaningful change in urban transportation behaviors.

The backbone of this entire system is blockchain technology. Blockchain ensures that every transaction, from the earning of tokens to their redemption, is transparent, secure, and immutable. Each transaction is recorded on a public ledger that is visible to all users but cannot be altered or

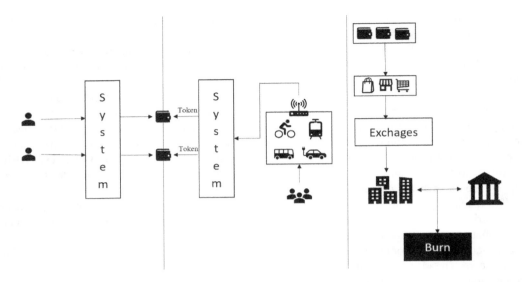

FIGURE 15.1 Flowchart illustrating the token distribution and utilization process within integrated systems.

deleted. This transparency builds trust among users, as they can see exactly how many tokens they have earned and how they have spent them. Moreover, the decentralized nature of blockchain means that no single entity has control over the system, making it resistant to fraud and manipulation.

This decentralized framework offers a comprehensive, blockchain-based solution to incentivize sustainable urban mobility. From the moment a user creates an account to the point where they redeem tokens for real-world rewards, every step is designed to promote sustainability, backed by the security and transparency of blockchain technology. Figure 15.1 gives an overview of a basic system design.

15.6.4.2 Benefits (Sustainable Development Goals [SDGs])

For Individual Users

- *Incentivized sustainable behavior.* The cornerstone of this blockchain-based system is the incentivization of sustainable behavior. When users opt for greener modes of transportation, be it cycling, walking, carpooling, or using public transit, they are awarded digital tokens. These tokens are not merely symbolic; they have tangible value and can be redeemed for various goods, services, or even further transit options. The immediate gratification of earning tokens serves as a powerful psychological incentive, encouraging users to make eco-friendly choices repeatedly. Over an extended period, this reward mechanism could instigate a profound behavioral shift among urban commuters, steering them away from fossil fuel–dependent options and reducing the overall carbon footprint of the city. The long-term implications of such a shift are enormous, ranging from decreased pollution levels to a more sustainable urban infrastructure.
- *Incentivizing sustainable transportation.* The token-based system is designed to directly incentivize users to opt for more sustainable modes of transportation. When users choose eco-friendly options like cycling, walking, or public transit, they earn tokens. These tokens serve as a tangible reward that can be redeemed for goods or services, making the act of choosing sustainable transport financially beneficial. This financial incentive is a powerful motivator that can significantly influence user behavior. Over time, the accumulation of these tokens can represent a substantial value, making the choice to go green not just an ethical decision but also a financially prudent one.

- *Promoting public health.* The system does not just encourage eco-friendly behavior; it also has a direct impact on public health. By incentivizing walking and cycling, the system promotes physical activity. Regular physical exercise has numerous health benefits, including improved cardiovascular health, better mental well-being, and a reduced risk of chronic diseases like diabetes and obesity. These health benefits translate into long-term cost savings for individuals, as healthier lifestyles can lead to fewer medical bills and less need for ongoing medical care. In essence, the system serves a dual purpose: it improves environmental health while also contributing to the physical health of individuals.
- *Financial rewards.* The tokens earned in this system are not just abstract points; they have real-world value. Users can redeem these tokens for a variety of services or products, ranging from discounts on future public transport tickets to special offers at local businesses that are part of the network. This creates a financial feedback loop that further encourages sustainable behavior. For example, a user who has accumulated a significant number of tokens could redeem them for a month's worth of free public transport, thereby saving money that they might have otherwise spent on fuel for a car. The financial rewards serve as an additional layer of incentive, making it even more appealing for users to engage with the system.

For Transport Sector

- *Increased public transport usage.* The token-based incentive system is poised to drive up the usage of public transport services. When individuals are rewarded with tokens for choosing buses, trams, or trains over personal cars, there is a compelling reason for them to make that choice regularly. This increased ridership not only makes public transport services more economically viable but also justifies investment in expanding and improving these services. More passengers translate into higher revenue, which can be reinvested into the system to make it more efficient, reliable, and user-friendly. Over time, this creates a virtuous cycle where improved services attract even more users, further boosting ridership and revenue.
- *Data-driven improvements.* One of the most underrated benefits of implementing a blockchain-based system in the transport sector is the wealth of data it can provide. The blockchain's transparent and immutable ledger can capture a wide array of data points, from the frequency of service usage to peak travel times and preferred routes. This data is invaluable for transport authorities for planning and decision-making. For instance, if the data shows that certain bus routes are consistently underutilized, resources can be reallocated to busier routes to better meet demand. Similarly, if there is a surge in token redemptions for late-night services, it might justify extending operating hours. This data-driven approach allows for dynamic, real-time improvements to the system, making it more responsive to the actual needs and behaviors of its users.
- *Reduced traffic congestion.* The shift from personal cars to public transport does not just benefit the environment; it has a direct, positive impact on the quality of the transport services themselves. Fewer cars on the road mean less traffic congestion, which, in turn, allows public transport vehicles to operate more efficiently. Buses and trams can stick to their schedules more reliably, and the reduced likelihood of getting stuck in traffic jams makes public transport a more attractive option for users. This efficiency is not just about speed; it also translates into fuel savings and reduced wear and tear on vehicles, lowering operational costs. In the long term, this could lead to lower ticket prices, creating yet another incentive for users to choose public transport.

For Environment

- *Reducing air pollution.* The token-based incentive system has a direct impact on air quality by encouraging the use of more sustainable modes of transportation. When people opt for public transport, cycling, or walking, they effectively reduce the number of cars on the road. Cars, especially those running on fossil fuels, are significant contributors to air pollution, emitting harmful substances like carbon monoxide, nitrogen dioxide, and particulate matter. By reducing car usage, the system can substantially decrease these emissions. Improved air quality has a cascading effect on public health, reducing respiratory issues and other pollution-induced ailments. Over time, this could lead to a significant decrease in healthcare costs related to pollution, making the city more livable and potentially attracting more residents and businesses.

- *Lowering carbon footprint.* The environmental benefits of the system extend beyond just air quality; they also contribute to lowering the city's overall carbon footprint. Transportation is one of the largest sources of greenhouse gas emissions, particularly carbon dioxide. By incentivizing the use of low-emission or zero-emission modes of transport, the system can make a meaningful contribution to global efforts to combat climate change. This is especially crucial in the context of international agreements aimed at reducing carbon emissions, such as the Paris Agreement. Cities adopting such a system could potentially receive credits or funding for their efforts to reduce emissions, further incentivizing the adoption of sustainable practices.

- *Resource conservation.* Another often-overlooked benefit of reducing car usage is the conservation of material resources. Roads and other public infrastructure undergo significant wear and tear due to the constant stress from vehicular traffic. Fewer cars on the road mean less degradation of this infrastructure, reducing the frequency and scale of repairs needed. This not only conserves material resources like asphalt, metal, and concrete but also translates into financial savings for the city. These funds could then be redirected to other essential services or used to further improve and expand sustainable transportation options.

For Government

- *Alignment with policy goals.* The blockchain-based incentive system for sustainable urban mobility is inherently aligned with many governmental policy objectives, particularly those related to environmental sustainability and public health. Governments worldwide are under increasing pressure to meet carbon reduction targets and improve the quality of life for their citizens. Implementing a system that incentivizes sustainable transportation choices can serve as a cornerstone in a broader policy framework aimed at achieving these goals. By adopting this system, governments can demonstrate a tangible commitment to sustainability, which could make it easier to secure both political and financial support for other related initiatives. Furthermore, the success of such a program could serve as a model for other cities and countries, potentially leading to broader systemic change.

- *Public health benefits.* The public health implications of a more sustainable transportation system are profound. Reduced air pollution leads to fewer respiratory issues, less heart disease, and a decrease in other pollution-related health problems. This, in turn, can lead to a significant reduction in healthcare costs, relieving a financial burden on public health systems. The promotion of physical activities like walking and cycling also has a direct impact on public health by reducing obesity rates and associated health problems like diabetes and heart disease. These benefits are not just individual but collective, creating a healthier workforce and potentially boosting productivity. The financial savings from reduced healthcare costs can be reallocated to other critical public services or used to further incentivize sustainable behaviors, creating a positive feedback loop.

- *Regulatory leverage.* One of the most innovative aspects of the system is how it can be integrated into existing regulatory frameworks. Governments can require companies, particularly those in environmentally impactful industries, to buy and "burn" tokens as a form of carbon offset. This not only provides a financial underpinning for the token but also creates a mechanism for these companies to contribute to broader sustainability goals. The more a company engages in buying and burning tokens, the more regulatory benefits or incentives they could receive from the government. This could range from tax breaks to preferential treatment in government contracts, creating a virtuous cycle that encourages companies to contribute more actively to sustainability efforts.

15.6.4.3 Implementation

15.6.4.3.1 Account Abstraction (AA)

Account abstraction (AA) is a concept that can significantly enhance the user experience in blockchain-based systems by abstracting away some of the complexities associated with blockchain transactions. In the context of a decentralized system for incentivizing sustainable urban mobility, account abstraction can serve as a crucial component for improving usability and encouraging widespread adoption.

15.6.4.3.2 Gas Fees and User Experience

One of the major barriers to entry for average users in blockchain systems is the concept of gas fees, small transaction costs required to execute operations on the blockchain. These fees can be confusing and off-putting for users unfamiliar with blockchain technology. Moreover, if users are expected to pay these fees to participate in a system designed to reward them for sustainable behavior, the financial incentives could become less appealing, thereby reducing the system's effectiveness.

15.6.4.3.3 Account Abstraction as a Solution

Account abstraction can solve this problem by allowing the system to pay the gas fees on behalf of the users (Figure 15.2). When a user creates an account and registers their sustainable transportation methods, the system can generate a wallet for the user and automatically sign a set of predefined UserOperations. These signed operations serve as templates for common actions the user will take within the system, such as reporting their location, identifying nearby users, or specifying the type of transport used.

15.6.4.3.4 Automating UserOperations

By having these UserOperations pre-signed, the system can automatically execute these actions on behalf of the user without requiring additional transactions or gas fees from the user

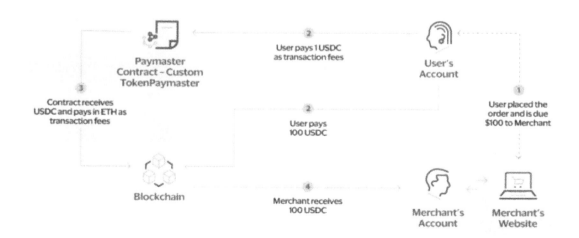

FIGURE 15.2 Paymaster facilitating the use of ERC-20 tokens for transaction fees.

(see Figure 15.3). For example, if a user takes a bus ride, the system could automatically detect this action based on the user's GPS location and the proximity to a registered bus stop. A pre-signed UserOperation could then be executed to award the user tokens for this sustainable action, all without requiring the user to initiate a transaction or pay a gas fee.

15.6.4.3.5   *Financial Sustainability*

This approach not only improves the user experience but also enhances the financial sustainability of the system. Traditional methods of covering gas fees, such as distributing free gas to users, are not sustainable in the long term and can be subject to abuse. Account abstraction provides a more elegant and sustainable solution by integrating the cost of gas fees into the overall system economics. The tokens awarded to users for sustainable actions could be slightly adjusted to cover the cost of gas fees, ensuring that the system remains financially viable without compromising the incentives for users.

In the system designed for sustainable urban mobility, the blockchain serves as the core infrastructure that enables a transparent, secure, and decentralized platform. The back-end architecture is built around the blockchain, leveraging its capabilities to create a robust and efficient system (Figure 15.4).

Smart contracts. The business logic of our system is encapsulated in smart contracts deployed on the blockchain. These contracts handle the core functionalities, such as token issuance, rewards distribution, and account management. For example, when a user opts for a sustainable mode of transportation like cycling or public transit, the corresponding smart contract is triggered to issue tokens as rewards. These tokens are then securely transferred to the user's blockchain wallet.

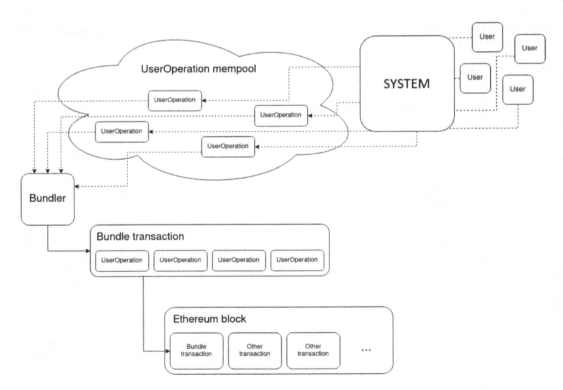

FIGURE 15.3   Diagram depicting the workflow of UserOperations (in AA) from system initiation.

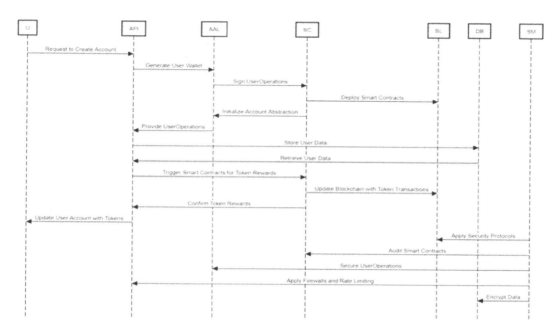

FIGURE 15.4 Back-end architecture sequence diagram of component interaction flow (*user* as U, *block-chain layer* as BL, *smart contracts* as SC, *account abstraction layer* as AAL, *APIs and microservices* as API, *database* as DB, *security measures* as SM).

Account abstraction layer. To make the system more user-friendly and to remove the complexities of blockchain transactions, we employ an account abstraction layer (AAL). This layer automatically signs UserOperations, allowing the system to pay for transaction fees (gas) on behalf of the user. This ensures that users can interact with the system without worrying about the intricacies of blockchain transactions or the need to hold cryptocurrency for gas fees.

Data storage and retrieval. While the blockchain stores all transactional data, we also maintain a traditional database for storing user profiles, preferences, and other non-transactional data. This hybrid approach ensures that while all critical and sensitive operations are securely and transparently handled by the blockchain, the system remains efficient for read-heavy operations.

APIs and microservices. Our back end exposes a set of APIs that allow for seamless interaction between the front-end application and the blockchain. These APIs are responsible for triggering the smart contracts based on user actions. For example, when a user completes a journey using sustainable transportation, the front-end application sends a request to the back end via an API, which in turn triggers the smart contract for token issuance.

Security measures. Security is a paramount concern, especially when dealing with financial transactions and rewards. Our smart contracts undergo rigorous security audits to ensure they are free from vulnerabilities. Additionally, the account abstraction layer employs advanced cryptographic techniques to securely sign transactions, ensuring that malicious actors cannot forge transactions.

Scalability. Given that urban mobility is a large-scale concern, our back-end architecture is designed for scalability. The smart contracts should be optimized for low gas consumption, ensuring that the system can handle a large number of transactions without incurring exorbitant fees. Moreover, the APIs and microservices are designed to be stateless and horizontally scalable, allowing us to easily add more computing resources as the user base grows.

Our system fundamentally diverges from existing solutions in its approach to decentralization, transparency, and user autonomy. Most current systems operate on a custodial basis, functioning much like centralized exchanges where the platform has full control over user assets and transactions. This centralized approach inherently lacks transparency and poses risks related to security, data privacy, and system downtime.

In contrast, our system employs account abstraction (AA) to create a non-custodial environment. In this setup, users have complete control over their assets and transactions, as they are the sole owners of their private keys. The AA layer allows the system to pay for transaction fees (gas) on behalf of the users without ever taking custody of their assets. This not only enhances user experience by removing the complexities of gas fees but also ensures that users have full ownership and control over their tokens and data.

The use of AA also contributes to greater transparency. In a non-custodial system, all transactions are recorded on the blockchain, visible to anyone who wishes to verify them. This is a stark contrast to custodial systems, where transactions are often obscured behind the walls of centralized databases. The transparent nature of our system, backed by blockchain's immutable ledger, fosters trust among users and stakeholders. It ensures that the rewards distribution is fair, auditable, and free from manipulation.

Moreover, the non-custodial nature of our system significantly enhances security. In custodial systems, the centralized storage of assets and data makes them lucrative targets for hackers. Our system mitigates this risk by ensuring that assets are stored in individual user wallets, secured by their private keys. Even if the system were to experience a security breach, user assets would remain untouched, as the system never takes custody of them.

15.6.4.4 Use Case Scenario: Alice's Journey to Sustainable Urban Mobility

15.6.4.4.1 Account Creation and Initial Setup

Alice, a tech-savvy resident of a smart city, hears about a new decentralized application (DApp) that leverages blockchain technology to incentivize sustainable transportation. Intrigued by the concept, she downloads the dApp onto her smartphone and proceeds to create an account. During this phase, the system generates a unique blockchain wallet for *Alice, secured by cryptographic keys* (see Figure 15.5).

To tackle the issue of gas fees for blockchain transactions, the system employs account abstraction (AA). During the account creation process, a set of UserOperations are pre-signed by Alice's private key. These pre-signed transactions are stored in a secure smart contract, known as the

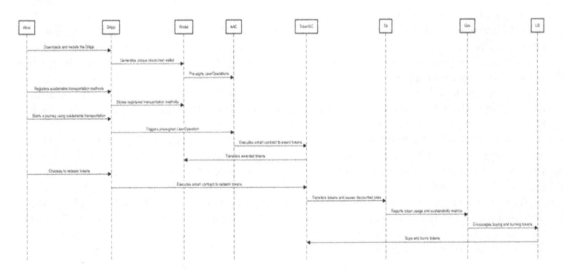

FIGURE 15.5 Use case scenario: Alice's journey to sustainable urban mobility (Alice as user, DApp as mobile app, wallet as blockchain wallet, AAC as account abstraction contract, TokenSC as smart contract for tokens, TA as transportation authority, LB as local businesses, gov as government).

account abstraction contract (AAC). This allows the system to pay for the gas fees on behalf of Alice for specific actions, such as earning tokens, thereby removing the financial barrier to entry for users.

15.6.4.4.2   Registering Sustainable Transportation Methods

Once her account and blockchain wallet are set up, Alice is prompted to register her sustainable transportation methods. She owns a bicycle and frequently uses public transportation. To register these methods, she scans the QR codes on her bicycle and public transportation pass. These QR codes are linked to unique identifiers on the blockchain, ensuring the validity of the registered transportation methods.

15.6.4.4.3   Earning Tokens through Sustainable Choices

The following day, Alice decides to cycle to her workplace. As she starts her journey, the dApp activates the GPS and sensor data on her smartphone. Her movement and choice of transportation are detected and verified against the blockchain identifiers for her registered methods. Upon verification, a pre-signed UserOperation from the AAC is triggered. This operation initiates a smart contract that awards Alice a certain number of tokens for her sustainable choice. The tokens are securely transferred to her blockchain wallet, and she receives a real-time notification on her app.

15.6.4.4.4   Redeeming Tokens

After accumulating tokens over a week through various sustainable transportation choices, Alice decides it is time to redeem them. She browses through the DApp and finds that she can get a 20% discount on her next monthly public transportation pass. She initiates the redemption process, and the corresponding smart contract is executed. The tokens are transferred from her wallet to the transportation authority's blockchain account, and she receives her discounted pass, all recorded transparently on the blockchain.

15.6.4.4.5   Data-Driven Improvements in the Transport Sector

On the back end, the transportation authorities have access to anonymized, aggregated data from the blockchain. This data reveals patterns in sustainable transportation usage, such as increased cycling on specific routes. Armed with this data, the authorities can make data-driven decisions like optimizing bus routes or installing new bike lanes, thereby making sustainable options even more convenient for the public.

15.6.4.4.6   Environmental and Governmental Impact

The system's success catches the attention of the local government, which sees it as a viable method to achieve their carbon-neutrality goals. They decide to buy and "burn" tokens, effectively removing them from circulation, to further incentivize sustainable behavior. Environmental companies are encouraged to do the same, and they receive tax benefits for each token burned, creating a virtuous cycle that benefits both the environment and the economy.

15.6.4.4.7   Government and Regulatory Leverage

The government, seeing the success of the program, decides to buy and "burn" tokens to further incentivize sustainable behavior. Companies that invest in sustainability are also encouraged to buy and burn tokens, receiving tax benefits in return, thereby creating a virtuous cycle of sustainability.

15.6.4.5   Challenges

Implementing such a system is not without challenges:

- *User adoption.* One of the biggest challenges is to get a sufficient number of users to adopt the system for it to be effective. This could require significant marketing efforts, partnerships, and perhaps even initial incentives to attract users.

- *Data privacy.* Ensuring the privacy of users' data is crucial, especially when the system relies on tracking users' locations and behaviors. GDPR and other privacy regulations must be adhered to.
- *System security.* The blockchain and the associated smart contracts must be secure to prevent hacking, fraud, and other types of attacks that could compromise user data or the token economy.
- *Scalability.* As the number of users grows, the blockchain network must be able to handle an increasing number of transactions without significant delays or increased costs.
- *Regulatory compliance.* The system must comply with transportation laws, financial regulations related to token issuance and trading, and any other applicable laws.
- *Interoperability.* The system needs to be compatible with existing transportation systems and payment methods to provide a seamless user experience.
- *Cost of implementation.* Developing a secure, scalable blockchain-based system requires significant investment, both in terms of technology and human resources.
- *Tokenomics.* Designing a token economy that is both attractive to users and sustainable in the long term is a complex task that requires deep understanding of both economics and user behavior.
- *Environmental impact.* Ironically, blockchain networks, especially those that use proof of work (PoW), can be energy-intensive. This could partially offset the environmental benefits gained through more sustainable transportation.
- *Public–private partnerships.* For the system to be most effective, collaboration between public transportation authorities and private businesses is essential, and such partnerships can be complex to negotiate and maintain.
- *Data accuracy.* The system relies on accurate data for tracking sustainable actions, calculating rewards, and issuing tokens. Inaccurate data could undermine the system's effectiveness and user trust.
- *User experience.* The system must be user-friendly to encourage widespread adoption. This includes not just the mobile app interface but also the process of redeeming tokens and integrating with existing transportation services.
- *Accessibility.* The system should be designed to be inclusive, catering to users with varying income levels and technical expertise.
- *Public awareness.* Public education campaigns and partnerships with local organizations could be instrumental in raising awareness about the system's benefits.

15.7 TECHNICAL REQUIREMENTS AND CONSIDERATIONS

Table 15.3 provides a comprehensive comparison of various implementation aspects, highlighting the differences between traditional centralized systems and blockchain-based decentralized systems. It serves as a guide for decision-makers and developers in choosing the appropriate technology stack for their specific needs. This table offers a succinct evaluation of traditional and blockchain-based systems across multiple criteria. It aims to provide stakeholders with a quick yet comprehensive understanding of the inherent trade-offs between the two paradigms, thereby aiding in informed decision-making.

The comparative table between traditional and blockchain-based systems for urban mobility offers a nuanced view of the strengths and weaknesses of each approach across multiple dimensions. At a glance, it becomes evident that blockchain technology holds significant promise in areas such as security, scalability, and user privacy. Its decentralized architecture not only ensures data integrity but also allows for a more democratic and transparent system. This is particularly important in an urban mobility context, where multiple stakeholders ranging from city planners and transport providers to end users need to interact seamlessly.

However, the table also highlights the challenges associated with implementing blockchain-based solutions. The initial setup cost and time are notably higher, primarily due to the specialized

TABLE 15.3

Comparative Analysis of Implementation Aspects between Traditional and Blockchain-Based Systems

Implementation Aspect	Traditional Systems	Blockchain-Based Systems
Initial setup	Requires centralized servers and databases	Requires setting up a decentralized network of nodes
Development time	Can be quicker due to existing frameworks	May take longer due to the need for smart contracts and decentralized architecture
Cost	Lower initial costs but higher maintenance due to intermediaries	Higher initial costs for setting up a blockchain but lower ongoing costs
Technical expertise	Requires expertise in database management and web services	Requires expertise in blockchain technology, cryptography, and smart contracts
Data migration	Easier if within the same centralized framework	Can be complex due to the immutable nature of blockchain records
User onboarding	Generally straightforward through centralized platforms	May require users to set up digital wallets or become familiar with blockchain interfaces
Regulatory approvals	Established pathways for compliance	May require new types of approvals due to the novel nature of blockchain
Scalability	Requires additional servers and infrastructure	Can be more easily scaled by adding nodes to the network
Security measures	Requires firewalls, SSL certificates, and other centralized security measures	Built-in cryptographic security, though smart contract vulnerabilities need to be carefully managed
Software updates	Easier to implement but require downtime	More complex due to decentralized nature but can be done without downtime
Community engagement	Typically managed by a central authority	Often involves a community of users who can propose changes or vote on aspects like fees or rules
Performance monitoring	Centralized analytics and reporting tools	Requires decentralized analytics tools, possibly custom-built
Backup and recovery	Centralized backup solutions	Data is inherently backed up across multiple nodes, offering robustness against data loss
Interoperability	May require complex APIs and data-sharing agreements	Easier due to the open nature of blockchain, allowing for seamless integration of services
User privacy	Managed by central authority, potential for misuse	Enhanced user control over personal data

skills required and the nascent stage of the technology. Regulatory hurdles are another significant concern, given that blockchain is still a relatively new technology and lacks a standardized legal framework. This could potentially slow down the adoption rate and make it less appealing for municipalities operating under tight budgets and regulatory scrutiny.

Traditional systems, while lacking in areas like data integrity and user privacy, offer the advantage of being well-understood and quicker to deploy (see Table 15.4). They are often seen as less-risky options, especially for smaller cities or for projects with limited scope. However, they usually incur higher ongoing costs and may not offer the same level of scalability and interoperability as blockchain-based systems. This could be a significant drawback as cities grow and the demand for integrated, multimodal transport solutions increases.

Moreover, the table underscores the importance of considering long-term implications. While traditional systems might be easier and cheaper to set up, their ongoing costs and limitations in

TABLE 15.4

Evaluation Criteria for Traditional vs. Blockchain-Based Systems

Criteria	Traditional Systems	Blockchain-Based Systems
Initial cost	Low	High
Ongoing cost	High	Low
Setup time	Short	Long
Scalability	Moderate	High
Security	Moderate	High
User privacy	Low	High
Regulatory hurdles	Low	High
Data integrity	Moderate	High
Interoperability	Low	High
User engagement	Centralized	Decentralized
Software updates	Easier	Complex
Backup and recovery	Centralized	Decentralized
Performance monitoring	Centralized	Decentralized
Community involvement	Low	High

terms of scalability and security could make them less sustainable in the long run. On the other hand, while blockchain systems require a higher initial investment, their lower ongoing costs and superior scalability could offer a better return on investment over time.

15.8 CARBON CREDITS AND BLOCKCHAIN

The concept of *carbon credits* has emerged as a pivotal mechanism in the global strategy to mitigate climate change. Essentially, carbon credits are tradable certificates that represent the reduction of 1 ton of carbon dioxide emissions. These credits can be bought and sold on various marketplaces and are often used by companies to offset their own carbon emissions. However, the carbon credit ecosystem is fraught with challenges, such as lack of transparency, inefficiency, and fraud. Blockchain technology, with its inherent characteristics of decentralization, transparency, and security, offers a promising solution to these challenges (Mollick, 2014).

15.8.1 TRANSPARENCY AND TRACEABILITY

One of the most significant advantages of using blockchain technology in the carbon credits system is the enhanced transparency and traceability it offers. Each transaction on a blockchain is recorded on multiple nodes that are spread across a decentralized network, making it nearly impossible to alter or delete transaction data once it has been added to the blockchain. This ensures that the issuance, transfer, and retirement of carbon credits are transparently recorded and easily auditable (Manski, 2017). This level of transparency can instill greater confidence among stakeholders and can potentially increase participation in carbon credit trading.

15.8.2 EFFICIENCY AND COST-EFFECTIVENESS

Traditional systems for trading carbon credits often involve multiple intermediaries, including brokers, auditors, and regulators, which can make the process slow and costly. Blockchain can streamline this by automating many of these processes through smart contracts. Smart contracts are self-executing contracts with the terms of the agreement written into lines of code. They can be designed to automatically issue carbon credits when certain verifiable conditions are met, such as the successful planting of a specific number of trees (Tapscott & Tapscott, 2016). This automation can significantly reduce the time and cost involved in trading carbon credits.

15.8.3 Fraud Prevention

Fraudulent activities, including the double-counting of carbon credits, have been a significant concern in the carbon trading market. Blockchain's immutable and transparent nature makes it extremely difficult for any single entity to manipulate the system. Once a carbon credit is issued, transferred, or retired, the transaction is recorded on the blockchain, making double-counting virtually impossible (Mertz, 2020).

15.8.4 Interoperability and Standardization

The carbon credits market often suffers from a lack of standardization, with various countries and organizations operating their own separate and often incompatible systems. Blockchain can offer a standardized platform where different types of carbon credits can be traded. This interoperability can make the market more liquid and could even pave the way for a global, unified carbon trading system (Zheng, Xie, Dai, Chen, & Wang, 2017)

15.8.5 Regulatory Compliance and Reporting

Blockchain can also simplify the complex and often cumbersome process of regulatory compliance and reporting. Smart contracts can be programmed to automatically enforce regulatory requirements, and the transparent nature of blockchain makes it easier for regulators to audit transactions (Christidis & Devetsikiotis, 2016).

15.9 REGULATORY AND POLICY IMPLICATIONS

Tokenization can also create new opportunities and challenges for the regulation and governance of mobility services, such as:

- *Data privacy.* Tokenization can enhance the data privacy of users by allowing them to control and monetize their own mobility data using blockchain-based tokens. This can empower users to decide how their data is collected, stored, shared, or used by mobility service providers or third parties. However, this also raises the question of how to ensure the data quality and validity of tokenized mobility data, as well as how to balance the data privacy rights of users with the data access rights of regulators or other stakeholders (Kshetri, 2017).
- *Consumer protection.* Tokenization can improve the consumer protection of users by allowing them to verify the identity and reputation of mobility service providers or other users using blockchain-based tokens. This can reduce the risk of fraud or malpractice in the provision or use of mobility services. However, this also raises the question of how to ensure the compliance and accountability of tokenized mobility service providers or other users with the relevant laws and regulations, as well as how to resolve disputes or conflicts that may arise from tokenized transactions (Kshetri, 2017).
- *Environmental sustainability.* Tokenization can promote the environmental sustainability of urban mobility by allowing users to measure and reduce their carbon footprint using blockchain-based tokens. This can encourage users to adopt more eco-friendly transport modes or behaviors, as well as enable carbon offsetting or trading schemes for mobility services. However, this also raises the question of how to ensure the accuracy and reliability of tokenized carbon emissions data, as well as how to align the

environmental goals of tokenized mobility services with the broader climate change policies and targets (Kshetri, 2017).

15.10 POTENTIAL IMPACT

The integration of blockchain technology into urban mobility and carbon credit systems presents a transformative approach to addressing some of the most pressing environmental and societal challenges of our time. The potential impact of such a system is multifaceted, affecting various stakeholders, from individual users to governments and corporations. This section aims to elucidate the potential impact of implementing a blockchain-based system for incentivizing sustainable urban mobility and carbon credit trading.

- *Economic impact.* From an economic standpoint, the system has the potential to create new markets and revenue streams. For instance, the tokenization of carbon credits and sustainable behaviors can lead to the emergence of new financial products and services. Companies can leverage these tokens to offset their carbon footprint, thereby enhancing their corporate social responsibility profiles and potentially increasing their market value. Moreover, the system could reduce the economic burden on public transportation infrastructures by optimizing their usage through data analytics, thereby making these services more economically viable.
- *Social impact.* On the social front, the system could significantly influence public behavior towards adopting more sustainable modes of transportation. By providing tangible rewards in the form of tokens, individuals are more likely to opt for public transport, cycling, or walking over using personal cars. This shift not only reduces the carbon footprint but also fosters a culture of sustainability. Additionally, the system could contribute to public health by encouraging physical activities like walking and cycling, thereby reducing healthcare costs in the long run.
- *Environmental impact.* Environmentally, the system could be a game changer. By incentivizing sustainable transportation and facilitating transparent and efficient carbon credit trading, the system has the potential to significantly reduce greenhouse gas emissions. This aligns well with global efforts to combat climate change and could contribute to achieving the targets set in international agreements like the Paris Accord (Le Quéré et al., 2018).
- *Policy and governance.* From a policy perspective, the system offers governments a robust and transparent mechanism to achieve sustainability goals. The blockchain's immutable ledger ensures that companies cannot cheat the system, thereby making regulatory compliance more straightforward (Manski, 2017). Moreover, governments can leverage the system to implement dynamic policies that adapt to real-time data, thereby making governance more effective.
- *Technological innovation.* The system could also serve as a catalyst for technological innovation (Abbas et al., 2021). The integration of Internet of Things (IoT) devices for tracking sustainable behaviors, coupled with blockchain's secure and transparent ledger, could lead to the development of new technologies and methodologies for data collection and analysis (Zheng, Xie, Dai, Chen, & Wang, 2017).
- *On user behavior.* The blockchain-based system for incentivizing sustainable urban mobility has the potential to significantly influence user behavior. By tokenizing eco-friendly actions, the system can provide immediate, tangible rewards that make sustainable choices more appealing. This aligns with behavioral economics theories that suggest immediate rewards can effectively encourage desired behaviors (Thaler & Sunstein, 2008). Over time, these rewards can shift societal norms, making sustainable transportation not just an economic choice but a social one as well. This could lead to a long-term change in user behavior, making sustainability a default choice rather than an active one (Ariely, 2008).

- *On sustainability.* From a sustainability perspective, the system offers a multi-pronged approach to reducing carbon emissions and promoting eco-friendly living. By incentivizing public transport and non-motorized modes of transport like walking and cycling, the system directly contributes to reducing a city's carbon footprint. This is crucial in the context of global climate change and the urgent need for sustainable development (Sachs, 2015). Moreover, the system's potential to integrate with carbon credit markets can create a more efficient and transparent mechanism for companies to offset their emissions, thereby contributing to broader sustainability.

- *On urban mobility.* The system's impact on urban mobility could be transformative. By encouraging the use of public transport and other sustainable transportation options, it can alleviate some of the most pressing issues cities face, such as traffic congestion, air pollution, and noise. This has a cascading effect on the efficiency of a city's entire transportation network, making public transport timelier and reducing the economic costs associated with traffic congestion (Litman, 2014). Furthermore, the data collected through the blockchain could provide city planners with invaluable insights into transportation patterns, enabling more effective urban planning (Batty, 2013).

15.11 CHALLENGES AND LIMITATIONS

15.11.1 TECHNOLOGICAL CHALLENGES

The implementation of a blockchain-based system for sustainable urban mobility is not without its technological hurdles. One of the primary challenges is scalability. As the number of transactions increases, the blockchain network must be able to handle the increased load without compromising speed or security (Croman et al., 2016). Additionally, the integration of various data sources like GPS and vehicle sensors into the blockchain poses challenges in data integrity and validation (Zheng, Xie, Dai, Chen, & Wang, 2017). Moreover, the use of account abstraction for gas payments adds another layer of complexity, requiring robust smart contracts to ensure seamless transactions (Buterin, 2020).

15.11.2 USER ADOPTION

For the system to be effective, it requires widespread user adoption. Behavioral inertia and resistance to change are significant barriers to adoption (Rogers, 2003). While token incentives can drive initial interest, long-term engagement will depend on the perceived value and ease of use of the system (Davis, 1989). Furthermore, the system must be inclusive, catering to users with varying levels of technological literacy to ensure widespread adoption (Vanheusden, van Dalen, & Mingardo, 2022)

15.11.3 ETHICAL CONSIDERATIONS

The system also raises several ethical considerations. Data privacy is a significant concern, especially given the sensitive nature of location data (Nissenbaum, 2009). While blockchain offers enhanced security, the immutable nature of the technology could potentially make it difficult to rectify any erroneous or misleading data entries (Maurer, Nelms, & Swartz, 2013). Additionally, the tokenization model could inadvertently create a divide between those who can afford to participate and those who cannot, raising questions about social equity.

15.12 CONCLUSION

The investigation into the utilization of blockchain technology for fostering sustainable urban mobility has yielded several key insights that hold substantial promise for the future of transportation.

At its core, the system leverages the decentralized and immutable nature of blockchain to create a transparent and secure environment for all transactions. This is particularly crucial in building trust among users, who can be assured that their efforts toward sustainable transportation are accurately recorded and rewarded.

Certainly, one of the most noteworthy findings in our exploration is the incorporation of account abstraction (AA) to enhance the system's usability. Traditional blockchain systems often require users to pay for gas to submit transactions, a feature that could deter widespread adoption. AA offers a solution to this by allowing the system to pay for gas on behalf of users. This not only removes a significant barrier to entry but also enhances the user experience by eliminating the need for users to manage gas fees.

Moreover, AA allows for the automatic signing of UserOperations at the time of user wallet creation. These UserOperations can trigger various actions in the user's wallet, such as gathering location data, identifying nearby users, and determining the type of transport used. By automating these processes, the system reduces its dependency on user signatures, thereby streamlining the user experience and making the system more robust and efficient.

Tokenization, another cornerstone of the proposed system, emerges as a compelling mechanism to drive behavioral change. By converting sustainable actions into digital tokens, the system provides a tangible and immediate reward, thereby making eco-friendly choices more appealing. This aligns seamlessly with broader societal and governmental objectives, such as the reduction of greenhouse gas emissions and the promotion of public health through increased physical activity. The token-based incentives could serve as a catalyst for a paradigm shift in urban mobility, moving away from fossil fuel–dependent modes of transportation to more sustainable options like public transit, cycling, and walking.

However, it is crucial to acknowledge that the system is not a panacea and comes with its own set of challenges. Technological issues, particularly those related to the scalability of blockchain networks, could pose significant hurdles. As the system gains more users, the blockchain must be able to handle an increasing number of transactions without compromising on speed or cost.

User adoption is another critical factor that could make or break the system. While the token rewards are designed to incentivize sustainable behavior, the system's success ultimately hinges on widespread adoption. This involves not just initial uptake but sustained engagement over time, which could be influenced by various factors ranging from the perceived value of the rewards to the ease of use of the application.

Lastly, ethical considerations cannot be overlooked. The system's data collection methods, aimed at tracking sustainable actions, must be designed to respect user privacy and data security. Moreover, the system must be inclusive, ensuring that it is accessible to people from diverse socio-economic backgrounds.

As cities continue to grapple with the challenges of urban mobility, the proposed system offers a novel approach to fostering sustainable behaviors. However, the implementation of such a system is in its nascent stages, and several areas warrant further research:

- *Scalability solutions.* Future research could focus on optimizing the blockchain for high transaction volumes, possibly through layer-2 solutions or sharding mechanisms (Nakamoto, 2008).
- *User experience.* Studies could be conducted to understand user behavior and preferences better, thereby informing system design for increased adoption (Venkatesh et al., 2012).
- *Ethical frameworks.* Ethical guidelines need to be developed to address data privacy and social equity concerns.
- *Policy integration.* Research could also explore how the system could be integrated into existing governmental policies for urban planning and sustainability.
- *Economic models.* Further studies could delve into the economic viability of the tokenization model, exploring various avenues for token utility and value stabilization (Tapscott & Tapscott, 2016).

By addressing these areas, the system has the potential to serve as a cornerstone for sustainable urban mobility, contributing to a greener, healthier, and more efficient urban environment.

REFERENCES

Abadi, A., Rajabioun, T., & Ioannou, P. (2015). Traffic flow prediction for road transportation networks with limited traffic data. *IEEE Transactions on Intelligent Transportation Systems, 16*(2).

Abbas, K., Tawalbeh, L., Rafiq, A., Muthanna, A., Elgendy, I., & Abd El-Latif, A. (2021). Convergence of blockchain and IoT for secure transportation systems in smart cities. *Security and Communication Networks, 2021.*

Ahmadjee, S., Mera-Gómez, C., Bahsoon, R., & Kazman, R. (2022). A study on blockchain architecture design decisions and their security attacks and threats. *ACM Transactions on Software Engineering and Methodology, 31*(2).

Anderson, S., & de Palma, A. (2004). The economics of pricing parking. *Journal of Urban Economics, 55*(1).

Ariely, D. (2008). *Predictably irrational: The hidden forces that shape our decisions.* HarperCollins Publishers.

Arnott, R., & Small, K. (1994). The economics of traffic congestion. *American Scientist, 82*(5).

Batty, M. (2013). *The new science of cities.* MIT Press.

Bell, M., & Ebisu, K. (2012). Environmental inequality in exposures to airborne particulate matter components in the United States. *Environmental Health Perspectives, 120*(12).

Bento, A., Goulder, L., Jacobsen, M., & Von Haefen, R. (2009). Distributional and efficiency impacts of increased US gasoline taxes. *American Economic Review, 99*(3).

Block, M., & Calderón-Garcidueñas, L. (2009). Air pollution: Mechanisms of neuroinflammation and CNS disease. *Trends in Neurosciences, 32*(9).

Buterin, V. (2014). Ethereum white paper: A next generation smart contract & decentralized application platform. *Etherum*(January).

Buterin, V. (2020). *Ethereum 2.0: A complete guide.* https://blog.chainsafe.io/ethereum-2-0-a-complete-guide-d46d8ac914ce.

Buterin, V. (2021). *ERC4337: Account abstraction without Ethereum protocol changes.* September. https://medium.com/infinitism/erc-4337-account-abstraction-without-ethereum-protocol-changes-d75c9d94dc4a.

Catalini, C., & Gans, J. (2020). Some simple economics of the blockchain. *Communications of the ACM, 63*(7).

Chester, M., Horvath, A., & Madanat, S. (2010). Parking infrastructure: Energy, emissions, and automobile life-cycle environmental accounting. *Environmental Research Letters, 5*(3).

Christidis, K., & Devetsikiotis, M. (2016). Blockchains and smart contracts for the internet of things. *IEEE Access, 4.*

Clancy, L., Goodman, P., Sinclair, H., & Dockery, D. (2002). Effect of air-pollution control on death rates in Dublin, Ireland: An intervention study. *Lancet, 360*(9341).

Croman, K., Decker, C., Eyal, I., Gencer, A., Juels, A., Kosba, A., . . . Wattenhofer, R. (2016). On scaling decentralized blockchains. In J. Clark, S. Meiklejohn, P. Ryan, D. Wallach, M. Brenner, & K. Rohloff (Eds.), *Financial cryptography and data security. FC 2016.* Lecture Notes in Computer Science (Vol. 9604, pp. 106–125). Springer. https://doi.org/10.1007/978-3-662-53357-4_8

Davis, F. (1989). Perceived usefulness, perceived ease of use, and user acceptance of information technology. *MIS Quarterly: Management Information Systems, 13*(3).

Diamond, D. (2009). The impact of government incentives for hybrid-electric vehicles: Evidence from US states. *Energy Policy, 37*(3).

Duranton, G., & Turner, M. (2011). The fundamental law of road congestion: Evidence from US cities. *American Economic Review, 101*(6).

Eliasson, J. (2014). The stockholm congestion charges: An overview. *Centre for Trnasport Studies, Stockholm, 7.*

EPA, U. (2021). *Nitrogen dioxide (NO2) pollution.* U.S. Environmental Protection Agency(2).

EPA. (2018). *Volatile organic compounds' impact on indoor air quality.* EPA.

Fagnant, D., & Kockelman, K. (2018). Dynamic ride-sharing and fleet sizing for a system of shared autonomous vehicles in Austin, Texas. *Transportation, 45*(1).

Fisch, C. (2019). Initial coin offerings (ICOs) to finance new ventures. *Journal of Business Venturing, 34*(1).

Gillingham, K., & Palmery, K. (2014). Bridging the energy efficiency gap: Policy insights from economic theory and empirical evidence. *Review of Environmental Economics and Policy, 8*(1).

Glaser, F. (2017). Pervasive decentralisation of digital infrastructures: A framework for blockchain enabled system and use case analysis. In *Proceedings of the Annual Hawaii International Conference on System Sciences, 2017-January* (pp. 1543–1552).

Gössling, S., & Hall, C. M. (2006). An introduction to tourism and global environmental change. In *Tourism and global environmental change* (pp. 1–33). Routledge.

Government, U. (2015). *Distributed ledger technology: Beyond blockchain*. Government Office for Science.

Graedel, T. (1992). Corrosion mechanisms for silver exposed to the atmosphere. *Journal of The Electrochemical Society, 139*(7).

Graham-Rowe, E., Skippon, S., Gardner, B., & Abraham, C. (2011). Can we reduce car use and, if so, how? A review of available evidence. *Transportation Research Part A: Policy and Practice, 45*(5).

Guo, Z., & Ren, S. (2013). From minimum to maximum: Impact of the London parking reform on residential parking supply from 2004 to 2010? *Urban Studies, 50*(6).

Hardman, S., Chandan, A., Tal, G., & Turrentine, T. (2017). The effectiveness of financial purchase incentives for battery electric vehicles – A review of the evidence. *Renewable and Sustainable Energy Reviews, 80*.

Hensher, D. (2017). Future bus transport contracts under a mobility as a service (MaaS) regime in the digital age: Are they likely to change? *Transportation Research Part A: Policy and Practice, 98*.

IEA. (2023a). *Global status report for buildings and construction 2019 – Analysis—IEA*. IEA 2023.

IEA. (2023b). Tracking SDG7: The Energy Progress Report, 2023, IEA, IRENA, UNSD, World Bank, WHO. 2023. Tracking SDG 7: The Energy Progress Report. World Bank, Washington DC. © World Bank, Paris. https://www.iea.org/reports/tracking-sdg7-the-energy-progress-report-2023, Licence: CC BY NC 4.0

INRIX. (2023). INRIX global traffic scorecard. *INRIX Research* (February).

IPCC. (2018). Global warming of 1.5°C: An IPCC special report. *Ipcc—Sr15, 2*(October).

Javed, A., Shahzad, F., Rehman, S., Zikria, Y., Razzak, I., Jalil, Z., & Xu, G. (2022). Future smart cities requirements, emerging technologies, applications, challenges, and future aspects. *Cities, 129*.

Javier, B., & NOMMON. (n.d.). *New mobility options and urban: Challenges and opportunities for transport planning and modelling*. Momentum, Ref. Ares(2019)7704805 - 16/12/2019, https://h2020-momentum.eu/wp-content/uploads/2020/01/MOMENTUM-D2.1-New-Mobility-Options-and-Urban-Mobility.pdf

Kahneman, D., & Tversky, A. (2018). Prospect theory: An analysis of decision under risk. *Experiments in Environmental Economics, 1*.

Khan, M., Du, J., Anwar, F., Khan, H., Shahzad, F., & Qalati, S. (2021). Corporate social responsibility and the reciprocity between employee perception, perceived external prestige, and employees' emotional labor. *Psychology Research and Behavior Management, 14*.

Kshetri, N. (2017). Can blockchain strengthen the internet of things? *IT Professional, 19*(4).

Le Quéré, C., Andrew, R. M., Friedlingstein, P., Sitch, S., Hauck, J., Pongratz, J., . . . Zheng, B. (2018). Global carbon budget 2018. *Earth System Science Data, 10*(4), 2141–2194. https://doi.org/10.5194/essd-10-2141-2018

Lovett, G., Burns, D., Driscoll, C., Jenkins, J., Mitchell, M., Rustad, L., . . . Haeuber, R. (2007). Who needs environmental monitoring? *Frontiers in Ecology and the Environment, 5*(5).

Manski, S. (2017). Building the blockchain world: Technological commonwealth or just more of the same? *Strategic Change, 26*(5).

Maurer, B., Nelms, T., & Swartz, L. (2013). "When perhaps the real problem is money itself!": The practical materiality of Bitcoin. *Social Semiotics, 23*(2).

Merkle, R. (2016). DAOs, democracy and governance. *Cryonics Magazine, 37*(4) (July–August).

Mertz, C. (2020). *Blockchain in carbon credit markets: Ensuring transparency and preventing double-counting*. Climate Action Data Trust. Retrieved from https://www.climateactiondatatrust.org

Mollick, E. (2014). The dynamics of crowdfunding: An exploratory study. *Journal of Business Venturing, 29*(1).

Morkunas, V., Paschen, J., & Boon, E. (2019). How blockchain technologies impact your business model. *Business Horizons, 62*(3).

Mougayar, W. (2016). *The business blockchain: Promise, practice, and application of the next internet technology*. John Wiley & Sons.

Nakamoto, S. (2008). *Bitcoin: A peer-to-peer electronic cash system, October 2008*. Cited on.

Nallet, C. (2018). *The challenge of urban mobility: A case study of Addis Ababa Light Rail, Ethiopia*. IFRI: Institut Français des Relations Internationales. Notes de l'Ifri, février 2018. Retrieved from https://policycommons.net/artifacts/1406335/the-challenge-of-urban-mobility/2020600/ on 08 Jul 2024. CID: 20.500.12592/cp4g64.

Nissenbaum, H. (2009). *Privacy in context: Technology, policy, and the integrity of social life*. Stanford University Press.

Ostrom, E. (2015). Governing the commons: The evolution of institutions for collective action. *Land Economics, 68*(3), 354–357. https://doi.org/10.2307/3146384

Pannia, P. (2023). Effects of air pollution on children"s health. *Archivos Argentinos de Pediatria, 121*(1).

Pelgander, L., Öberg, C., & Barkenäs, L. (2022). Trust and the sharing economy. *Digital Business, 2*(2).

Poon, J., & Buterin, V. (2017). Plasma: Scalable autonomous smart contracts. *Whitepaper*.

Reijers, W., O'Brolcháin, F., & Haynes, P. (2016). Governance in blockchain technologies & social contract theories. *Ledger*, *1*.

Rogers, E. M., Singhal, A., & Quinlan, M. M. (2014). Diffusion of innovations. In *An integrated approach to communication theory and research* (pp. 432–448). Routledge.

Sachs, J. D. (2015). *Incentivizing public transport and non-motorized modes of transport for sustainable development*. Sustainable Development Knowledge Platform. Retrieved from UN Sustainable Development.

Schär, F. (2021). Decentralized finance: On blockchain-and smart contract-based financial markets. *Federal Reserve Bank of St. Louis Review*, *103*(2).

Schrank, D., Eisele, B., & Lomax, T. (2021). *2021 Urban mobility report*. Texas A&M Transportation Institute (June).

Shaheen, S., Cohen, A., & Zohdy, I. (2016). Shared mobility: Current practices and guiding principles. *Fhwa-Hop-16–022 2* (Washington D.C.).

Shoup, D. (2006). Cruising for parking. *Transport Policy*, *13*(6).

Sierzchula, W., Bakker, S., Maat, K., & Van Wee, B. (2014). The influence of financial incentives and other socio-economic factors on electric vehicle adoption. *Energy Policy*, *68*.

Sims, R., Schaeffer, R., Creutzig, F., Cruz-Núñez, X., D'Agosto, M., Dimitriu, D., ... Tiwari, G. (2014). Transport. In O. Edenhofer, R. Pichs-Madruga, Y. Sokona, E. Farahani, S. Kadner, K. Seyboth, ... J.C. Minx (Eds.), *Climate change 2014: Mitigation of climate change. Contribution of Working Group III to the Fifth Assessment Report of the Intergovernmental Panel on Climate Change* (pp. 599–670). Cambridge University Press. Retrieved from IPCC.

Small, K., & Yan, J. (2001). The value of "value pricing" of roads: Second-best pricing and product differentiation. *Journal of Urban Economics*, *49*(2).

Somuyiwa, A., Fadare, S., & Ayantoyinbo, B. (2015). Analysis of the cost of traffic congestion on worker's productivity in a mega city of a developing economy. *International Review of Management and Business Research*, *4*(3).

Swan, M. (2015). *Blockchain: Blueprint for a new economy*., O'Reilly Media, Inc.

Szabo, N. (1997). Formalizing and securing relationships on public networks. *First Monday*, *2*(9).

Tapscott, D., & Tapscott, A. (2016). *Blockchain revolution: How the technology behind bitcoin and other cryptocurrencies is changing the world*. Penguin.

Thaler, R., & Sunstein, C. (2008). *Nudge: Improving decisions about health, wealth, and happiness*.

US EPA. (2020). Carbon monoxide (CO) pollution in outdoor air. *January 19, 2017 Web Snapshot*.

US EPA. (2021). *Ozone pollution and your patients' health*. United States Environmental Protection Agency.

US EPA. (2022). *Volatile organic compounds' impact on indoor air quality | US EPA*. United States Government.

Vanheusden, W., van Dalen, J., & Mingardo, G. (2022). Governance and business policy impact on carsharing diffusion in European cities. *Transportation Research Part D: Transport and Environment*, *108*.

Venkatesh, V., Thong, J. Y. L., & Xu, X. (2012). Consumer acceptance and use of information technology: Extending the unified theory of acceptance and use of technology. *MIS Quarterly*, *36*(1), 157–178. https://doi.org/10.2307/41410412

Weinberger, D., Harboe, Z., Sanders, E., Ndiritu, M., Klugman, K., Rückinger, S., ... Lipsitch, M. (2010). Association of serotype with risk of death due to pneumococcal pneumonia: A meta-analysis. *Clinical Infectious Diseases*, *51*(6).

White, K., Habib, R., & Hardisty, D. (2019). How to SHIFT consumer behaviors to be more sustainable: A literature review and guiding framework. *Journal of Marketing*, *83*(3).

WHO. (2020). *Ambient air pollution: Health impacts*. World Health Organization.

Xie, J., Tang, H., Huang, T., Yu, F., Xie, R., Liu, J., & Liu, Y. (2019). A survey of blockchain technology applied to smart cities: Research issues and challenges. *IEEE Communications Surveys and Tutorials*, *21*(3).

Zhang, K., & Batterman, S. (2013). Air pollution and health risks due to vehicle traffic. *Science of the Total Environment*, *450–451*.

Zheng, Z., Xie, S., Dai, H., Chen, X., & Wang, H. (2017). An overview of blockchain technology: Architecture, consensus, and future trends. *Proceedings—2017 IEEE 6th International Congress on Big Data, BigData Congress 2017* (pp. 557–564). Honolulu, HI, USA, 2017, doi: 10.1109/BigDataCongress.2017.85. keywords: {Bitcoin;Peer-to-peer computing;Organizations;Contracts;Blockchain;decentralization;consensus; scalability}.

Zheng, Z., Xie, S., Dai, H., Chen, X., & Wang, H. (2018). Blockchain challenges and opportunities: A survey. *International Journal of Web and Grid Services*, *14*(4).

Zohar, A. (2015). Bitcoin: Under the hood. *Communications of the ACM*, *58*(9).

16 Blockchain Technology for Smart Contracts

S M Nazmuz Sakib

16.1 INTRODUCTION TO SMART CONTRACTS AND BLOCKCHAIN TECHNOLOGY

Smart contracts and blockchain technology have emerged as promising tools for revolutionizing the supply chain industry. *Blockchain technology* is a distributed ledger system that enables secure and transparent transactions without the need for intermediaries. Smart contracts are self-executing contracts that automatically execute the terms of an agreement when the conditions specified in the contract are met. These contracts are stored and executed on a blockchain network, making them immutable, transparent, and secure [1].

Blockchain technology and smart contracts have the potential to significantly improve supply chain management by providing real-time visibility, improving traceability, enhancing security, and reducing costs. With these technologies, supply chain stakeholders can track and trace products throughout the supply chain, from raw materials to finished goods. They can also ensure the authenticity and quality of products, prevent counterfeiting and fraud, and streamline the entire supply chain process [2].

In this chapter, we will provide an overview of blockchain technology and smart contracts and explore their role in supply chain management. We will also discuss the benefits, implementation considerations, and potential limitations of using smart contracts in supply chain management. Finally, we will discuss the future outlook and potential developments in the use of smart contracts and blockchain technology in supply chain management.

16.2 OVERVIEW OF THE SUPPLY CHAIN AND ITS CHALLENGES

Supply chain management is the process of managing the flow of goods, services, and information from the point of origin to the point of consumption. The supply chain includes all the activities and processes involved in bringing a product or service to the end consumer. The supply chain industry faces a number of challenges, including:

- *Lack of transparency.* The supply chain industry often lacks transparency, making it difficult to track and trace products from the point of origin to the point of consumption.
- *Counterfeiting and fraud.* Counterfeiting and fraud are common issues in the supply chain industry, which can lead to significant financial losses and damage to brand reputation.
- *Inefficiency.* The supply chain industry is often inefficient, with delays and bottlenecks in the flow of goods and services.
- *Quality control.* Ensuring the quality and authenticity of products throughout the supply chain can be challenging, especially for products that are highly regulated or require strict quality control measures.
- *Data management.* The supply chain industry generates a large amount of data, which can be difficult to manage and analyze effectively.

DOI: 10.1201/9781003450306-18

These challenges can lead to increased costs, reduced efficiency, and damage to brand reputation. In the next section, we will explore how blockchain technology and smart contracts can help solve these challenges in supply chain management [3].

16.3 HOW BLOCKCHAIN TECHNOLOGY CAN HELP SOLVE SUPPLY CHAIN CHALLENGES

Blockchain technology has gained significant attention for its potential in revolutionizing supply chain management. Blockchain is a distributed ledger system that enables secure and transparent transactions without the need for intermediaries. The technology offers a number of benefits, including real-time visibility, improved traceability, enhanced security, and reduced costs. In this section, we will explore how blockchain technology can help solve supply chain challenges and improve the overall efficiency and transparency of the supply chain [4].

16.3.1 TRANSPARENCY AND TRACEABILITY

One of the biggest challenges in the supply chain industry is the lack of transparency and traceability. This makes it difficult to track and trace products from the point of origin to the point of consumption. Blockchain technology can help solve this challenge by providing a secure and transparent ledger system that allows supply chain stakeholders to track products throughout the supply chain [5].

Each transaction in the blockchain is recorded and cannot be altered, making it easy to trace the origin and movement of products. This feature is particularly useful for products that require strict quality control measures or those that are highly regulated. With blockchain, supply chain stakeholders can ensure the authenticity and quality of products, prevent counterfeiting and fraud, and streamline the entire supply chain process [6].

16.3.2 REDUCED COSTS

Another challenge in the supply chain industry is the inefficiency of the supply chain process. Delays and bottlenecks in the flow of goods and services can lead to increased costs and reduced efficiency. Blockchain technology can help reduce these costs by eliminating intermediaries and automating the supply chain process [7].

Smart contracts are self-executing contracts that automatically execute the terms of an agreement when the conditions specified in the contract are met. These contracts are stored and executed on a blockchain network, making them immutable, transparent, and secure. With smart contracts, supply chain stakeholders can automate the supply chain process, reducing the need for intermediaries and minimizing delays and bottlenecks [8].

16.3.3 ENHANCED SECURITY

Security is another challenge in the supply chain industry, with counterfeiting and fraud being common issues. Blockchain technology can help enhance security by providing a secure and tamper-proof ledger system. The decentralized nature of blockchain ensures that data is not controlled by any single entity, making it difficult for malicious actors to manipulate the data [9].

In addition, blockchain uses advanced cryptography to secure the data, making it virtually impossible to hack. With blockchain, supply chain stakeholders can ensure the security and privacy of their data, prevent counterfeiting and fraud, and improve the overall security of the supply chain process [10].

In conclusion, blockchain technology offers a number of benefits that can help solve supply chain challenges and improve the overall efficiency and transparency of the supply chain. By providing real-time visibility, improving traceability, enhancing security, and reducing costs, blockchain can revolutionize the way the supply chain industry operates. While there are implementation considerations and potential limitations that need to be addressed, the potential benefits of blockchain technology in supply chain management are undeniable. The adoption of blockchain technology in the supply chain industry is expected to grow rapidly in the coming years, and it will be interesting to see how this technology will transform the supply chain landscape in the future.

16.4   USE CASES OF BLOCKCHAIN TECHNOLOGY IN SUPPLY CHAIN MANAGEMENT

Blockchain technology has the potential to revolutionize the way supply chains operate by providing a transparent, secure, and efficient platform for managing the flow of goods, services, and information. Blockchain is a distributed ledger system that allows secure transactions without the need for intermediaries. With its immutability and transparency, blockchain technology can help address some of the key challenges faced by the supply chain industry, such as lack of transparency, inefficiencies, fraud, and counterfeiting [11].

In this section, we will explore some of the key use cases of blockchain technology in supply chain management.

16.4.1   Track and Trace

One of the primary use cases of blockchain technology in supply chain management is track and trace. With blockchain, it becomes possible to track and trace products throughout the supply chain, from the point of origin to the point of consumption. This is made possible by the immutability of the blockchain ledger, which ensures that each transaction is recorded and cannot be altered [12].

This level of traceability can help improve supply chain transparency and provide greater visibility into the movement of goods. For example, blockchain technology can be used to track the origin of raw materials, ensuring that they are ethically sourced and comply with environmental and social standards. It can also be used to track the movement of finished products, providing greater transparency into the supply chain process [13].

16.4.2   Supply Chain Financing

Blockchain technology can also be used to improve supply chain financing. Supply chain financing is a financing method that provides financing to suppliers based on their outstanding invoices. With blockchain technology, it becomes possible to automate the supply chain financing process, reducing the need for intermediaries and improving the speed and efficiency of the process [14].

Smart contracts, which are self-executing contracts that automatically execute the terms of an agreement when the conditions specified in the contract are met, can be used to automate the supply chain financing process. Suppliers can create invoices on the blockchain, which are then automatically verified and settled once the conditions of the contract are met. This can help improve the cash flow of suppliers and reduce the risk of default [15].

16.4.3   Counterfeiting and Fraud Prevention

Counterfeiting and fraud are common issues in the supply chain industry, which can lead to significant financial losses and damage to brand reputation. Blockchain technology can help prevent counterfeiting and fraud by providing a secure and transparent ledger system that allows stakeholders to verify the authenticity and provenance of products [16].

With blockchain technology, it becomes possible to create a digital identity for each product, which is then recorded on the blockchain. This digital identity can include information such as the origin of the product, the materials used in its production, and any certifications or quality control measures. This information can then be verified by supply chain stakeholders, such as suppliers, manufacturers, and retailers, ensuring the authenticity and quality of the product [17].

16.4.4 Supply Chain Optimization

Blockchain technology can also be used to optimize the supply chain process. By providing real-time visibility into the movement of goods, blockchain technology can help identify inefficiencies and bottlenecks in the supply chain process [18]. This can help supply chain stakeholders optimize the supply chain process, reducing costs and improving efficiency.

For example, blockchain technology can be used to track the movement of goods from the point of origin to the point of consumption, providing real-time visibility into the supply chain process [19]. This can help supply chain stakeholders identify bottlenecks and delays in the process, allowing them to take corrective action to improve efficiency [20].

16.4.5 Compliance and Regulatory Compliance

Blockchain technology can also be used to ensure compliance and regulatory compliance in the supply chain industry. With blockchain, it becomes possible to create a tamperproof record of all supply chain transactions, which can be used to ensure compliance with regulations and standards [21].

For example, blockchain technology can be used to ensure compliance with environmental and social standards. By creating a digital identity for each product on the blockchain, supply chain stakeholders can track the origin of raw materials and ensure that they meet environmental and social standards [22]. This can help reduce the risk of non-compliance and ensure that supply chain stakeholders meet their obligations under local and international regulations.

16.4.6 Supply Chain Visibility

Another use case of blockchain technology in supply chain management is supply chain visibility. *Supply chain visibility* refers to the ability to track the movement of goods and information throughout the supply chain process. With blockchain technology, it becomes possible to provide real-time visibility into the movement of goods and information, improving supply chain transparency and reducing the risk of fraud and counterfeiting [23].

Blockchain technology can be used to create a digital record of all supply chain transactions, which can be accessed by supply chain stakeholders in real time. This can help improve collaboration and communication between supply chain stakeholders [24], reducing the risk of miscommunication and delays.

16.4.7 Sustainability and Environmental Impact

Blockchain technology can also be used to promote sustainability and reduce the environmental impact of the supply chain industry [25]. With blockchain, it becomes possible to create a digital record of the environmental impact of each supply chain transaction, which can be used to monitor and reduce the environmental impact of the supply chain industry.

For example, blockchain technology can be used to track the carbon footprint of each supply chain transaction, providing greater visibility into the environmental impact of the supply chain process [26]. This information can then be used to identify opportunities for reducing carbon emissions and improving the sustainability of the supply chain industry.

In conclusion, blockchain technology has the potential to revolutionize the way supply chains operate, providing a transparent, secure, and efficient platform for managing the flow of goods, services, and information. By providing real-time visibility into the movement of goods and information, blockchain technology can help address some of the key challenges faced by the supply chain industry, such as lack of transparency, inefficiencies, fraud, and counterfeiting.

The use cases of blockchain technology in supply chain management are many and varied, ranging from track and trace to supply chain financing, counterfeiting and fraud prevention, supply chain optimization, compliance and regulatory compliance, supply chain visibility, and sustainability and environmental impact. By leveraging the power of blockchain technology, supply chain stakeholders can improve the efficiency, transparency, and sustainability of the supply chain industry, reducing costs and improving customer satisfaction.

16.5   BENEFITS OF USING SMART CONTRACTS IN SUPPLY CHAIN MANAGEMENT

Supply chain management involves coordinating the flow of goods, services, and information between multiple stakeholders, which can be time-consuming, inefficient, and prone to errors. Smart contracts, which are self-executing contracts with the terms of the agreement being directly written into lines of code, offer a number of benefits to supply chain management, including increased efficiency, transparency, and security. They automate many manual processes, reduce intermediaries, and streamline the supply chain process, resulting in faster transaction times, lower costs, and increased efficiency [27]. Smart contracts also provide a transparent and tamperproof record of all supply chain transactions, improving supply chain transparency and helping reduce the risk of fraud and counterfeiting. They are based on blockchain technology, which provides a secure platform for managing supply chain transactions, reducing the risk of fraud and counterfeiting. Real-world examples of smart contracts include tracking food products for food safety issues, tracking the movement of goods in the logistics industry, tracking the origin and movement of diamonds, and automating the process of financing supply chain transactions [28]. While there are challenges to implementing smart contract–based systems, such as interoperability and scalability, the benefits are clear and will continue to drive the adoption of this technology in the years to come.

16.6   IMPLEMENTATION CONSIDERATIONS FOR USING SMART CONTRACTS IN SUPPLY CHAIN MANAGEMENT

Smart contracts offer numerous benefits to supply chain management, including increased efficiency, transparency, and security. However, implementing smart contracts in supply chain management can be a complex and challenging process. In this section, we will discuss the implementation considerations for using smart contracts in supply chain management.

16.6.1   INTEROPERABILITY

One of the primary considerations for implementing smart contracts in supply chain management is interoperability. Smart contracts are designed to be self-executing and self-enforcing, but they must also be able to interact with other systems in the supply chain. This requires a standardized protocol for communication and data exchange between different systems [29].

Interoperability can be a challenge in supply chain management because there are often multiple stakeholders involved, each using different systems and data formats. To overcome this challenge, it is important to establish clear standards for data exchange and communication, such as the use of open APIs and standardized data formats [30].

16.6.2 Scalability

Another consideration for implementing smart contracts in supply chain management is scalability. Smart contracts are designed to be executed on a decentralized network, which means that the processing power is distributed across multiple nodes [31]. This can limit the scalability of smart contract–based systems, particularly when processing large volumes of data.

To address scalability issues, it may be necessary to implement a hybrid approach that combines decentralized and centralized processing [32]. For example, a smart contract–based system could use a centralized processing engine for certain functions, such as data validation and verification, while still leveraging the benefits of decentralized processing for other functions [33, 34].

16.6.3 Security

Security is a critical consideration for implementing smart contracts in supply chain management. Smart contracts are designed to be secure and tamperproof, but they can still be vulnerable to attacks if not implemented correctly [35]. This includes attacks such as hacking, data breaches, and other forms of cybercrime [36, 37].

To ensure the security of smart contract–based systems, it is important to implement robust security protocols, such as encryption, access controls, and regular security audits [38] [39]. It is also important to have a clear incident response plan in place to respond quickly to any security breaches or other incidents [40–42].

16.6.4 Regulatory Compliance

Regulatory compliance is another important consideration for implementing smart contracts in supply chain management. Many industries are subject to strict regulations around data privacy, security, and other issues, and smart contract–based systems must comply with these regulations to ensure legal compliance [43].

To ensure regulatory compliance, it is important to work closely with regulatory agencies and legal experts to understand the specific requirements for your industry. This may involve implementing additional security measures, such as encryption and access controls, or ensuring that data is stored and transmitted in compliance with local and international regulations.

16.6.5 Integration with Legacy Systems

Finally, integrating smart contract–based systems with legacy systems can be a challenge. Many supply chain management systems are built on legacy technologies that may not be compatible with smart contract–based systems. This can make it difficult to integrate data and processes between these systems.

To overcome this challenge, it may be necessary to develop custom integration solutions that bridge the gap between legacy systems and smart contract–based systems. This may involve using middleware or APIs to facilitate data exchange between different systems or implementing custom integration solutions to address specific integration challenges.

Implementing smart contracts in supply chain management can be a complex and challenging process, but it offers numerous benefits, including increased efficiency, transparency, and security. By considering the implementation considerations outlined in this section, supply chain stakeholders can successfully implement smart contract–based systems and realize these benefits. This includes establishing clear standards for data exchange and communication, addressing scalability issues, implementing robust security protocols, ensuring regulatory compliance, and developing custom integration solutions to bridge the gap between legacy systems and smart contract–based systems [44].

16.7   CHALLENGES AND LIMITATIONS OF USING SMART CONTRACTS IN SUPPLY CHAIN MANAGEMENT

Smart contracts offer numerous benefits to supply chain management, including increased efficiency, transparency, and security. However, like any new technology, there are also challenges and limitations to using smart contracts in supply chain management. In this section, we will discuss the challenges and limitations of using smart contracts in supply chain management.

16.7.1   COMPLEXITY OF SUPPLY CHAIN PROCESSES

One of the primary challenges of using smart contracts in supply chain management is the complexity of supply chain processes. Supply chains can involve numerous stakeholders, including suppliers, manufacturers, distributors, retailers, and consumers, each with their own processes and data requirements [45]. This complexity can make it challenging to design smart contracts that can effectively address all the different processes and requirements.

To overcome this challenge, it is important to carefully map out supply chain processes and data requirements to identify areas where smart contracts can provide the most value. This may involve developing custom smart contracts for specific processes or stakeholders, rather than trying to create a one-size-fits-all solution.

16.7.2   LIMITED DATA INPUT CAPABILITIES

Another challenge of using smart contracts in supply chain management is the limited data input capabilities of smart contracts. Smart contracts are designed to be self-executing and self-enforcing based on predetermined rules, but they are limited in their ability to process external data.

This can be a challenge in supply chain management, where data inputs can be highly variable and subject to change. To overcome this challenge, it may be necessary to develop more complex smart contracts that can process a wider range of data inputs or to integrate smart contracts with other systems that can provide additional data inputs.

16.7.3   INTEGRATION WITH LEGACY SYSTEMS

Integrating smart contracts with legacy systems can be a challenge. Many supply chain management systems are built on legacy technologies that may not be compatible with smart contract–based systems. This can make it difficult to integrate data and processes between these systems.

To overcome this challenge, it may be necessary to develop custom integration solutions that bridge the gap between legacy systems and smart contract–based systems. This may involve using middleware or APIs to facilitate data exchange between different systems, or implementing custom integration solutions to address specific integration challenges.

16.7.4   REGULATORY COMPLIANCE

Regulatory compliance is another challenge of using smart contracts in supply chain management. Many industries are subject to strict regulations around data privacy, security, and other issues, and smart contract–based systems must comply with these regulations to ensure legal compliance.

To ensure regulatory compliance, it is important to work closely with regulatory agencies and legal experts to understand the specific requirements for your industry. This may involve implementing additional security measures, such as encryption and access controls, or ensuring that data is stored and transmitted in compliance with local and international regulations.

16.7.5 LACK OF STANDARDIZATION

A lack of standardization can be a challenge when using smart contracts in supply chain management. Smart contracts are still a relatively new technology, and there is not yet a standardized set of best practices or protocols for using them in supply chain management.

To overcome this challenge, it is important to stay up-to-date on the latest developments in smart contract technology and to participate in industry efforts to develop standardized protocols and best practices for using smart contracts in supply chain management.

16.7.6 LIMITED SCALABILITY

Smart contracts are designed to be executed on a decentralized network, which means that the processing power is distributed across multiple nodes. This can limit the scalability of smart contract–based systems, particularly when processing large volumes of data.

To address scalability issues, it may be necessary to implement a hybrid approach that combines decentralized and centralized processing. For example, a smart contract–based system could use a centralized processing engine for certain functions, such as data validation and verification, while still leveraging the benefits of decentralized processing for other functions.

While smart contracts offer numerous benefits to supply chain management, there are also challenges and limitations that must be addressed to realize these benefits. These challenges include the complexity of supply chain processes, limited data input capabilities, integration with legacy systems, regulatory compliance, lack of standardization, and limited scalability.

To overcome these challenges, it is important to carefully map out supply chain processes and data requirements, develop custom smart contracts for specific processes or stakeholders, and integrate smart contracts with other systems that can provide additional data inputs. It may also be necessary to develop custom integration solutions that bridge the gap between legacy systems and smart contract–based systems, and to work closely with regulatory agencies and legal experts to ensure regulatory compliance [46, 47].

In addition, staying up-to-date on the latest developments in smart contract technology and participating in industry efforts to develop standardized protocols and best practices can help address the lack of standardization challenge. Finally, implementing a hybrid approach that combines decentralized and centralized processing can help address scalability issues.

Overall, while there are challenges and limitations to using smart contracts in supply chain management, the potential benefits make it well worth the effort to overcome these challenges. By leveraging smart contract technology, supply chain managers can achieve greater efficiency, transparency, and security, ultimately leading to improved business outcomes.

Some of the challenges and limitations of using smart contracts in supply chain management include the following.

The need for reliable and trustworthy data sources (oracles) to trigger the execution of smart contracts. Depending on the type and complexity of the oracle, there may be issues with data quality, availability, security, and cost.

The difficulty of integrating smart contracts with existing legacy systems and processes that may not be compatible or interoperable with blockchain technology.

The legal uncertainty and regulatory compliance of smart contracts, especially across different jurisdictions and industries. There may be conflicts or gaps between the code and the law, as well as challenges in enforcing and resolving disputes involving smart contracts.

Some of the benefits of using smart contracts in supply chain management include:

The ability to automate transactions and processes that are otherwise manual, time-consuming, and error-prone. Smart contracts can reduce transaction costs, improve operational efficiency, and enhance customer satisfaction.

The ability to increase transparency and traceability of supply chain activities and events. Smart contracts can provide real-time visibility and accountability of the flow of goods, information, and money throughout the supply chain.

The ability to enhance security and trust among supply chain partners. Smart contracts can prevent fraud, tampering, and unauthorized access by using cryptography and consensus mechanisms to ensure data integrity and authenticity.

To realize these benefits, supply chain managers need to evaluate their supply chain maturity and readiness for adopting smart contract technology. They also need to assess the sustainability impacts of smart contracts on their supply chain performance and stakeholders. A possible framework for doing so is proposed, which maps the relationships between organizational development, sustainability, and technology. According to this framework, smart contracts can contribute to the economic and social development of networked value chains and Society 5.0 by enabling efficient and transparent governance and collaborative self-coordination of human and non-human actors. However, there are also trade-offs and challenges that need to be addressed, such as ensuring data quality, privacy, ethics, and social inclusion [48].

In conclusion, smart contracts offer a promising opportunity for supply chain management to achieve higher levels of efficiency, transparency, security, and sustainability. However, they also pose significant challenges and limitations that require careful consideration and adaptation. Supply chain managers need to assess their current situation and future goals, as well as the potential impacts of smart contracts on their supply chain operations and stakeholders. By doing so, they can leverage smart contract technology to improve their business outcomes and contribute to social good.

16.8 FUTURE OUTLOOK AND POTENTIAL DEVELOPMENTS IN THE USE OF SMART CONTRACTS AND BLOCKCHAIN TECHNOLOGY IN SUPPLY CHAIN MANAGEMENT

The use of smart contracts and blockchain technology in supply chain management has already shown great promise, but the potential for future developments and advancements is even more exciting. In this section, we will explore some of the potential future use cases and developments for smart contracts and blockchain technology in supply chain management.

16.8.1 INTEROPERABILITY AND STANDARDS

One potential area of future development is the establishment of interoperability and standards between different blockchain networks. Currently, different blockchain networks use different protocols and standards, which can make it difficult for businesses to collaborate and share data. However, efforts are underway to develop cross-chain interoperability solutions, which would enable data and assets to be exchanged across different blockchain networks.

Another potential area for standards development is the creation of standardized smart contract templates that can be easily adapted for use in different supply chain processes. This would enable businesses to more easily and efficiently implement smart contracts and would also promote greater consistency and transparency across different supply chains.

16.8.2 MACHINE LEARNING AND ARTIFICIAL INTELLIGENCE

Another potential development is the integration of machine learning and artificial intelligence (AI) with blockchain and smart contract technology. By analyzing data from different points in the supply chain, machine learning algorithms can help identify patterns and optimize supply chain processes. For example, AI could be used to predict demand patterns, optimize production schedules, and identify potential supply chain disruptions before they occur [47, 49].

16.8.3 Supply Chain Finance

Smart contracts and blockchain technology could also revolutionize supply chain finance by enabling automated payments and reducing transaction costs. Currently, the financing of supply chains involves multiple parties and complex payment arrangements, which can result in delays and high costs. However, smart contracts could be used to automate payment processes, eliminating the need for intermediaries and reducing transaction costs.

16.8.4 Environmental and Social Sustainability

Blockchain technology could also be used to promote environmental and social sustainability in supply chains. For example, blockchain could be used to track the carbon footprint of products, enabling businesses to make more sustainable sourcing and transportation decisions. It could also be used to promote fair labor practices and ethical sourcing by providing greater transparency into supply chain operations.

Smart contracts and blockchain technology have the potential to transform supply chain management, providing greater efficiency, transparency, and security. However, there are still challenges to be addressed, such as regulatory compliance and scalability issues. Nevertheless, the potential benefits of this technology are too great to ignore, and we can expect to see continued advancements and developments in the coming years. By staying up-to-date on the latest developments and exploring new use cases, businesses can leverage smart contracts and blockchain technology to create more efficient and sustainable supply chains.

16.9 CASE STUDIES OF COMPANIES THAT HAVE SUCCESSFULLY IMPLEMENTED SMART CONTRACTS IN THEIR SUPPLY CHAIN MANAGEMENT

Smart contracts and blockchain technology have the potential to revolutionize supply chain management by improving efficiency, transparency, and security. While the technology is still in its early stages, there are already companies that have successfully implemented smart contracts in their supply chain operations. In this section, we will examine some case studies of companies that have successfully implemented smart contracts in their supply chain management [50–56].

16.9.1 Walmart

Walmart, one of the world's largest retailers, has been a pioneer in the use of blockchain technology and smart contracts in its supply chain operations. In 2016, Walmart began piloting a program to use blockchain technology to track the origin of pork in China. By using blockchain technology, Walmart was able to track the pork from the farm to the processing plant, and then to the store shelves [57, 58].

Following the success of the pilot program, Walmart has expanded its use of blockchain technology to track other products in its supply chain, such as leafy greens, mangoes, and strawberries. By using smart contracts to automate the tracking process, Walmart has been able to improve supply chain transparency and reduce the time it takes to track products in the supply chain [59].

16.9.2 Maersk

Maersk, the world's largest container shipping company, has also been experimenting with blockchain technology and smart contracts in its supply chain operations. In collaboration with IBM, Maersk has developed a blockchain-based platform called TradeLens, which aims to improve transparency and efficiency in the global shipping industry [60, 61].

By using smart contracts to automate the processing of shipping documents, TradeLens has been able to reduce the time it takes to process documents from days to minutes [62, 63]. This has enabled Maersk and its customers to more easily track shipments and reduce the risk of lost or delayed shipments [64].

16.9.3 DE BEERS

De Beers, the world's largest diamond producer, has also been exploring the use of blockchain technology and smart contracts in its supply chain operations. In collaboration with other members of the diamond industry, De Beers has developed a blockchain-based platform called Tracr, which aims to improve transparency and traceability in the diamond supply chain.

By using smart contracts to automate the tracking and certification process, Tracr has been able to improve supply chain transparency and reduce the risk of fraud and counterfeiting in the diamond industry. The platform has also enabled De Beers and other members of the industry to more easily track the origin of diamonds and ensure that they are ethically sourced.

16.9.4 PROVENANCE

Provenance, a UK-based startup, has developed a blockchain-based platform that enables businesses to track and verify the origin of products in their supply chain. By using smart contracts to automate the tracking and verification process, Provenance has been able to improve supply chain transparency and enable businesses to make more informed decisions about sourcing and sustainability.

One example of a company that has successfully implemented Provenance's platform is Co-op, a UK-based food retailer. By using Provenance's platform to track the origin of its fish products, Co-op has been able to ensure that its products are sustainably sourced and that they meet the company's ethical standards.

These case studies demonstrate the potential of smart contracts and blockchain technology to revolutionize supply chain management by improving transparency, efficiency, and security. While the technology is still in its early stages, these companies have shown that it is possible to successfully implement smart contracts in the supply chain [65, 66]. As more companies explore the use of blockchain technology and smart contracts in their supply chain operations, we can expect to see continued advancements and developments in the coming years. By staying up-to-date on the latest developments and exploring new use cases [67], businesses can leverage smart contracts and blockchain technology to create more efficient and sustainable supply chains [68, 69].

16.9.4.1 Ethical Considerations in Using Blockchain Technology in Supply Chain Management

Blockchain technology has emerged as a promising solution to address supply chain challenges, such as improving traceability, reducing fraud, and increasing efficiency. However, as with any technology, there are also ethical considerations that need to be taken into account when using blockchain in supply chain management. In this section, we will explore some of the ethical implications of using blockchain in supply chain management and how companies can navigate them [70].

16.9.4.1.1 Transparency and Privacy

One of the key benefits of blockchain technology is its ability to provide transparency, allowing all parties in the supply chain to track products and transactions from the point of origin to the point of consumption. However, this also raises concerns about privacy and data protection. For example, if blockchain is used to track sensitive information, such as personal data or trade secrets, there is a risk that this information could be exposed to unauthorized parties [71].

To address these concerns, companies should implement measures to ensure that only authorized parties have access to sensitive information. This can include using encryption and access control mechanisms to limit access to the blockchain, as well as implementing privacy-enhancing technologies, such as zero-knowledge proofs, which allow parties to prove the validity of data without revealing sensitive information [72].

16.9.4.1.2 Environmental Impact

Blockchain technology is based on a distributed ledger, which requires a significant amount of computing power and energy to operate. This has raised concerns about the environmental impact of blockchain, particularly as the technology becomes more widely adopted.

To address these concerns, companies can explore alternative approaches to blockchain, such as using more energy-efficient consensus algorithms or transitioning to more sustainable energy sources. Companies can also consider offsetting their energy usage through carbon credits or other sustainable practices.

16.9.4.1.3 Fairness and Inclusivity

Another ethical consideration when using blockchain in supply chain management is the potential impact on fairness and inclusivity. Blockchain technology has the potential to create more transparent and fair supply chains, but it can also reinforce existing power structures and exacerbate inequalities.

To address these concerns, companies can ensure that all parties in the supply chain have equal access to the benefits of blockchain technology. This can include providing training and resources to ensure that all parties have the skills and knowledge to participate in blockchain-based supply chains. Companies can also work to promote diversity and inclusion within their supply chains and engage with stakeholders to ensure that the benefits of blockchain are distributed fairly.

As with any technology, there are ethical considerations that need to be taken into account when using blockchain in supply chain management. These considerations include privacy and data protection, environmental impact, and fairness and inclusivity. Companies can address these concerns by implementing measures to ensure the privacy and security of sensitive information, exploring more sustainable approaches to blockchain, and promoting fairness and inclusivity within their supply chains. By addressing these ethical considerations, companies can unlock the full potential of blockchain technology to transform supply chain management [73].

16.9.4.2 The Role of Internet of Things (IoT) Devices in the Implementation of Smart Contracts in Supply Chain Management

The Internet of Things (IoT) is the connection of devices and machines to the Internet, which can range from simple sensors to complex machinery. The adoption of IoT in various industries has increased due to its potential for enhancing efficiency and productivity. IoT devices play a critical role in the implementation of smart contracts in supply chain management, which are self-executing contracts that operate on a blockchain network. By integrating IoT devices with smart contracts, supply chain processes can be automated, and stakeholders can easily track the movement and condition of products throughout the supply chain, thereby reducing the risk of delays and product spoilage [74]. Additionally, the use of smart contracts and IoT devices in supply chain management enhances security, as all transactions are recorded in a tamperproof manner. However, challenges such as standardization of IoT devices and data privacy and security need to be addressed. Finally, the use of IoT devices and smart contracts can provide benefits for supply chain management, such as enabling real-time tracking and monitoring of goods and assets, reducing the risk of theft or loss, improving the accuracy of delivery times, and streamlining supply chain operations [75–79].

16.9.4.3 The Potential Impact of Smart Contracts and Blockchain Technology on Logistics and Transportation

The food and beverage industry is one of the largest and most complex supply chains in the world, with a variety of stakeholders involved. Blockchain technology and smart contracts can help prevent food contamination and safety issues by increasing transparency and traceability throughout the supply chain. Smart contracts can also be used to automate certain processes in the supply chain, such as payment and quality control, and reduce the need for intermediaries. Another potential use case for smart contracts is in the area of sustainability [80, 81].

The use of blockchain technology and smart contracts in the food and beverage industry has the potential to revolutionize the way food products are tracked and traced throughout the supply chain, providing greater transparency, efficiency, and accountability. Companies such as Walmart and Nestlé have implemented blockchain-based systems for tracking the origin of certain food products, such as mangoes and pork in China. However, there are several challenges that must be addressed, such as ensuring interoperability between different blockchain systems and data privacy and security [82]. These technologies can help prevent food safety issues and provide consumers with more information about the sustainability and quality of the products [83].

In conclusion, the use of smart contracts and blockchain technology in the food and beverage industry has the potential to revolutionize the way food products are tracked and traced throughout the supply chain. By providing greater transparency, efficiency, and accountability, these technologies can help prevent food safety issues and provide consumers with more information about the sustainability and quality of the products they consume. However, there are also challenges that must be addressed in order to ensure the widespread adoption and success of these technologies in the industry.

REFERENCES

1. Khan, S. N., Loukil, F., Ghedira-Guegan, C., Benkhelifa, E., & Bani-Hani, A. (2021). Blockchain smart contracts: Applications, challenges, and future trends. *Peer-to-Peer Networking and Applications*, 14(6), 2901–2925. https://link.springer.com/article/10.1007/s12083-021-01127-0
2. Taherdoost, H. (2023). Smart contracts in blockchain technology: A critical review. *Information*, 14(2), 117. www.mdpi.com/2078-2489/14/2/117
3. IBM. (n.d.). *Benefits of blockchain.* www.ibm.com/topics/benefits-of-blockchain
4. Kouhizadeh, M., Saberi, S., & Sarkis, J. (2021). Blockchain technology and the sustainable supply chain: Theoretically exploring adoption barriers. *International Journal of Production Economics*, 231, 107831. www.sciencedirect.com/science/article/pii/S0925527320302012
5. Sweeney, E. (2022). The big challenges for supply chains in 2022. *The Conversation.* https://theconversation.com/the-big-challenges-for-supply-chains-in-2022–174420
6. Hayes, A. (2022). Blockchain facts: What is it, how it works, and how it can be used. *Investopedia.* www.investopedia.com/terms/b/blockchain.asp
7. Hobbs, B. (2019). Supply chain inefficiencies can crush customer experience and cost you millions. *Forbes.* www.forbes.com/sites/forbesbusinessdevelopmentcouncil/2019/09/30/supply-chain-inefficiencies-can-crush-customer-experience-and-cost-you-millions/
8. Frankenfield, J. (2023). Smart contracts and their advantages. *Investopedia.* www.investopedia.com/terms/s/smart-contracts.asp
9. Ghadge, A., Duck, A., Er, M., & Caldwell, N. (2021). Deceptive counterfeit risk in global supply chains. *Supply Chain Forum: An International Journal*, 22(2), 87–99. www.tandfonline.com/doi/full/10.1080/16258312.2021.1908844
10. McKinsey. (2022). *What is blockchain?* www.mckinsey.com/featured-insights/mckinsey-explainers/what-is-blockchain
11. Saberi, S., Kouhizadeh, M., Sarkis, J., & Shen, L. (2019). Blockchain technology and its relationships to sustainable supply chain management. *International Journal of Production Research*, 57(7), 2117–2135. www.tandfonline.com/doi/full/10.1080/00207543.2018.1533261
12. Kshetri, N. (2018). Blockchain's roles in strengthening cybersecurity and protecting privacy. *Telecommunications Policy,* 42(10), 843–852.
13. Tian, F. (2016). An agri-food supply chain traceability system for China based on RFID & blockchain technology. *2016 13th International Conference on Service Systems and Service Management (ICSSSM)*, 1–6. https://ieeexplore.ieee.org/document/7538424
14. Gaiha, A., & Gaur, V. (2020). Building a transparent supply chain. *Harvard Business Review*, 98(3), 102–109. https://hbr.org/2020/05/building-a-transparent-supply-chain

15. Enkronos. (2020). *What is a smart contract? Advantages and disadvantages.* https://content.enkronos.com/what-is-a-smart-contract-advantages-and-disadvantages/

16. Vandevelde, P. (2018). Using blockchain technology to fight counterfeiters. *Development Asia.* https://development.asia/case-study/using-blockchain-technology-fight-counterfeiters

17. Accenture. (n.d.). *Blockchain for digital identity.* www.accenture.com/us-en/services/blockchain/digital-identity

18. Asmussen, C. G., & Charles, A. (2020). Blockchain technology in supply chain management: Insights on adoption barriers and enablers. *Management Accounting Research, 47,* 100–113. https://doi.org/10.1016/j.mar.2019.07.002

19. Higgins, M. (2021, November 8). Blockchain in supply chain. *Forbes.* www.forbes.com/sites/forbestechcouncil/2021/11/08/blockchain-in-supply-chain/

20. Khan, M. (n.d.). Revolutionizing the supply chain: How blockchain technology is enhancing efficiency and transparency. *LinkedIn.* www.linkedin.com/pulse/revolutionizing-supply-chain-how-blockchain-enhancing-maaz-khan-

21. Gaur, V., & Singh, S. (2020). Blockchain technology for supply chain compliance. In *Blockchain technology for industry 4.0* (pp. 1–22). Springer, Singapore. https://doi.org/10.1007/978-981-15-4814-7_1

22. Zhang, Y., & Liu, X. (2021). The effect of blockchain technology on supply chain sustainability: A review. *Sustainability, 13*(4), 1726. https://doi.org/10.3390/su13041726

23. Lee, K., & Kim, J. (2019). Blockchain technology for enhancing supply chain resilience. *Business Horizons, 62*(1), 35–45. https://doi.org/10.1016/j.bushor.2018.08.012

24. Rejeb, A., Keogh, J. G., Simske, S. J., Stafford, T., & Treiblmaier, H. (2021). Potentials of blockchain technologies for supply chain collaboration: A conceptual framework. *The International Journal of Logistics Management, 32*(3), 1005–1026. https://doi.org/10.1108/IJLM-02-2020-0098

25. Kouhizadeh, M., Saberi, S., & Sarkis, J. (2020). Blockchain practices, potentials, and perspectives in greening supply chains. *Sustainability, 12*(21), 8692. https://doi.org/10.3390/su10103652

26. Saberi, S., Kouhizadeh, M., & Sarkis, J. (2021). Blockchain technology and its relationships to sustainable supply chain management. *International Journal of Production Research, 59*(3), 621–643. https://doi.org/10.1080/00207543.2018.1533261

27. Kamble, S. S., Gunasekaran, A., & Gawankar, S. A. (2018). Sustainable Industry 4.0 framework: A systematic literature review identifying the current trends and future perspectives. *Process Safety and Environmental Protection, 117,* 408–425. https://doi.org/10.1016/j.psep.2018.05.009

28. Groschopf, W., Dobrovnik, M., & Herneth, C. (2021). Smart contracts for sustainable supply chain management: Conceptual frameworks for supply chain maturity evaluation and smart contract sustainability assessment. *Frontiers in Blockchain, 4,* 506436. https://doi.org/10.3389/fbloc.2021.506436

29. Bottoni, P., Gessa, N., Massa, G., Pareschi, R., Selim, H., & Arcuri, E. (2020). Intelligent smart contracts for innovative supply chain management. *Frontiers in Blockchain, 3,* 535787. https://doi.org/10.3389/fbloc.2020.535787

30. Pan, S., Trentesaux, D., McFarlane, D., Montreuil, B., Ballot, E., & Huang, G. Q. (2021). Digital interoperability in logistics and supply chain management: State-of-the-art and research avenues towards Physical Internet. *Computers in Industry, 128,* 103435. https://doi.org/10.1016/j.compind.2021.103435

31. Musyoka, J. (2022). Role of smart contracts in supply chain management. *LinkedIn.* www.linkedin.com/pulse/role-smart-contracts-supply-chain-management-john-musyoka

32. Solaiman, E., Wike, T., & Sfyrakis, I. (2021). Implementation and evaluation of smart contracts using a hybrid on- and off-blockchain architecture. *Concurrency and Computation: Practice and Experience, 33*(1), e5811. https://doi.org/10.1002/cpe.5811

33. Gotskind, A. (2021). Decentralized finance and the power of smart contracts. *Research Blog.* https://researchblog.duke.edu/2021/12/13/decentralized-finance-and-the-power-of-smart-contracts/

34. Amazon Web Services. (n.d.). *What is decentralization in blockchain?* https://aws.amazon.com/blockchain/decentralization-in-blockchain/

35. Casper, R. H., Lazaro, J. A., Wang, E., & Wegrzyn, K. E. (2021). Smart supply chains using smart contracts. *Manufacturing Industry Advisor.* www.foley.com/en/insights/publications/2021/09/smart-supply-chains-using-smart-contracts

36. Kshetri, N. (2018). Blockchain's roles in strengthening cybersecurity and protecting privacy. *Telecommunications Policy, 42*(10), 843–852. https://doi.org/10.1016/j.telpol.2017.09.003

37. Pinsent Masons. (2020). How smart contracts can enable better supply chains. *Out-Law.* www.pinsentmasons.com/out-law/analysis/smart-contracts-better-supply-chains

38. ConsenSys. (n.d.). Smart contract security best practices. *GitHub.* https://github.com/ConsenSys/smart-contract-best-practices

39. Zhang, Y., Li, Y., & Liu, J. (2021). Smart contract security: A practitioners' perspective. In *2021 IEEE/ACM 43rd International Conference on Software Engineering (ICSE)* (pp. 127–138). IEEE. https://doi.org/10.1109/ICSE43902.2021.00127

40. Li, J., & Zhang, Y. (2022). How do smart contracts benefit security protocols? *arXiv preprint*, arXiv:2202.08699. https://arxiv.org/abs/2202.08699

41. Alharby, M., & van Moorsel, A. (2017). Blockchain-based smart contracts: A systematic mapping study. *arXiv preprint*, arXiv:1710.06372. https://arxiv.org/abs/1710.06372

42. Luu, L., Chu, D.-H., Olickel, H., Saxena, P., & Daian, A. (2016). Making smart contracts smarter. In *Proceedings of the 2016 ACM SIGSAC conference on computer and communications security* (pp. 254–269). ACM. https://doi.org/10.1145/2976749.2978309

43. Grunert, E. W., & Pinsent Masons. (2018). Regulatory compliance in the global supply chain. *Out-Law*. www.pinsentmasons.com/out-law/analysis/regulatory-compliance-global-supply-chain

44. IT Exchange Web. (2022). *Smart contracts for innovative supply chain management*. www.itexchangeweb.com/blog/smart-contracts-for-innovative-supply-chain-management/

45. Wang, S., Li, D., Zhang, Y., & Chen, J. (2019). Smart contract-based product traceability system in the supply chain scenario. *IEEE Access, 7*, 115122–115133. https://doi.org/10.1109/ACCESS.2019.2935873

46. Queiroz, M. M., Telles, R., & Bonilla, S. H. (2020). Blockchain and supply chain management integration: A systematic review of the literature. *Supply Chain Management: An International Journal, 25*(2), 241–254. www.emerald.com/insight/content/doi/10.1108/SCM-03-2018-0143/full/html

47. Alraja, S. M. A., & Alraja, M. A. (2021). Smart contracts and supply chain management using blockchain. *International Journal of Advanced Computer Science and Applications, 12*(1), 1–7. www.researchgate.net/publication/365027511_Smart_Contracts_and_Supply_Chain_Management_Using_Blockchain

48. Kouhizadeh, M., & Sarkis, J. (2021). Smart Contracts for sustainable supply chain management: Conceptual frameworks for supply chain maturity evaluation and smart contract sustainability assessment. *Frontiers in Blockchain, 4*, 506436. https://doi.org/10.3389/fbloc.2021.506436

49. Javaid, N., & Khan, I. (2019). Blockchain-based Secure data sharing platform for research data rights management over the Ethereum network. In *2019 IEEE 5th international conference on engineering technologies and applied sciences (ICETAS)* (pp. 1–6). IEEE. www.researchgate.net/profile/Nadeem-Javaid/publication/334696593_Blockchain-based_Secure_Data_Sharing_Platform_for_Research_Data_Rights_Management_over_the_Ethereum_Network/links/5d3aa69e92851cd04686d625/Blockchain-based-Secure-Data-Sharing-Platform-for-Research-Data-Rights-Management-over-the-Ethereum-Network.pdf

50. Lee, J.-H. et al. (2019, May). A blockchain-based smart contract design for supply chain management. *Symmetry (Basel), 11*(5), 635. www.mdpi.com/2073-8994/11/5/635

51. Naz, S., & Al-Zahrani, A. (2019). A secure data sharing platform using blockchain and smart contracts. In *2019 IEEE 5th international conference on engineering technologies and applied sciences (ICETAS)* (pp. 1–6). IEEE. www.semanticscholar.org/paper/A-Secure-Data-Sharing-Platform-Using-Blockchain-and-Naz-Al-Zahrani/45e5f96cd89f6da12710133b946b85a88d567475

52. Zhang, Y., & Zhang, Y. (2020). A blockchain-based secure data sharing scheme for cloud storage. In *2020 IEEE international conference on communications workshops (ICC Workshops)* (pp. 1–6). IEEE. https://ieeexplore.ieee.org/stamp/stamp.jsp?arnumber=9329051

53. Li, J., & Li, J. (2023). A blockchain-based secure data sharing scheme for cloud storage [Journal article]. *Security and Communication Networks*, 2023, Article ID 9998433, 10 pages. www.hindawi.com/journals/scn/2023/9998433/

54. Chen, X., & Wang, Y. (2021). A blockchain-based secure data sharing scheme for cloud storage [Journal article]. *Journal of Cybersecurity and Information Intelligence, 1*(2), 15–22. www.mdpi.com/2674-1032/1/2/15

55. Liang, X., Liang, Q., & Gao, F. (2022). Blockchain technology in supply chain management: A review of applications and challenges in operations and logistics management contexts [Journal article]. *Sustainability, 14*(3), Article ID 1470. www.mdpi.com/2071-1050/14/3/1470

56. Liu, J., & Zhang, X.-L. (2021). Research on the application of blockchain technology in supply chain finance [Journal article]. *Journal of Industrial Engineering and Engineering Management, 35*(4), 107–116. https://kns.cnki.net/kcms/detail/detail.aspx?doi=10.14132/j.cnki.1673-5439.2021.04.013

57. Hyperledger. (n.d.). *Walmart case study* [Web page]. www.hyperledger.org/learn/publications/walmart-case-study

58. Walmart Global Tech. (2022, January 12). *Blockchain in the food supply chain* [Web page]. https://tech.walmart.com/content/walmart-global-tech/en_us/news/articles/blockchain-in-the-food-supply-chain.html

59. Harvard Business Review. (2022, January). *How Walmart Canada uses blockchain to solve supply-chain challenges* [Web page]. https://hbr.org/2022/01/how-walmart-canada-uses-blockchain-to-solve-supply-chain-challenges

60. A.P. Moller—Maersk. (2022, November 29). *A.P. Moller—Maersk and IBM to discontinue TradeLens, a blockchain-enabled shipping solution* [Web page]. www.maersk.com/news/articles/2022/11/29/maersk-and-ibm-to-discontinue-tradelens

61. Reuters. (2022, November 29). *Maersk, IBM discontinue shipping blockchain platform* [Web page]. www.reuters.com/technology/maersk-ibm-discontinue-shipping-blockchain-platform-2022-11-29/

62. IBM. (2018, August 9). *TradeLens, how IBM and Maersk are sharing blockchain to build a global trade platform* [Web page]. www.ibm.com/blogs/think/2018/11/tradelens-how-ibm-and-maersk-are-sharing-blockchain-to-build-a-global-trade-platform/

63. IBM Corporation. (2018). *TradeLens, a Maersk and IBM solution, delivers* [PDF file]. www.ibm.com/common/ssi/rep_ca/4/897/ENUS218-524/ENUS218-524.PDF

64. Tappert, C., & Srinivasan, S. (2019). *Emerging information technologies II, CSIS, Pace University* [PDF file]. http://csis.pace.edu/~ctappert/srd2019/d2.pdf

65. CoinGeek Backstage—CoinGeek. (n.d.). Retrieved March 25, 2023, from https://coingeek.com/news/tag/coingeek-backstage/?gclid=EAIaIQobChMIpfHI5sb5_QIVyTUrCh1FyAXgEAMYAiAAEgJ0a_D_BwE

66. Difrancesco, R. M., Meena, P., & Kumar, G. (2022). How blockchain technology improves sustainable supply chain processes: A practical guide. *Sustainability, 14*(1), 7894. www.ncbi.nlm.nih.gov/pmc/articles/PMC9797894/

67. Zhang, Y., Li, X., & Wang, Y. (2020). A review on the applications of blockchain technology in international trade and finance. *Frontiers of Engineering Management, 7*(4), 445–458. https://doi.org/10.1016/j.tbench.2022.100073

68. DHL Customer Solutions & Innovation. (2018). *Blockchain in logistics: Perspectives on the upcoming impact of blockchain technology and use cases for the logistics industry.* www.dhl.com/content/dam/dhl/global/core/documents/pdf/glo-core-blockchain-trend-report.pdf

69. Khan, S., & Khan, S. (2023). Impact of technological advancements on international trade and finance. *Modern Diplomacy.* https://moderndiplomacy.eu/2023/03/23/impact-of-technological-advancements-on-international-trade-and-finance/

70. Tokkozhina, U., Martins, A. L., & Ferreira, J. C. (2021). Use of blockchain technology to manage the supply chains: Comparison of perspectives between technology providers and early industry adopters. *Journal of Theoretical and Applied Electronic Commerce Research, 17*(4), 82–100. https://doi.org/10.3390/jtaer17040082

71. Agi, M. A. N., & Jha, A. K. (2022). Blockchain technology in the supply chain: An integrated theoretical perspective of organizational adoption. *International Journal of Production Economics,* 108458. https://doi.org/10.1016/j.ijpe.2022.108458

72. Sedlmeir, J., Lautenschlager, J., Fridgen, G. et al. (2022). The transparency challenge of blockchain in organizations. *Electron Markets, 32,* 1779–1794. https://doi.org/10.1007/s12525-022-00536-0

73. Sharif, M., & Ghodoosi, F. (2022). The ethics of blockchain in organizations. *Journal of Business Ethics, 178*(4), 1009–1025. https://doi.org/10.1007/s10551-022-05058-5

74. Schoentgen, A., & Wilkinson, R. (2011). The WTO's trade policy review mechanism: How to create political will for compliance? *The World Economy, 34*(11), 1897–1925. www.econstor.eu/bitstream/10419/238052/1/Schoentgen-Wilkinson.pdf.

75. OECD. (2019). *2019 OECD global blockchain policy forum: Summary report* (Report No. 9789264633230). www.oecd.org/finance/2019-OECD-Global-Blockchain-Policy-Forum-Summary-Report.pdf

76. Bergström, A. (2020). *The role of social media in crisis communication and crisis management* [Doctoral dissertation, University of Gothenburg]. www.diva-portal.org/smash/get/diva2:1574301/FULLTEXT01.pdf

77. Alharby, N., & Moorsel, A. V. (2018). *Internet of Things security with blockchain technology: A state-of-the-art review.* www.researchgate.net/publication/365584843_Internet_of_Things_IoT_Security_with_Blockchain_Technology_A_State-of-the-Art_Review

78. Kshetri, N., & Voas, J. (2018). On the internet of things, blockchain technology for supply chain management IoT. *IEEE IT Professional, 20*(4), 15–21. https://doi.org/10.1109/MITP.2018.043141660

79. Alharby, N., & Moorsel, A. V. (2021). Blockchain-based IoT security: A comprehensive review of architectures and challenges. *Future Generation Computer Systems, 122,* 1–16. https://doi.org/10.1016/j.future.2021.07.015

80. Alharby, N., & Moorsel, A. V. (2013). Blockchain-based IoT security: A survey. *Computers & Security*, 88, 101614. www.sciencedirect.com/science/article/abs/pii/S0045790623000198

81. Tracefood.io. (2020). *Benefits of blockchain in food supply chain industry.* https://tracefood.io/benefits-of-blockchain-in-food-supply-chain-industry/

82. Blockhead Technologies. (2019, October 16). *How blockchain is revolutionising food supply chains.* https://blockheadtechnologies.com/how-blockchain-is-revolutionising-food-supply-chains/

83. QSales. (2020, August 19). *How blockchain is being used today in the food & beverage industries.* https://qsales.com/how-blockchain-is-being-used-today-in-the-food-beverage-industries/

17 Blockchain Technology for Digital Vehicle Passport

Alberto Butera and Valentina Gatteschi

17.1 INTRODUCTION

Today, more than ever before, the digitalization process is sweeping across an increasing number of fields, transforming business processes, products, and customer experience, among other aspects. Even in the automotive industry, digitalization has had a significant impact on both production and use, revolutionizing business processes, products, and customer experiences (Rachinger, 2019). For example, digitalization has enabled the use of advanced sensors, cameras, and software that can allow the implementation of self-driving vehicles, optimize the performance of electric motors in electric vehicles, and let vehicles communicate with each other and with the infrastructure by exchanging data. Another example of how digitalization can change the automotive industry is the introduction of digital passports for vehicles. A digital passport is a secure and verifiable record of a vehicle's identity, history, and ownership that can be accessed through a smartphone app or a web portal. Digital passports can provide benefits, such as simplifying the registration and transfer of ownership processes, enhancing the security and transparency of vehicle transactions, and enabling new services such as personalized insurance and maintenance. Digital passports can also facilitate the integration of vehicles with other smart devices and platforms, such as smart homes, smart cities, and smart grids. Digital passports are an emerging technology that still requires much research and development. There are no official and operational implementations yet, only proposals, guidelines, and prototypes to test and define standards.

Although the digitization process is well underway in this sector, there are still some aspects where further digitization could bring greater efficiency, reliability, and sustainability, such as using blockchain technology to facilitate traceability and prevent fraud, digitizing new data types to perform advanced analytics, and developing augmented reality systems to improve the testing phase and customer experience.

In particular, this book chapter focuses on the application of blockchain technology to create digital passports for vehicles. By using blockchain technology, digital passports can enable new services and functionalities (tracking vehicle's life cycle, performances, quality, real-time data, and so on) for vehicle owners, manufacturers, and service providers, while leveraging the advantages of this technology, such as reliability, transparency, and security. This book chapter presents the state of the art of blockchain-based digital passports for vehicles, comparing and analyzing different existing solutions and frameworks. It also evaluates the potential benefits and challenges of implementing digital passports in the automotive industry and provides some recommendations and best practices for future developments.

This chapter is organized as follows. In Section 2, we review the current literature and solutions on the implementation of blockchain-based digital passports for vehicles and evaluate their strengths and weaknesses. In Section 3, we perform a detailed analysis and comparison of the solutions proposed in the literature, focusing on technical aspects, such as the type of blockchain, the data storage method, and the privacy protection for sensitive data. In Section 4, we discuss the advantages and disadvantages of implementing digital passports for vehicles from an economic and social perspective. In Section 5, we conclude the chapter with a summary of what we have discussed and some concluding remarks.

DOI: 10.1201/9781003450306-19

17.2 LITERATURE OVERVIEW

The goal of this section is to give a thorough overview of the latest developments and trends of digital passports for vehicles through blockchains. However, since this field is still in its infancy and has many aspects to explore, it is essential to have a clear understanding of the general idea and implementation of digital passports in other domains and contexts. Exploring how digital passports have been implemented in other domains can inspire and inform the design and development of digital passports for vehicles, by learning from the best practices and lessons learned from other contexts.

Therefore, the first part of this section presents a brief introduction to digital passports, explaining their definition, purpose, and scope, as well as some examples of existing applications and initiatives in various fields. The second part of this section focuses on the state of the art of the related scientific works that have addressed the topic of digital passports for vehicles.

17.2.1 DIGITAL PASSPORTS

Before analyzing some examples of the implementation of digital passports in different contexts, it is worth clarifying what is meant by this technology and what are its main characteristics.

A digital passport is an electronic document that contains information and characteristics about an asset, which can be a person, a physical object, or a digital asset itself. This information is used to identify or enable the asset to perform certain functions or access certain spaces, as in the case with traditional passports. However, a digital passport has the advantage of being able to interact with other existing digital systems, thus extending the possibilities of use and improving the services offered.

A digital passport can be implemented in different ways, depending on the needs and purposes of its users. For example, this book focuses on an implementation based on blockchain technology, which provides security, transparency, and data traceability. In addition, a digital passport can be equipped with additional features, such as biometric verification, digital signature, or geolocation, which increase the level of authentication and personalization of the document.

17.2.2 APPLICATIONS IN OTHER FIELDS

During the years, the idea of having a digital passport to store and track information has been applied to different fields beyond vehicles. Some of these fields include healthcare, travel and immigration, and circular economy.

In the healthcare field, digital passports have gained attention as a potential solution for improving patient care and communication between patients and healthcare professionals. Several studies have proposed blockchain-based platforms for recording and sharing COVID-19 vaccine passports. These platforms utilize blockchain's distributed nature to ensure data integrity and privacy. For example, in Razzaq (2022), authors proposed a blockchain-based platform for digital health passports (DHP). This platform incorporates decentralized storage using interplanetary file systems (IPFS) and smart contracts constructed and tested with Ethereum. The use of blockchain technology ensures the immutability and integrity of the DHP, while smart contracts enable prompt and trustworthy responses from medical authorities. This approach addresses the need for secure and tamperproof documentation of COVID-19 test results and vaccination certificates. Also, Barati (2021) proposed a new platform architecture for creating, storing, and verifying digital COVID-19 vaccine certifications. The platform makes use of IPFS to guarantee there is no single point of failure and allow data to be securely distributed globally. Blockchain and smart contracts are also integrated into the platform to define policies and log access rights to vaccine passport data while ensuring all actions are audited and verifiably immutable. The proposed platform realizes general data protection regulation (GDPR) requirements in terms of user consent, data encryption, data erasure, and accountability obligations.

Some other studies have been performed in the travel and immigration field. For example, in Jahan et al. (2023), authors have designed and implemented a new way to manage digital passports for travelling using Hyperledger Fabric (a framework for developing permissioned blockchains) and IPFS. The paper suggests that using a private blockchain and a distributed file system can provide more effective, faster, and safer transactions for digital passport verification. The paper also explains how these technologies work and how they can protect the private passport information and biometric data of the users. Another example is Gao (2022), which proposes a new way of issuing and verifying immunity passports using a dual-blockchain architecture. The paper claims that the current methods of implementing immunity passports are not very effective or secure, and that they face many challenges, such as vaccine controversies, privacy issues, and passport forgery. The paper introduces a scheme that uses two blockchains, one for storing the vaccination records and one for authenticating the passport holders. The paper also uses searchable encryption and anonymous authentication to protect the users' privacy and prevent unauthorized access. The paper shows that the scheme is more efficient and secure than other authentication schemes, and that it can facilitate the international travel of people who have been vaccinated.

The work described in Panchamia and Byrappa (2017) presents a vision of digitizing passport, visa, and immigration documents using blockchain technology. The paper proposes a solution based on distributed ledger for storing and retrieving information, which will help in streamlining and simplifying passport and visa issuing, renewing, revoking, verification, and validation process. The paper also claims that this framework will help do away with fake passports and visa, unauthorized and repetitive data verification process, and improve efficiency and potentially lower costs at all levels.

Finally, in our literature review, we discovered some relevant studies that focused on the development and implementation of digital passports for products to promote circular economy. For example, in Nowacki et al. (2023), authors describe a system design for digital products passports (DPPs), which are digital documents that store and carry data about the life cycle of individual products. The paper explains that DPPs are introduced in the EU Green Deal as a tool to facilitate the transition to a circular economy and introduces a DPP use case framework. This paper also presents a technical architecture for DPP systems based on distributed ledger technologies and smart contracts and provides the code for a working prototype. Another work related to digital product passports is Navarro et al. (2022), where the authors present a project that aims to create digital product passports for ICT products using blockchain technology. The project explores how to design, implement, evaluate, and operate a verifiable registry for digital product passports and how to deliver these services efficiently and at scale. In this work, the authors claim that digital product passports can help the ICT sector to become more transparent and accountable, and to contribute to the climate change goals.

The preceding overview, which has been summarized in Table 17.1, shows the research that has already proposed blockchain-based solutions for digital passports in three domains, where we found the highest number of papers related to digital passports which are different than the automotive sector.

TABLE 17.1

Papers about Digital Passports in Fields Different Than the Automotive Sector

Paper	Units
(Razzaq, 2022)	Healthcare
(Barati, 2021)	Healthcare
(Jahan et al., 2023)	Travelling
(Gao, 2022)	Travelling
(Panchamia and Byrappa, 2017)	Travelling
(Nowacki et al., 2023)	Supply chain
(Navarro et al., 2022)	Supply chain

17.2.3 Applications in the Automotive Field

As noted at the beginning of this section, the topic of digital vehicle passports is still under-researched and requires further study and development by researchers and practitioners. As a result, the current state of the art is limited and incomplete. However, the potential benefits and applications of digital vehicle passports are many and promising. For example, one possible use case could be to extend the use case of digital passports for products to track the history and life cycle of vehicle components, thereby promoting the circular economy process and reducing environmental impacts. At this purpose, the work described in Berger et al. (2021) presents a study that explores how to use digital product passport (DPP) technology to support sustainable and circular management of electric vehicle batteries (EVBs). The study proposes a preliminary concept of the information model of an EVB's DPP, which contains data about the EVB's life cycle and environmental impacts. The study also identifies some use cases for the DPP, such as conducting a dynamic life cycle assessment or deciding on an EVB's potential second life.

Another application of digital passports in the automotive sector is to provide a kind of digital identity card for vehicles. This ID card can contain information about the vehicle's technical specifications, changes of ownership, condition, and repairs or maintenance performed over time. This information can be useful for ensuring the traceability, safety, and quality of vehicles, as well as facilitating sales, purchases, insurance, and recycling transactions. Some examples of digital passport–based solutions for vehicles have been proposed in the literature, such as in Alessandria and Vizzari (2021), where the authors propose a software application that uses blockchain technologies to improve the management of car accidents. The application runs on smartphones and allows the driver to fill in the CID (amicable statement of accident) using self-sovereign identity (SSI) credentials and the car's digital passport, which are both stored on the blockchain. The application aims to reduce the time, costs, and frauds involved in the data exchange between the driver and the insurance company after a car accident.

Certainly, original equipment manufacturers (OEMs) are among the major players interested in implementing and using digital passports for vehicles, as they can benefit from both efficiency and innovation. For this reason, some of them are already experimenting with blockchain-based solutions. For example, VeChain and BMW have created a digital passport called VerifyCar (BMW, 2019) for each vehicle that allows customers to verify the odometer and maintenance history of a vehicle. The project aims to increase transparency and trust for the car owners and buyers. Similar projects have been carried out by Renault (Cointelegraph, 2017) and Hyundai (Hyundai, 2023). Another example is the vehicle identity (VID) standard Mobi (2022) developed by Mobility Open Blockchain Initiatives (MOBI), a nonprofit alliance that develops and promotes blockchain standards for the mobility sector. The VID standard provides a digital document that links a specific vehicle to its digital twin and contains key events in the life of a vehicle, such as odometer readings, repairs, and accidents, and can be used to verify existence, manage access control, and confirm ownership history. The VID standard also enables vehicles to securely interact with infrastructure, consumers, and digital currency, facilitating transactions with the external world. The VID standard has two versions: VID I, which provides a "birth certificate" for vehicles, and VID II, which provides a "trusted trip" credential for vehicles. This standard is supported by a global and multi-stakeholder project led by MOBI, which includes some of the world's largest OEMs, technology firms, and others. The VID standard is expected to bring benefits, such as reducing fraud, improving safety, lowering costs, and enhancing user experience in the mobility sector.

The works cited earlier show that the growing interest of the major OEMs in the development of digital vehicle passports is an indication of how promising this technology could be for the future of mobility. Indeed, many of them are investing time and resources in developing innovative solutions based on this technology, which would enable the creation of integrated and secure digital ecosystems in which vehicles can communicate with each other and with the infrastructure. However, to realize this scenario, it is necessary to identify the best technologies and techniques that can be used to implement digital passports effectively and reliably, which is why research and development in this area are crucial.

17.3 ANALYSIS OF THE IMPLEMENTATION DETAILS

To implement digital passports for vehicles, there are several possible solutions, which we tried to identify through a literature review. Since we found that the topic of digital passports in the automotive field is still little covered in the literature, we expanded our research to different contexts, such as healthcare, travelling, and supply chain, to analyze the different techniques used in these sectors. We also looked at solutions proposed by some leading automotive OEMs that have already developed prototypes or proof of concepts (POCs) of digital passports for vehicles. In this section, we want to delve into the characteristics of the solutions identified in the state of the art, comparing them with each other and evaluating their advantages and disadvantages. Table 17.2 shows a summary of the technologies used by the works cited in Section 2. In this way, we aim to provide the reader with a clear and comprehensive overview of the different techniques available for implementing digital vehicle passports, highlighting the strengths and weaknesses of each solution. In addition, we will add some considerations on the use of techniques not used in the articles mentioned in the previous section, to prove whether they can be viable alternatives or not.

17.3.1 BLOCKCHAINS COMPARISON

One of the most important technical decisions when implementing digital vehicle passports through blockchain is the type of blockchain to be used. In fact, there are different types of blockchains that differ in various aspects, such as cost, performance, permissions, decentralization, and security. Blockchains can be divided into two main categories: public blockchains and private blockchains. However, there are also two more categories that combine the characteristics of the first two: hybrid blockchains and consortium blockchains. Let us see what these types of blockchains consist of and what their advantages and disadvantages are:

- *Public blockchains.* These are blockchains that are open to anyone who wants to participate, either as a node or as a user. They do not require permission to access or write to the blockchain and are therefore highly decentralized and transparent. However, this also comes with high transaction costs due to consensus mechanisms and network congestion. In addition, public blockchains have limitations in terms of scalability and speed, as they need to handle a large number of transactions and nodes.
- *Private blockchains.* These are blockchains that are closed to a small group of participants, who must have permissions to access or write to the blockchain. They are therefore more

TABLE 17.2
Summary of the Technologies Used by the Works Analyzed

Paper	Blockchain	Storage	Privacy
(Razzaq, 2022)	Ethereum	IPFS	Encryption
(Barati, 2021)	Ethereum	IPFS	Encryption
(N. Jahan, 2023)	Hyperledger	IPFS	NDF
(Gao, 2022)	Consortium-based	IPFS	Pseudo-anonymization Encryption
(S. Panchamia, 2017)	Hyperledger	On-chain	NDF
(S. Nowacki, 2023)	IOTA	On-chain	NDF
(Navarro et al., 2022)	IOTA	Hybrid	DID
(Alessandria and Vizzari, 2021)	Hybrid-based	Hybrid	SSI
OEMs solutions	VeChain	NDF	NDF

Note: NDF, *not defined.*

centralized and controlled by an authority or organization. This reduces transaction costs because the consensus mechanism is based on different, more efficient algorithms. In addition, private blockchains have greater scalability and speed because they need to handle fewer transactions and nodes. However, this also results in less transparency and security, as data can only be accessed by authorized participants and can be modified or deleted by the central authority.

- *Hybrid blockchain.* These are a type of blockchain technology that combines the features of both public and private blockchains. They aim to achieve the benefits of both types, such as security, transparency, scalability, and privacy, while avoiding their drawbacks, such as high costs, low performance, or lack of control. This provides a trade-off between decentralization and centralization.
- *Consortium blockchain.* These blockchains are neither completely public nor completely private but have characteristics in between. They do require permissions to access or write to the blockchain, but those permissions are granted by a consortium of participants rather than a central authority. This provides greater decentralization and transparency than private blockchains, but also greater privacy and security than public blockchains.

In addition to choosing the type of blockchain to use, it is also necessary to consider the specific characteristics of each blockchain belonging to the same category. In fact, there are significant differences between different blockchains that may affect the performance, functionality, and compatibility of digital vehicle passports.

For example, among public blockchains, there are different consensus algorithms which directly affect the security and the performances of the blockchains. Consensus algorithms are the methods that allow the nodes of a blockchain network to agree on the validity and order of transactions. So they are essential for ensuring the security, reliability, and decentralization of a blockchain. Different consensus algorithms have different advantages and disadvantages in terms of efficiency, scalability, energy consumption, and resistance to attacks. Some of the most common algorithms are proof of work (PoW) and proof of stake (PoS). In addition, some public blockchains (such as Ethereum) are characterized by the ability to execute code through smart contracts, which are programs that are automatically activated when certain conditions occur. This allows the creation of decentralized applications (dApps) that can interact with the blockchain and users, providing advanced services and features. Other examples of public blockchains include Bitcoin, which is the world's first and most widely used blockchain but has limited functionality to handle monetary transactions, and Cardano, which is a third-generation blockchain designed to be scalable, sustainable, and interoperable.

In terms of private blockchains, however, Hyperledger Fabric, Corda, and Quorum can be mentioned. Hyperledger Fabric is a modular and flexible blockchain that allows the creation of private networks tailored to the needs of participants. It also offers the ability to use different programming languages for smart contracts and different consensus algorithms. Corda is a blockchain designed for the financial sector, offering a solution for managing legal agreements between parties. It uses a consensus mechanism based on digital notarization and allows blockchain data to be integrated with existing systems. Quorum is an Ethereum-derived blockchain that retains its smart contract and dApps functionality but adds layers of privacy and permissions for transactions. It also uses a consensus algorithm that is more efficient and faster than the Ethereum's one.

In light of the previous considerations, let us go on to analyze the implementation choices made by the solutions identified in the state of the art. Among them, there are some solutions that have opted to use public blockchains, such as Ethereum (Razzaq, 2022; Barati, 2021) or IOTA (Navarro et al., 2022; Nowacki et al., 2023). Among the advantages is the ability to guarantee that any user can read the data recorded on the blockchain at any time. This can be useful for various use cases, such as the buying and selling of used cars. Indeed, thanks to digital passports based on public blockchain, potential buyers can easily verify the history and condition of the vehicle without having to rely on intermediaries. In addition, the public blockchain ensures data immutability and transparency, making it more difficult to commit fraud or forgery. However, one of the disadvantages is the issue of privacy. Indeed, if the data recorded on the public blockchain is accessible to everyone, the rights and preferences of users who own vehicles could be violated. For this reason, public blockchain-based solutions must be complemented with techniques to ensure the protection of personal and sensitive data.

Moreover, Ethereum is the most popular and established blockchain for developing dApps due to its ability to execute code through smart contracts. However, it still has scalability issues that limit the number of transactions it can handle and increase transaction costs. This could be an obstacle for a use case like the secondhand vehicle market and the insurance management, which requires frequent and rapid interaction between users and the blockchain. Therefore, it may not be the most efficient and cost-effective solution at the moment. IOTA, on the other hand, is an innovative technology based on a directed acyclic graph (DAG) that does not use an actual blockchain but a structure called a tangle. Designed for the Internet of Things (IoT), IOTA offers greater scalability, speed, and lower cost than Ethereum. It also recently introduced the ability to program smart contracts, expanding its functionality and potential. However, IOTA is still an evolving and experimental technology that has not reached the maturity and security of Ethereum and still relies on a central coordinator, which reduces its level of decentralization and autonomy.

Other works base the implementation of their solution on private blockchains, such as Jahan et al. (2023) and Panchamia and Byrappa (2017), which rely on Hyperledger. This choice has advantages and disadvantages, depending on the use case. The pros include the fact that private blockchains offer greater scalability and lower transaction costs than public blockchains, as well as greater privacy and data protection, as they are only accessible to authorized users. On the downside, private blockchains lose the advantage of decentralization and immutability typical of public blockchains, as they are managed by a central authority or organization that can modify or delete data at will. This could be a problem for some use cases, such as buying and selling used cars. Indeed, in this scenario, the potential buyer may not trust the data recorded on the private blockchain, since it could be changed or deleted by the authority that controls the blockchain.

If the use case concerns the tracking of its vehicles by an individual OEM and its customers, then a private blockchain could be a viable solution, as it offers greater privacy, scalability, and lower costs. In this case, the OEM would be the authority that manages the blockchain and authorizes users to read and write data. Customers, on the other hand, would be the users who can access the data about their vehicles and use the services offered by the OEM. However, this solution would also have drawbacks, such as the lack of interoperability between services when creating an ecosystem based on digital passports. In fact, if each OEM used its own private blockchain, there would be no communication or data sharing between different blockchains, and thus digital passports would only be valid within the OEM's network. This would limit the opportunities for interaction and collaboration between users and mobility organizations.

Consortium-based blockchain solutions, such as the one implemented in Gao (2022), partially solve the problem of centralization of private blockchains, as it is not based on a single authority or organization managing the blockchain but on a group of entities forming a consortium and sharing the interests and goals of the project. In this way, the validation of transactions on the blockchain is more decentralized and transparent, as it requires the consensus of a majority of the consortium participants. However, consortium blockchains still have drawbacks, such as less openness and interoperability than public blockchains, as data is only accessible to users authorized by the consortium. In addition, consortium blockchains may have governance and coordination problems among the different entities that are part of the consortium, as conflicts or disagreements may arise among consortium members.

Finally, other works have proposed hybrid blockchain-based solutions. For example, in Alessandria and Vizzari (2021), the authors implemented their work using an off-chain network, citing the Raiden network as an example. The Raiden network is an off-chain scaling solution that enables near-instantaneous, low-cost, and scalable payments. The network is an infrastructure layer on top of the Ethereum blockchain that uses payment channels to transfer value off the blockchain without involving the blockchain for each transaction. Payment channels are bi-directional connections between two nodes that allow the exchange of ERC20-compliant tokens (type of digital currency that can be created and used on the Ethereum blockchain). Nodes can also connect to each other through a channel network, creating a routing network that allows payments to be made between any pair of nodes. The Raiden network is still under development but aims to provide stateful channel technology, define protocols, and develop reference implementations. This type of solution offers advantages in terms of speed of transaction execution and anonymity for parties not directly involved, but it also has limitations. In effect, it executes all transactions off-chain and stores only the initial and final states on-chain. Therefore, the only operations tracked are those of opening and closing channels, which may not be sufficient to ensure transparency and verifiability of data. Arguably, such a solution does not fit all those use cases of digital vehicle passports, whose primary objective is to track the history of vehicles and their operations in order to prevent fraud, theft, and counterfeiting.

As another example of hybrid blockchain-based solutions, some of the leading OEMs, including BMW and Renault, have decided to develop their own POCs using VeChain. VeChain is a public blockchain platform designed to improve supply chain management and business processes, which also enables the development and execution of smart contracts. However, there are a certain number of master nodes that must be authenticated and are responsible for reaching consensus on transactions in the VeChain blockchain, while anonymous nodes are not allowed, and disclosure of identity is an essential requirement to become an authority master node.

This system differs from other public blockchains, which require all nodes to vote on a transaction before reaching consensus, so we define it as hybrid. Indeed, the master node system centralizes voting in a decentralized system. But the founders of VeChain have said that their goal in designing this protocol is to achieve a balance between centralization and decentralization. So again, depending on the use case, using this type of blockchain could be a viable choice. At the moment, as the solution that some of the major players in the automotive industry have moved toward, it could be a de facto standard for digital vehicle passports. However, as mentioned at the beginning of this chapter, as digital vehicle passports are still in their infancy, future studies and research could explore other, more efficient and effective alternatives.

17.3.2 DATA STORAGE COMPARISON

In the previous paragraph, we discussed the importance of choosing the right type of blockchain based on the use case being implemented, and how this choice can determine the performance, cost, security, and privacy of the solution.

In this paragraph, we will examine the importance of choosing how and where to store data for a digital vehicle passport, again analyzing the work cited in Section 12.2.

First, when developing a blockchain-based project, there are three different solutions for data storage: on-chain, off-chain, and hybrid.

- The on-chain solution involves storing all data directly on the blockchain, taking advantage of its security, immutability, and transparency. This method ensures maximum reliability and traceability of data, but it also has drawbacks, such as high storage costs, limited scalability, and potential data breaches.
- The off-chain solution involves storing data outside the blockchain, on external systems, such as databases, clouds, or local devices. This method reduces storage costs, increases scalability, and protects privacy, but also requires additional security and verification mechanisms to ensure data integrity and authenticity.

- The hybrid solution involves storing data selectively, choosing which data to store on the blockchain and which to store on external systems. This method attempts to balance the advantages and disadvantages of the previous two solutions, offering greater flexibility and adaptability to the specific needs of the project.

Having outlined the possible implementation choices for data storage, we move on to analyze the choices made in the aforementioned works.

Works such as Razzaq (2022), Barati (2021), Jahan et al. (2023), Gao (2022) have chosen IPFS as their data storage warehouse. IPFS is part of off-chain data storage solutions. However, unlike standard solutions, it is distributed storage, which is a data management system without a central server, based on the principles of content addressing and peer-to-peer networking. Content addressing is a fundamental concept of IPFS. Instead of using URLs to identify files, IPFS uses cryptographic hashing to create a unique identifier for each file. This identifier is called a CID (content identifier) and is used to retrieve the file from the IPFS network. The CID is created using a cryptographic hash function such as SHA-256. This hash function takes the contents of the file as input and returns a unique hash that identifies the contents of the file. The CID is then created by concatenating the prefix "Qm" with the hash of the file contents. Thus, IPFS provides greater efficiency, scalability, and resistance to censorship because the data is distributed across network nodes and identified by a unique code.

However, despite the benefits of IPFS, there are also challenges and risks, particularly with respect to privacy. In fact, data stored on IPFS is publicly available and may contain sensitive or personal information. Therefore, if the solution requires the storage of sensitive data, it is necessary to incorporate privacy protection techniques, such as encryption, anonymization, or data fragmentation, to protect user data on the IPFS.

Other solutions, such as Panchamia and Byrappa (2017) and Nowacki et al. (2023), have chosen to store information directly on blockchains. In general, this practice is considered the most secure and reliable, as data stored on the chain benefits from all the properties of blockchains, such as immutability, transparency, and verifiability. However, this practice also has drawbacks, such as high storage costs, limited scalability, and potential privacy violations. In the case of Panchamia and Byrappa (2017), the authors used Hyperledger Fabric's private blockchain to store digital passport information. This limits the risks associated with privacy breaches, as only authorized users have access to read the data. However, in the case of an OEM, the authorized users could be the various customers, so additional techniques would be needed to protect privacy. In the case of Nowacki et al. (2023), on the other hand, the authors used IOTA's decentralized public ledger to store the information, which is then exposed to everyone and does not guarantee privacy if not handled properly.

The solutions presented in Navarro et al. (2022) and Alessandria and Vizzari (2021) are based on a hybrid storage system that combines blockchain with off-chain storage. The blockchain stores non-sensitive information, while off-chain storage protects the privacy of sensitive information. This approach has advantages and disadvantages for both the on-chain and off-chain parts. The on-chain part has the same characteristics as the previous two works, with the difference that the data on the blockchain is theoretically non-sensitive and therefore does not require additional privacy protection. The off-chain part, on the other hand, offers greater privacy, but also greater vulnerability to attacks or failures of the server hosting the data. Both solutions assume the use of a centralized server, which is a single point of failure and therefore a threat to data availability.

Unfortunately, we did not find sufficient information on how the major OEMs have implemented the solutions, so we cannot analyze how they have chosen to handle the digital passport data of their vehicles.

To conclude the analysis of different ways to store information, let us look at some thoughts on the use of digital passports in the automotive sector. In general, regardless of the use case, this is sensitive data, so a solution that stores all data on the chain may not be suitable for privacy reasons.

Also, on some public blockchains, the volume of data to be stored could significantly increase the cost of operation. A hybrid solution may be best, allowing a distinction to be made on an as-needed basis between data to be stored on the blockchain and data to be stored off-chain. In addition, choosing distributed storage would reduce the risk of service disruptions that centralized servers are exposed to. Of course, it is important to use techniques known to protect privacy.

17.3.3 PRIVACY TECHNIQUES COMPARISON

In the previous section, we looked at the different ways of storing digital passport data and emphasized the need to protect personal information to ensure privacy. In general, when it comes to privacy, the most important techniques are encryption, anonymization, and pseudonymization:

- *Encryption* is a process that converts data into a format that can only be read by those with the decryption key. This makes the data inaccessible to unauthorized parties.
- *Anonymization* is a process that removes or modifies data that can be traced back to an individual, making it unrecognizable. In this way, the data cannot be associated with a specific individual.
- *Pseudonymization* is a process that replaces data that identifies an individual with codes or symbols but maintains a correlation between the original and pseudonymized data. In this way, the data can be used for specific purposes but cannot be used to identify an individual.

To protect the privacy of blockchain-based digital passports, several advanced techniques derived from the general principles described earlier can be applied. One such technique is decentralized identity, which gives individuals control over their own identity or personal information without relying on central authorities, such as governments or corporations. Decentralized identity relies on encryption and anonymization protocols that ensure the security and confidentiality of data. For example, self-sovereign identity (SSI) is a digital identity protocol that allows individuals to create and manage their own identities without having to register them with third-party entities. This means that individuals can independently and securely control what identity information they share, and with whom. SSI is based on blockchain technology, which ensures that identities are decentralized, transparent, and tamperproof. One of the main components of this protocol is the decentralized identifier (DID), which is a unique and persistent identifier that represents an entity (person, organization, device, etc.) and can be resolved into a DID document that contains the information and public keys associated with the entity. Added to this is the verifiable credential (VC) component, which is a digital credential that confirms a certain quality or property of an entity, such as name, age, education, and so on. In addition, VC allows people to share their identity information in a verifiable way without revealing personal or sensitive information. Proving one's identity or personal information without revealing or sharing it is possible through cryptographic techniques, such as zero-knowledge proof (ZKP). This technique is useful for protecting the privacy of identity information because it allows a VC to be verified without having to share the contents of the VC itself. ZKP is also a technique that can be incorporated into the VC standard, as it allows VCs to be created with the proof property, which allows the holder to derive a verifiable representation that reveals only the information it intends to reveal. To make the use of decentralized identity protocols for digital passports effective, it is essential to define a common standard among different blockchain platforms, identity providers, and all services that would benefit from them. This would ensure interoperability, compatibility, and scalability of decentralized identity systems. To this end, initiatives have already been launched by organizations such as W3C, DIF, and IETF, which have proposed some standards for the definition and management of decentralized identities. These standards are constantly evolving and improving thanks to the input of various stakeholders, including companies, institutions, researchers, and developers. The goal is to create an open, secure, and inclusive decentralized identity ecosystem that can support the implementation of digital passports and other identity-based services.

Among the papers we analyzed, not all made explicit their approach to privacy management. However, among those that did, we found several solutions. Some papers, such as Razzaq (2022) and Barati (2021), while referring to SSI, simply encrypted sensitive data before storing it on IPFS. Specifically, Razzaq (2022) encrypted the data and then stored the encrypted version on IPFS, while Barati (2021) stored the plaintext data on IPFS and applied encryption to the CID identifying the data. While this method is easy to implement, it requires careful and secure management of the encryption system. In addition, encrypting only the CID makes the verification process faster because there is less data to encrypt and decrypt, but at the same time, it exposes the plaintext data on IPFS, which is a public store accessible to all. In the work of Gao (2022), passport data is encrypted before being stored in the IPFS, but a pseudonymization system is also used, which increases the privacy level of the whole system by removing the direct link between the subject and the associated data. However, even in this case, in addition to the need to carefully manage the encryption system, care must be taken in how the pseudo-anonymization is implemented, as it is not based on well-defined and tested standards, and therefore the risk of making mistakes is high.

Some papers did not propose a privacy management system. For example, Panchamia and Byrappa (2017) and Nowacki et al. (2023) left the implementation of a viable and efficient privacy management system to future work. Instead, Jahan et al. (2023) made no reference to privacy management. This could be a problem, because even though their implementation is based on Hyperledger, which is a permissioned blockchain and therefore only accessible to authorized users, it could still be vulnerable to cyberattacks and thus exposed to privacy risks. In addition, this solution also stores data on IPFS, which, if sensitive, should be properly protected.

Finally, some work, such as Navarro et al. (2022) and Alessandria and Vizzari (2021), used well-known privacy standards in their solutions. In particular, Navarro et al. (2022) drew inspiration from the W3C standard for implementing a decentralized identity–based system so that no personal or sensitive information is stored on-chain or off-chain. A similar approach has been taken by Alessandria and Vizzari (2021), which instead proposes to use the entire protocol of SSI, leveraging both decentralized identity and VCs, allowing users to share only the information they want without having to expose private information. Certainly, relying on standards is the best solution, because they are already tested and, more importantly, allow you to make your implementation compatible with all other services that use the same standards. However, most of these standards are still in the research and development phase, so there may be some unidentified risks.

Again, as in the previous section, we found no detailed information on how privacy is protected in the solutions implemented by OEMs.

17.4 ADVANTAGES AND DISADVANTAGES OF ADOPTING DIGITAL PASSPORTS

In the previous section, we explored the various technical and operational options for implementing digital vehicle passports based on blockchain technology. We considered the various aspects related to the type of blockchain, the method of data storage, and the protection of sensitive data. In this section, however, we want to assess the potential impact that digital vehicle passports could have on the transportation sector and society in general. We will analyze what possible advantages and disadvantages could result from the adoption of this innovation, both economically and socially. We will also discuss the challenges and opportunities for stakeholders, such as vehicle manufacturers, regulators, consumers, and service providers.

The benefits that digital vehicle passports could offer are manifold and cover several areas. The first benefit is that the immutable and distributed nature of the blockchain increases the transparency and reliability of information about a vehicle's history, condition, and performance. This means that digital vehicle passport data, once recorded on the blockchain, cannot be changed or deleted, and is shared and verified by all participants in the network. This prevents fraud, forgery, and data manipulation and ensures greater trust among the various parties involved, such as sellers, buyers, insurance companies, and government agencies. This benefit can lead to greater safety and quality of vehicles, greater ease, and convenience in buying and selling transactions, and greater empowerment of owners.

The second benefit is to reduce the cost and time of managing vehicle sales, purchases, rentals, insurance, and maintenance by simplifying and digitizing processes. In fact, the introduction of digital vehicle passports would make it possible to eliminate or reduce the need for intermediaries, paper documents, manual checks, and third-party verification, and to automate and expedite transactions and contracts between parties through the use of smart contracts. This reduces operational and administrative costs and increases efficiency and convenience for customers. This benefit can lead to increased competitiveness and innovation in the transportation sector, increased accessibility and flexibility of services, and increased consumer satisfaction.

The third benefit is improved road safety and air quality through the ability to monitor and incentivize compliance with regulations and emission limits. This is because digital vehicle passports could also be used to collect, analyze, and transmit data on driving behavior, technical conditions, and vehicle emissions to the relevant authorities in real time. In this way, violations such as traffic violations, overdue inspections, and unpaid taxes can be prevented and punished, and responsible practices such as safe driving, regular maintenance, and the use of alternative fuels can be encouraged and rewarded. These benefits can lead to greater public safety and health, environmental sustainability, and social awareness.

Finally, another benefit that digital vehicle passports could bring is the development of new business models and customized services by using digital vehicle passport data to create innovative, customer-focused solutions. Indeed, digital vehicle passports could potentially provide a source of valuable and up-to-date information about vehicles and their owners, which can be used to offer tailored and differentiated services, such as pay-per-use insurance, peer-to-peer rental, shared mobility, preventive maintenance, and vehicle personalization. This creates new market and value creation opportunities for vehicle manufacturers, service providers, and consumers. These benefits can lead to greater diversification and personalization of offerings, increased customer loyalty and satisfaction, and greater collaboration and integration among industry players.

The introduction of digital vehicle passports could mean the digitization of new types of data, some of which have not yet been converted to digital format. This process has the potential to significantly improve the transport sector and benefit society. However, the potential offered by this advanced technology is not without challenges and risks. It is therefore important to proceed with careful evaluation and management of any drawbacks. In the following, we present some of the critical issues that the implementation of digital vehicle passports may entail.

The first disadvantage is that it creates privacy and data protection risks due to the potential exposure or misuse of sensitive information contained in digital vehicle passports. This means that if digital vehicle passport data is not properly secured and encrypted, it could be accessed or used by unauthorized parties who could violate the privacy of vehicle owners or exploit the data for illegal or harmful purposes. This could compromise the security and trust of customers and violate privacy regulations and rights.

The second drawback is the difficulty of interoperability and standardization, due to the multiplicity of existing blockchain platforms and protocols and the lack of internationally harmonized regulations. Indeed, as seen in the previous section, if digital vehicle passports are based on different blockchains, they may not be compatible or communicate with each other, which could lead to disputes or uncertainty about applicable regulations and responsibilities. This could limit the functionality and effectiveness of digital vehicle passports and create barriers or conflicts between different stakeholders, such as vehicle manufacturers, regulators, consumers, and service providers.

The third disadvantage is the need for investment and technical expertise, due to the complexity and novelty of blockchain technology and the need to adapt existing infrastructure and systems. This means that in order to be efficiently and securely implemented and managed, digital vehicle passports will require skilled economic and human resources to develop and maintain blockchain platforms and protocols, and to integrate and upgrade existing infrastructure and systems. This could increase the cost and difficulty of implementing and adopting digital vehicle passports.

Finally, another disadvantage is that it generates resistance to change and disintermediation due to the potential loss of power and revenue for some traditional actors in the transport sector, such as dealers, mechanics, and authorities. This means that digital vehicle passports, due to their transparency and automation, could reduce or eliminate the role and value of some intermediaries or controllers, who could see their influence and profitability diminish. This could lead to opposition or resistance from these actors, which could hinder or slow down innovation and progress in the transport sector.

17.5 CONCLUSIONS

In this chapter, we delved into the topic of digital vehicle passports based on blockchain technology, exploring the technical and operational details of possible solutions. We compared the different options available in the literature, highlighting the criteria for choosing between blockchain types, data storage methods, and privacy protection methods. We also assessed the potential economic and social impact of digital vehicle passports, analyzing the advantages and disadvantages that could result from their adoption.

In conclusion, we can say that digital vehicle passports are an innovative and promising technology that could lead to a radical transformation of the transportation sector and a number of societal benefits. However, this technology also poses challenges and risks that require careful evaluation and responsible management. Therefore, a collaborative and participatory approach among the various stakeholders is essential to ensure the functionality, reliability, security, and sustainability of digital vehicle passports. In addition, a harmonized and appropriate legal and regulatory framework is needed to promote interoperability, standardization, data protection, and consumer rights. Only in this way can digital vehicle passports reach their full potential and contribute to the progress and well-being of society.

ACKNOWLEDGMENTS

This study was carried out within the MICS (Made in Italy – Circular and Sustainable) Extended Partnership and received funding from the European Union Next-GenerationEU (PIANO NAZIONALE DI RIPRESA E RESILIENZA (PNRR) – MISSIONE 4 COMPONENTE 2, INVESTIMENTO 1.3 – D.D. 1551.11-10-2022, PE00000004). This manuscript reflects only the authors' views and opinions, neither the European Union nor the European Commission can be considered responsible for them.

BIBLIOGRAPHY

Alessandria, M. L., and Vizzari, A. (2021). Self-Sovereign Identity and Blockchain applications for the automotive sector. *AEIT International Conference on Electrical and Electronic Technologies for Automotive (AEIT AUTOMOTIVE)* (pp. 1–6). Torino, Italy.

Barati, M. B. (2021). A privacy-preserving platform for recording covid-19 vaccine passports. *CloudAM: 10th International Workshop on Cloud and Edge Computing, and Applications Management.* arXiv preprint arXiv:2112.01815.

Berger, K., Schöggl, J.-P., and Baumgartner, R. J. (2021). Concept of a digital product passport for an electric vehicle battery. *Resource Efficient Vehicles Conference, Centre for ECO2 Vehicle Design* (pp. 224–251). Resource Efficient Vehicles Conference – rev2021, Online , Sweden. Available at: https://kth.diva-portal.org/smash/record.jsf?pid=diva2%3A1604250&dswid=-3666

BMW. (2019, April 22). *Tratto da VerifyCar – Vehicle digital passport on the VechainThor Blockchain.* https://vechaininsider.com/news/vechain-summit-2019-bmw-announces-verifycar-powered-by-vechain/

Cointelegraph. (2017, April 27). *Groupe Renault innovates with VISEO and Microsoft on the Blockchain.* Tratto da https://cointelegraph.com/news/renault-uses-blockchain-to-store-car-passport-details

Gao, H. H.-y. (2022). An immunity passport scheme based on the dual-blockchain architecture for international travel. *Wireless Communications and Mobile Computing, 2022*(1), 5721212.

Hyundai. (2023, September 23). *Hyundai to track used car history through blockchain project with Blocko.* Tratto da www.newcoint.com/hyundai-to-track-used-car-history-through-blockchain-project-with-blocko/

Jahan, Nusrat, Reno, S., and Ahmed, M. (2023). Securing E-passport management using private-permissioned blockchain and IPFS. *International Conference on Electrical, Computer and Cmmunication Engineering (ECCE).* Chittagong, Bangladesh.

Mobi. (2022). *Blockchain for vehicle identity: Business White Paper.* Tratto da https://dlt.mobi/wp-content/uploads/2023/05/MOBI-VID0001WP2021_Version-2.1.pdf

Navarro, L., Cano, J., Font, M., and Franquesa, D. (2022). Digital transformation of the circular economy: Digital product passports for transparency, verifiability, accountability. *Manuscript submitted for publication.*

Nowacki, S., Sisik, G. M., and Angelopoulos, C. M. (2023). Digital product passports: Use cases framework and technical architecture using DLT and smart contracts. *19th International Conference on Distributed Computing in Smart Systems and the Internet of Things (DCOSS-IoT)* (pp. 373–380). Pafos, Cyprus.

Panchamia, S., and Byrappa, D. K. (2017). Passport, VISA and immigration management using blockchain. *23RD Annual International Conference in Advanced Computing and Communications (ADCOM)* (pp. 8–17). Bangalore, India.

Rachinger, M. a. (2019). Digitalization and its influence on business model innovation. *Journal of Manufacturing Technology Management,* 1143–1160.

Razzaq, A. a.-K. (2022). Blockchain in healthcare: A decentralized platform for digital health passport of covid-19 based on vaccination and immunity certificates. *Healthcare,* 2453.

18 WBSA with QR Code for Efficient Usage of Metro/ Bus Services Using Private Cloud Infrastructure

Sangeeta Gupta, Y. Ramadevi, S. Durga Devi,
P. Akshay, K. Hrithik Pawan, and K. Rohit

18.1 INTRODUCTION: SIGNIFICANCE OF WALLET-BASED SMART APP (WBSA)

The tickets in most metro stations use QR code–based paper tokens to swipe and pass through to board the train. There is a possibility of the paper-based tokens to be damaged due to multiple reasons, or they may get lost, leading to unexpected delays. It is a tedious task for the commuter to remember the identity code to pass through. Also, if the smart card that provides access to pass through and board the metro is lost, if it is not realized by the commuter that he lost the card, then there is a scope for an intruder to gain unintended access. Hence, it is essential to safeguard against such unavoidable circumstances. Toward this end, a wallet-based smart app (WBSA) is developed in this work that includes an initial phase of login via the onetime password (OTP) sent to the mobile of the customer. This login enables the customer to proceed with various facilities, like storing smart card credentials in a wallet, storing quick response (QR) code credentials, cloud-based private key generator, etc., to enable the passengers to commute efficiently. The proposed work is aimed to provide convenience to passengers to enable them to overcome the difficulties when a smart card, token, or smartphone is either lost or damaged and to prevent unintended access to the card. It is identified from the results that the time taken to carry out various activities such as login, ticket scan, fetching the scanned tickets and the time taken to fetch details such as QR code, entry and exit time and booked time of single ticket, retrieval of fares, showing past journeys using QR limited to about 50, and also recording single journey details all achieve better performance with the proposed model, where the application and the server run on the same network rather than the Ngrok-based tunnel mode.

18.1.1 Smart Card Access

Metro is used as a daily commute means from source to destination by the people in urban areas, particularly to overcome delays, get rid of pollution, and enjoy the ride in the metro during humid weather conditions. Most of the daily commuters use smart cards to board the metro, which saves time by overcoming queuing at the ticket counters to get tickets. This also reduces the probability of missing a train due to huge crowds at the counters. However, there are instances where people miss their trains due to the less frequency between the arrival and departure of trains, if stuck in huge crowd. At the other end, people who travel randomly from one corner of the city to another use the metro facility by purchasing tickets at the time of travel [1, 2].

DOI: 10.1201/9781003450306-20

Smart cards play a prominent role in enabling passengers to pass through barricades at metro stations to overcome unnecessary delays. However, to ensure the service quality during their transit, a huge set of inconveniences may be experienced due to a variety of reasons, such as damage of the card, unknown usage of the card (i.e., difficulty finding the appropriate position to swipe in), improper functioning of the machines to swipe card, or even the presence of huge crowd. All these situations pose a great difficulty for passengers.

The existing systems, as quoted in the literature, are designed in such a way that if the smart card is lost or damaged, a new one must be purchased without the leftover balance of the lost one appended to the new one, incurring loss to the passengers. There is even no means to integrate the smart card with personal gadgets instantly. Also, the tokens purchased are valid only for a stipulated time period, and passengers have to spend drastic amounts of time waiting in long queues for the issuance of another token. This may cause them to miss out on high-priority tasks when running late.

All these situations pose a great difficulty for the passengers. An estimate of reduction of wait time using various mathematical and fuzzy models to improve the service quality during transit is developed by the authors in [3]. Also, the methodology adopted is not applicable to various difficult levels faced by the passengers, and the solutions may vary from one location to the other. Particularly, if it is an IT hub, then there are a greater number of educated and well-trained techies who can deal with the aforementioned difficulties in a better way than other arenas.

At the other end, the time taken by the passengers to commute from one location to another in urban areas has a major impact on the cognitive and psychomotor skills of the commuters. This arises as they may have to spend time waiting to overcome unforeseen delays due to technical issues. Hence, it is essential to provide alternate solutions to the tracks chosen by the metro trains in case of a hurdle in transit. The smart card data not only enables to retrieve passenger details like name, card number, etc. but also helps one understand the rate at which steps are taken by the passengers to board the train. This data enables us to categorize users based on their age groups and provide efficient services accordingly. This also helps overcome long wait times for the passengers that can be efficiently utilized to carry out value-added tasks. However, if the card falls into the wrong hands, then the data may be misused and tampered with by the intruders, thereby leading to unintended consequences.

To deal with the difficulties, a wallet-based smart app (WBSA) is developed in this work. The chapter is organized as follows: Section 1 draws various scenarios pertaining to the difficulties faced by the commuters while travelling via metro, and an essence for the proposed work is presented. Section 2 drives through the existing works and highlights their limitations. Section 3 draws a discussion on the proposed framework with module-wise explanation, while Section 9.4 presents the steps followed for the implementation of the proposed framework, with a discussion on the results achieved in terms of response times recorded for various activities. And finally, Section 9.5 concludes the work.

18.2 LITERATURE SURVEY

The smart card (SC) in the existing systems is designed using a wide set of domains pertaining to IoT, cloud computing, and data mining [4]. However, it is essential to ensure the security mechanisms to prevent unintended actions during a "lost or damaged SC" incident. The layer at which security is imposed also varies based on the level of complexity. The length of the encrypted code and the size of the SC are the parameters that must be considered while designing a security mechanism. Various focus points during implementation of security, such as performance, rate of retrieval, data loading, etc., play a prominent role in assessing the strength of the design.

A mechanism to detect anomalies in the smart cards swiped by the passengers at entry and exit points in metro stations is developed. If the behavior of any passenger is identified to be malicious, then their details are retrieved via swiped cards stored in the metro database. Pre-processing steps are applied on incomplete data items to retrieve accurate data pertaining to the passengers

[5]. However, an analysis made using fixed time intervals seems to be static in nature and may be inefficient to clean the voluminous big data. Also, if the passenger is misinterpreted to be guilty, then it is a risk at the authorities' end, and the confidential data of the passengers may be stolen for commercial benefits. At the other end, the time taken by the passengers to commute from one location to another in urban areas has a major impact on the cognitive and psychomotor skills of the commuters. This arises as they may have to spend time waiting to overcome unforeseen delays due to technical issues. Hence, it is essential to provide alternate solutions to the tracks chosen by the metro trains in case of a hurdle in transit [6].

The smart card data not only enables the retrieval of passenger details, like name, card number, etc., but also helps one understand the rate at which steps are taken by the passengers to board the train. This data enables us to categorize users based on their age groups and provide efficient services accordingly. This also helps overcome long wait times by the passengers that can be efficiently utilized to carry out value-added tasks [7]. However, if the card falls into the wrong hands, then the data may be misused and lead to unintended consequences. Hence, security threats are always prominent to prevent the card from being lost or stolen. Big data analytics in amalgamation with machine learning techniques like regression, classification, and prediction serve as a major driving factor to analyze the flow rate of passengers using various pass-through options in a metro. These mechanisms can also be used to infer the type of passenger, like normal, malicious, etc., when intended to estimate their behavior in "lost or stolen smart card" incidents [8].

Also, the data associated with smart cards enables us to predict the arrival time, reduce the wait time, and enable to make predictions based on the passenger preferences. Particularly, for advertisement agencies, it is an easy mechanism to extract the passenger's data, provided that the data should not fall into the wrong hands. However, the data collected via smart card is not in a structured format. Pre-processing steps must be carried out on the data to perform any suitable analysis [9]. However, when using a smart card (SC) to swipe and pass through, the burden on the user toward the need to remember user identity and password for secure credential-based access is greatly reduced. This will be more impactful in preventing the card from falling into the wrong hands. A simple solution to deal with lost cards is to block the card by calling the corresponding customer care. The time taken by customer care may be wide enough due to either technical or network issues and hence may cause the credentials of the victim to be hacked and misused. These difficulties can be overcome when integrating user SC credentials into a cloud-based secure environment [10, 11]. It is essential to design solutions to overcome the aforementioned problems in a cost-effective manner to reduce the computational overhead [12]. Various focus points during implementation of security, such as performance, rate of retrieval, data loading, etc., play a prominent role in assessing the strength of the design [13].

A QR code–based ticket booking system is adopted in the current trend to overcome long queue-based waiting hours and reach the destination in confined time. This system is preferred by most working youngsters travelling from one location to another to reach their workplace without incurring any delays. To utilize this kind of service, only a smartphone is required to scan the code and pass through the barricades [14]. However, if the phone is lost, then there is no alternative way to extract the details but rather get disappointed. If the smartphone that has all credentials is lost or stolen by the intruder, then the only way to prevent unauthorized access is to block the sim card. If the commuter realizes very lately, then they might lose their hard-earned money.

The aforementioned difficulties can be overcome when integrating user smart card and mobile credentials into private cloud-based secure environment proposed as an inventive step in the proposed work. It is also essential to design solutions in a cost-effective manner to reduce computational overheads.

18.3 PROPOSED WORK

Smart card (SC) plays a prominent role in enabling passengers to pass through barricades at metro stations to overcome unnecessary delays. However, to ensure the service quality during their transit, a huge set of inconveniences may be experienced due to a variety of reasons, such as damage to the card, smart card being lost, or the mobile that stores all credentials itself being lost. All these situations pose a great difficulty for the passengers.

The WBSA framework design, as shown in Figure 18.1, integrates various secure facilities for the efficient commute of passengers, thereby overcoming unprecedented delays. The framework

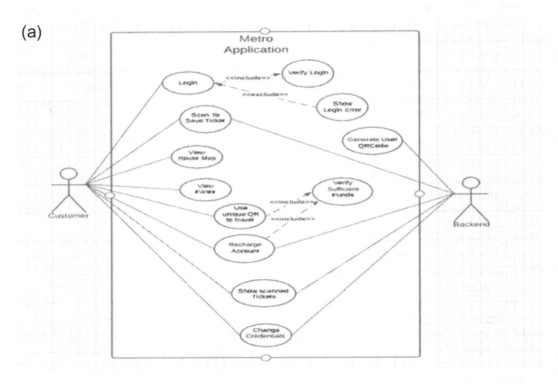

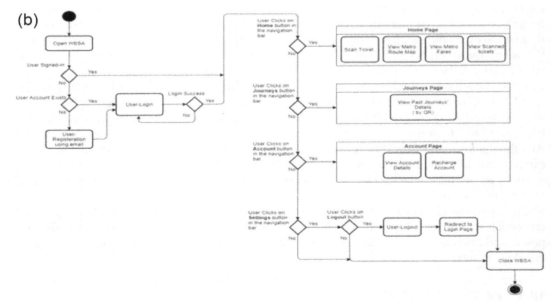

FIGURE 18.1   (a) WSBA process flow and (b) diagram.

includes the initial phase of login via a onetime password (OTP) sent to the mobile of the customer to proceed further with the procedure, like smart card credentials, quick response (QR) code credentials, cloud-based private key generator [15], wallet credentials integrated into the smartphones, and other additional facilities like balance viewer, journey planner. The security is double-ended prevention of both the tampered and damaged SC, respectively.

18.3.1 MODULE DESCRIPTION

The modules developed in the proposed work are presented as follows.

18.3.1.1 User Registration

Initially, the user must get through the verification process to access the services. So a verification email is sent to the registered mail ID as provided by the user to utilize the metro app services. Once the login is successful, various services available in the app can be utilized.

18.3.1.2 Home Page Access

After the user registers through the mail, they will be redirected to the home page, where they can perform a wide set of operations, like scanning the ticket, checking for details on the metro route map, showing fares related to travel from various source to destination platforms, etc.

18.3.1.3 Ticket Scan

Tickets issued to the commuter can be scanned with their smartphone. With this, the QR code associated with the ticket and other details will be displayed [16]. In addition, the information about the tickets previously booked can also be viewed to overcome double bookings. The app is developed in such a way that multiple tickets can be scanned at once [17]. Also, a ticket scanned once will be added to the user's account.

18.3.1.4 Wallet-Based Account Page

In the proposed model using the wallet-based QR code, if the card is lost, then further attempts to access the card through other devices will be disallowed. Invalid attempts made to access the card through varying credentials will be identified with the very first access made, and the user will be logged out from the system. In turn, it will be regarded as invalid access. In addition, the leftover balance amount will be diverted back to the user's account with which they have registered, upon recovery.

18.3.1.5 Unique QR Access

To proceed with the travel, a minimum balance should always be maintained in the wallet. To overcome unintended delays, instead of using the smart card (with the fear of being lost), a unique QR associated with the user will be scanned to enable the user to pass through the entry and exit barricades. Once the scanning process is completed, a billing statement will be generated to permit the travel. The final account balance after deducting the fare for the journey will be updated and stored in the wallet.

18.3.1.6 Password Recovery

In this step, to ensure account safety, the access by the user through an unregistered device will be disabled. This event may take place when the user loses their mobile device and they are making an attempt to access their wallet through some other device. The user needs to reset the password by selecting the "forgot password" option. This will enable the user to create a new access to utilize the metro services again, thereby preventing malicious attempts.

18.3.2 WSBA SYSTEM ARCHITECTURE

The WBSA process flow design, as shown in Figure 18.1, integrates various secure facilities for the efficient commute of passengers, thereby overcoming unprecedented delays. The framework includes the initial phase of login via a onetime password (OTP) sent to the mobile of the customer to proceed with access to several other services, such as scanning QR, viewing route map, viewing ticket fares, recharging, etc., all integrated into the app, which can be accessed through smartphones; also, other additional facilities, like balance viewer and journey planner, are available [18]. If the login credentials are incorrectly entered by the user, then access to the app will be blocked. If the login is valid, then the user can access various services of the app. This design is applicable to any ticket-based journeys either using rail routes or roadways to commute from one location to another, thereby eliminating the need to store paper-based tokens.

(a)

(b)

The explanation for WSBA flow is as follows.

Initially, the user opens the app. If the user has already signed in previously, they will be redirected to the home page; else, the user will be shown the login page. Here, the user must enter the credentials and click on the Login button. On successful login, the user is redirected to the home page. If the user does not have an account, then they must register by clicking on the "Create a New Account" link. In the home page, the user can perform the following activities:

- Scan ticket (to link to their account)
- View metro route map
- Get metro fares
- View the list of scanned tickets

In the "journey" page, the user can access the details about their past journeys for which they have paid using their smart wallet (i.e., using the unique QR).

In the account page, users can view the account information and the balance amount. The users can also recharge their account.

The settings page contains the Logout button, which upon clicking will clear user data from the device and redirect the user to the login page.

18.4 DISCUSSION AND RESULTS

The work is developed in Python 3 environment, and the packages installed on the virtual environment to run the back end are Flask, Flask-Bcrypt, Flask-Mail, Flask-SQLAlchemy, Pillow, pyzbar, qrcode, qrtools, SQLAlchemy, bcrypt, itsdangerous, Markupsafe, as shown in Figure 18.2. A database is created to store the back-end-related models.

Initially, user registration should be done by opening the application and clicking on the "Create a New Account" button. Then, the user should fill in the details and click on Register. Once this process is complete, the user will receive a mail (as entered by the user during registration) with a

```
* Serving Flask app "metro_app_backend" (lazy loading)
* Environment: production
  WARNING: This is a development server. Do not use it in a production deployment.
  Use a production WSGI server instead.
* Debug mode: off
* Running on http://0.0.0.0:5000/ (Press CTRL+C to quit)
```

FIGURE 18.2 Environment setup.

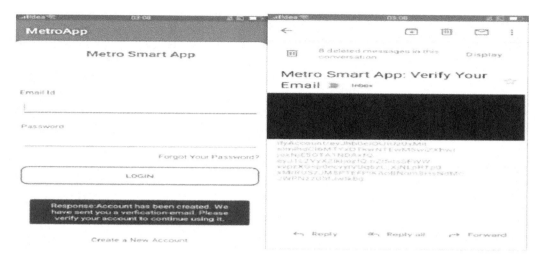

FIGURE 18.3   Email verification for registration.

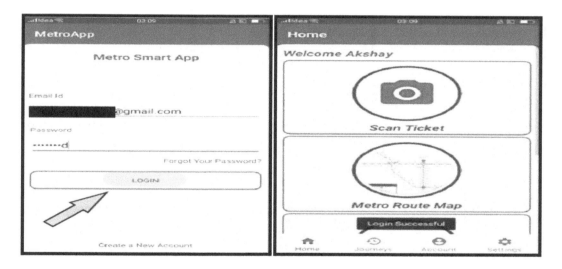

FIGURE 18.4   Options for user access.

link. Clicking on the link will enable the user to complete the registration process. This process is as shown in Figure 18.3.

Once the user logs in, different icons such as for "scan ticket," "route map," "fare details," etc. are available, as shown in Figure 18.4. The user can choose a particular one to navigate, with a set of actions associated with it. For example, the ticket created is stored in the database, mapping a source to destination, making it easy for the user to view the reservations made by them, as shown in Figure 18.5, respectively.

The QR code on the ticket should be scanned and linked with the user's account to retrieve it in the event of losing the ticket. The user should choose the station and upload the QR image in the emulator website, which is equivalent to scanning the QR on the phone at the entry gate at a metro station, as shown in Figure 18.6, respectively.

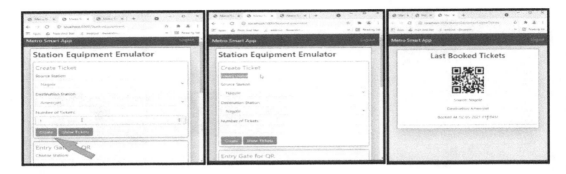

FIGURE 18.5   Reservations details.

FIGURE 18.6   QR code–based access.

FIGURE 18.7   Metro app fare calculator.

Once this process is completed, the fare calculator will generate the fare toward the journey commuted by the user from source to destination, as shown in Figure 18.7, in terms of account balance that is displayed after deduction of the commuted journey fare.

Tables 18.1–7 record the response times as computed for the server running on the local network [19] compared against the use of Ngrok to create a tunnel to Localhost. The results are recorded against four runs, mentioned as attempt 1 through attempt 4 in all the tables. It is identified from the results that the time taken to carry out various activities, such as login, ticket

TABLE 18.1
Login Time

No. of Attempts/Runs	Time Recorded during Various Runs (in Seconds)			
	1st Attempt	2nd Attempt	3rd Attempt	4th Attempt
Proposed app on local network	1.01	0.73	0.563	0.732
NgrokTunnel–based network	1.456	1.424	1.427	1.406

TABLE 18.2
Time Taken for Scanning a Ticket

No. of Attempts/Runs	Time Recorded during Various Runs (In Seconds)			
	1st Attempt	2nd Attempt	3rd Attempt	4th Attempt
Proposed app on local network	0.251	0.204	0.178	0.168
NgrokTunnel-based network	3.01	2.531	3.45	2.584

TABLE 18.3
Scanned Tickets

No. of Attempts/Runs	Time Recorded during Various Runs (In Seconds)			
	1st Attempt	2nd Attempt	3rd Attempt	4th Attempt
Proposed app on local network	0.091	0.095	0.084	0.078
NgrokTunnel-based network	1.308	1.12	0.954	0.958

TABLE 18.4
Time Taken to Fetch Details (QR Code, Entry/Exit Time, Booked Time) of Single Ticket

No. of Attempts/Runs	Time Recorded during Various Runs (In Seconds)			
	1st Attempt	2nd Attempt	3rd Attempt	4th Attempt
Proposed app on local network	0.157	0.144	0.139	0.169
NgrokTunnel-based network	2.161	1.933	1.75	1.646

TABLE 18.5
Get Fare

No. of Attempts/Runs	Time Recorded during Various Runs (In Seconds)			
	1st Attempt	2nd Attempt	3rd Attempt	4th Attempt
Proposed app on local network	0.248	0.135	0.108	0.112
NgrokTunnel-based network	1.070	1.143	1.128	1.101

TABLE 18.6
Show Past Journeys Using QR

No. of Attempts/Runs	Time Recorded during Various Runs (In Seconds)			
	1st Attempt	2nd Attempt	3rd Attempt	4th Attempt
Proposed app on local network	0.060	0.063	0.143	0.093
NgrokTunnel-based network	1.104	0.949	1.240	0.977

TABLE 18.7
Show Single Journey Details

No. of Attempts/Runs	Time Recorded during Various Runs (In Seconds)			
	1st Attempt	2nd Attempt	3rd Attempt	4th Attempt
Proposed app on local network	0.187	0.111	0.141	0.129
NgrokTunnel-based network	1.614	2.02	2.156	1.690

scan, fetching the scanned tickets, time taken to fetch details such as QR code, entry and exit time and booked time of single ticket, retrieval of fares, showing past journeys using QR limited to about 50, and also recording single journey details, all achieve better performance with the proposed model, where the application and the server run on the same network rather than the Ngrok-based tunnel mode.

18.5 CONCLUSION AND FUTURE WORK

The tickets in the majority of metro stations use QR code–based paper tokens to swipe and pass through to board the train. There is a possibility of the paper-based tokens to be damaged due to multiple reasons, or they may get lost, leading to unexpected delays. It is a tedious task for the commuter to remember the identity code to pass through. Also, if the smart card that provides access to pass through and board the metro is lost, if it is not realized by the commuter that he lost the card, then there is a scope for the intruder to gain unintended access. Toward this end, in the proposed WSBA app, there is no need for the user to carry tokens or tickets while communting from one end to another, to prevent unintended delays when the token is lost. The generation of false tickets is avoided as the developed system does the entire fare calculation automatically to maintain consistent balance in the user's account. The WSBA design is applicable to any ticket-based journey, either using rail routes or roadways to commute from one location to another, thereby eliminating the need to store paper-based tokens. In the future, more enhancements in terms of key based match to overcome wallet thefts can be developed. This work can be contributed to the government to make hassle-free commute to passengers utilizing metro services.

REFERENCES

[1] S. Lei, J. Zhou and J. Zhou, "Age-Friendly Public Transport: Evidence from Travel Behaviors of Older Adults in Hong Kong's Metro Station," *2023 Smart City Symposium Prague (SCSP), Prague, Czech Republic*, pp. 1–8, 2023, doi: 10.1109/SCSP58044.2023.10146218.

[2] J. Zhong, Z. He, J. Wang and J. Xie, "A Hierarchical Framework for Passenger Inflow Control in Metro System With Reinforcement Learning," *IEEE Transactions on Intelligent Transportation Systems*, vol. 24, no. 10, pp. 10895–10911, 2023, doi: 10.1109/TITS.2023.3274817.

[3] J. Li, X. Xu, Z. Yao and Y. Lu, "Improving Service Quality With the Fuzzy TOPSIS Method: A Case Study of the Beijing Rail Transit System," *IEEE Access*, vol. 7, pp. 114271–114284, 2019, doi: 10.1109/ACCESS.2019.2932779.

[4] S. Gupta and R. Aluvalu, "Pre-Processed Tweets for Secure Capital Market Analysis Using Cloud," *International Journal of Sociotechnology and Knowledge Development*, vol. 13, no. 1, 2021, doi: 10.4018/IJSKD.2021010101.

[5] W. Yu, H. Bai, J. Chen and X. Yan, "Anomaly Detection of Passenger OD on Nanjing Metro Based on Smart Card Big Data," *IEEE Access*, vol. 7, pp. 138624–138636, 2019, doi: 10.1109/ACCESS.2019.2943598.

[6] W. Li, Q. Luo and Q. Cai, "A Smart Path Recommendation Method for Metro Systems With Passenger Preferences," *IEEE Access*, vol. 8, pp. 20646–20657, 2020, doi: 10.1109/ACCESS.2020.2969075.

[7] W. Li, X. Yan, X. Li and J. Yang, "Estimate Passengers' Walking and Waiting Time in Metro Station Using Smart Card Data (SCD)," *IEEE Access*, vol. 8, pp. 11074–11083, 2020, doi: 10.1109/ACCESS.2020.2965155.

[8] K. Zhu, P. Xun, W. Li, Z. Li and R. Zhou, "Prediction of Passenger Flow in Urban Rail Transit Based on Big Data Analysis and Deep Learning," *IEEE Access*, vol. 7, pp. 142272–142279, 2019, doi: 10.1109/ACCESS.2019.2944744.

[9] Y. Zhang and T. Cheng, "A Deep Learning Approach to Infer Employment Status of Passengers by Using Smart Card Data," *IEEE Transactions on Intelligent Transportation Systems*, vol. 21, no. 2, pp. 617–629, February 2020, doi: 10.1109/TITS.2019.2896460.

[10] Sangeeta Gupta et al., "IoT Data Management Using Cloud Computing and Big Data Technologies," *International Journal of Software Innovation*, vol. 8, no. 4, doi: 10.4018/IJSI.2020100104.

[11] Sangeeta Gupta, G. Narsimha, "Secure NoSQL for the Social Networking and E-commerce Based Bigdata Applications Deployed in Cloud," *International Journal of Cloud Applications and Computing*, vol. 8, no. 2, April 2018, doi: 10.4018/IJCAC.2018040106.

[12] Z. Ali et al., "ITSSAKA-MS: An Improved Three-Factor Symmetric-Key Based Secure AKA Scheme for Multi-Server Environments," *IEEE Access*, vol. 8, pp. 107993–108003, 2020, doi: 10.1109/ACCESS.2020.3000716.

[13] E. B. Sanjuan, I. A. Cardiel, J. A. Cerrada and C. Cerrada, "Message Queuing Telemetry Transport (MQTT) Security: A Cryptographic Smart Card Approach," *IEEE Access*, vol. 8, pp. 115051–115062, 2020, doi: 10.1109/ACCESS.2020.3003998.

[14] B. Pretty, "Online Ticket Booking Using Secure QR Code," *International Journal of Research in Engineering, Science and Management*, vol. 1, no. 12, December 2018, ISSN (Online): 2581-5792.

[15] S. Gupta, "Performance Evaluation of Unstructured PBRA for bigdata with Cassandra and MongoDB in Cloud," *International Journal of Cloud Applications and Computing*, vol. 8, no. 3, July 2018, doi: 10.4018/IJCAC.2018070104.

[16] https://telanganatoday.com/qr-code-based-e-ticketing-launched-for-hyderabad-metro, last accessed October 2021.

[17] www.consumerismcommentary.com/best-mobile-payment-apps/, last accessed September 2021.

[18] www.qr-code-generator.com/qr-code-marketing/why-should-i-use-qr-codes/, last accessed October 2021.

[19] O. O. Ajibola, T. E. H. El-Gorashi and J. M. H. Elmirghani, "Disaggregation for Energy Efficient Fog in Future 6G Networks," *IEEE Transactions on Green Communications and Networking*, vol. 6, no. 3, pp. 1697–1722, September 2022, doi: 10.1109/TGCN.2022.3160397.

19 Three Decades of Recommendations Systems in Vehicular Ad Hoc Network

Open Issues, Challenges, and Research Opportunities for the Future

Richa and Amit Kumar Tyagi

19.1 INTRODUCTION

In today's era, the exponential increase of information in the web increases the complexity of decision-making for users. The information-filtering approach helps deal with the information overload problem. Recommender systems are an information-filtering approach that assists the end user in the decision-making process [1]. The broad categorization of recommender system is divided into three broad categories: collaborative filtering, content-based filtering, and hybrid approach. A collaborative filtering approach works based on the idea that if two people have shared the interest in the past, then they might share the same in the future as well. It is further categorized into user-based collaborative filtering and items-based collaborative filtering [2]. The user-based collaborative filtering discusses the similarity between two users' rating pattern, whereas the item-based collaborative filtering helps deal with two items' rating pattern [3]. A content-based approach helps deal with the content of the items rather than the user's rating pattern [4]. Let us consider a book recommender system where the books are recommended to the user based on the genre of the book. For example, if the user has read a book which belongs to the genre fantasy, then more fantasy books or novels might be a good choice for the user.

A hybrid approach combines more than one or more approaches of recommendation. For example, collaborative and content-based approaches are combined to remove the problem related to both approaches and include the advantages of the approaches [5].

The general methodology involved in the recommendation commences by collecting the user's information. The user information incorporates the rating behavior or demographic details of user. Based on user interest, the system starts calculating the similar user as per the target user. Once the neighborhood for the target user has been shortlisted, then the system calculates the prediction for those items that are not yet seen by the target user but have been seen and rated by the neighborhood. Now, the top-n items from the predicted items are provided to the target user as recommendation (refer to Figure 19.1).

The recommendation approach can be formulated as:

$$UserXItem = Rating$$

To improve the recommendation process, many e-commerce websites have incorporated contextual aspects into the process. Many researchers have focused on the contextual information of users,

DOI: 10.1201/9781003450306-21

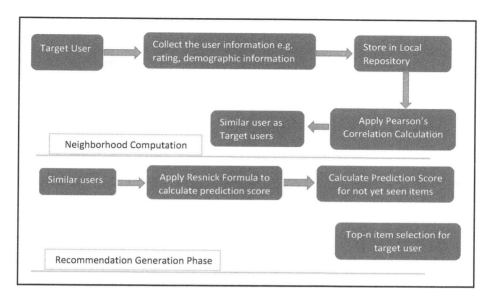

FIGURE 19.1　General model of recommendation generation.

which has been thoroughly explored in context-aware recommender systems. The context-aware recommendation system focusses on targeting the evolving preferences of users in terms of contextual requirements [6].

It can be stated as follows:

$$UserXItemXcontext = Rating$$

The context-aware recommender system is divided into context pre-filtering, post-filtering, and contextual modelling. Contextual pre-filtering is the approach that filters the items which contain the contextual preferences of the user. Once the items are filtered, then the traditional approach of recommendation can be applied to get the recommendation for the target user. The post-filtering approach of recommendation applies the general approach of recommendation and then filters out the items based on the contextual requirement of the user. This provides the final set of items that match and fulfil the user's perspective of context. The third approach of context-aware recommendation includes the context into the model itself. The first two approaches have been widely explored by various researchers [7]. The preceding three can be demonstrated as follows (refer to Figure 19.2).

There are many scenarios where the recommendation provided to the group of users rather than individual user is preferable. For example, in coffee shops, it is important to play music of general interest rather than individual choices, or to provide recommendations of travel places that are famous among users for a group of users. Providing recommendation to a group of users can be done by collecting the individual choices and then making the intersection of the users' interest [8]. Group recommendation has been connected to many other approaches to improve the approach. A cross-domain-based group recommendation has been presented by [9] to handle the cold start problem in group recommendation by using the advantages of the cross-domain approach. They have included trust and reputation to provide the influential users in order to provide more personalized recommendations (refer to Figure 19.3).

Knowledge graph recommendation involves graph-based approaches with the recommender system [10]. The knowledge graph (KG) is a collection of entities, namely, objects, events, or concepts.

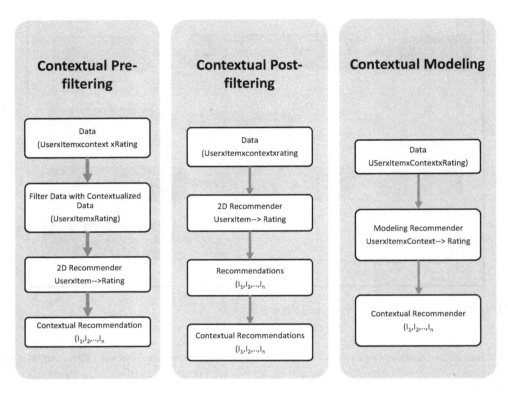

FIGURE 19.2 Context-aware recommender system.

The framework for data integration, analytics, unification, and sharing is provided by the knowledge graph when it puts the data into the context. It is based on the semantic network that helps compute the semantic similarity between two entities. A graph is used to form the information using the structure of the node, which represents entities, and the edges represent the connection between the two edges. The knowledge-based recommender system contributes to reducing the problem of data sparsity and explanation.

Explanation-based recommendations are an important factor which helps generate the explanation for the presented recommendations. Once it is combined to the serendipitous recommendation, then it has the capability to present the recommendations that can surprise the user and, at the same time, explanation that helps boost user acceptance toward the generated list of items [11].

The importance of trust, reputation, and recommendation in vehicular ad hoc network (or transportation sector) and in other sectors: trust, reputation, and recommendation are important factors in many sectors, including the transportation sector and vehicular ad hoc networks (VANETs). Here are some reasons:

- *Trust*. Trust is essential in VANETs because vehicles need to rely on information received from other vehicles to make decisions about driving. For example, if a vehicle receives information from another vehicle about an upcoming obstacle, it needs to trust that the information is accurate and reliable. Trust is also important in the transportation sector because customers need to trust that the transportation provider will deliver them to their destination safely and on time.
- *Reputation*. Reputation is important in VANETs because it helps vehicles determine which other vehicles to trust. A vehicle with a good reputation is more likely to be trusted than

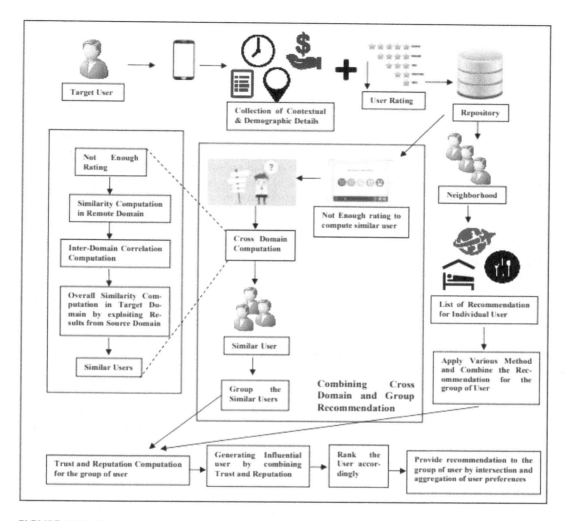

FIGURE 19.3 Cross-domain group recommender system.

a vehicle with a poor reputation. Reputation is also important in the transportation sector because customers rely on the reputation of transportation providers to make decisions about which provider to choose.

- *Recommendation.* Recommendation is important in both VANETs and the transportation sector because it can help vehicles and customers make better decisions. For example, if a vehicle receives a recommendation from another vehicle about a route to take, it can use that information to make a better decision about which route to take. Similarly, if a customer receives a recommendation from another customer about a transportation provider, it can use that information to make a better decision about which provider to choose.

In summary, trust, reputation, and recommendation are important in many sectors, including the transportation sector and VANETs, because they help individuals and organizations make better decisions and build more effective networks.

Section 2 discusses about related work. Section 3 discusses about issues raised in recommender systems. Further, challenges for the recommender system in transportation and other sectors are discussed in Section 4. Section 5 discusses about future research opportunities toward recommender systems. And lastly, in Section 6, this work is concluded in brief.

19.2 RELATED WORK

The recommender system has spent almost three decades among researchers as of now. There are many different domains where recommendations have been applied, such as movies [12], music [13], research [14], e-commerce [15], tourism [16], and many more. In recent years, neural network–based algorithms have gained immense popularity among researchers due to their accuracy and preciseness. It also helps the traditional approach of recommendation systems to improve and surpasses the accuracy of the traditional approach. A survey has been provided by [17] that aims to summarize the work on neural recommender systems model. To reduce sparsity problem, an enhanced multi-stage user-based collaborative filtering approach is proposed by [18]. They have utilized the concept of active learning that is incorporated to use unknown rating for the target users. Collaborative filtering has also been combined with a deep learning–based approach [19]. A time-aware deep collaborative filtering approach has been proposed by [20] that combined short-term preferences with long-term ones to present a dynamic user preference model.

In the group recommendation, each member of the group is important, and to incorporate their opinion, a model is proposed by [21] that uses weighting members according to the degree of importance. To analyze the importance of each member, a matrix factorization technique has been proposed. The sparsity problem, which is considered as one of the major issues of the recommender system, is resolved by the method that uses an SVM technique, as suggested by [22]. In another effort, an opinion dynamics–based group recommender system [23] is proposed that considers the rigidness among the aggregation and overlooks certain group features. The involvement of individual users and aggregating their preferences or recommendations help generate the recommendation for the group rather than individuals. It needs various issues to be tackled while presenting recommendations to the group of users, as mentioned in [24]. To generate quality in the group recommendation, [25] has proposed Cascade TOPSIS. It selects the group recommendation from the group, which consists only those members that provide a good quality of recommendation.

The collaborative approach of recommendation, along with trust-based recommendations, has been found effective to alleviate cold start problems [26]. They have proposed a hybrid collaborative approach of recommendation that includes the user–item trust record, which includes the user trust into the existing collaborative filtering approach. Another trust- and distrust-based recommender system is given by [27] that mentions the involvement of distrust as important as the trust between users. In [28], the authors provide a survey on the knowledge graph–based recommendation. They have mentioned the use of KG as an embedding-based method, path-based method, and unified method. The involvement of knowledge graph gets more accurate recommendation and interpretability. [29] has provided a detailed analysis of trust-aware recommender systems (TARS). This analysis involves eight different implicit trust metrics with respect to the various properties of trust. In [30], the authors have incorporated ALS algorithm where they have mentioned a new loss function, and the issue is solved by determining the similarity joins between items and users. In different iterations, by comparing the root mean square, we get the algorithm output results with the other existing collaborative filtering techniques. The world of recommendation has reached three decades to this date. Nowadays, e-commerce websites have shown a huge interest, and various algorithms have been utilized to improve the recommendation systems as per the requirement. RSs have become an integral part of e-commerce websites.

19.3 POPULAR ISSUES IN RECOMMENDER SYSTEMS

Although, recommender systems have been taken into consideration in the past three decades, there are still many issues that exist in this area. One of the major issues is cold start problem, which is further divided into user cold start problem and item cold start problem [31]. User cold start problem deals with the scenario where there is no personalized recommendation for the user because of the unavailability of user information. A similar scenario occurs for the new item cold start problem, where the item is new to the system and thus does not have enough rating that could be used to send them as recommendation to users. Another issue with the recommendation system is sparsity problem. Sparsity is a major issue that has been targeted by many researchers in the past, but still it needs attention [32]. The problem appears because there are millions of users and items in the catalogue, which is nearly impossible to be rated by the customer.

One issue in recommendation is scalability of the system. Another problem is mentioned in the literature as gray sheep problem. This problem occurs due to the unavailability of data to generate personalized recommendations [33]. The reason behind this is that the system is not able to find out similar users as per the target user despite the user providing a few ratings. But the ratings given by the user do not match with that of other users, so the system is not able to provide a neighborhood for the target user.

Cross-domain recommender systems are found to be a potential solution for the issue of cold start problem by various researchers. In this approach, two or more than two domains are involved, which make use of a user's information from one domain into another domain. It is divided into four types: attribute-level, type-level, item-level, and system-level [34]. The attribute-level cross-domain considers the recommendation in the same domain. For example, on the basis of genre of the movie, a system can generate recommendation. The type-level cross-domain provides the recommendation across the two domains, for example, the rating of the movie domain can be used to generate the recommendation in the book domain. The item-level cross-domain approach provides the analysis of utilizing two different domains, where many of the attributes differ. System-level cross-domain deals with the same items which are provided in different ways, for example, two different movie recommender systems: one is Netflix [53], and another is MovieLens [54].

Another approach that has been suggested to handle the problem of sparsity is matrix factorization technique. This approach has been found as superior in comparison with the traditional nearest-neighbor technique [35]. It also incorporates the additional information of the product, such as implicit feedback, confidence level, etc., to get the product recommendation. Another important factor for the recommender systems is personalized recommendation. To enhance the user acceptance and to transfer the most appropriate recommendations to the user, trust and reputation play an important role [36].

Trust is defined as the positive encounter between the users in the literature, whereas *reputation* is considered as the opinion of the community for a single user (see Figure 19.4). Instead of providing recommendations based only on user similarity or item similarities, it has been found that trust

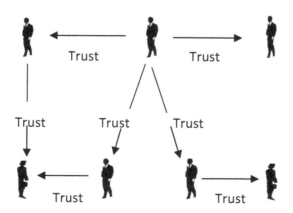

FIGURE 19.4 Web of trust.

factor improves the accuracy of the presented recommendations. Another work has claimed [37] to improve personalized recommendation by incorporating a trust relationship between users. They have used an axiomatic approach, which works on a voting and ranking system.

19.4 OPEN ISSUES AND CHALLENGES FOR RECOMMENDER SYSTEM IN TRANSPORTATION AND OTHER SECTORS

In the recent years, deep learning has gained an immense popularity in various areas, including recommender systems. It is capable of handling the nonlinear relationship between user and item that helps handle and enhance the system as compared to the traditional approach of recommendation [38]. Another survey has been presented by [34] that provides the detailed analysis of the effectiveness of deep learning–based information retrieval and recommendation-based research. The current trends and future perspectives on this new and emerging field have been analyzed. Both literatures have provided a comprehensive review of the recommendation system based on the deep learning approach.

There are many scenarios where there are challenges and scope of improvement in terms of many factors, such as scalability. Collaborative filtering has been enhanced using the neural network, where the authors have used self-organizing map (SOM) neural networks [39]. They have utilized the demographic details of the user and made a cluster using the preference of items using the mentioned neural network. The collaborative approach is applied on the cluster created using the SOM approach.

The challenge of personalization and effectiveness of recommendations has been noted by various researchers. A suitable method, knowledge-based recommendation, has been mentioned in the literature as a potential solution for the mentioned issues. Incorporating knowledge along with ontology-based recommendation has been carried out by [40, 41]. They have claimed that the hybridization of ontology and knowledge-based recommendation aims to enhance the effectiveness of the recommendations and improve the quality of the presented list. A knowledge-based recommender system has been incorporated with social web, aimed to provide information about the social elements and services of user interest. Semantic technology is considered as reliable and consistent to deal with the data at various levels and claimed to enhance the quality of presented items significantly [42].

A different recommendation than the conventional recommender system in this area are sequential recommender systems (SRSs). It is an emerging area that has gained attention in recent years. It includes many aspects, such as user context, intent, and goals, which result into a more accurate and precise recommendation. A systematic review has been presented by [43] summarizing the literature for the SRSs and categorizes the key challenges in this area, including the long-term preferences to evolve over time by combining user–item and item–item interactions. A two-layer hierarchical attention network has been presented by [44, 45] that aims for long-term user preferences that utilize the historical evidence of the interest of the user. Now, issues and challenges in general, and required sectors (including other sectors), will be discussed in detail.

19.4.1 POPULAR ISSUES AND CHALLENGES IN THE TRANSPORTATION SECTOR

The transportation sector is essential for the efficient movement of people, goods, and services. However, this sector faces many challenges and issues that can affect its effectiveness, sustainability, and safety. Some of the popular issues and challenges in the transportation sector include:

- *Traffic congestion.* Traffic congestion is a common problem in cities, leading to wasted time, increased fuel consumption, and air pollution. It can cause significant delays for commuters, transportation of goods, and emergency vehicles.

- *Infrastructure maintenance.* Transportation infrastructure, such as roads, bridges, and tunnels, require regular maintenance to remain safe and functional. However, funding for maintenance is often insufficient, leading to deteriorating conditions and increased risk for accidents.
- *Environmental concerns.* Transportation is a significant contributor to greenhouse gas emissions, air pollution, and noise pollution. These environmental concerns affect public health, quality of life, and the sustainability of the transportation sector.
- *Safety.* Transportation accidents, including road crashes and train derailments, can cause serious injuries, fatalities, and property damage. Safety concerns also extend to security issues, such as terrorism and cyberattacks.
- *Equity.* Access to transportation is not equal for all communities, leading to disparities in mobility and economic opportunities. Rural areas, low-income communities, and people with disabilities often face significant barriers to transportation access.
- *Emerging technologies.* The transportation sector is undergoing significant changes due to emerging technologies, such as autonomous vehicles, electric vehicles, and alternative fuel sources. These changes present opportunities for innovation and sustainability but also pose challenges for infrastructure, regulation, and workforce training.
- *Funding.* Transportation projects require significant funding, and funding sources are often limited or uncertain. This lack of funding can limit the implementation of necessary infrastructure improvements and limit access to transportation for underserved communities.
- *Security and privacy.* These terms need to be considered as primary objective to protect during the implementation of recommender systems in the required sector.

Addressing these challenges and issues in the transportation sector requires collaboration among government agencies, private industry, and the public to create sustainable, equitable, and safe transportation systems.

19.4.2 Popular Issues and Challenges in Other Sectors

Here are some popular issues and challenges faced by other sectors:

- *Healthcare sector.* The healthcare sector faces challenges such as rising healthcare costs, access to care, and the aging population. There is also a need to ensure healthcare services are inclusive, equitable, and of high quality.
- *Education sector.* The education sector faces challenges such as access to quality education, student debt, teacher shortages, and the need for effective use of technology in the classroom.
- *Technology sector.* The technology sector faces challenges such as cybersecurity threats, data privacy concerns, and the need to address the digital divide that limits access to technology and broadband connectivity in underserved communities.
- *Energy sector.* The energy sector faces challenges such as the transition to renewable energy sources, energy efficiency, and reducing greenhouse gas emissions to address climate change.
- *Agriculture sector.* The agriculture sector faces challenges such as the need for sustainable and efficient use of natural resources, food security, and ensuring the safety of the food supply chain.
- *Manufacturing sector.* The manufacturing sector faces challenges such as automation and the need for upskilling workers, global competition, and supply chain disruptions.
- *Finance sector.* The finance sector faces challenges such as the need to adapt to changing consumer preferences and expectations, cybersecurity threats, and managing risks associated with financial products and services.

Hence, these challenges require innovative solutions and collaboration across different sectors and stakeholders to address the needs of the society and the environment while also promoting economic growth and prosperity.

19.4.3 POPULAR ISSUES AND CHALLENGES IN TRANSPORTATION AND OTHER SECTORS IN IMPLEMENTING RECOMMENDER SYSTEMS

Recommender systems are widely used in various sectors to provide personalized recommendations to users. However, there are some challenges and issues that need to be addressed when implementing recommender systems in transportation and other sectors. Here are some popular issues and challenges:

- *Data privacy.* Recommender systems often rely on collecting and analyzing user data to provide personalized recommendations. This raises concerns about data privacy and the need to ensure that user data is collected and used in an ethical and transparent way.
- *Data quality.* The accuracy and quality of the data used to train and test recommender systems are crucial to the effectiveness of the system. In transportation, for example, recommender systems need to rely on accurate and up-to-date traffic data to provide useful recommendations.
- *User engagement.* Recommender systems rely on user engagement to provide personalized recommendations. However, users may not always engage with the system, leading to less-effective recommendations.
- *System complexity.* Recommender systems can be complex to implement, requiring expertise in data science, machine learning, and software development. This can pose a challenge for organizations without the necessary skills and resources.
- *Bias.* Recommender systems can be biased, resulting in recommendations that are unfair or discriminatory. This is particularly relevant in transportation, where recommendations could impact access to services and opportunities.
- *Explainability.* Recommender systems can be difficult to explain, making it challenging for users to understand how recommendations are generated. This can lead to a lack of trust in the system.

Addressing these challenges requires a careful consideration of the design, implementation, and evaluation of recommender systems. Organizations need to ensure that they collect and use user data ethically and transparently, improve the quality of the data used, and engage users effectively. They also need to ensure that recommender systems are free of bias and provide explanations of the recommendations generated. Finally, organizations need to ensure that they have the necessary skills and resources to implement and maintain recommender systems effectively.

19.5 FUTURE RESEARCH OPPORTUNITIES TOWARD RECOMMENDER SYSTEMS

Recommender systems have become an integral part of our lives, providing personalized recommendations for a variety of products and services, such as movies, music, books, and even groceries. As the amount of data generated and consumed by users continues to grow exponentially, there are several exciting research opportunities toward improving recommender systems. Some of these opportunities include:

- *Explainability and interpretability.* One of the biggest challenges in recommender systems is the lack of transparency and interpretability. Often, users are presented with recommendations without knowing why they were recommended. To improve user trust and adoption, future research should focus on developing explainable and interpretable recommender systems that can provide users with clear explanations of the recommendations.

- *Context-aware recommender systems.* Traditional recommender systems consider only the user's historical interactions with the system and do not take into account the context in which the user is making the request. Future research should focus on developing context-aware recommender systems that can take into account the user's current situation and preferences, such as time of day, location, and mood.
- *Personalization at scale.* As the amount of data generated by users continues to grow, recommender systems need to be able to handle and process large-scale data in real time. Future research should focus on developing scalable recommender systems that can personalize recommendations for millions of users in real time.
- *Diversity and serendipity.* Traditional recommender systems tend to recommend popular items, which can result in homogeneity and lack of diversity in the recommended items. Future research should focus on developing recommender systems that can balance between recommending popular items and providing diverse and serendipitous recommendations that can surprise and delight users.
- *Cross-domain recommendations.* Recommender systems have traditionally been developed and deployed in specific domains, such as movies, music, or books. Future research should focus on developing cross-domain recommender systems that can leverage data from multiple domains to provide personalized recommendations across a wide range of products and services.
- *Privacy-preserving recommender systems.* The use of personal data in recommender systems raises privacy concerns. Future research should focus on developing privacy-preserving recommender systems that can provide personalized recommendations without compromising users' privacy.

In summary, future research in recommender systems should focus on developing more personalized, interpretable, and scalable systems that can provide diverse and serendipitous recommendations while preserving users' privacy.

19.6   FUTURE RESEARCH OPPORTUNITIES TOWARD RECOMMENDER SYSTEMS IN THE TRANSPORTATION SECTOR

Recommender systems have become increasingly popular in various sectors, including transportation. These systems are designed to suggest the most suitable transportation modes or routes to users based on their preferences, past behavior, and other factors. Some future research opportunities toward recommender systems in the transportation sector are:

- *Personalized route recommendation.* Developing personalized route recommendation systems that can suggest the most suitable route for individual users based on their specific needs, such as time constraints, cost, and preferred mode of transportation.
- *Multimodal recommender systems.* Developing recommender systems that can provide users with recommendations for multiple modes of transportation, such as public transit, ride-sharing, and bike-sharing.
- *Real-time prediction.* Developing real-time prediction models that can provide users with accurate recommendations for transportation modes and routes based on current traffic conditions and other factors.
- *Collaborative filtering.* Developing collaborative filtering techniques that can leverage the collective knowledge and behavior of users to make better recommendations for transportation modes and routes.

- *Explainable recommender systems.* Developing explainable recommender systems that can provide users with clear explanations for why a particular mode of transportation or route is recommended, which can improve users' trust in the system.
- *Privacy-preserving recommender systems.* Developing privacy-preserving recommender systems that can protect users' sensitive information, such as their location and travel patterns, while still providing accurate recommendations.
- *Context-aware recommender systems.* Developing context-aware recommender systems that can provide recommendations based on users' current context, such as weather conditions, time of day, and the availability of transportation modes.
- *Machine learning–based recommender systems.* Developing machine learning–based recommender systems that can leverage advanced algorithms and techniques, such as deep learning and reinforcement learning, to provide more accurate and personalized recommendations.
- *Multilingual recommender systems.* Developing multilingual recommender systems that can provide recommendations to users in different languages, which can improve the accessibility and usability of these systems for users from diverse backgrounds.

Hence, these research opportunities have the potential to improve the performance and usability of recommender systems in the transportation sector, which can ultimately lead to more efficient and sustainable transportation systems [46–52].

19.7 CONCLUSION

In the last three decades, information overload has increased exponentially. To help the end user in the decision-making process, the recommender system came into existence. Due to the abundance of information available on the Internet, it helps to make personalized recommendations to the user. There are many approaches that improve the accuracy of the presented recommendations to the end user. Cross-domain recommendations help target the cold start problem, whereas the inclusion of trust awareness provides more personalized recommendations. The incorporation of neural network–based approaches has targeted many issues, such as sparsity and preciseness of the presented list. The chapter has focused on the mentioned issues in the recommendations and the solution of the systems.

REFERENCES

1. Resnick, Paul, and Hal R. Varian. "Recommender systems." *Communications of the ACM* 40, no. 3 (1997): 56–58.
2. Schafer, J. Ben, Dan Frankowski, Jon Herlocker, and Shilad Sen. "Collaborative filtering recommender systems." *The Adaptive Web: Methods and Strategies of Web Personalization* (2007): 291–324.
3. Zhao, Zhi-Dan, and Ming-Sheng Shang. "User-based collaborative-filtering recommendation algorithms on Hadoop." In *2010 third international conference on knowledge discovery and data mining*, pp. 478–481. IEEE, 2010.
4. Aggarwal, Charu C., and Charu C. Aggarwal. "Content-based recommender systems." *Recommender Systems: The Textbook* (2016): 139–166.
5. Burke, Robin. "Hybrid recommender systems: Survey and experiments." *User Modeling and User-adapted Interaction* 12 (2002): 331–370.
6. Adomavicius, Gediminas, and Alexander Tuzhilin. "Context-aware recommender systems." In *Recommender systems handbook*, pp. 217–253. Springer US, 2010.
7. Richa and Punam Bedi. "Parallel proactive cross domain context aware recommender system." *Journal of Intelligent & Fuzzy Systems* 34, no. 3 (2018): 1521–1533.
8. Felfernig, Alexander, Ludovico Boratto, Martin Stettinger, and Marko Tkalčič. *Group recommender systems: An introduction.* Cham: Springer, 2018.
9. Richa and Bedi, Punam. "Combining trust and reputation as user influence in cross domain group recommender system (CDGRS)." *Journal of Intelligent & Fuzzy Systems* 38, no. 5 (2020): 6235–6246.

10. Burke, Robin. "Knowledge-based recommender systems." *Encyclopedia of Library and Information Systems* 69, no. Supplement 32 (2000): 175–186.
11. Richa, Chhavi Sharma, and Punam Bedi. "Explanation-based serendipitous recommender system (EBSRS)." In *International conference on innovative computing and communications: Proceedings of ICICC 2021, Volume 3*, vol. 1394, p. 1. Springer Nature, 2021.
12. Kumar, Manoj, D. K. Yadav, Ankur Singh, and Vijay Kr Gupta. "A movie recommender system: Movrec." *International Journal of Computer Applications* 124, no. 3 (2015).
13. Schedl, Markus, Peter Knees, Brian McFee, Dmitry Bogdanov, and Marius Kaminskas. "Music recommender systems." *Recommender Systems Handbook* (2015): 453–492.
14. Beel, Joeran, Corinna Breitinger, Stefan Langer, Andreas Lommatzsch, and Bela Gipp. "Towards reproducibility in recommender-systems research." *User Modeling and User-adapted Interaction* 26 (2016): 69–101.
15. Schafer, J. Ben, Joseph Konstan, and John Riedl. "Recommender systems in e-commerce." In *Proceedings of the 1st ACM conference on electronic commerce*, pp. 158–166. New York: Association for Computing Machinery, 1999.
16. Bedi, Punam, Sumit Kumar Agarwal, and Vinita Jindal. "Marst: Multi-agent recommender system for e-tourism using reputation based collaborative filtering." In *Databases in Networked Information Systems: 9th International Workshop, DNIS 2014, Aizu-Wakamatsu, Japan, March 24–26, 2014. Proceedings 9*, pp. 189–201. Springer International Publishing, 2014.
17. Guo, Q., F. Zhuang, C. Qin, H. Zhu, X. Xie, H. Xiong, and Q. He. A survey on knowledge graph-based recommender systems. *IEEE Transactions on Knowledge and Data Engineering*, 34, no. 8 (2020 October 7).
18. Gupta, S., and S. Nagpal. Trust aware recommender systems: A survey on implicit trust generation techniques. *International Journal of Computer Science and Information Technologies* 6, no. 4 (2015): 3594–3599.
19. Xie, Li, Wenbo Zhou, and Yaosen Li. "Application of improved recommendation system based on spark platform in big data analysis." *Cybernetics and Information Technologies* 16, no. 6 (2016): 245–255.
20. Wu, Le, Xiangnan He, Xiang Wang, Kun Zhang, and Meng Wang. "A survey on accuracy-oriented neural recommendation: From collaborative filtering to information-rich recommendation." *IEEE Transactions on Knowledge and Data Engineering*, 35, no. 5 (2022).
21. Wang, Wei, Guangquan Zhang, and Jie Lu. "Member contribution-based group recommender system." *Decision Support Systems* 87, no. 1 (2016): 80–93.
22. Ghazarian, Sarik, and Mohammad Ali Nematbakhsh. "Enhancing memory-based collaborative filtering for group recommender systems." *Expert Systems with Applications* 42, no. 7 (2015): 3801–3812.
23. Castro, Jorge, Jie Lu, Guangquan Zhang, Yucheng Dong, and Luis Martínez. "Opinion dynamics-based group recommender systems." *IEEE Transactions on Systems, Man, and Cybernetics: Systems* 99 (2017): 1–13.
24. Masthoff, Judith. "Group recommender systems: Aggregation, satisfaction and group attributes." In *Recommender systems handbook*, pp. 743–776. Springer, 2015.
25. Dixit, Veer Sain, Harita Mehta, and Punam Bedi. "A proposed framework for group-based multi-criteria recommendations." *Applied Artificial Intelligence* 28, no. 10 (2014): 917–956.
26. Wang, Fan, Haibin Zhu, Gautam Srivastava, Shancang Li, Mohammad R. Khosravi, and Lianyong Qi. "Robust collaborative filtering recommendation with user-item-trust records." *IEEE Transactions on Computational Social Systems* 9, no. 4 (2021): 986–996.
27. Richa, and Punam Bedi. "Trust and distrust based cross-domain recommender system." *Applied Artificial Intelligence* 35, no. 4 (2021): 326–351.
28. Guo, Q., F. Zhuang, C. Qin, H. Zhu, X. Xie, H. Xiong, and Q. He. "A survey on knowledge graph-based recommender systems." *IEEE Transactions on Knowledge and Data Engineering* (2020 October 7).
29. Gupta, S., and S. Nagpal. "Trust aware recommender systems: A survey on implicit trust generation techniques." *International Journal of Computer Science and Information Technologies* 6, no. 4 (2015): 3594–3599.
30. Xie, Li, Wenbo Zhou, and Yaosen Li. "Application of improved recommendation system based on spark platform in big data analysis." *Cybernetics and Information Technologies* 16, no. 6 (2016): 245–255.
31. Lam, Xuan Nhat, Thuc Vu, Trong Duc Le, and Anh Duc Duong. "Addressing cold-start problem in recommendation systems." In *Proceedings of the 2nd international conference on Ubiquitous information management and communication*, pp. 208–211. New York: Association for Computing Machinery, 2008.
32. Yin, Hongzhi, Qinyong Wang, Kai Zheng, Zhixu Li, and Xiaofang Zhou. "Overcoming data sparsity in group recommendation." *IEEE Transactions on Knowledge and Data Engineering* 34, no. 7 (2020): 3447–3460.

33. Gras, Benjamin, Armelle Brun, and Anne Boyer. "Identifying grey sheep users in collaborative filtering: A distribution-based technique." In *Proceedings of the 2016 conference on user modeling adaptation and personalization*, pp. 17–26. New York: Association for Computing Machinery, 2016.
34. Cremonesi, Paolo, Antonio Tripodi, and Roberto Turrin. "Cross-domain recommender systems." In *2011 IEEE 11th international conference on data mining workshops*, pp. 496–503. IEEE, 2011.
35. Koren, Yehuda, Robert Bell, and Chris Volinsky. "Matrix factorization techniques for recommender systems." *Computer* 42, no. 8 (2009): 30–37.
36. Ozsoy, Makbule Gulcin, and Faruk Polat. "Trust based recommendation systems." In *Proceedings of the 2013 IEEE/ACM international conference on advances in social networks analysis and mining*, pp. 1267–1274. New York: Association for Computing Machinery, 2013.
37. Andersen, Reid, Christian Borgs, Jennifer Chayes, Uriel Feige, Abraham Flaxman, Adam Kalai, Vahab Mirrokni, and Moshe Tennenholtz. "Trust-based recommendation systems: An axiomatic approach." In *Proceedings of the 17th international conference on World Wide Web*, pp. 199–208. New York: Association for Computing Machinery, 2008.
38. Mu, Ruihui. "A survey of recommender systems based on deep learning." *IEEE Access* 6 (2018): 69009–69022.
39. Zhang, Shuai, Lina Yao, Aixin Sun, and Yi Tay. "Deep learning based recommender system: A survey and new perspectives." *ACM Computing Surveys (CSUR)* 52, no. 1 (2019): 1–38.
40. Lee, Meehee, Pyungseok Choi, and Yongtae Woo. "A hybrid recommender system combining collaborative filtering with neural network." In *Adaptive hypermedia and adaptive web-based systems: Second international conference, AH 2002 Málaga, Spain, May 29–31, 2002 Proceedings 2*, pp. 531–534. Springer Berlin Heidelberg, 2002.
41. Perumal, Saravanakeerthana, Siddhi Rawal, and Richa. "Handling cold-start problem in restaurant recommender system using ontology." In *Proceedings of Emerging Trends and Technologies on Intelligent Systems: ETTIS 2022*, pp. 319–329. Springer Nature Singapore, 2022.
42. Tarus, John K., Zhendong Niu, and Ghulam Mustafa. "Knowledge-based recommendation: A review of ontology-based recommender systems for e-learning." *Artificial Intelligence Review* 50 (2018): 21–48.
43. Carrer-Neto, Walter, María Luisa Hernández-Alcaraz, Rafael Valencia-García, and Francisco García-Sánchez. "Social knowledge-based recommender system. Application to the movies domain." *Expert Systems with Applications* 39, no. 12 (2012): 10990–11000.
44. Wang, Shoujin, Liang Hu, Yan Wang, Longbing Cao, Quan Z. Sheng, and Mehmet Orgun. "Sequential recommender systems: Challenges, progress and prospects." *arXiv preprint*, arXiv:2001.04830 (2019).
45. Ying, Haochao, Fuzhen Zhuang, Fuzheng Zhang, Yanchi Liu, Guandong Xu, Xing Xie, Hui Xiong, and Jian Wu. "Sequential recommender system based on hierarchical attention network." In *IJCAI international joint conference on artificial intelligence*. New York: Association for Computing Machinery, 2018.
46. Tyagi, A. K., G. Rekha, and N. Sreenath (Eds.). (2021). *Opportunities and challenges for blockchain technology in autonomous vehicles*. IGI Global. http://doi.org/10.4018/978-1-7998-3295-9
47. Tyagi, A. K., S. Kumari, T. F. Fernandez, and C. Aravindan. "P3 Block: Privacy preserved, trusted smart parking allotment for future vehicles of tomorrow." In Gervasi, O. et al. (Eds.), *Computational science and its applications – ICCSA 2020*. ICCSA 2020. Lecture Notes in Computer Science, vol. 12254. Springer, 2020. https://doi.org/10.1007/978-3-030-58817-5_56
48. Tyagi, A., S. Niladhuri, and R. Priya. "Never trust anyone: Trust-privacy trade-offs in vehicular Ad-Hoc networks." *Journal of Advances in Mathematics and Computer Science* 19, no. 6 (2016): 1–23. https://doi.org/10.9734/BJMCS/2016/27737
49. Tyagi, A. K., and Sreenath Niladhuri. "Providing trust enabled services in vehicular cloud computing." In *Proceedings of the international conference on informatics and analytics (ICIA-16)*, Article 3, 1–10. Association for Computing Machinery, 2016. https://doi.org/10.1145/2980258.2980263
50. Tyagi, A. K., and N. Sreenath. "Providing trust enabled services in vehicular cloud computing." In *2016 International Conference on Research Advances in Integrated Navigation Systems (RAINS)*, pp. 1–7. 2016. https://doi.org/10.1109/RAINS.2016.7764391.
51. Tyagi, A. K., A. M. Krishna, S. Malik, M. M. Nair, and S. Niladhuri. "Trust and reputation mechanisms in vehicular Ad-Hoc networks: A systematic review." *Advances in Science, Technology and Engineering Systems Journal* 5, no. 1 (2020): 387–402.
52. Tyagi, A. K., and N. Sreenath. Security, privacy, and trust issues in intelligent transportation system. In *Intelligent transportation systems: Theory and practice. disruptive technologies and digital transformations for society 5.0*. Springer, Singapore, 2023. https://doi.org/10.1007/978-981-19-7622-3_8
53. https://www.netflix.com/in/
54. https://grouplens.org/datasets/movielens/

Index

Note: Page numbers in *italics* indicate a figure and page numbers in **bold** indicate a table on the corresponding page.